本丛书出版得到广东省高水平大学重点学科建设项目支持

系统功能语言学文献丛书

丛书主编：彭宣维 黄国文

语篇功能与语篇分析

——理论探讨与应用

TEXTUAL FUNCTION AND DISCOURSE ANALYSIS

Theoretical Exploration and Application

方 琰 ◉ 著

上海外语教育出版社
外教社 SHANGHAI FOREIGN LANGUAGE EDUCATION PRESS
www.sflep.com

图书在版编目(CIP)数据

语篇功能与语篇分析：理论探讨与应用 / 方琰著.
—上海：上海外语教育出版社，2020
(系统功能语言学文献丛书)
ISBN 978－7－5446－6144－7

Ⅰ. ①语…　Ⅱ. ①方…　Ⅲ. ①功能(语言学)—研究　Ⅳ. ①H0

中国版本图书馆 CIP 数据核字(2020)第 022580 号

出版发行：上海外语教育出版社
（上海外国语大学内）　邮编：200083
电　　话：021-65425300（总机）
电子邮箱：bookinfo@sflep.com.cn
网　　址：http://www.sflep.com
责任编辑：李健儿

印　　刷：上海市崇明县裕安印刷厂
开　　本：635×965　1/16　印张 34.5　字数 546千字
版　　次：2020 年 9月第 1版　2020 年 9月第 1次印刷
印　　数：1 100 册

书　　号：ISBN 978-7-5446-6144-7
定　　价：108.00 元
本版图书如有印装质量问题，可向本社调换
质量服务热线：4008-213-263　电子邮箱：editorial@sflep.com

系统功能语言学文献丛书

编委会名单

总　序

彭宣维　黄国文

初学者对文献的重要性往往缺乏足够的认识，想写文章的时候绞尽脑汁却一筹莫展，勉强凑一个东西出来却不入流：缺乏研究背景，缺乏研究问题，缺乏研究方法，缺乏创新观点，缺乏学科用语，缺乏组织策略，也缺乏格式规范。

确定一个研究方向，可先从汉语文献中选择自己感兴趣的章节入手，再及英文著述，半年一年，便会有所心得；三年五载，自当独树一帜。实践表明，知识来源于文献，己见发端于文献，学科推进更是少不了文献。文献的重要性由此可见一斑。

为此，我们组织汇编了这套"系统功能语言学文献丛书"，方便后学查阅细读，揣摩审视。丛书中既有综述介绍，也有前沿研究；有独著，也有合作；作者之中，有德高望重的耄耋长者，有硕果累累的学派中坚，也有勤奋精进的青年才俊。我们想借此机会感谢各位师友积极配合。

本丛书的内容涉及系统功能语言学理论与应用的各个方面，既体现了各位学者在学术领域孜孜不倦的研究历程，也凝结了中国系统功能语言学团队的集体智慧，代表了中国学人在这一领域的研究水平。读者可以看到，其中有不少高水平的成果发表于国外知名期刊，走向了国际学科前沿；有理论开拓，也有应用尝试。

今后，除了国际化和理论探索，本土化与应用研究仍将是一个需要集体努力的基本方向。从理论上看，除了语篇语境、词汇研究和语音书写，研究者还需放眼其他学派和其他学科领域，协同求进，积极从议题上做超学科思考。我们希望，应用研究能够成为各位同仁的责任意识，在诸如翻译理论与操作框架、语言生态视角、外语教育学、汉语系统描写、辞书多元义项梳理、语言过程的计算表征、语言的生理神经机制、语言的脑成像实证研究、语言病理、国家话语等等领域，打开全新的研究局面，取得丰硕的研究成果。

我们衷心感谢上海外语教育出版社对本丛书出版的鼎力支持，感谢各位责编的精心付出。

目　录

第一部分　汉语研究

第二部分　语篇分析

第三部分　语类分析及教学实践

Contents

Part One Studies on Chinese

Part Two Discourse Analysis

PART THREE GENRE ANALYSIS AND TEACHING PRACTICE

图表目录

我的学术生涯

（自序）

1. 引　言

学习和研究系统功能语言学(以下简称 SFL)是我学术生涯的转折点,虽然在此之前,我对语法并无兴趣。记得大学三年级上过一门英语语法课,使用的是苏联语法学家编撰的教科书,一个学期的学习只留下了"枯燥无味"的印象。1982 年我有幸成为教育部第四批公派留澳访问学者,到悉尼大学语言学系学习。出发前我十分忐忑不安,因为觉得与很多学者特别是学长胡壮麟之间有很大的差距:他们的英语基础比我强,在出国之前对语言学已有一定的了解,而且对语言学的研究也有很大的兴趣,因而学习目的非常明确。鉴于我的英语水平较差,也因为大学时期仅有的一点负面体验,似乎语言理论不可能引起我的兴趣,所以我给自己设定了两个可能达到的学习目的:(1) 提高自己的英语水平和英语交际能力;(2) 学好与英语教学相关的理论课程,提高对英语教学的认识,以便回国后能更好地从事英语教学工作。在悉尼大学期间,虽然我认真学习了各门必修课和选修课,而且成绩也不错,但是对语法理论或语言学理论认识仍然相当肤浅。记得在学《普通语言学》这门必修课时,有一次老师留了一个作业,要我们对斯瓦希里语音的特点做一个归纳。我完成了作业,而且也都做对了,但是心里对这种看似与英语教学无关的东西很有抵触,觉得没有什么用处。殊不知这是训练语言学研究者必须做的功课!当然更加突出的例子,就是在韩礼德(M.A.K. Halliday)教授提出由他指导我做硕士论文，在我的课程论文的基础上继续研究汉语的“主位-述位”时，我竟然会说出“我对语言学理论不感兴趣”的话来。现在用什么语言来形容我当时的愚钝都毫不过分！与很多学者不同，“我真正迈进系统功能语言学研究的大门是从教学实践中逐渐领悟出来的”——在《迈进功能语言学的门槛》（见黄国文等 2011）一文中，我比较详细地叙述了我是如何通过讲授研究生的几门课程，才逐渐领悟到语言学理论的实际应用价值的，又如何开始自己的学术研究的，这里不再赘述。本文主要回忆对我学术道路影响至深的两位学者，我与其他一些学者之间的友谊以及他们对我的影响，补充叙述参加国内外学术交流、组织研讨会活动以及教授几门课程和学术研究的情况，最后谈谈对 SFL 发展的个人看法，文中也会谈及经历的一些趣闻逸事。

2. 对我影响至深的两位学者

对我的学术道路影响最大的两位学者先后是胡壮麟教授和韩礼德教授。胡老师是我认识的第一位 SFL 专家。1981 年底经别人介绍，“我去拜访了胡老师，坦率地谈到了我出国留学的多种顾虑。胡老师说了许多鼓励的话，让我打消顾虑，坚定信心，而且建议我一定要攻读应用语言学硕士学位，这样才不会在澳洲白白浪费两年的宝贵时间。这是我第一次见到胡老师，他对我的启示、他的平易近人以及他和蔼可亲老大哥的形象开始印在我的脑海里。回国之后，通过与他的接触，拜读他许多的文章，尤其是与他多年来在功能语言学会的共事，对他有了更深的了解。了解越深对他的为人和学识越加佩服”（见黄国文 2010）。这里主要谈谈协助他举办第一次功能语言学研讨会和第 22 届 SFL 国际大会的情况。

1988 年前后，胡壮麟和徐盛桓两位教授商量在华南师大举办中国第一届功能语言学研讨会。由于他担任北大英语系系主任行政工作非常忙，有些事情就委托我具体与徐老师联系。徐老师代表华南师大积极筹备。但是到了 1989 年初，徐老师来信说经费实在困难，办不成了。但是胡老师还是毅然决定7月份在北大召开这次研讨会，邀请了学术泰斗季羡林、李赋宁、许国璋参加这个具有里程碑意义的学术会议。他们均发表了热情洋溢的讲话，给大家很多鼓励。参加会议的有三十几位学者（胡壮麟1990），包括杨潮光、周光亚、朱永生、张德禄、乐眉云、周晓康、林纪诚、赵建成、王寅、罗建生、王振亚、徐雅琴等。我也带了第一个研究生郑海兰参会。大家在风景秀丽的临湖轩热烈研讨，会议开得很成功。

我对胡老师的为人和他的行政工作领导能力，在1995年举办的第22届国际SFL大会的筹备工作中有了更深的了解。

当时的中国高校经费非常紧张，要解决召开一个有几百人参加的国际会议的经费真是一个头痛的问题。按照国际惯例，大会之前还要举办一个短期培训班，也需要一笔不小的经费。怎么办？幸好，胡老师之前认识了香港理工大学的Terence Lo。我们一起商量，由三所学校共同举办两个活动。胡老师代表北大牵头，大会在北大举行，我代表清华大学举办暑期短训班，Terence Lo负责解决经费问题。我得到当时我校外语系主任程慕胜教授的全力支持。培训班和在北京大学召开的第22届国际SFL大会都举办得很成功，对推动SFL在我国和其他国家的发展产生了积极的影响。会后胡老师和我共同编辑了论文集《功能语言学在中国的进展》（1997）。以后我和胡老师除了在中国的功能语言学和语篇分析会议期间见面之外，我会经常打电话向胡老师请教很多问题，他都耐心地一一回答。2000年之后，我和胡老师两家又都搬到同一个小区居住，交流更加方便。除了通话，我们还经常在小区锻炼或散步时见面聊天，我有时还向胡老师的夫人陈大夫讨教烹饪技巧。陈大夫对人非常和善热情，她不仅是胡老师的"私人保健医生"，我也把她看作我的好朋友和保健、烹饪"顾问"。胡老师虽然已八十几岁，但是他仍然勤奋耕耘在SFL和各个不同的学术领域，不断推出新著，令人钦羡佩服！他永远是我学习的榜样！

韩礼德是我的老师，我的学术领路人。在悉尼大学语言学系，我上了他的两门课程——"功能语言学概论"和"语言学入门"，开阔了我的眼界，也为我以后迈进功能语言学的大门做了铺垫。记得我们所有的中国访问学者都去旁听了"语言学入门"。这是一门语言学系本科生一年级的必修课，内容涉及很广，韩礼德从世界一些古老文字的发展到语言的种类、语言的共性和区别做了详细的介绍。我很喜欢韩礼德的教学方式。虽然是几百人的大课，他的课不但条理清晰、生动有趣，他还很注意与学生的交流。比如讲到中国的民族和语言的情况，他问我们这些中国听众他讲的对不对，我们不知如何回答，因为当时我们自己不甚了了，只好一言不发，真觉得难为情！“功能语言学概论”理论性较强，为了让同学们理解基本要点，他会分析许多小句或短小的语篇，实际上就是在实践他创导的将功能语言学的理论，用于语篇分析的宗旨（Halliday 1985）。他鼓励大家提问，或者对某个问题展开讨论。“他赞赏学生提出具有挑战性的问题。我在研究生中是属于比较喜欢提问的，提出一些问题有时很难回答。他不但不生气，反而觉得我肯动脑筋。在撰写他的《功能语言学概论》课程论文期间，我经常带着问题去请教他，以致他称我为‘a basket of questions’”（黄国文等 2011）。

虽然韩礼德当时已经名震国际语言学界，但是他为人非常谦和，仅举两个例子。记得上他课的澳大利亚或外国学生都直呼其名，称他“Michael”。中国学生包括我自己都非常不习惯，我不管在什么场合均称他为“Professor”。过了相当一段时间，他有一次跟我说：“You are the only one who calls me ‘Professor’”，我只好勉强改口。不过这样也似乎真的拉近了我们之间的距离，慢慢地我将他看作像自己父亲一样的好朋友。还有一件小事也让我念念不忘。1983 年秋，他在离开中国三十几年后再次访问中国，应邀在北外和上外做学术访问。记得期间我收到他专门写给我的一封信，谈到他愉快的访问经历，还提到在北外讲学时碰到我的一位清华同事。收到信我很惊喜，根本没有想到他会给我写信，我也回了一封信表示感谢，可惜他寄给我的这封信没能保存下来。

20 世纪 90 年代初，我读到一篇三位学者贡特尔·克雷斯（Gunther Kress）、韩茹凯（Ruqaiya Hasan）和詹姆斯·马丁（James R. Martin）对韩礼德的采访（*Social Semiotics*, 1992）全文。韩礼德细述了他的学术经历，尤其是他为什么对中国和汉语情有独钟，为什么会走上语言学研究的道路，使我对他有了更深的了解。他谈到在四五岁时就梦想到中国来，就对中国非常向往，让我倍感亲切。这样的采访形式也启发了我邀请他与胡壮麟和朱永生两位教授，在第 36 届 SFL 国际大会上就学派的现状和发展进行了对话（2010），谈话给大家留下了深刻的印象，黄国文教授还撰文解读（2010），为大家理清了思路。

这里要补充 1995 年在清华举办暑期短训班发生的两件逸事。一件是我主观地认为韩礼德一定能流利地使用中文，因为他本科就开始学习中文，而且在20世纪40年代末在中国师从王力、罗常培学习过三年，所以我没有跟他商量，就安排了请他做一个多小时的中文报告。他一听就急了，发了脾气，真把我吓了一跳。后来经韩茹凯慢慢劝慰，他才同意这个安排，最后做了一个非常精彩的讲座。记得当时来听讲座的还有我校中文系的袁老师（现在已转到北大中文系），讲座之中他还提了问题，与韩礼德用中文交流，袁老师很高兴，大家反应也很好，我这才松了口气。但是我确实对他三十几年没有机会使用过中文，一定会有很多困难体谅不够，心里很抱歉。还有一件就是有关他于1987年退休的事。他的学生们都认为他才62岁就退休，太早了；而且他退下来之后，系主任工作由年轻的没有行政工作经验的詹姆斯·马丁接替，结果影响了SFL在悉尼大学的发展，使我们这些原来喜欢这个系的学生都非常失望。我在短训班期间去宾馆看望他和韩茹凯时，就直截了当地询问，他为什么那么早退休让别的学派占了上风，他一时不知如何回答，最后还是韩茹凯说了什么，缓和了气氛。给我的印象，似乎这个问题也真触动了他。

以后韩礼德多次访问北京，我与他在不同场合多次见面，一有机会我就会邀请他来清华大学讲学。最让我难忘的是2003年春我和黄国文教授商量，由中山大学和清华大学共同邀请韩礼德和韩茹凯到我们两校讲学一事。刚刚商定不久，就发生了非典。还邀请他们来吗？几经商量，最后还是让他们来了。不料他们到广州以后，非典形势越来越严重，我非常着急，真害怕出现意外。黄老师后来告诉我，他每天都收到胡老师原来的澳洲学生马爱德的电子信件，催促他马上让韩礼德夫妇回国，否则发生意外，不好向国际语言学界交代。可是韩礼德夫妇却从容不迫，没有丝毫惊恐。他们不仅在中山大学成功做了学术访问，还兴致勃勃游览了广西桂林。我非常担心他们的身体，几乎每天电话询问他们的身体状况，回答都是"Very well"。后来两位还到云南大学作讲座，吸引了多达500多位听众。接着他们又受西安外国语大学杜瑞清教授的邀请飞往西安，在那里做了学术报告，还兴致盎然地参观了兵马俑和其他名胜古迹。他们后来告诉我，那是一次最好的游览，因为非典，景点几乎没有别的游客。可是他们的访问只能止步于西安。如果来京，将会马上隔离，根本谈不上做什么学术报告。这样，他们只好回国了。我感到非常遗憾，让清华和北京几所高校的师生们失去了一次向他们学习的好机会。但他们非典时期在中国访问期间的从容态度也真让我敬佩！

韩礼德虽然不是我硕士学位论文的导师，但是在过去三十年中他对我的学术研究一直非常关心，也非常提携。无论是国际还是国内会议，如果有我的发言，不管是主题报告还是分会场的发言，他必定到场，有时还提出问题，对我是莫大的鼓励。比如 2004 年我们都参加了日本京都第 31 届 SFL 国际大会，我在分会上作了"功能语言学与电影语篇分析"的发言；2005 年我回到悉尼大学参加第 32 届 SFL 国际大会，并在分会上作了有关《论语》语篇分析的发言（Fang Yan，2006），他都坐在观众席上认真听取而且不时记录。这里特别要提到两次在香港城市大学做主题报告的情况，因为都与韩礼德教授有关。2006 年香港城市大学成立了由卫真道（Jonathan Webster）教授牵头的"韩礼德语言研究智能应用中心"（下称"韩礼德中心"），中国几位学者胡壮麟、黄国文、朱永生和我应邀出席并做主题发言。我的题目是"A Study of Topical Theme in Chinese: An SFL Perspective"。我报告时大家提了不少问题，还有的学者很坦率地对我说："做汉语研究吃力不讨好。"我也感到自己的研究不很深入，心情不太好。但是韩礼德却亲切地跟我说："学术研究上出现争论，没有关系，如果发现问题，以后还可以修正。"他宽慰我的一席话给了我很大的鼓励，让我至今念念不忘。会后我又认真读了有关的资料、做了更加深入的研究，最后成文，被收集于卫真道（Jonathan Webster）主编的 *Meaning in Context* 一书中（2008）。2007 年，韩礼德中心成立之后举办了第一次比较大型的会议，会议的主题是：Becoming a World Language: The Growth of Chinese, English and Spanish。我受到韩礼德本人的特别邀请代表中国做主题发言，这是给我的极大荣誉，同时我也感到有很大的压力。我的发言题目是："The Growth of Chinese: A Systemic Functional Perspective on the Expansion of Meaning Potential"。后来将题目稍作修改，收于黄国文等主编的论文集（2011）。大会发言受到韩礼德和韩茹凯两位教授的肯定和来自不同国家学者的鼓励，让我受到很大的鼓舞。韩礼德还就个别英语措辞给我提出建议，我非常感激。

2015 年是韩礼德教授的九十诞辰，北师大功能语言学研究中心在召开第十四届中国功能语言学研讨会期间，为他举办了盛大的庆祝活动。我应邀就"Warm Memories of My Academic Advisors"做了发言，表达对韩礼德和韩茹凯两位教授多年来给我学术指导的深切感谢；我参加了"韩礼德—韩茹凯语言学国际基金"成立的报告会；还在他的生日晚宴上唱了一首20世纪30年代就在美国工人运动中流行的英语歌"We Shall Not Be Moved"。我将歌词稍作修改(将原来的 With the union behind us, we shall not be moved. 改为 With Michael behind us, …!),以表达我们将永远行进在 SFL 研究道路上的决心,也表达了祝愿韩礼德教授身体安康、健康长寿的祝福!

3. 与其他学者的深厚友谊

首先要提到的是,我与 SFL 著名学者韩茹凯、詹姆斯·马丁、克里斯蒂安·马蒂森(Christian Matthiessen)之间的友谊和他们对我学术研究的影响。

虽然韩茹凯教授不是我的老师,但我一直是她的仰慕者,是一位在我学术成长的道路上给过我多方面帮助和指导的学者。认识韩茹凯教授始于1984年。韩礼德邀请她给我们研究生做了一次精彩的学术报告,至今我还保留那次报告的照片,可谓弥足珍贵!1984年暑假我们中国留学生受到韩礼德夫妇的邀请到他们家做客,受到他们的热情款待;2005年的第32届 SFL 国际大会后,我们又受到韩礼德夫妇邀请,与许多参会者一起到他们的新家做客。这两次聚会,她都亲自下厨,做了很多有南亚风味的美食,至今令人回味。特别让我难忘的是1995年,她接受我代表清华大学的邀请,与韩礼德及其他两位国际著名学者到我校在"功能语言学暑期研讨班"上做了三个星期的学术讲座,为中国培养了一批当今在功能语言学界都很有影响的学者。令我感动的是,由于我申请不到经费,是他们两位自掏腰包购买的往返机票,才使这次学术活动能顺利进行。我还要感谢她于1992年部分资助我参加了她主持的第19届 SFL 国际大会,并将我的论文"On Theme in Chinese: From clause to discourse"收入由她和弗里斯(Peter Fries)主编的 *On Subject and Theme: A discourse functional perspective* 一书之中(Hasan & Fries, 1995)。其间她与我频繁联系,提出了许多宝贵意见。以后在多次的学术会议中她都对我的发言给予鼓励,并提出中肯的意见和建议，让我心中充满了深深的谢意。可能由于我们都是东方女性，性格又都比较直爽，所以几次接触之后就成为好朋友。她在中国作学术报告，我很荣幸多次为她主持。2011 年，她提议由我为她的《韩茹凯应用语言学自选集》撰写中文序言，让我深感荣幸。2015 年，彭宣维教授又提议让我为她的《韩茹凯论语言》的中译本写序，我不仅感到荣幸还感到压力山大。我尽力尽为，但愿没有让她失望，只愿我对她渊博的知识、深邃的洞见、严谨的科研作风的敬佩之情能充分表达出来。

"韩茹凯对中国怀有深厚的感情，一直对中国功能语言学的发展非常关心，曾给予过多方面的指导。自 20 世纪 90 年代，她与韩礼德一起参加过在杭州、苏州、北京、上海、南昌、厦门的中国功能语言学和语篇分析会议，还应邀在清华大学、中山大学、北京师范大学、云南大学、西安外国语大学、北京科技大学做过学术报告，2006 年后还担任中国香港城市大学'韩礼德中心'研究规划主任，对推动中国功能语言学的发展做出了贡献，在中国功能语言学者中产生了很大的影响"（方琰，见韩茹凯，2011）。彭宣维教授跟我提到，"韩礼德—韩茹凯语言学国际基金"事实上就是由她提议建立的，而且她和韩礼德捐助了第一笔款项。但是由于她病重，不能来京出席庆贺典礼，很是遗憾。参会的所有她的朋友惦念她的健康，寄去了一封签有大家名字的明信片。但是不幸的是她一病不起，没能痊愈。2015 年 6 月 24 日下午，我突然接到彭宣维教授电话，告诉我韩茹凯教授因肺癌不幸去世。听到噩耗，我非常难过，好些天都沉浸在悲痛之中。她的离世不仅让韩礼德失去了他钟爱的生活伴侣和学术知音，也让世界语言学界，痛失一位"热衷于社会研究的语言学家"。国内外许多学者都表达了对她的敬佩和悼念之情，我也马上给韩礼德教授发去唁电。韩茹凯教授度过了美好的一生，为系统功能语言学做出了杰出的贡献。她将永远活在我们心中！

除了韩礼德夫妇对我的深刻影响，我必须要提到国际上两位杰出的语言学家，一位是詹姆斯·马丁教授，一位是克里斯蒂安·马蒂森教授。马丁是我悉尼大学求学期间的老师，当时他是一位带有一些叛逆性格的很帅气的年轻人。记得我和他住在同一条街上，回家的路上常常会看到他戴着头盔，骑着自行车飞驰而过的身影。我至今忘不了的是，他给我们研究生上"语言学流派"的情况。当时的教室里没有电子设备，只有黑板。他用左手在黑板上画的各个学派相互联系的树形图至今历历在目，这个图帮助我理清了杰弗里·桑普森(Geoffrey Sampson)1980年出版的《语言学流派》一书中提到的各个学派之间的关系和它们之间的异同,也为我回国后讲授"语言学流派"打下了很好的理论基础。在这里我要向马丁教授深深致谢。他还是一位烹饪高手,记得1992年我在悉尼参加第19届SFL国际大会之后,受到他的邀请到他家做客,品尝到他亲自下厨做的鲜美的饭菜。之后,他陆续给我寄来他的新作,包括《英语文本:系统与结构》(*English Text: System and Structure*, 1992)、《功能语法实探》(*Working with Functional Grammar*,与Matthiessen和Painter合著,1997)、《语篇实探》(*Working with Discourse*,与Rose合著,2003)等,使我及时了解学术研究前沿,为我的教学和科研提供了宝贵的资源。随着新世纪的到来,马丁开始了他对中国的学术访问,加强了与中国学者的交流。2001年,在加拿大开会期间,我推荐李战子到他那里做访问学者,他很爽快,欣然同意。2012年我在北京三个不同的学校——清华、北大、北师大为他组织了每次一周的高级研修班(详见4.1)。此时他的讲课风格有了很大的改变,他更注重与学生之间的交流,更注重与学生们讨论SFL有关语篇语义学最前沿的理论和实践问题,更注重启发学生的思维,让学生自己对小句或语篇做出具体分析。一个星期的研修讨论,学生们收获颇丰。马丁还是珍惜时间的典范,他每次都是开讲的前一个晚上到达,最后一次课的第二天立即启程回国,是一心扑在科研上的学者,值得钦佩!

马蒂森教授是我在1989年3月参加西安交通大学举办的"The International Conference on Text and Language Research"的会议上认识的。会议由郝克琦教授和荷兰著名学者赫尔曼·布卢默(Hermann Bluhme)发起和主持。有相当多的来自欧洲的学者,包括马蒂森。他与约翰·贝特曼(John Bateman)一起向大会作了"Uncovering the Text Base",我也就汉语的主位与述位做了大会主题发言(Keqi Hao, H. Bluhme, Renzhi Li, 1993)。1991年和1993年我们又都参加了杭州大学外国语学院任绍曾院长主办的中国第一、第二届语篇分析研讨会。1993年会后,本来说好我请他到我的家乡千岛湖游览,可是因为我因患心脏病刚刚出院身体较弱,没能成行,很是遗憾。马蒂森教授是个脾气温和的学者,很容易沟通,很快我们就变成了好朋友。1992年,他和澳中友协出资让我在参加第19届SFL国际大会之后,在悉尼大学做了两个月的科学研究,让我再一次享受在悉尼大学Fisher Library阅读的机会。当时弗里斯(Peter H. Fries)夫妇也在悉尼大学访问,就住在他家。记得我和马蒂森教授的一个中国学生一起包了很多饺子,虽然面和得有点软,但大家似乎还是很喜欢。第二年,他写了一本很厚的书 *Lexicogrammatical Cartography*,由居住在日本的一位华人学者联系在日本出版,这位朋友还与我联系,看是否能在中国出版,我几经打听,出版费太高,没有办成,很是遗憾。马蒂森教授给我寄来了原稿的复印件,让我有幸成为第一批阅读的学者,使我对他的"修辞结构"(rhetoric structure)理论、对语言系统的概念有了更深的理解,为我的教学和科研提供了珍贵的资料。后来他还寄来了与约翰·贝特曼合著的 *Text Generation and Systemic-functional Linguistics: Experiences from English and Japanese*(1991),让我对语言生成的可能性有了具体的认识,也让我更加佩服他在计算语言学和语言类型学方面的学识。后来我和马蒂森教授经常通过电子邮件交往,也邀请他到清华做过报告。他移居香港担任理工大学外语系主任之后,因为传统上清华大学外文系与他们有学术往来,每年都轮流组织英语教学研讨会,因而他也经常访问我们校园。2009 年在清华举办的第 36 届 SFL 国际大会之前,他很热心地向我提出过许多建议,还接受我的邀请在大会上作了精彩的报告。马蒂森教授是系统功能学派内理论研究最深的学者之一,同时又是通晓计算语言学的专家。他做的电子课件让所有人折服,无人可匹敌。我们现在并不经常通信,只在各种会议上见面,但仍然是很好的朋友。

可能因为我参加国际会议较多,又担任过两届国际 SFL 执行委员会副主席(2002－2008),因而在国际上认识的学者也比较多。比如,罗宾·福西特(Robin Fawcett)教授就是我参加 1992 年第 19 届悉尼 SFL 国际大会上认识的。尽管我对他的像灯笼一样的理论图解方式了解不深,但他执着的科研精神、他真诚热情对待朋友的态度给我留下极深的印象。记得我请他详细地介绍了 SFL 研讨会发展的脉络,因为他是最初会议的发起人。我也详细记录,打算回国后撰文介绍。后来因为种种原因,没有成文,很是遗憾。但是我们也成了很好的朋友。他有理由为 SFL 会议从很小规模的讨论会,变成了每年在四大洲轮流举办的年会做出的贡献感到自豪! 而且他培养了像黄国文等一批出色的中国学者,很值得他骄傲!

我还与四位国际功能语言会执行委员会主席打过交道。2001 年在加拿大开会期间,当时的主席克里斯廷·戴维泽(Kristin Davidse)突然找我谈话,出乎我的意料,她问我是否愿意担任下一届的副主席。考虑到自己的资历太浅，我婉拒了。但是第二年在利物浦的年会上还是被当选了。之后我代表中国担任了两届副主席，先后与两位主席——美国学者切奇利娅·科隆比（Cecilia Colombi）教授和澳大利亚学者杰夫·威廉姆斯（Geoff Williams）教授共事，让我对学会的管理和流程有了更深的了解，通过后来与他们在不同场合的交往，也加深了我与两位学者的友谊。2008年执委会改选，英国的杰夫·汤普森（Geoff Thompson）教授被选为主席，黄国文教授代表中国担任副主席。汤普森是2002年利物浦大学国际年会的主办人。我记得非常清楚，整个会议都是由他和他优雅热情的夫人苏姗操办的，效率令人佩服！在准备2009年的第36届SFL国际大会过程中，我也得到汤普森的大力支持，很多有关会议的事项都是与他协商之后才决定下来的。会后他又给了大会很高的评价，在给我的贺信中说到，本次会议是"成功而令人愉快的"，"许多年以后，人们会依然记起它，尤其是作为中国系统功能语言学发展史上的一个里程碑。"

下面我必须提到的就是香港城市大学的韩礼德语言研究智能应用中心主任卫真道教授。他不仅邀请我两次在他主办的研讨会上做主题发言，还代表他的学校与清华大学共同主办了第36届大会。包括大会的标志设计、邀请主要发言人、日程、经费等事宜，都是我们共同协商决定的。他行政工作的高效率、组织能力令人敬佩！虽然他很遗憾不能来参加会议，但是他同我一起主编了 *Developing Systemic Functional Linguistics*（Fang & Webster, 2014），收集了大会主要发言者的论文，展现了最近十几年这个学派的最新成果。

当然我不可能忘记温迪·鲍切尔（Wendy Bowcher），一位澳籍女学者。她曾多年旅居日本，在东京学芸大学任教，并一度担任日本系统功能语言学会（JASFL，"日本機能言語学会"）主席。2005年，受到她的邀请，我参加了在东京学芸大学举办的JASFL年会，并做大会发言。现在她受邀任中山大学外国语学院教授。2008年，我在厦门大学第十届语篇分析会上做过分析《清明上河图》的大会发言，她似乎很感兴趣，邀请我撰写有关这幅长卷的多媒体论文"A Multisemiotic Analysis of Chinese Long Scroll Painting"，收于她编辑的 *Multimodal Texts from Around the World: Cultural and Linguistic Insights*（Bowcher 2012）。她的编辑工作极其细致、深入，从文字到画面都给我提出了许多宝贵意见和建议，令人难忘。非常感谢她给了我一个与五大洲学者在书中交流的机会。

国内的学者,因限于篇幅,我只提三位教授——张德禄、朱永生、任绍曾。张德禄是我留澳的同班同学,比我小十五岁,1982 年才 27 岁,是一个令人羡慕的年龄。他给人的印象是不善言辞、老实憨厚。因为毕业于一所名不见经传的地方院校,因而开始学习阶段受到一些阻力。澳大利亚规定只有名校毕业的学者才能直读硕士学位,所以他只能从预备生读起。可是这并没有消减他攻读语言学的热情。由于他出色的学习成绩,第二年很快就赢得了韩礼德的赏识,不仅顺利拿到学位,而且从此以后一心一意钻研学问,在语言学的理论和应用方面做出了令人钦羡的成绩。回忆在一起的两年时光,我们不仅同时上课,还经常相互切磋,他也给了我不少帮助;我们还一起参加了许多澳中友协组织的活动,一起游览了悉尼、墨尔本、阿德雷德,一起度过的快乐时光令人难忘!

朱永生比我们晚来澳大利亚一年。他最初被"发配"到澳洲南部的一座小城阿德雷德的大学做访问学者,令他非常不快。他随即给韩礼德教授写信要求转到悉尼大学,他诚挚的申请得到了韩礼德的同意,成为我的同学和好朋友。虽然我们在一起学习的机会不多,但他给人的印象深刻:英语口语流利、发音准确,中英文的写作能力都很强。而且他才思敏捷、领会理论的能力很突出。我们在澳洲相处一年,也度过了一段值得回忆的时光。他现在是中国 SFL 杰出的语言学研究者之一,他在多次会议上的发言令我印象深刻,也让我佩服。

任绍曾教授是我另一位老大哥。和他的结缘始于 1991 年他召开的全国第一届语篇分析会议。那时他是杭州大学外语学院院长,邀请了弗里斯做客座教授。弗里斯也是一位系统功能语言学家,是他力促举办了这个语篇分析会议。这次研讨会,任绍曾教授邀请了复旦大学的程雨民教授和广东外语外贸大学的桂诗春教授做主题报告,两位老先生的治学态度和深厚的语言学和应用语言学功底让人敬佩。此后任老师又连续在杭大举办过全国功能语言学第二届研讨会和第二次语篇分析会议。后来于 1997 年,任老师和我分别代表澳门大学和清华大学在澳门共同举办过一次国际语篇研讨会,邀请了韩礼德夫妇、克里斯蒂安·马蒂森等著名学者做大会发言。任绍曾教授不仅是中国语篇会议的发起人,也是我国研究叶斯柏森(Otto Jespersen)的著名专家,在国内多个一流语言学刊物上发表过很有分量的论文,还培养了许多优秀的外语人才。无论是他的学识还是他的为人都令我非常尊敬。

4. 参加会议及学术交流情况

4.1 参加与组织国际、国内会议

参加学术研讨会、与同行学者交流,不仅让我加深了对相关领域的理论和实践的认识,更重要的是扩大了我的视野,促进了我的学术研究。国内我只参加两个学术研讨会:功能语言学和语篇分析。一是因为本人精力和学术水平都有限,不能像胡老师和其他一些学者那样积极参与多个学术团体的活动;二是因为这两个研讨会关系密切,前者侧重研讨功能语言学的理论与应用,后者着重应用功能语言学理论或其他理论,分析和阐释语篇语义;更重要的是功能语言学派内部团结,学者们互相学习、互相谦让,很好共事。

除了在东北和内蒙古举办的两次会议,我记得出席了几乎所有有关这两个研讨会的会议,包括在北京大学、杭州大学、苏州大学、复旦大学、洛阳解放军外院、湘潭师院、西南师大、重庆大学、澳门大学、山东大学、燕山大学、河南大学、厦门大学、绍兴文理学院、江西师大、南京师大、华中师大、同济大学、清华大学、中山大学、长安大学、北师大、宁波大学举办的各届会议,并在大部分的会上作过主题发言。此外我还两次参加了香港城市大学《韩礼德语言研究智能应用中心》举办的研讨会,并分别作了主题报告。

作为韩礼德的学生,后来又在教学中得益于 SFL 理论的指导,我觉得应当与有兴趣的同行们分享自己的体会,应当为传播 SFL 尽一份义务。因此,我比较积极参与组织国内的一些学术活动或在一些院校作学术报告。如前所述,我参与了 1995 年第 22 届国际大会的一些组织工作,并负责举办会前的暑期培训班。我还于 1997 年代表清华大学与当时在澳门大学任职的任绍曾教授,共同举办了一个国际语篇分析研讨会。2009 年又代表清华大学举办、主持了第 36 届 SFL 国际大会暨第 11 届全国功能语言学研讨会,于 2012 年为马丁在北京组织了三次高级研修班。下面着重介绍 1995 年大会会前的暑期培训班、2009 的第 36 届 SFL 国际大会、

2012 年的高级研修班。

1995 年的暑期培训班，邀请了韩礼德、韩茹凯及玛格丽特·贝里（Margaret Berry）和艾佳·文托拉（Eija Ventola）四位国际知名学者轮流作了十几天的讲授，130 多名学员来自 10 个国家和地区，包括现在一些国内外语言学界的领军人物如马蒂森以及杨永林、李战子、高一虹、刘世生、张克定等，为推进功能语言学做了一点自己的贡献。

2009 年 7 月 14 日至 18 日在清华大学，我主持召开了第 36 届 SFL 国际大会暨第 11 届研讨会。我领导和参与了全过程的策划、组织工作。大会的主题是“系统功能语言学在理论和实践上面临的挑战”。参加会议的正式代表共 300 多人，来自世界五大洲的 22 个国家和地区，共宣读论文 250 余篇。议题主要涉及 SFL 在理论上的发展、在不同语言、领域和语境中的应用及其所面临的挑战（庞玉厚、方琰、刘世生 2010；方琰 2010）。关于这次国际大会，想补充几点体会。第一，举办国际会议是一项非常复杂的事情，而且有时会遇到预想不到的情况。2009 年春天发生了 H1N1 流感，北京的形势相当紧张。清华外办不鼓励召开国际会议，但是我们会议的准备工作已经进行了一大半，而且参会者已经开始了报名，国外学者非常踊跃，有的已经将会费汇了过来，弄得我们骑虎难下。会议团队讨论了好几次，最后决定按原计划进行，但是我们采取了内松外紧的做法：在会议举办的宾馆内加强消毒防疫，做好物资准备，一有情况马上采取措施。期间发生了一段很有趣的插曲。那次流感始发墨西哥，清华外办要求一定要阻止墨西哥学者参会。记得当时真有一位叫纳塔利娅（Natalia）的俄籍墨西哥学者坚持要来，我给她写了好几封电子邮件劝阻她，告诉她如果来，下了飞机马上就会隔离。可是她说因为参会的款项已经拨下来了，她的领导要她一定来，她夹在中间不知如何是好。有一段时间，我们几乎天天电子邮件来往，我婉拒，她坚持，我真不知该如何收场。后来她想出了一个办法——提早九天来京，如果发生情况她隔离后还可参会。我没有办法，只好同意，结果她不但来了，还带来她的家人，而且一切顺利。我们见面时，大家哈哈一笑，还成了好朋友！第二，会议的主办单位，不仅要考虑会议的经费问题，还要考虑会议的主要发言人、时间地点、收费标准、紧急事件的处理办法等细节安排。对于主题发言人应广泛征求国内外学者的意见。我们这次大会邀请了有影响力的九位学者，但是忽略了我们是代表亚洲的举办国，应当邀请更多的亚洲有代表性的学者做主题报告。

第三,这次大会还出现了有少数中国学者不按时到场或不宣读自己论文的现象,使一两个分会场不能按计划进行,打乱了会议的安排。这是我们事先没有预料到的。2015 年北师大功能语言学研讨会,想出为每位发言的学者颁发证书的主意,是个积极鼓励的措施,可以有效避免此类事情的发生。

2012 年我与北大的高一虹教授和北师大的彭宣维教授合作,在三个不同的学校——清华、北大、北师大为马丁教授分别组织了每次一周的高级研修班。马丁拟定了比较详细的计划,要求研修班成员最好固定不变,都能参加每一期的学习。研修班第一期四月在清华举办,第二期安排于九月在北师大,最后一次十二月在北大,每次相隔几个月,好让参加者读书、消化、吸收。这个学术活动也是一波三折。本来似乎清华有可能搞到一笔经费成立"适用语言学中心",马丁听了非常高兴。我与他积极筹备,通过大量的电子信件来往,但是后来经费成了问题,就只好仅仅举办高级研修班了。好在研修班进行顺利,三个星期的研修讨论,学生们收获颇丰。

我可能是国内参加 SFL 国际会议比较多的学者,先后参加过 1992 年第 19 届(澳大利亚麦考利大学)、1995 年第 22 届(北京大学)、2001 年第 28 届(加拿大卡尔顿大学)、2002 年第 29 届(英国利物浦大学)、2004 年第 31 届(日本京都)、2005 年第 32 届(澳大利亚悉尼大学)、2007 年第 34 届(丹麦欧登塞大学)、2009 年第 36 届(清华大学)、2013 年第 40 届(中山大学)举办的各届国际会议。此外,2005 年我还应温迪·鲍切尔的邀请,参加在东京学芸大学举办的 JASFL 年会,并作大会主题报告。

4.2 作学术报告及参与其他学术交流活动

我知道自己的理论和实践水平都有限,因而我为自己确定了学术报告的目的是普及这个学派的理论与实践。先后分别在北京大学、中山大学、西南师大、重庆大学、香港理工大学、香港城市大学、北师大、北科大、深圳大学、广西大学、绍兴文理学院、北京信息工程学院、西安外国语大学、兰州铁道学院(现兰州交通大学)、成都理工大学和浙江海洋学院(现浙江海洋大学)等院校做过学术报告。自 2003 年至 2007 年,我接受浙江海洋学院的聘请担任了该校外国语学院的名誉院长,之后我仍为他们的客座教授。其间,每年都会去一次或数次。我给自己设立了两个任务:一是帮助他们建立起一支学术队伍,积极开展各种学术活动;二是在教师中推广功能语言学理论和语篇分析。第一年我去了三次,成立了不同的科研小组,以后每年在学院内组织学术报告,交流科研心得。从 2005 年开始,我和这个学院的老师一起应用语类教学理念,做了十几年的写作教学实验,取得了一些成绩。每次有机会去,我不仅作学术报告,汇报我自己在 SFL 理论或语篇分析取得的成果,还聆听参加实验课老师的各类课程,与实验团队研讨总结取得的进步、存在的问题、改进的措施。平常还通过电子邮件与他们交流,也为他们修改过好几篇论文,发表在核心刊物上。其他各个科研小组也开展了自己的活动,与十几年前相比,这所院校的科研面貌发生了很大的变化,让我感到非常欣慰。

5. 教授的课程和研究生培养

1985 年我们系开始招收硕士生班,系里要我担任一些研究生的课程,我决定开设两门课程:"功能语言学概论"和"语言学流派"。后来考虑我本身特点,我改上"功能语言学概论"和"应用语言学"两门课程,同时还先后上了本科生高年级的阅读课和写作课。教学中我特别注重把 SFL 的研究成果应用到教学中去。

5.1 "功能语言学概论"和"应用语言学"

跟所有教授"功能语言学概论"的老师一样,我使用的教科书是韩礼德编写的第一版 *An Introduction to Functional Grammar*(1985)。90 年代以前,我担任恢复英语专业的第一任主任(清华大学 1952 年院系调整之后,取消了英语专业,主要教授都去了北大和北外。清华大学从一所综合性大学变成了一所理工科大学。英语专业 1983 年复建,1984 年初我一回国就被任命为专业主任)。当时的人力资源非常有限,管理一个新的专业几乎占据了我全部的时间,没有充裕的时间让我准备研究生的课程,我只能利用假期和周末备课。除了教科书,我后来还参考了多部有关书籍,例如 *An Introduction to Systemic-Functional Linguistics*(Eggins 1994)、*Introducing Functional Grammar*(G. Thompson 1996)、*Working With Functional Grammar*(Martin, Matthissen & Painter 1997)等。我自己还编写了一本近 100 页的教材,用简单的语言总结出教科书每个章节的要点,并补充有关系统的概念。我学习韩礼德的教学方法,先把基本要点讲解清楚,然后举例说明,将理论与语篇分析结合起来。为了给《功能语言学概论》提供语篇分析的素材,我和两位同事编写了一本教材《经典影片精彩片段语言评析》(方琰等 2001)。我尝试应用功能语言学的理论,用通俗的语言分析了从每部经典英语影片(包括 *The Sound of Music*、*Casablanca*、*Roman Holiday*、*On Golden Pond*、*Forrest T. Gump* 等十部)中选择的四五个片段的精彩对话。由于"功能语言学概论"的学时有限,我就将它与"应用语言学"结合起来进行教学。除了把"应用语言学"的基本概念讲清楚之外,我会在课堂上引导学生做比较多的语篇和句子分析,以巩固有关功能的概念。

教授这两门课的体会是:首先自己要把主要的概念搞懂,尽量使用通俗的、清晰的语言讲授,后来又配以制作较好的演示文稿,让学生们感受到语言和语言学的魅力。这些年来,我多次听到有些院校的师生反映说,语言学教学仍然非常"boring"或"没有一点意思"。我想主要的原因恐怕有两个:(1)教师没有完全明白主要的概念或内容,要么课堂上照本宣科,要么教学充斥了自己都没弄懂的专业术语;(2)教师授课方式或使用的语言恐怕不够得当。如果学生认为语言学就是"枯燥无味",这是教学的极大失败,非常影响学生对语言学的学习和研究兴趣!我自己的科研成果不突出,但是值得自己自豪的是,我的课多年来一直都受到学生的好评,并得到过学校的嘉奖。

5.2 "高级英语"和高年级"写作课"

"高级英语"课正好是我实践语篇分析的好机会。我把功能语言学的理论和分析方法应用到阅读课教学中,改变了逐词逐句教学的传统。教学的目的是让学生了解语篇表达的语义通过哪些手段来实现、达到了什么效果。根据不同课文的语类,我和学生一起分析了每篇课文的功能特点,有的分析主位分布与课文主题的关系,有的分析情态、意态词汇用法的变化对塑造人物的作用,有的观察衔接手段与连贯之间的关系,有的分析课文中出现的动词及物系统的特点和产生的特有语义等等。后来我把自己的教学体验写在了论文"Applications of Functional Grammar to the Teaching of the Advanced Reading Course"(朱永生 1993)中。为了更好地教授研究生课程和高级阅读课,我还对语篇分析的研究步骤和方法做了一点探讨,写了"系统功能语法与语篇分析"(2005)一文。

在高年级写作课中,我实验使用韩茹凯的 GSP 理论(H & H 1985),让学生学写不同语类的作文,了解不同语类语篇的语义成分、语义成分的排序顺序以及必要成分与可选成分的差异或区别,培养学生的语类意识。之后又指导一名硕士研究生在非英语专业的学生中继续试验,也取得了较好的结果。这是我后来在浙江海洋学院推行语类教学法(见本文 4.2)的基础,这里不再赘述。我的研究兴趣和科研情况在"迈进功能语言学的门槛"(见黄国文等 2011)一文中有比较详细的介绍,本文上面几个部分也多有涉及,不再单独叙述。

6. 对系统功能语言学在中国发展的几点思考

"从韩礼德教授 1955 年完成他的博士论文《元朝秘史》提出他对语言学的初步构思,至今整整过去了六十年;从他于 20 世纪 60 年代初创建系统功能语言学,迄今也走过了半个世纪的路程"(方琰,见韩茹凯 2015)。如今这个学派已发展成国际语言学界的主流学派之一。自 80 年代起,由胡壮麟等语言学家将 SFL 引入中国至今也有三十几个年头,它也成为中国语言学界一支颇有影响力的语言学派。在看到 SFL 蓬勃发展的同时,我们更应该清醒地看到发展中面临的种种挑战。我在"迈进功能语言学的门槛”（见黄国文等，2011）一文中阐述了几点看法：（1）要充分认识语言的复杂性，因为“Language is probably the most complex phenomenon in the universe”（Halliday，“Interview” 2010），这会在很大程度上影响我们研究语言采取的态度和方法。（2）中国的 SFL 研究者应当从我们的祖先所创造的哲学思想中汲取宝贵的营养，指导我们对语言学的研究。将西方不断解剖、分解的思维方法与中国注重整体的、宏观的思维方法结合起来研究语言，因为一个整体很可能往往大于各个部分的总和。（3）加强对语篇分析的研究，特别要注重踏踏实实的实证研究工作。（4）用 SFL 理论探索汉语的特点，为汉语语言学理论框架的建立做出自己的贡献。下面补充两点。

首先，我们对韩礼德的语言学理论的实质应有更深的理解。韩茹凯教授在她的“韩茹凯论语言”（2015）中指出，“语言学的目的就是要‘发展分析语义的方法’；语言研究必须分析人类活动的‘语义性质’，必须认识到语言在认知过程中的‘关键中介作用’，因为它能通过意义解释人类的活动经验，而意义交流才是语言在人类生活中最重要的功能”，这可能就是为什么韩礼德一再强调“语言是一种意义潜势”，“语言是最重要的社会符号”（social semiotic）的原因所在。韩礼德的这个语言观“奠定了 SFL 关于语言层次、语境学说、语言功能、语言系统、语篇生成、语篇分析、衔接与连贯、语言教学的认识基础，也是区分这个学派与其他一些语言学派，尤其是形式语言学的核心理念”（方琰，见韩茹凯 2015）。

第二，要加强对语言系统的分析、描述和建构。记得我在悉尼大学学习期间，每次到韩礼德的办公室，都会看到在右面墙上挂了一张很大的英语语言系统分析图，几乎占了整个墙面。当时是一个包含 800 多个子系统的网络，可见韩礼德对系统的研究是多么重视！但是这距离整个英语语言系统的构建还差得很远。中国的语言学研究者应当大踏步赶上我们国际上的同行，特别要向在这方面做了杰出贡献的韩茹凯和马蒂森等学者学习和借鉴，从构建小的系统开始，逐步扩展到较大的系统；从构建英语系统开始，逐步扩展到其他语言，包括汉语。希望“总有一天能‘实现韩礼德将整个语言形式都变成语法系统进行描述的梦想’”（韩茹凯，2015）。

最后表达一个愿望：希望中国最终能建立起独立的语言学系或语言学研究学院，利用汉语专家和各种语言的研究专家的综合资源，培养出具有良好语言学素质的又有多种语言基础的语言学研究人才。这不仅有利于汉语的系统研究，也一定会促进我们对其他国际上有影响力的语言的研究，促进我国少数民族语言的学习、研究、维护。这可能也是我国提出的“一带一路”倡议的战略发展纲要，给我国语言学工作者带来的新的研究课题。设立跨语种的语言学专业是语言学研究的迫切需要，但愿这个愿望能早日实现！

0

意义至关重要

——系统功能语言学简史[*]

詹姆斯·马丁[①](James Martin)撰

方琰　译

0.1　之前与以后

韩礼德[②]1961年刊于《词》(*Word*)的论文《语法理论范畴》,被普遍认为是发展为系统功能语言学(后称SFL)的奠基性论文。源于该文的图0-1,勾勒出该理论的基本构架——在这个阶段被称为"阶与范畴"语法。该框架给人的第一印象,似乎综合了叶尔姆斯列夫(1961)关于"形式"和

* 本章原文刊登于《词》(*Word*)第62卷第一期,第35至58页。可在网址http://dx.doi.org/10.1080/00437956.2016.1141939上查阅。文章由马丁于2016年4月21日从网上下载。文中提及的著作未收录到本书的"参考文献"之中。

① 马丁为澳大利亚悉尼大学语言学系教授、中国上海交通大学"适用语言学马丁中心"教授。电子信箱:james.martin@sydney.edu.au

② 这是M. A. K. Halliday自己起的中文名字。还有两位学者有自己起的中文名字:Ruqaiya Hasan—韩茹凯,Jonathan Webster—卫真道。译文中一律将原名译为中文,除国内常见约定俗成的以外,均按照原名本族语的发音、根据新华社各语种译名手册音译。详见篇末所附译名对照表。

“实体”层次，与弗斯（1957a）关于语境层次（当代语言学读者可能会期待其与语义学有些关联）的理念；事实上，韩礼德也确实在脚注里引用了这两位学者的论述。后来，韩礼德等学者（1964：18）对这个理论框架稍做了进一步阐述，比如将音位层解读为形式与音素实体之间的关系，将语境解读为形式与情境之间的关系。

图 0－1 勾勒出的语言层次的独特概念，提出了有关语言家族史和语言繁衍的问题。我在本文中将简要论述 SFL 的语言学史。若想了解 SFL 进展的详细论述，请参阅马蒂森（2007a；2007b；2009；2010；2015），也可参阅下列学者关键评论的论文集：韩茹凯等（2005；2007）、韩礼德与卫真道（2009）、卫真道（2015）、巴莱特及奥格莱蒂（2017）以及汤普森等（2019）。基础性的论文收集在马丁和多论的论文集中（2015a；2015b；2015c；2015d；2015e）（包括韩礼德、韩茹凯、马丁编撰的三本论文集的参考文献）；马丁（2013a）收集的韩礼德访谈录也颇具启迪性，马蒂森（2010）等则提供了关键术语的索引词表。

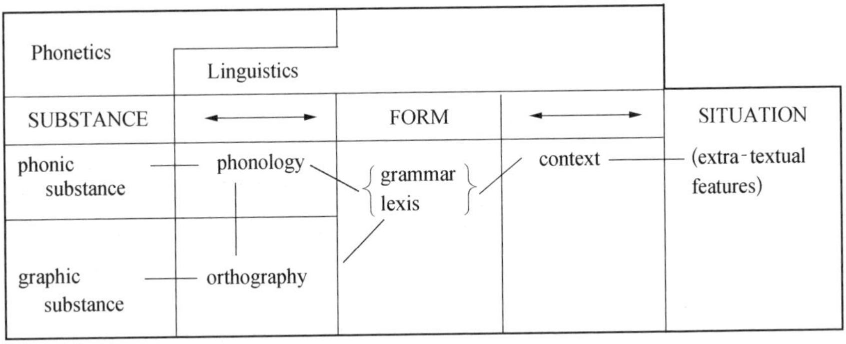

图 0－1　语言的层次①（韩礼德 1964：244）

① Phonetics：语音学；linguistics：语言学；substance：实体；form：形式；situation：情景；phonetic substance：语音实体；phonology：音位学；grammar：语法；lexis：词汇；context：语境；extra-textual：语篇之外的；graphic substance：字体实体；orthography：正字法

0.2 作为符号意义[①](semiotic)系统的语言

SFL 一个著名的概念是将语言视为符号意义系统，这体现在韩礼德(1978)的专著《作为社会符号意义的语言》的书名上。这就意味着，我们的简史有必要从索绪尔(1916; 1966)开始，首先回顾他将符号视为“所指”(signifié)与“能指”(signifiant)之间密不可分的联结关系概念。我用阴阳之间的象征性关系，将这种联结模式用图 0－2 展示出来。我这样做是出于对索绪尔提出的三种类比的尊重，他用符号的通常观念，来替代某些事物(比如替代人脑中的一个概念，或替代人世间的一个参照物)。他将符号类比为一枚钱币，或为一张纸，或为水中的波浪。对每种类比，索绪尔都竭力强调符号是语音实体与思想的耦合，不是钱币的正、反两面，而是两面的结合；不是纸的正、反两面，而是两面的结合；不是水或风，而是两者的结合(即波浪)。因而语言如同其他符号意义系统，也被构想为一个符号系统。

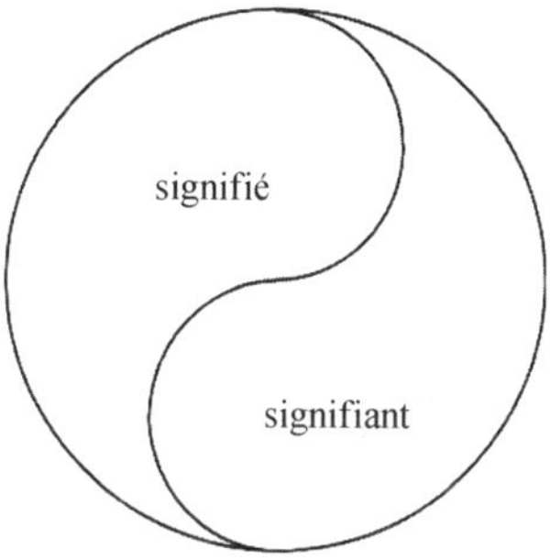

图 0－2　索绪尔的符号概念

叶尔姆斯列夫(1961)忠实于索绪尔这个经典说法，也同样强调语言是一种形式而不是实体。而且他更进一步阐明，语言不是一个简单的符号意义系统(如动物的交际系统，婴儿的原始语言)，而是一个有层次的符号意义系统。表 0－1 勾勒出他著名的形式相对于实体、内容相对于表达之间的交汇关系。在这个清晰的表中，语言包含了内容形式层次和表达形式层次(他的内容和表达平面)，其中任何一方均不优于另一方。将其与图 0－1 对比，图 0－1 中的内容形式(即韩礼德的语法和词汇)是处于中心的位置，而音位学像语境一样被视为层际层次。

① 韩礼德曾多次指出，“semiotics”应理解为“意义学”。鉴于国内学者将其译为“符号学”的传统，本文将“semiotic”译为“符号意义”。

表 0-1 叶尔姆斯列夫的形式/实体与内容/表达的交汇

内　容	表　　达	
形式	内容形式	表达形式
实体	内容实体	表达实体

在 SFL 中,内容形式(content form)与表达形式(expression form)之间的关系,一般会被解释为一个等级体系,艾伦清晰地阐明了这个观点(这与弗斯相反,弗斯不认为任何一个层次优于其他层次。)。这个观点后来在兰姆和格利森发展层次语言学时,放在了突出的位置(这两位学者对 SFL 的发展,有着直接的影响;见马丁 2014)。至少在马丁和马蒂森(1991)看来,这个等级系统曾用两个同圆表示出来(韩礼德的建议)。圆环从右下角表达形式开始,逐渐向上移动到上面靠左较高的层次。圆环在上升的过程中越变越大,反映了分析的中心单位逐渐增大的趋势(如图 0-3 中的音节对应于小句①)。层次之间的关系,反映了语言作为动态、开放的系统,不断出现的复杂性;其中较抽象的系统可用较低层次系统的范式来解释(这种"范式的范式"的动因,被莱姆基称为隐喻重复,1995)。

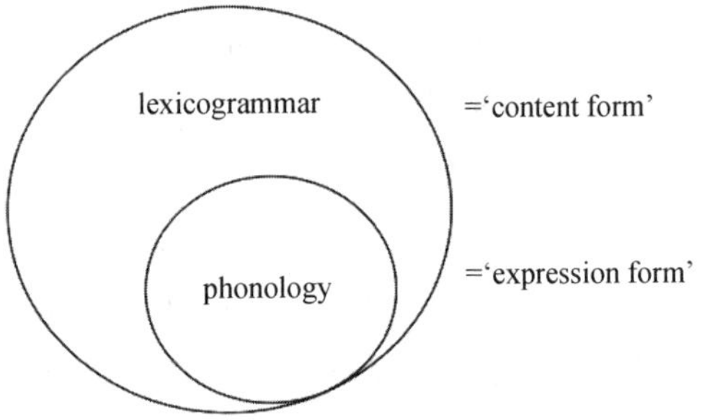

图 0-3 传统的 SFL 语言层次表达方式

20 世纪 80 年代,韩礼德进一步将叶尔姆斯列夫的内容平面,划分为词汇-语法层和语义层(图 0-4)。这就意味着,语言被构想为具有两个意义生成的层次——词汇-语法层(主要关心小句的意义生成潜力);语义层(重心放在语篇的意义生成潜力上)。语法被视为意义生成源泉的观点,

① 原文如此。根据图 0-3,应该是作为表达形式的音位(phonology)对应于作为内容形式的小句的词汇-语法(lexicogrammar)。

是 SFL 有别于其他学派的特点之一。如果考虑到 SFL 语法构架能用来描述语言的丰富性,这个特点被人欣赏就不难理解了(韩礼德在《功能语言学概论》1985、1994、2004、2014 年的各种不同的版本中,对英语的描述就是杰出的例证)。这个模式可与图 1 做非常有益的对比。在图 0 - 1 中,弗斯将形式和与之相关的作为语境的情景,单独划分为一个层次,就反映了他将意义解释为语境中的功能。事实上,语义层作为一个层次,最先出现在 1964 年韩礼德等学者的著作中(1964: 18),语义学(semantics)被视为一个具体的层际层次。我们将在 0.7.1 节中再讨论语义学和语境的关系。

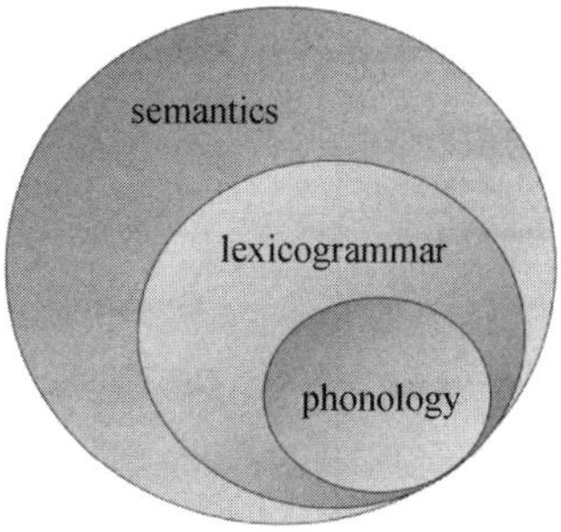

图 0 - 4　韩礼德有关语言作为不同层次的符号系统的表达

0.3　系统语法

上面已经勾勒出 SFL 逐渐形成的语言符号意义系统的层次概念,现在我们要回到 SFL 继承索绪尔的另一个关键线索,这就是索绪尔的值(Valeur)的观念。索绪尔主张,用一个普通的含义替代符号的意义,提出了到底符号是什么意思的问题。在这方面,索绪尔将符号与钱币类比的例子可能最具启发性,因为任何钱币的值,明显取决于它与其他钱币之间的关系。索绪尔非常强调这个符号值的观念。他认为,语言中只有差异,没有绝对的表达方式(1916: 120)。叶尔姆斯列夫(1947)使用交通信号灯为例,解释索绪尔有关值的概念。我本人改进了他的阐述,在下面建立了一个有三对相互对立符号的意义系统网络:停止/红灯,加速/黄灯,放行/绿灯。在选用表示相互对立的符号时,我选用了能将“所指”和“能指”耦合的词汇来表示,以避免再次使用索绪尔竭力反对的有关意义概念的表达方式(图 0 - 5)。

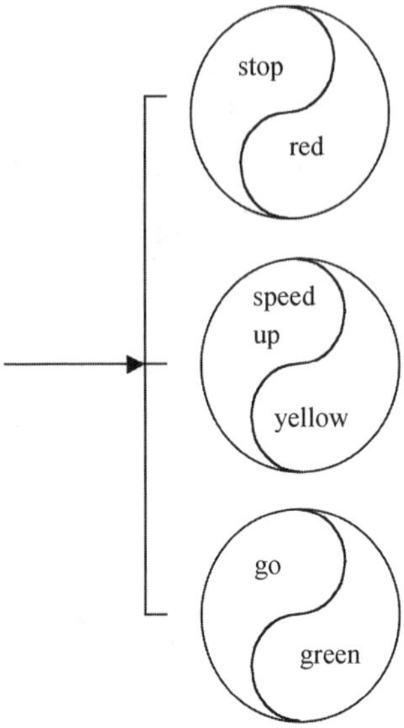

图 0-5 交通信号灯：简单符号系统中的值

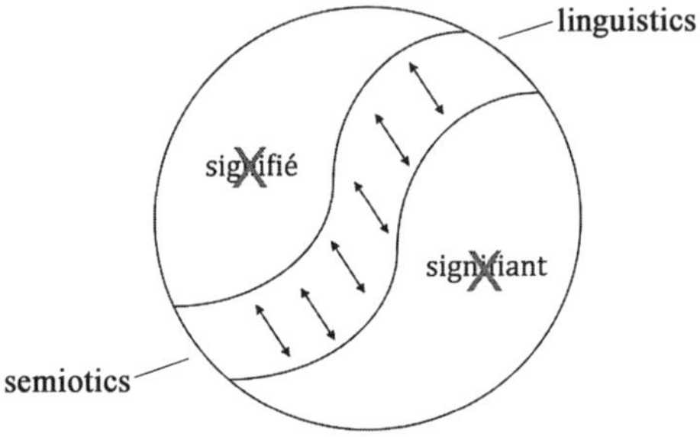

图 0-6 “所指”与“能指”的黏合关系——语言学和符号意义学的研究目标

索绪尔和叶尔姆斯列夫两位学者有关语言作为关系网络的观念，被兰姆在发展他的层次语言学的过程中，放在了最首要的位置上，包括在形式化的过程中，描述是用纯粹的“关系”术语来表示（如兰姆 1966；洛克伍德 1972；马凯及洛克伍德 1973；加西亚等 2017）。正如索绪尔指出的，“语言学在声音和思想成分结合的边界上起作用：它们的结合产生了形式，而不产生实体。”（这是他在 1916/1966：113 的论述中所强调的。）在图 0-6 中，我就是沿着这样的思路，将注意力放在“所指”与“能指”之间的黏合关系性质上，来解释语言学和符号意义学的。就是这个关系网络，构成了两位学者研究的目标；其中，就构成关系网络的绘图而言，层次和值被视为关键的基石。图 0-6 中，符号 x 意在加深索绪尔/叶尔姆斯列夫/兰姆的传统观点，即认为语言学（linguistics）和符号意义学（semiotics）关注形式，而不关注实体，这就是 SFL 与他们共享的基本理论方向。

SFL 简史的另一个关键基石，就是我们现在所谓的组合关系和聚合关系（索绪尔称之为组合关系和关联关系）。这是索绪尔划分的、我们一直追随叶尔姆斯列夫区分的两个关系。这些关系对索绪尔和叶尔姆斯列夫（以后对兰姆）而言，如同弗斯的结构和系统一样，后来被视为相互补充的，无所谓哪个更为优先。但在 SFL 中，就像这个学派的名称所示，系统被认为优先于结构；也就是说，就黏合"所指"和"能指"的关系网络而言，系统被视为基本的组织原则，结构是对系统选择的结果。SFL 用系统网络将这些聚合关系形式化。图 0-7 中，英语人称代词系统诠释了这个论点。圆括号逻辑上表示"以及"，方括号表示"或者"。下指斜箭头将系统和结构相连（图 7 中仅指英语单数第三人称代词）。要了解这种形式化，要了解结构实现和选择聚合关系动因的途径（即 SFL 的纵轴），请参阅马蒂森和韩礼德（2009）以及马丁（2013b）。

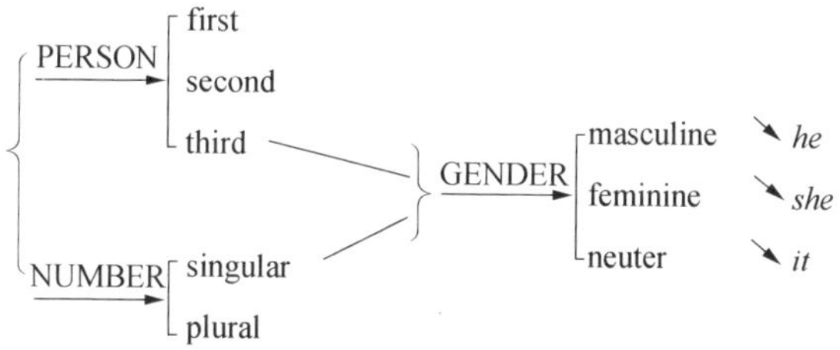

图 0-7　英语人称代词的聚合关系

0.4　功能语法

要欣赏 SFL 有关聚合关系的视角，很重要的一点，就是重温通过聚合关系所实现的丰富的组合结构的描述。为了阐述 SFL 这方面发展的历史，我们必须提及沃尔夫的研究工作。对沃尔夫而言，在语言学的描述中，重要的是区别"phenotypes"和"cryptotypes"；"phenotypes"他视为显性呈现的范畴，尤其在语言形态学方面；"cryptotypes"指的是隐性范畴，但它可在结构以特别的方式改变了的情况下显现出来。沃尔夫以英语的形容词为例，认为它用不同的次类构成了两种隐性结构……其中一组含有"固有属性"……具有一种"反应"属性，使它比……不具有固有属性的另一组，可放在更接近名词的位置上（1942/1956：93）。因而表面上看起来似乎同属一个词类的形容词……

a **pretty** girl

a **French** girl

……实际上属于两个的词类,反映在它们相互结合时的“反应”属性中:

a pretty French girl

*a French pretty girl

费尔默引用了沃尔夫有关“隐性”的概念,创建了他的“格语法”,让人们关注下列小句中的“affectum/effectum”(情绪性/效应性)的区别。比如:

John ruined **the table**.

John built **the table**.

这种情况下,我们用“do to”来审问小句的动词过程时,相关的“反应”属性就显现了出来:

What did John do to the table?

Ruined it.

What did John do to the table?

*Built it.

格利森讨论他所谓的“对称性”和“非对称性”时,就将“反应”属性变化的现象的探索形式化了(“对称性”大概的意思是:相同的结构,不同的词汇;“非对称性”大概的意思是:不同的结构,相同的词汇)。应用沃尔夫例子,下面的小句结构被视为“对称”的:

a pretty French girl

a pretty Spanish girl

a pretty Australian girl

但是下面这几对却是“非对称”的:

a pretty French girl

a very pretty French girl

a pretty Spanish girl

a very pretty Spanish girl

a pretty Australian girl

a very pretty Australian girl

沃尔夫觉得对隐性属性的分析,是语言学描述至关重要的一环,特别是想要探索分析、报告语言中被凝固为"时尚的话语"经验的方法、而这样的经验又跨越了典型的语法分类的时候。这种"时尚"可能涵盖词汇、词素、句法,但它们又以非常不同的系统,按某种框架结合在一起(1942/1956: 158)。

这种对语法描绘扩展的视野,是韩礼德语法分析的基本方法。对于韩礼德来说,区分"固有的"和"非固有"特质的一个关键"反应"属性,可能就是"等级性"(gradability)(注意:下列各对短语中,只有在 French 和 Australian 被读为具有非固有属性时,第二组名词词组才合乎语法):

a very pretty girl

*a very French girl

A very lovely girl

*a very Australian girl

与其引进基于这些或者其他"反应"属性的无数形容词次类,韩礼德采取的策略,是将功能(一个词项在结构中的作用)和词类(是什么样的词项)区分开来,即将功能标识(即关系)和词类标识(即范畴)区别开来。因而,pretty、French 及 Spanish 在下面的分析中就被划分为形容词(因为这两类词,在像 *She's French/Spanish* 的关系定语小句中,看来均可作为描述词),而同时又可在性质形容词^类别形容词的结构中做功能解释(因为它们在说明女孩的类型时不能分级)。

	A	***pretty***	***French***	***girl***
功能	指示词	性质形容词	类别形容词	事物
词类	限定词	形容词	形容词	名词

	A	***pretty***	***Spanish***	***girl***
功能	指示词	性质形容词	类别形容词	事物
词类	限定词	形容词	形容词	名词

这从一个方面说明，SFL 在描述语法时是功能性的——因为这些描述区别了功能和词类，因而也就区别了组合体（词类的顺序）和结构（功能的构建）。功能和词类的互补性，使得词类可完成一个以上的功能（比如，a red dress 相对于 some red wine），也能使功能以用不同的词类得以实现（比如，*some red wine* 对应于 *some sparkling wine*）。这样，“反应”属性的范围可能变得很宽泛，而成为产生不同功能结构的动因。举一个可与费尔默解释上述“格语法”相应的例子：韩礼德对英语的功能描述，区分了动词词组⌃名词词组的组合体，其中名词词组“补语”（complement）会受到动词词组的影响，但在其他可与之相比的组合体中，这个成分却没有受到影响。费尔默建议的“do to/do with”的反应作用①，适用于解释下面足球比赛例句中，非对称性的语篇和人际功能的变化：

Messi kicked the ball.
What Messi kicked the goal (making the score 3 – 2 for Barcelona).

What Messi did with the ball was kick it.
*What Messi did with the goal was kick it.

What did Messi do with the ball?
Kicked it.

What did Messi do with the goal?
*Kicked it②.

这就是导致韩礼德区分“过程目的结构”（Process Goal structures）和“过程范围结构”（Goal Scope structures）的部分隐性推理因素，虽然这两个结构可被同样的组合体实现。

① 有趣的是，韩礼德在描述英语时，并没有应用这样的“反应”属性，来区分情绪性功能结构和效应性功能结构，虽然“反应”是区别物质过程创造类型和规则类型聚合结构的部分动因（两者都涉及一个概括出来的“目标”功能）；反映这种创造类型和规则类型相对立的、更加精细的功能结构，当然是有可能的。
② 除非我们要表达像“踢门柱”这样的意思。

	Messi	*kicked*	*the ball*
功能结构	动作者	过程	目标
词类序列	名词词组	动词词组	名词词组

	Messi	*kicked*	*the goal*
功能结构	动作者	过程	范围
词类序列	名词词组	动词词组	名词词组

SFL 的隐形语法,沿着这样的推理思路,对具体语言的语法,提供了典型的、丰富的功能解释。这就提出了功能结构如何相互关联的问题。下面我们将回答这个问题(也就是说,SFL 认为,语法并不是由通过一个序列的组合体实现的序列结构;产生这些结构的聚合关系才是最重要的)。

0.5　系统功能语法

如上所述,SFL 继承了索绪尔、叶尔姆斯列夫和弗斯的聚合关系和组合关系的互补性,但在两者之间更重视聚合关系。如何做到这一点呢?说明这一点最好的方法,莫过于观察英语的语气(Mood)。众所周知,英语是首先,而不是滞后,实现它小句的协商性(很像他加禄语,而不像韩语或日语,将其放在终点,滞后实现协商性)。与大多数语言不同,英语在过程小句中,分成两部分来实现小句的协商性——一半是主语(名词协商性核心),一半是限定动词(动词协商性术语)。还有一点与大多数语言不同,英语是以主语和限定动词的功能顺序或者是否缺失,来区别语气的。因而,韩礼德提出了下列功能结构,区分基本的英语语气类型:

[陈述语气]	*Real Madrid*	*have*	*stopped*	*Messi*
	主语	限定词	述词	补语
	名词词组	动词词组		名词词组

[疑问语气]	*have*	*Real Madrid*	*stopped*	*Messi*
	限定词	主语	述词	补语
	动词……	名词词组	……词组	名词词组

[命令语气]	***stop***	***Messi***
	述词	补语
	动词词组	名词词组

从聚合关系的角度来看，declarative（陈述语气）和 interrogative（疑问语气）可放在同一组（为 indicative，直陈语气），因为两者均包含主语和限定动词功能[与 imperative（命令语气）完全不同，命令语气在非标志结构中，没有这两个功能]。可用主语和限定动词功能的排列顺序，将陈述语气与疑问语气区别开来。（为使讨论简便化，我们将不考虑 wh-特殊疑问句）。左边的图 0－8 网络系统，将这些相关的选项（作为按精细化程度划分的系统特征）形式化，并指明每个选项对英语语气结构所做的贡献（+S 的意思是：插入主语；S ^ F 的意思是：主语放在限定动词之前）；详细介绍，请参阅马丁等(2013)。

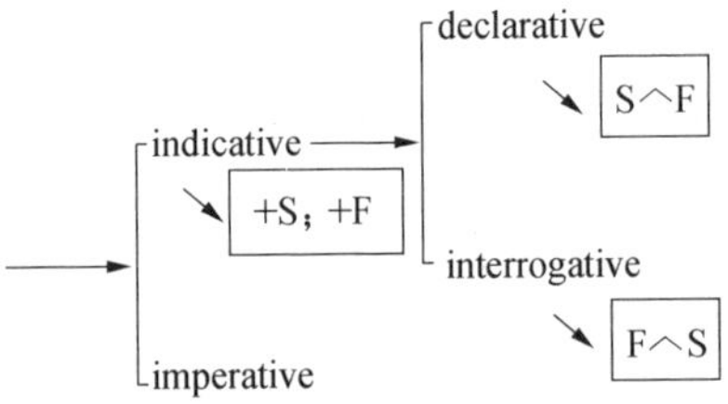

图 0－8　语气系统与实现语气的功能结构

这种视角的形式化工作，主要由马蒂森和他的同仁们完成（比如马蒂森及贝特曼 1991；马蒂森 1995；以及韩礼德的《功能语言学概论》第三、四版）。在系统和结构之间更突出系统的思路，最重要的意义在于：在词项组合体和功能结构（不论表现为序列或树形），让我们看到语言应用的具体实例的地方，系统网络提供了一个纵观全局的视角，来观察语言整体的意义潜势。这就能使 SFL 将作为意义资源的语言，以构图的形式（而不是规则的目录）将语言模式化，这样就可以最终解释 SFL 既是系统的也是功能的原因，以及这样的模式能做些什么。

也许体现 SFL 理论和描述方面，将聚合关系视为基本组织原则最强有力的动能，就是韩礼德著名的纯理功能概念的出现。奠基性的论文包括韩礼德常常被引用的（但是我怀疑并不常常被阅读）"Notes on transitivity and theme in English"（关于英语中的及物性及主位的说明）

(1967a; 1967b; 1968),以及"Functional diversity of language as seen from a consideration of modality and mood in English(从英语的情态和语气的角度看语言功能的多样性)(1970a)",及更容易读到的"Options and functions in the English clause"(英语小句中的选项和功能)(1969);这些思想在韩礼德(1970c)一文中得到进一步普及。1969 年的论文实际上是在捷克共和国出版的,意在强调韩礼德确认他的功能观,与布拉格学派在这方面有相似性[特别是达内什(1964)的研究工作;可与费尔玻斯(1964)、瓦谢克(1964;1966)的著作相比较]。韩礼德最初观察是基于系统网络中的系统束,这些系统束是他和他的伦敦同事们,为描写各种语言(包括英语、法语、恩泽玛语①、姆奔贝语②)发展起来的。他们观察到,小句的级(rank)系统表现出不同程度的内在互联现象,这样的互联现象倾向于将系统组织为三组,反映了对通常被称为及物性、语气、主位系统的选择。韩礼德认为,这些系统束,就概念、人际、语篇意义而言,反映了语言的内在功能组织。这些纯理功能被认为存在于各个级和层次当中,其中,概念(ideational)功能资源解释我们周围的世界(以及我们的内心世界),人际(interpersonal)资源规定了社会关系,语篇(textual)资源组成语篇。随着科研的进展,这些纯理功能被认为与不同的结构实现类型相联系——概念意义与粒子结构相关联(序列的或轨道的结构),人际意义与韵律结构相关联,语篇意义与周期结构相关联(韩礼德 1979;马丁 1996)。

这就突出了 SFL 功能性的第二个主要的含义:就语言功能解释世界、规定社会关系、组成语篇的互补性而言,语言的系统和结构可视为固有的组织结构。但请注意:这个纯理功能视角,与第四节中讨论的功能结构并不是没有关系。没有那里介绍的隐性语法推理促成功能结构,就不可能出现构成 SFL 的"深层语法"丰富的聚合关系网络。而没有对这个丰富的聚合关系网络的深入探索,就不可能有韩礼德纯理功能的设想。曾经提出过多个不同的动机,促成了跨越级和层次的语言纯理功能组织的设想(比如:韩礼德的《功能语言学概论》第三版封面上,跨切层次横排的

---

① Nzema
② Mbembe

有色的纵列)。图 0－9 列出了这个跨类的粗略轮廓①,勾勒出跨越层次的纯理功能。

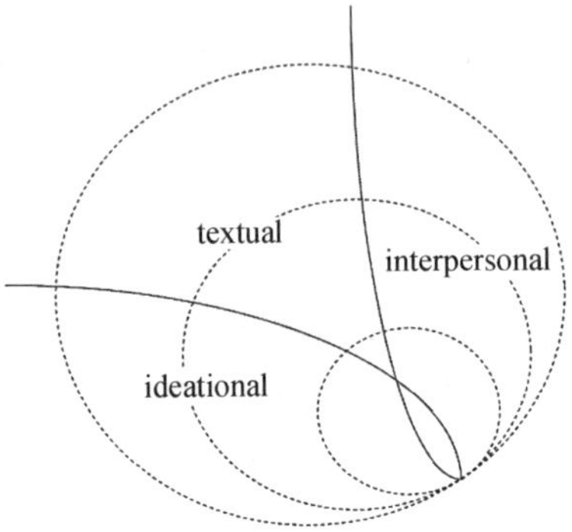

图 0－9　SFL 跨越层次的纯理功能的线路图

0.6　系统功能语言学

正如图 0－9 所突出的那样,SFL 是一种语言理论,并不只是语法[虽然很多语言学家仍然追随乔姆斯基围绕语法这个术语,使用了这个很不幸的含义模糊的词汇——把整个语言的性质看成被这些语法规则所支配,而不是语言的一个层次——因而 SFL(系统功能语言学)就被称为 SFG(系统功能语法)]。我将在此对音位学、词汇学、(语篇)语义学做一些评述。

SFL 继承了弗斯研究音位学的自上而下的独特视角,他是第一位重点研究表达形式跨成分范围方面的学者(帕尔默 1970),而且他强烈批评以音位为基础的方法,他认为这种方法是基于字母写作系统的音位学,而

① 图 0－9 里最小圈子(表达形式)中的曲线所包围的空间无关紧要,它只不过是在我们从一个层次移动到下一个层次时,可在图中给每个纯理功能更加平等的分量(即面积),这样的意图只得到部分成功。

不是建立在声音系统本身的区分特征之上(Firth 1957b)。韩礼德从 SFL 的视角发展了弗斯的研究,他有关汉语音节(1992)和英语的节奏和语调的研究(韩礼德 1967c;1970b;韩礼德与格雷夫斯 2008),最突出地体现了这一点。有关具有应用价值的 SFL 表达形式的研究论文集,见特伦奇(1992)、鲍切尔与史密斯(2014)。

从弗斯那里,SFL 还继承了将词汇视为语言学的一个层次的关注(韩礼德 1966;对比图 0－1)。弗斯对词汇搭配的兴趣,主要由辛克莱和他的同事们,在语料库语言学的研究中得到发展(如 1966;1991),也在 SFL 中得到发展,虽然与之相比较少了一些。韩礼德早期的研究中,就认可了词与词项的区别,认可了需要从组合的角度,看待词项之间的预期关系;持这样观点的背景,往往建立在把词汇看成精细语法的兴趣之上(韩茹凯 1987;及其他学者追寻的“语法学家的梦想”)。他们的想法是:在小句和词组层次上,不那么精细的系统网络中的系统,往往可以通过结构和功能词汇得到实现;而比较精细的区分则要通过词项来实现。尽管韩茹凯倡导了这个想法,但在追随这个梦想中,SFL 学者发展“反应”推理方法一直很缓慢。即使这个不易掌握的事业是可行的,也不清楚是否可以避免需要像语料库语言学那样对搭配进行研究。正如贝特曼(2008b)所警告的那样,如果 SFL 过于强调聚合关系,那就会有缺陷。这需要比某些 SFL 实践,更注重对组合关系的研究加以平衡。塔克(2007)参与了这场辩论,发表了不少论著,试图调和韩礼德(作为精细语法的词汇)和辛克莱(搭配范式)之间的工作分工。

至于对语法以外的意义探讨,SFL 最著名的著作当属对衔接的研究(如韩礼德和韩茹凯 1976)。韩礼德在概述英语语法时,通常将衔接概念定位为语篇功能的非结构组成成分(比如,韩礼德 1970c①)。韩茹凯(在韩礼德及韩茹凯 1980;1985: 82;1989 等著作中)将这方面的研究朝着语义学的方向推进,包括她的所指、替代、省略、词汇衔接、连接词的框架,以

① 韩礼德和韩茹凯(1976: 29),实际上将这样的图形看作英语语义学的轮廓,衔接被放在与大家熟悉的及物性、语气和主位系统并列的位置上。我只把这视为韩礼德试图向读者描述他的丰富的语言学的一种方法。那是语言学的麦卡锡主义时期,那时除了乔姆斯基形式化的美国结构主义直接成分分析法,其他的语言学研究工作一律被排斥。1980 年代,与其可比的功能/阶模型往往都被视为语法资源图谱,而不是语义学资源图谱。

及对毗邻对、连续体、平行结构的贡献、主位-述位发展及已知-新信息组织的研究(进一步讨论,请参阅马丁 2017 及印刷中)。马丁(在 1992 年的著作中得到进一步巩固)综合了格利森(如 1968)、韩礼德和韩茹凯(1976)的研究工作,将衔接重新构建为语篇语言学。在马丁的框架中,衔接手段被重新解释为语篇结构(用莱姆基的术语来说,主要指的是共同变体手段);语篇语义系统由纯理功能恰如其分组合而成——概念与连接对应于概念语义;协商与评价对应于人际语义,识别与周期性对应于语篇语义(寓意这是一个联合体,这个联合体中,概念与连接构成粒子结构、协商与评价构成韵律结构、识别与周期性构成周期结构)。这个语篇语义学的模式大纲以及它包含的结构动因均列在图 0-10 中;对图 0-10,马丁和罗斯(2003;2007)提供了一个容易理解的介绍。将衔接重新构建为语篇语义系统和结构的做法,有着重要的意义:它为评价的发展提供了空间,评价为 SFL 中的评估模式(包含价值、立场、障碍、增强等等),有关的基础性介绍见马丁和怀特(2005)。如塔克(2007)所指出,就生成意义而言,评价分析重新重视了对词项和词汇搭配研究的重要性;贝德纳德(如 2006;2007;2008)一直追随这条研究路线,开展了以语料为基础、语料为动力的语言评估研究。

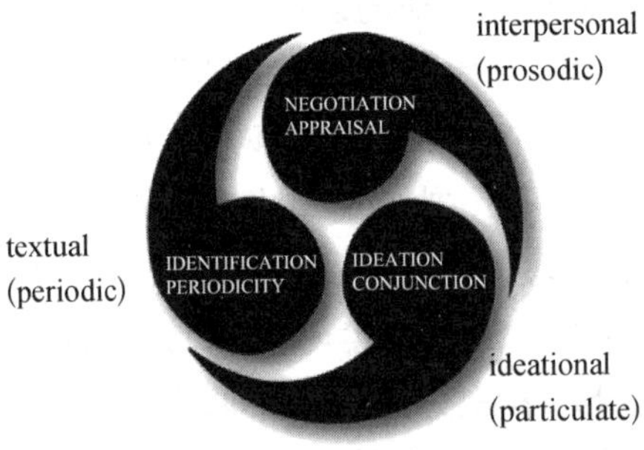

图 0-10　马丁的语篇语义系统模式(以及所涉及的结构)

在 SFL 之内,对语义学研究与此相异的路子,往往建立在对小句语义的研究上,而不是对衔接的再语境化。韩茹凯发展了特纳和韩礼德(如特纳 1973)较早时期,在精细语义网络方面有关社会语义学网络的工作,用以支持她对母亲与他们的学前子女对话编码方向的研究,将重点放在性别与社会阶级之间的变量上(在韩茹凯 2009 年的著作中得到巩固)。比较有名的关于这些网络的研究(比如,韩茹凯 2009: 283)可以被理解为突出人际意义的语义学研究;随着对这个网络更精密的研究,网络提供了性别和阶级之间非常敏感的细微差别(进一步讨论,可参阅韩茹凯等 2007)。

韩礼德本人倾向于突出语法隐喻理论，意在证明在 SFL 理论中，有必要设立有层次的内容平台。他有关语言科学进化的著作（收集于韩礼德 2004）将焦点放在了概念隐喻，以及对将作为参与者、过程、和环境成分的实体、事件、联系者进行常态性和隐喻编码的可能性。他对复合句之间做了基础性的对比，比如 *they played poorly and so were eliminated* 与 *their poor play led to their elimination*。这项研究，在 SFL 的各个应用领域产生了主要的影响，特别是在教育领域（比如，韩礼德和马丁 1993；马丁和梅顿 2013）。有关概念隐喻的研究，在韩礼德和马蒂森（1999）的论著中得到了最全面的展示。韩礼德（1984）重点关注的是人际隐喻的互补现象，首次提供了清晰的、归纳出来的独特的语义学模式和语法范式——即**言语功能**语义网络，它通过语气的常态和隐喻的方式得以实现。就需要一个有层次的内容平台而言（比较图 1 和图 9），如需阅读易懂的推理概论，请参阅韩礼德《功能语言学概论》任何一个版本有关语法隐喻章节；如需做更详细的研究，请参阅西蒙-范登博根等学者的著作（2003）。

0.7 系统功能符号意义学

0.7.1 语域及语类

在这个节点上，让我们再回到图 1 和图 4，我们看到不同的语言模式造成了矛盾的紧张状态。在图 1 中，弗斯以某种方式与叶尔姆斯列夫得到了调和：语言被建构为有着互补性的表达和内容两个平台（叶尔姆斯列夫的遗产），其中语境是作为连接语法-词汇和语篇之外特点的层际联系层（弗斯的遗产）。这个模式尊重了弗斯将意义视为语境中的功能的研究方向，这是他从马林诺夫斯基那里继承来的视角（1923；1935；比较弗斯 1957a；1957c）。而在图 0－4 中，我们看到了一个有层次的模式，展现了一个有层次的内容平台（即音位学层/字系学层，词汇-语法层，语义层）。很显然与弗斯相比，更突出了兰姆的影响（很可能反映了韩礼德与层次语言学的对话结果;这是自 1960 年代后期,他做耶鲁大学访问教授时发展起来的)。然而就有关语境的研究工作而言,这个语言的三层次模式,给了我们一幅误导 SFL 发展的图片;如韩礼德的《作为社会符号意义学的语言》的论文所显示的那样(韩礼德 1978),特别是第六、第七、第十章。他的这些论文清晰地阐明,图 4 中的词汇-语法层和语义层,涉及了叶尔姆斯列夫的内容形式层次,而不是一个直接用语义层来代替作为层际联系层的语境层次①。

韩礼德(1961)有关语境的观念,最初在韩礼德等的著作中(1964),发展为语场、语旨、风格(style)。语场指的是正在发生的事,语式指的是语言在这个活动中起的作用,风格指的是参与者之间的关系。为了避免与文学作品中的术语"风格"的含义想混淆,他在后来的著作中采用了格雷戈里的术语"语旨"(首次使用于斯潘塞和格雷戈里 1964)。请注意,这个语境三重模式的形成稍早于 SFL 在 1960 年代发展起来的纯理功能——作为深层语法的聚合关系的形式化。然而至少在韩礼德看来(如,在 *The First LACUS Forum* 中发表的论文《作为符号意义学的语言》),语境的三个维度——语场、语式、语旨,分别与概念、语篇、人际功能有着对应关系,而且相应地,与外在的功能性也有对应关系;这些外在的功能性(如语境范畴),被描述为被"被反映在……里、决定了、激活了、被联系与、通过内在的功能性得以实现(即纯理功能)"。表 0-2 勾勒出这些对应相关性。

表 0-2　SFL 的语域(语场、语式、语旨)及纯理功能的钩链(hook-up)

外在的功能性(语境)'被反映在……里'内部的功能性(纯理功能)
语场用……来解释概念资源 语式由……组成语篇资源 语旨由……规定人际资源

① 根据韩礼德(1961)图 13 的脚注阐明,图 0-1 中的模式选择语境这个术语,是因为语义学这个术语,通常被理解为试图将语言形式与概念相联系(也就是说,将可观察到的与没有观察到的联系在一起);而语境的研究往往将焦点放在语言形式与语言之外可观察到的抽象概念的关系上面。

马丁和马蒂森(1991)使用同圆切面动因,将语境构建为意义的附加层面模式,反映了 SFL 逐渐对将语场、语式、语旨网建成语言学范式的范式的关切(要了解这个议题,参阅韩礼德在 2002/2005: 255 - 256 中清晰的阐述)。在叶尔姆斯列夫的术语中,语境被视为内涵符号意义,语言(本意符号意义)是它的表达平台。韩礼德沿着这样的思路(马丁 2013a: 215),特别对将语境看作一个更加抽象的意义层面做了评述。他是这样说的:"我们能不能对语境的模式、语境所代表内容、语境的解释,视为在通常涉及的框架中的一种语言的理论呢?弗斯那时认为你可以那样想,而我现在就这么想,如果只因为这是你得到的最好机会"。图 0 - 11 呈现了图 0 - 4 勾勒出的将语境与语言模式相关联的概念。

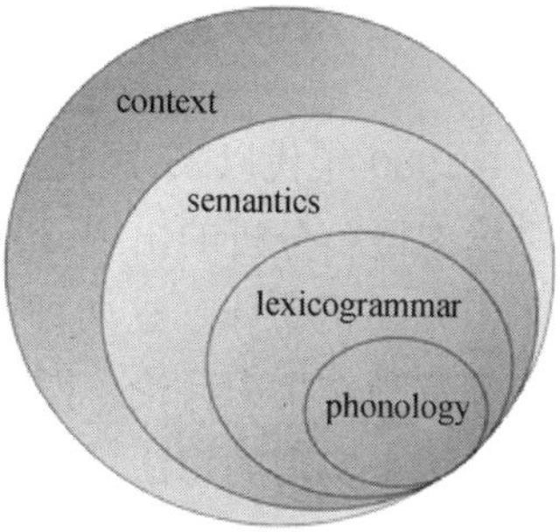

图 0 - 11 作为意义层次的语境

(与叶尔姆斯列夫的内涵与本意符号意义学相关的概念)

1960 年代发展起来的另外一些模式提出了四个变量,而不是三个。格雷戈里(1967)提出了语场、语式、个人语旨、功能语旨的建议;埃利斯及尤尔(1969)(也参阅尤尔和埃利斯 1977)提出了语场、语式、礼仪和角色。福西特(1980)稍后提出了题材、渠道、关系目的、语用目的。每个建议中前三个变量,均自然而然地与韩礼德所追随的纯理功能相匹配。"目的"变量(即功能语旨、角色、语用目的)与纯理功能的相应关系不那么清楚。部分就是这个原因,促使马丁和他的学生们在 1980 年代,发展了语境的层次模式,其中作为比较抽象变量的语篇的社会目的,就是通过语场、语式和语旨得以实现的——见图 0 - 12。这个模式在马丁(1992)的著作中得到进一步巩固(见马丁 1999;2001,印刷中的 c 作了进一步的阐明);在这个模式中,语境被划分在语类的层次上,通过语域得以实现(语域是作为语场、语式、语旨系统的覆盖术语)。马丁和罗斯(2008)专注于这些高层的语类系统研究,语类被视为超越语域系统所呈现出来的复杂层面(换句话说,它是语场、

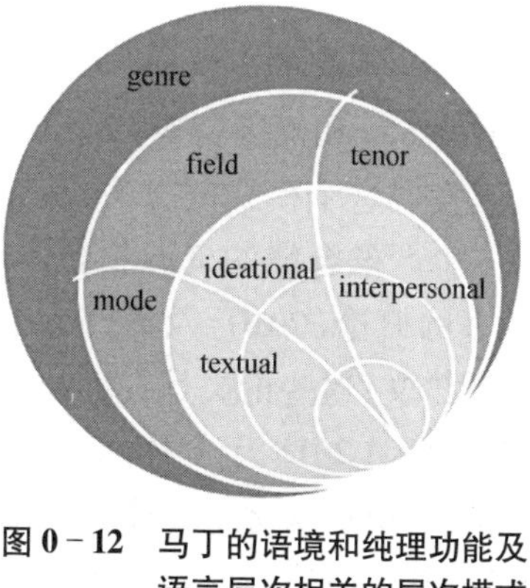

图 0 - 12 马丁的语境和纯理功能及语言层次相关的层次模式

语式、语旨范式的隐喻重复范式)。马丁(1984)就是为语言教育工作者所撰写的这个模式的普及版。

0.7.2 多模态

1980年代以来,系统功能意义学的另一条发展主线(后称SFS),就是多模态语篇分析的出现,最初的灵感来自克雷斯和范利文(1996)及奥图尔(1994)的著作。这两种创始灵感均将纯理功能当作关键出发点。克雷斯和范利文集中讨论了图像,提出了概念、人际、语篇系统,通过不同的图像结构来实现的想法;马蒂内(2005)和奥哈洛伦等学者(2015)回顾了从SFL汲取了灵感的这股研究思潮,将单一、静态的图像的研究,向外延伸到作为符号意义系统的画册、电影、体现行为、辅助语言、音乐及声音、雕塑、建筑及印刷版面模式的建构。在这方面,SFS圆满完成了索绪尔和叶尔姆斯列夫的前瞻思维;他们对语言之外的一系列作为符号意义系统的交际模态,做出了恰当的解释。这个研究事业的关键步骤,就在于SFL突出了聚合关系,使得系统功能符号意义学者,能够驰骋在广阔的模态领域中,这些领域通过非常不同的"结构"资源产生了意义。有关这些关键发展的评论,请参阅马丁(2011);也可见贝特曼所做的评论性介绍(2014)。

SFS学者这方面的研究工作彻底改变了语篇分析,将它对语篇中语言范式的分析,推进到必须考虑对伴随语言的多种模式的分析。图0－1重构了无限大比例被称之为"语篇之外的现实";这个现实被视为符号意义系统。这就使得"语篇之外的现实"成为可控,既能使分析本身易于操作,也能用相当程度丰富了我们对社会符号意义学理解的方法,来考虑语言问题。关键的多模态实例,可参阅贝特曼(2008a)和佩因特等(2013)。这项研究面临的主要理论上的挑战,是要找到发展这个模式的方法,从而能使一个语篇中体现的不同的模态,发展为一个严丝合缝的资源集合体。对应这个挑战的建议,可参阅贝德纳德和马丁的概论(2010)及汤普森编撰的《语篇与谈话》(*Text and Talk*, 2013)里的论文;这些论文是在韩礼德90岁诞辰的前夕,作为生日献礼发表在特别双刊上(2015年4月)。这里有争议的论点,是SFL关于实例概念(系统与语篇的关系)与抽象等级(层次与上面介绍的纯理功能)之间关系的某种解决方案。对这个解决方案的关键评述,就是韩礼德将实例视为一个连续体,而不是语言和言语的对立的视角——他受到叶尔姆斯列夫的影响,重新审视了索绪尔关于这两者的关系(比如,韩礼德 2008b 关于语言互补性的论述)。

0.8 意义至关重要

这样一篇简短的回顾论文,当然不可能对 SFL 发展中所有意义重大的时刻和运动,做出公允的评价。令人遗憾的是,我没有提及跨越多种语言和语言家族的艰辛的描述工作。卡法雷德等(2004)在这方面提供了一个窗口(也请参阅马蒂森等 2008;特鲁亚和马蒂森 2015)。这些研究对翻译工作的影响也没有提及。重要的研究,请参阅斯坦纳和亚洛普(2001);德索萨(2010)。另外还需说明,本文中我注重理论,而不是应用,因而没有讨论理论和实践之间重要的辩证关系,比如 SFL/SFS 学者在教育语言学、法律语言学、医诊语言学等各种领域里,展开的实践行为研究。第一节提及的评论文章和基础性的论文,审视了这些方面的原创精神。罗斯和马丁(2012)包含了其中最著名的一个方面——所谓的“悉尼学派”以语类为基础的读写大纲(马丁 2012,收集了有关这个行为研究的一些关键论文)。

这个短短的纵览,只可能做到将 SFL 的学术研究家谱做一个巡视。正如我们这里读到的,我们巡视了欧洲和北美洲各种流派,后来这些流派在南半球和亚洲的知识界得到令人鼓舞的繁荣发展。正如马蒂森(2015)所指出的那样,这里评论的许多基础概念,在刚开始引进时,并不时尚;但是随着时光的流逝,却被更广泛地接受了。他列出的范例转移包括:

——对语法和词汇的关系持有一个更加融合的视角(对应于隔离的模本)

——对语言或然性的研究兴趣逐渐增强(对应于明确的规则目录)

——在聚合关系和组合关系之间,显示了更加平衡的研究路子(对应于主要侧重结构研究的路子)

——对音位学的研究,采取的是更注重韵律研究的路子,突出了对“长

成分”，即节奏、语调的研究（对应于对“特点模式”组成的单个音位的研究）

——对于语言的发展，持社会互动的视角（对应于受先天制约的习得视角）

——接受理论与实践之间的辩证观点（对应于语言学和应用语言学属于完全相异的学科观点）

也许 SFL 的最后一个特点，就是韩礼德 1964 年在乔治城（Georgetown）圆桌会议上，发表题为“句法与消费者”的论文时，发出的信号。这个发言显然并没有得到重视，只被付之一笑，因为他说：“或许只能有一种真正的语法理论”（马蒂森 2015：196）。韩礼德最近又回到了这个历经艰难的主题（2008a：7），将它正式命名为“适用语言学”；他将其描述为综合的、理论上强大的语言模式；正因为它所具备的综合性和它所呈现的强大有力，它就可能被应用于解决科研问题和实际问题，而这些问题是现代社会中，人们以各种方式使用语言时，会面对的问题。

但是现在，我想不会再有什么语言学家蔑视这个远见卓识了。现在有太多的人行走在世界各地，他们或致力于研究应用中的语言，或在社区内处理各种实际的交际问题。然而要使这个奋斗目标取得成功，你不仅要有良好的愿望，你必须要有一个不断进化的语言的功能理论和符号意义学理论，在你前行的路上让你获得力量。我们的这些前行同伴，能通过什么样的互补的、叠盖的世系脉络，才能为找到发展、描述这个理论所需要的方法呢？

处置声明：

作者没有报告与任何一方有潜在的利益冲突。

姓氏译名对照表

原　名	译　名	原　名	译　名
Allen	艾伦	Martinet	马蒂内
Barlett	巴利特	Matthiessen	马蒂森
Bateman	贝特曼	O'Grady	奥格雷迪
Bednard	贝德纳德	O'Hallonran	奥哈洛伦
Bowcher	鲍切尔	O'Toole	奥图尔
Caffared	卡法雷德	Palmer	帕尔默
Chomsky	乔姆斯基	Parmer	帕默
Daneš	达内什	Painter	佩因特
De Souza	德索萨	Rose	罗斯
Doran	多兰	Saussure	索绪尔
Ellis	埃利斯	Seiner	赛纳
Fawcett	福西特	Simon-Vandenbergen	西蒙-范登博根
Fillmore	费尔默	Sinclair	辛克莱
Firbus	费尔玻斯	Smith	史密斯
Firth	弗斯	Spencer	斯潘塞
Garcia	加西亚	Steiner	斯坦纳
Gleason	格利森	Teruya	特鲁亚
Greaves	格雷夫斯	Thompson	汤普森
Gregory	格雷戈里	Trench	特伦奇
Halliday, M. A. K.	韩礼德	Tucker	塔克
Hasan, Ruqaiya	韩茹凯	Turner	特纳
Hjelmslev	叶尔姆斯列夫	Ure	尤尔
Kress	克雷斯	Vachek	瓦谢克
Lamb	兰姆	Van Leeween	范利文
Lemke	莱姆基	Webster, Jonathan	卫真道
Lockwood	洛克伍德	White	怀特
Makkai	马凯	Whorf	沃尔夫
Martin	马丁	Yallop	亚洛普
Maton	梅顿		

第一部分

汉语研究

Part One

Studies on Chinese

1

主位和述位初探*

1.1 引　言

自从意念功能法被推荐为全国理工大学的外语教学法以来，引起了很多争论，这无疑对于推动我国公共外语的教学和学术研究是十分有益的。在这个众说纷纭的问题上，意念功能的利弊以及我国贯彻这个教学法的条件是否成熟，更是争论的焦点。意念功能法的提出与社会语言学的发展，尤其与功能语言学①的问世有着非常密切的关系，因而我们有必要学习和研究功能语言学的一些基本理论，这有助于探讨在中国是否要推行这个教学法，也有助于我们公共外语教师在吸取外国经验教训的基础上，去开创自己的路子。

本章不直接涉及意念功能法本身，而是学习和探讨韩礼德的功能语言学中的语篇功能——主位-述位结构。这个理论之所以引起我们的兴趣，是因为它不仅可以帮助我们冲破传统语法的束缚，还因为它对于语序

---

* 本章曾发表于《大学英语教学研究》1986 年第二期。有少许改动。

① 根据 1983 年韩礼德在当时的北京外国语学院学术讲座录音，美国功能语言学的代表是肯尼斯·派克（Kenneth Pike）；在欧洲功能语言学有四派，即捷克的布拉格学派、丹麦的哥本哈根学派、法国学派以及伦敦学派。

的研究、对于阅读、翻译和写作的教学有着十分重要的实际意义。

半个多世纪以来,尤其是 20 世纪 80 年代以后,国内已有好几位语言学家撰文介绍和探讨主位-述位结构。他们分别就俄语、英语主位-述位的定义、在句中和在连贯话语中的划分与模式,以及这个结构在教学上和语言研究上的运用都进行了探讨。本章除了进一步讨论主位-述位结构的定义和划分、主位与述位的关系等问题之外(前四节),将着重讨论主位-述位结构在科技语体中的特点和模式,以及这个结构在教学中的应用(后二节)。

1.2 主位和述位

韩礼德从功能的角度,提出可对话语进行切分的理论,即一句话或一段话语可划分为主位(Theme,常标作 T)和述位(Rheme,常标作 R)(Halliday 1985)。例如:

[1] We (T) do not call them university towns (R). *①

韩礼德把主位定义为信息的出发点,例[1]中"we"就是主位。主位实际上就是起了"as for ..."或"as far as ... concerned"的功能,例[1]的主位表达了"As for us"或"As far as we are concerned"的意思。

述位的定义是信息的其余部分,是发展主位的部分(the remainder of the message, the part in which the Theme is developed)。

韩礼德认为,主位-述位是包括英语在内的许多语言的话语结构方式(Halliday 1985)。英语中的主位是由句中的位置来表示的:由于主位是信息的出发点,因而决定了它总是出现在句首。

① 本章中带 * 的例句均选自清华大学外语系编写的理工科公外英语教材,其余例句选自其他来源。

1.3 主位-述位结构的实质

1.3.1 简单的历史回顾

主位-述位结构理论最初是由捷克语言学家马泰休斯(Vilem Mathesius)于1929年创立。他对主位的定义是"在一定的语言环境中已知的内容,或至少是显而易见的内容,是说话者作为出发点的内容"(That which is known, or at least obvious, in the given situation, and from which the speaker proceeds in his discourse. 见 Halliday 1985)。

这个定义包含了两个特点:(1)在一定的语言环境中,主位是已知信息(known)或者显而易见(obvious)的信息;(2)说话者把已知信息作为说话的出发点。

换句话说,马泰休斯认为主位既是已知信息,又是说话的出发点。例[1]中的We就是说话的出发点,同时从一定的上下文或语言环境中对于双方又是已知的信息。

马泰休斯的这个理论自问世以来,引起了很多语言学家的兴趣,韩礼德就是其中之一。但与马泰休斯不同,他主张把主位和已知信息看作两个不同的概念。他仍借用马泰休斯的主位-述位术语,但他关于主位的定义与马泰休斯并不完全相同。他认为主位是说话者的出发点,已知是听话者已知的信息,它们是两个既有联系又有区别的概念。

1.3.2 主位-述位结构与已知-新信息结构

主位-述位结构属于语法范畴,而已知-新信息则是信息结构(information structure)。信息结构具有以下特点:

(1)每个信息单位由已知和新信息两部分构成,在口语中属于一个语调群,或者下降(falling),或者上升(rising),或者下降上升(falling-rising),或者上升下降(rising-falling)。语调重音落在信息焦点

(information focus)的成分上,这个信息焦点成分往往是新信息的高潮或结束,含有意料之外或强调的意思。

(2) 信息单位一般的顺序是:已知⌃新信息。此时已知与主位叠合(mapping),新信息与述位叠合。例如:

[2] At that time (T) many of the students were very young (R). *

此句主位"at that time"在课文中指上一段中的1226年,是已知的信息;新信息的高潮,或信息焦点是处于句尾的"young",是述位的一部分,可用音调标出。但是带有语调重音的信息焦点不一定都在句子结尾,信息单位的顺序可以变成"新信息⌃已知",此时新信息与主位叠合,已知与述位叠合。例如:

[3] Very young (T) were many of the students at that time (R).

句中"very young"是主位,又可是标有语调重意的新信息。

[4] With what (T) shall we mend it (R)?

"With what"在句中既是主位又是新信息。

有时,新信息与主位和述位的一部分叠合。例如:

[5] If you (T) suggest it's beautiful (R) they (T) see it as beautiful (R). (见 Halliday 1985).(这个复合句有两个信息单位,语调重音分别落在 suggest 及 see 上。)

"If"从句中的新信息包括"If you"及述位的一部分"suggest",在主句中新信息包括主位"they"及述位的一部分"see"。

很清楚,主位-述位结构与已知-新信息结构属于两个不同的概念。不应将它们混为一谈。它们的区别与心理学有关。句子划分为主位和述位是以说话者的心理判断为依据的。思维的过程总有一个出发点,主位就是思维的出发点,是"我想说的事"。有些语言学家认为,思维通过已知的信息将新信息与客观事物或现象联系起来(王福祥 1984)。韩礼德等语言学家则主张主位-述位结构是"说话者功能"(speaker-oriented function),以说话者为中心;而已知信息和新信息是说话者从听话者的角度出发(listener-oriented)组织的信息结构,以听话者为中心(Halliday 1985)。在通常情况下,说话者需要考虑听话者的心理,将对于听话者的已知信息放到句首主位的位置,而将新信息放到句尾(见例[2])。但往往由于某种原因(见本章第7部分),说话者把新信息当作思维或说话的出发点,使新信息与主位或部分主位叠合(见例[3]、[4]及[5])。

1.4 主位和主语

1.4.1 主语

首先必须区别传统语法与功能语法对主语的定义。

传统语法中的主语,没有明确的定义,主语在不同的句子中起不同的作用。19世纪下半叶人们开始用心理主语、语法主语、逻辑主语来区别主语在句子中的不同作用(Halliday 1985)。例如,下句中三个类型的主语都是"the boy"。

[6] **The boy** gave me this book.

心理主语

语法主语

逻辑主语

然而,将该句变为被动句,并将词序重新安排,三个主语就不再叠合。

[7] This book I was given by the boy.

This book	I	was given by	the boy.
心理主语	语法主语		逻辑主语

由于这三个主语在句中起了不同的作用,韩礼德用三个不同的术语取而代之:

心理主语 = 主位

语法主语 = 主语

逻辑主语 = 动作者

因而例[7]中的This book为主位,I为主语,the boy为动作者。

以下提到的主语仅指语法上的主语。(分析以下句子时，T = Theme，R = Rheme，S = Subject，C = Complement，P = Predicator，A = Adjunct。)

1.4.2 主位和主语

1.4.2.1 陈述句中的主位和主语

英语是一个有固定词序的语言(Halliday 1985)，陈述句通常的词序是：主语(subject) + 限定动词(finite verb) + 述词(predicator) + 补语(complement) + 附加语(adjunct)。

主位总是出现在句首，因此在陈述句中常与主语叠合，这样的主位称为无标记主位(unmarked theme)。例[1]中的 we 和例[6]中的 boy 都是无标记主位。再如：

[8] A meeting of technical and commercial translation (S, T)* was taking place in Britain (R).

[9] What used to be wrong (S, T) becomes right (R).*

例[8]和[9]中的画线部分，主位与主语叠合，都是无标记主位。

前面已指出，主位与主语在句中起不同作用，它们也可不叠合，此时主位与其他成分叠合。这样的主位称为标记主位(marked theme)。例如：

[10] Later (A, T) Cambridge became a centre of learning (R).*

[11] The presence of your husband's cheeses in her house (C, T) she would, I instinctively feel, regard as a put down (R). (*College English* III - 1 - Lesson 13)

[12] In case of failure (A, T) their position would be perilous in the extreme (R); and fail (P, T) they (S) surely would (R), … (*College English* III - 2 - Lesson 14)

例[10]中的 Later 是副词附加语充当主位；例[11]中的句首是补语充

当主位;例[12]中的前一句的主位由作为附加语的介词短语充当。但是最具标记主位的是后一个小句中的 fail,它是述词作为句子的主位,英语中比较少见。

1.4.2.2 感叹句中的主位和述位

感叹句中的无标记主位是 what 和 how 引出的感叹成分,因而主位和主语一般不叠合。例如:

[13] What tremendous easy questions (T) you (S) ask (R)!

1.4.2.3 疑问句中的主位和述位

在一般疑问句中:其无标记主位由限定动词 + 主语构成,主语是主位的一部分。例如:

[14] May I (S, T) speak to Mr. Parsons (R)?*

特殊疑问句中:其无标记主位由疑问词构成,主位和主语一般不叠合(who 除外),如例[4]。

1.4.2.4 祈使句中的主位和述位

有两种祈使句,即带主语的祈使句与不带主语的祈使句。

带主语的祈使句中的主语就是主位,两者叠合。例如:

[15] You (S, T) keep quiet!

不带主语的祈使句可有主位,也可为零位主位;而带限定词 do 的祈使句中,do 是主位。例如:

[16] Do (T) keep quiet!

在 let 祈使句中,let 及其补语是主位。例如:

[17] Let me (T) get a bit of paper (R)!*

在表示否定的祈使句中,don't 是主位。例如:

[18] Don't (T) try to drive through Cambridge during the five minutes between lectures (R).*

零位主位,如:

[19] (T) Stop in some safe place, and wait (R)! *

1.5 单项主位、复项主位、句项主位

1.5.1 单项主位

单项主位由一个语义成分组成,如例[1]中的 We 和例[8]中的"a meeting of technical and commercial translators",它们分别是两个句子中的主语。

1.5.2 复项主位

韩礼德认为一切自然语言都是由三种语义功能构成的,即一个句子可同时表达概念功能(ideational)、交际功能(interpersonal)及语篇功能(textual)。

概念功能是语言对主客观世界的事物和过程的反映,以及事物与事物之间关系的表达。

交际功能表示交际者在一定的语境中,以某种身份、某种态度参加言语活动,用叙述、询问、建议、劝告和命令等方式表达自己对客观现象的意见、态度和评价,表达交际者之间的关系。

语篇功能与话语的形式、言语活动的结构有关。通过这个功能使语言实现同一定的上下文和语境相关联,从而,使言语活动成为可能,使说写者能够创立语篇,使读者能够理解语篇。

复项主位就是由这三种功能语义成分组合而成。复项主位内部各成分的排列顺序是语篇^交际^概念。语篇成分包括:(1) 持续成分(continuative),如 well、oh、now 等;(2) 结构成分(structural),如 and、 but、when、in case 等;(3) 连接成分,如 therefore、finally、on the other hand 等。交际成分,包括(1)呼语(vocative),如 Tom、ladies and gentlemen;(2) 情态成分(modal),如 in my opinion、honestly、by chance;(3) 限定动词,如 do、won't、should;(4) WH 成分,如 why、what、how。概念成分包括主题成分(topical),即主语、补语或环境附加语(circumstantial adjunct)。下面句中的主位是一个包括这三种语义成分的复项主位:

[20] Well, but in that case Ann surely shouldn't everybody (T) have the same chance (R). (Halliday, 1985)

句中,"well"和"but"为语篇成分,"Ann""surely""shouldn't"为交际成分,"everybody"是句子的主语,为概念成分。

复项主位中的语篇成分和交际成分可有可无,但一定要有概念成分。若三种成分同时存在,语篇和交际成分的顺序可颠倒,但概念成分总是在主位部分的最后。比如例[20]中的 everybody 和[21]中作为概念成分的 you,它们都位于语篇成分和交际成分的后面,处于复项主位的最后位置。

[21] Ah, well, Tom, you (T) turn to the right and then go straight on (R).*

1.5.3 句项主位

句项主位是复合句中的从句或主句。

(1) 句项主位可由主句充当。例如:

[22] Men always shake hands (T) when they are introduced to another man (R).*

(2) 句项主位可由从句充当。例如:

[23] If you want to pronounce a word correctly (T), first you must hear it correctly (R).*

复合句的主句和从句还可继续划分为主位和述位,如例[22]和[23]可进一步切分为:

[22] Men (T) always shake hands (R) when they (T) are introduced to another man (R).

[23] If you (T) want to pronounce a word correctly (R), first you (T) must hear it correctly (R).

1.6 科技英语中的主位-述位结构特点

1.6.1 结构特点

在不同文体的话语中,主位和述位的成分结构有不同的规律。为了说明科技英语主位和述位的特点,先将十二篇科技英语读物[①]中的主位与口语作一比较。

1.6.1.1 陈述句

口语中最常见的无标记主位是 I,因为交际双方的话题最经常涉及自己,其次是人称代词 you、we、he、she、it、they 以及 it 和引导词 there,最后是名词和名词词组(Halliday 1985)。

与口语形成鲜明的对照,书面体的科技英语多以名词和名词词组为主位。在这十二篇文章中,这样的主位占全部主位的二分之一到四分之三,其次是 it,人称代词很少充当主位。原因是显而易见的:科技文章所涉及的一般不是我们自己或他人,而是我们周围的世界、客观存在的事物和现象。例如:

[24] Science (T) has many characteristics (R), and to understand what science is (T) requires a detailed examination of these properties and peculiarities (R).

---

① 出处同第 28 页脚注。

1.6.1.2 疑问句、感叹句和祈使句

口语是交际双方面对面的交流，应用大量的疑问句、感叹句和祈使句；书面科技语很少出现疑问句和祈使句，基本不出现感叹句（上述教材中的前六篇仅有一个一般疑问句，二个 WH 疑问句和三个祈使句，无一例感叹句），因而很少出现这三类句式中的主位-述位结构。另外书面科技英语中的祈使句多以 Let us（consider）、suppose 一类词和短语充当主位。

1.6.1.3 复项主位的成分

英语科技文章和口语都存在大量的复项主位，然而构成语篇-交际-概念的成分在这两种语体中有些区别：

语篇成分中的持续成分（continuative）如：well、yes 等词在口语中是交谈双方进行交际的手段，被频繁使用，而在书面体的科技英语中基本不出现。

四种交际成分（见 1.5.2）在口语中经常使用，但在科技文章中基本不用呼语，很少用情态成分，因为科技文章描述客观事实，一般不涉及作者的感情。科技文章中由于很少出现疑问句和感叹句，自然很少用限定动词与 WH 充当主位。

1.6.2 英语科技文章中主位-述位结构模式

上面分析的都是以句子为单位的主位和述位。现在我们来分析和研究大于句子的连贯话语，涉及一篇科技文章中的句子与句子如何通过主位-述位相互联系、衔接、照应、过渡的问题，这样的探讨可以揭示文章如何把具有内在联系的句子连接起来表达一个复杂的思想。

参考徐盛恒（1982）、黄衍（1985）提出的话语结构模式，笔者分析了上述十二篇科技文章，提出六种模式。

模式 1：各句均以第一句的主位（T1）为主位，引出不同的述位，从不同的角度发展同一个主位。可用下式表示：

T1……R1
T2（= T1）……R2
.
.
.
Tn（= T1）……Rn

例如：

[25] Science（T1）is, indeed, concerned with nature …（R1）. Science（T2）is much more than knowledge of elusive high-speed subatomic particles, …（R2）. Science（T3）embraces all of nature, and expresses our best ideas …（R3）.

[26] The Moon, the Sun, and the individual planets（T1）also follow as identifiable objects in the same realm（R1）. Though each（T2）is unique, demanding a field of study all to itself（R2）, each（T3）is also an example of a general thing（R3）.

模式 2：第一句述位（R1）成为以后各句的主位，即后面句子的主位都围绕这个述位的思想展开讨论。可用下式表示：

T1…… R1
T2（= R1）……R2
.
.
.
Tn（= R1）……Rn

例如：

[27] In the course of constructing the idealized mathematical model for any given engineering problem（T1）, certain approximations will always be involved（R1）. Some of these approximations（T2）may be mathematical（R2）, whereas others（T3）will be physical（R3）.

模式 3：第一句的述位成为第二句的主位，该主位又引出新的述位，这新的述位又成为下一句的主位，如此延续下去。可用下式表示：

T1……R1

T2（=R1）……R2

.

.

Tn（=Rn-1）…… Rn

例如：

[28] To measure velocity (T1) we have to measure time at different points in space (R1). To do this (T2) we need to test that clocks remain synchronized ... (R2). To carry out this test (T3), we require knowledge of the velocity of light (R3).

模式4：各句均以第一句的述位（R1）为述位，各句不同的主位都归结为同一个述位（R1）。可用下式表示：

T1……R1

T2 ……. R2(=R1)

.

.

.

Tn …… Rn(=Rn)

例如：

[29] While we (T1) are on the subject of conceptual things (R1), let us (T2) attempt a fine distinction between what we may call physical conceptual things and mathematical conceptual things (R2). The utopium billiard ball (T3) is a physical concept (R3) .... The point – particle (T4) is a mathematical concept (R4).

模式5：第一句的主位（T1）为第二句的主位（T2），第二句的述位（R2）为第三句的主位，第三句的主位（T3）为第四句的主位（T4），第四句的述位为第五句的主位（T5）。可用下式表示：

T1……R1

T2（= T1）……R2

T3（= R2）…… R3

.

.

.

Tn（= Tn-1）… Rn

Tm（= Rm-1）… Rm

例如：

［30］The world science（T1）comes to us from a Latin word *scire*, which means "to know"（R1）; loosely, then, science（T2）is simply what we know: the total of all human knowledge（R2）. But the definition of science as all knowledge（T3）would not be a workable one（R3）, …

模式 6：各句的主位-述位无明显联系。可用下式表示：
例如：

［31］… but why（T1）concern ourselves with conceptual things（R1）when there（T2）are many real identifiable things to be investigated and their nature understood（R2）. Unfortunately one（T3）cannot avoid a large degree of abstraction（R3）.

笔者同意黄衍(1985)指出的，"后一句的主位或述位，不一定非要逐字逐句重复原来的词句。"后一句使用的主位或述位，大致有以下几种情况：(1) 完全重复同一词语，如例［25］中的 science；(2) 用代词代替，如例［26］中的 each 代替"the Moon, the Sun, and the individual planet"所包含的每一个单项；另外，还可用部分重复的方法(partial repetition)，这种部分重复可以是形式上的，也可以是语义内容上的，如例［27］中的"some of these approximations"就是形式上的重复；例［30］中的"total of all human knowledge"指的就是"to know"；例［28］的"to do this"语义上与"we have to measure time at different points in space"相同。

在分析这些科技文章中，笔者发现黄衍(1985)指出的以下两点也是非常正确的:“在语言的实际运用中,由于思想表达的复杂性,往往是几种模式搭配交替使用。”“一般话语,不一定都按原思路径直发展下去,而是可能有曲折、有迂回、有波澜。反映在句子之间的联系上,就是主位-述位的衔接发生一些变化。”但是由于科技文章一般不涉及作者态度或感情的变化,因而表现在主位-述位上的变化比口语或文学作品要少。

1.7 主位-主位结构在教学上的应用

徐盛桓(1985)曾撰文探讨这个结构在教学上的应用,比如,有助于语言材料的组织,进行有条理的、合乎逻辑的叙述;可用以指导制作提示卡片,帮助组织口头作文;可应用于指导翻译实践。

本节着重讨论主位-述位结构对加深阅读理解和指导作文可能发挥的作用。

1.7.1 主位-述位结构与语篇阐释

主位-述位结构可揭示一些传统语法不能解释的语义现象,帮助学生加深对连贯话语的理解。以下仅举四个方面的例子。

(1) 可用来解释 A is B 与 B is A 在语义上的细微差别。用传统语法分析下面两个例子,它们的结构分别是:

[32] His other favorite sport　is　boxing.*

主语　系词　表语

[33] Boxing　is　his favorite sport.

主语　系词　表语

显然,有些词在句中的语法作用有了改变,如例[32]中的 boxing 是表语,在例[33]中却变成了主语。至于这两句话的语义差别,传统语法无法做出回答。而用主位-述位结构理解分析这两个句子,内含的语义差别可得以区别。例[32]的主位是 His favorite sport,含有“我将告诉你有关他的另一项喜爱的运动”;而在例[33]中 Boxing 处于主位的位置,含有“我将告诉你有关拳击的事”。两句话的不同点在于他们的出发点不同,关心的内容不同,表达了两个不同的信息。

(2) 可用来解释被动态与主动态语句的差别。

在分析主位-述位结构实质时,我们已经指出主位-述位在一般情况下与已知和新信息叠合,这是为了让听话者把注意力放到有语调重音的新信息上。例如:

[34] That (T) is Mary (R). Mary (GIVEN) sailed the boat (NEW).

例[34]第二句话的出发点是已知成分 Mary,新信息是落在有语调重音的述位结构部分 boat 上。

若要强调动作者 Mary,英语有三种方法:

其一,在口语中把重音放到 Mary 上,即:

Mary (T) sailed the boat (R).

此时,Mary 成为无标记主位。

其二,用 It is Mary who sailed the boat 这样的句型。

其三,将原句变成被动态:

[35] The boat (T) is sailed by Mary (R).

这就是说,若要强调动作者,根据上下文,可把句子变成被动态,将动作者放到介词之后。不过,例[35]最好出现在下列语境中:

That (GIVEN) was a boat (NEW). It (GIVEN) was sailed by Mary (NEW).

此时,Mary 既是落有语调重音的新信息,又是述位的结束。

(3) 可用于解释连贯话语各句之间如何衔接、照应、过渡(H & H 1976),揭示各句在语义上的内在联系。引导学生用模式 1-6 来分析连贯话语,无疑有助于学生了解作者如何将句子有机地组织成章,从而提高他们的阅读能力。

(4) 可用来解释英语的语序变化在语义上的含义。

前面已经谈到,英语是一种有固定词序的语言(见第 3 节)。通常,陈述句中的主位与主语叠合,为无标记主位;句子的其他成分也可充当主位,为标记主位。

最常见的标记主位是在句中起附加语作用的副词和介词短语,如例[2]、[4]、[10];句子的补语(包括介词补语)有时也做主位,如例[11];在特殊情况下,也可将述动词放到主位的位置上,如例[12]。

韩礼德(Halliday 1985)指出,英语非主语成分放到主位的位置上,必须有充足的理由(good reason):

其一,使连贯性话语各句之间更好地衔接。比如例[2]"At that time"是句子的主位,是为了能与上句结尾的年代1226年更紧密地衔接、呼应(属模式3)。

其二,为了加强语气,强调某个成分。比如例[11]中的补语"The presence of your husband's cheeses in her (landlady's) house"是该句的主位。从上下文我们得知说话人竭力反对对方将奶酪带到他租用的公寓,理由是房东太太会大加阻挠。说话人把这一补语放到句首,因为这是他最关心的问题。又例如[12]"fail they surely would"一句中,fail成为主位的一部分,因为作者想强调在敌人发觉的情况下,失败是注定的。

其三,为了表达某种感情,比如激动、赞美、惊讶、遗憾等感情,或表达同意、反对的意义(见王福祥1984)。这一点最充分地体现在感叹句的语序排列上,见例[13]。

疑问句和祈使句的语序排列也有语义上的原因,但与阅读理解关系不大,故略。

理解标记主位带来语序变化的原因和内在含义,可以帮助读者深刻理解作者的意图,使理解更加准确。

1.7.2 主位-述位结构与作文能力的提高

首先,掌握主位-述位结构规律有助于帮助学生将语言材料组织成为条理清楚、合乎逻辑的连贯性话语。

写好作文的一个重要因素是如何将语言素材组织起来成为一个有机的整体。假如学生能熟练掌握上述1~6个模式,将处于零散状态的句型组织成连贯性的话语，那么文章的条理性和逻辑性自然会大大地加强。否则就会出现句子互相不衔接或衔接不当的现象。例如：

[36] Classes have been set up to offer professional training which will enable the disabled to earn their own living. We will continue to offer these classes.

显然，这两句话的衔接不自然。原因有二：

(1) 语态不一致，第一个句子是被动语态，第二个句子是主动语态；

(2) 两句话的出发点转换不自然。第一句话的出发点是 classes，但是正当读者头脑里建立起 classes 是谈话中心的时候，突然第二个句子的话题变成了 we，而 classes 却成了述位的一部分。这种思想上的跳跃，即主位-述位的迁移变化很不自然，不符合人们头脑里逻辑思维的发展。例[36]可改为：

Classes have been set up to offer professional training which will enable the disabled to earn their own living. Such training courses will continue to be held.

或

We will set up classes to offer professional training which will enable the disabled to earn their own living. We will continue to offer such classes.

其次，英语语序通常情况下的固定结构以及它的变化规律，也是写好作文应当遵循的重要原则。同样，原因有二：

(1) 学生必须清楚，一般情况下，没有充足的理由，写的句子的主位与主语应当是一致的，不能毫无理由地将句子的任一成分放到句首。尤其在决定是否将补语或述动词变成标记主位时更要慎重，比如例[3]、[11]、[12]只有在一定的语境中才能出现。

(2) 但是为了达到某种效果，比如为了更好地与上下文衔接，为了加强预期或强调某个成分，或为了表达某种感情，学生也应当学会把不是主语的某个成分放到句首的位置上，比如例[11]和[12]。

主位-述位结构在教学上的应用探讨刚刚开始，有待进一步深入研究。

2

浅谈汉语的“主语”
——“主语”“施事”“主位”*

2.1 前　言

随着国外各种不同流派的语言学理论被纷纷介绍到国内，中国语言学界的气象耳目一新。对国外的语言学，特别是普通语言学理论，我们的态度应当是“好好研究，大力提倡。”当然，“我们学习语言学理论，并不是为了理论而理论”（王力 1982）。学习的目的是应用，是开辟新的研究领域。目前，中国的语言学工作者或许可以在两个方面应用语言学理论：

第一，以语言学理论为指导，研究某种外语的特点，并把研究的成果应用于教学或其他方面。比如英语，这是在中国学习人数最多的一门外语。中国的语言工作者有责任用语言学的理论，进一步研究英语的语音、语法、语义系统的特点，特别是语篇结构的特点，进而研究在中国这个特定的语境中，教授英语应当遵循的规律和方法。许多外语教师在这方面做了大量的工作，随着语言学的深入学习和研究，相信这方面的成果会更

* 本章原为 1989 年在第一次中国功能语言学研讨会上的发言，辑录于北京大学 1990 年出版、胡壮麟主编的论文集《语言系统与功能》第 53－62 页。

加突出。

第二,王力先生(1982)一再强调:“我们极需用语言学理论指导我们研究汉语和少数民族语言。”面对汉语研究的落后状况,他一针见血地指出:“我们天天说汉语,但却研究得很不够,不但汉语的历史研究得不够,就是汉语的现状——现代汉语也研究得很不够。”他认为汉语的研究,有着广阔的前途,指出:“学习了语言学理论和欧美语言学家有关语言研究的著作,回过头来考虑我们的汉语研究,就能开辟许多新的园地,甚至可以产生新的理论。”

对于汉语的研究,可以采取不同的方法,目前比较流行的是用比较语言学的研究方法,即将汉语与其他语言进行比较。这种方法的好处是,研究者可以借鉴国外语言学的研究成果,从新的角度对汉语进行剖析,开创出崭新的研究领域。

本章就是遵循王力先生的主张,在学习了韩礼德功能语言学理论的基础上,将汉语与英语相比较,对汉语“主语”这个概念进行讨论,提出自己的粗浅看法。

2.2 对“主语”概念的不同理解

下面这些句子当中,哪个成分是“主语”,不同的语法学家,从不同的角度有着很不相同的理解。

[1] 北京我没有到过。
[2] 这个字我不认识。
[3] 自行车骑走了。
[4] 电灯修理好了。
[5] *a*. 窗台上摆满了鲜花。
b. 窗台上鲜花摆满了。
[6] 审判员审判罪犯。

[7] 罪犯被我们判处五年徒刑。

[8] 这个人头脑清楚。

[9] 他脸色不大好。

[10] 老王,我昨天还见到他。

[11] 祖国这是多么庄严的名字。

笔者拜读了吕叔湘(1984;1985)、朱德熙(1984)等语言学家的语言学著作。归纳起来,这些学者对“主语”的概念和主谓语的划分提出了三种不同的看法。

1. 按照主语谓语的相对关系划分主、谓语。主语是“被陈述的对象”,谓语是用来“陈述”主语的部分,它的主要成分是谓语动词。根据这种看法,例[1]、[2]句中的“我”,[3]、[4]句中的“自行车”“电灯”,[5b]中的“鲜花”,[6]、[7]句中的“审判员”和“罪犯”,[8]、[9]句中的“头脑”“脸色”以及[10]、[11]句中的“我”“这”就分别是句子的主语,因为它们都是被谓语陈述的对象。

2. 按施受关系划分主谓语。主动句中施事(者)就是主语,被动句中受事(者)为主语。比如[1]、[2]中的“我”,[6]、[7]、[10]句中的“审判员”“罪犯”以及“我”均为各句的主语,它们或是施事(者)或是受事(者)。

3. 按前后位置或从说话人表达的角度来划分主谓语。朱德熙(1984)、胡裕树(1987)把这样的主语称为“话题”或“话题主语”;吕叔湘(1985)则称它为“句子陈述的起点”或“起语”。根据这个看法,各句句首的词都可作为各句的主语,因为它们是话题,是陈述的起点。

有些语法学家认为,例[1]、[2]、[8]、[9]各句中均有两个主语同时存在,前者为话题主语,又称为“大主语”,后者为“小主语”。有些学者则将“老王”及“祖国”称为句子的“提示主语”,起提示或强调的作用。

事实上,关于主语的定义和地位,自20世纪50年代以来在语法学界一直存在着分歧。李临定(1985/1994)认为“它是一个令人头痛的问题”。他在从语义到形式诸方面考察了主语的特点之后,认为“主语形式贫乏,语法地位不重要,在语法分析中不需过于重视。”他还认为应当更重视“施事”“受事”以及和谓语动词发生关系的其他各种词性成分,因为“这些成分在语句结构中起重要作用”。这里他似乎将主语和施事两个概念区分了开来,而且提出了要重视对施事或与之地位相当的成分的研究,这无疑是有一定意义的。但是重视对施事的研究并不能完全解决主语概念的问题。事实上，有相当多的句子没有施事，却有主语，如例[8]、[9]和[11]。主语和施事是两个在语言功能上不相同的概念，它们在功能上不能相互替代，也不应被混淆。

2.3 主语、施事(者)、主位

韩礼德认为，任何一种语言同时具有三种功能，即概念功能、人际功能和语篇功能(Halliday 1985)。所不同的是，在不同的语言中，实现这些功能的手段或方式不同。用这个观点来观察上面提到的三种不同概念的主语，似乎可以找到一条解决这个"令人头痛的问题"的出路。从功能语言学的角度来看，这三个不同的主语概念体现了三种不同的功能。

第一种对主语的理解，着眼于主语与谓语，特别是主语与谓语动词之间的相对的语法关系，体现出语言是用来进行交际的工具，语言帮助说话者之间进行信息的交流。这时，主语是"被陈述的对象"，谓语是用来陈述主语的。换句话说，没有主语或者没有谓语(省略句除外)，说话者之间就不可能达到交流的目的。

第二种对主语的理解体现了主客观世界在语言结构中的反映，语言用来表示主客观世界，用来表达一定的内容，因而具有"概念功能"。这时，完成动作者称为施事者或施事，动作所及对象称为受事者或受事。由于主客观世界所具有的复杂性，还存在与施事地位相当的功能，如"感觉者""载体"等。

第三种按前后位置划分主谓语的看法，反映了语言具有语篇功能。这时，说话者将句子看作表达信息的手段。吕叔湘(1984)认为这样划分的主语，是"遵从某一种心理指示"来进行的，他称之为"心理主语"。

将上面三种不同的概念，三种不同的功能都称之为主语，显然是把三个不同语法平面上的概念混淆在一起了，这样就难免出现问题，很难自圆其说。为使语法概念更加科学化，本章建议不妨借鉴韩礼德的理论

(Halliday 1985),采用他的三个不同的术语,即“主语”、“施事”(或相当于这个功能的其他术语)和“主位”来代替原来的“主语”这一笼统的概念。这样做或许可以比较科学地客观地反映语言的本质。这三个术语的定义分别是:

主语——被谓语陈述的对象

施事——动作者

主位——信息的出发点或起点

将汉语与英语进行比较,有几点需要说明:

第一,汉语与英语的主语在功能上有相当大的差异。英语主语的主要功能在于它是实现不同语气的主要成分之一。英语中语气的变化主要是通过主语与定谓成分(谓语中对动词起限定作用的成分)的位置变化来实现的,比如在陈述句和祈使句中,主语必须置于定谓成分之前;而疑问句的语序一般为:定谓成分+主语+……,也就是说,疑问语气是通过这两个成分位置相互交换来实现的(Halliday 1985)。而在汉语中,主语与谓语动词的位置相对固定,不同语气句子的语序都是:主语+谓语动词+……。疑问语气是依靠其他手段来实现的,比如句尾的语气词,口语中不同的语调,书面语言中的标点符号等等。

第二,汉语的主语不像某些西方语言具有“格变”,主语没有其他形式。另外,谓语动词也不必随着主语人称的变化进行变位。这也许就是为什么李临定先生认为汉语主语“形式特征贫乏”,进而断言它的“实际的语法地位就不那么重要”的原因吧!

第三,通常情况下,主位、施事(或受事)、主语三者重合,或者主位与施事(或受事)、或主位与主语重合。现分析上述各个例句(均借用韩礼德的术语:T=Theme,主位;S = Subject,主语;V= Verb,A=Actor,施事;G=Goal 目标或受事,C=Carrier,载体;R = Rheme,述位,它是句子的其余部分,其功能是发展主位):

[6] 审判员(T/S/A)审判罪犯。

[1] 北京(T)我(A/S)没有到过。

[2] 这个字(T)我(A/S)不认识。

[3] 自行车(T/G)骑走了。

[4] 电灯(T/G)修理好了。

[5b] 窗台上(T)鲜花(S)摆满了(V)。

但在被动句中：

[7] 罪犯(T/S/G)被我们(A)判处五年徒刑。

对[5a]有两种不同的分析方法。根据吕叔湘(1984)的看法，汉语可以有VS语序，此句可以分析为：

窗台上(T)摆满了(V)鲜花(S)。

但如果参照朱德熙(1984)认为主语应置于谓语动词之前的观点，那么鲜花应为宾语(object)，即：

窗台上(T)摆满了(V)鲜花(O)。

另外，汉语为了强调某个成分，可将其变为提示成分放在句首，后面在一定的位置上重复相应的名词或代词。这时，句子的主位就是这个提示成分。它相当于英语中"As for ..."或"as far as ... concerned"短语的功能，可视为提示主位(Preposed Theme，见M. Berry 1977)。因而：

[10] 老王(PreT)，我(S/A)昨天还见到他。

[11] 祖国(PreT)这(S/C)是多么庄严的名字。

例[8]和[9]可以根据语调的不同，有两种不同的语义和两种不同的划分主语和主位的方法：

[8a] 这个人(T)头脑(S/C)清楚。

当"这个人"重读时，它是句子的出发点，是主位；"头脑"是被谓语陈述的对象，是主语，连同"清楚"二字构成述位。

[8b] 这个人头脑(T/S/C)清楚。

"头脑"被重读时，"这个人"被当成定语，修饰"头脑"，可以理解为"这个人的"。同样：

[9a] 他(T)脸色(S/C)不大好。

当"他"重读时，就成为句子的起语或出发点，是主位；"脸色"是说明的对象，是主语。

[9b] 他脸色(T/S/C)不大好。

“脸色”被重读时,“他”相当于“他的”,修饰“脸色”。

下面想说明一下为什么建议用一个新的术语“主位”代替“话题”。

张斌指出汉语中存在“话题主语”,但没有给“话题”下明确的定义(见胡裕树 1987)。胡裕树(1987)则认为“话题是个广泛的概念,凡是句子叙述的起点,几乎都可看作‘‘话题’’”。这里,胡裕树所谓的话题与韩礼德对于主位的定义相仿。但是,对于许多语言学家来说,“话题”和“主位”并不等同,话题是与 Comment 即“述题”相对应的(Chao 1968),它的范围并没有像胡裕树说的那么广泛。严格地说,第一,话题只是主位的一部分;第二,它通常仅指“已知”的信息部分(Halliday 1985)。

韩礼德指出,主位可分为简单主位与复合主位。简单主位除指由各词词组体现的“话题”成分(Topical element)外,也可以是由其他词组或短语体现的语气、情态或环境成分等。同样,复合主位除了必须包括“话题”成分之外,还可包括语篇成分(Textual element)和人际成分(Interpersonal element)。下面参照韩礼德(Halliday 1985)关于英语复合主位的分析,比较下列句子(Cont = Continuative,连续语;M = Modal,情态成分;Voc = Vocative,呼语;Exclam = Exclamatory,惊叹语;Inter = Interpersonal,人际成分;Text = Textual,语篇成分;Topic = Topical,话题成分):

[12] On the other hand maybe on a week day it would be less crowded.

<table>
<tr><td>Cont.</td><td>M</td><td rowspan="2">Topic</td><td rowspan="3">Rheme</td></tr>
<tr><td>Text</td><td>Inter</td></tr>
<tr><td colspan="3">Theme</td></tr>
</table>

[13] 昌林哥,玉翠嫂子,你们两位 同意不?

<table>
<tr><td>Voc</td><td rowspan="2">Topic</td><td rowspan="3">Rheme</td></tr>
<tr><td>Inter</td></tr>
<tr><td colspan="2">Theme</td></tr>
</table>

[14] 好，　　就这样决定。

<table>
<tr><td>Cont</td><td rowspan="3">Rheme</td></tr>
<tr><td>Text</td></tr>
<tr><td>Theme</td></tr>
</table>

“好”暗示新的行为的开始，是“语篇成分”，作为主位的一部分。这句话的话题主位成分“咱们”被省略。

[15] 啊呀，天，　你　长得多结实啊！

<table>
<tr><td>Exclam</td><td rowspan="2">Topic</td><td rowspan="3">Rheme</td></tr>
<tr><td>Inter</td></tr>
<tr><td colspan="2">Theme</td></tr>
</table>

[16] 你瞧　　这些孩子的嘴　多巧！

<table>
<tr><td>Exclam</td><td rowspan="2">Topic</td><td rowspan="3">Rheme</td></tr>
<tr><td>Inter</td></tr>
<tr><td colspan="2">Theme</td></tr>
</table>

“你瞧”表示说话者的惊讶，以引起对方的注意，是人际成分，作为主位的一部分。

[17] 看起来，　我们有些同志，对于马克思、列宁所说的
　　　　　　　　　　　　民主集中制，还不理解。

<table>
<tr><td>Modal</td><td rowspan="2">Topic</td><td rowspan="3">Rheme</td></tr>
<tr><td>Inter</td></tr>
<tr><td colspan="2">Theme</td></tr>
</table>

“看起来”表示推测和估计，是人际成分作为主位的一部分。

[18] 毫无疑问，　我们　应当批评各种各样的
　　　　　　　　　　错误思想。

<table>
<tr><td>Modal</td><td rowspan="2">Topic</td><td rowspan="3">Rheme</td></tr>
<tr><td>Inter</td></tr>
<tr><td colspan="2">Theme</td></tr>
</table>

“毫无疑问”表示强调、肯定的语气，是人际成分作为主位的一部分。

[19] 不用说，两个人的劲头 都绷得像梆子戏上的琴弦。

<table>
<tr><td>Modal</td><td rowspan="2">Topic</td><td rowspan="3">Rheme</td></tr>
<tr><td>Inter</td></tr>
<tr><td colspan="2">Theme</td></tr>
</table>

“不用说”表示肯定的语气，是人际成分作为主位的一部分。

可以看出，上面这些句子当中，“话题”成分仅是简单主位的一种选择，也仅是复合主位的一部分。

最后谈谈“话题”与“已知”的关系。在通常情况下，一个句子就是一个信息单位，它包含两个部分：“已知”（Given）与“新信息”（New）。在口语中，它们属于一个语调群，重音一般落在“新信息”上。一般情况下，“已知”出现在“新信息”之前，语序为“已知”^“新信息”。此时，“话题”指“已知”。但有时为了强调“新信息”，或者为了上下文衔接的需要，作为标记的“新信息”可置于“已知”之前，语序为“新信息”^“已知”。由于话题必须出现在句子的开始，而它同时又必须指“已知”（Halliday 1985），有时就出现了分析上的困难。而使用“主位”这个术语，就不会出现这样的问题。因为它不仅可以与“已知”重合，也可以与“新信息”重合。因而这个术语比“话题”更恰当。例如（Gn = Given，已知；N = New，新信息）：

[20] 我（T/Gn）已经知道这件事（R/N）。

[21] 这件事（T/N）我已经知道（R/Gn）。

总而言之，目前汉语语法对主语的定义缺乏科学性，它的含意不够明确，包含的内容太多太杂，担负了太多的语法功能。本章建议用“主语”表示被（谓语）陈述的对象，“施事”表示动作者，用“主位”表示信息的出发点，即用三个表示不同功能的术语来代替原来的“主语”。这或许是一条解决这个难题的出路。

3

A Contrastive Study of Theme and Rheme Structure in English and Chinese*

3.1 Introduction

Halliday (1985) assumes that in all languages "the clause① has the character of a message". In English, the clause is organized as a message by having two parts — Theme and Rheme. He defines Theme as "the element which serves as the point of departure of the message: it is that with which

---

* This chapter combines two papers, one with the same title presented at the conference with the theme "Text and Language" hosted by Xi'an Jiaotong University in 1989, and then collected in *Proceedings of the International Conference on Text and Language* published in 1993 by Xi'an Jiaotong University Press and edited by Keqi Hoq, Hermann Bluhme and Renzhi Li, and the other entitled "试论汉语的主位述位结构—兼与英语的主位述位相比较", published in *Journal of Tsinghua University*, 1989(2).

① A "clause" in Halliday's terminology is approximately an independent sentence in many cases as understood by most people. In the analysis of Chinese, we will use the term "sentence".

the clause is concerned". Rheme, by definition, is "the remainder of the message, the part in which the Theme is developed."

Halliday further states that in English, Theme can be identified as "that element which comes in first position in the clause" (*ibid.*) and in Japanese it is the part before an auxiliary word. Since the beginning of the 20th century, many linguists have described this structure in quite a few languages. Actually, this division was first put forward by the Prague School linguist Mathesius (1929), using Czech as his analytical language. Up to 1970, there had been more than 600 papers discussing the Theme-Rheme structure in Russian (Wang Fuxiang, 1984).

Is a Chinese sentence also structured as a message by having the two parts — Theme and Rheme? If so, does Theme take the initial position as in English? And what are the similarities and differences in the Theme-Rheme structure between the two linguistic systems?

This chapter is an attempt to answer these questions. We shall offer a comparison of the thematic elements in declarative, interrogative and complex sentences in the Chinese and English languages, prefaced by a discussion of the necessity of introducing the concept of "Theme" to the grammatical analysis of the Chinese language and that of the thematic elements in different sentence structures in this language.

3.2 Theme-Rheme structure in the Chinese language

The definitions of the grammatical category "subject" given by various scholars and especially Lü Shuxiang's criteria for identifying the "subject" of a Chinese sentence convince me that the Theme-Rheme structure is also followed in the organization of a Chinese sentence into a message.

Lü (1984) established four criteria for identifying the subject of a sentence in Chinese:

(i) According to the relationship between the doer and the affected;

(ii) According to the sequence of elements;

(iii) According to relative subjectivism;

(iv) According to absolute subjectivism.

Comparing the above criteria with the three types of "subjects", namely, "logical subject", "psychological subject" and "grammatical subject", existing in the Western languages as classified by the 19th century Western grammarians (Halliday 1985), we find that the subject identified according to (i) and (iv) is equivalent to the "logical subject", and the ones following (ii) and (iii) will be the "psychological subject" and "grammatical subject" respectively. In other words, as in English, there also exist three different subjects in the Chinese language, which perform different functions in different sentence structures or patterns. To avoid confusion, we follow Halliday's terminology and label the above three subjects as "Doer", "Theme" and "Subject" respectively. This will provide us with a better framework for the analysis of the different functions taken on by the traditional "subject".

Lü cited the following sentences as examples:

[1] 本科① 探花② 点 了 个 旗人。
*benke *tanhua dian le ge qiren。
Benke tanhua point (ASP) (MEAS) Manchu
Benke tanhua is assigned to a Manchu.

[2] 榻上 坐 着 个 老子。
ta shang zuo zhe ge lao zi。
couch on sit (ASP) (MEAS) old man
On couch is sitting an old man.

① a form of royal exam

② This title was given to the one who came out the third in the royal exam held annually in the Qing Dynasty.

Analyzing the two sentences according to Lü's first criterion, [1] has no subject as the doer① is not made explicit, while [2] takes "老子" (*lao zi*, old man) as the subject since it is the doer of the verb. However, dividing the two sentences in accordance with Lü's second criterion — the sequence of elements, we have "本科探花" (*benke tanhua*) and "榻上" (*ta shang*) as the subjects of the two sentences. As pointed out by Lü, this analysis follows a kind of "psychological clue", so the two subjects are actually the psychological subjects. The definition for this kind of subject can be: "a full word which is closely related to, but put before the verb and is the starting point of a statement" (Lü 1984). He argues that this grammatical category could be termed as "the starting element" rather than "subject". This term approximates Halliday's "the point of departure of the message" or "Theme" (1985). Accordingly, "本科探花" (*benke tanhua*) and "榻上" (*ta shang*, on couch) may be said to be "the starting elements" or the "themes" of the sentences.

Lü Shuxiang argues that the sequence in Chinese can follow these syntactic patterns: SVO, SOV, OSV, VS and VO (1984: 447 - 465). The author of this chapter has analyzed some sentences according to these patterns and found that Chinese sentences can be indeed divided into two parts — Theme and Rheme. At first, she thought that this could be a strong influence on Chincse coming from English in the past decades, for "among all the Western languages, English is the language which exerts the strongest influence on Chinese." (Wang Huan 1986) However, having observing these data closely and considered Lü's "position" criterion, she would assume that the Theme-Rheme structure may be an inherence characteristic of the Chinese textual structure.

Please look at the themes in the following syntactic patterned sentences (T = Theme, S = Subject, O = Object, A = Adjunct, V = Verb, R = Rheme, asp = aspect, meas = measure word, part = particle, prep = Preposition):

① The terms "theme", "subject", "doer" and etc. are capitalized when used abstractly but not in examples.

(1) In the SV (O) pattern:

[3] 孔雀(T, S)东南 飞(R, V), 五 里(T, A)一 徘徊(R, V)。
kongque dongnan fei, wu li yi paihuai。
peacock southeast fly, five (MEAS) a flight back
(The peacock flies southeastward, and paces up and down every five *li*.)

[4] 凤凰(T, S)出(R, V), 百鸟(T, S)朝(R, V)。
fenghuang chu, bai niao chao。
phoenix come out, all birds worship.
明君(T, S) 有德(R, VO), 凤凰(T, S)乃来(R, V)。
ming jun you de, fenghuang nai lai。
enlightened ruler have virtue, phoenix appear.
(When the phoenix comes out, all birds will worship it; when an enlightened ruler is virtuous, the phoenix will appear.)

[5] 我(T, S)认识 您(R, VO)。
wo renshi nin。
(I know you.)

[6] 有白色 眼角 的 眼睛(T, S), 流露出 愉快的神色(R, VO)。
You baise yanjiao de yanjing, liuluchu yukuai de shense。
White corner (ASP) eyes betray pleasant (ASP) look
(The eyes with white corners betray a pleasant look.)

(2) In the SOV pattern:

[7] 他(T, S)言(O)也 不 答(R, V), 头(O)也 不 回(R, V),……。
ta yan ye bu da, tou ye bu hui,
He word (NEG) reply, head (NEG) turn, ...
(He did not reply nor did he turn his head; ....)

[8] 你(T, S)什么(O)也 不用 管(R, V)。
Ni shenme ye buyong guan。
You what also (NEG) care
(You need not care about anything.)

[9] 他 呀(T, S), 天(O) 不怕(R, V), 地(O) 不怕(R, V)…….
Ta ya tian bu pa di bu pa
He (PART) sky (NEG) fear earth (NEG) fear ....
(He fears nothing ....)

[10] 我(T, S) 牛马(O) 也做 了 几十年 了(R, VA)。
Wo niuma ye zuo le jishinian le。
I ox horse also do (ASP) decades (ASP)
(I have labored like a beast of burden for decades.)

(3) In the O (S) V pattern:

[11] 姑娘 的心事(T, O), 我们(S) 也都 知道(R, V)。
guniang de xinshi, women ye dou zhidao。
Maiden (ASP) mind, we also all know
(The maiden's mind we all know too.)

[12] 北京人 的 影子(T, O) 我(S) 铰 好 了(R, VA)。
beijingren de yingzi wo jiao hao le。
beijingnese (ASP) shadow I cut well (ASP)
(I have cut out the shadow of a Bejingnese.)

[13] 一 只 孔雀(T, O), 也 没 看见(R, V)。
Yi zhi kongque ye mei kanjian。
One (MEAS) peacock also (NEG) see
((We) did not see a single peacock.)

(4) In the (A) VS pattern:

[14] 晚 间(T, A), 挤 了(V) 一 屋子的 人(R, S)。
wan jian, ji le yi wu zi de ren。
evening (IN), crowd (ASP) (MEAS) room people
(In the evening the room was full of people.)

[15] 我们 的 后头(T, A) 走着(V) 个 姓 白 的 伙计(R, S)。
Women de houtou zouzhe ge xing bai de huoji。
We (ASP) behind walk (MEAS) name bai (ASP) guy.
(Behind us walked a guy with the family name Bai.)

[16] 羊群 里(T, A)跑出(V) 骆驼来了(R, S)。
Yangqun li pao chu luotuo laile。
Sheep crowd (PREP) run out (ASP) camel (ASP)
(From among the crowd of sheep ran out a camel!)

[17] 去 了(T, V)穿红 的(S, R),还有(T, V)挂 绿 的(R, S)。
Qu le chuan hong de haiyou gua lü de
Go (ASP) wear red (ASP) also have hang green (ASP)
(Gone are those in red but there are still those in green.)

[18] 冒出 了(T, V)你这个 小兔崽子(R, S)。
Maochu le ni zhege xiaotuzaizi。
Crop out (ASP) you this little rabbit son
(Cropped out you, the son of rabbit!)

(5) In the VO pattern:

[19] 下(T, V)雨了(R, O)。刮(T, V)风了(R, O)。散(T, V)会了(R, O)。……
Xia yu le gua feng le sanhui le。
Rain (PART) blow wing (PART) end meeting (PART)
(It was raining and blowing. The meeting was over and ....)

[20] 有(T, V)个 凤丫头(R, O),就 有(T, V)个 你(R, O)。
You ge feng yantou jiu you ge ni 。
Have (MEAS) feng girl (ASP) have (MEAS) you
(Wherever there is the girl Feng, there is a you!)

[21] 少(T, V)一个心上才郎(R, O),多(T, V)一个脚头丈夫(R, O)。
shao yige xinshang cailang duo yige jiaotou zhangfu 。
Lack one (MEAS) sweetheart more (MEAS) foot husband
(Without a sweetheart, she would have a heart-to-heart husband.)

An analysis of the above examples further testifies that the Theme-Rheme structure is also governing the organization of a Chinese sentence into a message. Sequentially and psychologically, a Chinese sentence can be cut into the two parts: Theme and Rheme, a feature inherent in the Chinese language.

3.3 A comparison of the Theme-Rheme structure in English and Chinese

3.3.1 The position of Theme in Chinese and English

As pointed in Section I (Introduction), Theme in English always occupies the initial position of a sentence (Halliday 1985). Similarly, the Theme-Rheme structure in Chinese is also expressed by the sequence in which the elements occur in the sentence, as shown in the above examples. Halliday says "it seems natural that the position for the Theme should be at the beginning, rather than at the end or at some other specific point." (*ibid.*) This may account for the Theme occupying the first position in both languages.

3.3.2 Theme in declarative sentences (Theme = Psychological subject; Subject = grammatical subject)

3.3.2.1 Theme in the SVO and SOV structures

The structure or pattern of SVO is the most basic one in both English and Chinese (Lü 1984) while SOV may be rarely found in English. We discuss Theme in these two structures because they share one similarity in Chinese and English: Subject functions as the starting point, or the theme of a sentence. In other words, the Theme is often found to be conflated with the Subject in these two structures in both languages. Compare the coincidence frequencies of Theme and Subject in the two languages in the following Table 3 – 1①:

① The figures are obtained from Chen Naochong's MA thesis " A Study of Subject in English and its Functions", unpublished.

Table 3 - 1 Coincidence Frequencies of Theme and Subject in English and Chinese

Total number of sentences	Sentences in which S&T coincide	Percentage of sentences in which S&T coincide
	(English)	
News report: 36	20	55.6%
Travelogue: 238	80	33.6%
Short story: 154	96.5	62.7%
	(Chinese)	
News report: 16	11	68%
Travelogue: 69	34	49%
Short story: 86	46	53%

The statistics demonstrate a rather high coincidence frequency of Subject and Theme in both languages though they vary with different genres of discourses. This fact reinforces Halliday's statement (*ibid.*): "The Subject is the element that is chosen as Theme unless there is a good reason for choosing something else." The mapping of Theme onto Subject is termed as the Unmarked Theme.

Two points are worth our notice:

(1) The English personal pronouns I, you, he, she, it, they and nominal groups are often found to act as unmarked Themes (Halliday 1985). This feature is shared by the Chinese language as exemplified in the above examples in the two patterns, and also in the descriptive essay "孔雀开屏" (*kongque kai ping*— The Peacock Opens its "screen"①). Out of the 62 sentences in this essay, 54 have personal pronouns or nominal groups as Unmarked Themes.

(2) A Theme in Chinese may be a Subject consisting of V+ O. This is

① A descriptive essay published in a journal in 1982, which provided the data I used for writing my course paper on theme and rheme; but unfortunately the name of the journal and the publisher cannot be found now.

similar to a gerund group in English acting as both Subject and Theme. Compare [22] and [23]:

[22] 说到他们的死(T, S = V + O)使人愤恨 那个 残忍的封建社会。

shuo dao tamen de si, shi ren fenhen nage canren de fengjian shehui 。

speak(PREP) their death make person hate that (MEAS) cruel feudal society

(Speaking of their death makes people hate that cruel feudal society.)

[23] Learning a second language (T, S = V + O) extends one's vision and expands the mind (R).

3.3.2.2 Theme in the OSV structure

This structure is regarded as the inverted structure of SVO (Lü 1984: 452), with Object taking the initial position of the sentence (see examples [11], [12], [13]). The purpose is to put stress on the Object of the verb (or Complement, as termed by Halliday, *ibid.*), or to make it the focus of the information structure. This is the marked structure of the sentence. Frequently, such expressions as "若论","关于","至于","这" or "那" before the subject are omitted. The functions of these expressions are more or less similar to those of the English expressions "As for" or "As far as ... concerned" (*ibid.*).

3.3.2.3 Theme in the VS structure

Strictly speaking, there are two sub-structures:

Examples [2], [14], [15], [16] are under the same category: being in the pattern (A) VS, in which "榻上","晚间","我们的后头" and "羊群里" all act as Adjuncts. Lü (1984) regards this group as an interesting one: the subjects inherently appear after the verbs; therefore they are in the unmarked position. Verbs used in this pattern are restricted to those such as

“坐”,“立”,“来”,“到” or “出(来)”,“进(来)”,“下(来)” (Lü, 1984: 156 - 157). This pattern is similar to the English one applying the verbs “come” and “go”:

[24] Here (T, A) comes (V) the bus (R, S).

[25] There (T, A) goes (V) the bell (R, S).

The other structure is in the “real” V + S pattern, as exemplified in [17] and [18], with verbs denoting the meaning either of “appearing” as in [17] or “disappearing” as in [18] and followed by the particle “了” (*le*) (Lü 1984: 457 - 458). Here the speaker makes the action of “appearing” or “disappearing” as the point of departure; thus, the verbs function as the unmarked themes of these sentences.

Verbs act as themes can also be found in English, where a verb is being emphasized and foregrounded, though the verbs are not confined to those denoting “appear” or “disappear”. This structure, however, is very rare, thus highly marked. For example:

[26] In case of failure their position would be perilous in the extreme; and fail (T, V) they surely would (R). (*College English III* - 2 - Lesson 14)

In which “fail” is fronted because the speaker wishes to predict the certainty of failure. It seems that this structure is more often found in Chinese than in English. However, it needs further research to verify this as we do not have statistics to support the argument.

3.3.2.4 Theme in the VO structure

This structure may be analyzed in two ways:

First, it could be regarded as the elliptical structure of SVO (see [19]. The Subject in such a structure may be taken as indicating an indefinite entity or worked out from the context. It refers to “the sky” as understood by both the speaker and the hearer because in Chinese we can also say 天下雨了…… (*tian xia yu le*; literally, “The sky is raining”.). We find no Theme with the subject being omitted. There is no such structure in English, which needs a formal subject when referring to "weather": It is raining; it is snowing, etc. Here the pronoun "it" is both the Subject and Theme of the sentence.

Second, such a structure in Chinese can be said without Subject as it may not be worth mentioning (See Examples [20] and [21]). The verbs are the starting points, thus functioning as the Themes of the sentences.

3.3.2.5 Adv. group and prep. phrase as Theme

In a declarative sentence, we need to pay attention to the position and the function of an adverbial group and a prepositional (shortly, PREP.) phrase.

Unlike English in which an adverbial group is the most usual Marked Theme (Halliday, 1985), adverbial groups in Chinese sentences can occur in two positions: either before or after the subject. Some adverbials must come after the Subject, e.g. 也(*ye*, also), 还(*hai*, still), 都(*dou*, all), etc., as in [27]:

[27] 我们(T/S) **都** 认为 这个 办法很好(R)。
women **dou** *renwei zhehe banfa hen hao*。
We all consider (MEAS) method very good
(We all consider this method very good.)

Under no circumstances can they be Themes of sentences. However, adverbials such as 后来(*houlai*, later), 然后(*ranhou*, then), 现在(*xianzai*, now), 以前(*yiqian*, before) or those denoting time sequence, etc, may function as conjunctions and tend to be in the thematic status in Chinese though they may also appear after the subject (compare (a) and (b) in [28]). However, there is still another group of adverbials such as modal adjuncts, such as 可能(*keneng*, maybe), 也许(*yexu*, perhaps), etc., which usually appear after the Subject, but when necessary, they can come initially and thus become Marked Themes. Compare (a) and (b) in [29]:

[28] *a.* **后来** (T/A), 我 在 学校 里 读书, ……(R)
houlai, wo zai xuexiao li dushu ...
Later, I (PREP) school (IN) study ...
(Later I studied in school.)

b. 我(T/S) **后来** 在 学校 里 读书, ……(R)
wo houlai zai xue xiao li dushu ...
I later (PREP) school (IN) study ...
(I studied in school later.)

[29] *a.* 他(T/S) **可能** 会 来(R)。
ta keneng hui lai。
(He may come.)

b. **可能**(T, A) 他 会 来。
keneng ta hui lai。
(Probably he will come.)

Similarly, although a prep. phrase is also "the most usual form of Marked Theme" (Hailiday 1985) in English (see [30], their Chinese counterparts may have different positions when acting as Adjuncts: also before or after the Subject. When before the Subject, it is the Theme of the sentence as in [31]:

[30] With sobs and tears (T, A), he sorted out those of the largest size (R).

[31] 自古 以来(T/A), 人们 最喜欢 的是凤凰(R)。
zi gu yi lai, renmen zui xihuan de shi fenghuang。
Ancient time (PREP) people most like be phoenix
(Since ancient times, what people most like is the phoenix.)

Although the prep. phrase "自古以来" (*zi gu yi lai*, since ancient times) does not come under the category of "conjunction", it functions as a cohesive tie, connecting this sentence and the previous one. It can be considered to be the unmarked theme in this sentence.

But in contrast to the above, a large group of prep. phrases usually come after the Subject though they can take the thematic position.

Compare *a* and *b* in [32]:

[32] a. 孟板加　　王子　　召树屯(T/S)在　湖　边　爱　上　了第七个姑娘,……(R)

Mengbanja wangzi Zhaoshutun zai hu bian ai shang le diqige guniang ...

Mengbanja prince Zhaoshutun (PREP) lake fall in (PART) love with seventh girl ...

(Prince Zhaoshutun of Mengbanja fell in love with the seventh girl by the lake.)

b. 在　湖边(T, A)孟板加　　王子……(R)

zai hu bian　　Mengbanja wangzi ...

(PREP) lake Mengbanja prince ...

(By the lake Prince Zhaoshutun of Mengbanja ....)

Sentences [32a] and [32b] differ in their choice of the Theme; the concern of [32a] is with 召树屯(*Zhaoshutun*), which is the Unmarked Theme, while the other the location where he fell in love with the girl, which functions as the Marked Theme of the sentence; thus the two sentences are carrying two slightly different messages.

For some prep. phrases, their position is always at the beginning of the sentence — naturally in the thematic status (see [33]):

[33] 全　厂　　里(T, A),我　是　典型(R)。

quan chang li,　　wo shi dianxing.

whole factory (PREP),　I　be "model"

(I am the model for the whole factory.)

This sentence would sound awkward if the position of the prep. phrase is changed.

3.3.2.6 Conjunction as Theme

English and Chinese share another similarity: both can have a conjunction as part of the Theme (a Textual Theme). Compare the conjunction of "so" with those of "虽然" and "但" in the following sentences:

[34] **So** that (T) is why you are late(R).

[35] a. **虽然**孔雀(T = Conj. + S)不再 在 这个 地方 成群 地 生长……(R)
suiran kongque bu zai zai zhege difang chengqun de shengzhang …
Although peacock (NEG) more (PREP) this place groups (POSS) grow …
(Although peacocks do not grow in large groups in this place any more, …)

[36] **但** 傣族 人民(T = Conj. + S)个个 喜爱孔雀……(R)
dan Daizu renmin gege xiai kongque … (dan = danshi)
But Dai people everyone like peacock …
(But every one of the Dai likes the peacock.)

However, there is a difference: while conjunctions in English always occur first, those in Chinese can be divided into two groups. Some such as 但(*dan*) or 但是(*danshi* ,but) and 可是(*keshi* ,but) must come initially whereas others can either follow or precede the Subject, e.g. 虽然(*suiran* , though), 因为(*yinwei* , as).

[35] can also be written as

(b) 孔雀(T) 虽然 不 再 在 这个 地方……
kongque suiran bu zai zai zhege difang …
Peacock although no more in this place …
(Although peacocks do not grow in large groups in this place any more …)

In [35b], the peacock is what the writer intends to talk about whereas in [35a] it is both the concession and the peacock that are the main concern of the writer.

In short, in declarative sentences, English and Chinese exhibit quite a number of similarities as well as differences in the Theme-Rheme structure.

The similarities and differences are summarized as below:

Similarities

(A) Theme takes the first position.

(B) Theme and Subject are often conflated.

(C) Personal pronouns and nominal groups frequently function as unmarked Themes.

(D) Theme may be patterned as V+O.

(E) Conjunctions can be part of Theme.

Differences

(A) Adverbial groups and prepositional phrases in English are the usual marked Themes. Although some of their Chinese counterparts can be marked Themes, others will always come in the first position while still others can never be foregrounded.

(B) Some conjunctions in Chinese must come initially but others can either follow or precede the Subject.

(C) While the most marked types of Theme are Object or Complement and Predicator (realized by Verb) in English, these elements may be unmarked themes in Chinese.

3.4 Theme in interrogative sentences

3.4.1 In general questions

In English Theme is formed by the finite verb + subject, which differs from Chinese, whose Theme element is the same as that in declarative sentences. Compare:

Declarative Interrogative

[37] 您(T, S)不 认识 我。您(T, S)认识 我 吗?
nin bu renshi wo. nin renshi wo ma?
You (NEG) know me. you know me (PART)?
(You don't know me.) (Do you know me?)

In both sentences, "您", a personal pronoun, is the Theme and the Subject.

3.4.2 In WH questions

In English, as Halliday explains, the WH element is usually what the speaker is concerned about, hence the Theme. On the other hand, interrogative expressions (inter. exp.) such as "怎么样" (*zenmeyang*, how), "为什么" (*weishenme*, why), etc. in Chinese can occur before or after the subject, in a way similar to that of adverbial groups. These inter. expressions act as the theme when they occur in the initial position. Compare [38a] and [38b] in the following:

[38] *a.* 您(T, S)怎么 修 没 了(V, R)?
Nin zenme xiu mei le?
You how repair (NEG PART)
How come that what you are repairing is missing?

b. 怎么(T),您 修 没 了(S + V, R)?
zenme nin xiu mei le?
How you repair (NEG PART)
How come that what you are repairing is missing?

"怎么" (*zenme*, how) in [38b] functions as the theme while the word in [38a] does not.

3.5 Thematic organization in complex sentences

A subordinate clause in English can either come before or after the main clause; therefore, we may have both (a) α ^ β or (b) β ^ α(α = the main clause, β = the subordinate clause) structure, where α in (a) is the unmarked Theme while β in (b) the marked Theme (Halliday 1985). But the thematic organization in Chinese is quite different (see [39], [40], [4]):

[39] 油　多(T, β),就　得　用　一 个　大桶(R, α)。
you duo,　jiu dei yong yi ge　da tong。
(If) oil much,　then must use　one (MEAS) big barrel
(If much oil is needed, then (we) must use a big barrel.)

[40] 没有　底(T, β),那多少　油也　装　不满　哪(R, α)。
meiyou　di,　na duoshao you ye zhuangbu man na。
(Barrel)(NEG) bottom,　then however much oil can　(NEG) fill up (PART)
(If the barrel has no bottom, then no matter how much oil cannot fill it up.)

[4] 凤凰出(T, β),　百鸟朝(R,α)。
fenghuang chu,　bai niao chao。
Phoenix come out, all birds worship
(When the phoenix comes out, all birds worship.)

明　君　有德(T, β),凤凰　乃　来(R, a1)。
ming　jun　you de,　fenghuang nai lai.
enlightened ruler have virtue,　phoenix　come.
(When the enlightened ruler is virtuous, then the phoenix will come.)

Three features warrant our attention:

(A) The position of the subordinate clause is fixed: it always stands before the main clause, hence the unmarked Theme.

(B) In spoken and classical Chinese, frequently no conjunction is used to connect the main and subordinate clauses. The sequential indicators "就" (*jiu*, then), "便" (*bian*, then), "那么" (*name*, then), "乃" (*nai*, then), etc. show the existence of a subordinate clause and function as cohesive ties to connect the two clauses. For example, in [39] and [40], the β clause "油多" (*you duo*, oil much) or "没有底" (*meiyou di*, no barrel) is equivalent to an English "if" clause ("If much oil is needed" or "If there is no barrel"). "要是" (*yaoshi*) or "假如" (*jiaru*), both of which mean "if", could precede the two Chinese expressions.

Two complex sentences are found in [4], which is written in the classical language. In both sentences, β serves as the subordinate clause of condition. No conjunction is employed to connect the β clause and α clause.

(C) The structure of the complex sentence in modern Chinese has been influenced to a certain degree by the English language. Conditional clauses such as "当……时候" (*dang ... shihou*) and "如果 ..." (*ruguo...*) or "假如 ..." (*jiaru...*) or "……的话" (... *de hua*) could be the translation of "when ..." and "if ..." clauses. In classical Chinese, no subordinate clause can go after the main clause; in the modern language, it can, however, when in its marked position. For [39], we can have another version: 那多少油也装不满哪 (*na duoshao you ye zhuang*(NEG) *man* (MOOD PART), then no matter how much oil cannot fill it up), (要是)没有底(R, β) (*yaoshi*(NEG) *di*, (if) (the barrel) has no bottom). But then the message would have a slight different meaning. "(要是)没有底" (*yaoshi*) *meiyou di*) serves as an afterthought or a complement rather than a condition as in the first version. In this case, the α clause functions as the marked Theme.

3.6 Conclusion

So far the chapter has discussed the existence of Theme and Rheme in Chinese and made a comparison of similarities and differences of this structure in the declarative, interrogative and complex sentences in both English and Chinese. We find that: 1) a Chinese sentence can also be divided semantically and functionally into two parts — Theme and Rheme; 2) in the declarative sentences: i) in the SVO and SOV patterns, where Theme and Subject are overlapped, Subject acts as unmarked Theme; ii) "the most marked type of Theme is complement" or Object or Predicator, which is true both in English and Chinese, as is exemplified in the OSV pattern; iii) in the VO pattern, Adjunct and even Verb may function as Theme of the sentence, which is marked in English while in Chinese in many cases, unmarked; 3) Subject and Theme in the interrogative sentence in Chinese remain the same as in the declarative sentence because there is no change of the word order; and 4) in the complex sentence, the "β" clause always precedes the "α" one, thus functioning as the Theme of the sentence though the "α ^ β" structure is also possible in modern Chinese, but that is the marked version.

We have cited many examples from both oral and written modes and in both classical and modern language. It is not, however, an exhaustive study of the Theme and Rheme structure in these two languages. Further research is expected to be done in the comparison of this structure in sentences and discourses in the two linguistic systems.

4

汉语主位进程结构分析*

4.1 前　言

自从马泰修斯(Mathesius 1929)提出主位概念以来,许多学者都参与了主位-述位的分析和研究。但就目前来看,对汉语主位-述位的分析描写基本上还是停留在语篇以下的语法层面上。为了从更高的语法层角度进一步描述汉语主位-述位结构的特点,我们选择了 10 篇不同语类的汉语语篇进行分析,希望能为分析探讨汉语语篇主位进程结构做一点贡献。

4.2 相关理论

主位是话语的出发点(Halliday 1985: 28),这也是本文句子主位的定

* 本章原与艾晓霞合写,刊于《外语研究》1995 年第 2 期,已略作修改。

义。为了表达完整的思维过程或阐述某一事件，任何一位说话者均会从某一点出发讲出一连串语句。如果这些语句能够为受话者理解，则各个语句间不仅从语义上相互呼应，而且从语法上也会相互联系。主位发展模式就是将一连串语句结合成语篇的实现手段之一，这也就是达内什（František Daneš）的“主位进程（thematic progression）”（Daneš 1974：118－119）理论。达内什的三个主要模式分别为：

（一）简单的线型顺序：第一句话的述位（Rheme）是第二句话的主位（Theme）：

T1 -------R1

T2（= R1）......... R2

Tn（= Rn−1）......... Rn

［1］我们（T1）主张积极的思想斗争（R1），因为它（T2 = R1）是达到党内和革命团体内的团结使之利于战斗的武器（R2）。

（二）一个主位连接着多个不同述位，即不同的述位发展同一个主位：

T1 --------R1

T1 --------R2

T1 --------R3

T1 --------Rn

［2］自由主义者（T1）以抽象的教条看待马克思主义的原则（R1），他们（T1）赞成马克思主义（R2），但是（他们）（T1）不准备实行之（R31），或不准备完全实行之（R32），（他们）（T1）不准备拿马克思主义代替自己的自由主义（R4）。这些人（T1），马克思主义是有的（R51），自由主义也是有的（R52）。

（三）具有派生主位的顺序：个别句子的主位是由一个总主位派生出来的。

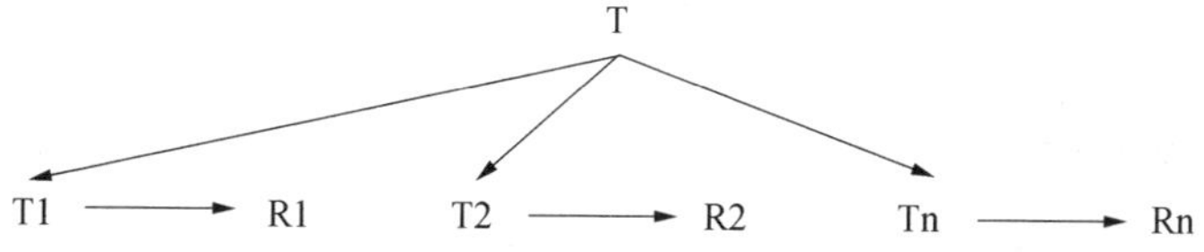

［3］说的（T1）是马克思主义（R1），行的（T2）是自由主义（R2）；对

人（T3）是马克思主义（R3 = R1），对己（T4）是自由主义（R4 = R2）：

上述各主位的中心主位（T）都是自由主义者。

中国学者发展了达内什式的模式（徐盛桓 1982；黄衍 1985；方琰 1986），并指出"在语言的实际运用中，由于思想表达的复杂性，往往是几种模式搭配交替使用"（黄衍 1985）。

马丁（James Martin）在《英语语篇：结构与系统》（*English Text: Structure and System*，1992）一书中对英文语篇进行了透彻的分析研究，并在此基础上提出了一些很有见解的理论观点，其中对本文有重大影响的观点之一是 macro-Theme 和 hyper-Theme。马丁将这两个术语定义如下：

macro-Theme：语篇主位，一般为引言段落
hyper-Theme：段落主位

这两个术语的提出有着重要的意义。马丁认为，一般来说，在写作中，语篇主位预示着段落主位的出现，相应地，段落主位又预示着一连串句子主位的出现，这是语篇组织（texture）的一个重要方面，缺乏这种相互预示作用模式的语篇可能不会很连贯（In writing，the use of macro-Themes to predict hyper-Themes，which in turn predict a sequence of clause Themes is an important aspect of texture；and texts which do not make use of predicted patterns of interaction in this way may be read as less coherent ）（*ibid.*：437）。其实也是对达内什第三个模式的发展更为明确的阐述。

我们所选择分析的 10 篇语篇与马丁在该书中选择的语篇不很相同，这体现在：第一，我们所选语篇仅限于书面语体，而马丁的还包括口语语体；第二，我们所选语篇均有标题（有的还有小标题），而马丁的却没有。考虑到这两点不同，我们在马丁对 macro-Theme 和 hyper-Theme 定义的基础上，自创了一些术语。在我们的语篇中，语篇主位为 text-Theme，而 macro-Theme 成了段落主位（即马丁的 hyper-Theme）。其他的术语，可见下节另述。

我们使用主位-述位链（Fang & Ai 1995）这个术语，因为这一概念对本文的语篇分析有重要意义。在分析汉语的主位结构时，不仅应分析小句（Clause）和复合句（Clause Complex）的主位，还应运用句群（钱乃荣 1990）的概念分析主位-述位链。汉语与西欧语言区别之一就是复合句以

上的语法单位，这是由于汉语逗号的用法与西方语言不同，形成了汉语的句法特点（申小龙 1993）。因而在分析汉语时，这个特点必须考虑在内。分别举例如下：

单句：非标记主位，如：我们（Actor =T）主张积极的思想斗争（R）。

标记主位，如：命令（Goal =T）不服从（R）。

复合句：我们主张积极的思想斗争（α =T），因为它是达到党内和革命团体内的团结使之利于战斗的武器（β =R）。

句群：它（T1）（自由主义）是消极的东西（R1），（它）（T2）客观上起着援助敌人的作用（R2），因此敌人（T3 =R2）是欢迎我们内部保存自由主义的（R3）。

句群作为一个语法单位，是组成汉语语篇不可缺少的一部分（钱乃荣 1990）。实际上在长篇幅的语篇里，句群非常之多。而通常主位-述位链即由句群组成。

总之，本章应用的理论包括：

（1）韩礼德关于主位的定义（1985）；

（2）达内什的主位进程模式（1974）；并将马丁（1992）和达内什关于主位的论述结合起来。即马丁的语篇主位预示段落主位，段落主位预示句子主位的论断；

（3）钱乃荣关于句群的概念（1990）以及方琰等（1995）提出的主位-述位链的分析方法。

4.3 语篇主位进程结构分析实例

我们分析了 10 篇不同语类的汉语语篇。选择不同语类语篇的目的在于通过分析这些语篇，希望能发现不同语类语篇的结构特点，同时扩大分析的广度。这 10 篇语篇分别为：新闻报道、物理实验指令、前言、后记、图书馆简介、名山胜概、菜谱、政府要人发言、议论文及作者简介（类似人物传记）。

本章所使用的有关主位的术语以及主位分析层次如下：

text-Theme(语篇主位→语篇主位或语篇中心思想)

macro-Theme(段落主位)[显现 / 隐含]

即段落主位既可显现,也可隐含在这个段落中。隐含主位是这一段的中心思想的总结。

T-R chain(主位-述位链)>>>[句群的主位-述位 / 复句的主位-述位 / 单句的主位-述位]

注:>>> 由……组成,即主位-述位链可由单句、复句和相互不同的句群组合构成。

语篇表达的意思比较复杂时(这时一般语篇的篇幅也比较长),还需要以下术语:super macro-Theme(超段落主位)——几个段落表达同一个中心意思,即几个段落主位都说明这一个中心意思。

由于篇幅所限,我们在此仅举一个议论文语篇主位进程结构分析的例子,这就是毛泽东同志于 1937 年发表的著名的《反对自由主义》。我们将分析选文的 text-Theme、super macro-Theme、macro-Theme 以及每一段中句群的 T-R chain。

反对自由主义

tex-Theme(语篇主位):题目即《反对自由主义》

super macro-Theme 1:对思想斗争的态度(包括 macro-Theme 1,macro-Theme 2)

Para 1:macro-Theme 1:思想斗争是有力武器

T-R chain — T1:我们……斗争(α)
t:我们
r:主张……斗争
R1:因为它……　武器(β)
t:因为它
r:是……武器。
— T2:每个……分子,
R2:应该……武器。

Para 2：macro-Theme 2：自由主义对思想斗争的态度及后果

T-R chain — T：（α）但是……主张……和平（β）
t：但是自由主义
r1：取消……
r2：主张……和平。
R：结果是……起来（α）
t：结果是……发生（β）
r：使党……起来（α）。

注：详细的主/述位分析略。

super macro-Theme 2：自由主义的表现和危害（macro-Theme 3→macro-Theme 17）；

super macro-Theme 3：进一步揭示自由主义的来源及性质，并呼吁反对自由主义（macro-Theme 18 … macro-Theme 22）。

4.4 主位进程结构

这篇语篇的分析给我们两点启示：

（一）证实了马丁的观点，即语篇主位通过不同的段落主位得到体现，而段落主位又可以由一连串句子主位-述位所组成的主位-述位链得以实现。图 4－1 所示文中分析这篇议论文整个语篇的主位进程可以说明这一观点。

（二）语篇主位是通过主位进程模式不断向前推进的。前述达内什的三个主要主位-述位进程模式，在本文所分析的议论文中都得到了体现。其中最为常用的模式为第二种：一个主位连接着多个不同的述位，即同一个主位由不同的述位得到发展。再者，从整个语篇的主位进程发展来看，为了阐述语篇主位反对自由主义，作者从对思想斗争的态度，自由主义的表现和危害，以及自由主义的根子及性质等三个方面，即三个超段

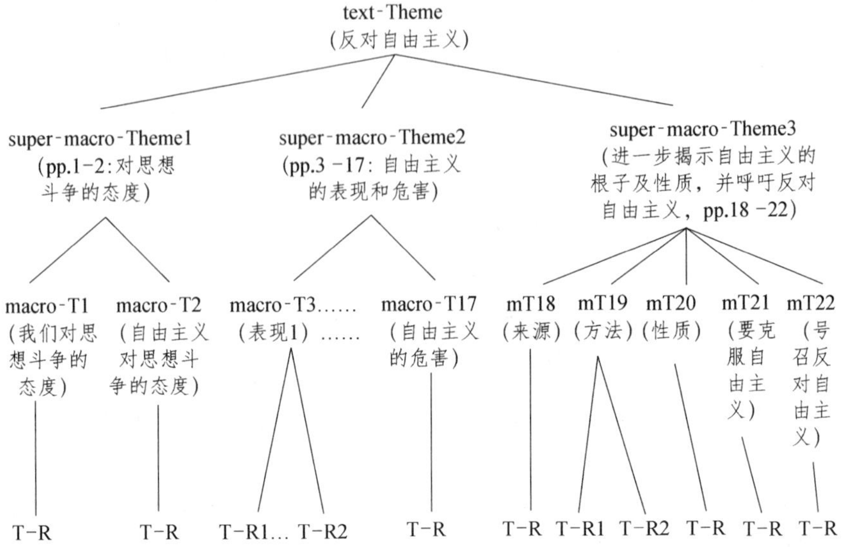

图 4-1 《反对自由主义》的主位进程

落主位入手，层层深入，进行剖析。每个超段落主位，又由不同的段落主位进行阐述。考虑到文中所分析议论文的主旨，就不难理解作者这样做的目的了：为了反复强调某一观点(T)，作者必然会从不同的角度对其进行阐述(R_n)，从而使文章的思想鲜明突出，层次清晰。通过主位分析，我们从语法角度，试图解释毛泽东同志的这篇文章的中心思想非常鲜明突出的原因，以及他是如何达到这种效果的。

在 10 篇语篇分析的基础上，我们总结出汉语议论文语篇主位进程结构，如图 4-2 所示：

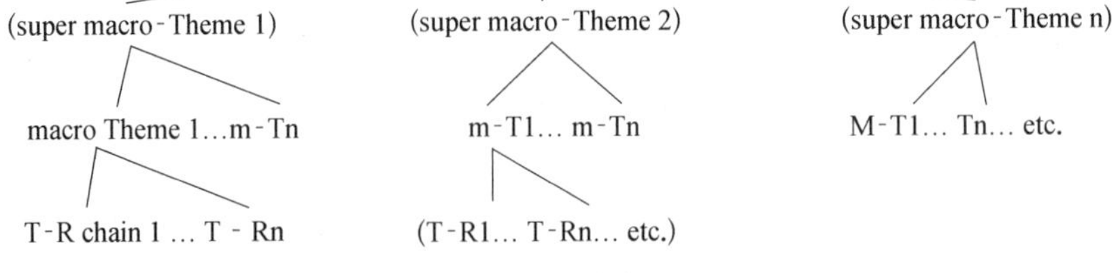

Note: m-T: macro-theme; T-R: Theme-Rheme chain

图 4-2 汉语议论文语篇主位进程结构

每一具体的议论文语篇,其语篇主位进程结构可以比这个结构简单,即圆括号内的成分可以不出现。也可以比较复杂,层次更多。然而,无论简单或复杂,无一例外,一个议论文语篇的主位进程结构必然有语篇主位、段落主位和主位-述位链这三个成分。我们对其他类型语篇的分析也论证了主位进程结构对形成语篇的重要贡献。

4.5 结　论

本章运用功能语法中主位进程的模式,对一篇议论文语篇进行了分析,可以得出以下结论: 这样的语法分析有助于对语篇内容的理解,有助于了解语篇表达内容的手段,也有助于初步领略文章成功的原因(韩礼德 1985: XI)。当然要对文章作出全面的评价,还需从语境和其他角度进行分析,这已超出本文的范围。

上述对主位-述位在汉语语篇主位进程结构分析中的讨论,希望能为探讨分析汉语语篇主位-述位结构做出一点贡献。由于时间有限,我们仅仅分析了 10 篇语篇,而本章也只能列举其中一例。这些不足之处都有待于进一步的研究探讨。

5

A Tentative Thematic Network in Chinese*

5.1 Introduction

This chapter is intended to generalize a tentative Thematic Network in Chinese based on the analyses of 10 written texts in various genres, namely, a news report, an instruction, a preface, an epilogue, an introduction to a library, an introduction to a famous mountain, a recipe, a political speech, an argumentative article and a biography.

There are several reasons why it is significant to do research in the description of the **Theme** system in Chinese. To start with, in the past few decades, paradigmatic relations in Chinese have been ignored. Excessive stress has been put on syntagmatic relations, due to the extensive influence of American Structuralism (Chomsky 1957), which emphasizes structure than

---

* This chapter is much revised on the basis of a paper written by Fang Yan and Ai Xiaoxia collected in *Language*, *System*, *Structure* edited by Ren Shaozeng and Ma Bosen and published by Hangzhou University Press in 1995. Due to the short of space, the texts for detailed analysis are not included in this book.

system. In contrast to American Structuralism, Systemic-Functional Grammar, whose outstanding exponent is Halliday (1985), regards system as the basis, and structure as the product, which is the result of the choices made from among various paradigms. Therefore, to achieve a comprehensive understanding of a language, it is both necessary and important to illustrate the underlying aspect of the language — the system. In the second place, working out the **Theme** system will help to provide part① of a grammatical framework for Chinese text generation and machine translation.

Producing a tentative thematic network requires an appropriate research method. The current study is based on text analysis for the following two reasons. First, text will bring us meaningful interpretations of the linguistic features of the language produced and utilized in the Chinese culture and in its various situational contexts. The data for text analysis are genuine rather than purposely created, for the texts used here are selected from printed materials in real life. Second, analysis of instantial texts in different registers or genres will provide insights into the resource of a language (Matthiessen 1993) so that generalization of a thematic network will become possible.

This chapter owes the theoretical findings to the following linguists:

1) Halliday — Theme-Rheme theory, and the notion of system (1985);

2) Martin — concepts of the following terms: Hyper-Theme, Macro-Theme, and their relations; and his views on register and genre (1992);

3) Hasan — Generic Structure Potential (GSP), which offers the criteria for judging the genre of a text selected for this study (Halliday & Hasan 1985);

① The complete grammatical system of a language should include its theme system, interpersonal system and transitivity system.

4) Daneš — Thematic Progression (TP) (1970; 1974);

5) Fries — Method of Development of Text (1992);

6) Matthiessen — the notion of system and English systems (1995);

7) Fang, McDonald and Cheng — On Theme in Chinese: from Clause to Discourse (1995);

8) The theories of some other famous Chinese grammarians and their theories on Chinese grammar, e.g. Wang Li (1985), Qian Nairong (1990), Shen Xiaolong (1991), Li Linding (1985/1994).

5.2 Principles for the Analysis

5.2.1 The mode of text for analysis

Halliday and Hasan define text as "a semantic unit" (1976), which implies that a text may consist of utterances or sentences so long as they make a meaningful unit no matter what form the text takes (*ibid.*).

Although we agree to their definition, yet in this chapter, the texts we have analyzed are restricted to written ones, which usually have a title and occasionally a sub-title. The formation of text is represented as Figure 5 - 1:

Please look at the following example in Table 5 - 1: (The text cited here consists of two paragraphs, with the first made of a clause complex in the paratactic relation and two sentence clusters and the second of a clause complex in the hypotactic relation.)

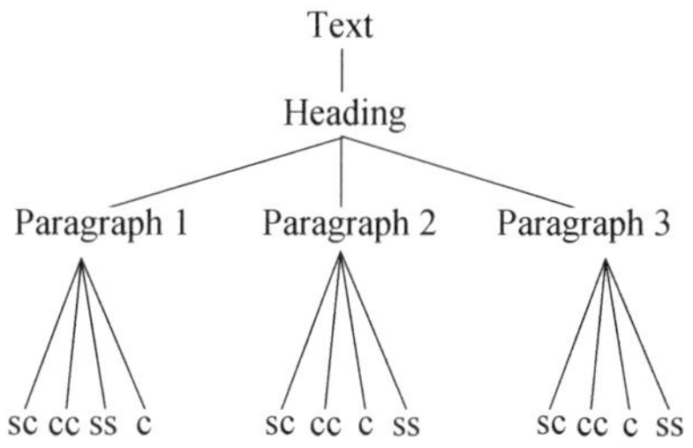

Figure 5－1　Formal Structure of a Text

(Note: SC means Sentence Cluster(s)①; CC means Clause Complex(es)②; C means Clause(s)③; SS means Simple Sentence(s)④.)

Table 5－1　An Example of the Formation of a Text

TEXT			
编辑后记(Heading)			
Para.1		**Para. 2**	
(parataxis) Clause complex 《中国现代语法》是王力教授早年的语法学著作，出版于1943年(上册)和1944年(下册)。	Sentence Cluster 1 作者从汉语的特点出发，对汉语的语法构造进行了详细的分析和描写，创见颇多；对当时和以后的语法研究，产生过很大的影响，是《马氏文通》以后在汉语语法史上有着重要地位的一部书。	Sentence Cluster 2 1954年，中华书局曾据商务厚纸型熏印。这次我们编辑汉语语法丛书，即据1954年本重排，并请作者校阅过，现合为一册出版。	(hypotaxis) Clause Complex 为了便于翻检，我们编了词语索引，附于书后。

① A sentence cluster usually consists of two or more than two sentences or clause complexes. It is a complete and independent semantic unit, whose structuring is governed by a central meaning (Qian 1990: 275). A paragraph may contain more than one sentence cluster.

② A clause complex usually consists of two or more than two clauses, either in the relation of hypotaxis patterned as $\beta \wedge \alpha$ or $\alpha \wedge \beta$, or of parataxis following the pattern $1 \wedge 2$ (Halliday 1985: 131) or $1 \wedge 2 \wedge 3 \wedge 4 \wedge \ldots \wedge n$. One noticeable phenomenon is that the last paratactic pattern is frequently found in Chinese.

③ A clause may consist of Actor(or its equivalents) +Process [+other element(s)]. In writing, it is separated from another one by a comma patterned as x, y.

④ A simple sentence has the same form as a clause; however, in writing, it ends with a full stop (cf. Halliday 1985: 131).

5.2.2 Definitions of "Theme" and "Rheme"

"Theme" is "the point of departure of a message" (Halliday 1985), which sets the orientation for communication. A thematic element may consist of a topical element (simple Theme); or the combination of a topical and/or a textual, and/or an interpersonal element (multiple Theme) (*ibid.*). "Rheme", by definition, is "the remainder of the message, the point in which the theme is developed" (*ibid.*). Compare:

[1] 《语言学概论》是《普通语言学》的基础理论部分。
Theme (TOPICAL) ---------Rheme ----------
(Carrier)-----(P) -----------------------

[2] **如果** 你所用的钩码每个的质量是 50 克……
Theme 1 Theme 2
(Textual) (Topical)

5.2.3 Identification of Theme

1) In a clause or simple sentence: the simple Theme is unmarked when conflated with "Actor" or its equivalents (e.g. carrier, sensor, etc. See Halliday 1985. Chap. 5); otherwise marked.

Compare [1] and [3]:

[1] 《语言学概论》是《普通语言学》的基础理论部分。
Theme (TOPICAL) ---------Rheme ----------
(Carrier)-----(P) ------------------------

where 《语言学概论》 is an unmarked Theme.

[3] 这个字 我 不认识。(Fang 1990)
Theme
Phenomenon Sensor Mental: Cognition Process

where 这个字 is a marked Theme.

If the initial element of a clause includes a LOCATIVE (or: domain) and/or a TEMPORAL component and the Actor with their sequence of occurrence being "(TEMPORAL) + (LOCATIVE) + Actor" or "Actor + (TEMPORAL) + (LOCATIVE)", all of the three will be counted as the clause Theme. This is because in Chinese, the unmarked position for an Adjunct (realized by TEMPORAL and/or LOCATIVE elements) is usually before or after the Actor, whereas in English, Adjunct usually is put at the end of a clause so that once it moves to the initial position, it becomes the marked Theme (Halliday 1985). This means that in a Chinese clause Theme may include more than one element or we may call it a multiple TOPICAL Theme. Therefore, in the following clauses, the Actor "赖尚龙" and a LOCATIVE or a TEMPORAL element are both counted as Theme, though they are separated by a comma (Berry 1977). See Examples [4] and [5]:

[4] 联合国经济社会发展……赖尚龙博士 在不久前的一个学术研讨会上,

Theme 1 (Actor/Sayer)-------------Theme 2 (LOCATIVE)------

Multiple TOPICAL Theme (unmarked)

作了"从中国台湾的经验,中国内地发展的模式……的发展"的发言。

(P) --------------------(Reported)----------------

[5] 在谈到中国发展模式时,**赖尚龙**说……

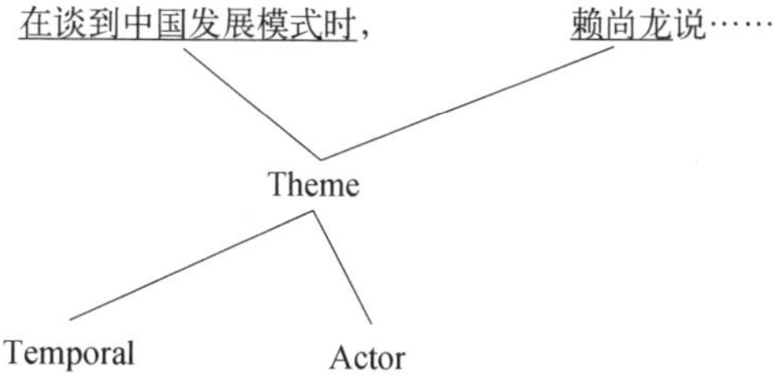

In discussing what element is "typically chosen as Theme in an English clause", Halliday (1985: 44) states that in "a declarative clause, the typical pattern is one in which Theme is conflated with Subject". Here Subject is a functional term, which, together with Finite, realizes the selection of mood in the clause in English (*ibid.*: 74). Yet in Chinese, Subject is a confusing term and has been "a headache" for Chinese linguists who have argued about its definition since the 1950s without finding a solution. For there is not a definite form to decide which element is Subject in a clause (Li Linding 1983). Therefore, when identifying what element is typically chosen as Theme in a Chinese clause, we turn to terms such as Actor and its equivalents at the transitivity level. It seems that there have been fewer disputes about the definition of Actor among Chinese linguists (Li Linding 1983; Shen Xiaolong 1991).

The Thematic pattern for a clause (a simple sentence) is: T-R

2) **In a clause complex**, which consists of a main clause and a subordinate clause, the pattern is either β ^ α or α ^ β (Fang Yan 1993).

a) **In its unmarked form**, the Theme is conflated with "β" and the Rheme with "α", the pattern being β ^ α. For example:

[6] (由于)书中没有一一注明(β),在此向有关作者表示谢意。(α)
Theme ----------------, --------- Rheme ---------------

b) **In its marked form**, the Theme is usually conflated with α and the Rheme with β, the pattern being α ^ β. For example:

[7] 就其性质而言,是交叉学科(α),因为它……。(β)
Theme -------------------, --- Rheme ---------

However, there exist two exceptions to this norm as Wang Li (1985: 63 - 64) points out: when the subordinate clause denotes "result" or "purpose", the unmarked sequence of the clause complex may be α ^ β. For example:

[8] 书末附"现代语言学讲座"(α),供读者参考(β)。(purpose)
Theme ----------- ------, Rheme -----------------

[9] 山回溪折，折复绕山（α），环结成"曲曲山回转，峰峰水抱流"的九曲之胜（β）。(Result)

Theme -------------,-----------Rheme ----------------

The unmarkedness and markedness in Clause complexes (CC) are confirmed by the following two tables:

Table 5-2 Number of Clause Complexes Appearing in the 10 Texts

Total	57
Time	12
Supposition	21
Condition	4
Cause	15
Purpose	2
Result	3

Table 5-3 Patterns of Clause Complexes

Type of CC \ Type of Pattern	β ^ α	α ^ β
Time	16	0
Supposition	19	0
Condition	1	0
Cause	13	3
Purpose	0	2
Result	1	2

The Thematic pattern for a clause complex (subordinate conjunction: when, what, before, after, if, although, since ...) is:

t1 ... r1 t2 ... r2 *Or* t1 ... r1 t2 ... r2

β ^ α α ^(β) α ^(β) β ^ α

In a clause complex, which consists of two main clauses, the Theme-Rheme pattern is 1 ^ 2 or:

T1 ... R1 | T2 ... R2

1 ^ 2

3) In a T-R chain:

The most possible candidate for a T-R chain is a sentence cluster; however, sometimes a clause/a simple sentence or a clause complex alone can also constitute a T-R chain, the prerequisite being that the clause/simple sentence or clause complex functions as a paragraph or it represents a complete meaning separate from the meanings of other clauses/sentences within a paragraph.

The pattern for a sentence cluster may be a T-R chain:

T1 … R1
T2 … R2
.
.
.
Tn … Rn

5.2.4 Terms for analysis

The Themes in a text will be analyzed at various levels, which include: text, paragraph, sentence cluster, clause complex, and clause. In doing so, it will be helpful to bring in some terms. First, we think it necessary to introduce several terms proposed by Martin, since it is on the basis of his concepts that we have defined our own terms. Those notions Martin puts forward are: Daneš's hyper-Theme, and his own term macro-Theme on the basis of hyper-Theme (For detailed information, please refer to his work: *English Text: Structure and System*, 1992). In order to be consistent with the levels at which the Themes in a text will be analyzed, our terms include:

text Theme → Head or Title or the main idea of the whole text

macro-Theme → Main idea of a paragraph [explicit / implicit]

(Note: macro-Theme may be either explicitly or implicitly stated.)

T-R chain >>> [sentence cluster(s) / clause complex(es) / clause(s)/simple sentence(s)]

Note:
Theme-Rheme :: clause (occasionally clause complex, if the analysis need not go further);
theme-rheme :: subordinate/embedded clause: expansion of T or R or both;
theme′-rheme′ :: clause in which t′ and r′ are expansions of t or r or both.
"→" means "refers to"; ">>>" means "consists of"; " :: " means "used in describing".

Where a text is of extreme complexity (in terms of the meaning it conveys, and most possibly also its length), several extra terms are needed, such as the following:

super-macro-Theme → main idea of a set of paragraphs which expresses several meanings (owing to the space limitation, we are unable to cite examples here.)

sub-macro-Theme → a central meaning conveyed by more than one paragraph (*ibid.*)

5.3 System

Analyzing the thematic elements in the ten texts, we arrive at two figures representing 1) the thematic network in clause and 2) the thematic network in clause complex with two clauses. Please look at the examples and their related figures (T = Theme; A = Actor; C = Carrier; S = Senser; P = Process; G = Goal; Ad = Adjunct; Cir = Circumstance; Pheno = Phenomenon; Cont. = Context; Str. = structure; Tex = Textual; Exp = Experiential; n.g. = Noun Group; CAd = Circumstantial Adjunct; Att. = Attribute):

Thematic Network in Chinese Clause [Clause (See Figure 5 - 2) / Clause Complex with two clauses (See Figure 5 - 3)]

- Thematic Network in Chinese (clause)
  - Simple Theme
    - Unmarked
      - T/A in APR/G or AR/GP stc. (example [4], [5])
      - T/C in CPAtt stc. (example [1])
      - T/S in SPPH stc. (example [12])
      - T/PG in P′G′PAtt. Stc. (example [13])
    - Marked
      - as proposed Theme, patterned as n.g. +A+P+others+Rep of n.g. (example [17])
      - as predicated Theme, structured as 是+A/Cir/comp. (example [18])
      - as Theme matter realized by 关于,至于 etc. (example [19])
      - as transitivity role
        - Process theme in the PA stc. (example [20])
        - Goal in GAP (in cont) (example [3])
  - Multiple Theme
    - Multiple Topical Theme ... T/CAd, A in CAP stc. where Cad represents either
    - Time or Place or both Theme/Topical (example [14], [15])
    - Multiple theme-T/Text+Exp. (example [2], [16])

Figure 5 - 2 Thematic Network in Chinese Clause

Examples I (Clause)

Unmarked:

[10] See Example [1] (C + P)

[11] See Example [4] (A + P + R).

[12] 他们认为,中国现在的改革……

--S—P ----- --------Pheno --------

[13] **加强** 同第三世界国家的团结与合作(T)**是**我国对外政策的基本点……(R)

--P′ -------- G′ -------------- P -------Att. ---------

[14] <u>昨天他</u>…………………………出差了。

Multiple Topical Theme (Cir. + A) + P

[15] <u>在清华园</u>,你……………………… **可以** 看到很多的自行车。

Multiple Topical Theme (Cir. + S) ----(P)-- ----(Pheno)

[16] <u>因为他</u>……………………………… 打了你……

Textual+Topical = Theme (Cad + A) (P) —(G)----

Marked:

[17] <u>老王</u>**我** 昨天还见到**他**。

n.g. T R repetition of n.g.

[18] 是**他**跟我说的。

A (Theme)

[19] (至于)正徽同志垦荒之劳,**人们** 是不会忽视的。

Matter (Theme) Actor Rheme

[20] 下雨了。

P (T)

- Thematic Network In Chinese Clause Complex With Two clauses
  - Paratactic
    - A in 1 or 2 patterned as T1 - R1 / T2 - R2 (example [21], [22])
    - conj. + A in both 1 and 2 str. as T1 (或者/不是+A) - R1 / T2(或者/就是+A) - R2 (example [23])
    - (A) in 1 conj. +A in 2 str. as T1 - R1+T2 - R2 in which 但/可是/而且/也 may be used (examples [24], [25])
    - P1A1+P2A2 (example [26])
  - Hypotactic
    - Unmarked
      - β ^ α when β =cause, time, condition or concession (examples [27], [28], [29])
      - α ^ β when β =purpose, result (example [30])
    - Marked - α ^ β when β =cause, time, condition or concession (example [31])

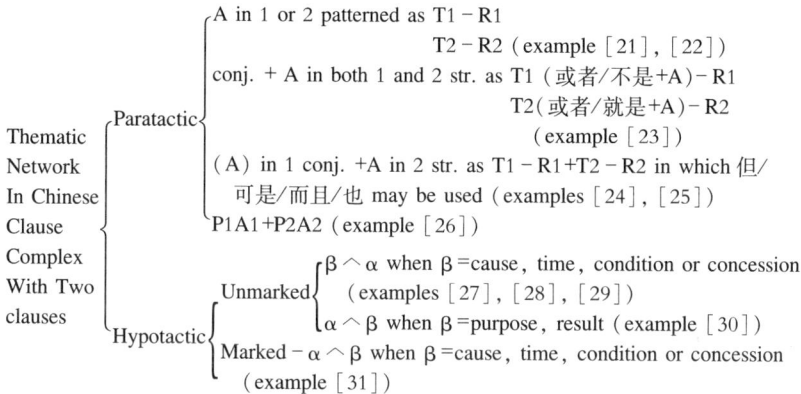

Figure 5 - 3 Thematic Network in Chinese Clause Complex

Examples II (Clause Complex)

Paratactic:

[21] 中国的改革(T1)要求在稳定中前进(R1),这(T2)非常重要(R2)。(pattern: 1 ^ 2)

[22] 中国的改革(T1),不是中国台湾地区的经验 (R1),[中国的改革] (T2) 也不是亚洲“四小龙”或日本的经验可以代表的 (R)。(pattern: 1 ^ 2)

[23] 或者你说错了,或者我叫错了。

T1 R1 T2 R2 (pattern: 1 ^ 2)

[24] 音乐不但能使人快乐,而且能陶冶情操。

T1 R1 T2 R2 (pattern: 1 ^ 2)

[25] 不是我不会,而是他不愿意让我做。

T1 R1 T2 R2 (pattern: 1 ^ 2)

[26] 去了 穿红的,还有 挂绿的。

P1 (T1) A1(R1) P2(T2) A2 (R2)(pattern: 1 ^ 2)

Hypotactic:

[27] 每搓一个钩码(β: T),都用短横线在白纸条上记下指针的位置(α)(time)。(β ^ α)

[28] (在别的名山胜地),要观赏山景(β: T),通常是免不了登山之劳的(α)(condition)。(β ^ α)

[29] See Example [6] (cause) (β ^ α).

[30] See Example [9] (result) (α ^ β).

[31] 就其性质而言,是交叉学科(α: T),因为它不仅涉及相关的语言学科,而且与心理学、逻辑学、……等交叉(β)(cause)。(α ^ β)

5.4 Conclusion

This chapter has been devoted to the thematic analysis of Chinese written texts and to the generalization of a crude thematic network in Chinese. Yet the study is by no means an exhaustive one; for research in thematic analysis and system is still very much in its infancy. It is quite possible that some of our findings may not even be accepted by some Chinese linguists. It is hoped, however, that this study provokes thinking and stimulates more extensive research at a more profound depth.

6

On Theme in Chinese

— From Clause to Discourse [*]

6.1 Introduction: The descriptive problem

The syntactic analysis of Chinese in this century, since the introduction of Western-style linguistics, has been hampered by the perception that Chinese is a language "without grammatical signals" (Li & Thompson 1978); and by the consequent, and seemingly unresolvable debates on problems like the nature of subject in Chinese (Tsao 1980: 7). We believe that approaching Chinese grammar from the point of view of its textual function, in particular the systems of THEME and INFORMATION (Halliday 1985) (see especially chapters 3 and 8), can help us understand the types of grammatical patterning present in Chinese. Using this approach enables us not

* This chapter is based on the paper with the same title written by Fang Yan, Edward McDonald & Cheng Musheng collected in the book *On the Subject and Theme: A Discourse Functional Perspective*, edited by R. Hasan and P. Fries and published in 1995 by John Benjamins Publishing Company, Amsterdam & Philadelphia.

only to delimit the boundaries of the clause and explain the ordering of elements within the clause, but also to see how this sort of patterning operates in the organization of discourse. In this chapter, we will attempt to show how the insights about clause structure embodied in Chinese linguistics and Prague School linguistics can be more comprehensively developed within the framework of systemic functional theory (Halliday 1985). We will go on to show that the principles underlying the internal organization of the clause in Chinese can be generalized to account for the ordering of two or more clauses joined in a clause complex. Finally we will identify some ways in which these same principles operate in the construction of texts.

6.2 Background to the study: Theoretical traditions

Before setting up the framework for the current study, we will briefly review the two main relevant theoretical traditions: (*a*) theories of clause structure in Chinese; and (*b*) functional theories of clause structure.

6.2.1 Theories of clause structure in Chinese

In the Chinese descriptive tradition, one of the most controversial issues has been what element in the clause can be identified as subject. Generally speaking, those answering this question fall into two main schools: those who work with the notion of subject only; and, secondly, those who recognize subject and topic as two separate notions.

6.2.1.1 The subject only view

Zhu (1981: 95 - 96) gives a structural definition of the subject (*zhuyu*) in contrast to the predicate (*weiyu*): in most cases, the subject precedes the predicate, is marked off from it by an optional pause and/or particles, and may be omitted if understood from the context. Zhu then gives two interpretations of the subject-predicate relation: semantic, and expressive. Semantically, the subject may enter into a number of different relations with the predicate: e.g. agent, patient, recipient, time etc. This view diverges from that of a number of scholars such as, for example, Wang Li (quoted in Tsao 1980: 8) for whom the subject "denotes something (or some person) to which the behavior (active or passive), property or nature indicated by the predicate belongs", i.e. experientially it must be a participant rather than a circumstance (for more detail see 3.2.2 below.) Expressively, the relation of subject and predicate is explained as follows (Zhu 1981: 96): "What the speaker chooses as subject is the topic he is most interested in; the predicate is then a statement about the topic chosen." For example, in the following two clauses, the choice of agent or time as subject is explained by its expressive function:

[1] a. *Women* *zuotian* *kai* *le* *yi* *ge* *hui.*
We yesterday hold (ASP①) one (MEAS) meeting
Subject ---------**Predicate**---------
(We held a meeting yesterday.)

b. *Zuotian* *women* *kai* *le* *yi* *ge* *hui.*
Yesterday we hold (ASP) one (MEAS) meeting
Subject ---------**Predicate**---------
(Yesterday we held a meeting.)

Further, the predicate of a clause may itself be a "subject-predicate construction": thus, in effect the clause contains two subjects, the first being the subject of the whole clause, the second the subject of only the predicate part of the clause as illustrated in [2]:

① The key to abbreviations for grammatical words in these and following examples is given immediately following the main text.

[2] *Zhe ge re xinyan'r hao.*
this (MEAS) person heart good
----**Subject**--- ----**Predicate**----
Subject Predicate
(This person is kind-hearted.)

Chao (1968: 67–69, 78–80) defines subject and predicate structurally in a very similar way to Zhu, also allowing for the possibility of what he refers to as an "s-p predicate", exemplified by *xinyan'r hao* 'heart good-kind-hearted' above. Chao goes on to characterize the "grammatical meaning" of subject and predicate in Chinese as "topic and comment, rather than actor and action" (p. 69), explaining this as follows (p. 70): "The subject is literally the subject matter to talk about, and the predicate is what the speaker comments on when a subject is presented to be talked about." Furthermore, since "the subject sets the topic of the talk and the predicate gives the information by adding something new" (p. 76), there is a strong correlation between subject and "definite", and between "predicate" and "indefinite", as shown by the following examples:

[3] *a. Huo zhao le.*
fire start (ASP)
Subject **Predicate**
(The fire is lit.)
b. Zhao huo le!
start fire (ASP)
Subject **Predicate**
((There has) started a fire — there is fire!)

Chao (pp. 78–80) makes a further distinction between two types of predicate: the "grammatical" predicate, in other words the comment; and the "logical" predicate, i.e. the point of the message. The logical predicate is "normally located in the [grammatical] predicate" but "may be located in any part of the sentence" if marked by "contrastive stress". Chao notes that there is in fact a much stronger tendency in Chinese than in English for the two types of predicate to coincide, i.e. for the final element of the clause to be both grammatical and logical predicate (see also Gao 1984). In the following examples, the respective (logical) points of the two sentences are the equivalent "too many/ *tai duo*". In English it is expressed grammatically as a modifier to part of the grammatical predicate "are ... people here" as in [4a]; in Chinese it is the grammatical predicate (see [4b]):

[4] *a*. There are too many people here.

Subject ——**Predicate**——

b. *Zhe'r de ren* *tai duo*.

Here (SUB) person too many

Subject **Predicate**

(The people here are too many.) (= There are too many people here.)

6.2.1.2 The subject and topic view

In contrast to Zhu and Chao, for whom subject and topic are largely equivalent notions, Li and Thompson (1981: 85 - 92) consider these as entities of quite different kinds. They distinguish between the subject, "the noun phrase that has a 'doing' or 'being' relationship with the verb" (p.87), and the topic, "what the sentence is about" (p.86); for them, "a topic sets a spatial, temporal, or individual framework within which the main predication holds" (p.86). Structurally, they define topic in a very similar way to Zhu's and Chao's subject: it "always occurs in sentence initial position" and "can be separated from the rest of the sentence by a pause or by one of the pause particles" (p.86). Since topic and subject bear a distinct relationship to the rest of the sentence, their co-occurrence is independent of each other. Li and Thompson recognize four possibilities: (a) both topic and subject discretely present; (b) a topic identical to the subject; (c) topic present but not subject; or (d) neither topic nor subject present. We reproduce their original examples (Li and Thompson 1981: 88 - 90) as illustration, showing relevant items in bold; in [5a] the topic — *na zhi gou* — precedes subject *wo*; in [5b] *wo* is both subject and topic; in [5c] *nei ben shu* is simply topic, not subject; in [5d] the second clause in elliptical, with neither subject nor topic:

[5] ***a***. **+ Topic, +Subject**

Na zhi gou, wo yijing kan-guo le.

That (MEAS) dog I already look (ASP)(ASP)

(That dog, I've already seen.)

b. **Topic = Subject**

Wo xihuan chi pingguo.

I like eat apple

(I like eating apples.)

c. **+Topic, −Subject**

Nei ben shu chuban le.

that (MEAS) book publish (ASP)

(That book has been published.)

d. **−Topic, −Subject**

(Ni kan-guo Lisi ma?)

you look (ASP) Lisi (MOD)

(Have you seen Lisi?)

mei kan-guo.

(NEG) look (ASP)

(I) haven't seen (him).

Tsao (1980: 36–38) agrees in outline with Li and Thompson's analysis, but argues that topic and subject belong to different levels of grammatical organization. While subject is an element of sentence structure which "bears some selectional relation to the main verb of a sentence" (p.84), topic is a "discourse element" which "may ... extend its semantic domain to more than one sentence" (p. 88). In example [6], all three sentences share the topic *ta* "he" which is omitted after the first sentence (for a fuller justification for viewing *ta* as topic rather than subject in this example, see Tsao 1980: 11 – 13):

[6] *Ta* *duzi* *e*
s/he stomach hungry
you *zhao-bu-dao* *dongxi chi*
also seek (NEG) reach thing eat
suoyi tang-zai *chuang* *shang* *shui-jiao.*
So lie at bed on sleep nap
(He was hungry, and (he) couldn't find anything to eat, so (he) lay down on his bed and slept.)

6.2.1.3 Relevant features of Chinese clause structure

The above descriptions of clause structure in Chinese have drawn attention to the following four characteristics:

(1) The clause is commonly defined in "message" terms; in other words "the clause ... has some form of organization giving it the status of a communicative event" (Halliday 1985: 38);

(2) structurally, the clause divides into two parts: the first part, the beginning of the message; the second part, the continuation of the message;

(3) the different parts of the clause tend to have different information status: the first part known, definite; the second part new, indefinite; and

(4) the first part of the clause is significant in the creation of discourse.

6.2.2 Functional theories of clause structure

The concepts relevant to the "message" organization of the clause found in definitions of clause structure in Chinese were first introduced in the 1930s by Prague school linguists. Since then, they have been extensively applied in other functional schools, such as systemic functional theory (e.g. Halliday 1967b: see especially pp. 211 – 215). The relevant concept here is that of

Theme, which was first defined by Mathesius in 1929 as "that which is known or at least obvious in the given situation and from which the speaker proceeds" (see Fries 1981: 1). We briefly review the different ways in which this notion has been developed, and attempt to explain why the version current in systemic functional linguistics is most suitable for our purposes.

6.2.2.1 Theme in functional theories

Fries analyses Mathesius' definition of Theme as containing two distinct aspects: firstly, which is "known or obvious in the situation", and secondly, that "from which the speaker proceeds" (1981: 1). He then distinguishes two approaches to the concept of "Theme": the "combining" approach, which uses both of these criteria to define Theme; and the "separating" approach, which takes only the second as definitive of Theme. The difference between the two approaches to Theme is shown in Table 6-1, adapted from Fries (1981: 1-2):

Table 6-1 Combining and Separating Approaches to Theme

a) combining approach	
Theme:	That which is known or obvious in the situation that from which the speaker proceeds
b) separating approach	
Theme:	That from which the speaker proceeds (point of departure of the message)
Given:	That which is known or obvious in the situation

Commenting on the analysis of Theme in the English clause, Fries (1981: 3) sums up the differences between the two approaches as follows:

> The difference ... between the combining and the separating approach to the definition of Theme is that while the combiners either ignore the contribution of word order [to the realization of Theme as point of departure FY et al.] ... or treat it as contributing to the same

concept as the given-new distinction ... separators tease out and separate the contributions of word-order and of the distinction between given and new information, and they use the term theme to indicate the meaning of initial position in the clause.

Thematic progression

The separating approach assigns Theme to a particular position in the clause (in English, this is the initial position) and identifies it as the "point of departure of the message" (Fries 1981: 4; see also Cloran, in R. Hasan and Fries 1995). If Theme is defined as the point of departure of the message, then its significance can only be understood by seeing how it contributes to the progress of the message in texts. Fries, borrowing a term from Daneš, refers to this as the thematic progression. The patterns of thematic progression are identified by reference to the way a text moves forward from Theme to Rheme, within each clause, and between clauses (for some more discussion of this notion, see Fries and also Cloran in Hasan & Fries 1995). From this point of view, we can see the Theme-Rheme structure of each clause as textually motivated, organizing the text as a whole.

6.2.2.2 A multifunctional view of clause structure

If we refer back to Zhu's definition of subject in Chinese given in 6.2.1.1, we find that at least part of his definition corresponds very closely to the way Theme is defined for English in separating functional theories: i.e. Theme takes the initial position in the clause, and is a topic on which the predicate comments. While Zhu's definition works well in analyzing single clauses, it is not designed for analyzing extended stretches of text, and thus does not particularly help us to determine why particular elements are chosen as subject, apart from the vague formulation "what the speaker ... is most interested in" (Zhu 1981: 96). The notion of Theme does deal with the discourse considerations involved in the choice of clause Theme (Zhu's "expressive subject"); however, it fails to address Zhu's other main feature of subject, its "semantic" relationship with the predicate in terms of agent, patient, etc.

Systemic functional theory incorporates both of these types of meaning relation into a framework that explicitly recognizes the multifunctional nature of the clause as a "combination of three different structures deriving from distinct functional components" (Halliday 1985: 158). Two of these components, generalized abstract functions of language known as "metafunctions", correspond to Zhu's two interpretations of the meaning of subject in Chinese. The first, corresponding to Zhu's "semantic", derives from the ideational metafunction, which analyses the clause from the point of view of its "representational meaning: what the clause is about ... typically some process, with associated participants and circumstances" (Halliday 1985: 158). The second, corresponding to Zhu's "expressive", derives from the textual metafunction, which focuses on the "organization of the message: how the clause relates to the surrounding discourse, and to the context of situation in which it is being produced" (Halliday 1985: 158). The third component, not treated by Zhu, is the interpersonal metafunction, which is concerned with "interactional meaning: what the clause is doing, as a verbal exchange between speaker/writer and audience" (Halliday 1985: 158).

In the grammar of the clause in English, each of these three components or metafunctions "contributes a more or less complete structure, so that a clause is made up of three distinct structures combined into one" (Halliday 1985: 158). In Chinese, however, the interpersonal metafunction does not define a distinct clause structure in the same way the ideational and textual metafunctions do①. For this reason, in the discussion that follows we will

① Arguments for recognizing only two functional structures at clause rank in Chinese can be found in McDonald 1992: 437–440. In terms of Halliday's (1979) claim that each metafunction "typically generates different kinds of structural mechanism" (p.61), the system of Mood in Chinese is realized "prosodically" (p.66), by clause final modal particles and certain types of verbal group marking in conjunction with polarity.

focus mainly on the realization of the ideational and textual metafunctions in Chinese grammar.

In summary, if we adopt the multi-functional approach of a systemic functional grammar, we are able to (*a*) capture all the relevant types of meaning for the analysis of Chinese clause structure, and (*b*) take the analysis from the micro — i.e. clause-level, to the macro — i.e. discourse-level.

6.3 Framework for current study

In this study we aim to look at the textual organization of the clause from the point of view of its role in the formation of discourse. We will trace this organization from the level of single clauses to that of two or more clauses joined together in what in the systemic functional framework is known as the clause complex. We will also examine one example of a complete text in order to see how this same organization is manifested through a whole text. The analysis will involve two main types of textual organization: structural, and non-structural or cohesive.

6.3.1 Units of analysis

In the following discussion we will set up units of analysis on the basis of their textual organization: i.e. in terms of their Theme-Rheme structure. We will define two units, related to each other by constituency: a "clause complex" is made up of "clauses"①. The definition of these units also

① An earlier version of this research may be found in Fang 1989.

involves two other aspects of functional organization: for the clause, its experiential function: for the clause complex, its logical function (in systemic functional theory, these are known collectively as the ideational metafunction).

6.3.1.1 Clause

The clause in Chinese may be defined from two points of view. Firstly, from the point of view of its textual function, the clause is made up of Theme (starting point of message), and Rheme (continuation of message). This is characterized as the thematic structure of the clause. The Theme normally comes first in the clause, and may be marked off from the Rheme by a pause and/or a textual particle such as *a*, *ba*, *me*, *ne* (Chao 1968: 67; Zhu 1981: 95). The Rheme normally follows the Theme, and may itself be followed by an experiential (aspectual) particle and/or an interpersonal (modal) particle. The Rheme may precede the Theme only if the Theme is put in as an afterthought (Chao 1968: 69), with the aspectual/modal particles still following the Rheme:

[7] a. *Ni* *(a)* *gan* *ma* *(ne)?*
you (TEXT) do what (ASP)
Theme——Rheme——

b. *Gan* *ma* *ne,* *ni?*
do what (ASP) you
——Rheme——Theme
(What are you doing?)

Secondly, from the point of view of its experiential function, the clause divides into a Process (what is going on), one or more Participants (who/what are taking part), and associated Circumstances. This is known as the transitivity structure of the clause. From this viewpoint, the center of the clause is the Process, what is going on; different types of Process define different configurations of Participants and, to a lesser extent, Circumstances. There are a number of accounts of transitivity in Chinese in systemic functional terms (Tam 1979; Long 1981) as well as in comparable frameworks such as case grammar (Li 1971; Tang 1972) and Chafeian grammar (Teng 1975). Since this is not the main focus of the current study, we will not be treating transitivity in any detail here; the framework used will be the simplified one presented in McDonald 1992, which has the advantage that each of the three main Process types recognized, action①, state and relation, has a distinct kind of textual organization: that is, action clauses are textually very flexible, while state and relation clauses tend to have a more fixed thematic structure (see 6.4.1 below). In this framework, the example given above can be analysed as follows (particles omitted from transitivity analysis here):

[7] c. *Ni* *(a)* *gan* *ma* *(ne)?*
you (TEXT) do what (ASP)
Actor **Process** **Goal**
What are you doing?

A clause in Chinese is thus defined as the combination of a single thematic structure and a single transitivity structure. There are a couple of points that need noting here: first, the Process — particularly of the action type — may be realized by more than one verb. In that case the two verbs share the same thematic and transitivity structure; in other words, there is only one Theme-Rheme structure, and the two verbs share the same set of Participants and Circumstances as in [8]:

[8] *Ni* *gan* *ma* *qu* *le?*
You do what go (ASP)
Theme——Rheme——
Actor Pro- <Goal> cess
(What are you going (somewhere) to do?)

① In this framework, "action" subdivides into "material", "mental" and "verbal" (McDonald 1992: 440 – 441).

Secondly, the elements of the thematic and transitivity structures which define the clause are not necessarily isomorphic; what this means is that it is possible to have a thematic element which has no transitivity function in that clause. In [9], which is adapted from Tsao (1980: 104), *nei kuai tian* "that piece of land" does not function as an element of the experiential structure of the clause. If it had been part of the experiential structure, then as a Circumstance of location it would have needed to be in the form (*zai*) *nei kuai tian li* "in that piece of land". Here, while the reference to location in *nei kuai tian* is clearly related collocationally to the experience the clause is representing, structurally it merely serves as the starting point for the message:

[9] *Nei kuai tian*	*daozi*	*zhang*	*de*	*hen*	*da.*
That piece field	rice	grow	(EXT)	very	big
——**Theme**—		——**Rheme**———			
	Actor	**Process**	**Circumstance**		

((In) that field, the rice grows very large.)

6.3.1.2 Clause complex

A clause complex is made up of two or more clauses, and it may be described from two related points of view: the textual and the logical. From the point of view of the logical component of the ideational metafunction, clauses in a clause complex consist of one primary clause and one or more secondary ones. These are linked by two kinds of logical relations: interdependency relations of parataxis (coordination) and hypotaxis (subordination), and the logico-semantic relations of expansion or projection. The main categories of logical relation with their appropriate notations are displayed in Table 6-2 (For the definition and discussion of these, see Halliday 1985: 196-197):

Table 6 - 2 Logical Relations in the Clause Complex

Subtypes	Status of clauses	
(A) Interdependency relations		
	Primary	Secondary
Parataxis	1 (initiating)	2 (continuing)
Hypotaxis	α (dominant)	β (dependent)
(B) Logico-semantic relations		
I. EXPANSION		
a) elaboration	= (primary equals secondary)	
b) extension	+ (primary is added to secondary)	
c) enhancement	x (primary is multiplied by secondary)	
II. PROJECTION		
a) locution	"primary projects secondary as wording"	
b) idea	"primary projects secondary as meaning"	

From the textual point of view, two considerations appear important. First, the clauses in a clause complex may share a common Theme, though as illustrated by [6], the shared Theme may not occur overtly except in the first clause of the clause complex. Secondly, the clause complex as a whole has a point of departure, so that a thematic structure needs to be recognized which is specific to the clause complex as such and independent of the thematic structure of its constituent clauses. In the English clause complex, the initial clause is regarded as the Theme, with the remaining clauses making up its Rheme. The thematic structure of the clause complex is to a certain extent determined by the types of logical relations between its clauses. Specifically, some combinations of interdependency and logicosemantic relations may entail a fixed order for the primary and secondary clause: irrespective of this constraint; it is the initial clause that is automatically treated as the Theme of the clause complex. The justification for recognizing thematic structure in the clause complex lies in the fact that there do exist combinations of the two relations — interdependency and logico-semantic —

that permit variation in the order of clauses in a clause complex (Halliday 1985: 56 – 59). In these cases, it is the thematic progression of the text that determines which clause will occur initially, thus acting as Theme.

As Ouyang (1986: xi – xii) points out, the equivalent of clause complex in Chinese linguistics, *fuju* ("complex sentence"), does not make a clear distinction between interdependency and logico-semantic relations, nor does the notion of *fuju* cover the full range of possible relations between clauses in Chinese. In section 6.3.2.1, we will use Ouyang's classification of types of clause complex in Chinese, and give definitions and examples of the different types of interclausal relation. An example of a clause complex showing different kinds of interdependency and logico-semantic relations is given below:

[10] *a.* **1** *Mama* *mai le* *yixie* *taozi,*
mum buy (ASP) some peach
b. **+2x** β *chi-diao* *shiba* *zhi* *hou,*
eat up 18 (MEAS) after
c. 2α *hai* *sheng* *liu* *zhi,*
still remain 6 (MEANS)
d. **+3** *mama* *mai-lai* *duoshao* *zhi* *taozi?*
Mum buy come how-many (MEANS) peach
(Mum bought some peaches, after 18 were eaten, 6 still remained: mum bought how many peaches altogether?)

In example [10], we have both paratactic and hypotactic relations. The former has three terms, one initiating a paratactic relation, and hence shown as **1** in clause [10a], the remaining two continuing, show as **2**, **3**, [10b – 10d]. These terms are related by paratactic extension, shown as +; the relation is interpretable as temporal addition: i.e. **1** and then **2** and then **3**. The hypotatic relation occurs at the second term, which is itself made up of two parts, related by hypotactic enhancement, shown as **x**, with the dependent clause (β *chi-diao shiba zhi hou* "after eighteen were eaten") providing a precondition for the dominant clause (α *hai sheng liu zhi* "six still remained").

6.3.1.3 Textual organization through a text

Once we go beyond the boundaries of the clause or clause complex, we are dealing not with grammatical units, but rather with semantic units: in other words, with (parts of) complete texts (Halliday & Hasan 1976: 1–2). It is in this context that the concept of thematic progression really comes into its own. However, in order to understand the contribution of thematic progression to what Halliday and Hasan refer to as the cohesion of a text (1976: 4–6), in other words how the text hangs together, we need also to take into consideration the different functional varieties of language — or **registers** — and the different text types (or **genres**) that define particular texts. This would take us far beyond the present study; what we propose to do is to look at the thematic progression of one complete text — called Dreams — (see Appendix I), to see how some of the patterns we have identified at the level of the clause and clause complex contribute to the structure of text. The first three clauses of Dreams are analyzed below as an example [11a – 11c], to show how the pattern of thematic progression contributes to the introduction of the main information of the text:

[11] *a.* xβ *Dishang mei you gui,*

earth-on (NEG) exist ghost

Theme ——**Rheme**——

b. α *gui zai na'r?*

ghost be-at where

Theme ——**Rheme**——

c. *Gui dou zai renxin litou.*

Ghost all be-at people-mind inside.

Theme ---- **Rheme** ----

((If) there are no ghosts on the earth, (then) where are the ghosts? The ghosts are in people's minds.)

This extract from Dreams presents two main pieces of information: an entity (*gui* "ghosts"), and its various locations. The Theme of [11a] — (*dishang* " on earth") — is a location which sets the scene for the introduction of a new entity in the Rheme (*gui* "ghosts"). This entity then becomes Theme, functioning as the starting point for the next two clauses, while the main point of the paragraph, the location of the ghosts, is dealt with in the Rhemes of these two clauses.

6.3.2 Methods of analysis

The analysis① of textual organization in Chinese can be divided into two kinds: structural, and non-structural or cohesive (Halliday 1978: 133). The units of clause and clause complex were defined above according to structural criteria; once we begin to look at how clauses and clause complexes are formed into texts we need to consider cohesive criteria. As a preliminary step to the analysis, we will briefly review the implication of these two kinds of criteria.

6.3.2.1 Structural relations

Structural relations in the systemic functional framework are seen as multifunctional: that is, for any concrete structure, there will be more than one functional principle relevant to its interpretation. For the clause, different functional components define different abstract structures which interact with each other to determine the concrete ordering of the clause. For the clause complex, component clauses are linked to each other via different combinations of logical relations.

Structural relations in the clause

There are three grammatical systems which define distinct functional structures for the clause: the textual systems of THEME and

---

① Unless otherwise noted, all statements about structure etc. refer to Chinese, not English or any other language.

INFORMATION, and the experiential system of TRANSITIVITY. Strictly speaking, only the systems of THEME AND TRANSITIVITY have the clause as their structural unit. However, alongside the clause, we can recognize another structural unit, in this case not a grammatical one like clause, but rather a phonological one, the **tone group**, "the carrier of one complete tone contour" (Halliday 1978: 133). The tone group serves as the device for the realization of the **information unit**, which is defined as follows by Halliday (1985: 274-275):

The information unit is what its name implies: a unit of information. Information ... is a process of interaction between what is already known or predictable and what is new or unpredictable ... Hence the information unit is made up of two functions, the New and the Given.

While these two units are in principle distinct, we can take it as a general rule that "one information unit will be co-extensive with one clause" (Halliday 1978: 133), and we can therefore recognize Information structure also in written texts. This gives us the following distinct functional structures in a clause:

Table 6-3 Functional Structures in the Clause

System	Structural unit	Structural elements
THEME	clause	Theme, Rheme
TRANSITIVITY	clause	Pro, Participant(s), (Circ(s))
INFORMATION	information unit	Given, New

In the concrete structure of the clause, which is a realization of these three distinct functional structures, the different structures are conflated: i.e. in different contexts, the elements of these structures will map on to each other in different ways. The textual systems define two points of message prominence in the clause: Theme, which is the point of departure of the clause as message, and New, which constitutes the news in the clause as information. The Theme occurs at the beginning of the clause; the New normally falls at the end of the clause, i.e. within the Rheme. Fries (1992:

464) has coined N-Rheme (for New conflated with Rheme) as the term to refer to this "particular location in the clause"; in the present simplified description, we will assume that the last element of the Rheme is New unless otherwise stated. In characterizing clause structure in Chinese, we will, for the sake of simplicity, consider the conflation of different elements of transitivity structure with these two structural points, Theme and New, in the clause.

Structural relations between clauses

As noted in 3.1.2, underlying the syntagmatic structure of a clause complex are relations of two kinds: interdependency — parataxis and hypotaxis — and logico-semantic — expansion and projection. The intersection of these two types of relation is significant to the thematic structure of the clause complex. Thus, in a paratactic clause complex, the primary clause always comes first — precisely because the relation of parataxis is one based on the order of its constituents, with the initiating member followed by the continuing. So in a paratactic clause complex, whether expanding or projecting, the first clause will automatically be Theme of the clause complex: the structural order is fixed. The relation of hypotaxis, in contrast, is based on subordination between the primary and the secondary clauses. But the dependency may be expressed simply by the order of the constituent clauses. So in an expanding clause complex, the secondary clause normally precedes the primary, while in a projecting one the primary clause precedes the secondary. However, if this relation is marked by a structural device, clearly indicating which is the dominant and which the dependent clause, then variant ordering is possible.

Table 6-4 (adapted from Ouyang 1986: 18) presents the various possible combinations of interdependency and logico-semantic relations in the Chinese clause complex; where variant order is possible, the unmarked order is shown first. The table shows that variation in the structural order for thematic effect is possible only when the relation of hypotaxis combines with enhancement or projection. Where parataxis combines with projection, the structural order is invariant; what changes is whether the primary clause is projecting or projected.

Table 6 - 4 Types of Clause Complex in Chinese

Logico-semantic relation	Interdependency	Relation
I. EXPANSION	PARATAXIS	HYPOTAXIS
a) elaboration	1=2	
b) extension	1+2	$+\beta \wedge \alpha$
c) enhancement	1 x 2	$\{ x\beta \wedge \alpha$
		$\{ \alpha x \wedge \beta$
II. PROJECTION		
a) locution	1 "2	$\{ \alpha \wedge$ "β
	"1 2	$\{$ "$\beta \wedge \alpha$
b) idea	1 '2	$\{ \alpha \wedge$ 'β
	'1 2	$\{$ '$\beta \wedge \alpha$

6.3.2.2 Cohesive connections

On the basis of the structural relations already set up, we can identify further relations which act alongside structural relations, but unlike them are not confined to the clause/clause complex. These non-structural or "cohesive" relations extend over a whole text, serving to bind it together into a whole. Two main types of cohesive relations are relevant here: thematic progression, and cohesion proper.

Thematic progression

We have indicated above some of the different possibilities, in terms of the grammatical structures, for what is chosen as the Theme of a clause or clause complex. However, we have not explained why particular lexical material is chosen as Theme, nor how this fits in with the overall organization of the text. The notion of thematic progression (Fries 1981) is designed to provide a framework for answering this question. Following Fries (1981: 20), if we ask why a particular piece of information is chosen as the Theme of a clause, the answer is that the Theme of a clause is the point of departure of the message of that clause. As for the nature of the relationship between the information contained in the Themes of successive clauses in a paragraph or some significant segment of a text, it is suggested that this relation is what creates the method of development of that paragraph and/or textual segment.

Apart from these positive features, the choice of Theme also has a negative characteristic: that is, the choice of what information is not put in the Theme but rather in the Rheme is also significant. Theme of a clause, then again, we would suggest, following Fries (1981: 20 - 21) that a particular piece of information is put in the Rheme of a clause because it is the (main) point of the message of that clause. Further, the relationship between the information contained in the Rhemes of successive clauses is that together they form part of the (main) point of the paragraph. (See both Fries and Cloran in Hasan & Fries 1995; on the textual contribution of Rheme.) In Section 6.4, we will show some of the possible patterns of thematic progression in Chinese.

Cohesion

A cohesive relation may be defined as the "semantic relation between an element in the text and some other element that is crucial to the interpretation of it" (Halliday & Hasan 1976: 8). This sort of relation, as was pointed out above, exists alongside the structural relations found in clause and clause complex, and may be marked in various ways. The main types of cohesive relation (Halliday & Hasan 1976) are the following:

a) reference
b) substitution/ellipsis
c) conjunction
d) lexical cohesion

As explained above (6.3.3.1), a full treatment of text-forming relations, of which cohesive relations are only one part, would involve consideration also of the register (Halliday & Hasan 1976: 22 – 26) of the text, and would moreover require detailed analysis of actual texts. This takes us beyond the scope of the current study. We have included this brief discussion of cohesion for the sake of completeness; furthermore we have taken some account of cohesive relations in the analysis of the appendix text. Basically for this study, the point to be noted is that thematic progression always implies, at least, some lexically expressed semantic relations between the various clauses occurring in the text.

6.4 Textual organization in Chinese

In the following sections we will present a systematic overview of textual organization at and above clause level in Chinese. Our aim is to set out the different possibilities for the conflation of theme, transitivity and information structures in the clause and the clause complex. We are not presenting this as a comprehensive framework, but rather as an introduction to some characteristic textual patterns in Chinese. Large-scale text analysis, drawing from a wide range of different text types, will be needed to fill out and modify the outline given here. Most of the examples are extracts from actual (written) texts; in addition, we have provided one example of a complete (short) text in the appendices.

6.4.1 Clause

As noted in 6.2.2.1 above, the concrete structure of the clause in

Chinese can be seen as the conflation of three distinct structural functions which express the choices from three different systems. The basic, unmarked, structural functions associated with THEME, TRANSITIVITY, and INFORMATION are set out below in Table 6 – 5. The information provided in Table 6 – 5 is of course far from exhaustive, but it will suffice for our needs in this chapter.

Table 6 – 5 Clause Structures in Chinese

System	Functional structure
THEME	Theme ^ Rheme
TRANSITIVITY	
action:	Actor ^ Circumstance(s) ^ Process ^ Goal
state:	Carrier ^ Circumstance(s) ^ Process
relation:	Participant A ^ Circ(s) ^ Pro ^ Participant B
INFORMATION	Given ^ New

While every clause contains a Theme-Rheme and a Given-New structure, there are a number of different, mutually exclusive transitivity structures. The three main types of transitivity structure recognized in this framework, action, state and relation (McDonald 1992: 437 – 442), have different possibilities for ordering, and therefore for textual organization. As noted in 6.2.2.1 above, we discuss the textual organization in terms of the conflation of different elements of transitivity structure with Theme (initial position in the clause), and New (final position in the clause).

6.4.1.1 Textual organization in action clauses

Of the different clause types, action clauses tend to contain the largest number and variety of distinct functional elements. For most of these elements we can recognize a default or unmarked position in the clause, but they also have the possibility of being moved into positions of textual prominence[1]. This gives a two-fold choice for Circumstance, between initial position conflating with Theme, and post-initial position at the beginning of Rheme. Ignoring the function of Range in this simplified description, for Participant type roles — i.e. Actor and Goal — there is a three-fold choice: the element may occur in the clause initial position, thus conflating with Theme; or in post-initial position; or in a final position, thus, conflating with New. Process occurs in clause initial position either as a result of the ellipsis of a Participant function as in clause [20] of the Text in Appendix 1, or due to inversion as exemplified in [17] below. The first case would be analyzed here as one of ellipsed Theme while the second is treated as a case of Process conflating with Theme. Examples [12]-[17] illustrate these basic possibilities under headings a - f. The slash "/" shown in the heading titles — as in Actor/Theme, New/Goal — signifies that the elements on either side of the slash are conflated. Note that in the analysis of the examples, the function New is indicated not by entering the name of the element itself but by putting that transitivity function in bold italics with which the element New is conflated, e.g. ***Goal*** under heading **a**. in [12]:

a) *Theme/Actor, New/Goal*

[12] *Ta zuotian wanshang zuo-wan le zhe jian shi.*
S/he yesterday evening do finish (ASP) this (MEAS) matter
Th ————**Rheme**————————————————
Ac Circ Process ——***Goal***——————
(He finished doing this last night.)

---

① Halliday's discussion of Theme in the clause in English distinguishes "unmarked" and "marked" Theme according to its conflation with the various elements of Mood Structure (1985: 44-49). Since we are not recognizing a Mood structure at clause level in Chinese we are unable to use similar criteria; and moreover, the fact that almost any transitivity element of the clause can be conflated with Theme simply by moving it to initial position, without the need for any other structural changes, makes it very difficult to identify "basic" or "unmarked" Theme in the clause. For these reasons we have chosen not to characterize the various possibilities as marked or unmarked; further research may to establish a discourse basis for such a distinction.

b) ***Theme/Circumstance, New/Goal***

[13] *Zuotian wanshang ta zuo-wan le zhe jian shi.*
Yesterday evening s/he do finish (ASP) this (MEANS) matter
Theme ——**Rheme**————————————
Circ Actor Process ——Goal————
(Last night he finished doing this.)

c) ***Theme/Actor, New/Process***

[14] *Ta zhe jian shi zaojiu zuo-wan le.*
S/he this (MEANS) matter long-since do finish (ASP)
Theme——**Rheme**—————————————————
Actor ——Goal—— —Circ— ***Process***
(He finished doing this long ago.)

d) ***Theme/Goal, New/Process***

[15] *Zhe jian shi ta zaojiu zuo-wan le.*
this (MEAS) matter s/he long-since do finish (ASP)
Theme ————**Rheme**——————————
Goal Actor Circ ***Process***
(This, he finished doing long ago.)

e) ***Theme/Circumstance, New/Actor***

[16] *Huran pao-lai le yi zhi tuzi.*
suddenly run come (ASP) one (MEAS) rabbit
Theme ————**Rheme**————————
Circ Process ——***Actor***————
(Suddenly there ran out a rabbit.)

f) ***Theme/Process, New/Actor***

[17] *Qu le chuan hong de (hai you gua lü de.)*
go (ASP) wear red (SUB) still exist hang green (SUB)
Theme ——**Rheme**————————————————
Pro ——***Actor***——————————————————

((Though) gone were those in red, there still remained those in green.)

6.4.1.2 Textual organization in state clauses

In a clause with a state Process, the ordering of the (single) Participant (the Carrier of the state or property) and the Process is fixed, and only circumstantial elements may vary between initial (Theme) and post-initial position.

a) ***Theme/Carrier*, *New/Process***

[18] *Ni* *zuijin* *mang* *ma?*
you recently busy (MOD)
Theme ————**Rheme**————
Carrier Circ ***Process***
(Have you been busy recently?)

b) ***Theme/Circumstance*, *New/Process***

[19] *Zuijin* *ni* *mang* *ma?*
recently you busy (MOD)
Theme ————**Rheme**————
Circ Carrier ***Process***
(Have you been busy recently?)

The only exceptions to these two orderings are where an afterthought Theme is found (see 6.3.1.1 above):

[19′] *(Ni)* *mang* *ma,* *zuijin?*
you busy (MOD) recently
————**Rheme**———— **Theme**
Carrier Process **Circ**?
(Have you been busy recently?)

6.4.1.3 Textual organization in relational clauses

A relational clause structure always includes two participants (these were indicated as Participant A and Participant B in Table 6－5, p. 118); the type and ordering of these participants vary in the four subtypes of relational clause that have been recognized here. In a clause with a relation Process, ordering is part of the realization of transitivity structure. This implies that the Theme is always conflated with the same functional element, i. e. Participant A. In most cases the New is conflated with Participant B. In one subtype, viz. the existential, the New may be conflated with the Process.

a) ***existential clause: Theme/Location, New/Existent***

[20] *Dishang mei you gui.*
Earth-on (NEG) exist ghost
Theme ————**Rheme**————
Loc Process ***Existent***
((IF) there are no ghosts on earth ...)

b) ***locational clause: Theme/Existent, New/Location***

[21] *gui zai na'r?*
ghost be-at where
Theme ————**Rheme**————
Existent Pro ***Location***
(... (then) where are the ghosts?)

These two examples, from the opening clause complex of the first appendix text, show how in relational clauses, the use of different lexical verbs determines the textual organization, with the existential verb you "exist" and the locational verb *zai* "be located" defining transitivity structures that are mirror images of each other, and therefore placing textual prominence on exactly the opposite participant functions.

In an existential clause, the New may also be conflated with the Process. Furthermore, the Location may be omitted, in which case we have the equivalent of a Theme-less clause, with a distinction between Existent as New, or Process as New exemplified in [22] and [23], respectively:

[22] *(Zhe'r) you mei you niunai?*
here exist (NEG) exist milk
Theme ————**Rheme**————
Loc ——Process—— Existent
(Is there any milk (here)? i.e. do you sell milk here?)

[23] *(Zhe'r) niunai you mei you?*
Here milk exist (NEG) exist
Theme ————**Rheme**————
Loc Existent ***Process***
(Is there any milk (here)? i.e. do you have any left?)

c) *attributive clause: Theme/Carrier, New/Attribute*

[24] *Zhanggui shi yi fu xiong liankong,*
boss be one (MEAS) brutal face
Theme ————**Rheme**——————————
Carrier Process ————***Attribute***—————
(The boss had a brutal face ...)

A characteristic of attributive and equative relational clauses is that: either of the participants may be a clause or part of a clause embedded through nominalization with the subordinating particle *de*: Note that the embedded status of a clause, as *keyi huodong de* in example [25] is shown by enclosing it within double square brackets:

[25] *Ta de erduo shi [[keyi huodong de]].*
s/he (SUB) ear be can move (SUB)
Theme ———— **Rheme**———————————
Carrier Process ——Attribute———
(Its ears are moveable.)

d) *equative clause: Theme/Identified, New/Identifier*

[26] *Tamen bu shi gui*
they (NEG) be ghost
Theme ————**Rheme**————

Identified Process ***Identifier***

(They are not ghosts.)

[27] *Kepa de shi [[hai you ni mei jian guo ... de ren]].*

Frightening (SUB) be still exist you (NEG) see (EXP) (SUB) person

Theme ————**Rheme**————————————————

Identified Pro ————***Identifier***————————————

(The frightening thing is there are still people you've never seen.)

The lexical material of an equative clause may be reversed: in this case, the functional structure of the clause remains the same, i. e. Theme/Identified, New/Identifier as shown in [28]:

[26′] *Tamen bu shi gui.*

They (NEG) be ghost

Theme ————**Rheme**————

Identified Process **Identifier**

(They are not ghosts (they are something else.))

[28] *Gui bu shi tamen.*

Ghost (NEG) be they

Identified Process ***Identifier***

(The ghosts aren's them (the ghosts are something else)).

All types of relational clauses also admit Circumstances, with the same potential for either initial or post-initial position:

[29] *Yuanlai ta shi wode laoshi.*

originally s/he be my teacher

Theme ————**Rheme**—————

Circ Identified Pro ***Identifier***

(Originally she was my teacher.)

[30] *Ta yuanlai shi wode laoshi.*

s/he originally be my teacher

Theme ————**Rheme**————

Identified Circ Pro ***Identifier***

(She used to be my teacher.)

6.4.1.4 Possibilities of textual prominence for transitivity functions

Table 6 – 6 is designed to present a summary of the possibilities that are open to the different transitivity functions for conflation with either Theme — when they occur in initial position — or with New when they occur in final position; by comparison, the post-initial position usually means that an element has not been chosen as Theme of that clause, nor is it conflated with New. Note that certain positions are not open to certain functions in certain clause types. Thus, Process in action clauses, cannot occur in post-initial position, while in state clauses its position is the clause final one. In the table, those positions not open to a transitivity function in some clause type are indicated by a dash in the column. Of the transitivity functions, the two with the greatest potential for movement in the clause, are the participant functions Actor and Goal, which can occur in any of the three possible locations.

Table 6 – 6 Positions of Textual Prominence in the Clause in Chinese

Clause type	**Position of functions in the clause**		
	Initial/Theme	***Post-initial***	***Final/New***
action	Actor	Actor	Actor
	Circumstance	Circumstance	—
	Goal	Goal	Goal
	Process	—	Process
state	Carrier	—	Process
	Carrier	Carrier	—
	Circumstance	Circumstance	—
	—	—	Process
relation	Participant A	Participant A	—
	Circumstance	Circumstance	—
	—	—	Participant B
existential	Participant A	Process	Process
	—	Participant B	Participant B

6.4.2 Clause complex

The textual possibilities for ordering of clause complexes in Chinese may be viewed from two perspectives: the combinations of taxis and logico-semantic relations; and, secondly, thematic progression. A brief illustration of both is provided below in that order.

6.4.2.1 Basic combinations of parataxis/hypotaxis and expansion/projection

a) paratactic expanding clause complex, lexical material reversible:

[31] *a*. **1Theme** *Feng* *ye* *zhu* *le*,
wind also stop (ASP)
b. **+2Rheme** *yu* *ye* *ting* *le*.
rain also stop (ASP)
(The wind has stopped, the rain has stopped too.)

[31′] *a*. **1Theme** *yu* *ye* *ting* *le*.
rain also stop (ASP)
b. **+2Rheme** *Feng* *ye* *zhu* *le*,
wind also stop (ASP)
(The wind has stopped, the rain has stopped too.)

b) paratactic clause complex — [32b] and [32c] — nested inside first clause [32a]; note that the Rheme of [32a] follows the interrupting paratactic clauses:

[32] *a*. **1Theme** *Zhe* *ge* *ren*
this (MEAS) person
b. **=21** *ni* *bu* *zhidao*
you not know
c. **+22** *wo* *ke* *zhidao*
I really know

1Rheme *huai-tou* *le.*

Bad through (ASP)

(This person — you don't know, (but) I really know — is very bad.)

c) paratactic projecting clause complex, with either projecting or projected clause thematic:

[33] *a.* **1Theme** *Xiao Ming shuo*

young ming say

b. **"2Rheme** *"Wo mingtian bu qu shang xue".*

I tomorrow (NEG) go attend school

(Ming said: "I'm not going to school tomorrow.")

[33′] *a.* **"1Theme** *"Wo mingtian bu qu shang xue",*

I tomorrow (NEG) go attend school

b. **2Rheme** *Xiao Ming shuo.*

Young Ming say

("I'm not going to school tomorrow", said Ming.)

d) hypotactic expanding clause complex, with initial (subordinate) clause thematic to following (dominant) clause:

[34] *a.* **xβ Theme** *Tangshi gai de bu hao*

if revise (EXT) (NEG) good

b. **α Rheme** *duzhe keyi xie wenzhang piping.*

reader can write article criticize

(If (this book) is not well-revised, readers can write articles to criticize (it).)

e) hypotactic expanding clause complex, with initial (dominant) clause thematic to the following (subordinate) clause in [35] and the reverse in [35′]:

[35] *a.* **α Theme** *Tian yiding hen leng,*

sky definitely very cold

b. xβ **Rheme** *yinwei shui jie le bing.*
because water form (ASP) ice
(The weather must be very cold, because the water has frozen.)

[35′] *a*. **xβ Theme** *Yinwei tian hen leng*
because sky very cold
b. α **Rheme** *suoyi shui jie le bing.*
Therefore water form (ASP) ice
(Because the weather is very cold, (therefore) the water has frozen.)

f) hypotactic projecting clause complex, with either projecting or projected clause as thematic:

[36] *a*. α **Theme** *Women dou renwei*
we all consider
b. **xβ Rheme** *zhe ge banfa hen hao.*
This (MEAS) method very good
(We all think this is a good way of doing it.)

[36′] *a*. **xβ Theme** *zhe ge banfa hen hao,*
this (MEAS) method very good
b. α **Rheme** *women dou renwei.*
we all consider
(This is a good way of doing it, we all think.)

6.4.2.2 Thematic progression in the clause complex

In the following examples, for the sake of clarity, we have not shown the logical relations between clauses, and only the thematic structure of each individual clause (not that of the clause complex) has been indicated.

a) All clauses share common Theme/Actor, Theme is ellipsed after first clause; and Rhemes describe actions performed by Theme/Actor:

[37] **Theme** **Rheme**
a. *Ta qu-chu kapian,*
s/he take out card

b. *sai-jin* *yidou*,
stuff in pocket

c. *likai* *bangongshi*,
leave office

d. *congcong* *gan* *xia* *lou*,
hastily rush descend stair

e. *ti* *tade mishu* *ban* *shi* *qu le*.
for his secretary do matter go (ASP)

(He took out a card, stuffed it into his pocket, left the office, hurried downstairs and went to do some things for his secretary.)

b) initial and final clause share common Theme/Actor; *taozi* "peaches" is New in the Rheme of [38a]; it is the ellipsed Theme of [38b] and [38c]; and the following Rhemes specify amount of 'peaches'.

[38] **Theme** **Rheme**

a. *Mama* *maile* *yixie taozi*,
mum buy (ASP) some peach

b. *chi-diao* *shiba* *zhi hou*,
eat up 18 (MEAS) after

c. *hai* *sheng* *liu zhi*,
still remain 6 (MEAS)

d. *mama* *mai-lai duoshao* *zhi* *taozi?*
mum buy come how many (MEAS) peach

(Mum bought some peaches, after 18 were eaten, 6 still remained: mum bought how many peaches altogether?)

c) Theme of initial clause [39a] is elaborated in Rhemes of [39a]–[39d]; the Theme of [39a] is presupposed by ellipsis in [39b]–[39d]:

[39] **Theme** **Rheme**

a. *Laike* *ye bu shao*,
guest also not few

b. *you songxing de,*
exist see-off (SUB)

c. *you na dongxi de,*
exist bring thing (SUB)

d. *you songxing jian na dongxi de.*
exist see-off concurrently bring thing (SUB)

(There were quite a few guests also, there were those who came to see (them) off, there were those who came to carry things, and there were those who came to see (them) off and carry things as well.)

d) Initial clause [40a] has Theme/Circumstance (location); in its Rheme, New and Actor are conflated; the constituent realizing New/Actor consists of two nominal groups in coordination, each one extended in the separate following clauses:

[40] **Theme** **Rheme**

a. *Dongwuyuan zhong ji-man le daren xiaohai,*
zoo in crowd full (ASP) big-person small-child

b. *da de jiao,*
big (SUB) shout

c. *xiao de tiao.*
small (SUB) jump

(The zoo was full of grown-ups and children, the big ones shouting, the small ones jumping.)

e) expanding clause complex: with Actor/Theme in clause [41a]; in [41b] and [41c] conjunctions are thematic:

[41] **Theme** **Rheme**

a. *Ta hao bu rongyi de-dao le chu-guo huzhao,*
he very (NEG) easy gain reach (ASP) leave country passport

b. *dan yinwei youxie biyao de shouxu hai wei ban-hao*
but because some necessary (SUB) procedure still (NEG) do complete

c. rengran   mei you   huode   qianzheng.

Still   (NEG) have   obtain   visa

(He did, with some difficulty, get a passport, but because some of the necessary formalities had not yet been completed, he still has not obtained a visa.)

f) expanding clause complex, in which participants and enhancing conjunctions are thematic:

[42] **Theme   Rheme**

a. Zhanggui   shi   yi   fu   xiong   liankong,

boss   be   one   (MEAS)   brutal   face

b. zhugu   ye   mei   hao   shengqi,

customer   also   not-exist   good   humour

c. jiao   ren   huo-bu-de;

make   person   live not can

d. zhiyou   Kong Yiji   dao   dian,

only-if   Kong Yiji   arrive   shop

e. cai   keyi xiao   ji   sheng

only-then   can laugh   some   sound

f. suoyi zhijin   hai   jide.

So to-present   still   remember

(The boss had a brutal face, the customers were ill-humoured, making one miserable; it was only when Kong Yiji came to the shop that (we) could have a few laughs, and so today (I) still remember (him).)

6.4.3 Patterns of thematic progression

From the examples above, we can identify a number of different patterns of thematic progression in the clause complex. These are summarized below in terms of the movement of information between Theme and Rheme (thematic progression proper), and the general logico-semantic relations (see Table 6-4) between the clauses in the clause complex.

a) Participant introduced in Theme i; progression from initial Theme maintained by ellipsis throughout. Note in representing the thematic progression here, i-n refer to the number of the clause in the relevant clause complex (see the numbering system in examples [37]-[41]):

The clauses in clause complex [37a]-[37e] are related through extension, whereas those in [39a]-[39d] are related through elaboration. In both cases a simple linear pattern of thematic progression obtains:

[37]	Th *a*	Rh *a*	[39]	Th *a*	Rh *a*
	(Th *b*)	Rh *b*		(Th *b*)	Rh *b*
	(Th *c*)	Rh *c*		(Th *c*)	Rh *c*
	(Th *d*)	Rh *d*		(Th *d*)	Rh *d*
	(Th *e*)	Rh *e*			

b) In [40], the initial Theme of [40a] provides the setting; Rheme *a* of the complex introduces two participants; the Theme in [40b] and [40c] relate each to one of the two participants, extending them. The clauses of [40] are, thus, related by extension:

[40]	Th *a*	Rh *a* (participant 1)	Rh *a* (participant 2)	
	Th *b*	Rh *b*	Th *c*	Rh *c*

c) In clause complex [38], there are two main participants; the first is introduced in the Theme of [38a]. This participant is restated in the Theme of [38d]. The second participant is introduced in Rheme of [38a]; subsequently, it is the understood Theme of clauses [38b] and [38c]. Clauses [38a] and [38d] are related by extension; clauses [38b] and [38c] by enhancement:

[38]	Th *a*	Rh *a*	
		Th *b*	Rh *b*
		Th *c*	Rh *c*
	Th *d*	Rh *d*	

d) Participants are introduced in the initial Theme of [41] and [42]; some following Themes are realized by (enhancing) conjunctions; progression between Themes is by logical relation. The clauses of [41] are related by enhancement, while clauses [41a]-[41c] are related by addition and clauses [42d]-[42f] by enhancement:

[41] Th *a* Rh *a*
    Th *b* Rh *b*
    Th *c* Rh *c*

[42] Th *a* Rh *a*
  Th *b* Rh *b*
  Th *c* Rh *c*
      Th *d* Rh *d*
      Th *e* Rh *e*
      Th *f* Rh *f*

An analysis of thematic progression through a complete text is given in Appendix 2, using the same text — Dreams — introduced for thematic analysis in Appendix 1. In both appendices, for ease of presentation, the text has been divided into "paragraphs". The use of this term is simply to suggest convenient segments of text; we have not attempted to give a rigorous definition of "paragraph" here, since that would necessarily involve considerations of text structure that lie beyond the scope of the current chapter. It may, however, be noted that a change in thematic progression is often used to divide paragraphs from each other.

6.5 Conclusion

We have shown how it is possible to use the textual function of the grammar to define and explain the ordering of elements within clauses and clause complexes, and have identified some of the characteristic patterns of thematic progression in text. It has only been possible in this brief study to set up a preliminary framework: we hope that further research will be able to put our findings on a firmer footing. There is a need to carry out a systemic functional analysis of a wide range of text types in order to gain a better understanding of textual organization in Chinese.

Abbreviations

ASP	Aspect particle: perfective or imperfective (subtypes not indicated here)	MOD	Modal particle: interrogative, exclamative, etc. (subtypes not shown here)
CIRC	Circumstance	NEG	Negation adverb: neutral, perfective or potential (subtypes not shown)
DISP	Disposal marker: marks Goal as part of Given and moves it to front of clause	PRO	Process
EXT	Marks Circumstance of extent following Process	SUB	Subordinating particle: makes preceding group/clause into modifier of following nominal group
MEAS	Measure word (also known as classifier): obligatory for noun modified by numeral or demonstrative	TEXT	textual (pause) particle

Transcription

All Chinese examples and terms are given in the standard orthography of the People's Republic of China, Hanyu Pinyin; tone marks are omitted.

Appendix 1: The analysis of a complete text

The text, called Dreams, is presented through the analysis of Theme-Rheme at the rank of clause. Each ranking clause is numbered, and two columns are established, the left showing Theme, the right Rheme. The element New is shown by italicizing the constituent which realizes that function.

Theme **Rheme**

PARAGRAPH I

1. *Dishang mei you gui,*
   earth-on (NEG) exist ghost
2. *gui zai na'r?*
   ghost be-at where
3. *Gui dou zai renxin litou.*
   ghost all be-at person-mind inside

PARAGRAPH II

4. *Ni bu xin?*
   you (NEG) believe
5. *jiu kan meng.*
   then look dream

PARAGRAPH III

6. *Meng li name duo ren dou shi na'r lai de?*
   dream in so many people all be where come (SUB)
7. ——— *you ni ba,*
   ——— exist you father
8. ——— *you ni ma,*
   ——— exist you mother
9. ——— *you nide laoshi he tongxue,*
   ——— exist your teacher and classmate

10. ——— *you he ni zai yiqi shenghuo guo de ren,*
——— exist with you at together live (ASP) (SUB) person
11. ——— *ye you ni zhi tingshuo guo mingzi de ren,*
——— also exist you only hear (ASP) name (SUB) person
12. *zhe dou bu kepa.*
this all (NEG) frightening

PARAGRAPH IV

13. *Kepa de shi hai you ni mei jian guo,*
frightening (SUB) be still exist you (NEG) see (ASP)
mei ting guo, mei chi guo, mei wen guo,
(NEG) hear (ASP) (NEG) eat (ASP) (NEG) smell (ASP)
meng dou mei meng guo de ren.
Dream even (NEG) dream (ASP) (SUB) person
14. *zhe yi hui bu-qing-zi-lai le.*
This one time (NEG)-invite-self-come (ASP)

PARAGRAPH V

15. *Ni you bu neng wen:*
you again (NEG) can ask
16. *"Ni zi na'r lai?"*
you from where come
17. —— *"Yao dao na'r qu?"*
(you) want go where to
18. —— *jiushi wen le,*
just-be ask (ASP)
19. *ta ye bu shuo.*
s/he also (NEG) say

PARAGRAPH VI

20. —— *Zuo-wan le shi,*
do finish (ASP) matter

21. —— *hui shen jiu zou,*

turn body then leave

22. *na shi'r ni dao si ye mei jian-guo.*

That matter you do die also (NEG) see (ASP)

PARAGRAPH Ⅶ

23. *Ni shuo*

you say

24. *tamen bu shi gui*

they (NEG) be ghost

25. —— *shi shenme?*

Be what

PARAGRAPH Ⅷ

26. *Tian na, gui jiu zhu-zai women shenti li,*

heaven (text) ghost just live at we body in

27. *[xiang duo] ye duo-bu-kai.*

Want escape also escape-(NEG)-away

(If) on the earth there are no ghosts, (then) where are the ghosts? The ghosts are in people's minds. You don't believe (me)? Then take a look at dreams. In dreams, all those people come from where? There's your father, your mother, your teacher and classmates, there are people who have lived with you, there are also people you've only heard the names of, none of this is frightening. The frightening thing is there are also people you've never seen, never heard, never eaten, never smelt, never even dreamt of in dreams, this time they come without being asked. Nor can you ask (a ghost): "Where do you come from?" "Where are (you) going?" (You) just ask, and it doesn't say (anything). After (it) has finished doing something, it turns and leaves, that thing you'll never see in your whole life. (If) you say they're not ghosts, (then) what are (they)? My god, the ghosts live in our bodies, (if we) want to escape (them), (we) can't!

Appendix 2: Thematic Progression in Dreams

Note: ellipsed Themes are enclosed in round brackets e.g. in (5).

Theme	New
PARAGRAPH I	
1. **dishang** 'on the earth'	*gui* 'ghosts'
2. *gui* 'the ghosts'	*na'r* 'where'
3. *gui* 'the ghosts'	*renxin litou* 'in people's minds'
PARAGRAPH II	
4. *ni* 'you'	*xin* 'believe'
5. (*ni*) 'you'	*meng* 'dream'
PARAGRAPH III	
6. *meng li* 'in dreams'	*na'r lai de* 'come from where'
7. (same as 6)	*ni ba* 'your dad'
8. (same as 6)	*ni ma* 'your mum'
9. (same as 6)	*nide laoshi he tongxue* 'your teacher and classmates'
10. (same as 6)	*shenghuo-guo* (de ren) '(people) lived (with)'
11. (same as 6)	*tingshuo-guo mingzi* (de ren) '(people whose)' names (you)'ve heard'
12. *zhe* "this" (=6–11)	*(bu) kepa* '(not) frightening'
PARAGRAPH IV	
13. *kepa de* 'the frightening thing' = 'what is frightening'	*jian guo (de ren)* (people you)'ve seen' *ting guo (de ren)* '(people you)'ve heard' *chi guo (de ren)* '(people you)'ve eaten' *wen guo (de ren)* '(people you)'ve smelt'

	meng guo (de ren) '(people you)'ve dreamt of'
14. *zhe yi hui* 'this time' (contrast with clauses 7 – 11)	*bu-qing-zi-lai* 'come without being asked'

PARAGRAPH V

15. *ni* 'you'	*(bu neng) wen* '(can't) ask'
16. *ni* 'you' (different from 15)	*lai* 'come'
17. (same as 16)	*qu* 'go'
18. (same as 15)	*wen* 'ask'
19. *ta* 'it' (coreferential to 16 – 17)	*shuo* 'say'

PARAGRAPH VI

20. (same as 19)	*shi* 'thing, matter'
21. (same as 19)	*zou* 'leave'
22. *na shi'r* 'that thing'	*dao si* 'till death-all your life'

PARAGRAPH VII

23. *ni* 'you' (coreferential to 15)	*shuo* 'say'
24. *tamen* 'they'	*gui* 'ghosts'
25. (same as 24)	*shenme* 'what'

PARAGRAPH VIII

26. *tian na, gui* 'my god, the ghosts'	*women shenti li* 'in our bodies'
27. [*xiang duo*] 'want to escape'	*duo-bu-kai* 'can't escape'

7

A Study of Topical Theme in Chinese

— An SFL Perspective *

7.1 Introduction

In 2004 systemic functional linguists gathered in Kyoto for the 31st ISFC, discussing the directions and strategies of globalizing SFL. Today we are faced with the same issue — finding ways to propel Hallidayan linguistics in the world. Undoubtedly the official launching of the Halliday Centre in City University of Hong Kong, is a noteworthy symbol of this endeavour. The centre will certainly provide a platform for SF linguists coming from various countries to exchange views and to develop collaborations on "implementing intelligent applications of language studies".

---

* This chapter is collected in *Meaning in Context: Implementing Intelligent Applications of Language Studies*, edited by J. J. Webster, published by Continuum in 2008. I am grateful to Dr. Eden Li for reading the final draft and for giving critical comments.

In the past century since the publication of *Ma's Grammar* (1898/1983)[①], many researchers have been involved in the study of Chinese on the mainland of China. However, the main stream has been influenced by the formal approach, whether structuralism or generative-transformational grammar, which focuses on the study of form rather than meaning. In the last decade, however, more and more Chinese linguists have realized that the formal approach does not fit the Chinese language, which has "few formal signals" (Li & Thompson 1981), and that meaning should be taken as the basis for linguistics studies. This view is shared by the SF linguists who take meaning as the point of departure and form as the way to realize meaning. Articles taking this approach on various themes have appeared in great numbers in the leading linguistics journals and magazines on the mainland in the past decade. For example, there are over fifty on Topic and a dozen on Theme. Those on Topic either adopt the cognitive approach (Shen 1999; Shi 2001) or the various functional approaches including the SF linguistics (Fang 1989, 1990; Zhang & Fang 1994; Fang & Ai 1995). The dozen on Theme use the SFL framework in their discussions, among which, however, only a few on Topical Theme. These few articles define Topical Theme quite differently, and thus make it a controversial issue. I have chosen this topic in order to arouse interest in a more systematic study of Topical Theme and also to draw more SF linguists on the mainland of China and elsewhere to the study of Chinese grammar.

This chapter will address several issues. It will first discuss briefly clause structure, from both the traditional Chinese linguistics perspective, and the functional perspective, which will provide a basis for exploring Theme as part of the clause. Then it will deal with the concept of Theme in general but the focus will be on Topical Theme. Finally it will arrive at some conclusions.

① A grammar book titled *Mashi Wentong* (《马氏文通》) written by Ma Jianzhong (1845 – 1900), a Chinese official and scholar in the late Qing Dynasty. Literally the book title means "Basic principles for writing clearly and coherently by Mister Ma", and it was the first textbook of Chinese grammar written by a Chinese (there were already several grammars written by Westerners) published in 1898.

7. 2 Views on clause structure — From the Chinese linguistics perspective

Shi Yuzhi (2001: 82) states that there are mainly three views on clause structure in Chinese: the subject only view, the subject and topic view and the topic only view. However, Fang et al. (1995) believe that the second and the third views are similar in nature, which are able to be combined into one, as discussed below.

7.2.1 Subject only view

This view is represented by Zhu Dexi and Lü Shuxiang. Subject is defined structurally: Subject precedes predicate or "is the starting point of the clause" (Lü 1984), and is separated by an optional pause and/or particles; Subject may be omitted if understood semantically from the context. Yet, Subject and Predicate relation needs to be interpreted semantically and expressively. Semantically, Subject may be agent, patient, recipient, time, etc.; expressively, this relation can be explained as "Topic — Comment", and Predicate may be a "Subject Predicate construction", or there are two levels of Subject and Predicate (Zhu 1981: 95 - 96;). For example, in [1]

[1]	那块田	稻子	长	得	很	大。
	nei kuai tian	*daozi*	*zhang*	*de*	*hen*	*da*
	that piece field	rice	grow *V*	Adv	Adv	big
	Subject 1			Predicate 1		
		Subject 2		Predicate 2		

(In that piece of field, rice grows in big size.)

Both "那块田" (*nei kuai tian* or that piece of field) and "稻子" (*daozi* or rice) are defined as Subject in accordance with this view. However, two questions arise: do the two Subjects perform the same function? And if Subject is regarded as an element preceding Predicate, how should we analyze the following clause?

[2] 主席台上 坐着 个 老人。
zhuxitai shang *zuozhe* *ge* *laoren*
platform upon sit PROG MEAS old man.
(On the platform, sits an old man.)

where the circumstantial: location "主席台上" (*zhuxitai shang* "on the platform") appears initially and precedes the predicate, is it Subject? If it is, then it implies that there is no constraint put on the grammatical unit next below to realize the function of Subject. If it is not, then which element in the clause performs the function of Subject?

Actually, this type of analysis of clause structure and the confusion derived from the concept of Subject gave rise to heated nation-wide discussions on the classification of word classes and Subject/Object distinction during two linguistics conferences in the 1950s on the mainland of China. Subject has been regarded as "a headache" by some linguists (Fang & Shen 1997).

7.2.2 The Subject and Topic view

This view is maintained by Li and Thompson (1981), Shen Jiaxuan (1999) and Shi Yuzhi (2001), etc. Subject is defined as a "noun phrase that has a 'doing' relationship with the verb" while topic "sets a spatial, temporal or individual framework within which the main prediction holds." Further, Topic contrasts with Subject, which appears after Topic and does not overlap with Topic (Li & Thompson 1981). This view is shared by Chao Yuanren (1968) and Xu Tongqiang (1990) although there is a slight difference between them, which will not be elaborated here for short of space. Therefore, Example [1] would be analyzed as:

[1]	那块田	稻子	长	得	很	大。
	nei kuai tian	*daozi*	*zhang*	*de*	*hen*	*da*
	that MEAS field	rice	grow *V*	Adv	Adv	big
	Topic	**Subject**	Predicate			

(In that piece of field, rice grows in big size.)

where the first nominal group is Topic and the second Subject. In this clause both Topic and Subject are present, in which Topic "那块田" (*nei kuai tian* or that piece of field) "sets a spatial framework" for the "main predication", and Subject "稻子" (*daozi* or rice) has a "doing" relationship with the verb "长" (*zhang* or grow).

We can arrive at the following features relevant to Chinese clause structure from these views: 1) 'the clause is commonly defined in "message" terms; in other words, "the clause ... has some form of organization giving it the status of a communication event" (Halliday 1985/1994: 38); 2) structurally, the clause divides into two parts: the first part, the beginning of the message; the second part, the continuation of the message'; 3) 'the first part is significant in the creation of discourse' (Fang et al. 1995). There exists a problem, however, in the two views: There are other elements than Topic or Subject appearing initially in a Chinese clause in a certain context, such as [3]:

[3]	好,	我们	就	这样	决定	了。
	hao	*women*	*jiu*	*zheyang*	*jueding*	*le*
	Text	we	ADV	VADV	decide	VPART

(All right, let's decide in this way.)

In which only "我们" (*women* or we) is Subject or Topic (Referring to the above two views) while "好" (*hao* or all right) is not. Then what is it? The answer can be found in the SFL framework, which provides a multifunctional view of clause structure. We believe that approaching Chinese grammar from this view can help us solve the problem and "understand better the types of grammatical patterning present in Chinese" (Fang et al. 1995).

7.3 Clause structure in Chinese — An SF perspective

Mathesius (1929, see Fries 1981: 1) divides a sentence into two parts: Theme and Rheme from the functional perspective, which has had an impact on Halliday's functional approach in mapping out one of his meta-functions — Textual Function in organizing the constituents in a clause in a given context (Halliday 1985/1994). In what follows we will summarize in brief the multifunctional view represented by Halliday, and then elaborate on two models of clause structure.

7.3.1 A multifunctional view

Systemic functional theory incorporates three types of meaning relation into a framework that explicitly recognize the multifunctional nature of the clause as a "combination of three different structures deriving from distinct functional components" (Halliday 1985/1994: 158): the experiential structure, representing patterns of our objective and subjective experience in the world; the interpersonal structure, enacting interpersonal relationships in the social world, and textual structure, which is concerned with the organization of a message in a clause or a discourse. This multifunctional view is the basis for the study of clause structure in Chinese in this chapter.

7.3.2 Two models of clause structure

Fang et al. (1995) state "A clause in Chinese is the combination of a single experiential structure and a single thematic structure" as shown:

$$\text{Clause}\begin{cases}\text{Theme} \wedge \text{Rheme} \\ \text{Actor} \wedge \text{Predicator} \wedge \text{Goal}\end{cases}$$

This definition is made on the ground that the form, concept and function of Subject differ in Chinese from those in English. First, Subject is hard to recognize as it has no morphological inflections (Lü Shuxiang 1984); second, the concept of Subject given by different linguists differ a great deal, as mentioned in 7.2; therefore the status of Subject is indefinite; and third, Subject does not perform the function of realizing Mood as in English, in which the sequential positions of the finite verb and Subject are decisive in the making of Mood in a clause (Halliday 1985/1994). In Chinese, Mood is very differently realized — by the intonation and the mood particles. Compare:

In English:

The sequence of a clause in the Declarative Mood:

[4] **I finished my homework yesterday.**

in which Subject "I" precedes the Finite "did" fused with the Predicator.

The sequence of a clause in the Interrogative Mood:

[4′] **Did you finish your homework yesterday evening**?

in which the Finite verb "did" precedes Subject "you".

However, in Chinese:

The sequence of a clause in the Declarative Mood:

[5] 我 昨天 晚上 做完 作业 了。
wo zuotian wanshang zuowan zuoye le
I yesterday evening finish ASP homework VPART.
(I finished my homework yesterday evening.)

The sequence of a clause in the Interrogative Mood:

[5′] 你 昨天 晚上 做完 作业 了 吗?
ni zuotian wanshang zuowan zuoye le ma?
You yesterday evening finish ASP homework VPART MPART?
(Did you finish your homework yesterday evening?)

in which there is no change of word order as Chinese has no finite verb. The Interrogative Mood is realized by the mood particle "吗" (*ma*) and the rising intonation in spoken Chinese or the question mark in the written form. The second reason for this definition is that we find that Halliday's experiential functional structure and textual structure correspond to Zhu's semantic structure and his expressive structure (Fang et al. 1995).

However, further studies on the nature of dialogues reveal that Subject does play a role in making an interaction possible. For example,

[6] A: 谁 去 开门?

shei qu kaimen

Who go open door

Subject

↙

pronoun

(Who is going to open the door?)

B: 我 去 开门。

wo qu kaimen

I go open door.

Subject

↙

pronoun

(I will go and open the door.)

[7] A: 开会 你 去 不 去?

kaihui ni qu bu qu?

have meeting you go NEG go?

Subject

↙

Pronoun

(Are you going to the meeting?)

B：（我） 不去。
(wo) *bu qu*
(I) NEG go
Subject
↙
Pronoun
(I am not going).

In A and B of [6], the dialogue argues about who should be the person going to open the door; it is this element which makes the interaction between the interrogators possible. This element is realized by the pronoun "谁" in the interrogative clause, and "我" in the declarative clause. Different from [6] in structure, [7] has a verbal group taking the initial position, yet it is still the pronoun "你" (*ni*, or, you) or "(我)" (*wo*, or, I) being argued about between the two speakers. They are the elements which make the dialogue or interactive event valid or possible. All these pronouns function as Subject in the respective clauses. Semantically, Subject can be defined as the element performing the interactive function of making a proposition arguable (Halliday 1985/1994; Matthiessen 1995), or as the element responsible for the clause as an interactive event, and structurally, it usually precedes Predicator and is realized by a noun/nominal group or a pronoun.

Therefore, a clause in Chinese is the combination of a single experiential structure, a single interpersonal structure and a single thematic structure as shown:

$$\text{Clause}\begin{cases}\text{Theme} \frown \text{Rheme}\\ \text{Subject} \frown \text{Predicator} \frown \text{Complement}\\ \text{Actor} \frown \text{Process} \frown \text{Circumstance}\end{cases}$$

From the point of view of its experiential function, the clause divides into a process, one or more participants, and associated circumstances — an Experiential Structure. From the point of view of its interpersonal function, the clause divides into a Predicator, Subject and Adjuncts — an Interpersonal

Structure. From the point of view of its textual function, the clause is made up of Theme and Rheme — a Thematic Structure, the concept of which will be discussed in the next section.

7.4 The concept of Theme

As mentioned above, systemic functional theory recognizes the clause as a combination of three different structures (Halliday 1985/1994: 158): the experiential, interpersonal, and textual structures. The textual clause grammar provides resources to realize the experiential and interpersonal meanings as text organized in a succession of peaks of prominence followed by non-prominence elements, thus forming two different types of wave, namely thematic and information waves. The peaks represent two types of prominence — thematic prominence and news prominence, which are realized by Theme and New respectively (Halliday 1985/1994; Matthiessen 1992). This paper will only concentrate on the study of Theme, the realization of thematic prominence.

7.4.1 Definition of Theme

Mathesius (1929, see Fries 1981: 1) defines Theme as "that which is known or at least obvious in the given situation and from which the speaker proceeds."

In his earlier writings, Halliday gives the following definitions: Theme is "the point of departure of a message" (1967, 1985/1994), or "the starting-point for the message" (1985/1994: 39) or "the peg on which the message is hung" (1970), and also as "what is being talked about" (1967:

212), or "that with which the clause is concerned" (1985/1994). The two aspects of definition imply "whatever is chosen as Theme is put first", and Theme is "what the message is about" (Fang et al. 1995).

There are some differences between Mathesius and Halliday: the former holding the combining approach (Theme = Given) and ignoring the contribution of word order; the latter holding the separating approach (Theme may not be Given) and using the term Theme to indicate the meaning of initial position in the clause (Fang et al. 1995).

Halliday's definition has given rise to some criticisms. The major criticism comes from the argument that a point of departure may not be what the clause is about. While the experiential meaning may be what the clause is about, neither the textual nor the interpersonal has this connotation (Fries 1981; Wu Weizhong 2001). For instance, in [8]:

[8] 可是	说不准	明天	会	更	热。
keshi	*shuobuzhun*	*mingtian*	*hui*	*geng*	*re*
But	say NEG sure	tomorrow	MADV	ADV	warm
Text	Inter	Topic			
----- **Theme** -----			--------**Rheme** -----------		

(But I am not sure whether it will be warmer tomorrow.)

"明天" (*mingtian* or tomorrow) is Topical Theme (See next section) realizing the experiential meaning of the clause; however neither "可是" (*keshi*, or, but) nor "说不准" (*shuobuzhun*, or, not sure) has anything to do with expressing the experiential meaning or is concerned with the "aboutness" of the clause. In fact, the former, being a coordinate conjunction linking this clause with the previous one, performs Textual Function whereas the latter, being a modal element expressing the assessment of the speaker, performs Interpersonal Function.

Matthiessen (1995) describes Theme as "the resource for manipulating the contextualisation of the clause … for setting up a local context for each clause in a text". Halliday and Matthiessen redefine Theme later as "the point of departure of the message; it is that which locates and orients the clause within its context" (2004). There are two points noticeable in these two definitions: 1) They no longer mention the "aboutness" of a message; and 2) They highlight the role of context in defining this textual function, thus pushing the Hallidayan grammar a step further towards a "discourse grammar" (Halliday 1985/1994).

Chinese scholars provide various definitions of Theme in Chinese: some adopt Mathesius' view (Zhang & Fang, 1994); some only take the first part of Halliday's 1985/1994 definition (Wu Weizhong 2001); some follow Halliday's 1985/1994 concept literally in their earlier articles (Fang Yan, 1990).

Fang et al., in 1995 claimed: "Theme normally comes first in the clause, and may be marked off from the Rheme by a pause and/or a textual particle such as *a*, *ba*, *me*, *ne*." The reason why they stated that "Theme normally comes first in the clause" is because they believed that in spoken Chinese the position of Theme and Rheme may be reversible. The second half of the definition comes from their consideration of recognizing Theme formally. However, it seems now that the reversibility of Theme and Rheme needs to be further verified.

Referring to Fang et al. (1995) and Halliday and Matthiessen (2004), this chapter has revised a little of the definition of Theme in Chinese: **Theme is the point of departure of a message, and may be marked off from Rheme by a pause and/or a textual particle such as 啊 (*a*), 吧 (*ba*), 么 (*me*), 呢 (*ne*)**. Again take [8] as an example, in which "可是" "说不准" and "明天" are the point of departure of the message; these three elements provide respectively the ideational, interpersonal and textual context for the clause, and they may be separated by the textual particle 啊 (*a*) from the Rheme of the clause.

[8]	可是	说不准	明天	(啊)	会	更	热。
	keshi	*shuobuzhun*	*mingtian*	*(a)*	*hui*	*geng*	*re*
	But	say NEG sure	tomorrow	(Text P)	MADV	ADV	warm
	Text	Inter	Topic				
	-----	**Theme** -----------		---**Rheme** -----------			

(But I am not sure whether it will be warmer tomorrow.)

Halliday (1985/1994) argues that the Theme of a major clause extends up to the first element that has an experiential meaning. This gives rise to two major types of Theme: simple and multiple, which will be discussed in the following section.

7.4.2 Simple Theme and Multiple Theme

When we discussed [3] "好，我们就这样决定" (*hao, women jiu zheyang jueding*, or, All right, let's decide in this way.), we pointed out that "我们" (*women* , or, we) is the Topic but "好" (*hao*, or, all right) is not. Then what is it? We can find the answer from the concept of Multiple Theme. Halliday (1985/1994) claims that if there is only an element of the experiential mode of the ideational metafunction or Topical element in a clause, it is called Simple Theme. The Themes in the clauses of [1], [2], [5], [6] and [7] are Simple Themes. However, in [3], "好" and "我们" function differently though both appear at the beginning of the clause: "好" performs the function of "continuative" (Halliday 1985/1994: 53), thus labeled **as "Textual Theme"** as it connects this clause with the previous one in this context while "我们" is expressing its Topical meaning. To avoid confusion arising from the term Topic, which is associated with "only one particular type of Theme" (Halliday 1985/1994: 39), this chapter labels this function as "**Topical Theme**". Therefore this clause can be analyzed as:

[3]	好，	我们	就这样	决定。
	hao	*women*	*jiu zheyang*	*jueding*
	Continuative	we	ADV VADV	decide
	Text Theme	**Topical theme**		
	-------**Theme** -------		--------**Rheme** ----	

(All right, let's decide in this way.)

In the previous section, we pointed out that in Clause [8], there are three thematic elements simultaneously existing in the clause. More examples can be found in [9], [10] and [11]. The vocative elements "昌林哥, 玉翠嫂子" (*changlin ge, yucui saozi*, or, Changlin brother, Yucui sister) in [9] are used to bring closer the interpersonal relation between the speaker and the hearer; the exclamatory elements "啊呀, 天" (*a ya tian*, or, oh, heaven) in [10] to express the feeling of surprise of the speaker; and "不用说" (*bu yong shuo*, or needless say) in [11] to render the speaker's comment. Since all these elements appear initially, they are all Interpersonal Themes.

[9] 昌林哥, 玉翠嫂子, 你们两位 (啊) 同意不?

changlin ge yucui saozi nimen liangwei (a) tongyi bu

Changlin brother Yucui sister you two MEAS (Text P) agree NEG.

-----Vocative --------------------------------------

---**Interpersonal Theme** **Topical Theme**

--------------**Theme**------------ ----**Rheme**------

(Brother Changlin, Sister Yucui, don't you two agree?)

[10] 啊呀, 天, 你 (啊) 长得 多 结实 啊!

a ya tian ni (a) zhangde duo jieshi a

oh, heaven you (Text P) grow ADV sturdy MPART

Exclamatory

InterTheme **Topical Theme**

-------**Theme**----- --------**Rheme**----------------

(Oh, my God, how sturdy you have grown!)

[11] 不用说, 两个人 的 劲头(啊) 都 绷得 像 梆子戏 上的 琴弦。

buyongshuo lianggeren de jintou (a) dou bengde xiang bangzixi shangde qinxian

Needless say two MEAS people POSS look (Text P) ADV stretch like opera upon fiddle

Modal

InterTheme **Topical Theme**

--------------**Theme**--------- -------**Rheme**----------

(Needless to say, the two people are intensely stretched mentally like the fiddles being played in an opera.)

To sum up, in Chinese, a Simple Theme is made up only of Topical Theme while a Multiple Theme can comprise Textual Theme, and/or Interpersonal Theme and Topical Theme. A Textual Theme may consist of two types: (1) continuative, which is "one of a small set of discourse signalers" (Halliday 1985/1994: 53), such as 好 (*hao*, or, all right), 是的 (*shide*, or, yes), 不是 (*bushi*, or, no), which "signals that a new move is beginning" (*ibid.*) or indicates the speaker is ready to continue the interaction (Li 2007); (2) structural, including conjunctions and conjunctives (Halliday 1985/1994: 53), such as 虽然……但是 (*suiran... danshi*, or, although ...), 可是 (*keshi*, or, but), 其实 (*qishi*, or, in fact), 换句话说 (*huanjuhuashuo*, or, in other words), etc. These two types of Textual Theme function as a cohesive tie in the text, denoting a certain logico-semantic relationship between the neighbouring clauses. Interpersonal Theme may include: (1) an exclamatory element such as 啊呀 (*aya*, or, oh), 天 (*tian*, or, heaven), as in [10]; (2) a vocative, usually a personal name as in [9], which is used to identify the addressee in the interaction; (3) a modal element, such as 可能 (*keneng*, or, possible), 肯定 (*kending*, or, certain), 会 (*hui*, or, tend to), 应该 (*yinggai*, or, must), or 说不准 (*shuobuzhun*, or, not sure) as in [8] or 不用说 as in [11], etc. These modal elements are used to show the speaker's attitude towards the proposition or proposal expressed in the clause, either by means of modalization or of modulation (Halliday 1985/1994). Topical Theme is an ideational element, which is rather complex and will be elaborated in the next section. In other words, a Multiple Theme can contain all the three Themes or either Textual Theme and/or Interpersonal Theme plus Topical Theme. It follows, therefore, that there must be a Topical Theme in a clause although it can be omitted if the context is made clear, but a clause can go without one of the other two, as illustrated in examples [3], where there are Textual Theme and Topical Theme but without Interpersonal

Theme, and [9], [10] and [11], where there are Interpersonal Theme and Topical Theme but without Textual Theme. Similar to English, the sequence of the three elements when they all appear initially would usually be: Textual Theme ^ Interpersonal Theme ^ Topical Theme, which is well illustrated in [8]. However, a few conjunctions such as "虽然" can come before or after Topical Theme. For example, it is possible to choose either [12a] or [12b] to express similar meanings (hereafter we will omit the possible textual particle due to space limitation):

[12] *a.* 虽然 我 不知道 这事 是 谁 干的,
suiran wo buzhidao zheshi shi shui gan de
CONJ I NEG know this matter be who do VADV
Text Theme **Topical Theme**
但是 我 敢 肯定 与 他 有关。
danshi wo gan kending yu ta youguan
CONJ I MADV sure PREP he concern
Text Theme **Topical Theme**
(Although I don't know who did this, I am sure it has to do with him.)

b. 我 虽然 不知道 这事 是 谁 干的,
wo suiran buzhidao zheshi shi shui gande
I CONJ NEG know this matter be who do VADV
Topical Theme
但是 我 敢 肯定 与 他 有关。
danshi wo gan kending yu ta youguan
CONJ I MADV sure PREP he concern
Text Theme **Topical Theme**
(Although I don't know who did this, I am sure it has to do with him.)

Therefore, there are two positions for 虽然 (*suiran*, or, although) in Chinese, either before or after Topical Theme. Some linguists (Li 2007) argue that usually this kind of conjunction appears at the second initial position, and therefore, when it takes the initial position, it is in its marked position.

7.5 Topical Theme

This section will address several subtopics: definitions of Topic given by various linguists; two types of Topical Theme — Contextual and Experiential; the sub-categories of Experiential Theme — Marked Theme, Preposed Theme and Thematic Equative; functions of Topical Theme; and realization of Topical Theme.

7.5.1 Definition of Topic

We mentioned in the last section that Topical Theme originates from the term Topic but it has replaced the latter on the ground that it is only one type of a Theme in the SFL framework. Apart from this, the two terms share the basic concept.

The earliest definition of Topic comes from Hockett (1958), the linguist who initiates the concept of "discourse". He defines Topic as that "The speaker brings up something and goes on to talk about it", which is obviously a view based on the function performed by this element, i.e. providing the basis for the verbal act to continue. Different from Hockett, Chomsky gives a definition from the formal perspective (1965): Topic refers to the most left NP in a sentence in the surface structure, which defines this concept from the position it takes without giving attention to its function(s). Chao Yuanren (1968) combines the two approaches by stating that Topic is the most left NP, which provides Comment, and that the Subject and

Predication relation is one as "topic and comment rather than actor and action". For example, in [13], "我" is a pronoun and takes the most left position of the sentence, and it is the element which provides the ground for the comment. Hence it is the Topic of the clause.

[13] 我 头 疼。
wo tou teng
I head ache
Topic **Comment**
(My head aches.)

Li & Thompson (1981) proposes a definition which is frequently quoted: Topic "sets a spatial, temporal, or individual framework within which the main predication holds". Accordingly in [13], 我(*wo*, or, I) provides a setting for the main predication "头疼" (*touteng*, or, headache). Hence it is the Topic of the clause. Similarly, "那场火" (*nei chang huo*, or, that fire) in [14] sets a framework for the rest of the clause. It is regarded as the Topic of the clause.

[14] 那 场火, 幸亏 消防员 来 得 快。
nei chang huo, *xingkui xiaofangyuan lai de kuai*
That MEAS fire, fortunately fire-fighters come V AVD quickly.
Topic
[(As for that fire, it was fortunate that (as) the fire-fighters came quickly (it was put off.)]

Note that this Chinese clause is a simple one as there is only one verb process "来" (*lai*, or, come), yet the underlying meaning conveyed by the commentary adjunct "幸亏" (*xingkui*, or, fortunately) implies that logically there could be a hypotactic relation between "幸亏消防员来得快" (*xingkui xiaofangyuan laide kuai*, or, fortunately fire-fighters came quickly) and an omitted clause "it was put off", which is understood from the context. Chafe (1976) regards this type of Topic as "Chinese Topic".

Shen Jiaxuan (1999) maintains that Topic should have the following features:

a) It always appears at the beginning;

b) There is a pause or a mood particle after it;

c) It expresses given information;

d) It is a concept of discourse, which can govern the following clause(s) as well.

There are three characteristics in the four features: The first two take the formal features of Topic into consideration: its initial position and how it is parsed from the rest of the clause (as far as we are concerned, "is" should be replaced by "may be" and "a mood particle" changed into a textual particle as mood is not involved.); the third points out that it overlaps with given information (in an unmarked case); and the fourth states that it is a concept derived from discourse; therefore, Topic is also a discourse feature. Similarly, Shi Yuzhi (2001) claims that Topic is Given and appears initially; but he emphasizes that the topicalized elements are not only nouns, but also time, location, tool and beneficiary; however, in our view, these concepts are not on the same level: nouns are a notion of word class and the others notions of functions. Qu Chengxi (1999) defines Topic as a noun phrase or a pronoun or a zero anaphora appearing at the beginning of a clause and having the meaning of "aboutness". His definition restricts Topic as being realized by NP only, and having noticed the feature of zero anaphora appearing in a string of clauses in Chinese, he points out that it can also function as Topic in a discourse. Fang (1990) regards [in reference to Halliday (1985/1994)] Topic as "what the clause is about", and terms it as Topical Theme.

Referring to the above, this chapter defines Topical Theme as follows:

> Topical Theme is the point of departure of a message; it expresses the experiential meaning and/or provides a setting for the clause and may be marked off from Rheme by a pause and/or a textual particle.

There are three features in the definition:

a) It starts with the positioning of Topical Theme — as a point of departure of a message; therefore, it should usually appear initially;

b) It stresses the semantic meaning or function of this element — expressing the experiential meaning and/or providing a setting for the clause;

c) It formalizes Theme by stating how it may be parsed from Rheme — by a pause and/or a textual particle.

7.5.2 Types of Topical Theme

In 7.5.1 Topical Theme is defined as expressing the experiential meaning and/or providing a setting for the clause, which, accordingly, gives rise to two types of Topical Theme: Experiential Topical Theme and Contextual Topical Theme.

7.5.2.1 Experiential Topical Theme and Contextual Topical Theme

1) Experiential Topical theme: As mentioned above, when there is only one element in the Theme, we term it as Simple Theme, which performs the experiential function as Actor "我" (*wo*, or, I) as in [15] and as Location "学校里" (*xuexiaoli*, or, in school) as in [16]. This type of Topical Theme is termed as Experiential Topical Theme, or shortly, Experiential Theme; in the case of a Multiple Theme, the last thematic element is usually Experiential Theme as "明天" (*mingtian*, or, tomorrow) in [8], which expresses the experiential meaning of the clause as Carrier.

[15]
我	打算	去	北京。
wo	*dasuan*	*qu*	*beijing*
I	plan	go	Beijing.
Experiential Theme/Actor			
Theme	---**Rheme**	----------	

(I plan to go to Beijing.)

[16] 学校里 我见 过 他。
xuexiaoli wo jian guo ta
School in I see ASP he
Experiential Theme/Circumstance: Location
---**Theme**--- ---**Rheme**--------
(In school I saw him.)

[8] 可是 说不准 明天 会 更 热。
keshi shuo bu zhun mingtian hui geng re
But say NEG sure tomorrow MADV ADV warm.
Text Inter **Experiential Theme/Carrier**
---------**Theme**-------------- --**Rheme**-----
(But I am not sure whether it will be warmer tomorrow.)

2) Contextual Topical Theme: When two nouns or two nominal groups appear initially, both may be regarded as Topical themes. The first provides the setting for the clause, thus termed as Contextual Topical Theme or for short, Contextual Theme. Since the second noun usually performs the experiential and interactive functions, it may be regarded as Experiential Theme — the analysis is based on the consideration of Thematic patternings in a text, as shown in [1] and [14] below:

[1] 那 块 田 稻子 长 得 很 大。
nei kuai tian daozi zhang de hen da
that MEAS field rice grow VADV ADV big
Contextual Theme Experiential Theme ---Rheme----------
Subject/Actor
(In that piece of field, rice grows in big size.)

Note that "那块田" (*nei kuai tian*, or, that piece of land) is a nominal group, which should not be regarded as a circumstantial element or following an omitted coverb or preposition "在……里" (*zai... li*, or, in) structurally, although when rendered in English, it may be thought of as "在那块田里" (*zai nei kuai tian li*, or, in that piece of field).

[14] 那 场　　火，　幸亏　　消防员　　　来得快。
nei chang huo,　xingkui　xiaofangyuan　　laide kuai
That fire,　　fortunately　fire-fighter　come VADV quickly.
Contextual Theme　Experiential　Theme　　　Rheme
Subject/Actor
[As for that fire, it was fortunate that (as) the fire-fighters came quickly (it was put off.)]

Note that the concept of Contextual Theme resembles Topic given by Li and Thompson (1981) in two aspects: 1) Both stress its function of providing a setting for the clause; 2) Both regard the first initial noun/nominal group as Topic or its equivalent — Contextual Theme, which could be a "peripheral element" in front of the clause proper (Lü 1990: 120).

Matthiessen (1995) holds a similar view although he uses the term Absolute Theme. He argues that this Theme provides the textual "subject matter", and serves no role in the ideational and interpersonal metafunctions.

Some Chinese scholars claim that there could be two Themes in Chinese (Wu 2001). Li Yunxing (2002) labels them as Subject Theme & Topic Theme. Therefore, [1] and [14] can be analyzed as

[1]　那块田　　稻子　　　长　得　很　大。
nei kuai tian　daozi　　zhang　de　hen　da
that MEAS field　rice　　grow　VADV　ADV　big
Topic Theme　***Subject Theme***　---Rheme----------
(In that piece of field, rice grows in big size.)

[14] 那 场　　火，　幸亏　　消防员　　来得　　快。
nei chang huo,　xingkui　xiaofangyuan　laide　kuai
That fire,　　fortunately　fire-fighter　come VADV quickly.
Topic Theme　　　　***Subject Theme***
[As for that fire, it was fortunate that (as) the fire-fighters came quickly (it was put off)].

We can sum up the three versions for naming the two types of Theme, which are more or less equivalents:

Theme 1 = Topic Theme = Contextual (Topical) Theme

Theme 2 = Subject Theme = Experiential (Topical) Theme

Next, the chapter will elaborate on the sub-categories of Experiential Theme: Marked Theme, Preposed Theme and Thematic Equative. The primary contrast is between "Unmarked" Theme and "Marked" Theme.

7.5.2.2 Unmarked Theme and Marked Theme

In Chinese, "almost every functional component in the experiential metafunction can take the clause-initial position and can therefore be given thematic prominence". "Theme may conflate with any participant" (Li 2007). However, the frequency of the appearance in the initial position of these elements is different, which results in what is known as the distinction between Unmarked and Marked Theme. For example, Shi Yuzhi finds (2001) that the structure Actor + Verb + Patient, which is equivalent to the experiential structure Actor + Process + Goal in the SFL terminology, is the most important structure in Chinese. This implies that in most cases it is Actor which is given Thematic prominence. Li discovers (2007) from his data that "about 90% of thematic prominence is assigned to the 'participant' which is conflated with the Subject of the clause, a pattern which constitutes the 'unmarked' case". In classifying Unmarked Theme and Marked Theme, we may refer to either the Experiential Structure or the Interpersonal Structure or both. In the following, the chapter will discuss the two concepts in clauses of different types of mood.

1) In an indicative: declarative clause, the typical structure is **Subject ^ (Adjunct) ^ Predicator ^ (Complement) or Actor ^ (Circumstance) ^ Process ^ (Goal)**, which gives the ground for Shi (2001) and Li (2007) to state that Unmarked Topical Theme is usually conflated with Actor/Subject in the clause as in [17a]:

[17] *a*. 我 已经 知道 这 件 事。
wo *yijing* *zhidao* *zhe* *jian* *shi*
I ASP know DET MEAS matter.
Theme (Unmarked) -----Rheme---------
Actor/Subject Predicator/Process Complement/Goal
(I already know this matter.)

in which "我" (*wo*, or I) is Theme which is conflated with its role as Actor/Subject in the Experiential Structure and Interpersonal Structure. Hence it is Unmarked. When the Complement/Goal is given the thematic status, it becomes Marked Theme as in [17b]:

[17] *b*. 这 件 事 我 已经 知道。
zhe *jian* *shi* *wo* *yijing* *zhidao*
DET MEAS matter I ASP know
Theme (Marked) -----**Rheme**-------
Complement/Goal
(This matter I already know.)

However, the structure Complement^Subject^Predicator (or the OSV structure in traditional linguistics) is not infrequent in novels and spoken Chinese (Fang 1989). The markedness of Theme may have to do with genre. More research needs to be done on whether text types or genre would impose constraints on the markedness of a component in a clause. However, one thing is clear that Context contributes a great deal to the thematization of a component of a clause, which will be elaborated later.

In Chinese, an Adjunct denoting time or location typically appears at the second initial position (Shi 2001), which is its unmarked position. Its marked position would be at the beginning or at the end of a clause. Compare [18a], [18b] and [18c].

Unmarked position: as in [18a], the time adjunct "现在" (*xianzai*, or, now) takes the second initial position.

[18] *a.* 我 <u>**现在**</u> 不想 结婚。
wo *xianzai* *buxiang* *jiehun*
I now NEG want marry
Unmarked Position
(I don't want to get married now.)

Marked position: as in [18b], the same element appears initially, giving prominence to the time of the happening event, thus functioning as Marked Theme whereas in [18c] it takes the final position, functioning as Marked New.

[18] *b.* <u>**现在**</u> 我 不想 结婚。
xianzai *wo* *buxiang* *jiehun*
now I NEG want marry
Marked Theme
(Now I don't want to get married.)

[18] *c.* 我不想 结婚 <u>现在</u>。
wo buxiang *jiehun* *xianzai*
I NEG want marry now
Marked New
(I don't want to get married now.)

However, there is another clause structure in Chinese: **Adjunct** ^ **Predicator** ^ **Subject or Circumstance** ^ **Process** ^ **Actor** or the AVS (Adverbial ^ Verb ^ Subject) structure. Some Chinese linguists take it as a structure in the inverted order (Fang 1989), yet Lü Shuxiang (1984) disagrees by stating that it is common in this type of structure for Subject to take the final position, which is in the normal word order. Hence the Adjunct Theme in this structure is Unmarked as in [2] and [19]:

[2] <u>主席台上</u> 坐着 个 老人。
zhuxitaishang *zuozhe* *ge* *laoren*
platform upon sit PROG MEAS old man.
Adjunct (location) Predicator Subject
Theme (Unmarked)
(On the platform, sits an old man.)

[19] 羊 群 里 跑出 骆驼 来 了。
yang qun li pao chu luotuo lai le
Goat MEAS in run out camel come ASP
Adjunct (location) Predi- Subject -cator
Theme (Unmarked)
(Among the herds of goats ran out a camel.)

Note that verbs used in this structure are limited to a small group, such as "坐 (*zuo*, or sit"), "立" (*li*, or stand), "来" (*lai*, or come), "到" (*dao*, or arrive), "出 (来)" (*chu lai*, or come out), "进(来)" (*jin lai*, or enter), "下(来)" (*xialai*, or descend), etc. (Fang, 1989). Li (2007) terms this type of clause as "Existential". This chapter regards it as a sub-category of Material Process.

"Predicator is rarely thematized, thus 'extremely' marked" (Li 2007). However, it is not impossible. For example, in a given context, we may have a clause such as [20]:

[20] 失败 他们 将 肯定 会。
shibai tamen jiang kengding hui
Fail they ADV ADV MADV
Predicator Subject
Theme (Marked)
(… fail they certainly would.)

However, Fang (1989) finds that in the Chinese Experiential Structure, there exists the **Predicator ^ Subject** structure or the VS structure, where the verbs, usually "来" (*lai*, or come) or "去" (*qu*, or go) plus "了" (*le*, a particle denoting the completion of the verb process), have the connotation of "disappearance" or "emergence". Lü argues (1984: 457－458) that in this type of clause "the speaker would take the element denoting 'disappearance' as the starting point of the clause". Therefore, when a verb denotes either "disappearance" or "emergence", it would become the point of departure in this type of clause; hence Unmarked Theme as in [21]:

[21]	冒出	了	你这	个	小	兔崽子。
	mao chu	*le*	*ni zhe*	*ge*	*xiao*	*tuzaizi*
	emerge	PART	you DET	MEAS	little	rabbit son
	Predicator	Subject				
	Unmarked Theme					

(Emerge you, the son of rabbit.)

To sum up, the Circumstantial Adjunct or Predicator may be Unmarked Theme when taking initial position in some particular experiential structures. However, Circumstantial Adjunct is the most frequent Marked Theme in Chinese usually "followed by Complement and Predicator/Process" (Li 2007), as shown below:

Theme { Unmarked: Theme = Subject
Theme { Marked: Theme = Adjunct/Complement/Predicator

The primary means for a component to become Marked Theme is the change of word order as discussed above. In Chinese there are two other ways to thematize an element: by putting the preposition "对于" (*duiyu*), "关于" (*guanyu*), "至于" (*zhiyu*) ("as for" or "as to") or the copula "是 (*shi*, or, be)" in front of the element as in [22] and [23]. We follow Halliday's terminology (1985/1994) and take this construction as a Predicated Theme, that is, the Predicator "是" (*shi*, or, be) and its Complement are given thematic prominence, with "是" (*shi*, or, be) functioning as a marker of affirmation on the part of the speaker in a dialogue in which the hearer suspects about what has been said.

[22]	对于	波斯湾	战争,	我们	都	很	关心。
	duiyu	*bosiwan*	*zhanzheng,*	*women*	*dou*	*hen*	*guanxin.*
	PREP	Gulf	War,	we	ADV	VADV	concern
	Marked Theme			**Subject/Carrier**			

(As for the Gulf War, we are all very concerned about it.)

[23] 是　小王　看　完了　信。
shi　Xiao Wang　kan　wan le　xin.
be　xiao wang　see　finish ASP　letter
Marked Theme (Predicated)
Pre- Subject　-dicator
(It is Xiao Wang who has read the letter.)

2) In the indicative: interrogative clause, the structure generally is the same as that in the declarative. Yet there are two types of interrogative clauses: the polar- interrogative and that with WH type question words such as "为什么" (*weishenme*, or, why) or "怎么" (*zenme*, or, how), etc. In both types of clause, the element being queried would occupy the second initial position in the corresponding declarative clause. However, this element may be "assigned thematic prominence" when taking the initial position. "In this case, it is the element carrying both thematic and news prominence" (Li, 2007) as in [24a]:

[24] *a.*　为什么　他　还　没　来?
weishenme　ta　hai　mei　lai
Why　he　ADV　NEG　come
WH word
Marked Theme Subject/Actor
(Why has he not come yet?)

However, if there is an Adjunct, it will be the Marked Theme of the clause as in [24b]:

b.　昨天晚上　为什么　他　没　来?
zuotian wanshang　Weishenme　ta　mei　lai
Yesterday evening　why　he　NEG　come
WH-word
Marked Theme　Subject/Actor
(Yesterday evening why didn't he come?)

The system of Unmarked Theme and Marked Theme in an interrogative clause is summarized as follows:

Theme [Unmarked: Theme = Subject
Marked: Theme = Interrogative Element/Adjunct]

3) The sequence in the exclamatory and the imperative clause is the same as in the declarative. The principles for thematization in the declarative clause can be applied to both types of clause, except that Theme may be omitted in the imperative.

Example [25] is an exclamatory clause, in which "你" (*ni*, or, you) is Theme/Subject/Actor; in a particular context, the Adjunct "多结实" (*duo jieshi*, or, how sturdy) can be switched to the front functioning as Marked Theme. Compare [25a] and [25b]:

[25] *a*. 你 长得 多 结实 啊!
ni zhangde duo jieshi a
you grow ADV sturdy MPART
Unmarked Theme/Subject/Actor
(How sturdy you have grown!)

b. 多 结实 啊 你 长 得!
duo jieshi a ni zhang de
ADV sturdy MPART you grow
Marked Theme Subject
Exclamatory Element
(How sturdy you have grown!)

When there is an Adjunct appearing initially, it functions as Marked Theme as shown in [25c]:

[25] *c*. 那时候 你 长得 多 结实 啊!
na shihou ni zhangde duo jieshi a
DET that time you grow ADV sturdy MPART
Marked Theme
(How sturdy you grew at that time!)

The system of Unmarked Theme and Marked Theme in an exclamatory clause is summarized as follows:

Theme [Unmarked: Theme = Subject
Marked: Theme = Exclamatory Element/Adjunct

Example [26] is an imperative clause, in which Theme is omitted and there is only Rheme.

[26] (你) 走 吧!
(*ni*) *zou* *ba*.
(You) go MPART
(Theme) **Rheme**
[(You)'d better leave!]

An Adjunct may become Marked Theme in an imperative clause as in a declarative one when it appears initially.

[27] 现在 你 走 吧!
xianzai *ni* *zou* *ba*.
Now you go MPART
Marked Theme ----- Rheme -----
(Now you'd better leave!)

The system of Unmarked Theme and Marked Theme in an imperative clause is summarized as follows:

Theme [Unmarked: Theme = Subject
Marked: Theme = Adjunct

7.5.2.3 Preposed Theme

In Chinese, there is another way to thematize a noun or pronoun or a set phrase denoting a characteristic of a person or object: by preposing it so that it becomes a prominent element, and this element is referred to again later in the clause. This type of Theme is termed as Preposed Theme. A noun is usually referred to by a pronoun; a pronoun or a set phrase by a noun. For example in [28a], 这个人 (*zhe ge ren*, or this person), a nominal group, is preposed as compared with that in its normal position in [28b] and is referred to as the pronoun "他" (*ta*, or, him) later in the clause (Shi Yuzhi 2001):

[28] *a.* 这 个 人 我 跟他 通 过信。
zhe ge ren wo gen ta tong guo xin
This MEAS person I PREP *he* correspond ASP letter
Preposed Theme
(This person I exchanged letters with him.)

b. 我 跟 这 个 人 通 过 信。
wo gen zhe ge ren tong guo xin
I PREP this MEAS person correspond ASP letter
Theme
(I exchanged letters with this person.)

[29] 他 这 个 人 就 知道吃。
ta zhe ge ren jiu zhidao chi
He *this* **MEAS** *person* VAVD know eat.
Preposed Theme
(He is such a kind of person that all he knows is to eat.)

In [29], the Preposed Theme "他" (*ta*, or, he), which is a pronoun, is referred to as the nominal group "这个人" (*zhe ge ren*, or, this person) later.

[30] 通情达理,有求必应, 大家 都喜欢 这种 人。
tongqingdali, youqiubiying, dajia dou xihuan zhezhong ren
reasonable ready to help everybody VADV like this CLASSIFIER person
Preposed Theme
[(A person) is reasonable and ready to help; everybody likes such a person.]

where "通情达理,有求必应" (*tongqingdali, youqiubiying*, or, reasonable and ready to help) are two set phrases used to describe the characteristics of the nominal group "这种人" (*zhezhongren*, or, this type of person). They are fronted from their original positions before this nominal group. They are proposed because the speaker intends to impress the hearer first with the characteristic features of this person.

The system of Non-Preposed Theme and Preposed-Theme is summarized as follows:

Theme [Non-Preposed: Theme = Subject
Theme [Preposed-Theme: ↙Pronoun/Noun/Set Phrase

Some linguists argue that this type of clause may be "analyzed as having two layers of thematic structure" (Li 2007). For example, [28a] may be analyzed as:

[28] a. 这 个 人 我 跟他 通 过信。

Zhe ge ren wo gen ta tong guo xin

This MEAS person I PREP *he* correspond ASP letter

Theme 1 ----- **Rheme 1** ----------------------

Theme 2/Subject -----**Rheme 2**------

(This person I exchanged letters with him.)

7.5.2.4 Thematic Equative

In Chinese, there is an "A + 是 (*shi*, or, be) + B" construction, in which A is a nominal group or a nominalized verbal group ended with the particle 的 (*de*) while B is also a nominalized construction. A and B are linked by the copula 是 (*shi*, or be) or 就是 (*jiu shi*, with *jiu* as an intensifier), resulting in an identifying clause; the two parts are equative with the first thematized. This construction is thus labeled as Thematic Equative (Halliday, 1985/1994) as in [31]:

[31] 我 说 的 就 是 这 件 事。

Wo shuo de jiu shi zhe jian shi

I say PART INTEN be DET MEAS matter

Token **Value**

(Identifying)

Subject ***Predicator*** **Complement**

Theme-------- -----**Rheme**------------------

(What I said is this matter.)

Such clauses are usually reversible; however, in such a case the clause is possibly rendered in another wording as in [31′]:

[31′]	这	件	事	就是我说的	(那	件	事)。
	zhe	*jian*	*shi*	*jiu shi wo shuo de*	*(na*	*jian*	*shi)*
	DET	MEAS	matter	INTEN be I say PART	(DET	MEAS	matter)
	Value			**Token**			

(Identifying)

Subject Predicatior Complement

Marked Theme

(This matter is what I said.)

The system of Unmarked Theme and Marked Theme in a Thematic Equative clause is summarized as follows:

Theme
- Unmarked: Theme = Subject/Token (*de* construction)
- Marked: Theme = Subject/Value

In summary, we can arrive at the following system of Topical Theme:

Table 7-1 System of Topical Theme

- Topical Theme
  - Experiential
    - Simple Theme
    - Topic in Multi-Theme
      - Unmarked / Marked
      - Non-Preposed / Preposed
      - Non-Thematic Equative / Thematic Equative
  - Contextual

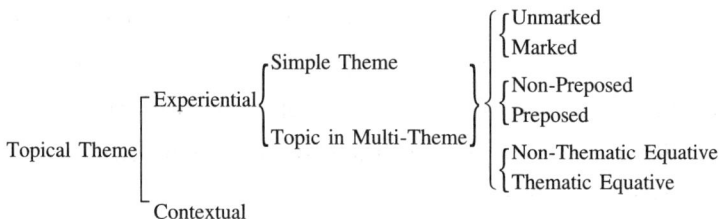

7.5.3 Functions of Topical Theme

Topical Theme may perform several functions: (1) aboutness function (Shi 2001); (2) clause-linking function (Chu 1997) as a cohesive tie; (3) providing a frame or setting of time or location; and (4) restricting a domain (Wu 2001), which will be illustrated below.

(1) Aboutness function

"对于波斯湾战争" (*duiyu bosiwan zhanzheng*, or, as for the Gulf War) in Clause [22] is what the speaker is concerned with or performs the aboutness function. More examples are as follows:

[32]	这盆	盆景,	叶子	很大,	花	太小,	不	好看。
	Zhepeng	*pengjing,*	*yezi*	*henda,*	*hua*	*taixiao,*	*bu*	*haokan.*
	this	bonsai,	leaves	ADV big,	flowers	ADV small,	not	good-looking.
	Carrier 1		Car.21	Attr.21	Car.22	Attr.22	Attribute 1	
	Theme 1					Rheme 1		
			Theme 21	Rheme 21	**Theme 22**	Rheme 22		

(As for this bonsai, the leaves are big but the flowers are small so it is not good-looking.)

This is a clause complex. Structurally, there are two layers: on the first layer is the main clause 这盆盆景不好看 (*Zhepeng pengjing bu hao kan*, or, This bonsai is not good-looking.). On the second layer, there are two clauses "叶子很大" (*yezi henda*, or, leaves are too big) and "花太小" (*hua taixiao*, or, flowers are too small), which are in the paratactic relation; however, semantically these two clauses could be regarded as giving the reason why the bonsai does not look good. 这盆盆景 (*zhepeng pengjing*, or, this bonsai) serves as the Experiential Theme — it is this element that the whole clause complex is about.

[33]	我	打算	去	北京。
	wo	*dasuan*	*qu*	*beijing*
	I	plan	go	Beijing.
	Theme/Actor	--------Rheme---------		

(I plan to go to Beijing.)

In [33], the Experiential Theme "我" (*wo*, or, I), is the element the speaker is concerned with.

(2) Clause-linking function in a Theme-Rheme Chain

We notice that in Chinese, there exists the structure: Topical Theme +

Rheme ^ comma ^ (01 Topical Theme) + Rheme ^ comma ^ (02 Topical Theme) + Rheme ^ comma ^ (0n Topical Theme) + Rheme ^ full stop, or Topical Theme ^ Rheme ^ [(Topical Theme) ^ Rheme] n], which is termed as a Theme-Rheme Chain. In a T-R chain, the first Thematic element is an Experiential Theme while the rest of the Themes realized by zero anaphora referring to the first. This chain of Topical Themes contributes to building up the cohesion among the clauses in a discourse as in [34]:

[34] 老吴　欠了　我　两百块钱,
Lao Wu　owe ASP　*I　200* MEAS *yuan,*
Theme 1　——Rheme 1 - - - - - - - - - - - -
0　一直　说　0　没有钱还。
always　say　NEG money repay
(**Theme 2**) Rheme 2 (**Theme 3**) Rheme 3
(Old Wu owes me 200 yuan, but he always says that he has no money to repay me.)

(3) Providing a frame of time or location

[35] 明天　我　打算　去　北京。
mingtian　wo　dasuan　qu　Beijing
Tomorrow　I　plan　go　Beijing.
Topical Theme (Contextual)
(I plan to go to Beijing tomorrow.)

The Topical theme in [35] provides the frame of the time when the actor will take the action.

(4) Restricting a domain or range

[36] 水果　我　只　吃一个。
shuiguo　wo　zhi　chi yige
fruit　I　VADV　eat MEAS.
Topical Theme (Contextual)
(As for fruit, I only eat one.)

In [36], the Contextual Theme "水果" (*shuiguo* or fruit) functions as the domain for the action to take place. In [37] it is 物价 (*wujia* or price) that provides the range for the comparison of prices.

[37] 物价　纽约　最　贵。
wujia　*Niuyue*　*zui*　*gui*
price　New York　CADV　expensive.
Topical Theme (Contextual)
(As for prices, the most expensive will be in New York.)

7.5.4 Realization of Topical Theme

Halliday maintains a multi-strata theory of language, in which the higher level is realized by the level next below (Halliday 1985/1994), as shown:

Semantics (meaning)
↙
Lexico-grammar (Wording)
↙
Phonology (Pronunciation)
Graphology (Writing)

Therefore, Topical Theme as a function at the semantic level may be realized by the choices made at the lexical — grammatical level. Concretely, it may be realized by a noun/nominal group, a verbal group/nominalized verbal group/clause, a prepositional phrase or a circumstantial element, which will be illustrated in this section.

1) Theme is realized by a noun, a pronoun or a nominal group as in [6]:

[6] 我　去　开门。
wo　*qu*　*kaimen*
Theme　Rheme
↙
pronoun
I　go　open door.
(I will go and open the door.)

2) Theme is realized by a verbal group as in [7]:

[7] 开会　　　　　你去不去?
kaihui　　　　　ni qu bu qu?
Theme (contextual)　Rheme
↙
verbal group
have meeting　　　　you go or not go?
(Are you going to the meeting?)

3) Theme is realized by a nominalized verbal group as in [38]:

[38] 一天　老　站着　　够累的。
yi tian　lao　zhanzhe　gou lei de
Theme　　　　Rheme
↙
nominalized verbal group
MEAS day ASP stand　　enough tire ASP
(Standing a whole day is tiring.)

4) Theme is realized by a down-ranked noun clause as in [39]:

[39] 他　一天　到晚　老　站在那儿,　真够累的。
ta　yitian　daowan　lao　zhanzai na'er　zhen gou lei de
he　all day　VADV　stand ADV that place INTEN　tire ASP
Theme　　--------Rheme------------------------
↙
Noun clause
(He is really tired standing there all day long.)

(5) Theme is realized by a circumstantial element of location/time, etc. as in [16]:

[16] (在) 学校　里 我 见　过　他。
(zai) xuexiao li,　wo jian　guo　ta
Theme　　　　Rheme --------
↙
Location (Cir)
(PREP) school in　　I see　ASP　he

(In school, I saw him.)

(6) Theme is realized by a prepositional phrase as in [22]:

[22] 对于 波斯湾 战争, 我们 都 很 关心。
duiyu Bosiwan zhanzheng, women dou hen guanxin.
PREP Gulf War, we ADV VADV concern
Theme --------- Rheme ------------------
↙
Prep. Phrase
(As for the Gulf War, we are all concerned about it.)

7.5.5 Theme and Context

The SFL model takes the concept of Context as indispensable in the study of clause structure (Halliday & Hasan 1985); Context puts constraints on which element should be Theme in a clause of a discourse and could be a decisive variable for the patterning of Thematic Progression (Fries 1981). We have mentioned that Matthiessen (1995), and Halliday and Matthiessen (2004) give a great deal of weight on the role of Context in defining Theme. Any of the clauses cited above would only occur within a given context. We mentioned that in Example [3], "好" performs the function of "continuative" and is a Textual Theme as it connects this clause with the previous one in the given context. One more example would suffice. Compare [36] and [40]. The Context would be a dialogue between two people talking about the habit of having fruit. **A** says:

[40] **A:** 我 每天 吃 两种 不同 的 水果。
Wo meitian chi liangzhong butong de shuiguo
I every day eat two MEAS different POSS fruit
Theme 1/Actor ----------- **Rheme 1** -----------
(I have two kinds of fruit every day.)

B, who keeps a different dietary habit of having fruit, takes part of the Rheme of [40] as the starting point for his part in the dialogue and says:

[36] **B**: 水果 我 只 吃一个。
shuiguo wo zhi chi yige
fruit I VADV eat MEAS.
Topical Theme 2 (Contextual) Rheme 2
(As for fruit, I only eat one.)

The patterning of Thematic Progression in this dialogue is Theme 1 - Rheme 1, part of which (水果, *shuiguo*, **or**, **fruit**) becomes Theme 2 (Contextual Theme) followed by Rheme 2. Due to the limit of space, this chapter will not give a more detailed discussion on the relation between Theme and Context, and on how Context imposes constraints on the choice of Theme in a longer discourse, or on how the patterning of Thematic Progression is folded in an extensive discourse. For the patternings of Thematic Progression, refer to Fang and Ai (1995).

7.6 Conclusion

This chapter has attempted to apply the Systemic-Functional model to dealing with clause structure in Chinese, mainly from the textual point of view, or in terms of Theme-Rheme structure. It has focused on the discussions on the features of Topical Theme.

However, this is only a brief study of this topic, which would not be able to cover every aspect of this concept. Chinese, as every other language, is a complex system, which has caused controversial views on some basic concepts such as clause structure, Subject, Theme, Topic or Topical Theme. Clarification and common ground can be reached only by conducting more research in a more extensive scope at both clause and discourse level. This, we believe, can only be achieved by building up a large corpus for a systematic study of Chinese and by establishing the collaboration of linguists from various institutions in different regions in the world, which, we are happy to see, is exactly the aim of founding the Halliday Centre of City University of Hong Kong.

8

A Functional Trend in the Study of Chinese*

8.1 Introductory Words

This chapter addresses itself to the verification of the hypothesis that a functional trend may exist in the study of Chinese — a language with few morphological inflections (Lü Shuxiang 1979), with a view to promote the setting up of a theory serving a better description of the Chinese grammar.

8.2 Concept of Functionalism

"Functionalism" in this chapter is used in a broad sense. It covers the

* This chapter is revised on the basis of a paper written by Fang Yan and Shen Mingbo, included in the book *Advances in Functional Linguistics in China*(《功能语言学在中国的进展》), published in 1997 by Tsinghua University Press, edited by Hu Zhuanglin and Fang Yan.

following aspects:

A) Language is an instrument of social interaction (Richards et al 1985; Halliday 1973; Scheffcyzyk 1986; Crystal 1991; Thompson 1992; Trask 1993; Lyons 1981).

B) Language is seen as multi-strata with semantics as the focus (Halliday 1985).

C) A language is interpreted as a system of meanings, accompanied by forms through which the meanings can be realized (Halliday 1985).

D) Text is the focus of study and is studied with reliance upon context (Lyons 1981; Halliday 1985).

E) Particular importance is attached to grammatical relations (Subject, Complement, etc.) and/or to semantic roles (Agent, Patient, Goal, etc.) (Trask 1993).

F) Each element in a language is explained by reference to its function in the total linguistic system (Halliday 1985; Crystal 1991; Trask 1993).

8.3 Development of Chinese Functionalism

We shall hereafter sketch the development of the functional trend in four periods in the tradition of Chinese linguistic study: the embryonic period, the imitation period, the reform period and the flourishing period, following Gong Qianyan (1987) in his *A History of Chinese Grammar.*

8.3.1 The embryonic period of Chinese linguistic study (475BC – AD1897)

This period is also referred to as the "prelinguistic period", attention being given to interpreting ancient texts (训诂学) with its focus on the study of lexical meaning such as synonyms, antonyms, and polysemy. But this does not mean that syntactic features were never studied. Some aspects of syntax such as function words and inversion were investigated, not for the study of form, but for explaining ancient texts, or for the study of meaning, as exemplified in the study of function words in *On the Structures of Chinese Characters* (Xu Shen 1989), and in the initial exploration into context. These can be seen as find traces of functionalism, despite their being fragmentary and unsystematic.

8.3.2 The imitation period of Chinese linguistic study (1898 - 1937)

The publications of *Ma's Grammar* (1898/1998) and Li Jinxi's *A New Chinese Grammar* (1992) marked the beginning of a systematic grammatical study of Chinese. These two books were modeled following the traditional Western grammars; as a result, many features unique of Chinese were ignored.

Chinese Functionalism, if there was any, still remained as an undercurrent. Traces of functionalism can be observed from two scholars' works in this period: Liu Fu grouped adjectives and verbs together as they were similar in function (Gong Qianyan 1987) and Ma Jianzhong realized the influence of context on word class (Ma Jianzhong 1988).

8.3.3 The reform period of Chinese linguistic study (1938 - 1949)

The reform period is characterized by an effort of Chinese linguists to shake off the fetters of Western grammars and probe into the unique features of Chinese. Chen Wangdao, Lü Shuxiang and Wang Li are three representative linguists of this period.

Chen Wangdao was the first to state explicitly the necessity to study Chinese in a functional way. He stated "In the study of Chinese grammar, many grammarians are wavering between a form-centered theory and a meaning-centered theory. Both theories have some weaknesses, which, in my opinion, can be counteracted by a function-centered theory." (1980) He suggested that function be used as a criterion to classify words. He defined function as the capacity of a word to combine with other words (*ibid.*). Here the meaning of function in Chen's term is similar to that of collocation. He extended function to the concept of word class in a sentence (1978). However, he didn't state clearly the relationship between meaning and function and his study was not yet systematic.

Chen's contributions to the functional view of grammar also lie in revealing the importance of context in studying Chinese. In his work *On Rhetoric*, he emphasized that "rhetoric must accord with context" (Chen Wangdao 1982). He further formulated the Theory of Six Wh-, referred to as "the six elements of context" (*ibid.*). Although Chen's study of context was limited exclusively to rhetoric, his recognition of the significance of context merits our notice.

In Lü Shuxiang's and Wang Li's works (1984, 1985) we can also see their functional bias. Since Hu Zhuanglin (1991) already discussed Wang Li's functional points of view at length, the following paragraphs will be devoted to discussing Lü Shuxiang's representative work *Essentials of Chinese Grammar* (1990 a & b) and some of his articles only.

8.3.3.1 Essentials of Chinese grammar

8.3.3.1.1 Linguistic outlook

1) Language as a social product

Functionalists hold that language is a product of social process; Lü Shuxiang expressed a similar idea in his works (1990a).

2) Meaning as the starting point

Functionalists interpret a language as a network of relations, with structures coming in as the realizations of these relationships; they take semantics as the foundation. What Lü wrote in the second part of *Essentials of Chinese Grammar* — "On Expression" coincides with this functional interpretation (1990b). In this part, Chinese is interpreted as a system of meanings, such as the systems of number, place and time, and the forms through which the meanings can be expressed are also studied.

Lü's approach to linguistics, therefore, is a combination of formal approach and functional one — both form and meaning are emphasized.

3) Language as a multi-level system

Lü shared the functionalist point of view of regarding language as a multi-level system, which is well manifested in his analysis of mood in Chinese. He said, "Mood can be expressed by both intonation and mood particles. Intonation is indispensable, while mood particles can sometimes be omitted." Thus, mood can be expressed at both lexico-grammatical level (by mood particles) and phonological level (by intonation) (1990a).

8.3.3.1.2 Grammatical concepts

1) Complement Theory

In discussing the narrative sentence, Lü pointed out that a word involved in an action plays a role in illustrating the action, and it is thus called a complement. There are mainly ten types of complements: initiator, terminal, beneficiary I, beneficiary II, co-initiator, means, location, time, cause and aim (English translations by the authors). Thus, a clause in the indicative mood can be analyzed from the angle of the relation between the verb and various complements. Bearing remarkable resemblance to Fillmore's Case Grammar (1968/2002) and Halliday's Transitivity System (1973), Lü's Complement Theory was proposed in 1942 (1979), over 20 years earlier than its Western counterparts.

2) Starting Word – End Word Theory

In his article "An Analysis of Chinese Sentence Patterns by Distinguishing Subject and Object" (1990b), Lü proposed his "Starting Word – End Word Theory". In this article, he summarized and analyzed 14 types of sentence patterns according to word order and the relation between actor and goal. The following are two types of sentence patterns which are of significance here.

[1] Sentence Pattern A: Goal+Actor+Verb

这个(G)我(A)不知道(V)。

[2] Sentence Pattern B: Verb+Actor

榻上坐着(V)一个老头子(A)。

Lü concluded that these two patterns were built on the same psychology: in Pattern A, something about which the hearer already knows is put at the beginning; in Pattern B, a circumstantial element is put at the beginning, while the new information is reserved to the end. In short, the information which is already known will precede the new information. Lü called the former "starting word" and the latter "end" word. The discourse, as shown below, provides another good example:

[3] *a*. Big fish (Starting word 1) eat small fish (End Word 1). Small fish (Starting Word 2) eat shrimps (End Word 2). Shrimps (Starting Word 3) hump their backs to eat mud (End Word 3).

which coincides with Theme and New in Prague School's terminology. The way he analyzed the discourse [3a] is similar to Danes' simple linear thematic Progression pattern (1974), as shown in [3b]:

[3] *b*. Big fish (Theme 1) eat small fish (Rheme 1 = New 1). Small fish (Theme 2) eat shrimps (Rheme 2 = New 2). Shrimps (Theme 3) hump their backs to eat mud (Rheme 3 = New 3).

in which Rheme 1 becomes Theme 2 and Rheme 2 functions as Theme 3, following the pattern:

T1 ... R1

T2 (=R1) ······ R2

Tn (=Rn−1)······ Rn

Nonetheless due to the influence of formal linguistics, Lü's approach to language is still different from that of functional linguistics. For instance, he analyzed 14 types of sentence patterns by following the traditional concept of the above mentioned article; in addition, his study of Chinese grammar was mostly organized around the sentence instead of the text.

8.3.4 The flourishing period of Chinese linguistic study (1949 –)

8.3.4.1 1949 – 1960s

This period saw the booming development of Chinese linguistic studies: 1) the publication of a great variety of linguistic works (for example, *A Guide to Grammar and Rhetoric* (1951) by Lü Shuxiang and Zhu Dexi); 2) two nation-wide discussions on linguistics (the Discussion on the Classification of Word Classes and the Discussion on Subject/Object Distinction). However, because of the weak basis of linguistic research in China, no systematic linguistic theories came into being in this period.

Though no functional theories took shape in China, the functional trend still manifested itself by taking meaning as the focus of study and by classifying word classes according to functions and contexts. The functional trend can also be witnessed by looking at the functional bias as manifested in some works, which laid a foundation for the development of Chinese Functionalism in the 1980s. Due to the limit of space, we shall elaborate on the functional bias only, the best example of which will be shown in *A Guide to Grammar and Rhetoric* by Lü Shuxiang and Zhu Dexi (1951).

First, the book took a pragmatic view of language, with the purpose of "correcting errors". Gong Qianyan (1987) pointed out, "this book played a great part in standardizing the Chinese language." Second, the authors provided a functional interpretation of punctuation marks. "Punctuation marks are an integral part of a language, rather than things added to the language. ... Each punctuation mark performs a specific role; therefore, it is reasonable to classify them as one type of function words. They should be treated in the same way as function words such as "的","呢", and "吗" … For instance, due to the use of the question mark, mood particles like "吗" and "呢" are often omitted." (Lü Shuxiang & Zhu Dexi 1951)

8.3.4.2 Late 1970s on

Having been suspended for more than ten years during the Cultural Revolution, Chinese linguistic study resumed only in the late 1970s.

In the following paragraphs, we shall sketch the development of functionalism in China in this period from two perspectives: development in theory and application of Western functional theories to the study of Chinese.

Development in theory

Chinese Functionalism was beginning to take shape in theory in the 1980s. The first one is called "the three-level theory", that is, grammatical analysis should be carried out on the levels of syntax, semantics and pragmatics (Wen Lian & Hu Fu 1984; Zhu Dexi 1985; Hu Yushu & Fan Xiao 1985).

Because of the space limitation, we shall focus our attention on Hu and Fan's article only. They (1985) distinguished the three grammatical levels corresponding to syntactic analysis, semantic analysis and pragmatic analysis respectively. Please look at the following examples (*ibid.*):

[4] 我读过《红楼梦》了。

[5]《红楼梦》我读过了。

Sentence [4], on the syntactic level, can be analyzed as "Subject + Predicate + Object" and on the semantic level, as "Actor + … + Goal" ("…" not specified). Sentence [5] has the same semantic structure as Sentence [4], while its syntactic structure is rather different from that of Sentence [4]. Why is the same semantic structure expressed by different syntactic structures? This question can be answered only when these sentences are analyzed from the pragmatic perspective. In Sentence [4],

"我"is Topic(主题), which the hearer already knows; in Sentence [5], however,"红楼梦"is Topic. Stress is put on "我"in Sentence [4], while "红楼梦" is the point of departure in Sentence [5]. At the end of this article, they pointed out that all these different but closely related levels must be studied in grammatical analysis. It is worth noting that Hu and Fan's pragmatic analysis bears much resemblance to Halliday's analysis of Theme-Rheme Structure. For instance, Hu and Fan defined Topic as "the point of departure" (*ibid.*), similar to Theme in Halliday's terminology, which is "the element serving as the point of departure of the message, ... the starting-point for the message" (Halliday 1985).

Along with this three-level theory is the contextual theory. In the 1980s, more and more Chinese linguists came to realize the importance of context in linguistic studies (Zhang Zhigong 1982; Li Chuanquan 1991; Shi Yunsun 1992). Li Chuanquan (1991) proposed a Form-Context Meaning Realization Model and discovered the"high-context"dependency characteristic of Chinese after a detailed analysis of the Chinese linguistic constituents, grammatical categories and word order. Li concluded that "Between English and Chinese, the former tends to depend more on form to realize meaning, while the latter on context" although the concept of context is important for both languages (*ibid.*).

Though immature, the contextual theory has been applied to many aspects of linguistic studies such as ambiguity in meaning, omission, rhetoric, and information processing. For example, Lü Shuxiang (1992) studied the role of context in eliminating ambiguity.

A word should be mentioned about Shen Xiaolong's work *Chinese Sentence Patterns* produced in 1988. According to Shen, the syntactic view of traditional philology is composed of three key elements: *judou* (phrase chunks) as noumenon, the logical arrangement of *judou* as pattern, expression fulfilled as sentence boundary. It is a function-prominent approach resting on a unity of meaning ("*sheng*") and form ("*qi*"). Shen applied this approach to the study of the Chinese grammar and classified Chinese sentences into three main types: Performance Sentences, which are sentences centering on verbs and have the function of narrating action and incident; Topic-Comment Sentences, which are sentences centering on nouns and have the function of commenting on certain topics; Relative Sentences, which have the function of expressing a logical relation between actions and incidents. However, Shen's views are open to discussion. For instance, he used an ancient text *Zuo Zhuan* as his object of study, a book written more than 2,000 years ago, which understandably would diminish its enlightening effect on modern Chinese due to the many changes of the language in the past centuries. In addition, his sentence patterns are a mixture of different grammatical levels.

Application of Western functional theories

1) The study of verbs

Due to the class of verbs lacking morphological inflections, many Chinese linguists in this period began to study verbs by turning to meaning and to explore cases in Chinese by referring to Halliday's Transitivity System (1985) and Fillmore's Case Grammar (1968). Among the well-known works are Li Linding's "Analysis of the Use of Object" (1994), "Actor, Patient and Grammatical Analysis" (1984) and "Instrumental Case and Objective Case" (1985); Xu Jie's "Instrumental Case and Sentence Patterns Containing Instrumental Case" (1986); and *Dictionary on the Use of Verb* by Meng Cong et al. (1987). We should also remember the contributions made by Lu Chuan and Lin Xingguang, who were engaged in the study of computational linguistics, having summarized 18 types of case relationships (1989).

Halliday's Transitivity System, which "specifies the different types of process that are recognized in the language, and the structures by which they are expressed" (Halliday 1985), provides us with a functional perspective of studying verbs. With meaning as the focus of study, it is especially beneficial to the study of verbs in Chinese, which are characterized by the lack of inflections. Zhou Xiaokang published her article "Initial Exploration into the Transitivity System of Chinese Verbs" in 1986 and "Verbs by Way of the

Transitivity System" in 1990. Some features unique to Chinese were found by applying Halliday's Transitivity System in her works. For example, it is known that sentence patterns applying "把" or "被" have peculiar features in Chinese. She argued that material processes can be changed into either sentence pattern containing "把" or "被", while mental processes cannot.

Halliday's functional theory has also seen its application in other fields such as Theme-Rheme System, Mood System and Cohesion.

Hu Zhuanglin made investigations in the word order and mood system in Chinese. He published "On the Word Order in Chinese from the Semantico-Functional Perspective" (1989) and "Mood and the Interrogative Mood System of the Chinese Language" (Li & Hu 1990) in succession. In these articles, he pointed out that word order of Chinese manifests three metafunctions: Ideational Function, Interpersonal Function and Textual Function at the same time. Fang Yan wrote articles on "Comparative Study of Theme-Rheme Structure in English and Chinese" (1989a), "A Tentative Study of Chinese Theme-Rheme Structure" (1989b), "On 'Subject' in Chinese — 'Subject', 'Actor' and 'Theme'" (1990) and some other articles. Huang Yan devoted himself to the study of lexical reiteration and published "Lexical Reiteration in Modern Standard Chinese" (1986), in which he reported that lexical reiteration occurs more frequently in Chinese than in English and that the function of lexical reiteration is for emphasis. It deserves our attention that Hu Zhuanglin, Zhu Yongsheng and Zhang Delu published in 1989 their joint work — *A Survey of Systemic-Functional Grammar*, in which they devoted a large space to a comprehensive study of Chinese in terms of the three metafunctions.

To sum up, Chinese grammarians have already begun to use Case Grammar and Halliday's functional theory in the study of Chinese grammar. They have not only applied these theories to the studies of Chinese, but begun to develop these theories in accordance with the characteristics of the Chinese language.

8.4 Conclusion

Our sketchy investigations into the diachronic linguistic research in China, we hope, can verify our initial hypothesis: there may be a functional trend in the study of the Chinese language — in the embryonic period, functionalism remained as a strong undercurrent; in the imitation period, it manifested itself sporadically despite the strong influence of Western formalism; in the reform period, Chinese Functionalism embodied itself mainly in the works of some prominent linguists; in the flourishing period, which still continues now, the functional approach has won recognition from the linguistic circle and exerted a strong impact upon different realms in Chinese linguistic studies. We anticipate the establishment of a systemic-functional theoretical framework for the study of Chinese in the 21st century.

9

A Systemic Functional Perspective on the Growth of Chinese*

9.1 Introduction

This chapter is inspired by Halliday's research on English in the paper "Written language, standard language, global language" (2003b), where he studies how English evolves from a local to a national and finally to a global language. He emphasizes that this evolution is a process of systemic expansion, having to do with "its total potential of meaning" (Halliday

* This chapter is based on a plenary presentation at the conference of "Becoming a World Language: the growth of Chinese, English and Spanish" in March of 2007 at the City University of Hong Kong, which was included in *Studies in Functional Linguistics and Discourse Analysis* (*Ⅲ*) published in 2011, edited by Huang Guowen et al. I express my sincere gratitude to Halliday for his valuable advice. He read and made suggestions on the draft outline of the paper, particularly on the choice of the title and the content of the paper. I am also thankful to Bai Xiaojing for her contribution to joining in writing the sixth part and particularly to the drawing of the two pies of (1) the three "circles" of Chinese speakers or learners and (2) the distribution of questionees' nationalities in my survey.

2014). Following Halliday, this chapter takes the systemic-functional perspective to study some aspects of the changes resulting from the growth of Chinese, focusing on whether the growth of this language in the historical and spatial dimension involves the expansion of the system network or the expansion of its meaning potential. It also addresses factors bringing about these changes and the causes giving rise to the changes as well as the effect of linguistic changes on social and ideological changes.

9.2 Halliday's theory on the expansion of meaning potential

The chapter mainly applies one of Halliday's most important theories concerning the nature of language — language as a system of meaning is forever changing. It also elaborates on the related theories such as factors contributing to the expansion of a language and the underlying causes giving rise to the changes in Chinese.

9.2.1 The nature of language

In the past decades, Halliday (2003a) has repeatedly stressed the basic concept of systemic-functional theory that "language is a semiotic system", and that "of all human semiotic systems, language is the greatest source of power. Its potential is indefinitely large" (2003a: 3). He also emphasizes that this system of meaning is "open, dynamic for ever changing", the "power of language comes from its paradigmatic complexity" and that this is its "meaning potential" (2003a: 9). In other words, he sees language as a resource, or as a system of meaning potential, which expands as a language grows under the pressure of demands arising from socio-political contexts.

He also argues that this meaning making system consists of several strata: semantics, lexicogrammar and graphology/phonology within the language, and cultural and situational contexts above it (1985/1994), and that changes of one stratum will give rise to changes of other strata and even affect the whole system network of the language.

9.2.2 Factors contributing to the expansion of a language

Halliday states (2003b) that there are several factors contributing to the changes or the growth of a language, which involve "not just new words, but new word-making principles"; "not just new words, but new word clusters (lexical sets)"; "not just new words, but new meanings"; "not just new words, but new registers (functional varieties)". He further points out that the changes not only involve the above factors but also the factor at the grammatical level because not only lexis but also grammar are "the motive power" (2003b: 413) or "the power house of language: the source of its semiotic energy" (2003a: 276), although the grammar or the "cryptogrammar" is "the slowest part of" language to change; however, it is "where the real work of meaning is done" (2003a). Therefore, we may assume that there are five factors mentioned by Halliday accounting for the growth of a language: the factors of new words and new word clusters, of new meanings, of new word-making principles, of new grammatical structures and of new registers or genres①.

Section 9.3 discusses in concrete terms the changes in these five aspects in Chinese.

---

① As they are both realized by the contextual variables (Hasan in H & H 1985; Martin 1992), register and genre are taken as equivalents in this chapter, which does not address their exact concepts or differences.

9.3 Systemic expansion of meaning potential in Chinese

As social factors constitute the driving force of the changes of language (See 4), the chapter will start with changes in registers, which is constrained by social factors (Halliday, in H & H 1985; Martin 1992). It is followed by the discussion of the changes from higher levels to the lower ones, going from the grammatical structural changes to changes at the lexical level.

9.3.1 Changes and expansions of registers/genres

With the eco-political and ideological changes in history, there have been changes of registers or genres in response to the changing cultural contexts. History has witnessed many cases of the decline and emergence of registers. Take a rather recent example of their decline. The register of the Big Poster Characters which appeared in the political movements in the 1950s in China and became popular during the Cultural Revolution disappeared almost overnight after the 1980s when the ideology of class struggle was replaced by that of market economy (Fang 1998). Though language changes inherently imply contraction or expansion, there is a stronger tendency for a language to expand than to contract if it is to survive (Halliday 2003a). This applies to the growth of Chinese, which is witnessed by the expansion of functional varieties or registers when history has developed from the ancient times to the present time. Fang (2003 in Qian Jun) has noticed when studying the most important official newspapers — *Renmin Ribao* or *The People's Daily* that on the whole there have been many more new registers or genres appearing in the present multicultural China as compared with those in the mono-cultural China 30 years ago. Their expansion in recent years can be evidenced in the boom of new registers such as stock exchange, internet communication, real estate, car transaction, fashions, ads of all kinds, etc. in Chinese, which had not existed at all before the 1980s, and which exhibit the signs of the "new 'modern' order" (of capitalism) (Halliday 2003b) or of the first stage of socialism.

9.3.2 Expansions of grammatical structures

In the past one hundred years or so, modern Chinese has experienced dramatic changes in syntactic or grammatical structure with the popularization of *Baihuawen* (vernacular Chinese) and perhaps also with influences coming from Western languages. This chapter only discusses two changes in the grammatical structure in this language.

9.3.2.1 New conjunctions making new forms of clause complexes

The unmarked clause structure in Chinese is patterned as $\beta \wedge \alpha$ (Fang, 1993) except when denoting purpose or result (Fang & Ai 1995). However, with the influence of Western languages, particularly English on Chinese, the $\alpha \wedge \beta$ clause structure appears and is used more and more frequently. One example from an email sent to me by one of my classmates majoring in English will suffice.

[1]《读书》第九期有两篇好文章值得一读(α),**如果**想多知道一些有关跨国公司和美国输出民主自由的情况**的话**(β)。

(*dushu di jiuqi you liangpian hao wenzhang zhide yidu, ruguo xiang duo zhidao yixie youguan kuaguogongsi he meiguo shuchu minzhu ziyou de qingkuang de hua*—

Two articles are worth reading in the No. 9 issue of *Dushu* (*Book Reading*), if you intend to know more about transnational companies and the export of the ideas of "democracy" and "freedom" by the Americans).

In this clause complex, "如果……的话" (= *if* clause) is a subordinate or β clause introduced by the conjunction "如果". What we have here is an α ^ β clause complex, which did not exist in classical Chinese.

9.3.2.2 Grammatical metaphor

Halliday and other scholars on GM

Since the 1980s, Halliday has frequently pointed out that in modern language, particularly in the register of scientific writings (1985; 1994; 2003a&b; 2005; 2014), one of the most powerful means to expand the system of meaning is by means of what he terms as Grammatical Metaphor, or for short, GM. This is a linguistic phenomenon resulting from a natural historical process under the "pressure to expand the meaning potential" (H & M 1999). By nature, it "involves cross-coupling between semantics and lexicogrammar" "because what it is being cross-coupled is not a word but a class" (Halliday 2003b). GM "opens up a new dimension of the semantic system in a language", and gives rise to the remapping of semantics and lexicogrammar (H & M 2004), which "plays two crucial roles": 1) "to carry forward the argument by packaging what has gone before so that it serves as logical foundation for what follows; and 2) to raise the argument to a theoretical level" "in taxonomic order". He states that "every language of science has followed the same route, reconstruing the human experience by exploiting the potential for metaphor in its grammar." (2003b) Halliday has studied this phenomenon not only in English but also in Chinese. He is among the first to associate "the reconstural of experience in the form of GM with the emergence of technical knowledge" in Chinese (Yang 2007), illustrating with examples the word-making principle of Chinese compound nouns or "hyponymic sets" by means of "hyponym + superordinate" (See 9.3.4.4).

Up to today, we are not clearly aware of when GM, involving the structural change systematically, appeared in Chinese. Very possibly it came into the language in the past hundred years when China began to learn from the West by introducing scientific writings into the academic fields.

Realization of grammatical metaphor

According to H & M (2004), GM involves creating "new patterns of structural realization". There are three types of GM: ideational, which expands "the meaning potential" by "downgrading the grammatical realizations of certain semantic units" to construe "our experience of the world"; interpersonal, which either provides "new meaning potential for negotiation between speakers of the same language" or expands "the method of making interpersonal assessment" by upgrading grammatical realizations (Yang 2007: 132) and the textual GM, the motivation of which lies in "construing Unmarked Theme as the point of departure in the form of nominalization" (*ibid.*). These types of GM are used to construct in Chinese everyday metaphors. The ba (把) structure (Halliday 2005: 332) is a good example of textual GM to create more "explicit" and more easily "accessible" "hyponymic sets" (than those in English) (337) and to objectify processes, participants and circumstances by means of nominalization, which is the most frequently used GM structure in scientific writings in Chinese.

Following Halliday, Yang Yannian makes the first comprehensive corpus-based study of GM in Chinese in his doctorial thesis (2007). He systematically addresses three main issues both in theory and practical discourse analysis: the identification, the categorization and deployment of GM in Chinese. He builds up a system of GM categories and that of GM syndromes, where he provides detailed examples of these systems.

For short of space, I shall not quote his examples. I shall only give one of my own examples of nominalization, which is one of the most important GM. It is obtained from a list of titles for applying research funds, the list provided by one of my friends working at a college in Zhejiang Province, shown as follows:

[2] 浙江省	高校	英语专业	英语教材	中跨文化	语用	意识
m8	m7	m6	m5	m4	m3	m2

培养的　**现状**　及　**对比研究**
m1　　head1　　head2

(The literal translation of the Chinese would be "Zhejiang Province higher learning institutions English Speciality English teaching materials cross-cultural language use awareness cultivation present situation and contrastive research", the meaning of which will be: **the present situation and a contrastive study** of the cultivation of the awareness of cross-cultural language use in English teaching materials by English Specialities in institutions of higher learning in Zhejiang Province)

There are eight nominal modifiers totaling 24 characters in different forms and functions arranged in a "sequence *a b c* ... di *n*" permitting "2^n-1 different bracketings" (Halliday 2005) going before the two nominal groups "**现状**及**对比研究**", whose meaning is very densely packed. This phenomenon frequently appears in academic writings and official documents.

9.3.3 Changes and the expansion of words and word clusters

The development of new words or vocabulary is "the most obvious outward sign of" the changes or "the expansion of the meaning potential" (Halliday 2003b). This is very true with Chinese in terms of the growth of characters and the expansion of words and word clusters, especially in recent years.

9.3.3.1 Steady growth of the stock of characters

The history of the Chinese language is a history of the growth of characters, which are words or the basis of words. First of all, it has witnessed a steady increase of the stock of characters. Historical relics have shown that in the Shang Dynasty (1600 B.C.- 1100 B.C.), there could be only a few thousand characters, as evidenced from the 4,600 characters discovered in Anyang, Henan Province, which were written on tortoise shells and animal bones called *Jiaguwen*(甲骨文) (Wang Shunhong 1998). Now the number of characters has reached about 60,000 used today (Wang Lijia et al. 1997: 173), as shown in Table 9 - 1:

Table 9 - 1 The Expansion of the Stock of Characters

Year	Title of the book	Number of characters contained
100 (AD)	说文解字 (*Explaining Texts and Interpreting Characters*)	9,353
1008 (AD)	广韵(*Extensive Rhyming Scheme*)	26,194
1716 (AD)	康熙大字典(*Comprehensive Kangxi Dictionary*)	47,043
1915 (AD)	中华大词典(*Comprehensive China Dictionary*)	Over 48,000
1968 (AD)	中文大词典(*Comprehensive Chinese Dictionary*)	49,905
1996 (AD)	汉语大字典(*Comprehensive Dictionary of the Han Language*)	Over 56,000

9.3.3.2 Speedy growth of words and word clusters recently

With the fast growth of registers and genres, there has been a speedy expansion of words and word clusters in recent years. According to the investigation on new words and expressions published in August 27th, 2006 (LAICNLC), their annual appearance is approximately 1,000, or more than three per day in the past few years. There appeared at least 171 dictionary items in 2006 alone (*Xinjing Bao*, August 17th 2007), for example.

These words usually do not appear in isolation but as collocations (Hu & Jiang 2006) or as "a set of words that are paradigmatically related" and arranged as "a hyponymic set" "in the taxonomic order", which is typical of Chinese (Halliday 2003b).

One concrete example will suffice. Yu Jiang (2005) points out that within five years, the words and the word clusters in the register of real estate have undergone the process of emergence and maturity, and now become important terms in people's daily usage, the speed of which has gone beyond everyone's expectation. They mainly involve seven semantic domains, namely, (1) those concerning the layout of the house or flat and their ancillaries, which amount to more than 30, e.g. *zhuwo*(主卧), *kewo*(客卧), *gongrenfang*(工人房), *shuangyongfang*(双佣房), *yangguangfang*(阳光房); *fushi*(复式), *yueshi*(跃式); *banshijiegou*(板式结构), *zhuanhunjiegou*(砖混结构), etc; (2) those concerning services, the number of which goes beyond 20: *wuye*(物业), *baoan*(保安), *shequ*(社区), *lühualü*(绿化率); *peitaolou*(配套楼), *yezhu*(业主), *huisuozhutihui*(会所主题会), *shangyechanglang*(商业长廊); *cheweibi*(车位比), *menjin*(门禁), *gongtanfeiyong*(公摊费用); (3) those concerning the real estate business, the number of which reaches more than 40: *fazhanshang*(发展商), *dichanshang*(地产商), *zhongjieloushi*(中介楼市), *ershoufang*(二手房), *fangchanpinggu*(房产评估); *fangling*(房龄), *yiqifang*(一期房), *fangbohui*(房博会), *shoulouchu*(售楼处), *louhua*(楼花), *ruzhulv*(入住(率)), *shouqikuan*(首期款); (4) those concerning types of houses/flats such as *shangpinfang*(商品房), *xiezilou*(写字楼), *jingjishiyongfang*(经济适用房), *danshengongyu*(单身公寓), *jiudianshigongyu*(酒店式公寓), *talou*(塔楼), *banlou*(板楼), *qunlou*(裙楼), *duhuzhuzhai*(独户住宅), *huayuanyangfang*(花园洋房), *lianpaibieshu*(联排别墅); (5) those concerning the names of houses/flats, mostly such names as *xx dasha*(××大厦), *xx huayuan*(××花园), *xx xiaoqu*(××小区), *xx guangchang*(××广场), *xx xincun*(××新村), *xx shijie*(××世界). *xx zuo*(××座), *xx ting*(××庭), *xx ju*(××居), *xx yuan*(××苑), *xx xuan*(××轩), *xx ge*(××阁), *xx wangfu*(××王府), *xx gongguan*(××公馆), *xx shanzhuang*(××山庄), *xx jun*(××郡), *xx lu*(××庐), *xx di*(××邸), *xx hui*(××汇), *xx shijia*(××世家), *xx wan*(××湾), *xx yinxiang*(××印象), etc.; (6) those concerning real estate ads, especially those of describing the house/flat: *jianzhuang*(简装), *jingzhuang*(精装), *haozhuang*(豪装), *mubenzhuang*(墓本装); *wudijingguan*(无敌景观),

zhutiyuanlin(主题园林), *sixianghuayuan*(私享花园), *qinshuihuayuan*(亲水花园), *zhinengxiaoqu*(智能小区), *shengtaishequ*(生态社区), *huangjinhuxing*(黄金户型), *hanguifashou*(罕贵发售), *mingxingloupan*(明星楼盘),etc., The number of domains 4,5 and 6 each amounts to more than 20; (7) those concerning some new phenomena describing the nature of real estate and the transaction of houses or flats, for example, *suoshuilou*(缩水楼), *lanweilou*(烂尾楼), *chaofang*(炒房), *erfangdong*(二房东), *yilouyanglou*(以楼养楼), *fuhedichan*(复合地产),etc.

9.3.4 Expansions of word-making principles

What is more worth noticing are the changes of the word-making principles. This part is the focus of Section 9.3.

We first make a comparison between Chinese and Western languages in this respect in order to see clearly the features of the expansion of word-making principles in Chinese.

9.3.4.1 In Western languages

A word in Western languages, such as in English, is usually made up either of a root or a compound word (root + root) or a derivation (root + affix), and this gives rise to the following word-making principles: invention, blending, abbreviation, acronym, analogical creation, borrowing, etc. (Hu & Jiang 2006).

9.3.4.2 In Chinese

Chinese, however, presents quite a different picture both in the definition of "word" and in the word-making principles though there are similarities too. In the ancient times, Chinese only recognizes characters, which are considered mono-syllabic morphemes. The concept of "word" almost did not exist. The distinction between "character" (字, *zi*) and "word" (词, *ci*) only appears at the beginning of the 20th century in a study of Chinese by Zhang Shizhao in 1907 (Lü 1990), who takes a character either as a monosyllabic word or part of a compound word, as shown below:

a character { a word (a monosyllabic morpheme)
part of a (compound) word

Now we find that a word may also be made of more than one character with multiple syllables, which, however, only makes one morpheme or one meaning. Accordingly, we either create a word consisting of one or more than one character (a monosyllabic or multi-syllabic morpheme) or a compound word (Wang Jiali et al. 1997: 200 - 206). Therefore, the meaning of a character is expanded as shown:

a character { a word (a monosyllabic morpheme)
part of a word (a multi-syllabic morpheme)
part of a compound word

9.3.4.3 Principles for the creation of a word with one morpheme

The creation of a character or a monosyllabic morpheme word is based on the features of "character", which is usually a combination of form, sound and meaning, and which always has a radical usually providing the semantic meaning of the word, and which renders the other part the rest of the form and maybe the sound of the word.

A word made of more than one syllable with one morpheme usually comes from transliterations by borrowing, for example, *luotuo* (骆驼, camel), *putao*(葡萄, grape), *boli*(玻璃, glass), *moli*(茉莉, jasmine), *jibei*(吉贝) or *gubei*(古贝), which is eventually replaced by *mianhua* (棉花, cotton), a semantic translation. These terms came into Chinese in the Han or the Tang Dynasties. During these periods, Chinese mainly borrowed words denoting objects from the Huns and the peoples to the west of China, almost no words involving economy, politics or technology because China was far more advanced in these fields (Xiang Xi 1993: 540).

9.3.4.4 Principles for forming a compound

We know little as to when compounding became one of the principles to form a word in Chinese. We only know that as early as in Confucius' time (551 B.C.- 479 B.C), there were already quite a few compound words. For instance, we find 远方 (*yuanfang*, a place afar), 礼节 (*lijie*, rites), etc, in the first few pages of *The Analects*, which takes down sayings by Confucius and other well-known figures (Xu Zhigang, 2000), though most words in the book are monosyllabic.

We believe that the proliferation of compounds very possibly results from the process of **borrowing through translation**.

Li Jiwei (2005) argues that there are three periods in creating new words and word clusters including compounds through borrowing foreign words. The first period is from the Han (206 B.C.) and Tang Dynasty (618 - 907) to the 18th century; the second from the 19th century to the middle of the 20th century; and the third in the past 30 years since the reform and the implementation of the open door policy. We shall deal with each period in detail.

The first period: from the Han and Tang Dynasty to the 18th century

There are four characteristics or principles in forming new compound words during this period: 1) Many words are the combinations of transliteration denoting a hyponym followed by its Chinese superordinate, arising from the need for the taxonomy order, an inherent feature of Chinese (Halliday 2005), such as *bocai* (菠菜, spinach), added into the hyponymic set of *cai* (菜, vegetable), the first character of which is a transliteration; or a transliteration functioning as a superordinate followed by a Chinese hyponym. It is found that a whole package of Buddhist terms were formed in this way after the Han Dynasty, which make a superordinate 佛 (*fo*, Buddha), a short for 佛陀 (*fotuo*), and its hyponymic set, such as 佛教 (*fojiao*, Buddhism), 佛士 (*foshi*, a Buddhist), 佛曲 (*foqu*, Buddhist music), 佛经 (*fojing*, Buddhist Scripture), etc. Therefore, the method is **transliteration (hyponym) + Chinese superordinate** or

transliteration (superordinate) + Chinese hyponym = a new item in a hyponymic set. 2) A few are a combination of both semantic translation and transliteration, for example, 西瓜 (*xigua*, water melon; refer to Xiang Xi 1993), in which the sound comes from "xeko" used in the original language by an ancient people to the west part of China but the compound word is formed by translating the second half under the taxonomy of 瓜 (*gua*, a kind of melon), functioning as the superordinate, and then rendering the first sound as *xi* (西), meaning west so that the whole compound means a kind melon produced in *xifang* (西方) or the west; hence the method is **semantic translation + transliteration**. 3) Chinese prefers making compounds with fewer syllables which are written more easily (See the first two principles above). 4) Chinese favors creating double syllabic words for producing rhythmic and aesthetic effects (See the first two principles above).

These four features in borrowing foreign words became important word-making principles later for creating new compound words.

The second period: from the 19th century to the Middle of the 20th century

This period saw many more words translated from the West, the number of which far surpassed those during the first period (Wang Li 1985). Apart from the principle of the combinations of transliteration denoting a hyponym + its superordinate and the other three principles (See above), which were widely applied, there appeared a new word-making principle — half transliteration and half semantic translation. Take 新泽西州 (*xinzexizhou*), which is a very interesting case where the first character has the semantic meaning "new", the two characters in the middle are the transliterations of "jersey" but the Chinese compound adds a taxonomic term 州 (*zhou*, meaning "state") as the fourth character, making it clear that it is a state in the USA; hence the method is **half transliteration and half semantic translation**.

The third period: in the past 30 years since the reform and the implementation of the open door policy

This period has seen a new word-making principle — foreign words directly coming into Chinese such as E-mail, PK (play and kill), NBA, etc. which are known as "字母词" (*zimuci*, letter words). They may also combine with a Chinese superordinate as exemplified in "Call 机" in which 机 (*ji*) means a kind of machine. Therefore, the method is **directly borrowing the letter words** which may or may not combine with a Chinese superordinate.

This period has also seen a proliferation of a lot of borrowed words created by applying the methods of **semantic translation, semantic translation + transliteration, and transliteration**, as shown below:

1) Words by semantic translation

Take 网络 (*wangluo* for Internet connection). The first character is a semantic translation of the English "net" and the second a Chinese word meaning connection, usually going with "联" (*lian*) to form a compound 联络 (*lianluo*, connection). This has brought about a whole hyponymic set related to the Internet: 网站 (*wangzhan*, Internet service station), 网民 (*wangmin*, Internet users), 网虫 (*wangchong*, those obsessed with the Internet), 网费 (*wangfei*, internet fee) etc.

2) Words by half transliteration + half semantic translation

"趴车" (*pache* for parking) very well exemplifies this principle in borrowing: "趴" is a transliteration of the pronunciation of "par" in "park" or "parking"; "车" is a superordinate in Chinese, generally referring to any kind of vehicle. When the two words come together, however, the new Chinese compound is more vivid in expressing the mode of parking: parking with the four wheels on the ground, arising from the meaning of the character "趴": "stay still with the four legs on the ground". I found it very interesting the first time when I heard it used by a Chinese American in 1996 in California. I thought it must have been created by the local Chinese in their active use in the interaction between English and Chinese.

3) Words by transliteration

There are many examples. The best known are perhaps 可口可乐 (*kekoukele*, Coca Cola), 麦当劳 (*maidanglao*, McDonald's), 的士 (*dishi*, taxi), 粉丝 (*fensi*, fans), which means very differently from its original meaning (a kind of noodle made of beans), etc.

Note that once it becomes a Chinese word through transliteration, it is often given meaning, usually similar or different from that in the original language and always having a much richer connotation in its Chinese context. 博客 is a very good example of this phenomenon. The pronunciation of 博 comes from the first consonant "b" of the English word "blog" while that of 客 from the consonant "g". "Blog" is a new word used in the Internet technology, referring to a space where writings can be published, or pasted, or transmitted on the Internet. Does 博客 mean the same as its English equivalent? 博 (*bo*) implies a wealth of knowledge while 客 (*ke*) means a guest or visitor in Chinese. Therefore, when the two characters go together to form a new compound word there is an additional meaning to "blog": a visitor of the Internet who has a wealth of knowledge in a certain area. Other examples are 奔腾 (*benteng* for Pentium) and 奔驰 (*benchi* for Benz). 奔腾 (*benteng*) is the transliteration of "pentium" but it renders the meaning of quickness, as quick as a racing horse. The same applies to 奔驰 (*benchi*), a transliteration of the brand name of the famous German car "Benz", implying the quick functioning capability of the vehicle. These examples illustrate that "every language enlarges its meaning range when it hosts translations of foreign texts ..." (Halliday 2003b)

Scholars agree that there is a rule governing a foreign word to become Chinese: it has to have the features of a Chinese character or word; in other words, it has to go through the process of "汉化" (*hanhua*) (Guo Xi, 1999: 75) or Sinolization. For example, phonologically, its number has to be fit into a Chinese word, preferably, a double syllabic word. However, scholars maintain different views about which would be the most important principle in making a Chinese word by transliteration. Some say (Wu Liquan 1994 in Yu Jiang 2005) that most words refuse to maintain their original sounds and prefer part transliteration or complete semantic rendering; or more accurately, there is a preference of semantic translation to half transliteration and half semantic translation, and that of half transliteration, and half semantic translation to total transliteration, and the least favored mode is the direct rendering of the original sounds or the use of letter words. Therefore this principle can be summarized as **semantic translation >**(> = is preferable to) **half semantic translation + half transliteration > transliteration > letter words.** However, others maintain that the above view best represents the present day preference(Li, Jiwei 2005), that the most favored mode in the ancient times was transliteration and that at first there would be different transliterations of the same foreign word. Sinolization has gone through a long time of evolution before a compound word has become what it looks like today (Hu Yushu 1987).

9.3.4.5 Principles for making a compound word in modern Chinese

Through thousands of years, Chinese has created some important word-making principles to form a large stock of compounds. According to modern Chinese linguists (Hu Yushu 1987; Wang Li 1985; Wang Jiali et al. 1997), the main principles for making a compound word in Chinese can be summarized as follows:

1) Bound morpheme + free morpheme or free morpheme + bound morpheme: 老师 (*laoshi*, teacher), 阿哥(*age*, elder brother), 桌子 (*zhuozi*, table), 木头 (*mutou*, wood) 创造性 (*chuangzaoxing*, creativity), 反法西斯主义者 (*fanfaxisizhuyizhe*, anti-fascist) etc.

2) Compounding two words: head + head

— by combining two synonyms: 树木 (*shumu*, tree), 语言 (*yuyan*, language);

— by combining two antonyms: 早晚 (*zaowan*, sooner or later), 始终 (*shizhong*, always), 开关 (*kaiguan*, switch);

3) Combining head + modifier or modifier + head

— as complementary type: 说明 (*shuoming*, explain), 看透 (*kantou*, see through), 船只(*chuanzhi*, boat), 人口 (*renkou*, population);

— as descriptive type: 头疼 (*touteng*, headache), 心细 (*xinxi*, very careful);

— as controlling type: 监工 (*jiangong*, overseer)

— by merging two words into one: 国家 (*guojia*, country), 兄弟 (*xiongdi*, brothers);

— by repeating a character or a word, or by following either the pattern AA or the pattern AABB: 姐姐 (*jiejie*, elder sister)、太太 (*taitai*, wife); 老老实实 (*laolaoshishi*, very honest); 家家 (*jiajia*, every family), 问问 (*wenwen*, ask), 说说笑笑 (*shuoshuoxiaoxiao*, chats and laughters);

— as acronyms: 劳模 [*laomo*, short for 劳动模范 (*laodong mofan*), model worker], 计生委 [*jishengwei*, short for 计划生育委员会 (*jihuashengyu weiyuanhui*), family planning committee], 厂矿 [*changkuang*, short for 工厂矿山 (*gongchang kuangshan*), plant and mine];

— as hyponym + superordinate or superordinate + hyponym (Halliday, 2005)

— by borrowing: Semantic translation; semantic translation + transliteration; transliteration; letter words, the last of which are not Chinese in the real sense.

To sum up, the expansion of word-making principles in creating mono-syllabic, multi-syllabic and compound words is one of the main factors for the expansion of the meaning potential in Chinese in the process of its evolution and spatial growth.

9.3.5 Creation of new meanings

The typical case of creating new meaning is that of old words rendered with new meanings. Chinese never stops seeing cases where old words are given new meanings in the course of its historical evolution and spatial expansion.

Take one recent example: 钉子户 (*dingzihu*). It was used in a negative sense about a household refusing to move house hoping to get a large sum of compensation from a local government or a building company but now it may be used in a positive sense for their courage to stay where they are for fighting for their lawful rights. Other examples are taken from real estate register, such as *huayuan*(花园,originally meaning "garden"), *guangchang*(广场, originally meaning "square"), *cun*(村, originally meaning "village"). Now they are used to refer to dwellings or residential areas.

Secondly, the meaning of a word may be expanded. This can be seen from borrowed words such as "拜拜" (*baibai*), a transliteration of "byebye" but now it can mean separation or divorce from one's love or spouse.

Thirdly, new meanings may be created when new grammatical structures appear. For example GM may bring about "new forms of authority" and the elite stratum (Halliday 2003b), which are discussed in Section 9.3.2 but the details will not be elaborated on for short of space.

9.4 Possible causes for the expansion of meaning potential in Chinese

There are several underlying reasons which give rise to the five factors causing the changes in Chinese.

9.4.1 Changes of socio-cultural contexts

That socio-political changes in both historical and territorial dimensions demand for the expansion of the meaning potential of a language is the most important reason for the growth of a language (Zhang & Liu 2006). Halliday argues that the systemic expansion or "the expansion of meaning potential" results from "a response to the changing ideology in different social contexts" (2003a). These changes "come about as a language takes on new cultural, economic and political responsibilities" (2003b). He states "As new social practices evolve, further semantic space is opened up; and variation occurs in the setting of grammatical probabilities in resonance with features of the semantic context" (*ibid.*). He also points out that the language system "tends to **evolve** towards increasing semantic complexity" "with the accumulating experience that constituted the human conditions" (2003a: 413). It then follows that the realization strata are to expand too in order to accommodate the increasing complexity of semantics. As a result, the phonological/graphological system not only becomes larger but also more delicate; and so are the lexical and the grammatical systems. This is evidenced by the historical evolution of Chinese. The economic-political evolution from the slave society into the feudal, then to the Republic of China, and now to the present day society in the age of globalization has brought about changes at all levels. Almost every historical period witnesses the appearance of large groups of new words and word clusters. For example, the 19th century is a period during which China underwent a great change in both material and spiritual life. Chinese absorbed words involving Western civilization covering areas such as socio-politics, economy, especially science and technology, as China was far behind the West in these fields (Wang Li 1985). In the past 30 years China has witnessed drastic changes in politics, economy, culture, science and technology, which have given rise to a large number of new words and new word clusters in Chinese (Please see the examples in the previous sections.).

9.4.2 Changes brought about by exchanges in culture and economy

"The demand for the use of language changes with the changes of interactions among people" (Zhang & Liu 2006). First, through daily interactions the standard dialect has been influenced by dialectical expressions. The best recent examples are found in many Guangdong dialectical words coming into Putonghua resulting from the more advanced commercial development exercised in Hong Kong SAR and the Pearl River Delta. Second, throughout its history, China has been in constant interactions with its northern and Western neighbors, many times involved in wars, in which the Han ethnic group (the main users of Chinese) never stops its cultural and economic exchanges with other ethnic groups, in the course of which, not only new words and mew word clusters appear but also some new word-making principles came into being (See Section 9.3.4). Third, with the expansion of international cultural exchanges, there have also been interactions between Chinese and other languages, which have resulted in the growth of the language system at both the lexical and the grammatical level. The best examples are the changes in the structure in clause complex and the phenomenon of GM (See 9.3.2.2). Fourthly, with Chinese being spoken by its immigrants and learned in other countries, a great many varieties spoken in different regions have enriched and had a great impact on Chinese through various channels (Guo Xi 2006). Here we just take two examples. One concerns the terms for Chinese music and the other for the different versions for taxi.

Table 9-2 Terms for Chinese Music (Wu Yingcheng 2006)

Chinese Mainland	Hong Kong SAR	Taiwan, China	Singapore
Hanyu/ putonghua	*Guoyu*/ putonghua	*Guoyu*	*Huayu*
民乐(*minyue*)	中乐(*zhongyue*)	国乐(*guoyue*)	华乐(*huayue*)

Table 9-3 Terms for Taxi (Wu Yingcheng 2006)

Number	Term	Hong Kong SAR	Shanghai, China	Singapore	Taiwan, China
1.	的士车(*dishiche*)	0	1	0	0
2.	的士(*dishi*)	95	0	0	6

(Continued on the next page)

Number	Term	Hong Kong SAR	Shanghai, China	Singapore	Taiwan, China
3.	出租车(*chuzuche*)	4	90	0	0
4.	计程车(*jichengche*)	1	6	2	94
5.	德士(*deshi*)	0	0	98	0
6.	打的(*dadi*)	0	3	0	0
	Total	100	100	100	100

Numerous examples can be found in the over 4,000 newspapers published in Chinese in 52 countries and in 230 journals produced in America, Europe and Singapore and elsewhere (Wang Lingling 2006).

9.4.3 The creative use of the language by writers/speakers

The expansion of meaning potential is also due to the creative use of Chinese by all the individual speakers and particularly writers of all types of discourses. Take the most famous example: the word 绿 (*lü* for green), which is usually used as an adjective, but was turned into a transitive verb in the line "春风又绿江南岸" (*chunfeng you lü jiangnan an*, or, The spring wind **greens** the river bank in the south.) by Wang Anshi in his poem "*Bo Chuan Guazhou*" (The Boat Stopped at Guazhou). Actually, everybody when using the language in a new way contributes to the expansion of the language system.

9.4.4 Technological advancements

It is well known that every new technology brings about a whole cluster of technical terms into the language, as exemplified by the terms arising from the four great innovations in Ancient China, particularly from the improved invention of paper by Cai Lun 2,000 year ago (Bai 2002), which makes it easier for written communication to expand largely. In modern times, the Western Industrial Revolution and the advancement in science and technology, particularly the present day information technology, have given rise not only to many new terms but to a new kind discourse in a new register, namely scientific writing, which highlights the use of GM, particularly nominalization "for the construal of processes into things" (Halliday 2003a). Halliday maintains when dealing with this phenomenon that this "was the major semiotic strategy for transforming technology into science" (2003a: 226).

9.4.5 Psychological changes

Another reason may be that of psychological changes arising from social and ideological changes. This is best exemplified in giving names to one's house/flat in the real estate register. In ancient times, Chinese used to give elegant names to their houses; now the real estate business under today's market economy has revived this tradition. Owners now adopt such terms as *yuan*(苑), *xuan*(轩), *ge*(阁), *lu*(庐), *di*(邸), *wangfu*(王府), *zhuangyuan*(庄园), etc. for naming their houses or flats, which sound elegant and dignified because by so doing the house/flat owners believe they may be regarded as belonging to the high class or their social status be enhanced. Note that quite a few extraordinary words are created in house transaction, such as 罕贵 (*hangui*, especially expensive) and 私享 (*sixiang*, for private enjoyment), for keeping in pace with the fashion and for catching the eyes of consumers.

In short, the growth of Chinese arises from socio-political changes in both historical and territorial dimensions (Zhang & Liu 2006), from "changes of interactions among people" (*ibid.*), from the creative use of the language by writers/speakers, from technological advancements and from psychological changes, among which the most important reason for the growth of Chinese comes from economic and socio-political changes, which call for the expansion of the meaning potential of the language. Halliday is right in arguing that the systemic expansion or "the expansion of meaning potential" results from "a response to the changing ideology in different social contexts" (2003a), and that "it is not improbable that the changes that take place reflect the vast range of new functions that languages are called upon to serve the increased demands on their overall semantic resources, a process that we are seeing again today as our language are further extended to cope with moving into the high technology age" (Halliday 2005: 328). This is evidenced by the historical evolution of Chinese discussed above though we lack space to discuss the changes in the phonological and graphological systems.

9.5 Language as an active agent in social changes

Halliday has always held a dialectic point of view on the relations between language and society. He argues that on the one hand, socio-political changes have a vital impact on the changes of a language; on the other, changes in a language also exercise a great influence on the socio-political and ideological changes in a society (2003a & b). Language is "itself the active agency in reality construction" (Whorf in Halliday 2003a: 244) or functions "as an active agent in these historical processes" (Halliday 2003b). Many examples can be found to show that Chinese is taking an active part in promoting the socio-political advancement in the country.

9.5.1 The effect of the "*Baihuawen* Movement"

First let us take a look at the effect of the "Baihuawen Movement" after the May Fourth Movement after World War Ⅰ. Before this movement, the learned used the classical form in the written mode which devoiced them from the mode spoken by the majority illiterate Chinese. In the 1920s, a group of progressive intellectuals in China advocated the use of "*Baihuawen*" (白话文, or plain language or a form based on the spoken mode) so as to raise the level of education of the population. News reporters and writers began to use this variety to write news and stories, teachers taught Chinese in this form in the classroom in addition to the classics, and magazines published articles with progressive ideas in this plain language. This not only raised the literacy level of the people but also created a new generation of youth with great influences on their ideology coming from the West such as equality between man and woman, democracy and freedom of speech, esp. Marxism, which paved the way for the revolution taking place later for political and ideological changes (Hu 1987; Gong 1987; Lu Jianming 2006).

9.5.2 The effect of popularization of "putonghua"

The second most influential event is the popularization of "putonghua". Actually the demand for a standard spoken form began with the Guoyu (国语) Movement, the mission of which was to popularize the speaking of the standard language among the broad masses, and it achieved successes after the 1930s. Putonghua was promoted as the standard dialect ever since 1956 when the State Council issued "The Decree of Promoting Putonghua" (Lu Jianming 2006). Through decades of promotion and popularization, 53.06% of the whole population speak it, and over 80% of people in the cities can communicate with it and 90% of all citizens hope they will learn it at present (BLAMME 2004). It is an institutionalized official dialect for media and instruction, and the standard form "taken over as second tongue by speakers of other dialects" (Halliday 2003b) and has become a mode learned by the minority ethnic groups and people from other countries, and a reference for *Huayu* for most overseas Chinese. The popularization of Putonghua has facilitated the communication among people speaking different dialects and to a large degree helped to promote the domestic economic, political and scientific and technological development, to push forward the standardization of the common language and to raise the level of education of the people (Lu Jianming 2006). It has, however, also brought about worries about the existence of local dialects and the relation between Chinese or Hanyu and other languages spoken by the minority ethnic groups (Lu Jianming 2006; Zhao Jinmin 2005; Zhou Qingsheng 2005).

9.5.3 The effect of the "script reform"

9.5.3.1 The popularization of *Pinyin*

Modern Chinese has seen attempts of "script reforms", the final goal being to Romanize the written form. This comes from the idea of popularizing education among the broad masses for the characters or the written system of Chinese is hard to learn by children and by the illiterate working class people. For this purpose, the mainland established "The National Reform Committee on the Characters" in the 1950s (Lu Jianming 2006). However, the reform has met with great difficulties so the committee changed its mission: to create a kind of script in reference to the Roman letters in order to promote the standard pronunciation which may lead to the convenience for education. By reference to the few systems of Romanization for the Chinese written form appearing earlier, for example, the Wade-Giles system, the Yale system, *Zhuyin Fuhao*, finally the committee succeeded in working out the *Hanyu Pinyin* system (汉语拼音系统, also known simply as *Pinyin* (the.freedictionary.com), which is the most common Romanization system for Standard Mandarin and the official system for the People's Republic of China, as well as for Singapore. It is claimed that Pinyin has at least three advantages over the other systems, namely, 1) it has only 26 letters, the number of which is identical to that of English, thus simple and concise; 2) it uses the Latin letters, thus convenient for information processing and internet communication; and 3) each letter or the combinations of letters can be phonemes, thus accurate and flexible (Wang, et al. 1997). Due to its being easy to learn, Pinyin is the first written form for children at school or the illiterate to learn Chinese, which functions as a useful tool for learning characters later or simultaneously. It is also very commonly used when teaching Mandarin or the spoken form to speakers of other languages in schools and universities in other regions or countries.

9.5.3.2 Simplification of characters

Actually the tendency of simplifying the characters began as early as the *jiaguwen* (甲骨文) time more than 3,000 years ago. The process accelerated after the May 4th Movement in the 1920s and 1930s. Going along with the creation of Pinyin, China issued four groups of simplified characters between 1956 and 1959; a revised version came out in 1964; and some adjustment was made in 1986 of a few of them. Now, the total number of simplified characters reaches 2,235. The idea of simplifying characters also arose from the need of raising the literacy level of the broad masses right after 1949 when the number of the educated had amounted to only 15%. The simplified system requires fewer strokes to write certain components and has fewer synonymous characters, thus easier for the laboring people to learn how to read and write. Yet now in retrospect, we have found some problems. For example, there have appeared pairs of simplified characters similar in form (扰 vs. 拢) and some simplified characters tend to lead to ambiguity in meaning as they have similarity in form (没有食堂 vs. 设有食堂). Therefore, Chinese linguists propose that there is the need to regulate the number, the forms and pronunciations of characters as well the sequences of the strokes of characters (Wang et al. 1997).

9.5.4 The effect of Grammatical Metaphor

Newton created a new register in writing, namely, scientific discourse realized mainly by GM "for codifying, transmitting and extending the new scientific knowledge" and for creating "a new reality loaded with a new ideology" (Halliday 2003a); and now, there is the threat of "technocratic discourse", a combination of bureaucracy with the scientific forms, which makes the language become "the high prestige" and "elitist language of the learned disciplines" (*ibid.*). Halliday (1998) is certainly very penetrating in arguing that "The use of ideational GM creates discourses of expert which will become a language of power and technological control" and which keeps out all those who know little of the game. This is especially obvious at the present time when language takes an active part in shaping the information society. In this sense, we are truly "at the mercy of" the language we speak (Sapir 1929: 209; in Sampson 1980). The phenomenon of nominalization in Chinese as an important form of GM has caused the problem of readability of textbooks and esp. items of mathematics and physics in the entrance exam for examinees. In a Chinese scientific work we see numerous noun groups organized in a "sequence a b c ... di n" permitting "2n − 1 different bracketings", where all the elements before "di" (Halliday, 2005) are modifiers belonging to different layers in a nominal group as Chinese does not allow postmodification. This causes enormous difficulties for the interpretation of the structure (Halliday, 2005: 342) because the meanings are very densely packed (2003b). The example "浙江省高校英语专业英语教材中跨文化语用意识培养的**现状及对比研究**" cited previously well illustrates this argument. There are eight nominal modifiers totaling 24 characters in different forms and functions going before the nominal group "**现状及对比研究**", whose meaning is very densely packed. It really takes time and energy for anyone to work out its meaning based on this grammatical structure. This is a good example of the "semiotic power" — only those learned can tackle such complex nominal structures.

9.5.5 The effect of new registers

Every year sees the appearance of new terms used in new registers. In a large sense, the new registers such as the real estate, the stock exchange, fashions and internet, etc. have exercised a great impact on the ideology of people in general, and to a large extent created a new generation of Chinese for the language used in these registers is loaded with particular ideologies, which helps in shaping their mind including their values, their way of thinking, their psychology (See Section 9.4), their likes and dislikes, etc.

9.6 Prospect on the future development of Chinese

9.6.1 The mode of expansion of Chinese

When a language expands, it may spread from local to national, and then, to international or even global. Halliday (2003b) defines a "global language" to be "a tongue which has moved beyond its nation, to become 'international'", and says "if its range covers the whole world we may choose to call it 'global'".

The expansion of a language has much to do with who its speakers are, and more specifically, how their political, economic, technological, cultural and military power is. The process of Western languages develops from national languages into international or even global is a very good example. That "Greek became a language of international communication in the Middle East over 2,000 years ago" is the result of the weapons used by "the armies of Alexander the Great". "Latin became known throughout Europe" with the expansion "of the Roman Empire". "Arabic came to be spoken so widely across northern Africa and the Middle East with the spread of Islam". "Spanish, Portuguese and French found their way into the Americas, Africa and the Far East through colonial policies set by the Renaissance kings and queens and implemented by armies and navies. English, the de facto global language right now, began its movement around the world with the expansion of British colonial power in the nineteenth century, and maintains its world position with the emergence of the United States as the leading economic power of the twentieth century" (Crystal 2003).

In a sense, the expansion of Chinese follows the similar trace, i.e. through those who speak it. However, the mode of Chinese spreading into other regions and countries differs from that of Western languages — through colonization, as there is a completely different history of Chinese speakers. The expansion of Chinese began in the Tang Dynasty, when Chinese technology and culture reached its zenith. The Chinese language was extensively borrowed into the languages of Japan, Korea and Vietnam through political, economic, technical and cultural exchanges. Further expansion of the language was promoted by the overseas Chinese. The Chinese people have had a long history of migrating overseas, which can be dated back to the Ming dynasty (1368 - 1644). In the 19th century, when the age of colonialism of Western countries was at its height, with many colonies lacking in laborers, a great tide of Chinese migration began. The language did not travel with the illiterate or poorly educated peasants and coolies either. It was those overseas Chinese, who later on integrated into the mainstream society of other countries, adopted the languages of the local languages while maintaining their own dialects. The elevated socio-economic status of 55 million overseas Chinese in recent years constitutes an important reason for the new wave of Chinese expansion. More importantly, China is back on the stage of world politics, economy and technology, which, together with the opening-up foreign policy, the long history of civilization and the newly initiated "Confucius Institute" Project, is providing a powerful impetus for the Chinese language to become an international language, attracting more and more learners outside the Chinese territory. The spread of Chinese around the world can be presented as the pie with three circles below in Figure 9 - 1. (We revised the concentric circles of Wu Yingcheng (2003) by stressing the size of each group with the area of the circle and the density of the dots.) The similarity between the three "circles" of Chinese and those of English as suggested by Kachru (1989) indicates the spread of Chinese from national to international. At present, the innermost circle takes the largest part and outmost the smallest. Will the number of learners of Chinese grow rapidly? Will Chinese go further to become global? Section 9.6.2 will give a brief discussion on this.

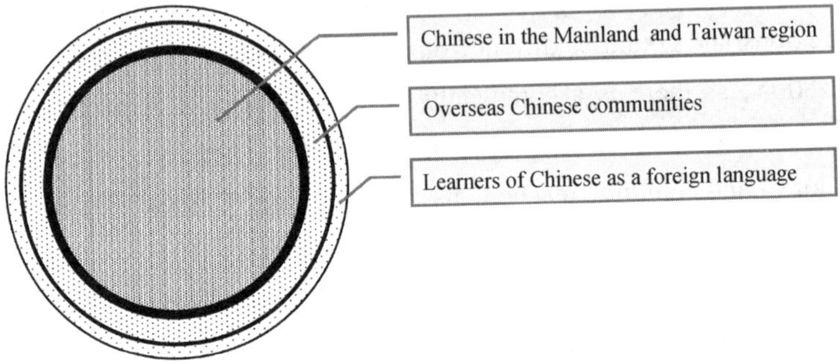

Figure 9 – 1 Speakers and Learners of Chinese Around the World

9.6.2 Chinese: international or global?

Chinese is the official language of the Chinese territory, both the Mainland and Taiwan region and one of the six official languages of the United Nations (alongside English, Arabic, French, Russian, and Spanish). In China, which is known to be the most populous nation in the world, 1.1 billion speakers take Chinese as their first language. There are also substantial numbers of Chinese speakers found in many other parts of the world. Besides, there is a growing tide to learn Chinese. It is reported that 30 million people in the world are learning this language and over 2,500 institutions of higher learning in 100 countries and regions have opened Chinese course (Yu Jin'en 2006). Considering the definitions provided by Halliday (2003b), we can say right now that Chinese is already an international or world language. Will it move on to become global? This has more to do with the institutional factors than the systemic ones that have been discussed previously. We would expect the globalization of the Chinese language going along with the ever-increasing influence of China on the world economy, politics, technology, culture, etc. but it would be a very long process. Due to the great strength of the United States and some of the other English-speaking countries, English, with such a long history of being used internationally and now globally, is making cross-language communication easy in almost every field: academia, education, information technology, business, media, entertainment, tourism, etc. It prevails in our real life and in the virtual space on the Internet as well. People from many non-English-speaking countries are now striving to make themselves heard by the rest of the world by the use of English. It could be said that for English, the population of the two outer circles as suggested by Kachru (1989) is much larger than that of the inner circle, while for Chinese, it is the contrary case, and the situation will remain the same for quite a long time.

To end our discussion, we would like to share some of our interesting findings from a survey among the international students of Tsinghua University. In recent years, there are a greater number of foreign students who come to China to learn Chinese. They are members of the two outer circles of the above chart, namely, descendants of overseas Chinese and learners of Chinese as a foreign language. Our survey was conducted among 57 Chinese learners, mainly of these two kinds, in Tsinghua University in order to have a glimpse of their attitudes toward Chinese and Chinese learning. (See Appendix for the English translation of our questionnaire.) Although our sample of survey is small, compared with the huge amount of Chinese learners from the two circles, our findings are still indicative of the corresponding issues on a large scale, especially the related situation in Beijing, capital of China.

The pie chart below in Figure 2 shows the distribution of our questionees' nationalities:

All of our questionees had learned Chinese before they came to Tsinghua for the further learning program in China. Among them, 47 percent have learned Chinese for more than three years. Their purposes of learning the language mainly include:

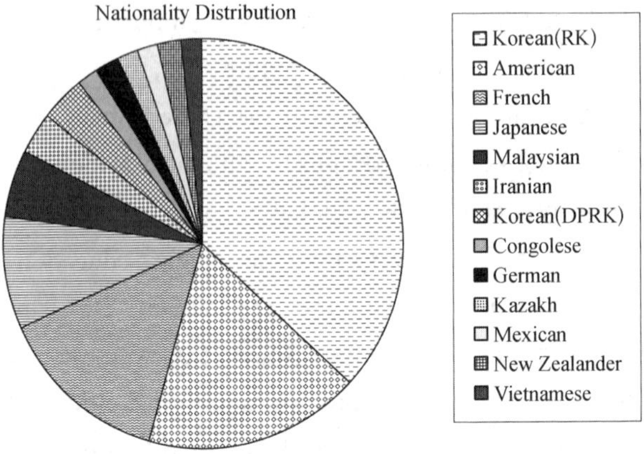

Figure 9 - 2 National Distribution of Chinese Learners of Our Survey

a) to develop their career potential;

b) to facilitate their education in China;

c) to pursue their interest in the Chinese language itself as well as China as a whole;

d) to trace their family origin and maintain their connection with China.

In response to the question "Do you think Chinese will become a global language like English?", 60 percent chose "not sure" or "no", while when asked about "Do you think there will be more people outside China to learn Chinese?", 93 percent chose "absolutely" or "yes".

We wonder whether the result of a research carried out by the British Council is indicative when it says that apart from English, Chinese, Spanish and Arabic will be the key languages of the 21st century (*Zhejiang Daily*, July 22, 2005).

9.7 Conclusion

From the above discussions, we can arrive at the following conclusions:

1) the semogenic power of Chinese grows along with the growth of the language, particularly in its paradigmatic complexity; 2) the expansion of the meaning potential of Chinese like other languages is realized through creating new words, new word clusters, new meanings, new word-making principles, new grammatical structures and new registers; 3) the expansion of meaning potential of Chinese arises from various causes including the sociopolitical, cultural, ideological, technological and other changes, and 4) whether Chinese will become a global language depends on China's development in all aspects. At present, we cannot clearly see the possibility.

We maintain that systemic changes of Chinese will never stop: the system will become more complex, and on the whole, will further expand, and the speed of the expansion will be accelerated with the speedy change of the society and with the temporal and spatial expansion of the language, and only those sub-systems which stop being useful will disappear.

Appendix：调查问卷（Questionnaire）

请填写或在选择的项目上划钩。(Please tick the chosen answer or write an answer.)

1. 你是哪国人？(What is your nationality?)

2. 你学过几年汉语？(How many years have you learned Chinese?)
   1) 一年 (one year)　　2) 两年 (two years)
   3) 三年 (three years)　　4) 四年或四年以上 (four years or more)

3. 你为什么学习汉语？(Why do you learn Chinese?)

4. 你觉得汉语难学吗？(Do you find it difficult to learn Chinese?)
   1) 不难 (not difficult)　　2) 有点难 (a little bit difficult)
   3) 难 (difficult)　　4) 很难 (very difficult)

5. 你觉得汉语最难学的是哪部分？(Which part do you feel the most difficult to learn?)

1）发音（pronunciation） 2）语调（tones）
3）语法（grammar） 4）写汉字（writing characters）
5）掌握语义（grasping the meaning）
6）使用汉语（using the language）

6. 你是从汉语拼音开始学习汉语的吗？（Did you learn Chinese by starting with *Pinyin*？）
   1）是（Yes）
   2）使用注音符号（using *Zhuyin*）
   3）使用其他符号（using other systems）
7. 你觉得汉语拼音是学习汉语的好方法吗？（Do you think *Pinyin* a good way to learn spoken Chinese？）
   1）非常好（very good）
   2）好（good）
   3）不太好（not very good）
   4）不好（not good）
8. 你认为有必要学写汉字吗？（Do you think it necessary to learn to write characters？）
   1）很有必要（very necessary）
   2）必要（necessary）
   3）不必要（not necessary）
   4）不太清楚（can't judge）
9. 你喜欢学写汉字吗？（Do you like practicing characters？）
   1）很喜欢（very much）
   2）喜欢（yes）
   3）不太喜欢（not very much）
   4）不太清楚（can't judge）
10. 你认为汉语会像英语一样成为全球性的语言吗？（Do you think Chinese will become a global language like English？）
   1）很肯定会（absolutely）
   2）肯定会（yes）
   3）不太肯定（not sure）
   4）不会（no）

11. 你认为在中国境外会有更多的人学习汉语吗?(Do you think there will be more people outside China to learn Chinese?)

1)很肯定会(absolutely)

2)肯定会(yes)

3)不太肯定(not sure)

4)不会(no)

12. 你能不能描述一下你们国家汉语学习的情况:学习目的、课程安排、学生学习的动机?(Could you describe the situation of Chinese learning in your country in terms of purpose, curriculum and the motivation of the students)?

第二部分

语篇分析

Part Two

Discourse Analysis

10

系统功能语法[①]与语篇分析[*]

10.1 引　言

黄国文在《语篇分析的理论与实践》(2001)一书中,成功地应用系统功能语法框架分析了广告语篇。他指出,这种语法比其他任何语言学框架"更适合用来分析语篇"。这是因为系统功能语法本身就是一种语篇语法,其"语法范畴可以被解释为对语义范式的实现",也就是说"其语法形式与所编码的意义自然相关联"(Halliday 1994: xvii)——这个语篇语法清晰地描述了语言各个层次及它们之间的实现关系;这是因为这个语法就是用来说明语言是如何使用的,即它提供了"洞察语篇的语义和语篇有效性"的方法(同上);这是因为系统功能语法系统清楚地描述了语言的三个纯理功能网络系统,以及它们的子系统的概念和应用的可能性;这还因为它将语篇分析的层次和步骤都清晰地勾勒了出来,应用这个语法框架分析语篇,可以使我们避免对语篇只作出主观的"随意的评论"(xvi)。

---

* 本章原刊登在《外语教学》2005 年第六期。

① "语法"一词有两个意义:狭义的"语法"仅指"句法";广义的"语法"指某个语言学(Halliday 1994),如"生成语法"指"生成语言学","系统功能语法"指"系统功能语言学"。

这一章有两个目的：进一步论证系统功能语法在语篇分析方面的应用性；提出一个更实际的应用这个语法框架分析语篇的方法或步骤。

下面，将首先讨论系统功能语法的主要理论方面——语言的层次和它们之间的实现关系（Halliday 1994）；然后提出"语境-语篇-评论"分析语篇的方法，分析时将提及有关的功能系统；最后将举例说明功能语法在语篇分析方面的应用价值。

10.2 功能语言学框架

10.2.1 语言的层次及语言的纯理功能系统

系统功能语言学认为语言是由三个纯理功能实现的意义潜势系统构成的，而这三个纯理功能又受制于情景语境和文化语境（Halliday 1994）。文化语境代表我们生活中各种社会活动的抽象意义，它涉及很多层面（Halliday 2002），至少涉及在某个文化中的观念形态和语篇类型（Martin 1992；Eggins 1994），因而是一个较抽象和笼统的概念；而一个语篇是实际社会交往中的一种形式，它必然发生在某一种文化的某个情景中。因而在分析一个语篇时，我们必须考虑它的情境变量：所发生的事或语场，话语的参与者或语旨，交际的形式或语式（H & H 1985；Huang 2001：72）。它们分别在语言中由概念功能、人际功能、语篇功能来实现。概念功能是代表或反映或解释世界的功能，人际功能是交际参与者分配角色和对语篇作出判断的功能，语篇功能是用各种语言手段将语篇中的各个句子连接成一篇连贯文章的功能（Halliday 1994）。语言和它的语境有五个层次：文化语境、情景语境、语义、词汇-语法、音系系统（口语）或拼写系统，它们之间的关系是实现的关系，即上面一个层次由下面一个层次来实现（Martin 1992；Eggins 1994），如图 10－1 所示（↙表示实现）：

Context of culture

↙

Context of situation

↙

Semantics (Meaning)

↙

Lexico-grammar (Wording)

↙

Phonology (Speaking)

Graphology (Writing)

图 10－1　语言及其语境层次

语篇的三个纯理功能系统如图 10－2 所示(由于篇幅有限,不能详细解释子系统的各个功能):

System of meta-functions
- ideational
  - transitivity
  - voice
  - polarity
- interpersonal
  - mood
  - modality
  - modulation
  - appraisal system
  - key
- textual
  - thematic structure
  - information structure
  - cohesion

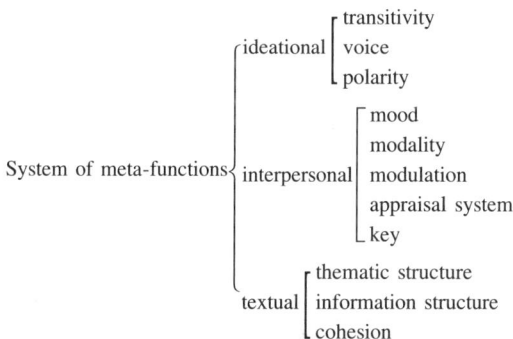

图 10－2　纯理功能系统

10.2.2　语篇分析的两个层面

韩礼德认为语篇分析涉及两个层面:第一个层次是对语篇的理解。这个层面要显示“语篇表达意义的方法和原因”。在理解语篇的过程中,“语篇的多层意义”(包括概念、人际、语篇意义以及它们子系统中的功能)和其他特征很可能被揭示出来(Halliday 1994: xv)。换句话说,第一个层次是一个描写和解释语篇意义的活动。第二个层面对语篇做出评价,涉及“语篇是否有效”“达到它的目的,语篇为什么达到或没有达到它所设置的目的——在什么方面语篇是成功的,在什么方面语篇是不成功或不那么成功”(Halliday 1994: xv)。这就是说第二个层面是一个说明和评价的活动。为了达到这个目的不仅要求分析语篇本身,还应分析它的语境(情景语境和文化语境)以及语境与语篇的关系(同上);这个层面的活动是要揭示语境变量如何用来建立语篇,或语篇如何受语境变量的制约。这就意味着分析者需要解码语篇的深层意义,需要对在一定的情景语境甚至文化语境中的词汇和语法的应用做出评论。

10.2.3 语篇分析的步骤

韩礼德提出分析语篇的三个步骤(Halliday 1994: xvi):

1. 分析词汇语法,这是分析的基础;

2. 评论这些词汇语法特点,将它们置于语篇的情景语境甚至文化语境中;

3. “联系其他社会意义系统进行分析”,“因为一个语篇是一个非常复杂的现象”。

在分析了30几个语篇(Fang Yan et al. 2001)的实践中,我们发现张传真和张德禄(1992)提出的用于外语教学的“情景(语境)—语篇—情景(语境)”的模式更为行之有效,这里我们将其更确切地称为“**语境—语篇分析—评论**(联系其语境变量)”模式:

1. 首先分析情景语境变量,为评论做准备(有了这一步,在评论时更易于将纯理功能的一些特点与语篇的情景语境联系起来);

2. 分析相关纯理功能的特点,即对词汇-语法进行分析;

3. 评论这些词汇语法特点,将它们放在语篇的情景语境甚至文化语境中进行解释和评论[一般情况下,只联系情景语境,因为情景语境是文化语境的实例(Halliday 2002)];

4. 如有必要应“联系其他社会符号系统进行分析”。比如,若分析《红楼梦》某一段王熙凤的话语,有可能要涉及清朝封建社会中复杂的家庭关系和当时的意识形态等方面因素。通常情况下,不必涉及这一步,因为会牵扯到很多复杂的文化因素(Halliday 1994: xvi),分析的篇幅会太长。

应当指出,在分析过程中,我们始终应当把注意力放在对语义的内涵进行解释方面,因为语篇分析的过程就是释义的过程。

10.3 语篇分析举例

10.3.1 The Middle Eastern Bazaar (第一段) (Mei & Wang, 1995)

10.3.1.1 语篇

The Middle Eastern Bazaar ***takes*** you back hundred — even thousand — of years. The one I **am thinking** of particularly ***is entered*** by a Gothic-arched gateway of aged brick and stone. You ***pass*** from the heat and glare of a big, open square into a cool, dark cavern which ***extends*** as far as the eye can **see**, ***losing*** itself in the shadowy distance. Little donkeys with harmonious **tinkling** bells ***thread*** their way among the throngs of people ***entering*** and ***leaving*** the bazaar. The roadway **is** about twelve feet wide, but it ***is narrowed*** every few yards by little stalls where goods of every conceivable kind ***are sold.*** The din of the stallholders **crying** their wares, of donkey-boys and porters ***clearing*** a way for themselves by **shouting** vigorously, and of would-be purchasers **arguing** and **bargaining is** continuous and **makes** you dizzy.

10.3.1.2 语篇分析

语篇分析目的: 从及物性动词过程(transitivity)类型看语篇的特点;

情景语境的变量:

语场: 描述中东集市及集市上的活动;

语旨: 作者与读者,社会距离最大;

语式: 正式的书写体英语;

及物性动词过程类型分析

及物性系统: 有六个过程: 物质过程、心理过程、话语过程、存在过程和关系过程;物质过程又可细分为动作过程和事件过程,如图 10 - 3 所示(Halliday 1994):

Transitivity system
- material process
  - action
  - event
- mental process
- verbal process
- behavioral process
- existential process
- relational process

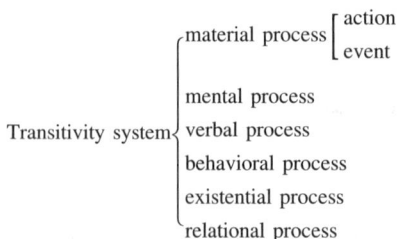

图 10－3 及物性系统

语篇中动词过程类型分析：

这段语篇共有 21 个动词(所有黑体字)，其中 11 个为物质(动作)过程，用来描述如“进入”“通过”“离开”“失去”“变窄”“踏着”“卖”等动作；5 个为话语过程，如“叮当”“喊”“讨价还价”“叫嚷”“争论”，用来描述集市里的嘈杂声；3 个为关系过程，如“是”(is)、“使”(makes)，用来描绘集市的容貌和气氛特点；还有 2 个是心理过程，即“看见”和“想”，反映作者的所见所想。

10.3.1.3 评论

占语篇主导地位的是物质：动作过程和话语过程。另外，由于作者和读者的社会距离很大，使用的是正式的书写体英语，因而有些动词采用了分词形式。21 个动词过程及它们的参与者和环境因素，用来描绘中东集市的特点：有大群的人和驴子出入，集市上人们正在忙碌着做生意，里面充满了叫卖声和买卖双方讨价还价的声音。总之，这些过程将这里**充满活力和嘈杂声音的气氛**成功地揭示了出来，这就是这段语篇的语义和文体特点。

10.3.2 Blackmail (Mei & Wang, 1995)

10.3.2.1 语篇

Duchess：“We **will** not pay you.” (modulation：inclination：insisting)

Ogivile：“Listen, lady ...”

Duchess: "I **will not** listen. (modulation : inclination : insisting) You **will** listen to me." (modulation : obligation : required) ...

Duchess: We **will not** pay you ten thousand dollars. But we **will** pay you twenty thousand dollars (modulation : inclination : insisting) ...

Duchess: You will drive our car north. (modulation : obligation : required)

10.3.2.2 语篇分析

语篇分析目的:从意态意义观察公爵夫人的性格特点;

情景语境的变量:

语场:讹诈撞车逃逸事件,就肇事小车开到北方讨价还价;

语旨:公爵夫人和饭店侦察员(Ogivile),前者是一个贵族,社会地位很高;而后者的社会地位极低,两者社会距离最大;

语式:公爵夫人和饭店侦察员之间的对话,口语体英语;

意态成分分析:

意态系统:有两个选择:倾向性或义务性,又分别有高、中、低三个程度不同的选择,用来表示说话人对事物的态度,如图 10-4 所示:

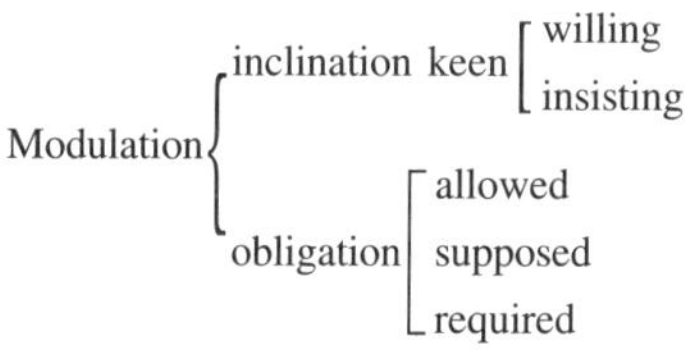

图 10-4 意态系统

语篇意态成分分析:

有 6 个表示意态的成分,如"一定要(will)""决不(will not)";如果包括与这段课文有关的其他 8 个意态成分,如"想要(want)""一定要""决不""意向(intended)""决然地(decisively)",一共有 14 个表示意态的成分,用来表示公爵夫人对待饭店侦察员对她和丈夫逃逸撞车事件讹诈的态度。

10.3.2.3 评论

意态成分的大量使用是这段语篇的语义和文体特点。这些意态成分显示了在与饭店侦察员讨价还价过程中，公爵夫人的决断个性和气势上所占的主导地位。饭店侦察员发现了她和丈夫逃逸撞车的行为，想讹诈一万美元，可是出乎他的意料，公爵夫人一定要给他两万，条件是要把他们的车开到北方（以逃脱警察的追逐）。她的居高临下的命令口吻，使对方渐渐处于被动地位。可以清楚地看出，这些"I/we will"和"you will"非常适合公爵夫人的生来居有的高傲气质，非常适合她来自贵族家庭的盛气凌人对待"下人"的态度。她的高贵身份使她不愿意在任何情况下处于劣势。因此，这些意态成分的巧妙使用，成功地刻画了公爵夫人精明、强干的性格，预示着这场讨价还价，她必然在气势上胜过饭店侦察员。

10.3.3 The Sound of Music (Fang Yan et al. 2001: 8-9)

10.3.3.1 语篇

(Sister Margaretta Tells Maria that she is expected by the Reverend Mother in her office. Maria follows her in.)

Reverend Mother: You've been unhappy, I'm sorry.

Maria: Reverend Mother.

R.M.: Why did they send you back to us?

Maria: They didn't send me back, Mother. I left.

R.M.: Sit down, Maria. Tell me what happened.

Maria: Well, I ... I was frightened.

R.M.: Frightened? Were they unkind to you?

Maria: Oh, no. I was, I was confused. I felt ... I never felt that way before. I couldn't stay — and I knew if I would be away from it, I'll be safe.

R.M.: Maria, our Abbey is not used to be as an escape. **What is it that you can't face?**

Maria: I can't face him again.

R.M.: **Him?** (*To Sister Margaretta*) Thank you, Sister Margaretta. (*Sister Margaretta leaves the room.*) **Captain Von Trapp? Are you in love**

with him?

Maria: I don't know, I don't know. The Baroness said I was. She said that he was in love with me, but I didn't want to believe it. Oh, there were times when we looked at each other. Oh, Mother, I could hardly breathe.

R.M.: Did you let him see how you felt?

Maria: If I did, I didn't know it. That's what's been torturing me. I was there on God's errand. To have asked for his love would have been wrong. I couldn't stay, I just couldn't. I am ready at this moment to take my vows. Please help me.

R.M.: Maria, the love of a man and a woman is holy too. You have a great capacity to love. What you ***must*** find out is how God wants you to spend your love.

Maria: But I've pledged my life to God. I've pledged my life to his service.

R.M.: My daughter, if you love this man, it doesn't mean you love God less. Now you ***must*** find out. You ***must*** go back.

Maria: Oh, Mother, you can't ask me to do that. Please let me stay. I beg you.

R.M.: Maria, these walls were not built to shut out problems. You ***have to*** face them. You ***have to*** live the life you were born to live. (*Then sings the song "Climb Every Mountain"*.)

10.3.3.2 语篇分析

语篇分析目的：从语气和意态成分的使用，观察院长嬷嬷如何劝说玛丽亚回到冯·特拉普舰长身边以及如何描写院长嬷嬷的性格特点；

情景语境的变量：

语场：玛丽亚回到修道院，院长嬷嬷与她谈话；

语旨：玛丽亚与院长嬷嬷；前者已经辞职，不再当家庭教师，希望成为修女；后者是位长者，担任修道院的最高职位；在修道院修女们好像生活在一个大家庭中，他们之间有社会距离但比较接近；

语式：玛丽亚与院长嬷嬷对话，口语体英语；

语气成分分析：

语气系统：陈述语气或祈使语气的区别；如果选择了陈述语气，还可进一步选择叙述语气或疑问语气；如果选择祈使语气，还可进一步选择是否包含说话者或不包括说话者，而且在每种情况下，说话者和听话者都担任不同的角色，如图 10－5 所示：

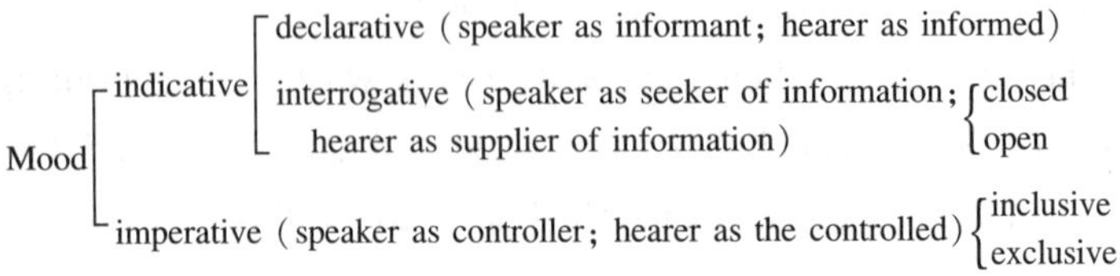

图 10－5　语气系统

语篇语气和意态成分分析：

这段对话中，院长嬷嬷使用了两个祈使句(Sit down, Please. Tell me what happened.)和八个疑问句(带有问号的句子)以及五次表示高量质义务的情态动词(三个“must”,两个“have to”)。

10.3.3.3　评论

祈使句和大量疑问句以及表示高量质义务的情态动词的使用，是这个语篇的语义和文体特点。院长嬷嬷是两个祈使句和八个疑问句的发话人，玛丽亚是动作的执行者和问题的回答者，说明两个参加对话的人的社会地位是不一样的：一个是修道院的院长，有较大的权力；玛丽亚是一名见习修女，处于较低的位置。正是通过这两种语气，院长嬷嬷掌握了他们对话的内容和走向；也正是通过这八个问题，她才了解了玛丽亚的内心活动，了解她苦恼的原因。这就是这两种语气在语篇中的语言功能。同时他们又是生活在修道院这样一个大家庭中，他们的关系就比较接近，比如他们相互称呼“母亲”和“女儿”，而且玛丽亚还把自己爱上了冯·特拉普的内心秘密告诉了院长嬷嬷。因而我们可以说，这两种语气和有关词汇的使用，成功地刻画了一个善良、有着丰富经验的修道院院长的性格和素质。另外，祈使语气和五次表示高量质义务的情态动词 *must*、*have to* 的使用，揭示了对话的另一个含义：虽然院长嬷嬷的话语很友好，但她的话却有着权威性，说话有很重的分量，她的语气会使玛丽亚感到她是代表上帝在说话，因而自己必须顺从上帝的意志，回到冯·特拉普的身边。

10.4 结 语

分析了三段对话，我们可以得出两个结论：第一，韩礼德的系统功能语法框架可以用来揭示语篇的深层含义，可以用来理解和解释语篇的语义和文体特点，这一点不仅对于阐释和赏析语篇至关重要，而且对于英语的阅读教学有着实际的应用价值；第二，“语境-语篇-评论”模式用来分析语篇是可行的。

有一个问题值得讨论：入项选择问题，即除了“分析者的目的和兴趣”（黄国文 2001；Halliday 2002：91；178；195）外，还有什么因素决定了语篇分析者选择某个或某些纯理功能对语篇进行分析？选择与语篇本身的语域和语篇类型以及其他特点有没有关系？国内外系统功能学者似乎都还没有做出明确的回答，有待通过进一步的研究找到答案。

11

Systemic-Functional Linguistics and Film Discourse Analysis*

11.1 Introduction

Huang Guowen (2001), after successfully analyzing discourses of advertisements following the systemic-functional linguistics (SFL) approach, states that this approach is "more suitable for discourse analysis (DA) than any other approaches". This is because this grammar is a "discourse-grammar" "with the grammatical categories explained as the realization of semantic patterns", and "the form of the grammar relates naturally to the meanings that are being encoded" (Halliday 1985/1994); this is because it is a grammar "designed to account for how the language is used" and a grammar, which provides "insights into the meaning and effectiveness of a text" (*ibid.*); this is also because the network of the three meta-functions with their sub-systems, and the levels and the steps for DA are rather

* This chapter is based on a plenary talk presented at a yearly international systemic-functional linguistics conference held in Japan in 2005.

explicitly mapped out. Applying this grammatical framework to DA will indeed enable us to avoid making only a "running commentary" (*ibid.*), which is not based on a discourse grammar.

There are three purposes for writing this chapter: firstly, to further verify the applicability of this linguistic framework to DA; and secondly, to propose a more practical procedure for DA; and thirdly, to illustrate through the analysis of some lively dialogues taken from a classical English film the usefulness of this linguistics theory in revealing the implied meanings of the texts to laymen and particularly to graduate students of linguistics so as for them to realize that the discipline of linguistics can be a very interesting one (or to rectify the wrong conception that it is a boring subject as I have often heard in the past 15 years of teaching SFL).

In the following, the chapter will first discuss the major theoretical aspects of this linguistic framework, i.e. the strata or levels of language and its contexts and their realization relationship, the two levels of and the steps for DA as advocated by Halliday (1985/1994), and then it will present the system of meta-functions and propose the pattern "Context-Text-Commentary in Context" for DA. Finally it will illustrate the application of this approach to analyzing three film dialogues taken from *The Sound of Music* before reaching some conclusions.

11.2 Systemic-Functional Linguistics Framework

11.2.1 Levels of language and the system of meta-functions

SFL regards language as a system of meaning potential realized by a system of three meta-functions constrained by context of culture and context of situation (Halliday 1985/1994). They are represented as five levels below. The relationship among the levels is that of realization: the level above is realized by the level below: context of culture is realized by context of situation, which is realized by semantics, which is, in turn, realized by lexico-grammar, which is, finally, realized by phonology in speaking or graphology in writing, as shown below (Martin 1992; Eggins 1994):

Context of culture
↙
Context of situation
↙
Semantics (Meaning)
↙
Lexico-grammar (Wording)
↙
Phonology (Speaking)
Graphology (Writing)

Figure 11 - 1 Strata of Language and Its Contexts

Context of culture, which represents an abstraction of social activities in our daily life, involves the ideology and various genres in a certain culture (*ibid.*). Therefore, it is a rather abstract and generalized concept. A discourse is a form for actual social communication, which must take place in a certain situation in a certain culture. Therefore, in analyzing a text or discourse, we must take into consideration the situation variables, namely, the content or the **field**, the participants or the **tenor**, and the form of communication or the **mode** (Huang 2001: 72). Concretely, the variable **field** refers to the subject matter or what activities are going on; **tenor** the interpersonal relations involved; and **Mode**: "what part the language is playing" (H & H 1985). They are realized in language at the lexico-grammatical level as **ideational** function, **interpersonal** function and **textual** function respectively (Halliday 1985/1994). Ideational function is the function of representing/reflecting/construing the world; interpersonal the function of assigning roles to the speaker/hearer and/or the reader/writer, and of making judgements of speeches and discourses; and textual the function of organizing different sentences into a coherent text by linguistic devices. Thus, a discourse can be analyzed in terms of the network of the three meta-functions as shown below (Due to the limit of space, we will not elaborate on the subsystems of the three meta-functions.):

- System of meta-functions
  - ideational
    - transitivity
    - voice
    - polarity
  - interpersonal
    - mood
    - modality
    - modulation
    - appraisal system
    - key
  - textual
    - thematic structure
    - information structure
    - cohesion

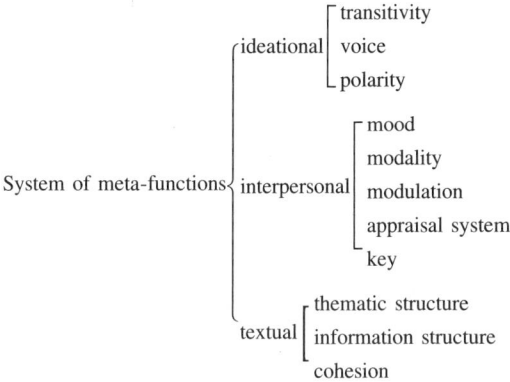

Figure 11 – 2 System of Meta-functions

11.2.2 Levels of DA

Halliday writes that DA can be conducted at two levels. Level One is a process of "the understanding of the text". It is a level to "show how, and why, the text means what it does". In the process of DA, "the multiple meanings" (ideational, interpersonal and textual and their functions in the sub-systems) and "other features are likely to be revealed" (Halliday 1985/1994: xv). In other words, Level One involves a descriptive and interpretive activity on the part of the analyst. The second level is to make an evaluation of whether the text is "effective" and "why it is or is not, an effective text for its own purpose" — "in what respects it succeeds and in what respects it fails or is less successful" (*ibid.*). Therefore, Level Two involves an explanatory and evaluative activity. For this purpose, it "requires an interpretation not only of the text itself but also of its context (context of situation and context of culture), and of the systematic relationship between context and text" (Halliday 1985/1994). This is an activity to reveal how the variables of the context of situation help to create a text or how the text is realized or constrained by the variables of the context. This implies that the analyst needs to decode the more profound meaning and conduct a critical or evaluative study of the text. For achieving this purpose, the analyst needs to make commentaries arising from the use of the lexico-grammatical features of the discourse under study in its context of situation and even in its context of culture.

11.2.3 Steps of DA

Halliday proposes three steps for DA (1985/1994):

1) "Grammatical analysis as the basis";

2) "Commentary in relation to its context of situation and context of culture";

3) "Semiotic analysis because a text is a highly complex phenomenon".

The actual steps involved in a DA may depend on the purpose of DA and the interests of the analyst (Huang 2001), and may also depend on the genre and field of the discourse but this assumption needs further verification. In our practice, we find the pattern **Context-Text-Commentary in relation to Context** is more feasible for film DA (See 10.2.3; Fang 2005).

It is worth noting that during the process of DA we should focus on interpreting the semantic implications as "The process of text analysis is one of interpretation" of meaning (*ibid.*).

11.3 Film Discourse Analysis

11.3.1 Materials

As mentioned before, this chapter will analyze three film dialogues taken from *The Sound of Music*. As a matter of fact, these are examples taken from a textbook entitled *Evaluations of Episodes in English Classic Films* (Fang Yan et al. 2001). In this book, we have analyzed over 30 dialogues taken from 10 films①. Concretely, every lesson of the book introduces a film, which consists of the following parts: introduction to the main characters, synopsis of the film, translation of the synopsis, representative dialogues and their translations, analyses of the dialogues in Chinese by applying the relevant theory of Systemic Functional Linguistics, a list of key words and expressions, and finally questions for discussion for the students. The task of the present writer for the book is to analyze these film dialogues by applying the SFL framework (For short of space, we cannot include the analysis of the other film dialogues in this chapter. We have taken some of them from four films — *Casablanca*, *Roman Holiday*, *Kramer Vs Kramer* and *On Golden Pond* and put them in the attachment.). But before that, let's discuss briefly some features of films in general.

11.3.2 Features of films

We find at least four features of the genre of film: 1) Film is recognized as a special genre in art and it has quite a few sub-genres: romance, musical, detective, fairy, moral, horror, thriller, spy, etc. 2) A film is the product by means of multi-media: visual, audio, linguistic, non-linguistic, etc. ... 3) A film is usually multiple-genre based, that is, it is realized by several genres at the same time. It may contain genres such as a list of film producers, dialogues, music, songs, narrations, dances, photography, actions, a list of the cast, etc. 4) A film is a composite of discourses.

A discourse can be defined as a "semantic unit" whose length is not

① The ten films are: *The Sound of Music*, *Thirty-nine Steps*, *Casablanca*, *The Wizard of Oz*, *Roman Holiday*, *Being There*, *Kramer Vs Kramer*, *On Golden Pond*, *Beauty and Beast* and *Forrest Gump*.

limited: a whole novel can be regarded as containing one text; a word may also be looked upon as a discourse so long as it expresses a complete meaning (H & H 1976). However, some linguists (Martin 2001) challenge this definition by saying that in a more accurate sense, a big discourse is a discourse network which contains more than one semantic unit, thus it being able to be looked upon as a composite discourse consisting of discourses. These discourses are linked by the constraint of expressing the main theme of the big discourse, in our case, of a film.

11.3.3 Focus and procedures

In this chapter we will focus on the analysis of some linguistic features in episodes of film dialogues from the SFL perspective.

We shall follow the procedures as below in analyzing film discourses (Hereafter, FD):

1) Analysis of the three variables of the context of situation, which is preparing for Step 3 [We find without this step, it would be hard to link features of some meta-functions to the context of situation when we make the commentary as proposed by Halliday (1985/1994)];

2) Grammatical analysis of some features in terms of meta-functions;

3) Commentary making: interpreting and evaluating the grammatical features by linking the phenomena of particular meta-functions with their context of situation and/or context of culture;

4) Semiotic analysis if necessary because "a text is a highly complex phenomenon" (Halliday 1985/1994). However in the analysis in this chapter, we shall not take this step as it will be very lengthy and involve too many cultural factors.

Concretely, we shall take the following steps:

Dialogue One and Dialogue Two:

1) Contextual Analysis of Dialogue One

2) Grammatical Analysis of Dialogue One

3) Contextual Analysis of Dialogue Two

4) Grammatical Analysis of Dialogue Two

5) Commentary (We make only one commentary as we are to compare the two dialogues.)

Dialogue Three:

1) Contextual Analysis of Dialogue Three

2) Grammatical Analysis of Dialogue Three

3) Commentary

11.3.4 Analysis of some features of the meta-functions of FD

We shall present the analyses of three film dialogues taken from the film *The Sound of Music* following the procedure mentioned above: first the analysis of the variables of the context of the dialogues, and then of some features of meta-functions of the dialogues, and finally, making commentaries based on the analysis by relating it to the particular context of situation of the dialogues.

Before we continue with the grammatical analysis, we need to mention a very important point: the choice of the meta-functions to be analyzed. Halliday states that every clause and every discourse construes three meta-functions, namely, ideational, interpersonal and textual; and if necessary we can analyze a clause or a discourse from all of the three functions, as he did in his book (1985/1994). Yet, it is practical to concentrate on one or two of them or even on some of the functional components (Halliday 1973; Huang 2001). We assume that the choice could also be closely related with the genre or register of a discourse. For example, if we analyze a detective film, which is full of actions, then perhaps we would concentrate on studying the features of the actions under the transitivity system of the ideational function. But with films full of dialogues to show the relationship between/among people, then we would naturally focus on disclosing the personal relationships by dealing with the interpersonal function. For example, in this chapter, as we shall illustrate the relations between Maria and Von Trapp (in the first two dialogues) and those between Maria and the Reverend Mother (in the third dialogue), we shall naturally focus on analyzing the mood and modal elements in the three dialogues. Therefore, before starting our analysis, we need to look at the Mood and the Modality systems: the Modulation and the Modalization respectively:

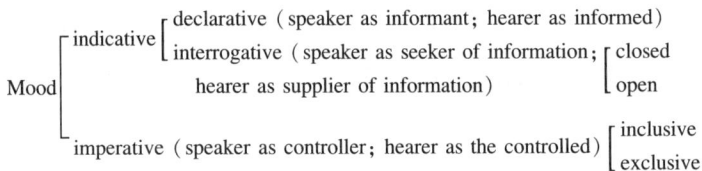

- Mood
  - indicative
    - declarative (speaker as informant; hearer as informed)
    - interrogative (speaker as seeker of information; hearer as supplier of information)
      - closed
      - open
  - imperative (speaker as controller; hearer as the controlled)
    - inclusive
    - exclusive

Figure 11 - 3 The Mood System in English

From Figure 11 - 3, we can see that the function of the speaker using the imperative mood is to control the orientation of the dialogue and that of the speaker using the interrogative mood is to seek information from the hearer, who, in an unmarked situation, has to supply the information being sought, and the function of the speaker using the declarative mood is to provide information to the hearer (Halliday 1985/1994).

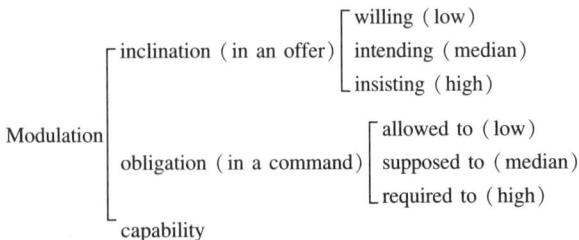

- Modulation
  - inclination (in an offer)
    - willing (low)
    - intending (median)
    - insisting (high)
  - obligation (in a command)
    - allowed to (low)
    - supposed to (median)
    - required to (high)
  - capability

Figure 11 - 4 The Modulation System

Figure 11 – 4 tells us that there are three options in the Modulation system: obligation, inclination and capability, and the sub-system of inclination and obligation render at least three degrees: high, median and low (*ibid.*).

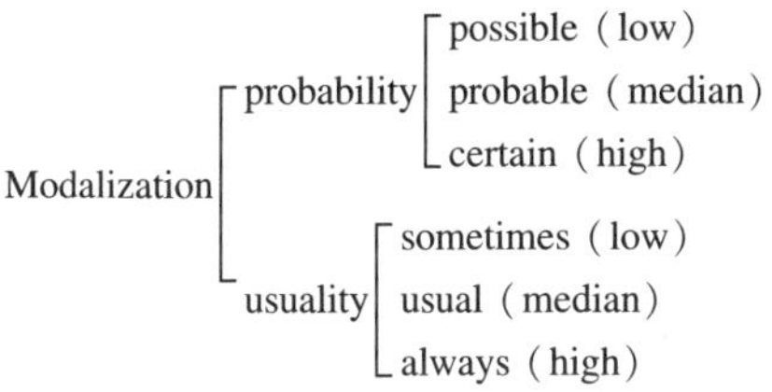

Figure 11 – 5 The Modalization System

Figure 11 – 5 indicates that there are two options in the Modalization system: probability and usuality, and each of them at least renders three degrees: high, median and low (*ibid.*).

11.3.4.1 Analysis of Dialogue One

Contextual Features

Field: the first meeting between Maria, the heroin, and Von Trapp, the hero, in the hero's lobby;

Tenor: Maria vs Von Trapp; the former is a young woman studying to become a nun at an Abbey and now she is assigned as the governess to the Von Trapp family whereas the latter a retired wealthy naval captain, the master of the house, and the father of seven children and widowed several years ago; the social distance between them being maximum, with Von Trapp in a more powerful social position;

Mode: a dialogue in English with clauses in ellipsis;

Contextual Configuration: Von Trapp tells Maria what are the proper things to do in the house (H & H 1985).

Grammatical Analysis

We shall compare the elements of mood of the two dialogues between Maria and Von Trapp in our commentary so that we may find the changes of the relationship between the two characters in the film. But first let's see the analysis of the grammatical features of Dialogue One. (Notice that the bold-faced words are the verb processes in the imperative mood, and the words in bold face and italics are indicating the use of a certain modal element).

(Scene One: First meeting between Maria and Von Trapp after Maria arrives at the latter's house.)

...

Von Trapp: I'm afraid you don't look very much like a governess. (Suddenly notices her dress) **Turn round, please**.

Maria: What?

V.T.: **Turn**. **Hat off.** The dress, you ***have to*** put on another one before you meet the children.

...

V.T.: Every morning you ***must*** drill the children in their studies. I ***will not permit*** them to dream away there on some other days. Each afternoon, they'***ll*** (**shall**) march on the ground, breathing deeply. ***Bedtime is strictly observed.*** No obsessions (**No obsessions are allowed**).

We have found that there are three imperative clauses with only one "please"; three modal verbs of high value (*have to*, *must*, *shall*) to show requirement; one modal verb of insisting (*will*) + a verb of obligation (*permit*); and two passive clauses stating rules to be followed.

11.3.4.2 Dialogue Two

Contextual Features

Field: Von Trapp expresses his love to Maria, who has returned from the Abbey;

Tenor: Von Trapp vs Maria, the distance becoming intimate, standing on an equal status;

Mode: first a dialogue in English and then songs sung to express their emotions;

Contextual configuration: Von Trapp is to propose to Maria.

Grammatical Analysis

(Maria and Von Trapp meet in the garden after Von Trapp calls off the engagement with the Baroness.)

V.T.: Hello, I thought (=**perhaps**) I just ***might*** find you here.

Maria: Was there ..., was there something you wanted?

V.T.: Hm, no, no. **Sit down**, please. Please ... *May* I? ... I *was just hoping* you *might perhaps*, *perhaps* change your mind?

In this dialogue, we have found one imperative clause followed by two "please"; one interrogative clause beginning with "may", asking for permission to sit down; the modal verb "might" denoting possibility; one verb "hope" in the past progressive tense expressing inclination and tentativeness; a mental process: cognition "thought", functioning as a grammatical metaphor denoting possibility and finally two "perhaps" also conveying the meaning of possibility and tentativeness.

Commentary

In Scene One, the use of the imperative mood (*turn*, *please*, *turn and hat off*), the model verbs of obligation of high value (*must*, *permit*, *shall*) and the passive structure, which states a rule to be observed in Von Trapp's family, shows that Von Trapp is the master of the house, or in total control of what should happen in the house; Maria is only a governess who should obey whatever he says. Then in Scene Two, the use of the two *please* (as a plea), the model verbs of "*may*" (obligation: allowed, here asking for Maria's permission), "*might*" (modalization : probability : possibility) and the verb "*hope*" (modulation : inclination : intending) and the hesitation tones (I thought) and the two "perhaps" expressing possibility is to denote the subtle change of Von Trapp's tone when speaking to Maria: being very polite and tentative, treating her as his equal because he is going to propose to Maria. So the change of the mood and the use of different types of Modality in the two dialogues imply the possible change of the relationship between the two main characters; or more accurately, the different types of modality reflect the change of Von Trapp's attitude towards Maria: from a naval captain who always gives orders into a nice and loving person who treats Maria as his equal and indeed has fallen in love with her.

11.3.4.3 Analysis of Dialogue Three

Contextual Features

Field: Maria has returned to the Abbey and the Reverend Mother has a talk with her;

Tenor: Maria and Reverend Mother; the former has resigned her work as a governess and wishes to become a nun; the latter is an elderly nun, holding the highest position in the Abbey, in which all are living in a family; the distance between them is rather close;

Mode: a dialogue in English with clauses in ellipsis

Contextual configuration: The R.M. persuades Maria to go back to Von Trapp's family.

Grammatical Analysis

We shall look at the interrogative and imperative mood and the modal verbs in the utterances by the R.M. in the dialogue:

(Sister Margaretta Tells Maria that she is expected by the Reverend Mother in her office. Maria follows her in.)

Reverend Mother: You've been unhappy, I'm sorry.

Maria: Reverend Mother.

R.M.: Why did they send you back to us?

Maria: They didn't send me back, Mother. I left.

R.M.: Sit down, Maria. Tell me what happened.

Maria: Well, I ... I was frightened.

R.M.: Frightened? Were they unkind to you?

Maria: Oh, no. I was, I was confused. I felt ... I never felt that way before. I couldn't stay — and I knew if I would be away from it, I'll be safe.

R.M.: Maria, our Abbey is not used to be as an escape. **What is it that you can't face**?

Maria: I can't face him again.

R.M.: **Him**? (*To Sister Margaretta*) Thank you, Sister Margaretta. (*Sister Margaretta leaves the room.*) **Captain Von Trapp**? **Are you in love with him**?

Maria: I don't know, I don't know. The Baroness said I was. She said that he was in love with me, but I didn't want to believe it. Oh, there were times when we looked at each other. Oh, Mother, I could hardly breathe.

R.M.: Did you let him see how you felt?

Maria: If I did, I didn't know it. That's what's been torturing me. I was there on God's errand. To have asked for his love would have been wrong. I couldn't stay, I just couldn't. I am ready at this moment to take my vows. Please help me.

R.M.: Maria, the love of a man and a woman is holy too. You have a great capacity to love. What you ***must*** find out is how God wants you to spend your love.

Maria: But I've pledged my life to God. I've pledged my life to his service.

R.M.: My daughter, if you love this man, it doesn't mean you love God less. Now you ***must*** find out. You ***must*** go back.

Maria: Oh, Mother, you can't ask me to do that. Please let me stay. I beg you.

R.M.: Maria, these walls were not built to shut out problems. You ***have to*** face them. You ***have to*** live the life you were born to live. (*Then sings the song "Climb Every Mountain"*).

In the analysis, we have found that there are two imperative clauses ("Sit down, Please." "Tell me what happened.") and eight interrogative clauses (those ended with the question marks); and five modal verbs denoting obligation of high level (3 "must" and 2 "have to")

Commentary

From the discussion of the tenor of this dialogue, we know that the two interlocutors are in different positions: the R.M. is the head of the Abbey, thus more powerful and Maria is practicing to be a nun, so in a much lower position, as revealed by the two imperative clauses and the eight interrogative clauses used by the Reverent Mother. It is through these two types of mood that the R.M. is able to control the content and the direction of the talk; and it is also through these questions, which Maria has to answer, that she is able to draw out Maria's innermost mind. Yet at the same time they are members of the same family in the Abbey, and therefore, their relationship is rather close as exemplified by the lexical terms "mother" and "daughter" and the confession made by Maria of her love to the R.M.. Thus, these two types of mood and the relevant lexical words have successfully fulfilled their functions in depicting the character of the R.M. as a kind and experienced church leader. Furthermore, the use of the imperative mood and the 5 modal verbs "must" and "have to" (expressing the highest degree in terms of modulation: obligation: required) reveals another phase of the dialogue: her words are cordial, yet at the same time authoritative as she was a representative of God, which would make Maria comply with the will of God — implying effectively the power of her words as a leader in the Abbey (Fang et al. 2001).

11.4 Conclusion

From the analyses of the three dialogues we can arrive at two conclusions: firstly, Halliday's systemic-functional linguistic framework is applicable to disclosing the profound meanings of film discourses and to understanding the semantic and stylistic features of these discourses, which is essential for the interpretation and appreciation of a discourse of this genre; and secondly, the "Context-Text-Commentary in relation to Context" analytical pattern is feasible for film discourse analysis. (For short of space, we cannot include the analysis of the other film dialogues in the chapter proper. We have selected some of them from four films — *Casablanca*, *Roman Holiday*, *Kramer vs Kramer* and *On Golden Pond* — in the attachment.)

There is an issue, however, arising from the process of analyzing film discourses, which needs further discussions. That is, since there could be smaller discourses within a big discourse as mentioned by Martin (2001), we may assume there are two levels of discourses: hyper-discourse and the discourses below it. If this assumption is accepted, then we may say that the linguistic representations in a film, for example, the narrations and the dialogues (the small discourses) are used to serve to reveal the theme of the hyper-discourse of the film. It then follows that the hyper-discourse of the film would have a hyper-field, a hyper-tenor and a hyper-mode. And in turn, each small discourse would have its own field, tenor and mode.

We know that different films deal with different subject matters so their fields would be different; the interpersonal relationship in films also varies with the types of films. Although all films share similarities in terms of mode: the utility of the audio-visual means, the main modes for presenting the films could be different, for example, in some, the music scenario only serves as the background, but in others as one of the main means to unfold the plot such as in musical films. Following the assumption made above that in every film, there could be a hyper-field, a hyper-tenor and a hyper-mode dominating the development of the film, we may further argue that as a film unfolds and the different small discourses are taking place in different situations, the field, tenor and sometimes mode in those situations would change, and it could be the dynamic changes of the three variables that push forward the development of the plot in the film. But this needs further studies to have it verified.

Another question worth noting and discussing is: what are the parameters for choosing particular meta-functions for the analysis apart from the purposes and the analysts' interests in a particular discourse? Would the nature of a text, for example the register or genre, also determine the choices, as shown in our discussions above? We are expecting further research on this issue.

12

经典英语电影精彩对话分析

12.1 引　言

2001年笔者曾与两位同事合作编写了一本高级听力教材，书名为《经典影片精彩片段语言评析》。我们选择了十部英美经典影片①作为教材，分成十章，每章的内容均包括主要人物介绍（英语）、故事梗概（英语及译文）、精彩对话、对话的词汇和表达方式、对话译文、对话分析、（电影歌曲原文）、口语练习、讨论的问题。除了统筹全书，我还负责应用系统功能语言学理论（Halliday 1985/1994），分析英语对话部分的语言特点及其含义。但是考虑到教材的使用者通常并不具备语言学的基础知识，所以笔者在分析中没有讨论理论问题，也避免使用难懂的学术用语，而是尽量用通俗的语言进行阐释。2004年我受邀参加了日本功能语言学年会，并作了主题报告，题目是"Systemic-Functional Linguistics and Film Discourse Analysis"（《系统功能语言学与电影语篇分析》，见本书第11章）。由于主题发言篇幅有限，只使用了《音乐之声》中的三个对话为例，作为对该理论

① 这十部影片是：《音乐之声》《三十九级台阶》《卡萨布兰卡》《绿野仙踪》《罗马假日》《就在那儿》《克莱默夫妇》《金色池塘》《美女与野兽》《阿甘正传》。

适用于语篇分析的佐证。为了更充分说明系统功能语言学对电影语篇分析的适用性,本文再选择原教材中的四部影片的对话分析,作为对上述一章的补充说明。这四部影片包括《卡萨布兰卡》《罗马假日》《克莱默夫妇》《金色池塘》。由于本书的篇幅有限,略去详细的对话原文。

12.2 经典影片对话分析

12.2.1 《卡萨布兰卡》(*Casablanca*)

选择的五段对话是情节发展中的几个关键场景,能大致揭示四个主要人物:**里克**(Rick — Richard Blain)、**伊尔萨**(Ilsa Lund)、**拉兹罗**(Victor Laszlo)、**雷诺**(Runo — Captain Louis Renault)之间的复杂关系,以及他们之间的矛盾和冲突如何得到解决或化解。这几段对话还集中勾画出**里克**这位反法西斯战士的高尚品质,揭示爱情和友谊的真谛。

第一段对话,提出了故事情节向前推进的主要矛盾:反法西斯战线的领导人**拉兹罗**,要从咖啡店老板**里克**手中得到出境证而遭到拒绝。

这一段对话的一个突出特点是:大量使用了表示人物身份和性格特点的动词现在时和过去时。在数十个主要动词中,这样的动词占了十几个(如 **Victor**:*Is* there some other place? It'*s* rather confidential, what I *have* to say .... It'*s* my privilege to be one of the leaders of the great movement. You know what it *means* to the work, to .... **Rick**:I'*m* not interested in politics. The problems of the world *are* not in my department. I'*m* a saloon keeper. ... **Victor**:... you *have* quite a record. *Isn't* strange that ... ? *Are* you enough of a businessman to ... There must *be* some reason ...)。这些动词说明了**拉兹罗**和**里克**的身份和他们各自的特点:**拉兹罗**是反法西斯运动的领导人,**里克**曾经站在被压迫人民的一边,但现在他自称只是一个咖啡店的老板,对政治毫无兴趣。这些动词与其他一些表示行为的动词如"*do*""*run*""*fight*"的应用,不仅描述了这两个人过去的

经历或现在正在从事的工作(**Victor**: You know what I'*ve been doing* .... You *ran* guns to Ethiopia. Isn't it strange that you always happen to *be fighting* on the side of the underdog?),而且也让作为自由战士、机智勇敢的**拉兹罗**,与表面玩世不恭、而实际上有着坚忍性格的**里克**,形成了鲜明的对照。对话一开始,**拉兹罗**就向**里克**说明,他逃离卡萨布兰卡去美国的原因并不是为了自己,而是为了成千上万的人民(You know what it means to the work, to the lives of thousands of thousands of people that I be free to reach America and continue my work.)。但当**里克**拒绝参与这件事之后,**拉兹罗**马上提起里克曾参加过反法西斯斗争(You fought against fascists in Spain),试图再次引起**里克**对被压迫者的同情,但**里克**表面上却无动于衷。此时,**拉兹罗**不得不将**里克**当作一名商人,想用金钱从**里克**手中买到出境证。这些不同手段的使用,表明**拉兹罗**是一位有着丰富斗争经验的战士,他知道如何去达到奋斗的目的。但出乎意料的是,所有这一切都丝毫没有打动**里克**,**里克**称妨碍**拉兹罗**获得出境证的正是他的妻子。

对话结束时,双方不断重复"*your wife*""*my wife*?""ask *your wife*",这两个词形成了这一段对话的信息焦点,不仅将获取出境证的关键人物**伊尔萨**推了出来,而且也制造了**里克**与**伊尔萨**之间关系的悬念,让观众去关注这三个人的关系将如何进一步发展。

第二段是**伊尔萨**与**里克**之间最精彩的对话之一。

在被告知她是妨碍丈夫获得出境证的人之后,**伊尔萨**设法单独与**里克**见面。她想尽办法说服**里克**帮助她丈夫,但都没成功。最后**伊尔萨**和盘托出她在巴黎与**里克**不辞而别的真实情况,**里克**才答应帮助**拉兹罗**,条件是**伊尔萨**必须离开**拉兹罗**跟他在一起。

这一段对话中,**伊尔萨**使用了一切能缩短他们感情距离的人际功能手段,要求**里克**帮助**拉兹罗**逃出卡市。充满深情的话语与表示高量质义务-要求的情态动词"*must*"、甚至命令的语气形成了明显的反差,但是这两种语气都是为了一个目的:为**拉兹罗**搞到出境证。

一开始她就称呼**里克**"Richard",这是他们两人相爱时她使用的称呼,而且一直保持到故事的结尾,可见**里克**在**伊尔萨**心目中占据了多么重要的地位。后来她一再向**里克**表达自己的感情,多次反复说"I loved you"或"I still love you",表达了她的一片真情。**伊尔萨**还一再表示不会再离他而去——“I know that I’ll never have the strength to leave you again.” “I ran away from you once. I can’t do it again.”，表达了她愿意与**里克**永远厮守在一起的决心。谈话结束时，她的一句“I wish I didn’t love you so much”更显得情真意切。但是对于她来说，最重要的莫过于帮助她的丈夫搞到出境证，能使他能继续从事反法西斯战争的伟大事业。一见面，她就要求**里克**“You must give me those letters.” “I must ask you to put your feelings aside for something more important.”。其中“must/have to(do)”是表示高量值义务-要求的情态动词，接近命令的语气，在这一段对话中先后出现三次(除了上面两个例子，还有“You have to think for both of us, for all of us.”)，可见**伊尔萨**要求的迫切。最突出的是 “Now I want those letters. Get them for me.” “... put them on the table”，将“要求”变成了“命令”，表现出她不达目的誓不罢休的决心。

表示动作、描述状态和事实的动词过去时和现在时/现在进行时的大量使用，是这一段对话的另一个重要语言特点。它们清楚地交代了**伊尔萨**的感情生活经历、她与两个男人之间的关系、她现在对他们的态度以及她对**里克**的深情（**Ilsa**：Richard, I *had to see* you. **Rick**：It’*s* “Richard” again. We’*re* back in Paris ... how you *feel* about me, ...? **Ilsa**：Richard, we *loved* each other once. If those days *meant* anything at all to you ... It *wasn’t* long after we *were* married that Victor *went* back to .... They *needed* him ... Then it *came* he *was* dead ... I *was* lonely ... Then I *met* you. **Rick**：... Why *weren’t* you honest with me? Why *did* keep your marriage a secret? **Ilsa**：It *was* not my secret, Richard. Victor *wanted* it that way .... **Rick**：... When *did* you first find out that he *was* alive? **Ilsa**：Just before you and I *were* to leave Paris together ... You see he *needed* me. I *wanted* to tell you, but I *didn’t* dare. I *ran* away from you once. I *can’t do* it again. I *don’t* know what’*s* right any longer. I *wish* I *didn’t love* you so much.”)。这些动词的使用也消除了**里克**对**伊尔萨**的误解，使他转变了对**伊尔萨**的态度。

第三段对话仍发生在**伊尔萨**与**里克**之间，是一个过渡段。此时**雷诺**正在检查**拉兹罗**的出境文件。**里克**仍未向**拉兹罗**说明他必须自己单独离境，**伊尔萨**焦急万分。**里克**要她相信他会妥善处理一切，**伊尔萨**表示完全信赖里克。但**里克**究竟会怎么样处理他们三个人之间的关系仍是一个悬念。**伊尔萨**说“*you were able to arrange everything for us*”用的是过去时态，意在提醒**里克**自己的保证，与上一段对话中里克说的“*I will*（*think for all of us*）”相互照应，是时态作为衔接手段的一个很好的例子。另外，“*all right*”重复数次，也值得注意。第一次是**伊尔萨**对**里克**说“*It is all right, isn't it?*”，在肯定的语气之后又加上了疑问的语气，是希望**里克**给予肯定的答复。**里克**则回答“*Everything is quite all right*”，使**伊尔萨**放下心来，于是她说“*All right*”。简单的两个词重复数次，却包含了不同的意思，而且也使上下文连贯起来。

第四段对话是描绘**里克**的为人的最重要的一个场面。有三点值得注意：第一，从**里克**与**拉兹罗**的对话中，我们了解**里克**实际上并不仅仅是一个咖啡店老板，他还是一个能不惜自己的生命和财产，去帮助战友的反法西斯战士。**拉兹罗**要付给他购买出境证的钱时，他只简单地回答“*Keep it, you'll need it in America.*”。虽然没有提到这笔钱的真正用途，但联系到第一段对话中**拉兹罗**告诉他自己去美国是为了“*the lives of thousands and thousands of people*”，不难看出**里克**行为的高尚。后来，他拔枪相助，更说明了他是一个与**拉兹罗**有着共同目标的战友。

第二，他也是一个有着丰富斗争经验的、既有胆识又懂得战略战术的战士。从表面上看，他似乎站在协助德国人的法国军官**雷诺**一边，他似乎可以为了爱情而出卖灵魂。**雷诺**说的“*Love seems to have triumphed over virtue*”，似乎是对**里克**本质的写照。但就在**雷诺**逮捕**拉兹罗**时，**里克**掏出了手枪对准**雷诺**（“*Louis, I wouldn't like to shoot you, but I will if you take one more step.*”）。话语中“will”表示决心，即一定会这样做，使这个法国军官吃惊不已（*You've taken leave of your senses?*）。**里克**还命令**雷诺**把枪放下，把手放在桌子上（*Keep your hands on the table.*），并且让他马上与监管飞机场的德国军官通话取得联系，以避免给**拉兹罗**出境带来麻烦。他的这一连串行动，无疑只有一个老练的战士经过深思熟虑、周密安排后才能做得出来。有一句话集中体现了他的干练与多智。当**雷诺**逮捕**拉兹罗**时，**里克**一边将手枪对准**雷诺**，一边说：“*Not so fast, Louis. Nobody is going to be arrested, not for a while.*”。一个“*not so fast*”，一个“*not for a while*”，一前一后，一个是谈话的出发点，一个是谈话的中心，加强了否定的语气。从他称**雷诺**为“*Louis*”并与不带任何感情色彩的中性名词“*nobody*”一起连用，起到了安定**雷诺**情绪、使他不至于太多疑的作用。也说明了他深知为了达到目的,在斗争中有时需要含糊其词,以迷惑对手。这句话还留下一个悬念:**拉兹罗**究竟能不能与他妻子一起离开,为以后情节的曲折发展做了铺垫。

第三,在这个场景中,**雷诺**的话语耐人寻味。开始他对**拉兹罗**的态度是非常坚决的,因为他认为自己做的事德国人肯定会高兴,而且他还以为自己是在帮**里克**的忙,使**里克**能与**伊尔萨**圆满结合。但他并不知道他是中了**里克**的圈套,所以当**里克**用手枪威逼他时,他着实吃惊不小。但作为法国军官他又不愿为德国人丧命,所以对里克的威逼没有丝毫的反抗。**雷诺**的这种态度折射出二战中法国统治阶层的软弱和两面性格。最后他似乎明白了**里克**的用意。在与德国军官通话时,他故意用了两句既表示客观存在又含糊其词的句式——"*There are two letters of transit for Lisbon Plane.*""*There's to be no trouble about it.*",既没有指明谁要登上飞机,又没有道出不要给谁造成麻烦,与上面提到的**里克**那句话(*Nobody is going to be ...*)前后呼应。**雷诺**使用客观的口吻显得自然、妥帖,看不出任何破绽。

第五段对话发生在机场。故事情节发展到了高潮,**里克**与**伊尔萨**、**拉兹罗**、**雷诺**的关系逐渐趋于明朗。

从**里克**的言谈之中,我们看到,他对**伊尔萨**的感情已从狭隘的两性之间的爱恋,升华到了一个更高的境界。他虽对**伊尔萨**依然一往情深,但这种感情远远超出两人终身厮守的愿望。他事事处处都为心爱的人考虑,不仅考虑**伊尔萨**若留下来可能遭遇的危险,而且还考虑到她未来的情感生活,可谓周到细心之极(*Last night ... You said I was to do the thinking for both of us. Well, I've done a lot of it since then, but it all adds up in one thing: you get on that plane with Victor where you belong to.*)。对**里克**来讲,**伊尔萨**曾经爱过他,而且在误会消除后,她仍然爱着他,这就足够了(*We'll always have Paris. We didn't have it. We lost it until you came to Casablanca. We got it back last night ... .*)。"We'*ll* always have Paris."是的,巴黎那段美好的感情生活将永远留在他们的记忆里。当**伊尔萨**说"*I said I would never leave you.*",**里克**肯定地回答"You never *will.*"。暗示**伊尔萨**,她的身影将永远伴随着他以后的生活。

对于他自己与**伊尔萨**和**拉兹罗**之间的复杂感情,**里克**表现出一个真正男子汉的坦荡与无私。他决定让**伊尔萨**跟随她丈夫一起逃走,不仅出于对**伊尔萨**安全的考虑，更重要的是他很清楚这样做，将有利于支持**拉兹罗**从事反法西斯斗争的伟大事业。他明白"*You're part of his work, the thing that keeps him going.*"。虽然他自称"*I'm not good at being noble.*"，而他的所作所为将他无私和高尚的情操充分展现了出来。为了消除可能因为他与**伊尔萨**之间的关系，在**拉兹罗**夫妇的未来生活中留下阴影，他在临别前特别告诉**拉兹罗**，他与**伊尔萨**之间的关系已经结束，再一次表现了他的真诚与坦荡。

在这个场景中，**里克**与**雷诺**的关系非常微妙。一方面**雷诺**是咖啡店的常客，从某种意义上讲，他是**里克**的老朋友，所以**里克**始终称呼他为"*Louis*"，而且在说话时避免使用带有敌意的语言。但另一方面，因为**雷诺**在政治上听命于德国人，**里克**又对**雷诺**保持着高度的警惕。他对**拉兹罗**说的一句话"*I'm staying here with him till the plane gets safely away.*"，表面上平淡无奇，丝毫没有火药味，而实际上却表达了另一层含义。这里表示动作过程的动词"*am staying*"是行为过程"*am watching*"的隐喻，这句话的潜在意思是"我将在这里一直看着他（**雷诺**），以免他去报告德国人"。**雷诺**是一个聪明的法国军官，他从**里克**一系列的言行中明白，**里克**为了帮助**拉兹罗**夫妇逃出卡市是做了充分的准备的。他的一句话"*You think of everything.*"中，表示心理过程的动词"*think*"与它的补语"*everything*"的连用，是对里克遇事均周密思考的准确评价。**雷诺**意识到与**里克**作对，对自己不会有任何好处，因而他事事顺从**里克**。当他终于明白，**里克**并不是一个感情用事的普通人，而是一名爱国者时，他又设法保护了**里克**，并决定与**里克**一同逃往刚果，因为那里是一个尚未被德军占领的法属殖民地。**雷诺**的这一决定也打动了**里克**，**里克**说："*Louis I think this is the beginning of a beautiful friendship.*"（见方琰等：Synopsis，2001），预示他们将同甘共苦，他们的相识将发展成真正的美好友谊。这句话也因此成为家喻户晓的至理名言。

在**里克**与**伊尔萨**、**拉兹罗**、**雷诺**的交谈中，我们不仅再一次领略到**里克**的干练与周到，而且看到了一个与咖啡店老板身份大不相同的、无私无畏的反法西斯爱国者的形象；从他对自己与**伊尔萨**和**拉兹罗**之间关系的妥善处理中，观众领略到了爱情的真正含意；从他与**雷诺**关系的戏剧性变化中，观众似乎懂得了真正友谊的内涵。

12.2.2 《罗马假日》(*Roman Holiday*)

这是一部经典的爱情故事片。影片讲述访问罗马的某个欧洲国家的公主**安**(Princess Ann),与一位美国记者**乔**(Joe Bradley)邂逅的故事。影片告诉观众,人们的社会地位往往决定他们的命运,包括他们的爱情生活。一个必须处处以国家利益为重的公主,必须牺牲对自由生活的向往和对美好爱情的追求。(当该国驻罗马大使询问她失踪的24小时的行踪时,她回答"Were I not completely aware of my duty to my country, I would not have come back tonight or indeed ever again.") 因此,她与一位平民之间的爱情,注定是一个悲剧的结局,这也是影片最感人之处。影片还告诉观众,真正的爱情是无私的,它不仅可以超越社会地位,而且也能超越世俗的欲望。刚开始,**乔**在得知**安**是一位公主时,马上意识到她的新闻价值,意识到对她的报道,可以给他带来巨大的经济利益,因而他与摄影师**欧文**(Irving)设了圈套,给**安**偷拍了许多照片,**乔**还对**安**的行踪做了详细的记录。但是他在爱上了**安**之后,便毅然放弃了对她报道的机会,最后冒着被解雇的压力,对报社老板说"I have no story"。他对**安**的感情也打动了摄影师**欧文**,在**安公主**召开的新闻记者会上,**欧文**将一叠她访问罗马的照片交还给了**她**。故事的结尾告诉观众,**安**和**乔**此后将各自回到现实的生活中去,他们短暂的爱情经历只能到此结束。

我们选择了四段在故事情节和语言的使用方面具有代表性的对话。

第一段对话发生在欢迎**安公主**访问罗马举行的舞会之后。**安**回到寝宫,宫廷侍女服侍她就寝,同时给她宣读第二天访问的活动安排。对话通过三组意义不同的词汇链以及某些词汇的重现这样两种手法,将**安**对宫廷生活方式的厌倦和她的逆反心理淋漓尽致地刻画了出来。

第一组词汇链包括:my night-gown(s) — my underwear — milk and cracker — tomorrow's schedule: breakfast — leave — be presented — inspection — present olive tree — new fondling home — preside over — trade relations — recent progress — lunch — wear — carry — very small pink roses — presentation — review 等等。从**安**的睡袍到睡前的饮食,从访问活动的具体安排到公主在某个场合的衣着和行为举止,都有着严格的规定,不能有丝毫的差错,而且日复一日,她必须说着同样的话,重复着

同样类型的活动，这样的宫廷生活让**安**感到窒息。

第二组词汇链包括：pajamas — there are people who sleep with absolutely nothing on at all — listen 等，代表**安**羡慕和向往的自由自在的、普通人的生活方式。

第三组词汇链：not two hundred years old — tired of sleep — not a sleep of a wink — thank you/no thank you — die — leave me — die 将她的厌倦情绪充分反映了出来，难怪她最后终于再也不能忍受，歇斯底里地哭了起来。

每一组词汇链都有着一定的象征意义，第一组代表严格规定的宫廷生活方式，第二组代表与之相反的另外一种不受任何拘束的生活方式，第三组代表她对宫廷生活的厌烦情绪和她内心的苦恼。

词汇的重现加强了对**安**的情绪的描述。谈话一开始**安**一连说了三句话，重复了三个"hate"，渲染了她对宫廷生活的厌倦情绪。后来当侍女谈到第二天的活动中会有人献礼物时，**安**机械地重复着通常在这种场合应该说的答谢词"Thank you"（三次），但是她并没有听清楚这是什么场合，当侍女纠正她不应该接受礼品时，她又毫不动脑子地说道"No, thank you"（三次），有时甚至连话都没听清楚就随便选择其中一个。当她实在忍受不了这种繁文缛节哭起来以后，侍女没有办法只能去请医生，**安**一连说了几句含有 *die* 或 *leave* 的话（I'm dying. Please let me die. Please let me die. Please leave me! Leave me! I'll die ...），这两个词的重复将她的疲倦、厌烦的情绪表现得淋漓尽致。

第二段对话的背景是这样的：**乔**将睡在街上的**安**带回自己的公寓，第二天上班，偶尔才知道在他屋子里睡觉的竟是一位公主。回到屋子，两人开始了一段非常有趣的交谈。两个使用的语言准确地表达了他们不同出身、身份和社会地位。

安的话语透露出她与众不同的生活习惯和特殊的身份。她在宫廷里的生活起居都是由身边的侍从人员和医生照料的，因而她在**乔**的屋中一醒来就问"Where is Dr. Banakou?" "Wasn't I talking to him just now?" 因为对前一天晚上发生的事毫无记忆，所以她又问"Have, have I had an accident?" 得知并没有发生意外事故，便说"Then quite safe without the doctor." 说明她的生活离不开宫廷医生。**安**是王位继承人，受到过良好的文化和语言教育。发现自己在一位陌生男子家中，便马上使用正式、客气的语言表达方式问**乔**"Would you be so kind as to tell me where I am?" 得知自己在**乔**的屋子睡了一个晚上,又用非常正式的语言向**乔**问候"How do you do?" 最明显暴露她身份的语言莫过于"You may sit down"——这是她习惯的上对下的说话方式,表示"我允许你坐下",令人忍俊不禁。她的言行举止都告诉观众,她出身于一个贵族家庭,她有着特殊的身份,受过良好的教育,因而说话礼貌、客气、有分寸。

乔是一个有经验的美国记者,当他知道了**安**的公主身份后,决定对**安**的活动进行报道。他的职业和他的这个决定,使他特别注意使用恰当的语言与**安**交谈,既能使**安**觉得他表现得体,又能准确地表达自己的意思。在告诉**安**这个不起眼的地方是他的公寓时,他说"Well, this is laughingly as my apartment." 此处"laughingly"有自贬、自嘲的意味,含有"不能与你的豪华宫殿相比"的言外之意。回答**安**询问她前一天晚上是否单独在这儿过夜时,他委婉地说"If you don't count me, yes."——意思是他们之间没有发生什么事,**安**没有受到任何伤害。接着**安**说"So I spent the night here, with you." 由于男女在一起过夜有着特殊的含意,因而**乔**客气地纠正她——"Well, now, I don't know if I'd use those words exactly (if I were you). But from a certain angle, yes." 前一句否认他们之间有不正常的关系,后一句很有礼貌地肯定他们确实在同一间屋子里度过一个晚上,遣词造句既准确又机智。

安不知道**乔**是个记者,也不知道**乔**将对她的行踪进行报道,因此,起床之后马上就要离开。为了稳住**安**,**乔**起初说"Why, what's your hurry. There're lots of time.";随后,又主动要为**安**准备洗澡水,以便在**安**洗澡时,他可打电话给摄影师**欧文**,让他做好准备为**安**拍照。这里,老练与狡黠的**乔**与不谙世俗的**安**形成了鲜明的对照。

乔与**安**在游艇舞会上与寻找**安**的秘密警察打了起来,一起落入水中,又一起在河对面上了岸。经过一整天的相处,他们相爱了。两人湿淋淋地回到**乔**的寓所,**安**冲了个澡,穿上了**乔**的浴袍。这就是第三段对话的背景。

双方说话的言外之意,将他们彼此相爱,但又都清楚现实中不能如愿的复杂的心情表现了出来。看到**安**穿着自己的浴袍,**乔**评论道"Suits you",后又加上了一句"You should always wear my clothes",表达了他希望**安**永远与自己在一起的愿望。**安**也心领神会,回答道"Seems I do."(It seems I always wear your clothes.） 接着，安表示她可以做点饭，乔说这里没有厨房，他天天在外面吃饭。安问了一句“Do you like that?” 乔的回答很微妙——“Life isn’t always what one likes, isn’t it?”，表面上是指吃饭，实际上是说，他们彼此相爱，但现实不允许他们随心所欲，安立即表示同意。乔又对安说“You had quite a day.” 安马上评论道——“A wonderful day.” 当然包括他们之间美好的感情。这时，收音机里传来有关安生病引起国内人民关注的消息。安说了一句“The news can wait’til tomorrow.”——说明安虽然没有明确告诉过乔她是公主，但她心里明白，这是不言自明的。这短短的一句话有两层含意——“You know who I am.”“I wish we could have more time together.” 后来乔问安是不是学过做饭，安回答说，她不仅能做饭，还会缝衣服、打扫房间、熨烫衣服，总之，“I’ve learned to do all those things”；后来又补上了一句——“It’s just as if I haven’t had the chance to do it for anyone.” 其中，泛指人称代词“anyone”，实际上指的是“you”，含有“I wish I could cook for you”的意思。乔明白此话的含意，立即说“It looks like I’ll have to move, and get myself a place with a kitchen.”——言外之意是“so that you can live with me and cook for me”，安马上表示同意。但是双方都明白这种愿望不可能实现。沉默了好一阵之后，安说她必须走了。此时乔想说些什么表达自己的感情，安阻止道：“No, please. Nothing（Please say nothing.）.” 然后她让乔开车将她送到住所附近。安离别前嘱咐乔：“Promise not to watch me go beyond that corner. Just drive away and leave me, as I leave you.” 这一段话意味深长，虽然他们两人对她的身份心照不宣，但安不愿让乔看到自己的住所，因为这里象征着她的身份的恢复，她愿意让乔在心里保持她平民的形象。

影片自始至终，没有说过一句表示彼此爱慕的话，但是每句话都意犹未尽。观众可以根据自己的理解，将未说出来的话补充进去。他们之间寓意深刻的用语打动了观众的心，为他们美好的情感到此结束感到深深的遗憾。

第二天，**公主安**召开了记者招待会，**乔**与**欧文**准时来到会场，站在第一排与其他记者一起静静地等候。这就是第四段对话的背景。

这一段对话，包括乔共有六位记者发了言。除了第一位代表大家向公主致意以外，其余五位记者都提了问题，询问安对欧洲联盟、国家之间的友谊、她最喜欢的城市等方面的看法，**安**均用正式的外交语言做出了恰当的回答。

对话涉及的内容和谈话的方式表现出招待会有很高的规格。招待会开始后，一名官员将**安**介绍给记者们，他使用了适合与这个庄重的场合的正式语言，并用王室的头衔“Your highness”(殿下)称呼公主。以后记者提问时，也都使用这个称呼，表示对**安**和她所代表的国家的尊重。在这个短短的对话中，“Your Highness”就频繁出现了七次，清楚地表明这是一场公主与记者之间的对话，有很高的规格。其次，记者招待会的庄重的氛围，也与记者们的提问和**安**回答问题时使用的语言表达方式密切相关，他们都使用似乎事先准备好的正式书面体语言。整篇对话共有 27 个主句和分句，其中 21 个是有着主语和谓语的完整句，占了 91%，这与平常朋友之间随意的谈话很不相同。比如在第三段对话中，影片的男女主人公是相互平等的朋友和恋人，虽然他们彼此的了解并不深，而且**安**因为长期生活在宫廷中，养成了说话比较正式的习惯，但他们谈话相对来说比较随便，对话中不乏主语或谓语或两者都省略或语法不规范的例子(Everything ruined? No, no. Suits you. Seems I do. Have a little wine might be good. No kitchen. Nothing to cook. Tired? A little. Did ya learn how in school? ... No, please. Nothing. Okey. Here? Can't think of any words.)。在第四段对话中，**乔**只说了两句话，第一句是在**安**回答第三位记者有关国家之间关系的问题之后，**乔**也像其他记者一样，称**安**为“Your Highness”，还使用了“May I ...”表示客气、礼貌的句型，加上完整的句子成分，符合他作为记者说话的身份。第二句是在**安**接见记者走到他面前时，他像其他记者一样作正式的自我介绍——“Joe Bradley. American News Service”。在这样一个气氛庄重的场合，人们都用正式的语言交谈，反映了**乔**与代表王室的**安**之间有相当远的社会距离，暗示着生活在两个截然不同的社会阶层中的**乔**与**安**之间，有着不可逾越的社会鸿沟。

安和**乔**之间简短的对话不仅具有正式书面语体的特点，而且通过语言所表达的感情只有他们两人才能意会。比如，一位记者问她“What, in the opinion of Your Highness, is the outlook for friendship among nations?” 她一边深情地看着**乔**，一边说：“I have every faith in it as I have faith in relations between people.” 这里的 people 不仅泛指人民，显然还特指她本人及**乔**。接着，**乔**又故意问了一句“May I say, speaking for my own press service, that we believe Your Highness' faith will not be unjustified."——他是想告诉**安**,他知道她有足够的理由说上面这番话,这理由就是他们之间的感情。安马上做出评论"I am so glad to hear you say so."——表面上似乎是一般的客套话,表达的却是她很高兴他们有着共同的看法。当第四位记者问**安**,在她所访问过的城市中,她最喜欢哪一座时,开始她看着**乔**不知如何回答,后来在别人提醒下,才按照事先准备好的回答说"Each in its own ways was unforgettable, it would be difficult to ....",但突然她把回答变成了"Rome, by no means, Rome." 这里 by no means 和重复的 Rome 加强了她肯定的语气,而且她还加上了一句:"I will cherish my visit here in memory as long as I live." 对在场的人来说,这只不过是一句对接待她的东道主的赞美,但其弦外之音只有**乔**听懂了,她是在告诉**乔**她将永远珍惜他们之间的感情,她将永远在心中保留这一段难忘的情感经历。记者招待会结束后,**安**与记者一一握手见面。她走到**乔**面前时,**乔**只作了简单的自我介绍,此时**安**说了一句"So happy, Mr. Bradley."——表达了她与**乔**相遇相爱的快乐心情。

在这样一个正式场合,他们必须努力控制自己,只能通过语言所传达的言外之意彼此交流感情,不可逾越的鸿沟给他们之间纯真的恋情,蒙上了一层淡淡的悲剧色彩,让观众产生了深深的同情。

12.2.3 《克莱默夫妇》(*Kramer versus Kramer*)

这是一部反映因快节奏工作导致夫妻离异、双方争夺孩子监护权的故事片。影片有三个主要人物:**克莱默**夫妇(Ted Kramer、Joanna Kramer)和他们的儿子**比利**(Billy Kramer)。选择的三段对话片段分别反映父子关系、法庭诉讼、母亲对儿子的深厚感情。

第一段对话的主要内容是**泰德**向儿子解释他妈妈离家出走的原因。

吃晚饭时,**比利**不听泰德的话,受到惩罚,父子之间的关系有些紧张。睡觉前,**泰德**来向儿子道晚安,**比利**对自己惹父亲生气表示道歉,**泰德**也觉得自己不应该发那么大的火,也向儿子表示歉意,紧张的关系得到缓和。紧接着**比利**问爸爸——"你也要离开吗?" 原来**比利**因为妈妈离去,产生了不安,生怕父母都将他抛弃。**泰德**明白,他们夫妻之间出现的裂痕深深伤害了儿子的心灵，所以他试图用幼小的孩子能听懂的语言反复解释，说妈妈离开家都是因为自己，与**比利**毫无关系。用不同的表达方式，向一个幼儿反复说明同一个意思，是**泰德**讲话的特点。

当**比利**问“Are you going away?”时，**泰德**说了三句话。他先用否定词“No”作了回答。接着用肯定的陈述句说“I'm staying right here with you.” 然后，为了让孩子安心又加上一句——“You're not going to get rid of me that easy.” 此句用“you”作为句子的出发点，**泰德**是想让孩子感到他是被关注的中心。**比利**又问是不是因为自己是个坏孩子，妈妈才离家出走的。这句问话本来可以放在一个复合句“Did Mammy leave because I was bad?”中，但**比利**说了两句话——“That's why Mammy left, isn't it?” “Because I was bad?” 这里，他将“Because I was bad”单独分出来，成为一个独立的句子，作为对自己问题的回答。这种方式使它成为新信息的焦点，是对“I was bad”语义的一种强调，也使情感向更深层次推进，在客观上提醒了**泰德**孩子所受伤害的程度。为此，**泰德**说了一大段话向**比利**解释。他先用两个包含“No/not”的省略否定句(“No, no. That's not it, Billy.”)，否定了**比利**的想法，马上又补充了一句“Your Mom loves you very much.” 然后，又用一个完整的句子再一次否定了孩子的想法(“The reason she left doesn't have anything to do with you.”)。几个否定句的应用达到了完全消除**比利**疑虑的效果。接着他开始解释**乔安娜**离家的原因。谈话中，他先后用了六个表示心理过程的动词“I *think*”或“I *thought*”(I think the reason … for a long time I'd kept trying to make her be a certain kind of person … And now I *think* about it, I *think* that … Just *thinking* about myself. I *thought* that if … But I *think* underneath she was very sad.)，对妻子离去的原因进行推测。**泰德**反复说，妈妈是因为自己对她不关心，她心里很痛苦，才离开的。在结束谈话前，**泰德**又一次说妈妈很爱他(she *loves* you so much)，并一再说妈妈的离去是因为忍受不了他自己，而不是因为**比利**(And the reason why Mammy couldn't stay any more was because she couldn't stand me, Billy. She didn't leave because of you. She left because of me.)。他告诉**比利**，如果不是因为妈妈爱他，她早就离开了(Mammy stayed longer than she wanted to, I think, because she loves you so much.)。**泰德**试图用简单的语言向一个七岁的孩子反复说明原因，可见他多么爱自己的孩子，生怕孩子的心灵再一次受到伤害。然

后，他们又用彼此非常熟悉的童话里的语言互道晚安，彼此都说"I love you"，足见父子情深！

第二段对话是**泰德**和**乔安娜**出席争夺孩子监护权听证会的情景。对话中主要有五个人，法官和书记官、双方的律师和作为起诉一方的第一个证人**乔安娜·克莱默**。五个人在法庭中的角色各不相同，说话的目的也不同，因此说话的方式和语言的应用也大相径庭。

代表法庭一方的法官和书记官，均按法庭程序规定的模式讲话。律师在与法官说话时、在打断对方律师讲话时，也要按一定的程式说话。例如，听证会开始时，书记官宣布："Persons having business with the Supreme Court, State of New York, special term Part 5. This court is in session. Judge Atkins presiding."，并要求全体起立（"All rise."）。后来，他在证人**乔安娜**提供证词前，又问她能否向上帝起誓只说真话——"Do you swear that you'll tell the truth, the whole truth, nothing but the truth, so help me God?" 所用的词语和表达方式是固定的、一成不变的。法官在法庭上的表达方式也是程式化的。听证会开始后，法官首先向起诉一方的律师发问——"Is the attorney for the petition ready?" 双方的律师发生争执时，法官必须用法庭规定使用的语言"overruled"或"I'll allow it"（反对无效或允许听证）。使用法庭的正规语言的主要目的，是维护法律的尊严和严肃性。

律师在听证会上的作用有三个：一是为自己的当事人辩护；二是通过对证人的提问，使其提供有利于本方的证词；三是通过向对方的证人的提问，贬低或损毁对方的形象。律师的第二和第三个作用往往是通过提问，为证人提供机会，陈述有利于自己的证词。利用语言产生的言外之意，赢得法官和陪审团对本方的同情和支持，或者使他们对对方产生不好的印象甚至反感，进而做出有利于本方的判决。因此律师提出的问题都是精心策划的，使用的语言和提问的方式都是经过反复推敲的。听证会上**泰德**和**乔安娜**的律师，分别对他们的提问就是很好的例证。**乔安娜**的律师向她提出的问题，都试图证明**乔安娜**一直爱着自己的孩子，而且现在经济上有能力监护自己的孩子，都意在证明**泰德**是**乔安娜**离家出走的根本原因。而**泰德**的律师向**乔安娜**的发问均是为了损毁她的名誉、贬低她的人格，使人们觉得她没有资格获得监护权。

乔安娜的律师一开始就向她提了两个问题：结婚有多长时间？是不

是幸福？目的是引出否定的回答。言外之意是，既然婚姻没有给她带来幸福，她的离家出走无可非议。接着律师又问她婚前是否工作过，**乔安娜**作了肯定的回答；律师又问她婚后是否继续工作，**乔安娜**予以否定，此时律师加上了一句“Did you wish to?”，巧妙的提示引发了**乔安娜**对**泰德**的抱怨，是**泰德**剥夺了她工作的权利（... he wouldn't listen. I remember once he said I probably couldn't get a job that would pay high enough to hire a baby-sitter.），然后律师又连续问她现在是否有工作，一年收入有多少，**乔安娜**的回答“I make thirty-one thousand dollars a year”，言外之意是自己经济上可以负担得起对孩子的监护。接着律师又问她为什么爱自己的孩子但选择了离开他，这个问题给了**乔安娜**大段解释自己婚后心理变化的机会。她说由于**泰德**只关心自己的事业，对她的愿望毫不理会，感情上离她越来越远，使她失去了自我尊严，甚至开始怀疑自己有病，怀疑自己不适于与孩子一起生活。后来经过心理医生的治疗，她才明白了自己并没有病。律师的最后一个问题是让**乔安娜**陈述为什么要争夺对孩子的监护权，这是诉讼最关键的部分，这个问题又给了**乔安娜**申述和解释的机会。她说当初离开他，是因为那样做可能对他最好，现在争取监护权是因为她爱自己的孩子。说话的开始她两次说：“I love him”，与结尾时重复说“I'm his mother. I'm his mother.”，加上她提到自己当了五年半的母亲，而**泰德**只当了十八个月的父亲，因而她更有资格获得监护权。话毕，她的律师说了一句“Thank you, Mrs. Kramer. I got no further questions.”，结束了他对**乔安娜**的提问，因为他认为，她的话对他们的起诉已经非常有利。

轮到**泰德**的律师向**乔安娜**提问了，他一连问了近十个问题：她的丈夫是否虐待过她？是否打过她？是否有不忠实于她的行为？是否养得起她？她打算在纽约待多长时间？曾有过多少男朋友？男朋友的数字是否在三个和三十三个之间？现在是不是有情人？是否会与这个情人保持长久的关系？前五个问题的目的，是想从**乔安娜**五个否定的回答中，证明**泰德**是个好丈夫，因而**乔安娜**没有离家出走的理由；后几个问题特别是关于她男朋友的问题，是想通过**乔安娜**的回答（I don't recall. Somewhere in between（即 between three and thirty-three）. Yes. I'm seeing someone.）使法官和陪审团对**乔安娜**产生不好的印象，意在证明她是个感情易变的女人，对孩子的未来会产生不良的影响，不适于对孩子监护，因而不应该得到监护权。

第三段对话发生在**泰德**与**乔安娜**。

法庭把孩子的监护权判给**乔安娜**,**比利**将与母亲一起生活。这一天终于来到了,父子难舍难分,**泰德**在做**比利**的工作,向他保证他们以后仍旧会常常在一起。这时电话铃响起,是**乔安娜**从楼下大厅里打来的。她要**泰德**单独来见她。**泰德**以为发生了意外,匆匆赶下楼。原来**乔安娜**一早醒来,反复考虑,觉得**比利**已经有了家,她不忍心让**比利**离开自己的家,她决定不把他带走。

从两个人的对话看出,虽然他们已经离婚,虽然他们曾面对公堂,争夺对孩子的监护权,他们仍然是朋友,见面时他们仍用名字相称,而且彼此间仍然相互关心。**乔安娜**要**泰德**下楼来,**泰德**马上问"Joanna, what's wrong? Tell me ...",语气关切。**乔安娜**决定不带走**比利**,但提出要去看看孩子,**泰德**马上同意,而且很体贴地补上一句"Listen, while you go upstairs and see him, I'll wait here.",让**乔安娜**和**比利**单独待一会儿,向**比利**解释改变决定的原因。**乔安娜**在上楼前问"How do I look?",**泰德**以赞赏的口吻说"Terrific!",可见**泰德**对自己的前妻仍怀有好感。

与**泰德**的对话中,**乔安娜**说了一大段话,传达了一个很重要的信息:她对孩子有着深深的爱。**乔安娜**的话一共包含了十几个分句,有两个特点。第一,有十一个分句是以我作为句子的出发点的(***I*** woke up ... ***I*** ... was thinking ... ***I*** was thinking ... (***I*** was) waking up ... ***I*** painted ... ***I*** thought ... ***I*** should ... But ***I*** realized ... ***I*** love him ... ***I***'m not ... Can ***I*** ...?),而且其中大部分的动词过程都表示她的心理活动,说明她考虑了很多,想了很多。第二,所有十几个句子都与**比利**有关,有三个是**乔安娜**设身处地地站在**比利**的角度来考虑他的未来,八个句子的新信息都是关于**比利**的(I was thinking of ***Billy***. I was thinking of ***him***. Waking up in ***his*** room. ***He*** was waking up at home. ... ***he*** already is home. I love ***him*** very much. I'm not going to take ***him*** with me ... Can I go upstairs and see ***him***?),可见在**乔安娜**的心中,**比利**是多么重要!正是由于"I love him very much.",才使她决定"not going to take him with me";正是由于爱自己的孩子,她才会问**泰德**"How do I look?",才会在乎外表在**比利**心中可能产生的印象。将"I"作为句子的出发点,而句子的信息中心却是关于Billy/his/him,让听者明白**乔安娜**事事都是从**比利**的角度来考虑,让听者明白她对孩子怀有多么深厚的感情!

12.2.4 《金色池塘》(*On Golden Pond*)

选择的三段对话描述了老年人之间的纯真爱情,反映了不同年龄段的人之间的友谊和矛盾。这三段对话发生在影片的几个主要人物之间(Norman Thayer、Ethel Thayer、Chelsea Thayer、Bill Ray、Billy Ray),是影片内容的浓缩。

对话给人印象最深的是,**诺曼**与**爱丝尔**这一对老年夫妻,对生活截然不同的态度。**诺曼**已年近八旬,对生活充满了悲观的情绪。他对周围的一切,对妻子、对邻居、对女儿、对**比尔**父子都怨气冲冲,甚至对他们嘲笑、挖苦。只有女儿与他的坦诚交谈、比利的天真,才唤起了他内心对生活的渴望,他对生活的态度才有所改变。与他相比,**爱丝尔**是一个天性乐观的人。她热爱生活,在她的眼里,世界美丽异常,小鸟、甚至小小的树叶、花草都能引起她对生活的兴趣。她甚至把一对洋娃娃比喻为"最美好的一对",诙谐、有趣。她喜欢邻居,与女儿、与**比尔**父子相处都十分和谐、融洽。

第一段对话中,29个表示属性特征或者身份的关系过程动词(**Norman**: Who the hell *is* this? (To Ethel) Someone'*s* at the door. **Ethel**: It'*s* me ... Oh, Norman, it'*s* so beautiful. ... Their name *is* Migliore, They *are* from Boston. They're a nice middle-aged couple just like us. **Norman**: If they'*re* like us, they'*re* not middle-aged. Middle age *means* the middle, Ethel. **Ethel**: Well, we'*re* the far edge of middle age, that'*s* all. **Norman**: We'*re* not, you know. We'*re* not middle-aged. You'*re* old and I'*m* ancient. **Ethel**: ... You'*re* in your seventies and I'*m* in my sixties. **Ethel**: (cries our when she sees her doll on the floor) Oh, no. Poor Elmer. He *was* my first true love, you know. **Norman**: I *was* the first in line. **Ethel**: No, you *were* rather a cheap substitute for Elmer. **Norman**: ... When my number'*s* up ... It'*s* not fascination. It just *crosses* my mind now and then. You must *be* mad...)和14个表示心理状态的动词(**Ethel**: I *saw* patch of little tiny flowers over the old cellar hole .... I *forget* what they're called. ... Well, *want* to help me with the dustcovers? Norman, what do you *think* I was doing? ... Italian, I *suppose*. ... Would you *like* to spend the rest ... We can if you *like*. I don't *know*. He *wanted* to kill himself. **Norman**: Maybe he *wants* to be cremated ... **Ethel**: ... Don't you have anything else to *think about*?),将**诺曼**与**爱丝尔**对生活不同的态度充分地表现了出来。特别是当**爱丝尔**向**诺曼**描述,她在拾柴的路上遇到了一对意大利邻居时,她使用的关系过程(be 动词)"They'*re* a nice middle-aged couple just like us",不仅将这一对意大利夫妻的特征点了出来,而且也反映出她乐观的生活态度。他们自己虽然已是六七十岁的人了,但在她看来,仍属中年(Well, we'*re* at the far edge of middle age, that's all.)。**诺曼**却不同意她的看法,比如,他不喜欢意大利邻居的名字(What sort of name is that?),接着又故意问"Do they speak English?" 关于他们的年龄,他认定"We're not middle-aged. You're old and I'm ancient",将他们归入垂暮的老年人行列。后来**爱丝尔**说这一对意大利邻居将邀请他们吃晚饭,他推脱自己的胃不好,不适应意大利食物,还造出一个意大利词"rigatani",表示不感兴趣。

这一段对话中,表示动作的动词 wake、meet、get 的现在时或过去进行时的运用(**Ethel**: Everything'*s just waking up*. I *was getting* wood. I *met* the nicest couple.),恰如其分地将忙忙碌碌的**爱丝尔**,和她眼中生机勃勃的自然景象生动地勾画了出来。这与"don't have anything else to do"的**诺曼**形成了鲜明的对照。除了想到死(When my number's up ...),**诺曼**此时对什么也没兴趣谈论(Nothing quite as interesting.)。

还有一段小小的插曲,将这两位老人对死亡的态度作了对比。**爱丝尔**看到自己的洋娃娃 Elmer 摔倒在地上时非常生气,因为"他"是自己的初恋(He was my first true love, ...)。听到这话,**诺曼**产生了妒意,争辩道,自己才是她的初恋(No, No, I was the first in line.),老人孩童般的心境被栩栩如生地刻画了出来。**诺曼**随即用嘲笑的口吻说,大概"他"想在得癌病之前被火葬(He *wanted* to kill himself. Maybe he *wants* to be cremated before he gets cancer or terminal or something.)。在这里两个表示心理过程动词 *want* 的使用反映了他悲观的情绪,他硬把生病死亡强加到洋娃娃身上。他还继而挖苦地评论道,这种死法也不错,他希望**爱丝尔**在他的日子临近时,也用同样的方法结束他的生命。不过**诺曼**有时也不乏幽默感,比如**爱丝尔**听烦了他的这些话,因而激将他——"Well, what's stopping you? Why don't you take your dive and get it over with it?"——省得他没完没了地叨叨。**诺曼**却幽默地回答："Leave you alone with Elmer? You must be mad."意思是："你让我死，好跟你的洋娃娃在一起，我才不干呢！"这句话也将他对妻子的真情充分地表达了出来。他们一辈子可能总是争争吵吵，但却相亲相爱。

第二段对话主要发生在**诺曼**与他女儿的男友**比尔**之间。**诺曼**起初不喜欢这个未来的女婿，但他并不明说，或者故意找碴儿，或者故意捉弄**比尔**。他们的谈话反映了两代人对一些问题的看法存在着明显的不同。

谈话一开始，**比尔**说他很喜欢**诺曼**的房子，这本来是一句客气话，可**诺曼**却故意说"这所房子并不出售"(It is not for sale.)。当**比尔**已经直呼其名，但还要问是否可以这样称呼，**诺曼**不高兴地说"I believe you just did"，言下之意是"你既然都这么叫了，还问我干什么?"当**比尔**问如何称呼**诺曼**的妻子，**诺曼**故意用商量的口吻问"How about Ethel?"，显然带有挖苦的味道，意思是"你既然已称我为**诺曼**，干吗还问我该怎么称呼我的妻子"。**比尔**后来提到他与**切尔茜**关系很好，还加上了一句"I'm sure you'd be pleased!"。对于**比尔**这种肯定的看法，**诺曼**不置可否，他环顾左右而言他，反问牙科医生**比尔**补一颗牙要花多少钱，言外之意很清楚，他不赞赏他们的关系。后来，**比尔**问**诺曼**对"we'd like to sleep together in the same room"的看法，这里"we"很清楚是指他与**切尔茜**，**诺曼**装着听不懂，故意跟他兜圈子(All three of you? You and Billy? Not Chelsea and Billy? That leaves Chelsea and you then)。后来他表面上同意，可是他又说记得**切尔茜**以前总是与自己的丈夫睡在一张床上，他自己也一直与自己的妻子睡在一起。这实际上是告诉**比尔**，只有结了婚的人才能睡在一起。他甚至用"violate"和"abuse"这样的词语，来形容**比尔**与**切尔茜**的关系。**比尔**逐渐明白**诺曼**是在拿他开心，把他当成了傻瓜(You're having a good time, aren't you? ... you like to have a good old time with people's heads ... making me feel like an ass hole) ...，终于渐渐明白了与**诺曼**交朋友不是一件容易的事。这一段对话的最后，**比尔**问**诺曼**附近是否有熊，**诺曼**又说了一句话(Oh, sure. Black bears and grizzlies. One came along here last month and ate an old lesbian.)，连**比利**都听出这是拿他开玩笑(He's just bullshitting you.)。两代人之间的差异还表示在对裸泳的看法上。**诺曼**的话"Permissiveness runs rampant here on Golden Pond"，表明他对裸泳极不赞成。

这一段对话,仍有不少地方反映了**诺曼**对年迈有病的悲观态度。在谈到他打算读一本新书时,他说道:“I can finish it before I'm finished myself.” 两个 finish 含意不同,前者指读完书,后者指他生命的结束,似乎死亡已经逼近他。悲观的处世态度,恐怕是导致他与周围世界格格不入的根本原因。

从第三段是**切尔茜**与**诺曼**的对话,发生在她与**比尔**去欧洲结婚度假回来以后。我们看到**诺曼**在**爱丝尔**的调解下,与女儿之间最后消除了误解,相互开始理解,恢复了父女之间的正常关系。

这一段对话的背景是:**切尔茜**在离开“金色池塘”,返回工作岗位以前,对母亲说她感到内疚,与父亲关系不好(I'm such an ass. I'm sorry.)。**爱丝尔**讲了两段劝慰的话,在调解父女关系中起了关键的作用。她对女儿说,**诺曼**对她是关心的,愿为她赴汤蹈火(He cares deeply. I know ... he'd walk through fire for you, too.),但他不愿意表现出来(It's just he's absolutely muck about telling anyone.);而且说**诺曼**已经快八十岁了,又有心脏病,记性也不好,女儿应该理解他,应当主动跟父亲谈心。这一番话表明她与女儿关系非常好,同时对自己的丈夫的内心世界也非常了解,不愧是好母亲、好妻子。

此时,**比利**与**诺曼**高高兴兴从海边回来。**切尔茜**抓住机会主动向父亲打招呼,看到**诺曼**头部受伤,她非常关切,然后她表示想与**诺曼**谈谈。这时她说话带有明显的口吃,表明她的心情极为紧张。然而**诺曼**却误解了女儿的用意,他用挖苦的口吻问**切尔茜**,是不是因为她对遗嘱感到担心(Eh, just in the nick of time, huh. Worried about the will, are you?),意思是:在我快死时你来恢复关系,安排得不错啊!接着他说会将所有的东西留给**切尔茜**的。这使**切尔茜**大为光火,表示她什么也不要,她只是觉得他们应该成为朋友。此时**诺曼**提了一个问题“Oh, does it mean you'll come around more often? You love your mother!”。前一句话表面上是一个问题,实际表达的是“I hope that you'll come around more often to see us.”,希望女儿能更经常回来看看自己,这两句话说明**诺曼**是一个自尊心很强的老人。**切尔茜**告诉他已与**比尔**结婚,**诺曼**又问**比利**是否将与他们一起生活。言外之意很清楚,他希望以后能经常看到**比利**,因为他喜欢这个孩子,特别是**比利**在他的指导下做了一个很难的后空翻跳水动作,使他非常高兴。交谈中,**诺曼**说了一句“You never were a great back flipper, were you?”——透露他对**切尔茜**不能做这个动作不大满意。为了让**诺曼**高兴，**切尔茜**虽然心里很害怕，但在父亲的鼓励下，她成功地做了后空翻跳水动作。**诺曼**极为兴奋，他说“She did it! She did it! You did it.”——三个 did 将他欢欣鼓舞的心情淋漓尽致地表现了出来。前两次是对**爱丝尔**说的，他为自己的女儿感到自豪，后一次是对**切尔茜**说的，一方面表示祝贺，一方面是向女儿表明，他为她的成功感到骄傲。此时，父女之间的误会完全消除，**诺曼**与**切尔茜**开始成为好朋友，恢复了父女之间的正常关系。

从这一段对话中，我们看到了**诺曼**的情绪发生了根本的变化。在**比尔**与**切尔茜**去欧洲旅行期间，**诺曼**与**比利**朝夕相处，他教**比利**钓鱼，他们还一块钓起一条名叫“Walter”的鱼，他们都认为应当把这条鱼放回水中，让“他”活下去。**比利**的活力和友谊，帮助**诺曼**逐渐消除了悲观消极情绪。在这一段对话中，我们几乎看不到他一贯对生活的抱怨态度。

这三段对话中，通俗的美式英语广泛使用，是这部影片语言上的另一个特点。这些通俗美式英语表达方式，将人物的形象活灵活现地勾勒了出来。例如，第一段一开头，**诺曼**听到有人从后门进来，就马上问“Who the hell is that?”其中，“the hell”决不会出现在作为教授的他和学生的交谈语言中。后来他发现，原来是**爱丝尔**从小树林回来，而且弄得脏兮兮的，她说“Oh, look at me! Quite a sight, aren't I?” 作为教授太太，在日常生活中居然也使用不规范的“aren't I”，而不使用规范的“am I not”！第二段**诺曼**与**比尔**的对话中，他说还要读一遍《金银岛》，因为“my mind is going”，这是“I am forgetful”的通俗说法。第三段对话中，**切尔茜**说自己很笨（I'm such an ass.），后来为了使父亲高兴，她决定“I'm going to do a goddam back flip”，“an ass”及“goddam”是典型的美式俚语。男性之间的对话尤为随便。第二段对话中，**比尔**对**诺曼**说，他明白**诺曼**喜欢拿人开心（You've been having a good time; You like to have a good old time with people's heads），并说自己懂得这些“crap”、“poopy”的含意。第三段对话中，**诺曼**对**比利**成功非常高兴，说“I got him doing the back flip just like a pro.”其中，“pro”是“professional”缩写，只用于非正式语言中。**比利**是一个在父母离异的家庭中生活的男孩，语言的运用更加随便，甚至还会用粗话，比如“He's just bullshitting you.”“We caught the son of a bitch.”这样的例子在整部影片中比比皆是。

12.3 结　语

本文补充分析了我们编辑教材中的四部影片的一些对话，试图进一步论证应用语言学理论分析语篇对揭示影片的内涵和描述人物性格的作用。教材中其余五部影片的对话分析，如果读者有兴趣，可参考原书。

13

Constructing a Harmonious World

— Linguistic Studies on *The Analects of Confucius* *

13.1 Introduction

The Analects is a book collecting sayings mainly of Confucius and also of a few famous scholars of his time. The book was compiled by their disciples in the third century B.C., 200 years after Confucius passed away. Known as a great work of philosophy, representing the essence of Confucianism, *The Analects* has been studied in the past centuries from various angles and for different purposes by both Chinese scholars and those of other countries. However, according to the nearly one million entries on the internet, there have been few linguistic studies and none from the

* This chapter is based on a paper presented first at the 32nd International Systemic Functional Linguistic Congress held at Sydney University in 2005 and later published in the *Journal of English Studies*, 2006(12).

Systemic-Functional (hereafter SF) perspective. Halliday points out "if a text is to be described at all, then it should be described properly; and this means by the theories and methods developed in linguistics" (2002: 4). He has shown that all discourses, whether literary or non-literary, spoken or written, scientific or poetic, short or long, can be analyzed by applying the theories and methods of the SF linguistic model (Halliday 2002). We will show in this chapter that this linguistic framework can also be applied to the revelation of some important semantic and linguistic features and of some basic ethics of *The Analects*. We shall first give a brief introduction to the social-cultural environment for the emergence of the book. Then our focus will be put on the linguistic analysis of some of its lexico-grammatical features, through which we hope to disclose the main gist and characteristics of the book. Finally we shall discuss the significance of Confucius' values and ethics contained in the book for the present China and world.

13.2 Analysis of *The Analects*

13.2.1 Contextual features of *The Analects*

13.2.1.1 The SFL framework

SFL regards language as a system of meaning potential realized by a system of three meta-functions constrained by the context of culture and context of situation (Halliday 1994). They are represented as five levels. The relationship among the levels is that of realization: the level above is realized by the level below: context of culture is realized by context of situation, which is realized by semantics, which is, in turn, realized by lexico-grammar, which is, finally, realized by phonology in speaking or graphology in writing, as shown in Figure 1 (↙ means "realized by") (Martin 1992; Eggins 1994; Halliday and Matthiessen 2004):

Context of culture
↙
Context of situation
↙
Semantics (Meaning)
↙
Lexico-grammar (Wording)
↙
Phonology (Speaking)
Graphology (Writing)

Figure 13 - 1 Levels of Language and Its Cultural and Situational Context

Following the five-level relationship among language and its cultural and situational contexts established by this figure, Fang proposes a three step analytical model for discourse analysis: Context-Text-Commentary in relation to Context (2005). In the following sections, we shall first tackle the contextual features and the purpose and then study the lexico-grammatical features and finally make some comments on the impact of this book.

13.2.1.2 Social contextual features and the purpose of *the Analects*

Halliday defines "context of culture" as "the socio-historical and ideological environment engendering, and engendered by, the text" (2002: 151).

Then what was the socio-historical and ideological environment for the engendering of *The Analects*, which appeared in the third century B.C.?

Confucius lived in the Spring and Autumn period (770 B.C. - 476 B.C.), an age when the country was split into many small states and thrown into a moral chaos. Wars broke out frequently among these states and the "law of the jungle" was predominant. Common values were widely rejected and Rites, which had been well established in the Western Zhou Dynasty (1100 B.C. - 771 B.C.), were simply disregarded. Under this social environment, many schools emerged, all intending to carry out reform schemes and restore peace and order in the society. Confucianism was one of the schools contending to become dominant so that the rulers may adopt and implement in their states. The time after Confucius is known as the Warring States Period (475 B.C.-221 B.C.), which was even worse — there were more wars and the principles of Rites totally destroyed (Xu Zhigang 2000). It was under this socio-historical and ideological circumstance that *The Analects* came into being. The purpose of the book was to help build up a harmonious society in which the Rites were restored and order established (*ibid.*).

The issue as to what kind of the socio-historical and ideological environment engendered by the book will be dealt with later in the chapter.

13.2.1.3 Features of situational context of *The Analects*

The context of culture is a rather abstract and generalized concept; it represents an abstraction of social activities, which is, as shown in Figure 1, embodied or realized by the features of the context of situation. A discourse is a form for actual social communication, which takes place in a certain situation in a certain culture. So in analyzing a discourse, we should take into consideration the variables of the context of situation: the **Field**, the **Tenor**, and the **Mode** (H & H 1985; Huang 2001: 72; also see Chapter 12, this book). Concretely, the variable **Field** refers to the subject matter or what activities are going on; **Tenor**, the interpersonal relations involved; and **Mode**, "what part the language is playing" (*ibid.*).

Applying the SF theoretical elaboration, we find the following contextual features in *The Analects:*

Field: delivering Confucius' philosophical beliefs on morality, politics, education, family, and comportment of the ideal man;

Tenor: Confucius and/or other Masters (who used to be his disciples) and his/their disciples, the former with an authoritative moral power over the latter, and the latter with an awe and respect for the former; sometimes their relations were closer as if they were good friends; but many times the receiver seems to be the reader, however; the relation between Confucius and the reader being one imparting knowledge and the other receiving it;

Mode: classical oral Chinese taken down in characters in the form of monologist sayings or statements by Confucius or other masters who were once his students, and sometimes dialogues between Confucius/other masters and his/their disciples.

From Figure 13 – 1, we know that these contextual features can be realized by lexico-grammatical features. Halliday (Halliday & Hasan 1985; 1994) has further pointed out that each of the contextual features is realized by a corresponding meta-function at the lexico-grammatical level (Halliday & Hasan 1985): field by ideational function, tenor by interpersonal and mode by textual. Then how are these features realized linguistically or at the lexico-grammatical level in the book?

13.2.2 Features of lexico-grammar in *The Analects*

13.2.2.1 Structure of the book

It contains 20 chapters with 11,000 characters consisting mainly of Confucius' sayings or statements, or sayings of other masters who were once his students. From the surface, each saying seems to stand only by itself; however, when examining the whole book, we find that all the sayings are connected by the motive of elaborating on the great Master's views on moral development, philosophy, education, politics, etc. Each chapter centers on one or two viewpoints.

13.2.2.2 Features of meta-functions

Halliday states that every clause and every discourse construes three meta-functions, namely, ideational, interpersonal and textual at the lexico-grammatical level, which realize the context of situation. Ideational function is the function of construing the world realities; interpersonal the function of enacting interpersonal relationship in the social world; and textual the function of organizing clauses into a coherent text by linguistic devices

(Halliday 1994; Halliday & Matthiessen 2004). Ideally, we should take a comprehensive study of all the functions utilized in creating the text. In practice, however, the choice of the functions for analysis depends very much on the purposes and the analysts' interests (Huang 2001), and sometimes on whether there is a feature foregrounded in the discourse (Halliday 2002). The analyst would often concentrate on the study of one or two of the meta-functions or even on some of the functional components (Halliday 1973; Huang 2001). In *The Analects*, one pattern and some words or characters repetitively appearing stand out as a prominent feature. Therefore, in this chapter, we will first study this feature — repetition, one of the lexical cohesive devices, which is a sub-function within the textual system. Then we will discuss linguistic features of processes and projection, mood and modulation in the book.

13.2.2.3 The function of repetition in *The Analects*

There are two ways to achieve texture in a discourse: structural and non-structural. Structural features are manifested in the Theme-Rheme structure and the Information structure while non-structural features in Cohesion. Cohesive ties are linguistic devices to link the different clauses into a cohesive whole in order that the discourse will be coherent. There are various cohesive ties: reference, illipsis and substitution, conjunction and lexical cohesion and each has sub-divisions (Halliday 1994). Due to the limit of space, we will not discuss them in detail. Here we will look at one particular lexical cohesive device — Repetition, which is foregrounded in this book.

The most frequently repeated pattern is **子曰:"x"** [*zi yue*: "x" — Confucius said: "x"], which has been repeated 363 times. 子 stands for 孔子 or Kongzi, 孔 or Kong being the family name; 孔 being omitted in the pattern shows that he was so well-known that it was not necessary to be mentioned. The repetition of the pattern establishes that Confucius is a scholar of authority; therefore whatever he teaches should be true. The most frequently repeated word or character is 仁 (*ren*). [Many believe that there is no proper translation equivalence of this word in English. Usually it is rendered as "benevolence" or "charity" or "humanity" or "humaneness" or "love" or "kindness", implying that Confucius' moral system was based upon empathy and understanding others. As far as we are concerned, it could embrace all the meanings of these words. In this chapter we will just use the original character 仁 (*ren*) so as to interpret it in a more comprehensive way.] This word has been repeated 109 times. It can be said that it is the device of repetition of 仁 (*ren*) that binds together the 20 chapters and individual sayings in the book. When discussing the function of repetition in poetry, Carter and Deidre claim (1982) that "The language of poetry is not necessarily powerful and magic, but the powerful and magic effect of a poem can be achieved by means of lexical items, esp. by means of repetition". Very often repetition is an effective way for poets or writers to express their love or hatred, pleasure or grief, or to create a certain aura and even to reveal the theme of a poem. Though *The Analects* is not a poetic collection, yet the employment of the device of repetition has achieved a similar effect — it is through the word 仁 (*ren*) which appears so frequently that Confucius successfully delivers the main message and central idea of the book, — to love people, to love one's parents, to love one's other family members, to love one's friends, or as Confucius puts it —"爱人*Aì rén*," or "love people" (*The Analects* XII: 22), which is the fundamental virtue of Confucianism. A few examples will suffice①.

[1] 子曰:"里仁为美。择不处仁,焉得知?"(*The Analects* IV: 1) (*zi yue: li ren wei mei, ze bu chu ren, yan de zhi?* — The Master said:"It is beautiful to live amid ren. If you choose to be apart from ren, how will you gain wisdom?)

[2] 子曰:"不仁者不可以久处约,不可以常处乐。仁者安仁,知者利仁。"(*The Analects* IV: 2) (*zi yue: bu ren zhe bu keyi jiu chu yue, bu keyi chang chu le. Renzhe an ren, zhizhe li ren.* — The master said "Those without the quality of *ren* can't endure

① All of the examples are taken from the translations by Brooks, 1998.

hardships, nor can they enjoy lasting happiness. Those with the quality of *ren* will be contented in practicing *ren*, and those with wisdom will be capable of using *ren*.)

[3] 子曰:"苟志于仁矣,无恶也。"(*zi yue: gou zhi yu ren yi, wu e ye.* — The master said: "When one truly aspires to practice *ren*, he will never do evils.)

But what are the means to attain 仁(*ren*)? Confucius states that it can be attained by practicing 礼 (*li*), 义 (*yi*), 忠 (*zhong*), 乐 (*yue*), 孝 (*xiao*), 悌 (*ti*), 恕 (*shu*) and other related virtues, which are naturally the next most frequently repeated words or characters: for example, 礼 (*li*) appears 66 times, 义 (*yi*), 10, 忠 (*zhong*), 13, 乐 (*yue*), 19, 孝 (*xiao*) 12, 悌 (*ti*), 5, 恕 (*shu*), 4 times. 礼 (*li*) means rites, that is, to form an appropriate attitude towards one's ancestors, superiors, parents, elders, subjects and friends. It involves studying and mastering the ritual forms and rules of propriety through which "one expresses respect for superiors and enacts his role in society in such a way that he himself is worthy of respect and admiration. Neglecting ritual, or doing rituals incorrectly, demonstrated a moral anarchy or disorder of the most egregious kind" (Creel 1949). 义 (*yi*) refers to right conduct, morality, righteousness. This means that rather than pursuing one's own selfish interests one should do what is right and what is moral. 忠 means loyalty to your ruler because he comes to the throne by the mandate of heaven. However, this does not mean a blind loyalty. Mencius, who developed Confucius' ideas later, states that the ruler who does not follow the practice of "*ren*" or no longer benevolent, by the mandate of heaven, should be overthrown, which may explain the phenomenon of one dynasty replaced by another in Chinese history. 乐 (*yue*) means practicing traditional and solemn music and dance in order to become an ideal person or gentleman with 德 (*de*) or "virtue". While rites show off social hierarchies, music unifies hearts in shared enjoyment (Fingarette 1972). 孝 (*xiao*) means filial piety and 悌 (*ti*), the love for one's younger brother and the respect for one's elder brother; 恕 (*shu*) means "forgiveness", which stresses the importance of "what you don't want yourself, don't do to others" (*Analects* XV: 24). Put in a systemic perspective, these words are standing in a hierarchy of two levels: the upper level is 仁 "*ren*", which is the ultimate goal for human beings to attain; the lower level involves the development of the necessary qualities or means to attain or realize the goal. But there is still another level: the ways to attain these values or qualities. Confucius states that they should be attained by learning and by following the good examples set up by the ancestors. One must cultivate oneself by learning six arts: ritual, music, archery, chariot-riding, calligraphy, and computation. The words standing for these two ways of acquiring the above-mentioned qualities are also frequently repeated. Learning or education is mentioned in 53 places and following the models set up by the ancestors in 22 places. Thus, repetition of key words at the three levels contributes, to a large degree, to establishing Confucius as a master of moral education and to elaborating on his basic philosophical moral doctrines, his ideal social model, and on the means to realize them. We may say that repetition is "a feature that is brought into prominent" in the book because "it relates to the meaning of the text as a whole" (Halliday 2002: 98). The figures of repetition discussed above are summarized in Figure 13 – 2.

Pattern/word repeated	Number of times for repetition
Confucius said: "x"	363
Ren 仁 (humaneness)	109
Li 礼 (rites)	66
Yue 乐 (music and dance)	19
Zhong 忠 (loyalty)	13
Xiao 孝 (filial piety)	12
Yi 义 (righteousness)	10
Ti 悌 (love of brothers)	5
Shu 恕 (forgiveness)	4

Figure 13 – 2 Figures of Repetition of Key Words

The realization relationship among them may be shown in Figure 13 - 3 below: ↙ means "realized by"

仁 *Ren*

↙

li 礼 *yue* 乐 *zhong* 忠 *xiao* 孝 *yi* 义 *ti* 悌 *shu* 恕

↙

学 Learning and 教 Education

Figure 13 - 3 Realization Relationship Among the Levels of Confucian Doctrine

13.2.2.4 Features of process, projection, mood and modality in *The Analects*

We have chosen Chapter 4 to study these four features to see how the variable of Field and Tenor are realized by ideational and interpersonal functions at the lexico-grammatical level, as this chapter deals with the main doctrine of Confucius — the concept of 仁 "*ren*".

A. Processes in the primary clauses

Halliday states (1994; Halliday & Matthiessen 2004) that transitivity is the grammar to construe what is happening in the world, which is a grammar denoting six processes: material, mental, relational, verbal, behavioral, and existential. With regard to the processes appearing in Chapter 4 of *The Analects*, we find **all the processes in the primary clauses are verbal**, following the pattern: 子**曰**: "x." (Confucius **said**: "x."), as exemplified by Examples [1]-[3]. In other chapters occasionally there is another pattern: a **问** b, 子**曰**"x" [a **asks** (Confucius) b, Confucius **said**: "x".], as exemplified by Example [4]:

[4] 孟懿子**问**孝,子**曰**:"x"(*Analects:* II: 5) [*mengyizi* ***wen*** *xiao*— Mengyizi **asks** (Confucius) (about) filial piety, Confucius **said**: "x"]

The dominance of the verbal process used in the primary clauses is an outstanding characteristic of the book, which establishes a particular relationship between a master and his disciples — the Master imparting knowledge to his disciples, or making statements of his moral principles, implying that the job of a master or a teacher is to offer explanations or 解惑 (*jiehuo*), and the job of a student to seek truth from his master.

B. Types of clauses

Examining the forms of the sayings, we have discovered two types of clauses in the whole book: 1) **statements** and 2) **dialogues**.

There are two kinds of statement. First, a statement is made on a certain point of view by Confucius with his name omitted or without the projecting clause. For example,

[5] 乡人饮酒，杖者出，四出矣。[*xiangren yinjiu, zhangzhe chu, si chu yi* — It is only after the old has left after drinking wine in the village, can one leave (*The Analects*, X: 13)].

Second, a statement in the form of "Confucius said: 'x'", as exemplified in Example [1], thus transmitting the voice of the Master directly in the quotation.

In the first kind of statement, apparently, there is only one voice and the source of the voice seems from the compiler of the book. In reality, there are also two voices: one from the compiler, the omitted projecting clause, and the other from Confucius, or what is projected in the clause. The omission of the projecting clause may lie in the fact that these statements are so well known to be Confucius' that there is no need to mention his name. Halliday states (1994) that the function of statements is to provide information; it is exactly through these statements that the book has achieved one of its purposes — to transmit Confucius Doctrine to his disciples and those who read it.

Dialogues are the second type of clauses in the book. Usually in these dialogues, a disciple would ask a question, which is either directly reported or indirectly reported, and then Confucius or some other master would provide the answer, as exemplified by Example [6]:

[6] ……子出，门人问曰："何谓也?"曾子曰："夫子之道忠恕而已矣。"

(*The Analects* IV: 14) (*zi chu, menren wen yue: "he wei ye?" zengzi yue: "fuzi zhidao zhongshu eryiyi."*— When Confucius went out, his disciples asked (Zengzi)): "What did he say?" Zengzi said: "Confucius' doctrine is nothing but loyalty 忠 (*zhong*) and forgiveness 恕 (*shu*)."

One thing worth noticing is that both types are arranged in clause complexes. Take Chapter 4. **All of the 27 clause complexes are in the paratactic: locution pattern 1″2** (Halliday 1994: 220; Halliday & Matthiessen 2004), as exemplified in [1], in which the projecting clause before the quotation is the primary clause 1 and after that, the projected clause ″2, as shown below:

[1] 子曰:"里仁为美。择不处仁,焉得知?" (*The Analects* IV: 1)
1 ″2

This pattern 1 + ″2 is a typical structure of clause complex in classical works. Actually there is not a single example of the pattern ″2 + 1 in this book, which is often observed in modern Chinese.

In short, a dialogue comprises two parts: a question and an answer, which perform different functions in language. The function of a question is to seek information from the speaker, and the function of an answer, which is usually a statement, is to give the information that the hearer hopes to get. Therefore, through asking questions by the disciples and the answers given by the Master, a philosophical view is clarified or transmitted.

C. Types of mood

In English there are four types of mood: the declarative, the interrogative, exclamatory and imperative (Halliday 1994: Chapter 4). It is also true of Chinese. Going through Chapter 4, we find that out of the 44 clauses, 40 are in the declarative mood consisting of statements made by Confucius, and 5 in the interrogative. There are two types of interrogative questions. The first type is of a rhetorical question put forward by Confucius in order to intensify the statements he has made, as illustrated in the second clause within the quotation ended with a question mark in [1]; the second type of real questions concerning an issue or a view asked by his disciples to Confucius or other Masters who then offered answers, as illustrated in [4]. There is not a single example of clauses in the imperative or exclamatory mood in this chapter, which, from another angle, strengthens the book as one of mainly giving information — imparting knowledge.

D. Features of modal elements

Halliday argues that a modal element would either denote polarity or modality, which can be further classified into modalization and modulation (Halliday 1994). Looking at Chapter 4, we find that out of the 44 clauses, 39 are sitting on either the positive or negative pole. There are only two clauses expressing modalization: possibility. For instance,

> [7] 子曰:"三年无改于父之道,**可**谓孝矣。"(*The Analects* IV: 19) [*zi yue: san nian wu gai yu fu zhi dao,* ***ke*** *wei xiao yi.* — Confucius said: "If a son has not changed the principles held by his father (after his father passes away) for three years, then he **can be** said to be filial."]

where "可" expresses modalization: possibility: probability.

There are three clauses expressing modulation: obligation. For example,

> [8] 子曰:"父母在,不远游,游**必**有方。"(*The Analects* IV: 18) [*zi yue: "fu mu zai, bu yuan you, you* ***bi*** *you fang.* — When parents are alive, (the son) does not go far; (if he has to do so,) he **must** have a definite place."]

where "必" expresses modulation: obligation: required, a high degree of obligation.

The dominance of using many modal elements denoting polarity or high degree of modulation: obligation demonstrates the affirmative belief on the part of the speaker, namely Confucius, in his own philosophical views or values. In other words, these are truths, which should not be doubted.

To sum up, the application of the verbal processes, the monologist or dialogic form, the 1 ^"2 logic pattern between the projecting and the projected clauses, the dominance of the declarative mood, and modal elements denoting polarity or high degree of modulation: obligation all work together to define the nature of the book as transmitting knowledge by a master to his followers, and to reinforce the power of Confucius as a master of teaching, to establish him as an authority of philosophy and to strengthen the truthfulness enshrined in his sayings.

13.3 Relevance of Confucianism to China and the present world

We have discussed above "the particular social and ideological environment" of the society which "engendered" *The Analects*. On the other hand the book has also exerted "the power' to change the environment that engendered it" (Halliday 2002: 196). This has to do with the impact that the book has exercised on the generations after it came into being. To evaluate its impact, we may apply the theory of appraisal.

Martin in his books elaborates on his appraisal system (1992; 2003) mainly in terms of the lexico-grammatical features of the text itself. However, a book of philosophy, written more than 2 500 years ago, needs to be evaluated also in terms of its historical impact and the possible impact it can exercise in the present world. It follows that the appraisal system should include these two aspects too if the evaluation is made on a classical work. This would be best done by analyzing the book itself and representative works commenting on the book; however due to the limit of space, we shall do this in other articles written later. Here we shall only briefly summarize our evaluative comments.

The Analects is a book by which Confucius proposed views hoping to find solutions to the social problems of his times. The wise saying by Confucius has helped many people learn about nature, the world, and the appropriate human behavior. Confucianism became, long after the master's death, the dominant Chinese philosophy both morally and politically, eventually transforming Chinese society with its values, and prevailing for centuries before 1911 when the last feudal dynasty was overthrown. Although Confucianism was very much criticized after 1919 when the May 4th Movement took place and after 1949 on the mainland of China, particularly during the "Cultural Revolution", its influence is still strongly felt among the Chinese people, especially in China's Hong Kong and Taiwan and in many East Asian countries. The recent revival of Confucianism in China has further intensified its impact. It can be said that it is *The Analects* that, to a great extent, has shaped the Chinese nation and "engendered" the particular social, political and ideological environment for the maintenance of the Chinese civilization (Leys 1998).

But can the values in *The Analects* or Confucianism engender an environment hopeful for the current world? The answer is "Yes."

First, they are relevant to our personality development. Confucius regards cultivation of the self as the basis of social and political order. His social philosophy largely revolves around the concept of 仁 (*ren*): to love others; to honor one's parents; to do what is right instead of what is of advantage. 仁 is a concept through which we can acquire traditional value or virtue so as "to achieve a state of orderliness and peace" (Hooker 2005).

Second, they are relevant to the management of a nation. Confucius believed that a ruler should learn self-discipline, should govern his subjects by his own example, and should treat them with love and concern or 仁. In the present day China, where occur frequent conflicts between different social strata we find this doctrine is particularly significant in "balancing the interests between different social groups, avoiding conflicts and making sure people live a safe and happy life in a politically stable country" (Wen 2005).

Third, they are relevant to raising the quality of education. The fundamental tenet held by Confucianism is "the unwavering belief in the perfectibility of human beings through learning" (Wilhelm 1970). Confucius was willing to teach anyone, whatever their social standing, which is best presented in his saying "有教无类" (*you jiao wu lei*— Teach anyone regardless of their social classes). He taught his students morality, proper speech, government, and the refined arts but he regards morality as the most important subject. This argument still holds true in the current world where morality is declining drastically. Confucius' pedagogical methods were also striking: he never spoke at length on a subject; instead he posed questions, cited passages from the classics, or used apt analogies, and waited for his students themselves to arrive at the right answers. Besides, he developed a dialectical view on the relation between learning and thinking. He said, "He who learns but does not think is lost. He who thinks but does not learn is in great danger." (*The Analects* II: 15)

Fourthly, they are relevant to the reconciliation of the international conflicts. Though Confucius lived over 2,500 years ago, yet "the truth and importance of his words still resonate today because his teaching was developed in reaction to the times in which he lived and our times are very much like his, where crime is on the rise, millions of people in poverty, regional wars and invasions are not infrequent" (Wilhelm 1970). We believe that the golden rule "what you don't do yourself, don't do to others" (*The Analects* VI: 28), which was first meant to help establish a proper personal social relationship, can also be applied to smoothening relations between countries with different cultural, religious and political backgrounds.

13.4 Conclusion

This chapter has made a linguistic study through which the main gist and the hierarchical structure of the ideas of Confucius have been disclosed. It puts stress on the linguistic phenomenon of repetition, arguing that this cohesive device contributes to the establishment of Confucius as a Master of philosophy and to the revelation of the essence of his teaching: the cultivation of the quality of 仁, which can be achieved by developing other related qualities through learning and following the models of our ancestors. The chapter has also discussed in brief the verbal processes, the monologist or dialogic form, the logic pattern in clause complexes and the dominance of the declarative mood and modal elements denoting polarity or obligation, which function to reinforce the power of Confucius as a master of teaching and to strengthen the truthfulness of his sayings.

This chapter has once again applied the three-step analytical model for discourse analysis (Fang 2005), which has further verified the applicability of this model. We have not only made an analysis of some important lexico-grammatical features, but also studied relevant factors of the cultural and situational contexts which engendered this book, which in its turn, has exerted a significant impact on the formation of Chinese culture and society.

The chapter is by no means a thorough study of *The Analects*, nor has it made a comprehensive evaluation. We have meant to point out that the essence of Confucianism still holds true. We believe that if China intends to continue on its embankment towards modernization, it not only has to revive Confucianism and other traditional values and ethics but also to develop them in the light of the new era. We also believe that the world is hopeful if we can construct a world of peace and harmony as envisioned by Confucius through creating "a multicultural context" and "a liberal atmosphere in which all the cultural forces and discourses", "whether Western or Eastern, could find their own sphere of function, and different opinions could thus encounter and carry on dialogues" (Wang 2004). In this sense, many of the good teachings by Confucius in the short but valuable book *The Analects* are still significant for the 21st century China and the 21st century world.

14

An Analysis of the "Attitudes" in a Discourse on Confucius*

14.1 Introduction

The chapter has taken from the internet for analysis a brief biological commentary on Confucius written by Richard Hooker (1996; updated 1999 & 2005). The choice of analyzing a text on Confucius has been inspired by Martin's point of view on PDA (positive discourse analysis, Martin & Rose 2003) that there are positive values embodied in human discourses such as this one that can be used as an attempt to change the world into a better one. There are, therefore, three purposes of this chapter: first, to see what positive attitudes the author adopts in evaluating Confucius; second, to see what rhetoric devices the author employs to align the reader into sharing his evaluation of Confucius; and third, to reveal the attitudinal implications invested in by the author with his types of attitudes.

---

* This chapter is based on a plenary presentation at the 10th National Discourse Analysis Conference held at Henan University, Kaifeng, Henan Province, 2006.

We adopt the "top-down" analytical model for our analysis. First we will define the genre of this text and divide it into several generic stages, and then we will analyze the features of the context of culture and those of the three variables of the context of situation of the discourse, namely, field of discourse, tenor of discourse and mode of discourse, in order to set our analysis against a clearly-defined background. The focus of the chapter, however, is on the discussion of the attitudinal orientations of the text by applying the appraisal theory (Martin & Rose 2003; Martin & White 2005), with particular concern over the interaction of appreciation, judgment, engagement and graduation, or over how evaluation is established, amplified, targeted and sourced. Finally, the paper will provide an evaluation of the semantic implications of these attitudinal orientations.

As mentioned above, the text for analysis is a brief biological commentary on Confucius, or a very brief introduction to the life and work of Confucius plus an evaluative commentary by the author on the personality of and contributions by Confucius. Therefore, the short text is to propose an argument for appreciation and admiration of Confucius and to evaluate his impact in history so as to promote the image of Confucius and popularize the philosophical ideas and way of thinking of Confucius among the potential readers, or to align the reader into positioning favorable attitudes towards this great scholar.

14.2 Theoretical parameters relevant to the analysis

There are several aspects of systemic-functional linguistic theory employed in this chapter: Halliday's concept of context of culture and that of context of situation (H & H 1985), and the concept of genre and the appraisal theory developed by Martin and his colleagues (Martin & Rose 2003; Martin & White 2005; Hood 2004). We will not elaborate on the concept of the context of situation here since it is very well known to all systemic-functional researchers. We will adopt Martin's argument concerning genre: "a staged, goal-orientated social process". Martin's concepts arise from the view that there are two strata making up the language: the outer language: genre, which constitutes the context of culture and the three variables: field, tenor and mode which make up the context of situation, and inner language, which performs three functions: ideational, interpersonal and textual, as shown in Figure 14 - 1 (Martin & White 2005):

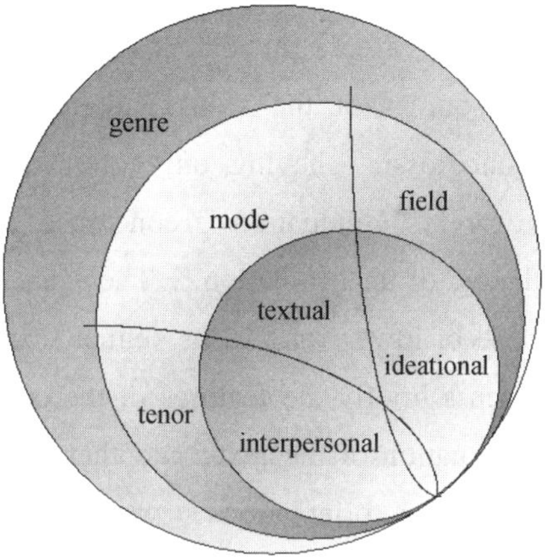

Figure 14 - 1 Strata of Language

Though we agree that genre may be one of the main variables constituting the context of culture, we believe that there are other factors such as the ideological variable that we should take into consideration. We think that Halliday's definition of context of culture as "the socio-historical and ideological environment engendering, and engendered by the text" developed as early as in the 1960s (2002: 151) can be applied for analyzing the context of culture of a discourse. In our analysis, therefore, we will follow this definition and also his concept of context of situation constituted of three variables: field, tenor and mode for disclosing the contextual features of the language.

The main analytical tool applied here, however, is the theory of appraisal, which is "one of the three major discourse semantic resources construing interpersonal meaning (alongside involvement and negotiation)" (Martin & White 2005: 34 - 35).

By definition, appraisal is concerned with the evaluation of "the kinds of attitudes that are negotiated in a text, the strength of the feelings involved and the ways in which values are sourced and readers aligned" (Martin & Rose 2003: 22). The system of appraisal consists of the sub-systems of attitude, engagement and graduation. Attitude conveys our "feelings, judgement of behavior and evaluation of things" (*ibid.*). It divides into three aspects: affect, judgement and appreciation. Engagement is concerned with the sources of the values implicated by the author, which can be either monoglossic (having only one voice) or heteroglossic (having multiple voices). "Graduation is concerned with gradability" or "with adjusting the degree of an evaluation". There are two kinds of graduation: force: either raise or lower, and focus: either sharpen or soften (*ibid.*). Next we will first discuss briefly the features of the context of culture and those of the context of situation of the text, and then work out the generic organization and the evaluative orientations, which are followed by analyzing how these evaluative orientations are realized stage by stage via certain rhetorical devices in the text.

14.3 Analysis of the Text

14.3.1 Features of the context of culture

What was the socio-historical and ideological environment for the engendering of this article in the late 1990s when Hooker wrote this commentary? It is clearly set against a modern world consisting of "different religions and different forms of governments" and a modern China whose way of thinking in many aspects "derived from" Confucius who lived more than 2,500 years ago (Hooker 1996).

14.3.2 Features of the context of situation

The **Field** of the discourse is a brief account of and commentary on the life of a person. The **Tenor** concerns the relation between the writer and the reader who maintain a maximum distance; the power relations between the two parties: the writer has a dominant power over the reader as he is the one who determines the content and attitudes towards the person evaluated, and also it is he who uses some rhetoric devices to express his values and attitudes with which he intends to influence the attitudes of the reader towards the person he evaluates. The discourse is in the written **Mode** from the third person perspective. As mentioned, the focus of the chapter is on discussing the features of Tenor and some rhetoric devices the author employs to align the reader into sharing his evaluation of Confucius.

14.3.3 Generic organization and stages

This is a short article containing only 283 words (see Appendix). It is a typical example of a brief biological commentary on a popular figure. Generically speaking, the text divides into three big stages: **impact of Confucius ^ life and work of Confucius ^ impact of Confucius' teaching method**, with the second stage further cut into four minor stages/phases: the **identity of Confucius and status of his family ^ a description of his names ^ experiences of his political life ^ his experiences as a teacher**. The composition of the stages is typical of this type of genre: it usually begins with a general evaluation of the importance of this person, which is followed by a very brief introduction to his birth, his family background, his life and work experience and then finally his unique contribution to a specific field of human civilization.

The purpose of dividing the stages is for detailed analyses of the attitudes inscribed or evoked by the author.

14.3.4 Evaluative orientations

The text is organized around the following three main evaluative orientations:

Appreciation: Confucius' impact on the way of thinking of Chinese and East Asians;

Sympathy: Confucius being born as an ordinary person at a hard time and his failure in realizing his political aspiration;

Admiration: Confucius' successful early political career as an administrator, and his natural talent in and method for teaching.

14.3.5 Analyses of the attitudes negotiated at each stage

Stage 1: Impact of Confucius

The author's appreciative attitudinal orientation is clearly expressed from the first three clauses right from the beginning:

> Confucius laid down a pattern of thinking followed by **more** people for **more** generations than **any other** human being **on the face of the earth**. **No matter** what religion, **no matter** what form of government, **the Chinese (and most other East Asian civilizations)** and their way of thinking can *in some way* be shown to have Confucian elements about them.

The author's positive appreciation and evaluation of Confucius' impact on the way of thinking among people is conveyed implicitly though objectively by the employment of the two "more"s and "any other" in the comparative clause "more ... than" [... **more** (intensifier : comparative : up-scaling : quality) ... people for **more** (*ibid.*) generation than **any other** (graduation : focus : sharpen) human being ...], which are further intensified and strengthened by the modifier "**on the face of earth**" amplifying the scope and space of Confucius' influence, implying that nobody else in the world can surpass his impact.

This intensified appreciation is further strengthened by the use of the two negative conjunctive expressions of "**no matter**" (counter-expectancy) (**No matter** what religion, **no matter** what form of government), though contracted or softened by the mentioning of the nationalities and regions which have felt his impact (**Chinese** and **most other East Asian** civilizations) and by the adverbial phrase "**in some way**" (graduation : focus : soften), which serves to moderate the evaluation of Confucius' impact.

This appreciative attitude at this stage is mainly rendered through the voice of the author. In other words, the impact of Confucius is constructed via the monoglossia as being "taken-for-granted" (Martin & White 2005). Thus "the reader who is being written into the text" (*ibid.*) from the start is one whose attitude may be affected by the author's appreciative tone and will tend to take a positive view of Confucius. This appreciation is further supported by another unknown voice via the verb "show" (engagement : proclaim : endorsement) in the passive construction, which functions to warrant the validity of this evaluation.

To sum up, we find at this stage an interaction between graduation: intensification and engagement of mainly the authorial voice supported by an unknown voice. By the use of the rhetoric devices of the comparative formulas and conjunctive pattern of counter-expectancy (though the tone is somewhat softened), the author succeeds in rendering a rather strong positive evaluation of Confucius' impact on a pattern of thinking on earth. This is mostly made via monoglossia, which is "endorsed" by the verb process "be shown" inviting a supporting voice from outside.

Stage 2: Life and work of Confucius

The sympathetic and admirable attitudinal orientation of the author is made through this short introduction to the experiences of the life and work of the person in question, which covers four minor stages: the **identity of Confucius and status of his family** ^ **a description of his names** ^ **experiences of his political life** ^ **his experiences as a teacher.** We will elaborate on these attitudes expressed in each of the minor stages.

Minor stage 1: identity of Confucius and status of his family

This part of the text goes as follows:

> But Confucius was no religious leader nor did he claim any special divine status (nor was any divine status claimed for him). He was, in fact, a relatively ordinary person; his family was from the lesser aristocracy that had fallen on extremely hard times when he was born in 551 B.C. in the province of Lu.

To begin with, the author provides Confucius' identity by using the negative polarity "**no**" and the negative conjunctives "**nor ... nor**" (**engagement: contract: disclaim**) to negate what kind of person he was not so as to define what kind of a person he was. The three negative expressions are resources for introducing an alternative positive position into the text or are presented as responding to such claims or beliefs that Confucius **was** a religious leader, and yet the employment of these formulations is for the purpose of rejecting such a position (Refer to Martin & White 2005: 117).

This first short clause complex gives a good example to illustrate the interaction between judgement: normality, and engagement. The identity of Confucius is actually made by heteroglossics or through three voices. The first is the authorial voice who makes the proposition that "Confucius was no religious leader", which is a firm assertion serving to counter an alternative position; the intention is to align the reader with the textual attitudinal judgement of Confucius' identity, and hence to enhance solidarity between the writer and the reader; the second from Confucius by the use of the verbal process "claim" (engagement : expand : attribute : distance) (nor did **he claim** any special divine status), which is intended to serve to support the author's assertion in the first clause as the claim was made from none other than Confucius himself; however, at the same time the word also distances the authorial stance from the proposition, thus "opening the dialogic space for alternative positions" (Martin & White 2005: 102); and the third voice from an unknown source by means of a nominal group plus the passive construction of "claim" (nor **was** any divine status **claimed** for him). The passive construction implies that the person who has made this proposition is unknown or the identity of the source is unimportant or the author intends to shift the responsibility of the proposition unto others. Again "claim" functions to separate the textual voice from the external unknown voice. The three sources of voices work together to identify Confucius as someone who was "no religious leader", and this identity is intensified by the repetition of the three negative polar expressions.

In the next clause the author describes what a person Confucius was (He was, in fact, a *relatively* **ordinary** person.). Here his sympathetic attitude towards Confucius is fully indicated through the adjective "ordinary", which denotes "judgment : normality" in the negative sense though the tone is softened by its modifier "**relatively**" (graduation : focus : soften).

This attitude remains in "his family was from the **lesser** aristocracy that had fallen on ***extremely*** **hard times** when he was born in 551 B.C. in the province of Lu." The use of the nominal group "hard times" denotes judgment: normality in the negative sense when he was born, which is intensified by the adverbial modifier "extremely" (graduation : intensifier : up-scaling : maximization), operating hyperbolically to convey a strong writer's investment in this proposition. The comparative "lesser" (graduation : intensifier : comparative : down-scaling : quality) is employed to contract or reduce the social status of his family. The verbal group "had fallen" (judgement : − normality) indicates the unfortunate declining of his family, clearly showing the authorial sympathy which intends to evoke a similar attitude from the reader. These negative judgments of his family status and economic position when he was born achieve the effect of making a great contrast between Confucius' impact and his ordinariness as a person at birth, thus being capable of arousing and evoking not only the sympathy but also a stronger admiration for him from the reader, who would not have expected a person from such an unfavorable family background could have achieved such a fame and produced such a great impact.

The admirable tone is further captured and strengthened by the conjunction "but" (contrast : disclaim), which signals a counter-expectation. For the reader might expect that the impact of Confucius mentioned previously could have been contributed to a special family background. However, this counter-expectation serves to reject this supposition and states that there was nothing special about him.

To sum up, there is an interaction among engagement : negative judgement, heteroglossia : disclaim, and up-scaling or down-scaling graduation : intensification. The proposition of "Confucius was no religious leader" is made through three voices: the author, Confucius and an unknown voice by the use of two "claim" (engagement : expand : attribute : distance), whose function is to distance the author from the proposition. The author expresses a sympathetic attitude towards Confucius' social status at birth by the adjectives "ordinary", "hard", the comparative expression "lesser", and this attitude is intensified by the adverb "extremely". This sympathetic attitude is turned into admiration for Confucius by the use of the conjunction "but" (contrast : disclaim) which rejects the expectation that Confucius would have come from a family of a high status with favorable conditions, and therefore strengthens the proposition that Confucius was the more worth admiring.

Minor stage 2: a description of his names

> He **was born** into the family of K'ung and **was given** the name Ch'iu; in later life he **was called** "Master Kung": K'ung Fu-tzu, from which the Latin form, Confucius, **is derived**.

This minor stage has an outstanding feature of engagement: heteroglossia: all the verbs are in the passive voice, implying that the names come from other sources than the author himself, who takes no responsibility of giving these names or that it is unimportant to provide the sources.

Minor stage 3: experiences of his political life

The author's admiration and sympathetic attitudinal orientation are given by the wordings of:

> He began a ***startlingly*** **successful** early political career as a young man, **rising *quickly*** in the administrative ranks, but **fell out of favor *fast.*** **Although** his intense personal goal was to restore peace and orderliness to the province, **he found himself dismissed** from government early on. He ***never*** returned to public life.

In the first two clauses, the author's appreciation and admiration of Confucius' achievement in his early political life are inscribed explicitly in the adjective "**successful**" (judgement : + capacity), whose effect is amplified by the adverb "***startlingly***" (graduation : intensifier : maximization : quality); this positive evaluation of his political career is further up-scaled by the lexical verbal expression "**rising**" (judgment : + normality), implying that as a young man Confucius did extremely well in politics; the force of which becomes stronger by the positive adverb modifier "quickly" (graduation : intensifier : up-scaling vigor), which stresses the speediness of the process of his promotion. However, soon he "fell out of favor" (judgment : − normality) and "dismissed" (judgment : − normality) from his high political position; both verbal groups were negative in sense, with the first intensified by the use of the adverb "fast" (intensifier : vigor) to show the quick speed of the action of his falling out of favor, and the second verb in the passive construction with the implication that he was forced to leave his position. Clearly, the two verbal expressions give a sympathetic tone from the author implying it was a great pity that Confucius was not given the chance to realize his political aspiration. The concessive conjunction "**although**" (engagement : counter : disclaim) is employed to soften the positive goal of Confucius. In the last clause, the polar adverb "**never**" (engagement : contract : disclaim) is used to strengthen the denial of the opportunity for him to achieve his political ambition in his later life.

There are two voices we can hear in the section: the main one is from the author (He began a ***startlingly*** **successful** early political career as a young man, **rising** ***quickly*** in the administrative ranks, but **fell out of favor** ***fast.*** **Although** his intense personal goal was to restore peace and orderliness to the province ...), whose mologlossical assertive appreciation and admiration of and sympathy for Confucius loaded with the above mentioned inscriptive expressions (***startlingly*** **successful; rising** ***quickly***) will very possibly invite the reader to share his evaluation and judgment. The other voice is conveyed by the expression "he found himself dismissed ...", which contributes the source to Confucius so as to show the unexpectedness and disappointment of Confucius in his unhappy political experience soon after his success. In addition, the negative adverb "never" (engagement : contract : disclaim) would counter the expectation from the reader with regard to his political career, thus further evoking the sympathy from the reader.

To sum up, the author makes a contrast between a positive judgement of Confucius' early political life and a negative appreciation and judgment of Confucius' political life in his later years. The positive judgement of Confucius' early political life is explicitly inscribed in the adjective "successful" and the verbal lexis "rising", whose effect is amplified respectively by the adverbs "*startlingly*" and "quickly"; while the negative appreciation and judgment of Confucius' political career in his later years is revealed by the use of the verbal phrases "fell out of favor", the speed and the degree of which is shown by the adverb "fast", the verb "dismissed" and the adverb "never".

Minor stage 4: his experiences as a teacher

The author's admiration of Confucius as a teacher is fully captured in this stage:

> Instead he turned to teaching, **hoping that** he could change the

world by changing its leaders at a young age. We have **many** accounts of his teaching and **all** his students **praise his natural talent** for **brilliant teaching**. These students recorded these teachings and this is what comes down to us as *The Analects*.

Here the author's admiration and positive appreciation of Confucius' personality and his talent in teaching are demonstrated in the second clause by the verb "**praise**" (appreciation : + reaction) and the noun "**talent**" (judgment : + capacity), which is modified by the adjective "**natural**" (judgment : + normality), stressing that this talent was born or bestowed with him, thus being distinctive from other talents which are only trained after birth. This orientation of admiration is highlighted by the adjective "**brilliant**" (judgment : + capacity and appreciation : + valuation) modifying the quality of his teaching. These positive judgment and appreciation are amplified by the adjectives "many" and "all", with "many" (graduation : intensifier : quantifier) to modify the records of his teaching, and "all" (*ibid.*) to strengthen the force of the praise by his students, implying that his students' unanimous agreement on the quality of their teacher is something very rare, as usually people are divided in their opinions in passing judgment on a certain person or a certain matter.

This stage is also a good example of using heterogrossia or multiple voices in presenting the sources of information. Apart from the authorial voice (he turned to teaching; we have many accounts ...; these students recorded ...), there are other two voices: from Confucius himself and from his students. In order to attribute the aspiration of changing the world coming from Confucius himself, the author projected the clause "hoping that he could change the world by changing its leaders at a young age", in which the logical agent is Confucius. The use of the "what clause" and "as + noun" form as a projected element within a clause is to indicate that the source is unknown or vague, thus shouldering no responsibility for the proposition made in the text.

To sum up, this stage is highlighted by the author's positive appreciation and judgment of Confucius' personality and his teaching quality via the use of positive content verb "praise", the nominal group "natural talent", the adjective "brilliant". This positive evaluation is amplified and intensified by the quantifiers "many" and "all", and projected by the projected clause "hoping that ...", "what clause" and "as" phrase to bring in other sources than the authorial.

Stage 3: The impact of his teaching method

In the last stage, the author has chosen the best representative field to which Confucius is known to have made a great contribution:

> The Confucian method characterizes just about **all** Chinese learning down to the present day; its **fundamental** tenet is the **unwavering belief** in the **perfectibility of human beings** through learning.

There are several rhetoric devices used by the author to evaluate Confucius' teaching method. The adjective "**all**" (graduation : intensifier : quantifier) as an amplifier is employed to strengthen the statement in the first clause implying that this is exclusive and there is no exception concerning "Chinese learning" in terms of applying Confucius' teaching method, though the tone is softened by the expression "just about" (graduation : focus : soften), thus making the positive values moderate. The use of the adjective "**fundamental**" which is a **positive appreciation : valuation**, on the other hand, stresses that it is Confucius rather than others who laid down the basic principles or foundation of education in China. The author also shows his admiration for Confucius' belief in education by the use of the adjective "**unwavering**" (judgment : + tenacity) to demonstrate Confucius' resolute belief that human beings can be educated to become a perfect person. The nominalization "**perfectibility**" (of human beings through learning) (appreciation : + reaction & graduation : intensifier : maximization : quality) defined as an ideal human quality able to be achieved through education has a cultural implication: it can be a challenge to the Christian belief that man is born evil and can never become perfect, and that the whole life of a person should be spent in repentance, and man's only hope lies in his afterlife when he is in heaven. Here Confucius provides an alternative philosophical belief which may bring about confidence in human beings themselves and thus Western readers would be invited to consider this alternative. The praise and the admiration are monoglossically asserted in these wordings so that there is no possibility of tolerance for alternative viewpoints; the purpose is to evoke the reader into sharing the author's attitude of positive evaluation of Confucius teaching method and belief in the significance of education.

To sum up, the author's positive appreciation of Confucius' contribution to and of his belief in education is made through the author's narration and by use of the adjectives "fundamental" and "unwavering", and of the nominalization "perfectibility". This positive appraisal of Confucius' impact on Chinese learning is strengthened by the use of the adjective "all" but then the tone is somewhat softened by the use of "just about".

14.3.6 Summary of the attitudes and rhetorical devices employed in the text

Our interpretation of the inscribed and evoked attitudes of this text is summarized in Table 14 - 1, and the rhetorical devices employed in Table 14 - 2 and 14 - 3 respectively. The summaries are made by following Martin and White (2005).

Table 14 - 1 Inscribed and Evoked attitudes of This Text

Appraising items	Appraiser	Affect	Judgment	Appreciation	Appraised
ordinary	Hooker		−normality		Confucius' family
lesser aristocracy	Hooker		−normality		Confucius' family
hard times	Hooker		−normality		Confucius' family
had fallen	Hooker		−normality		Confucius' family

(Continued on the next page)

Appraising items	Appraiser	Affect	Judgment	Appreciation	Appraised
successful	Hooker		+capacity		Confucius' early political life
rising quickly	Hooker		+normality		Confucius' early PL
fell out of favor	Hooker		−normality		Confucius' later PL
dismissed	Hooker		−normality		Confucius' later PL
praise	Hooker			+reaction	Confucius' teaching
natural	Hooker		+normality		Confucius' talent in teaching
brilliant	Hooker		+capacity		Confucius' teaching
fundamental	Hooker			+valuation	Confucius' impact on Chinese learning
unwavering	Hooker		+tenacity		Confucius' belief
perfectibility	Hooker			+reaction	Confucius' belief

Table 14－2 A Summary of the Features of Engagement in the Text

Stage One	Heteroglossia
	Show (proclaim : endorsement) from unknown
	No matter … (contract : disclaim) from the author
Stage Two: Minor Stage One	(No) … nor … nor (contract : disclaim) from the author, Confucius and unknown
	Claim (expand : attribute : distance) from Confucius
	Claim (expand : attribute : distance) from unknown
	But (contract : counter) from the author
Stage Two: Minor Stage Two	(Verbs in passive construction) from unknown
Stage Two: Minor Stage Three	Began … rising … fell out of … from the author
	Although (contract : disclaim : counter) from the author
	Found himself dismissed (expand : attribute : distance) from Confucius

(Continued on the next page)

	Never (contract : disclaim) from the author
Stage Two: Minor Stage Four	Hoping ... (expand : projection) from Confucius
	Many accounts ... from the author
	"What clause" and "as + noun" (expand) from unknown
Stage Three	From the author's voice

Table 14 – 3 A Summary of the Features of Graduation

	Force		Focus	
Stage	**Intensification**	**Quantification**	**Sharpen**	**Soften**
Stage One	more people		any other	in some way
	more generations			
Stage Two	lesser aristocracy			relatively
	extremely (maximizations)			
	startlingly (maximizations)			
	quickly (vigor)			
	fast (vigor)			
		many		
		all		
Stage Three		all		just about

We can observe from the three tables the following attitudinal features which are realized via various rhetorical devices:

1. There is no inscribed nor evoked "affect" conveyed by the author, which well fits the genre of the text as a biological commentary, usually involving no expressions of personal feelings or emotions.

2. There is a positive judgement of Confucius' personality, capacity and talent as well as a positive appreciation of his impact, contribution to education and his belief in perfectibility of human beings through learning (Table 14 – 1).

3. These positive judgements and appreciations are realized by the lexical and grammatical devices such as adjectives (successful, natural, brilliant, fundamental, unwavering), verb processes in different forms (rising, praise) and nominalization (perfectibility) (Table 14－1).

4. These positive stances are further reinforced and strengthened by intensifiers (more, startlingly, quickly) and quantifiers (many, all) (Table 14－3).

5. The author succeeds in evoking a great sympathy and a strong admiration for Confucius by providing negative judgement of Confucius' family background via adjectives such as "ordinary", "hard" times maximized by "extremely"; comparative formulas "lesser" when he was born, and his failure to continue his political career via the use of the verb processes "had fallen", "fell out of favor" intensified by the modifier "fast" and "dismissed" (Table 14－1 & Table 14－3).

6. One can detect three voices from the text (Table 14－2):

1) The authorial voice as a positive evaluative proposition which is being taken for granted, rendering no room for argument as to Confucius' impact, contribution to education and belief in perfectibility through learning.

2) This stance is supported either by the voice coming from Confucius himself (nor did he claim any special divine status; he found himself dismissed; hoping that ...)

3) or from another implicit source (be shown ...; nor was any divine status claimed for him; what comes down).

14.4 Conclusions

We can arrive at some conclusions from the above discussions. To begin with, our analysis of this text may help us to understand more profoundly the nature of a text in two aspects. First, it provides evidence that discourses or texts are both ideological and axiological (Bakhtin 1981; Martin & White 2005). For example, in this text, the author employs various lexical and grammatical items as rhetorical devices not only to construe experiential meanings, which have not been dealt with in the chapter, but at the same time convey the author's judgemental and evaluative attitudes towards the person under question. Second, any discourse or text is dialogic in nature (*ibid.*), or in any discourse or text the writer is in dialogue with the intended reader. This text appears to be a monologue, that is, we seem to hear only the author's voice, yet our analysis shows that there is an active interaction between the author and the reader not only through his own voice but also by inviting other voices so as to align the potential reader.

Secondly, our analyses of the attitudes and the rhetorical devices employed in expressing these attitudes demonstrate Martin's argument (Martin & Rose 2003) on how attitudes would function in a text: the "attitudinal values operate in combination to set up an evaluative prosody which resonates across an attitudinally loaded span" in the text and thus succeed in constructing an alignment and solidarity between the author and reader.

Thirdly, the chapter provides evidence for testifying the significance of PDA. In the current world, we not only need to use CDA (critical discourse analysis) as a tool to make critical analysis of discourses in order to reveal or expose the negative aspects existing in our lives, but more importantly, to examine the positive elements in positive discourses so that they may help us see positive elements in our society which may contribute to building up our confidence in constructing a hopeful society and a harmonious world.

However, there seems a question with regard to the appraisal theory. It seems to me that attitudes should permeate throughout a text: every word would either directly or indirectly imply the attitudes of the author. Should we only concentrate on the interpersonal meaning under the umbrella of "appraisal"? Should we not make evaluation of the ideology conveyed by the ideational meaning and the textual meaning via the lexis and grammatical structures employed in the discourse as well?

Appendix:

The text with indications of stages in brackets is presented below:

Confucius laid down a pattern of thinking followed by more people for more generations than any other human being on the face of the earth. No matter what religion, no matter what form of government, the Chinese (and most other East Asian civilizations) and their way of thinking can in some way be shown to have Confucian elements about them (**Impact of Confucius**). But Confucius was no religious leader nor did he claim any special divine status (nor was any divine status claimed for him). He was, in fact, a relatively ordinary person; his family was from the lesser aristocracy that had fallen on extremely hard times when he was born in 551 B.C. in the province of Lu. He was born into the family of K'ung and was given the name Ch'iu; in later life he was called "Master Kung": K'ung Fu-tzu, from which the Latin form, Confucius, is derived. He began a startlingly successful early political career as a young man, rising quickly in the administrative ranks, but fell out of favor fast. Although his intense personal goal was to restore peace and orderliness to the province, he found himself dismissed from government early on. He never returned to public life. Instead he turned to teaching, hoping that he could change the world by changing its leaders at a young age. We have many accounts of his teaching and all his students praise his natural talent for brilliant teaching. These students recorded these teachings and this is what comes down to us as the *Analects* (**Account of his life and work**). The Confucian method characterizes just about all Chinese learning down to the present day; its fundamental tenet is the unwavering belief in the perfectibility of human beings through learning (**Impact of his teaching**).

15

A Multisemiotic Analysis of a Chinese Long Scroll Painting*

15.1 Introduction

This chapter is an attempt to analyze the multimodal presentations of a long scroll painting *Along the River During the Qingming Festival* (*qingming shang he tu*, 清明上河图), produced more than 800 years ago in China's Northern Song Dynasty by Zhang Zeduan, as shown on the next page①:

---

* This chapter is based on Chapter 9 by Fang Yan from the book entitled *Multimodal Text from around the World: Cultural and linguistic Insights*, edited by Wendy L. Bowcher and published by Palgrave Macmillan in 2012.

① Refer to the website of the Beijing Palace Museum where this work is preserved: http://www.dpm.org.cn/www_oldweb/China/phoweb/Relicpage/2/R945.htm. Refer also to the brochure copy of the original painting printed in Kaifeng, which is the capital city of Henan Province, China (the publisher unknown) and to the book by Rong Bao Zhai Press (1999) entitled *The Scroll of 'Along the River During the Qingming Festival'*. Episodes of this painting can also be referred to on page 6 in the book written by Wang Bomin (2009) entitled *History of Chinese Painting*, published by Culture and Art Publishing House, Beijing (website accessed 21st February 2010).

There are several reasons to choose this painting as my analytical datum. To begin with, the painting itself, which depicts a few hundred people and many animals engaging in enormous number of activities, is invaluable for the study of Chinese cultural features and the life of people from different social strata on the occasion of "The Tomb-Sweeping Festival", a festival for paying tribute to one's ancestors, and also known as "the Qingming Festival"① (translated as "The Pure Brightness Festival"), a festival for people to enjoy the new spring season and for social gatherings and business transactions at fairs. Secondly, it has a high value as a work of art — it is considered by many to be one of the ten masterpieces in Chinese history; one of the postscript writers even regards it as a "神品" (*shen pin*) or a divine piece (Zhang 1962: 30). Thirdly, this work represents the typical practice of a Chinese painting, in which both verbal and visual elements are included. Usually a Chinese painting is composed of four genres, namely, a drawing, a calligraphic title, a stamp (seal) and sometimes a poem to accompany the artistic work. This painting does not have a poem but it includes the drawing, the calligraphic title and seals bearing the names of those who once had the fortune to own it. These features differ from those of paintings in other cultures. While the painting is a purely visual semiotic artefact, the title and the seals are considered to be both visual and verbal, being unique forms of Chinese art on the one hand, and presented graphically in Chinese characters on the other. This painting, for example, is said to have the title written by Zhao Ji or the Song Dynasty Emperor Huizong, one of the most famous calligraphers in Chinese history, and to have his double-dragon royal seal printed on this scroll②. Lastly, this work of art is a significant social semiotic in contributing to the understanding of the political, economic, technological, artistic, architectural and general social life of the Northern Song Dynasty (Zhang 1962).

The theory informing the analysis is that of Systemic-Functional Linguistics (SFL). The present study pioneers a social semiotic interpretation of this long scroll painting by applying the analytical tools of SFL theory.

---

① Qingming Festival falls usually on April 5th and sometimes on April 4th of the year, depending on the correlations between the solar and the Chinese lunar calendar.

② Refer to the website: http://baike.baidu.com/view/7998.htm dated 21st of February, 2010.

This chapter aims to identify the generic and semantic features of visual and verbal modes of this work in terms of the three metafunctions developed by Halliday (1994); to reveal how the semiotic resources work together to create meanings and to build up the texture to produce a coherent whole; and to explore the "cultural environment" for "engendering" this artefact and also its impact on China to the present day.

15.2 A Functional approach to an analysis of multisemiosis

Systemic Functional Linguistics (see for example Halliday 1994), originally developed for linguistic analysis, has been found by many to be an appropriate theory for interpreting other social semiotics such as visual, verbal or audio modes (O'Toole 1994; Kress & Leeuwen 1996; Lemke 1998; O'Halloran 2004). For example, Lemke (in Martinec 2005: 168) observes: "Michael Halliday's (1978) identification of three fundamental 'metafunctions' for language provides a useful framework for understanding the interaction of multiple semiotic modalities ...". This view is supported by O'Halloran who believes that "a systemic functional approach is useful for conceptualizing and analyzing multimodal semiosis across a range of domains ..." (in Martinec 2005: 160). Further, SFL scholars have developed a "visual grammar" (Kress and Leeuwen 1996) and "the language of displayed art" (O'Toole 1994), which provide models and dimensions for the analysis of multisemiotic discourse. The author adopts Halliday's terms *Ideational*, *Interpersonal* and *Textual* for the narratives and interpretations of the semantic features of both visual and verbal of this Chinese artistic work. For a well-grounded analysis, we have worked out a framework based on that of O'Toole's, which is characterized by analyzing the visual features along the hierarchical ranks (O'Toole 1994: 24) of Picture, Section, Episode, Figure and Member. We have also borrowed some terms and concepts from Painter and Martin (2011) such as "setting" when mentioning the visual background; "power", "social distance", "proximity", "visual affect" and "ambience" when discussing affected feelings and interpersonal relations, and "manner" when describing the behavior of a participant; "prominence", "salience" and "placement when analyzing the textual organization. Table 15 – 1 presents the framework for our analytical work based on O'Toole (1994: 24) with some terms borrowed from Painter and Martin, as mentioned above, for our analytical work although there is only selective discussion of some concepts in the analysis, due to space limitation.

Table 15 – 1 Functions and Systems Relevant to Paintings

Function / Rank	Ideational	Interpersonal	Textual
Picture	Main theme Main setting Participants	Orientation to reality	Genre/generic features Layout; proportion; frame Prominence and salience Rhythm relations Color cohesion
Section	Sub-theme Sub-setting Participants Actions/events/scenes	Perspective Rhythm Path Color Modality	Sub-layout Frame Placement of depicted elements within the frame Alignment
Episode	Sub-setting Actions/events/scenes Participants	Modality Interpersonal relations: power, social distance/proximity Visual affect Ambience	Horizontal; vertical; diagonal Placement of depicted elements within the frame Arrangement of focal points Coherence

(Continued on the next page)

Function / Rank	Ideational	Interpersonal	Textual
Figure	Character Acts/gestures Objects/clothing	Characterization Stance Manner	Relative position: front/back/profile Parallelism
Member	Parts of body Components of objects	Qualities and attributes	Cohesion Reference Parallelism Contrast

Table 15 – 1 displays the potential ranks for the purpose of making a concrete analysis. Based on the multi-strata concept (Halliday 1994; O'Toole 1994), it takes the lower stratum as constituting the higher; therefore, ideationally, "Member" constitutes "Figure", which, in turn, makes up "Episode", till we reach the highest rank "Picture". As shown in this table, we have added the rank "Section" because usually a long scroll may have sub-themes such as the one we analyze here; this rank actualizes "Picture". In our framework, we adopt the concepts of the three metafunctions developed by O'Toole, based on Halliday (1994). The Ideational Function is to "convey some information about reality" or "what the painting actually depicts"; it is concerned with "the subject matter" and "theme" of the work, (O'Toole 1994: 14), which is elaborated on at the different ranks, as shown in the table. The Interpersonal Function provides orientation to the viewer, reveals "the responses evoked in us by the systems of this function" (1994: 5) or the way "a painting engages or addresses the viewer" (1994: 5, 8) and is also concerned with the relations between/among the participants (Painter & Martin 2011). One point needs to be mentioned concerning the interpersonal function is the concept of Modality as explained by O'Toole: that of ambiguity or the degree of uncertainty of what is taking place in a painting or the possible relationships between or among the participants (1994: 9). The interpersonal meanings are also expressed such as at different functional ranks (Table 15 – 1). For example, orientation to reality on the level of Picture is constituted by "Perspective", "Rhythm", "Path", "Color", and "Modality" on the level of "Section", which is in turn constituted by "Modality", "Interpersonal relations", "Visual affect" and "Ambiance" on the level of "Episode", and so on till we get to the lowest level of "Member". The Textual Function is concerned with how "to structure" the ideational and interpersonal functions "into a coherent" whole, focusing on the "arrangement of forms within the pictorial space ..." (O'Toole 1994: 22). This is illustrated by the concepts under "Textual Function" in Table 15 - 1 (see O'Toole 1994, and Painter & Martin 2011, for detailed explanations of these notions).

Our analysis also refers to the figure offered by Kress & van Leeuwen (1996: 197) (reproduced here as Figure 15 - 1) when discussing dimensions of visual space. Figure 15 - 1 shows spatial locations which imply information value. We may interpret the figure as vertically, "Top is Margin and Ideal" and "Bottom is Margin and Real" while horizontally, "Left is Given" and "Right is New" and in both directions, "Center is Centrality", which may be understood as the most prominent point for the viewers. The horizontal spatial information distribution originates from Halliday's argument on the direction of information flow in language (Halliday 1994) based on the writing path from left to right in Western languages. However, does this model apply to cultures where people write from right to left as the ancient Chinese did? Does the argument that "Top is Margin and Ideal"

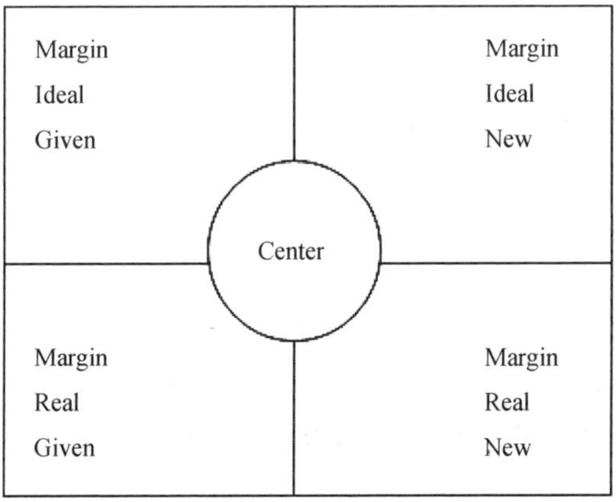

Figure 15 - 1 Dimensions of Visual Space

and "Bottom is Margin and Real" work for our painting? We shall try to find answers to these two questions and at the same time verify the claim "Center is Centrality" when we come to analyze this multisemiotic discourse.

15.3 Semiotic analysis

In this section we shall describe "what can actually be perceived as present in the 'text' of the work itself", which O'Toole considers "the first priority of any description" (1994: 213). Concretely, we shall analyze the functional and semantic features of the painting in detail, the title and the seals briefly and then relate them to the historical and cultural environment for the creation of this work.

15.3.1 Analysis of the visual elements

15.3.1.1 Analysis of the visual elements in the painting proper

In this section, we explore how the theme is construed and represented in the painting proper via visual elements with reference to Table 15 – 1. As it is impossible to examine the enormous activities carried out by the people and animals in many different settings in this long scroll, we shall discuss selectively some activities and events by mainly looking at the two higher levels "Picture" and "Episode". Our discussion also involves "Figure" (participants such as people and animals, and objects such as boats, trees, houses, etc.) and "Member" (expressions on people's faces, parts of a body, components of houses, etc.) — though without going into detail.

First we shall take a look at the ideational function or how the painting construes or represents the reality of that particular era. This is a picture drawn of the city of Bianjing (today's Kaifeng, one of the six ancient capitals, located in Henan Province) 800 years ago. It depicts over 550 humans, over 50 animals, more than 20 boats, about 20 vehicles and sedan chairs①, with the Bian River meandering through the entire length of the artwork. The whole picture enfolds from right to left and presents to the viewer a panoramic view of the suburban and urban areas of this city. On the right, we are presented with the spacious landscape of the rural areas, which serves as the preface to the painting identified as Section One, "Spring View of the Outskirts of Bianjing", where people and commodities are being transported by various means. The river is packed with fishing boats and passenger-carrying ferries, with laborers on the river bank pulling the larger ships. Then the viewer's eyes are drawn to more and more people till they light upon the most crowded place at the center of the painting, described as Section Two "the Busy Wharf of the Bian River", with the Rainbow Bridge located at the center of the painting. The viewer's eyes keep moving further left until they stop at the city gate which leads into "the Noisy Streets in the City", Section Three. We select one Episode from each section for our analysis (We shall take each display here as one episode though it may be further subdivided into more minor episodes.).

The outskirts of the city are taken as the setting of Episode I. It presents a scene of green trees, grass and crop fields, with thatched cottages scattered here and there and surrounded by trees, and a stream running on the far right with a simple bridge across it. Along the river, a team of unhurried rural folk and mules packed with charcoal are approaching the bridge. They are probably coming back towards these cottages or going to the city for the festival. On the left is a zigzag road on which people are seen walking or riding horses or mules from the city. Among them is a sedan chair carried by

① The number differ in the various sources: 550 people, over 50 animals, more than 20 boats, and 20 vehicles and sedans in Zhang Anzhi (1962: 14). This chapter takes the number from Zhang Anzhi.

two laborers and followed possibly by some servants. They are perhaps going from the city to the outskirts eastward to sweep their ancestors' tombs or to visit their relatives in the rural areas. This episode shows travelers amid a wooded countryside, presenting an interplay between actions such as walking, driving and riding in different directions, and the spacious tranquil bucolic scenery: see Illustration 15 - 1.

Illustration 15 - 1 Episode I: Outskirts of Bianjing

In contrast to the scenery in Illustration 1, Episode II, part of Section Two, depicts scenes across the gravity-defying but well-designed Rainbow Bridge (虹桥, *hong qiao*) spanning the Bian River, which by now has become a wide stream and functions as the artery of transportation (see Illustration 15 - 2). Along the southern bank, we see country cottages and roofs of one or two-storied mansions in big courtyards on the two sides of a very wide street running diagonally, where ox carts, mules and horses and people carrying goods with shoulder poles are coming to or going from the bridge. On the second floor of a big house beside one under construction on the left of the street, people are seen sipping tea or wine. What amuses the viewer is the scene on the slope of the bridge, where two men, each extending one hand in his direction, are beckoning to their food stand a gentleman wearing a robe and an official-like hat. On the opposite bank, to the left of the bridge, a horizontal street leads to the wharf, where several boats are moored and the laborers are busy loading cargo. Here we can see a row of small hotels and bars for the crew or laborers. The bridge is the busiest spot — filled with peddlers, pedestrians, and idlers coming and going or wandering among the two rows of vendors' stands extending all along the great bridge, which functions as a kind of fair where various kinds of daily necessities are being sold. Quite a few boats of different sizes are coming toward the bridge or going upriver, one being pulled by the laborers, walking with difficulty along the bank. A large boat full of people and goods is seen approaching at an awkward angle with its masts not completely lowered, threatening to crash into the bridge. The crew is hustling to lower the masts while the dozens of passers-by on the bridge and along the riverside are shouting or gesticulating, trying to steer it along to pass the bridge safely. One of them is seen throwing a rope from the bridge to the outstretched arms of one of the crew below.

Illustration 15 - 2 Episode II: The Rainbow Bridge

Episode III is labelled "The Busy Streets". Here we see the urban area of Bianjing bustling with noise and excitement (see Illustration 15 - 3). There are many activities going on in the wide horizontal street. On the right is the city wall, through whose gate people are coming in or going out. The most conspicuous scene is a team of camels, significantly stressing the importance of the city of Bianjing as the center of business because these camels are not local animals inhabiting in the middle of China; they must have traveled from the far west of China or maybe from one of China's neighbors along the "Silk Road" blazed around the 200 B.C. in the Western Han Dynasty. On the opposite street stands a quadrangle dwelling, a traditional housing structure with a courtyard surrounded by four houses, in the front of which a large group of people and beasts of burden are gathering. On each side of the big gate are two characters, one with "孙家" (*sun jia*) and the other "正店" (*zheng dian*), indicating it is a restaurant run by the Sun family, who are welcoming guests from all directions. Obviously this restaurant is doing a very good business with a houseful of guests. Beside an open ground in the front of the restaurant, peddlers are selling fruit or vegetables and quite a crowd is watching at martial arts or acrobatics. Opposite this group are also busy scenes with men leading horses or mules going along the diagonal street and three or four gentlemen are talking or chatting. What attracts our eyes is a long cart being driven by a row of horses and a few men walking in different postures and manners on both sides. In the busy street, we see two sedan chairs. A man seems to make some gestures to lead the front man carrying one sedan to the opposite side to his hotel. The other sedan chair seems to head for the city gate. Behind them is a group of three with two elderly people, one taking the hand of a child and the other carrying loads on a shoulder pole. They are followed by people in long ropes, who also look as if beckoning the passers-by to their hotels. Closest to the viewer along the diagonal street, four or five people are greeting very politely an elderly man, who seems to be showing off his grandchild in reddish brown. Beside him are a water-carrying mule cart and a private mansion owned by an official by the name of 王 (*Wang*). People in different styles of dresses and costumes are coming out or going into shops or wandering on the street. Here we can also see official buildings or private residences in various styles overlooking the street in the northern part. People from all ranks and walks of life are depicted: peddlers, jugglers, actors, paupers, beggars, monks, fortune tellers, officials and scholars.

Illustration 15 - 3 Episode III: The Busy Streets

Thus reality is construed level by level in a hierarchy. The grand setting of the spring time at the topmost level "Picture" enfolds the landscape in the outskirts and inner city along the Bian River and a panorama of activities, actions, events and scenes, which has the theme of celebrating the festive spirit and worldly commotion at the Qingming Festival; this level is constituted by the level below "Section"; each of the three sections has its particular setting, theme (depicting the festive ambience in that setting), participants and groups of actions and scenes; next below is "Episode", which is exemplified here also by three, each being set in a narrower setting and each depicting sub-actions and scenes involving clear descriptions of everyday activities, participants, scenes or interplay of activities and scenes; "Episode" is then actualized by the figures and members such as the person (Figure: character) throwing a rope to the "outstretching arm" (Member: part of body) of a crew member in order for the boat to avoid crushing into the bridge. We see this also in Episode II — the elderly person (Figure: character) showing off his grandchild to his friends and the man making a welcoming gesture with his hands (part of the body) to the man carrying sedan chair in Episode III.

As far as Interpersonal Functions is concerned, the focus is on the prominent elements, which may set the orientation for the viewer, the external and internal interpersonal relationships, the characterization and the attributes of characters and the attitude the artist displays toward the reality.

The prominent elements refer to those which engage or lead the eyes of the viewer: Perspective, Path, Rhythm, Color, and Modality at the ranks of Section and Episode. The whole picture takes a bird-eye view and a panoramic moving scattering perspective. It is as though the artist may have stood on a high point and his eyes may have swept over a vast space both vertically and horizontally, taking in all the scenes, activities and participants. A moving scattering perspective also means that the painter draws the scenes and participants as though in a continuous manner. In modern times, it could be likened to the way one may make a recording with a film camera; the picture shows what he has spotted no matter whether they are close or distant. The sections and episodes are extending with a waving and dynamic rhythm. Pathways are built up to guide the viewer's eyes to follow the traditional writing path from the right to the left and also to follow the rhythm of the routine of a day: from the morning tranquility of the countryside to the midday commotion on the Rainbow Bridge and along the city streets, although a viewer has the freedom to choose to appreciate this work of art from any direction or angle. These pathways may give the viewer a sense of co-presence as an observer looking at the festival scenes and merry-makers. Different shades of green tell of the spring season, which symbolizes the growth of life, the prosperity of a society, and people's hope and expectation for a good life.

Modality is an important variable for viewers to guess what activities are going on or what relations there are between or among the participants. For instance, in Episode II, we see boats carrying a lot of people rowing towards the bridge from the west or from where the city is located. Where are they heading? And what will the passengers do? It is unclear. Our guess is that very possibly they are going to sweep their ancestors' tombs or visit their relatives in the countryside. From the different ways of transportation and the styles of dresses worn by the people, we can guess their social positions. The horse or mule riders are most likely people of a higher social class, wearing ropes, round hats or in more decent clothes than the peasants with shoulder poles and wagon drivers dressed in shorts.

Also realistically and vividly reflected are the very different and complex interpersonal relations among the over 550 people, who are from different social, educational or family backgrounds. There are two types of interpersonal relationships: the external between the viewers and the painter; and the internal among the participants in the painting. Externally, there are special relationships between the first viewer Emperor Huizong of the Song Dynasty and other later viewers on the one hand, and the painter himself on the other, which will be touched upon in sections 15.3.1.2 and 15.3.2. Internally, the painter presents rich and abundant interpersonal relationships in visual images. A concrete example will suffice. Although the owners and sitters of sedan chairs in Episode III are unseen, their position can be easily identified: they must be people of power and influence, very possibly officials or merchants or landowners because in ancient times they were the people who could afford to have such a procession in public — with servants carrying them and with their faces hidden from the men in the street. This scene alone or in combination with other scenes significantly tells us about the social hierarchy since the Tang Dynasty (AD 618 – 907) (and which lasted until the end of the Qing Dynasty in 1911), when the ruling system in China was fully structured, with the highest rank being the Emperor and his officials, below them merchants and landlords and, at the bottom, farmers, known as peasants in the feudal society (Bai 2002).

From this artistic work, we can also detect the painter's positive attitude and high evaluation of the hard-working people of his era, characterized by the unprecedented active involvement of the urban inhabitants. People are the focus of the artist and the soul of the painting (Lei 2008: Chapter 9), and they are shown as the main driving force of the society. All the static elements such as houses, streets, waterways, ponds, trees and fields serve as the background or setting or stage for the dynamic show of the animate beings.

At the level of Figure and Member which concern the characterization and qualities and attributes of characters, the interpersonal function is also construed vividly in the visual mode. Although all the characters are very tiny, no more than 3 cm tall, yet each is drawn with their own characteristics and attributes. An outstanding feature is that there is not a single repetition in their acts, postures, gestures, stances, manners, or facial expressions. Take the man throwing a rope to the arms of the crew on the boat in Episode II. Applying a lens, we can tell his anxiety with his forward posture and eager facial expressions. Successful characterization is also exemplified in Episode III by the hotel waiter extending his two hands with one inviting his guest of the sedan chair and the other pointing toward the direction of his hotel.

Next we are faced with the question of how the painter has achieved such effects or what techniques he has used to actualize the ideational and interpersonal functions. This is concerned with what the Textual Function can contribute.

First, let's look at the size and the genre of this work. It can be identified as a light colored ink long scroll with a fine style painting on silk

(24.8 cm×528.7 cm). Differing from the Western-style oil painting, this work has several unique Chinese generic features. In terms of content, it is termed as "风俗画" (*fengsu hua*), a genre painting presenting social customs and folklores (Zhang 1962: 1) or "社会生活画" (*shehui shenghuo hua*), a painting depicting social life (Lei 2008: 100). Stylistically, it is a combination of three generic styles — naturalistic drawing of landscapes, realistic sketching of figures and animals, and explicit and exquisite depiction of the images of boats, bridges, carts and wagons, court houses, ordinary people's dwellings of various styles. The last style results from the skills known as the genre 界画 (*jie hua*) or fine-line drawing used by Chinese craftsmen for drawing architectural artifacts (Zhang 1962: 22). It is said that one of the reasons why this painting is famous is because of the degree of accuracy in the depiction of objects, structures and architecture. This may have much to do with the fact that the artist first specialized in fine-line drawing.

Second, if we look at the layout and the distribution of spatial information in reference to Figure 15 - 1, we find it support for Kress and van Leeuwen's (1996) argument regarding "Center is Centrality". In the painting, both horizontally and vertically, "Center is Centrality", evidenced by the most prominent scene of the Rainbow Bridge located at the center of the painting. This is what the eyes of the viewers are mostly drawn to, as it is the busiest place with the largest group of people involved in enormous number of actions and activities. This means that the highlight of the new information or salience appears at the center of this Chinese long scroll.

As this work follows the traditional writing path from right to left, the statement that horizontally, "Left is Given" and "Right is New" do not work for Chinese long-scroll painting. We are actually presented with a picture where "Right is Given", as there are fewer activities taking place here. However, that "Left is New" is only partially true in that on the one hand, the very left end of the work depicts "the Noisy Streets in the City", where there are many people and activities going on, making it a key local point, but on the other hand, compared with those on the bridge, the streets are less busy. Therefore the information seems to be distributed in progression, following the pattern as "Right is Given", "Center is Focus/New" and "Left is less New". Furthermore, on the one hand, the statement that "Top is margin" and "Bottom is margin" works well as on both top and bottom margins are only presented with water, roofs of houses and trees functioning as the settings. On the other hand, however, the demarcation between "Top is Ideal" and "Bottom is Real" does not fit this work. The painting has successfully taken in what is actually going on at the extensive space along the Bian River; therefore, everything is presented as Real and nothing as Ideal.

Thirdly, as a result of a rational layout, a well-balanced proportion of the three sections and information distribution is mapped in the "periodic or wave like" (Halliday 1994: 336) pattern in the painting, from which we observe a series of poetic rhythmic waves. This is contributed to by the building up of climaxes and ebbings away, and by the effective spacing of the scenes and internal framing of every section and every episode, each of which has a complete minor structure framed within a grander structure. The viewer is sometimes drawn to a scene with only a few people or animals against a vast spatial background of fields and water with a few houses and trees along a river bank. However, in many other scenes the viewer's eyes meet with big crowds and a variety of activities. There is also an effective placement and alignment of scenes, participants, actions and activities, and relative positioning of each figure, object and act in the settings if we refer to the concepts at lower ranks of Table 15 - 1. Everything is arranged so as to achieve a semiotic coherence for this occasion.

Fourthly, as far as Color is concerned, we cannot tell how many colors are applied because they are fading due to the lengthy exposure to the air in the past centuries. One thing is definite though: the dominant color is green as it is the color of the springtime and it is also suitable for a festival to honor the ancestors. With the passing of the time, however, this festival is less marked as such, but more as a festival for outdoor activities, relative-visiting and fair-going time. This is exactly why we do not actually spot one single scene depicting tomb sweeping. Therefore, while the main color is green in varying hues, which helps to construct a cohesive color pattern throughout, there is also the use of brighter colors such as blue and even reddish brown, which render a lively and energetic atmosphere, thus helping to construct a rhythmic color wave. We also see a skillful use of the Chinese soft brush and of the ink in different density to distinguish the distance from the viewer, and to mark the strength of the sketched participants and objects.

We have analyzed the three metafunctions of the painting proper separately. However, in the painting the three functions are interwoven in every activity, every event and every act. For instance, the depiction of the scene of the two sedan chairs in Episode III presents a scene in a street of the capital city, which, at the same time, reflects complex interpersonal relationships between the owners and their servants and also between the sitters and the on-lookers; and these two functions are brought to life by the textual function — the skillful layout of the sedan chairs in relation to their environment, the proper alignment of the servants and the other people in the street. It is the interaction of the three metafunctions in this artifact that succeeds in construing a flourishing society with a diversified lifestyle and in rendering the bustling festive ambience and worldly busy life at the Qingming Festival in a Chinese ancient capital city.

15.3.1.2 Analysis of the verbal and visual elements — the title and the seal

The title is mentioned by Zhang Zhu in his postscript, as being written by Emperor Song Huizong (Zhou 1997: 44). Verbally, the title "清明上河图" (*qingming shanghe tu*, translated as "**Along the River During the Qingming Festival**") is a nominal group, which can be analyzed as in Table 15-2:

According to Halliday, there are two structures of nominal groups in English (1994: 180-196).

Table 15 – 2 **Structure of the Nominal Group**

清 明	上 河	图
qingming	shanghe	tu
Qualifier 1	Qualifier 2	Thing
Noun	Noun	Noun
β1	β2	α
βα		

Experientially, the function of a nominal group is to specify 1) a class of things, and 2) "some category of membership within this class". Logically, the Thing is characterized by modifiers preceding and/or by qualifiers following it (Halliday 1994: 193). The structures of a nominal group in English and Chinese are similar in many cases though there are sometimes differences (compare Halliday 1994: 185, 191, with Hu 1987: 345; refer also to the subsequent sections of this chapter). Globally, Halliday's view on the structures of nominal groups in English can also be applied to analyzing nominal groups in Chinese. Experientially, this nominal group — *qingming shanghe tu*— specifies something about the painting (*tu*,图). There are two qualifiers in the nominal group. Together, the two qualifiers classify the painting by telling us the time and location of what the painting depicts — the Pure Brightness Festival (*Qingming*,清明) and along the section of the river at the place known as 上河[①](*shanghe*)(Lei 2008). Logically, *Tu*(图,painting) functions as the head α modified by β1 (清明,*Qingming*) and β2 (上河,*shanghe*) respectively, resulting in the βα structure. A notable feature is that there are three nouns. The first two function as Qualifiers and the last as the Thing. Therefore, ideationally, the title may function as a summary of the content of the painting, informing the viewer of what he may expect to see on that occasion.

① "上河"(*shanghe*) could have two interpretations: "up-river" or the name of a place. Here we take Lei Shaofeng's interpretation as the name of place (see Lei 2008).

Interpersonally, this nominal group does not contain any elements such as pronouns, possessives or epithets expressing judgement on the qualities of the work or the attitudes of the writer toward the work (see Halliday 1994: 191). Thus the title takes a non-personal involvement in evaluating the painting. However, the fact that it is said to be written by Emperor Song Huizong is significant interpersonally. The emperor was the highest in rank and was the most powerful person in the country while Zhang Zeduan was his subject and a court painter at his disposal. This means they were very distant in social status. But if we consider the fact that the emperor was a painter himself, an expert on depicting flowers and birds (Lei 2008: 121), then we may agree that they were equals in their status in the artist circle and that the act of the emperor writing the title was not so much as a condescension but a manifestation of his appreciation and high evaluation of this work of art. What is more, the slender calligraphic style ("*shou jin ti*", 瘦金体), in which the title was written, would doubtlessly enhance the artistic value of this work. Actually the calligraphy itself was valued as a visual artifact and this is perhaps why it was not present when the painting was discovered. It is thought to have been torn away from the painting for preservation as a treasure by an unknown person. The title imitating this style is shown here in Illustration 15－4 just to let the reader have a glimpse of what it might have looked like①.

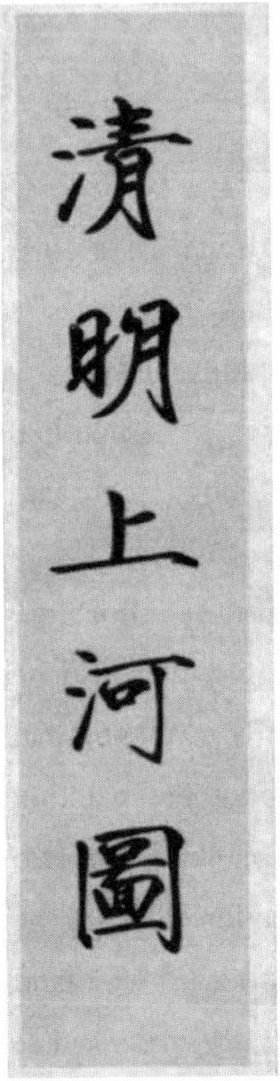

Illustration 15－4 The Possible Title Written by Emperor Song Huizong in the Style of "*shou jin ti*" (瘦金体)

Textually, we are concerned with 1) the ordering

① Refer to the title page of the brochure copy of the original painting printed by the "Garden of *Qingming Shanghe Tu*" in Kaifeng, Henan Province, People's Republic of China.

of the elements in the nominal group; and 2) the information distribution of these elements (Halliday 1994: 188). Firstly, differing from English, in which qualifiers are all post-positioned, all the elements in Chinese, either as modifiers or qualifiers, appear before the noun (Hu 1987: 345). Concretely, this nominal group can be translated literally in two versions: either as 1) "Qingming Shanghe Painting", in the same sequence as its Chinese equivalent; or as 2) "The Painting of the Qingming Festival at Shanghe", in an order almost the reverse of its Chinese equivalent. Secondly, we see from this example that the information focus falls on the last word/character in Chinese while in its English equivalents, either on the last salient syllable of the head noun, as in 1), or on the last syllable "*he*" in Shanghe, as in 2). The information distribution between the verbal and visual in this painting differs greatly: visually the focus falls on the center while verbally it is on the final word/character.

There are quite a few seals printed at the end or elsewhere on the painting. It is customary to have the painter's seal, which has only one verbal function — to give his identity as the creator. The ideational function of the emperor's seal on this painting is to give the emperor's identity as its owner; interpersonally, it reinforces his very positive valuation of the work. A seal is regarded usually as both verbal and visual discourse as it bears the name in characters, and as an artifact since the characters are usually carved on a piece of jade in a special style, known as "篆书" (*zhuan shu*) or a curve style dating from the Qin Dynasty (Meng & Wei 2008: 52). However, it is a pity that we cannot find the seal of the painter nor that bearing the name of the emperor. It is likely that these were lost due to the chaotic periods after the painting was revealed to the world. Most of the seals visible now on the work are shown as in Illustration 15 – 5. Ideationally those printed on the painting proper may have spoiled this work of art whereas all the seals, whether internal or external to the painting, perform one interpersonal function: to indicate who were once its masters or owners. Every time it changed hands, a new seal would be added behind which there may be stories of sad or unscrupulous events.

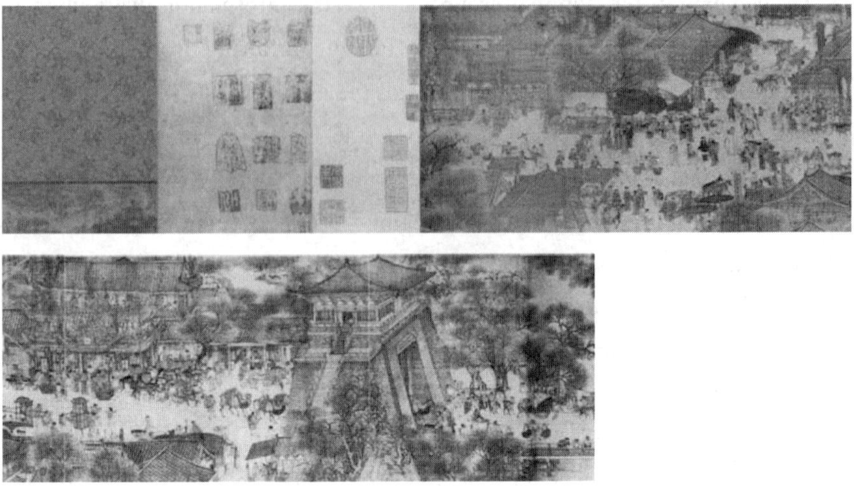

Illustration 15 – 5 Part of the Painting Showing the Seals

To sum up, although the three modes of semiotic discourse perform different functions, they are integrated to have successfully construed the reality of the 12th century China. The country at that time was well developed in the handicraft industrial economy, business transactions, urbanization, a multi-faceted culture and architectural designing of all types. The painting brings to life a diversified social life and a complex social interpersonal relationship along the social hierarchical strata and shows the painter's appreciation of the ways of living in that era as well as his very positive attitude towards the ordinary people who were, in the painter's eyes, the key force to make the reality possible. Furthermore, the painting brings to the present world the high level of artistic achievement attained by the skillful utilization of various means used in the process of creating this masterpiece. This is why almost all commentators and viewers have highly praised this ancient artistic work (Zhang 1962; Zhou 1997; Lei 2008). Undoubtedly, without the painter's highly artistic attainment, his long-time careful study and observation of the rural and urban life and of people from all walks of life as well as his exceptionally good memory, he could not have successfully attained these metafunctional goals (Zhang 1962: Chapter 5).

15.3.2 Context of culture

Having analyzed the features of the different modes of the painting, we go further to elaborate on the context of culture in which this great work of art was produced. But first we need to have a clear notion of this concept. We maintain that the definition given by Halliday (2002: 152) to this term, namely, "the socio-historical and ideological environment engendering, and engendered by the text" is also appropriate for interpreting the context of culture of this ancient multisemiotic text. This involves answers to the questions such as: what kind of person was the painter? Why did he create this work? Why did he dedicate his work to the emperor? What happened to the painting in the centuries after its creation? Where is it preserved?

Little is known of the painter Zhang Zeduan (张择端) except that he lived in the 12th century (1085 – 1145) when Song Huizong was on the throne, that he was a hard worker in learning designing and painting and that this work of art was created between 1111 and 1125 when he became a painter in 翰林院 (*Hanlinyuan*, equivalent to today's National Social Academy) (Zhou 1997: 44). We do not have records relating the reasons why he produced such a work and why it was presented to the emperor. There are different and even opposite views on this (Lei 2008: 116 – 17) although most agree that the artifact would be considered a way to eulogize the emperor for his successful ruling of the country and to show the painter's appreciation of the life style of his time, because the job of a painter of Hanlinyuan was supposed to please and entertain the ruler. This motif could be evidenced in this painting by the prosperous scenes of Bianjing in the spring season. With a population of more than one million, rivers and roads running through the city and a highly developed handicraft industry, Bianjing had become the center of politics, business and culture, an artery of road and water transportation and a representative of prosperity of the whole country. Scholars also argue that the emperor would be pleased to have a painting depicting the scenes on an occasion characterized by the two characters "清

明”(*qingming*, meaning “pure” and “bright”), an epithet describing an honest and upright ruler. These may perhaps be taken as the motifs or the socio-historical and ideological environments for the production of this work of art.

As for how it engenders the cultural environment, it is not an exaggeration to say that it has exerted an enormous impact upon generations of Chinese in later dynasties, even upon the present China. It is regarded as successful in portraying a society with peace, prosperity and a diversity of ways of living in the rural areas and a metropolitan city in China. This may be the very reason why in the 21st century China, it was chosen as the basis for an animated version bearing the same name to be shown to the visitors of the Shanghai Expo, 2010 on a screen of 100 meters-long at the Chinese Exhibition Hall. Its great influence is also felt by the very fact that court artists of subsequent dynasties have made many replicas, many of which are regarded as national treasures (Chinaonline.com). In addition, this painting has become a very important reference for the study of the Northern Song Dynasty in the domains of history, economy, society, culture, and folklore.

It is said that Zhang Zeduan created quite a few paintings but none of these remain except for this long scroll. But he would never have expected that his artifact would have to go through a very unusual experience for survival. When a neighbor of China, the state of Jin, conquered North China and its army captured the capital in 1126, this painting started its journey of changing hands. It was stolen four times out of the palace and brought back five times, being owned by dozens of court officials, painters and scholars. But the fact it survived the British soldiers in the Second Opium War of 1860, the Eight Nation Alliance during the Boxer Rebellion in 1900 and the Second World War is indeed miraculous. It is beyond the short space of this chapter to describe all these sad anecdotal accounts. But it suffices to say that in the 1950s the painting was discovered and evaluated by a group of experts under the auspices of Beijing Bureau of Preservation of Cultural Relics, who, after careful study and scrutiny, finally certified that this painting was the original one from among the many replicas. Indeed, it is remarkable that this masterpiece can have survived all the turmoil of wars and different dynasties to become one of the most treasured pieces preserved in the Palace Museum in Beijing (Ouyang 2010).

15.4 Conclusion

Many scholars and art commentators in the different periods of Chinese history have made appraisals of this remarkable work of art, yet none from a semiotic perspective①. Therefore, this chapter represents the first time the SFL multisemiotic theory has been applied to an analysis of a Chinese long scroll. This painting is used as an instantiation to illustrate the relationship among the different strata of visual images and wordings and to demonstrate in concrete terms that every metafunction has contributed to the meaning-making in the different modes of this artifact. ***Along the River During the Qingming Festival*** is a fine example of ideational representation of the social reality of an era in ancient China, the interpersonal revelation of the diversified social life of different social strata, and the textual actualization of the ideational and interpersonal meanings. Overall, it effectively brings together the ideational and interpersonal elements to achieve cohesion and coherence. This multisemiotic analysis has also shown the close relationship between semiotic meanings and the culture which engenders them. Indeed, the historical and cultural background for the appearance, the survival and the preservation of this work with unique Chinese generic features has testified that meanings attributed to verbal and visual information in a painting are to a large degree socially structured and "culturally bound" (Martinec 2005: 165).

① Refer to the commentaries at the back of the brochure copy of the original painting in Kaifeng, Henan Province. The publisher is unknown.

Although this is only a brief study, which needs deepening in all aspects, it has confirmed once more that the SFL theoretical model is an extremely useful and a very powerful analytical tool for exploration of the multi-faceted and multisemiotic meanings of an artistic work of any size, in any genre and in any culture.

16

中国长卷画的多符号分析框架与参数*

16.1 引　言

笔者曾于 2008 年厦门大学和 2010 年同济大学召开的第 11 届和第 12 届全国语篇分析的会上分别做过主题发言，用系统功能语言学的理论分析了张择端的《清明上河图》和黄公望的《富春山居图》。后又受中山大学温迪·鲍切尔（Wendy Bowcher）教授之邀，为她主编的 *Multimodal Texts from around the World: Cultural and Linguistic Insights* 写了一个章节，题为"A Multisemiotic Analysis of a Chinese Long Scroll Painting"，讨论了《清明上河图》的概念功能、人际功能、语篇功能和文化语境的一些特点。这本书于 2012 年由英国著名出版社 Palgrave 出版。2014 年 9 月在西安长安大学召开的全国第 14 届语篇分析大会上，笔者向大会做了"中国长卷画多符号、多模态分析的参数与框架"的汇报，比较详细分析了框架和框架中的各个参数。使用的分析素材主要是《富春山居图》，辅以《清明上河图》。使用这两幅长

* 本章基于 2014 年 9 月在西安长安大学召开的中国第 14 届语篇分析会议上的大会主题发言，做了一些修改。

卷做分析素材,不仅因为它们是中国长卷画的杰出代表(蒋勋 2012),不仅因为它们都有过极其坎坷的收藏经历(见 16.5),更主要的是,它们能为多模态、多符号分析提供很好的原始素材:除了绘画本身,还有题词或题跋和大量的印章,这是中国画与西方绘画的主要区别。西方以油画闻名于世,但没有长卷画,而油画只包括绘画本身,题词和绘画者的签字都在画面外,而且它们都没有什么艺术价值。对中国长卷画,研究者不仅可以剖析绘画的各个层面,还可以分析作为绘画一部分的题词和各个朝代收藏者写的题跋。题词或题跋往往代表各个朝代的书法艺术,因为收藏者往往都是当时的艺术界名人,有的就是著名的书法家。印章不仅印有绘画者和各个朝代收藏者的名字,是他们身份的象征,而且本身也是一种雕刻艺术品(Fang 2012)。

本章使用的理论分析框架来自系统功能语言学。迄今为止,多模态语篇分析者使用最多的就是这个理论延伸出来的分析框架(O'Toole 1994; Kress & van Leeuwen 1996/2006; O'Halloran 2004; Bowcher 2012)。第一节“引言”讨论素材及论文的内容和目的。第二节简述这个框架的性质,借鉴西方语言学家对西方油画和广告分析所使用的框架和参数,提出了自己的分析框架和分析参数。第三节具体分析《富春山居图》绘画部分,进一步论证本文提出的框架和参数,必要时会与《清明上河图》作对比分析。《富春山居图》发现时已分成了两个段面(见 16.5),我们从两个绘画段面中选取一个小节,对它们的概念功能、人际功能、语篇功能作较详细的分析。第四节分析题词、题跋和印章。第五节讨论产生这幅长卷的文化语境。文章的最后是简短的结语。

笔者对中国长卷有着深厚的个人研究兴趣,虽然只是个语言学研究者,对绘画是个地道的门外人。有几个研究目的:第一,从符号学的角度,通过使用系统功能语言学框架和基于这个理论框架产生的参数,对长卷做多符号、多模态分析,看看是否也能使行外人可以较好地赏析中国的艺术品。记得韩礼德教授曾提起过他创立这个语言学流派的初衷,就是想更好地解释经典文学作品。在学校学习古典文学作品时,他发现老师对这些作品的语言分析往往与作品本身没有丝毫的关系(“What they said made no contact with what was actually there”. “Interview” 1992)。后来他使用自己的理论分析了诺贝尔文学奖获得者威廉·戈尔丁(William Golding)的代表作《继承者》中的及物性系统,揭示了文学作品中的语义与文体特征的紧密联系(Halliday 1973)。他的分析成为文体学家分析文学作品的范文之一。通过分析确实让读者能够更好地欣赏文学作品，能够更深入地领会作品的深层含义，也为文体学的发展提供了一个理论框架。本章的第二个目的是试图揭示一幅成功的长卷画作品，如何使用不同的符号资源共同来构建作品的语义，又如何将不同的符号、模态成分编制成一个连贯的整体。本章的最后一个目的是想通过这个多符号、多模态分析，进一步论证韩礼德的观点：系统功能语言学是一种"适用语言学"(Halliday 2008a; Matthiessen 2014)，不仅可用来分析语言，也适用于分析其他符号的意义。

16.2 理论框架和分析参数

16.2.1 系统功能语言学框架

上面我们提到，多模态语篇分析者使用最多的就是系统功能语言学理论延伸出来的分析框架。为什么会出现这样的情况呢？这是因为，这个理论创立的目的就是为了"语篇分析"。学派创始人韩礼德特别强调：系统功能语法是一种"语篇语法"。作为"语篇语法"，它有两个目的：一是为了洞察语篇的语言意义；二是为了评判语篇是否有效地表达了语篇意义(Halliday 1985/1994)。另外，他认为，如果分析不包括语法，就根本不是语篇分析，充其量只不过是对语篇的随意评论：这种评论或者是基于"非语言学的传承看法"，或者是"找出了一些微不足道的语言的特点"(Halliday 1973)。这里所谓的"语法"，不仅包含词汇语法层，还包含了语义层和音系层，因而"语法"与"语言学"同义，即"系统功能语法"就是"系统功能语言学"。

笔者完全同意黄国文(2004)的观点：系统功能语言学比其他理论"更适合于语篇分析"，因为它的适用性"明显"，"可操作性强"。自系统功能语言学创始以来，已被很多学者用于语言的语篇分析(Martin 1992; Martin & Rose 2003/2007; Martin & Rose 2008; Thompson 1996/2004)。韩礼德本人带头在多部著作中对不同的语篇做过分析，堪称典范(Halliday 1973; 1978; 1985/1994; 2008)。他创立的语言学框架不仅可以用来分析文字语篇,也适用于对各种不同的社会符号的分析(2008a),因为他不仅是一位语言学家,更是一位符号学家。记得我于20世纪80年代,在悉尼大学听他的课"功能语言学概论"时,一次一个同学问他:"What are you?"他的回答是:"I am a social semiotist."。他明确指出,"存在于语码和例证/语篇之间的动态关系同样可以用来解释任何符号系统"(Halliday 1973)。事实上,90年代以来,许多西方学者已经将系统功能语言学用于分析视、听、说各个不同的模态(O'Toole 1994; Kress & van Leeuwen 1996/2006; O'Halloran 2004; Bowcher 2012)。莱姆基认为"说明语义生成的语言三大功能"完全"适用于所有符号系统"(Lemke 1998)。这个观点得到了许多学者的支持。而且,一些学者还提出了"视觉语法"(Kress & van Leeuwen 1996/2006)和"展示性艺术的语言"(O'Toole 1994)。他们均应用系统功能语言学的框架,发展了多模态、多符号的分析模式和分析方法。

系统功能语言学之所以"可操作性强"有很多原因。其中一个很重要的原因是它的框架明确了语言的三大功能(即概念功能、人际功能、语篇功能)和制约它们的文化语境之间的关系是实现与被实现的关系:文化语境由情景语境来实现;情景语境由语言的语义实现;语义由词汇-语法实现;口语表达时,要通过语音和语调来实现;用文字表达时,需要通过正字学的规则来实现。如下图:

文化语境
↙
情景语境
↙
语义
↙
词汇-语法
↙
音系/正字学
(↙意为被实现)

图16-1 语言的层次

这个模式可以用来分析语篇的语言素材。借鉴这个模式观察长卷画,我们发现它像语言一样,也存在不同的层次,这些层次之间的关系也同样是实现与被实现的关系。我们可以参照语言层次的模式,根据长卷画的特点,分析出长卷画的层次(见下图):

文化语境
↙
情景语境
↙
意义
↙
视觉语法 + 词汇-语法
↙
视觉形象+正字学(绘画 + 印章 + 书写规则)

图 16－2　长卷画的层次

语篇分析者只要把三大语篇功能和它们之间的关系解释清楚就完成了分析工作的很大一部分了。当然,对每个层次的分析还必须依据相应的具体参数逐步进行。

16.2.2　分析参数

本章参考了奥图尔(O'Toole 1994)和笔者(Fang 2012)的分析框架和分析参数,将视觉特征分成不同的层次来分析:长卷画——段——节——人物/景物——成员,并提出了更加适用的分析参数。

与奥图尔不同,描述视觉和语言特征时,我们仍采用韩礼德的术语“概念功能”“人际功能”“语篇功能”,这是为了在分析长卷画里各种模态或符号时均可使用同样的术语。另外,我们还借鉴了佩因特和马丁(Painter & Martin 2011)的一些术语和概念。比如,用“场景”(setting)来描述视觉背景;用“权力”(power)、“社会距离”(social distance)、“接近度”(proximity)、“视觉效应”(visual affect)及“氛围”(ambience)讨论人际关系及观者或鉴赏者的感受和产生的氛围;用“举止行为”(manner)描述参与者;用“凸显”(prominence)、“焦点显示”(salience)、“绘画成分分布”(placement of depicted elements)讨论绘画的组织建构。

表 16－1 显示了潜在的层面,将一幅长卷画分成段、节、人物/景物及成员五个层次,视野从宽逐渐缩小,描述也逐步从宏观到微观。

16.2.2.1　概念功能分析参数

如表所示,我们增加了“分段”层,因为通常一幅长卷会有次主题,各个分段的次主题共同构建整幅画的主题。本文采用了奥图尔的三大功能的概念。概念功能的定义是"表达有关现实的信息"或"画面描绘的东西"(O'Toole 1994：2)，即作品反映现实的主要信息及主题("... it is concerned with 'the subject matter' and 'theme' of the work")(1994：14)，可用表16－1所列出各个层次的相关参数详细描述。在画卷层次上，分析概念功能的主要参数是：主要现实信息、主题、主要场景和人物；分段层次的主要参数为：分段信息、分段主题、分段场景、分段中的人物/景物、行动/事件；分节层次的参数为：分节信息、分节主题、分节场景、分节中的行动/事件和人物/景物；人物/景物层次的参数为：具体人物及其行为、手势、穿着、具体的物体；成员层次参数为：身体部位、物体的组成成分。

16.2.2.2 人际关系参数

人际功能提供观赏者的倾向性，"揭示观赏者引起的反应参数"(O'Toole 1994：5)，或者"画面吸引观赏者的方法"(1994：5 &8)，同时还关注参与者之间的关系(Painter & Martin 2011)。这里必须说明，奥图尔使用的"Modality"用以表达事件的模糊性程度或人物之间可能的关系(that of ambiguity or the degree of uncertainty of what is taking place in a painting or the possible relationships between or among the participants)(1994：9)，可译为"可能性"。人际关系也在不同的层面上体现出不同的参数。例如，长卷中的"对现实的倾向性"通过分段中的"视角""节奏""路径""颜色""可能性"表现出来，而这些特点又通过分节上的"可能性""人际关系""接近度""视觉效应"和"氛围"参数具体体现出来。长卷中的"人际关系"通过分段和分节中的具体的人际关系得以实现。人物/景物层面上的具体参数则是：人物刻画、姿势、举止行为。最下层的"成员"的参数为：具体的特征及属性。

16.2.2.3 语篇功能参数

语篇功能关注的是如何将概念功能及人际功能建构成一个连贯的整体，重点是"在画面内布局好各个不同的形体成分的位置"(how "to structure" the ideational and interpersonal functions "into a coherent" whole, focusing on the "arrangement of forms within the pictorial space ...")(O'Toole 1994：22)。各个层次的主要参数为：长卷画层面的"长度、类

型/类型特点、整体框架的布局及比例、凸显及焦点、节奏关系、色彩衔接”；分段层面上的“分段框架、分段布局、分段框架中的成分分布”；分节层面上的“横向、纵向、斜向”及“成分分布、焦点排布、连贯”；人物/景物层面上的“相对位置：正面/背面/侧面/并列”；成员层次上的衔接：指向/平行性/对照等参数。表16－1列出了概念成分参数、人际成分参数和语篇功能参数：

表16－1 中国长卷画分析参数①

层次＼功能	概念功能	人际功能	语篇功能
画卷	主要现实信息 主题 主要场景 人物	对现实的倾向性 人际关系：权力，社会距离/接近度	长度、类型及类型文体特点 框架的布局、比例 凸显及焦点 节奏关系 色彩衔接
段	分段信息 分段主题 分段场景 人物 行动/事件	人际关系：权力、社会距离/接近度 视角、节奏、路径、颜色 可能性	分段框架 分段布局 凸显及焦点 分段框架中的成分分布
节	分节信息 分节主题 分节场景 行动/事件 人物	人际关系：权力、社会距离/接近度 可能性 视觉效应 氛围	横向、纵向、斜向 分节框架中的成分分布 焦点排布 连贯
人物/景物	人物 行为/手势 物体/穿着	人物刻画 姿势 举止行为	相对位置： 正面/背面/侧面/并列
成分	身体部位 物体的组成成分	特征及属性	衔接： 指向 平行性 对照

① 参考了方琰的文章“A Multisemiotic Analysis of a Chinese Long Scroll Painting”中的表15－1的参数(Bowcher 2012)，并做了适当的修改，使其更适合分析中国长卷画。

16.2.2.4 方位参数

本文的分析还参考了克雷斯和范律文有关视觉方位的图标和参数(Kress & van Leeuwen 1996：197)，如图 16－3 所示：

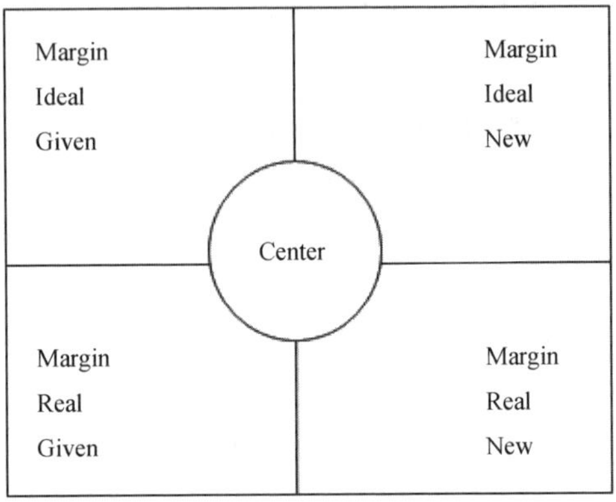

图 16－3 视觉方位

图 16－3 显示了具有信息量值参数的各个方位。纵向可以解释为："顶边为边界，表示理想状态"，"下边为边界，表示实际状态"；横向则为："左为已知"，"右为新信息"；而无论纵向还是横向，"中部都是中心"，观赏者可视为最凸显之处。这里的有关横向方位信息分布的观点源于韩礼德的语言信息流向的论点(1994)，而这个论点是基于西方自左向右的书写方式。然而，这个模式是否适用于书写方法自右向左的古代中国文化呢？"顶上为边界，表示理想状态"及"下边为边界，表示实际状态"的观点是否可以解释我们分析的中国长卷画呢？下文将试图回答这两个问题，同时也将确认"中部都是中心"的说法。

16.3 长卷分析

《富春山居图》是元朝末年黄公望的作品。长卷历经 600 多年坎坷的收藏经历，实际上已经分为两个分段：《无用师卷》和《剩山图》（见culture.china.com.cn）。《剩山图》自成一节，只有绘画，没有文字语篇。《无用师卷》可分为两节，第一节为绘画本体，第二节为文字语篇，主要由题跋构成，本文将其命名为“名家题跋”。由于篇幅有限，本文将着重分析绘画部分，文字语篇的分析只涉及绘画题词和黄公望的题跋。

下面将应用系统功能语言学的框架和表16－1和图16－3列出的参数，分析长卷的视觉形象（绘画、题跋、印章）。由于篇幅有限，只能有选择地集中讨论“画卷”、“分段”或“分节”两个层次的主要参数特点。必要时，也会涉及“人物/景物”和“成员”这两个层面。

16.3.1 概念功能分析

整幅长卷描绘了富春江沿岸一幅美丽的早秋景色。《剩山图》描绘了“一山、一水、一丘、一壑”（见culture.china.com.cn），如图16－4。

图16－4 《剩山图》

而《无用师卷》描绘的则是一幅多彩的画面：峰峦叠翠，松石挺秀，云山烟树，泉水茅亭，云烟掩映村舍，水波出没渔舟，如图16－5所示（见www.eshufa.com/html/21/n－18821.html 2011－06－02）。

整幅长卷和这两个分段的主题是：黄公望寻求远离社会的宁静隐居生活。整幅长卷呈现的就是**宁静**。这两个分段的不同，表现在人物/景物及成员层面上。《剩山图》展现的主要是一座挺拔的高山，及坐落在一片宁静水域旁的山丘、村舍、树林，没有一个人物，也没有任何活动；《无用师卷》不仅描绘了山丘、小桥、房屋、船只、泉水、茫茫江水，还出现了四个船人，其中两位分别在相隔不远的两片水域中垂钓，其他两位的船靠得很近，似乎在划着船向前慢慢行进，给画面带来了一丝动感。这些人物都像画家本人一样置身于繁忙的社会生活之外，享受世外桃源般的静谧生活。

16.3.2 人际功能分析

长卷的**倾向性**通过画家对**现实的态度**和描绘的**人际关系**表现出来。长卷中,自然景色是艺术家关注的中心,也是整幅画的灵魂。这些静止不动的自然景物似乎被当作抚慰一个脱离社会的孤独老人心灵的根本元素,也传达出古代文人士大夫的人生意趣。这种态度与张泽端在《清明上河图》中表达的完全不同。《清明上河图》描绘了五百多个来自不同社会阶层的人物,人物的活动是那幅画卷的关注焦点,自然风光被当作人物活动的舞台和背景,画家展示的是一幅繁荣的社会生活画面,表现了画家积极的生活态度和对美好的世俗生活的向往(Fang 2012),与黄公望在《富春山居图》表现的远离世俗社会的消极生活态度形成了鲜明的对照。

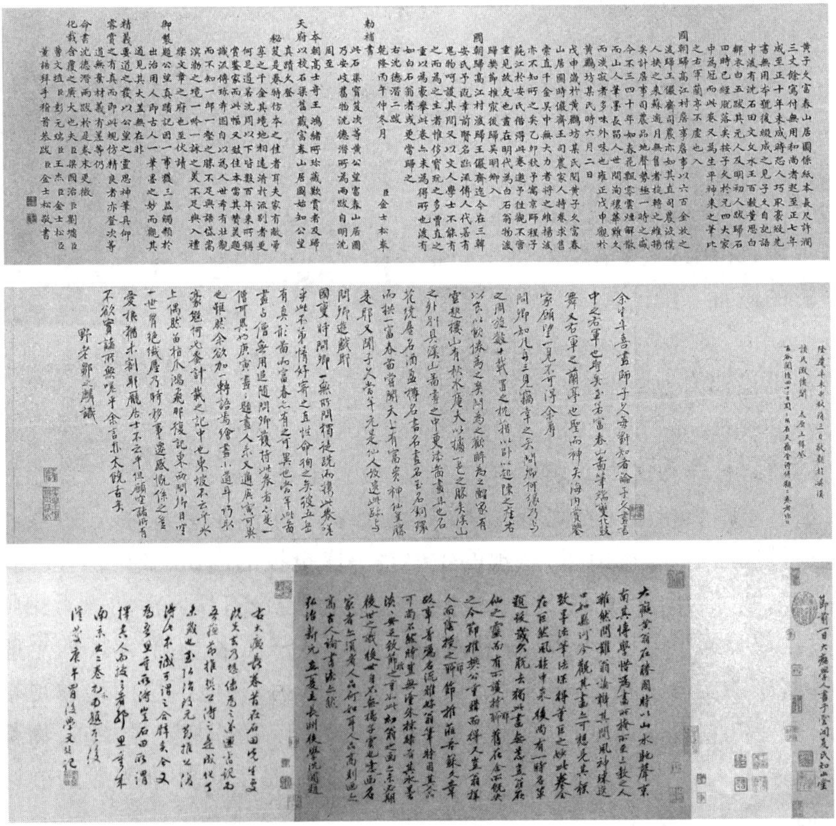

图 16-5 《无用师卷》

《富春山居图》展现了两个层次的人际关系：画外关系即观赏者与画家的关系，及画中人物之间的关系。长卷的画外关系可从画家的题跋找到印证（见 16.4 节）。画内的人物之间的关系不甚清晰。画面中的确有四个船人，但是他们分散在两片水域，尽管其中两位的船靠得很近，也许是好朋友相约垂钓，是画卷描绘的唯一的人际关系。

长卷对现实的倾向性态度也可从分段或分节中的视角、节奏和路径、视角效应、氛围表现出来。

《无用师卷》和《剩山图》的视角有些区别。前者似乎是画家沿着富春江一路漂流，记录下的不同场景的全景图；而后者似乎是画家站在河岸上，对着面前的山水拍下来的一幅实景图。但是它们所产生的视角效应和氛围都是一样的：呈现的都是秀丽的秋色和宁静、美丽的大自然。当然，考虑到画卷曾被烧为两段（见 16.5），全幅画卷的视角可能应与《无用师卷》相同。

起伏的丘陵与浩渺连绵的江南水色以及大片、大片的空白构成了画面的高潮、平落、低潮的节奏，不断变化的景色给观者带来极大的视觉享受。因为“路径”会涉及画面凸显的焦点，将在讨论长卷的布局时再提及。

至于在人物/景物和成员这两个层次上的特征，也许可以从两位垂钓人的姿势看出一些端倪：他们的姿势几乎完全一样，都戴着斗笠，握着鱼竿，身子向前倾斜，一动不动，好像凝固在江面上的两座雕塑，也给画面增添了宁静的氛围。而两位划船人的形象比较模糊，只用了线条勾勒出人形、桨和划船的姿势。

16.3.3 语篇功能分析

长卷的语篇功能表现在卷画的长度、类型及其文体特征、焦点凸显、色彩衔接和人物/景物的布局方面。

《剩山图》长约51.4厘米，宽31厘米；《无用师卷》长696.9厘米，宽33厘米，都为山水画或风景画。画家用自然的手法描绘了沿江的景色，同时在山丘、亭台、村舍和人物的塑造上又采用了抽象的、印象派的手法，并不追求对景物的现实主义描绘，呈现出“抽象”与“具象”的结合。山间丛树茂密，点缀着小桥、村舍、钓鱼人、泉沟、沙渚和连绵水域，布局疏密有致，衔接连贯，层次分明。艺术家用淡绛色描绘秋天的山色和水域，似乎带有一份淡淡的悲凉，也许反映了元朝末期乱世时期，画家一种孤独和无助的情怀。山石和树木的颜色有深有浅，与整幅画的山水颜色衔接连贯。长卷展示了画家各种优雅、娴熟的笔法。“山石的勾、皴，用笔顿挫转折，随意天成。”“长披麻皴，枯湿浑成”（见 culture.china.com.cn）。画家用“清润的笔墨，简约的意境”把江南山水的秋色表现得淋漓尽致（蒋锦彪2012）。另外，“景物由近向远，自然消失，将实与虚完美结合”（见 www.chinaqking.com），也表现了一种独特的东方审美。

中国的风景画一般不突出人物，景色是绘画的重点，人物只起到点缀的作用，《富春山居图》也不例外，上面已经提及，不再重叙。前面已经提到，画中的高山形成节奏的高潮，似乎是绘画的焦点所在。例如，《剩山图》的右边是一座高山，占据了三分之一的画面。山间的岩石和丛林树木清晰可见。高山的左后方是绵延的小丘，左边是密疏挺拔的树林，点缀着座座村舍。村落和小丘之间是一片水域，静静地躺着。绘画突出的就是这座气势恢弘的高山。《无用师卷》自成一幅长卷。如同中国古代采用的书写方式自右向左，长卷画也按照这个路径展开。画卷从右边题跋开始（见下文16.4节），慢慢向左边伸展。首先映入眼帘的是矮矮的小山，其中有几座乡舍，沙渚上成排的丛树，似乎是长卷的前奏。接着向左伸展隆起一座宏伟的高山，形成节奏的高潮。然后再向左绵延，山峦起伏，接着是一片长长的水域，水天一色，其间排布了星星点点的树木、村舍、茅亭、泉水，展现了一幅幅美丽的山水风景。接着是一座孤立的高耸入云的山峰，形成了一个次高潮。最后是一片空白，预示着长卷的结尾。这片空白似乎为收藏者的**“名家题跋”**留下空间。这个路径与西方自左向右的书写方式完全不同（见图16－3）。至于“顶边为边界，表示理想状态”，“下边为边界，表示实际状态”（图16－3）似乎也不适合用来解释中国长卷画，和《清明上河图》一样，画的上下边界均表达了现实状态。图16－3的横向“左为已知”,“右为新信息”,也不能用来诠释中国长卷,似乎画的两侧都为“已知”。右边为“前奏”,左边为“结尾”。长卷曾遭烧毁(见16.5节),“无用师卷”的前面可能还有一部分“前奏”被毁。清代一位收藏人代之以董其昌的题跋(王耀庭 2014),代表了众多鉴赏家对这幅画卷的评价。而“新信息”似乎坐落于长卷中“前奏”后不远的最宏伟的一座高山,也就是前面提到的节奏的“高潮”,观赏者可视为最凸显之处。对应图16－3中提及的“中部都是中心”,似乎可视为画卷的焦点。但是对于一幅曾遭烧毁,后来又分成两部分的风景画卷来说,究竟焦点在哪里,似乎很难确定。这与《清明上河图》的焦点就坐落在画卷中部的“虹桥”似乎不大相同(Fang 2012)。

以上分别分析了画卷的三大功能。画卷表达的概念功能(对现实的反映和表达的主题思想)和人际功能(画家对现实的倾向性态度和画中的人物之间的关系)是通过语篇功能的风景画特点、画面的布局、节奏的特征、焦点排布、色彩的衔接等参数得以一一落实,使画卷成为一个有机的整体;而且,长卷中这三大功能往往交织在一起去描绘各个美景,去刻画人物的行为、姿态。艺术品中三个功能的有机组合成功地反映了画家所追求的理想生活,以及画卷背后独特的道教人生哲学(蒋勋 2012)。

16.4 题词、跋、印章

16.4.1 题词

中国画除了画本身,一定会有画家本人的题词和印章,前者应该放在画的起首部分,后者会放在绘画之后。它们都是不同符号的艺术品,都是画作的一部分,共同构成作品的艺术价值。但是据台北故宫博物院原书画处处长、黄公望研究专家王耀庭考证(2014),《富春山居图》发现时,并没有黄公望的题词,很可能是被烧毁了,因为被烧毁的部分就在起首,非常令人遗憾。

16.4.2 题跋

《剩山图》没有题跋，所有的题跋都出现在《无用师卷》中。画卷中包括画家本人一共有七八位收藏家或鉴赏家（董其昌、黄公望、沈同、文彭、王稀登、邹之麟、金士松等）的题跋。“题跋”，顾名思义，应当放在卷尾。虽然这幅画卷中大部分的题跋都出现在了末尾，但是有两个例外。其中一个不知何故竟然出现在画中，虽然在空白处，但是还是破坏了画面，因为空白也是绘画的一部分。还有一个出现在卷首，是明朝画家董其昌的题跋。由于画卷的题词被烧毁，1652 年一位收藏人将董其昌的题跋切割下来，放在了“无用师卷”的卷首（王耀庭 2012），虽不是题词，但似乎可做“序言”，代表了所有鉴赏家对此画的高度评价。董其昌非常钦佩画家的绘画技术，赞叹道：“神韵超逸，体备众法，脱化浑融，不落畦径。”“一丘五岳，都具是矣！”由衷地称黄公望为“吾师乎！”

因为篇幅所限，本文不可能对所有的题跋作一一分析，只能简单讨论黄公望的题跋。

黄公望不仅是一位杰出的画家，还是著名的书法家。从他的题跋可见其书法功底绝非一般，达到了相当高的程度。

下面着重分析题跋的语篇特点。因篇幅有限，不能分析每个小句的概念功能、人际功能、语篇功能，只集中分析它的画外人际关系和语类（语篇类型）的结构特点。

首先请读跋的原文：

> 两至正七年，仆归富春山居，无用师偕往，暇日于南楼授笔写成此卷，兴之所至，不觉亹亹布置如许，逐旋填劄。阅三四载未得完备，盖因留在山中，而云游在外故尔。今特取回行李中，早晚得暇，当为着笔。无用过虑有巧取豪锐者，俾先识卷末，庶使知其成就之难也。十年青龙在庚寅歇节前一日，大痴学人书于云间夏氏知止堂。（见 culture.china.com.cn）

题跋写在作品之后，多对内容做出评价（见此卷的**“名家题跋”**）。而画家自己的题跋多提及与创作有关的事情，黄公望的题跋也是如此。鉴赏者可从语类结构的角度，分析其语义成分，也可了解画家和无用大师之间的关系。

题跋语类的语义成分包括：何时开始勾勒草图（两至正七年，仆归富春山居，——于 1347 年回到富春山安顿下来之后。）^如何作画（无用师偕往，暇日于南楼授笔写成此卷，兴之所至，不觉亹亹布置如许，逐旋填劄。——在无用大师陪伴下，闲暇心情好时，因大师的请求在南楼勤奋布局、一点点雕琢）^为何当时没有画完（阅三四载未得完备，盖因留在山中，而云游在外故尔。——三四年都未完成，因为画卷留在山中，而我却一直在外云游。）^跋的目的（无用过虑有巧取豪锐者，俾先识卷末，庶使知其成就之难也。——在未画完前，应无用大师之请写下此题跋，留给无用大师以防盗窃者）^如何继续作画（今特取回行李中，早晚得暇，当为着笔。——现在取回放在行李中，早晚有空继续着笔。）^书写跋的时间、地点、作者的身份（十年青龙在庚寅歜节前一日，大痴学人书于云间夏氏知止堂。——1350 年端午节前一天，大痴学人写于坐落在云雾中的夏氏知止堂。）

文中“无用过虑有巧取豪锐者，俾先识卷末，庶使知其成就之难也。”除了意图阻止有人可能会从无用大师手中夺走这幅他钟爱的画卷之外，还表明画家与大师的关系——他们既是好朋友也互为老师。黄公望在绘画方面是无用的老师，而无用大师是黄公望的传道人。据说这幅画就是为了感谢无用大师而创作的（蒋勋 2012），无用大师也是这幅画卷的第一位鉴赏者。这就是画卷外的人际关系。

16.4.3 印章

印章分布在画卷的各处，《剩山图》有十几个，《无用师卷》多达四五十个。画家黄公望在他的题跋后留下“黄子久”的篆刻印章（“子久”是他的“字”）。两段画卷中，在画前部、画中间、画末尾都有印章，都是收藏者或题跋者留下的。印章的主要功能是表明身份，表明他们或是画者，或是题跋人，或是收藏人，与现代社会的签字的作用相同。这里要特别提及“无用师卷”中间的三四个印章，它们出现在画卷烧毁后又被连接的地方，显然是拼接人的，表明他们的身份，还承担起拼接是否成功的责任。至于其他出现在画中的印章，本身有一定的艺术性，但对这幅画却起了破坏作用。当然，所有这些印章都是这幅画卷 600 多年以来历史沧桑的见证者——画卷在这漫长的动荡岁月中曾先后被几十个人拥有过。印章是一种独特的中国艺术,使用的字体主要是篆体,也可带有拥有者个人的风格。这里的每个印章的字体、风格均不相同,可能与拥有者的性格也不无关系。必须说明,只有黄公望即黄子久的印章才与画卷和他的题跋构成不可分割的艺术整体。

16.5 文化情境分析

本文不讨论情景语境,因为它往往与"意义"层面关联密切或交织在一起。事实上,表16-1已包含了情景语境的主要参数,比如主题、人际关系、画卷的类型、布局及其特点,这些参数都与情景语境密切相关。这里我们只讨论这幅画的文化情境,以便从整体上分析画卷。

本文采用了韩礼德有关文化情境的定义:"一定的社会历史和意识形态产生一定的语篇,而该语篇又产生一定的社会历史和意识形态"(the socio-historical and ideological environment engendering, and engendered by the text)(Halliday 1978)。

根据这个定义,我们可以对作品提出以下几个具体问题:

(1) 画家是个什么样的人?他生活在什么样的社会背景下,在什么样的历史意识环境之中创作了这幅画卷?
(2) 他为谁创作了这幅画?为什么创作?
(3) 这幅画以后在中国的历代经历了什么遭遇?现在保存何处?
(4) 这幅长卷对后代产生过什么影响?有什么社会意义?

根据考证(王耀庭 2014),黄公望(1269—1354)生活在蒙古人统治下的中国元朝末期。中年时期,曾任一地方小官,受到不公正的迫害,受冤入狱。之后,他对现实失去了信心,变成了一个道教信徒。他受道家大师郑无用之邀移居富春江的山丘之中,全身心信奉"全真道"并云游传播,自称"大痴学人",人们则称他"大痴道人"。

他于79岁即1347开始创作这幅画卷,1350年写了题跋留给郑无用,什么时候完成这幅作品,没有确切的日期。但是据王耀庭(2014)等研究者考证,大概完成于七年之后他离世之前。他写的题跋明示,这幅画是献给他的道教朋友郑无用的(见16.4)。他的作品反映了他的道教世界观:如果融入浩瀚的宇宙或大自然,人类可以过上一种脱俗、平淡的生活。也有学者认为:"元代社会的特殊性,使元代隐士只好借文学和艺术,来抚慰苦闷和压抑的心灵,在无奈中寻求闲适",也表达了他们对现实的不满(蒋锦彪 2012)。

这幅画卷为历代画家推崇。元代以后,凡有山水画的地方,皆有他的巨大影响所在。他的传统水墨写意的技巧发展趋向完美,真正做到了"抒情达意"(赵秋菊、曹春雷 2010)。长卷的成就将黄公望列入元朝末期的四大画家之首。长卷对后来的中国画家产生过深刻的影响,曾风靡清代将近三百年之久,被认为可以与王羲之的《兰亭序》媲美,被称为画界的"兰亭序",为"中国十大传世名画"之一(蒋勋 2012),是许多学画人学习的范本,曾被许多人临摹(王耀庭 2014),一些赝品甚至被错当原作,其中一幅甚至被品味颇高的乾隆皇帝误以为"真品"。这幅长卷不仅在画界影响深远,近年来被拍成了电影、编制为刺绣,还有艺术家以"山水画境,富春山图随想"为主题,创作成大型民族管弦乐演奏的曲目。

像《清明上河图》一样,这幅画卷经历坎坷,饱受摧残。它险些被它的第二个收藏者吴洪裕烧毁,成为殉葬品。就在被投入炉火的一刹那,吴洪裕的侄子将其救出,但是已经烧成了两段,"起首的那段被烧,到底画了什么,无从考证,引起人们无限遐想"。历经无数磨难,《富春山居图》现在被保存于中国两地。《无用师卷》保存于台北故宫博物院,而《剩山图》收藏于浙江省博物馆。2010年,时任国务院总理温家宝在"两会"记者见面会上表达了"我希望两幅画什么时候能合成一幅画;画之如此,人何以堪"的心愿。2011年6月1日,通过两地文化人的努力和中国中央政府的积极支持,人们终于在台北故宫博物院盼到了这幅完整画卷的展出。长期的隔离和其他种种原因,整幅画卷何时能在内地展出还是个未知数。两岸人民期盼有一天这幅长卷终能合璧,那一定是中国又一次实现了统一的一天,这个期盼表达了两岸中国人对祖国统一的强烈愿望。从这个意义上看,这幅画卷上附着了非常深刻的历史和政治意义。

16.6 结　语

本章通过对《富春山居图》的分析,揭示了这幅画卷如何使用绘画、题跋、印章这些不同的符号资源,共同构建作品的不同画面含义、画外含义和历史含义,它们又如何将不同的模态成分编制成一个连贯的整体,虽然有些符号,比如有些印章对画面并没有积极意义。文中也确认了笔者提出的基于系统功能语言学框架的分析参数的应用价值,这些参数可使一个门外人尝试讨论一幅长卷画作,没有系统功能语言学理论框架和这些参数作指导是不可能做到的。通过分析确实让笔者能够更好地、更全面地欣赏这幅作品,也能比较深入地领会作品的各个层次的深层含义。本文的这些参数也许对生动的描述没有多大的贡献,但是它们对作品可作有层次的、有系统的、有理论指导的分析。为了了解这幅画卷,笔者阅读了一些专业人士和网上的一些文章和著作(蒋锦彪 2012;蒋勋 2012;王耀庭 2014;赵秋菊、曹春雷 2010;culture.china.com.cn;hgw.fynews.com.cn),受益匪浅。但是笔者发现许多文章多讨论四个方面的问题:一是介绍画家的生平,二是讨论画面的内容,三是讨论画家的作画技巧,四是叙述它的历史经历,而其中画家的生平和画作的坎坷历史经历往往叙述得详细、生动,成为叙事的主轴,常常盖过了对作品本身有层次的、有系统的分析。有些只是文人轶事,与作品没有什么关系,似乎与韩礼德学习文学作品时老师的讲解相似(见 16.1)。笔者相信,如果这些分析者掌握一定的系统功能语言学的知识,他们的分析会更加深刻、更加贴切、更有层次感、更有系统性。对《富春山居图》的多符号、多模态分析再一次论证了系统功能语言学的"适用性",它的确是一种"适用语言学"。它的理论框架不仅可以有效地分析文字语篇,也同样可以有效地分析其他符号、其他模态的语篇。

笔者是国内第一个尝试用系统功能语言学理论解释中国长卷画的学者,也是第一个提出长卷分析参数的学者。由于自己的水平和文章的篇幅所限,本章无法对绘画、题跋、印章做更详细、全面、深入的探讨,只希望能起到抛砖引玉的作用。期待有更多同行参与对中国的多符号、多模态的艺术作品的研究当中。

17

为韩茹凯撰写的序言

17.1 《韩茹凯应用语言学自选集》中文序言[①]

凡是读过《英语的衔接》(*Cohesion in English*)一书的学者一定都知道韩茹凯(Ruqaiya Hasan,以前多译为哈桑)这个名字。该书是她和系统功能语言学创始人韩礼德(M. A. K. Halliday)的合著,是一本称得上是自20世纪70年代以来最有影响的语言学著作之一,在世界范围内对过去三十余年的语言学研究、语篇分析和英语教学产生了深刻的、积极的影响。

熟悉系统功能语言学的学者都知道,在韩礼德周围云集了一大批在国际上有影响的语言学家和应用语言学家,韩茹凯就是其中的佼佼者。自20世纪60年代以来,韩茹凯不仅在理论上发展了韩礼德创建的系统功能语言学,还在应用语言学的诸多领域中做出了杰出的贡献。理论方面,她对系统功能语言学的语境理论、语义学、词汇语法做了深入的、独到的研究;应用方面,她潜心探讨将系统功能语言学的框架应用到文体学、语

① 这是一篇笔者受韩茹凯之托为她的《应用语言学自选集》撰写的中文序言,英文序言为韩礼德撰写。她的自选集于2011年由外语教学与研究出版社出版。

篇分析、儿童语言发展等诸多方面的可能性。我们当然也不会忘记她曾参加伯恩斯坦(Beinstein)的多个研究项目,在社会语言学领域的理论和应用方面也取得了令人瞩目的成就。

由她本人精心挑选编辑成的这本应用语言学论文集,就集中展示了她在应用语言学中的研究成果。读者若想全面了解她的研究情况,可阅读由 Equinox 出版、香港城市大学教授卫真道(Jonathan Webster)编辑的她的七本论文选集。

本论文集包括了她自 1969 年以来在不同时期发表过的 14 篇论文,分成四个部分。

第一部分三篇论文主要讨论语言与社会的关系。她从系统功能语言学的视角,认为语言和社会之间存在着密不可分的辩证关系。回顾了语域、域码、社会方言的发展脉络,从理论上论证了这几个概念的区别,提出了语域和语码理论框架。她一再强调语言是一种意义潜势,语言学应当被看作为一种社会符号意义学,研究语言就必须涉及分布在语篇各个层次上的语言意义。这种对语言本质的探讨对应用语言学有着深刻的含意。

第二部分包括四篇论文,涉及与社会和语言有关的几个问题,强调语言学习和语言教学的社会实践性质。首先,通过分析 24 对母亲与孩子的日常交谈,探讨了母亲的说话方式在建构孩子的意识形态和价值观中所扮演的重要作用。第二,建立了学前儿童和母亲提问和回答方式两个语义系统网络。通过对原始材料的语义分析,说明母亲的提问和回答方式对孩子的知识取向、性格特征的形成有重要的引导作用。第三,分析了小学教育的开始阶段,教师在引导学生阅读图画读物时的说话方式在孩子中产生不同效果的原因,讨论了如何激活学生知识潜势发展的方式。第四,作者从社会符号意义学的角度,分析了无意识的传播知识的方式对儿童的生存方式、知识结构会产生相当大的影响。强调从事培训教师的工作人员必须认真考虑符号意义、社会、认知三者之间的关系。

第三部分四篇论文从语篇的功能角度讨论了与语篇有密切关系的几个问题。她反复强调语境在语篇研究中占有中心地位、情景语境与语篇之间存在着辩证关系。她还详细讨论了形成语篇的语篇纹理(texture)和语类结构潜势(Generic Structural Potential 或 GSP)这两个重要因素。阐述了语境配置与语域、语类和语篇结构之间的关系,讨论了必要成分与非必要成分在构成语篇中的作用,探讨了语类结构潜势的重要意义和广泛的应用价值。此外,她还分析了连贯与衔接和谐之间的关系,特别是被忽略的词汇衔接及几种词汇链的作用和互动情况。最后,她强调了语篇具有四种元功能,指出系统功能语言学的独特贡献在于说明语言具有这些元功能的原因。

第四部分三篇文章从社会符号意义学的角度,通过理论阐述、对传统文学评论方法的批评和对两篇诗歌和莎剧一个片段的分析,讨论了作者与读者、作者的创作意图与读者接收信息之间的关系;揭示了文体学的本质、语言学与文学的关系及社会、符号、意义之间的关系;讨论了文学作为一门学科的性质、特点,文学语篇与其他语篇的共性与区别以及文学的符号意义与其他符号意义及其他艺术活动的区别。提出了一个研究文学作品的三维研究模式,涉及词汇、语法在文学作品中的规则范式与前景化一致性的关系及前景化一致性与文学表达之间的关系等等深层次的问题。

韩茹凯的论文有几个特点:(1)她对使用分析的系统功能语言学框架,有着深刻的理解,使她的分析目标明确、方向清晰、结论可信度高;(2)她对研究的切入点把握准确,采用了科学、严谨的研究方法,对大量的原始资料做了深入、详尽的解析,为语篇分析和实证研究提供了范例;(3)她深厚的文学功底使她的语篇研究不仅包括日常生活的各种语类,还涉及了文学语类的多个子语类,提出了对文体学和文学语篇研究的真知灼见和研究框架。事实上,韩茹凯大学期间主修的是英国文学,攻读博士学位期间,她在教授文学课的过程中,就试图引导学生借助语言学寻找欣赏文学作品的理论依据,并将研究成果写成了探讨文体学的博士论文。从此,对文学语篇的关注从来没有离开过她的视线。相信她这方面的研究会对从事文体学、文学、文学作品分析的研究者有着深刻的启示。她的研究说明语言学研究者需要有扎实的文学功底才能对各种语篇做出深入的解析;同样,文学的研究人员则需要有语言学的基础才能使自己的研究避免仅仅停留在观察表面现象的层面,才能避免只重复别人的观点,才能做到尽可能深入到现象产生的原因和文学所表达的本质。

韩茹凯对中国怀有深厚的感情,一直对中国功能语言学的发展非常关心,曾给予过多方面的指导。自 20 世纪 90 年代,她与韩礼德一起参加过在杭州、苏州、北京、上海、南昌的中国功能语言学和语篇分析会议，还应邀在清华大学、中山大学、北京师范大学、云南大学、西安外国语大学、北京科技大学做过学术报告，现在还担任中国香港城市大学“韩礼德中心”研究规划主任，对推动中国功能语言学的发展做出了贡献，在中国功能语言学者中产生了很大的影响。

她不仅与中国功能语言学界有着深厚的渊源，而且还是我的好朋友，是一位在我学术成长的道路上给过我多方面帮助和指导的学者。第一次见到韩茹凯是我在悉尼大学韩礼德的语言学课堂上，聆听她给我们研究生作了一场精彩的学术报告。1984 年暑假我们中国留学生又受到韩礼德和她的邀请到他们家做客，受到他们热情的款待，她还亲自下厨，做了很多有南亚风味的美食，至今令人回味。特别让我难忘的是 1995 年，她接受我代表清华大学的邀请，与韩礼德及其他两位国际著名学者到我校在“功能语言学暑期研讨班”上做了三个星期的学术讲座，为中国培养了一批当今在功能语言学界都很有影响的学者。令我感动的是，由于我申请不到经费，是他们两位自掏腰包购买的往返机票才使这次学术活动能顺利进行。我还要感谢她于 1992 年部分资助我参加了她主持的第 19 届国际系统功能语言学大会，并将我的论文“On Theme and in Chinese: From Clause to Discourse”收入由她和弗里斯(Peter Fries)主编的 *On Subject and Theme: A discourse functional perspective* 一书之中(1995 由 John Benjamins Publishing Company 出版)。以后在多次的学术会议中她都对我的发言给予鼓励，并提出中肯的意见和建议。还要提及的是，她积极支持我主持的第 36 届国际系统功能语言学大会及在北京师范大学举行的会前系列报告会，并对我正在编辑的包括大会主要发言的论文集提出了很多宝贵的建议。

韩茹凯嘱我写序，我深感荣幸但实不敢当。我把它当成一次宝贵的学习机会，使我有幸成为第一个读者，通过仔细阅读受益匪浅。在此向她再次表示深深的谢意，同时对这本论文集在北京的出版表达诚挚的祝贺与衷心的推荐。

方　琰

2011 年 3 月

于清华园

17.2 《韩茹凯论语言》序①

从韩礼德教授1955年完成他的博士论文《元朝秘史》提出他对语言学的初步构思，至今整整过去了六十年；从他于20世纪60年代初创建系统功能语言学（以下称SFL），迄今也走过了半个世纪的路程。在这条崎岖不平的道路上有很多学者在前行，其中就有一位杰出的女性。她是韩礼德教授的伴侣，更是他的学术知音和并肩奋斗的战友。她就是SFL界一个响亮的名字Ruqaiya Hasan，她有一个儒雅的中文名字——**韩茹凯**。

20世纪60年代以来，韩茹凯教授不仅在理论上发展了韩礼德教授创建的SFL，还在应用语言学、社会学的诸多领域中做出了突出的贡献。要了解这位杰出的语言学家，最好的途径就是阅读由Equinox出版、香港城市大学教授卫真道（Jonathan Webster）编辑的她的七本英语论文选集，或者阅读由她本人精心挑选编辑成的、2011年外语教学与研究出版社出版的《韩茹凯应用语言学自选集》。相信阅读过她著作的广大读者一定收获颇丰，遗憾的是这七本选集因为没有中译本，使很多读者失去了一次学习的大好机会。现在，好消息终于来了——北京师范大学功能语言学研究中心主任彭宣维教授主持翻译的韩茹凯教授文选《韩茹凯论语言》终于出版了，多少填补了这方面的缺陷。

彭宣维教授2014年11月告诉我这个消息时，我真为韩茹凯教授感到高兴。彭教授还告诉我，选集的译者都是高校从事SFL研究的女性学者，我很感动，也感谢他为我国女性SFL研究者提供一个深入学习原著和展示自己才能的机会。他问我是否愿意为选集作序，我欣然答应。这不仅因为我一直是韩茹凯教授的仰慕者，更重要的是，我意识到出版她的中文选集是一件非常有意义的事情，它可以让更多的语言学研究者获益，也一定会推动我国的SFL理论和应用研究。能为这样一部译作写序，我深感荣幸。

这本选集从Equinox出版的七卷英文选集中挑选了23篇论文。最早

① 《韩茹凯论语言》于2015年由北京大学出版社出版。

的一篇写于1969年，最近的一篇2013年，前后跨越四十多年，代表韩茹凯教授各个时期勤奋耕耘的研究成果。

从接受写序的任务以后，我开始通读选集，做了笔记或摘要，有的文章、有的章节、有的段落反复阅读，仔细琢磨、思考良久。选集内容丰富、信息量大、理论深邃，以笔者的语言学水平，对有些内容的理解真的是不甚了了，更不可能对这部语言学著作做出中肯的介绍和评论。我真感到"压力山大"。只能勉为其难，权当是向读者汇报自己的学习心得，与读者做一次"心灵的沟通"吧！

韩茹凯教授始终站在各个时期研究的最前沿，积极参与探讨、辩论语言学研究涉及的"热门话题"。但是选集的主线是阐述和发展韩礼德教授创建的SFL理论，围绕语言性质的两个方面展开讨论：第一，**语言是一种社会符号**，而且是**最重要**的社会符号。韩茹凯教授完全赞同沃尔夫的"语言塑造现实"、"语言塑造社会"的观点，认为"语言资源是世界知识的主要建筑者，语言既可以用来做琐事，也可完成划时代的大事"。她认为"正是因为韩礼德教授将索绪尔符号两重性本质理论化，才解决了索绪尔理论的大部分矛盾"。有关语言符号学特性的论述是多篇文章的重要内容。韩茹凯教授肯定了维果茨基和巴赫金有关社会文化因素，尤其是语言符号对人类高级智力发展研究的贡献，赞同他们关于语言在创造、维系和改变社会关系、社会结构过程中的中心作用的论点。她揭示了现代社会与在符号中创造的认知之间的固有联系，让人们认识到智力需要社会、社会需要符号得以生存、发展、变革这一关键要素。她从社会符号学角度，坚持将语言变异纳入社会语言学研究范畴，她是提出这个主张的第一人；并讨论了与语言的变异现象相关联的多个问题，包括语义变体在产生、维系、改变言说者群体的社会语境中具有的特殊作用。她论证了信息时代语言符号在诠释经验意义、创作文学作品、表达抽象概念、创建理论时所起的中心作用。她强调，社会与符号的循环互动关系对塑造文化和塑造语言同等重要。她还将文学作品分析视为社会符号学的研究范畴。可以说，韩茹凯教授在为使系统功能语言学"发展为具有详尽解释能力的作为社会符号的语言理论"方面做出了不懈的努力。

第二，**语言系统是一种意义潜势**。韩茹凯教授反复强调，语言是"固有的可变的意义潜势"，"是创造信息的潜势"；语言学的目的就是要"发展分析语义的方法"；语言研究必须分析人类活动的"语义性质"，必须认识到语言在认知过程中的"关键中介作用",因为它能通过意义解释人类的活动经验,而意义交流才是语言在人类生活中最重要的功能。她认为成功的语言教学就是要能使学生"用词汇和语法产生适合语篇语境所需要的意义"。她深入探讨了将语言描绘成意义潜势的三个关键术语:"选择""系统""体现"。她认为,这三个术语一起工作,在"语言内部建构起大家都能接受的语义","使系统成为将语言描写成意义潜势的强大工具"。笔者认为,这是将索绪尔的"所指"表达为"能指"(意义)的有效途径。

"语言是社会符号"及"语言系统是意义潜势"的语言观,奠定了 SFL 关于语言层次、语境学说、语言功能、语言系统、语篇生成、语篇分析、衔接与连贯、语言教学的认识基础,也是区分这个学派与其他一些语言学派,尤其是形式语言学的核心理念。

韩茹凯教授在多个地方阐述了 SFL 的多层次观点。对各个层次通过"体现"建立起有机联系以及语言受制于文化语境和情景语境的观点,有鞭辟入里的解读。她指出,SFL 认为语义层和语法层是"自然关系":"不存在没有语言形式的语义,也不存在没有语义的词汇、语法形式";并且每个层次都代表了"不同的抽象概念",但都对"全面描述作为符号系统的语言同等重要"。她论证了语言是一个包含"四个层次"(语境、语义、词汇-语法、字音)的"复合编码系统",因而语言研究应当包括对四个层次的描述。

韩茹凯教授厘清了有关"语境"的许多概念。她指出,语言"扎根于人类生物学,但受文化的干预而发展",这是认识语境概念的基础。她阐述了语境创造语篇和解释语篇的"原动力"作用,详细说明了语境与语言性质以及语境、行为和文化之间的关系,建构了对话语篇和非对话语篇不同的语境模式;还审视了情景语境变量(语场、语旨、语式)之间的互动关系,分析了语境变量和语篇、语篇结构、语篇组织(texture)之间的关系。她认为教育者应当用伯恩斯坦的社会学视角审视文化教育和社会变革的相关性,应当看到语境因素在语言研究和语言教育中的重要性。

韩茹凯教授批驳了语言为镜像反映现象的论点。她认为,韩礼德教授"最有意义的贡献在于致力于探索为何要认可语言的三个**纯理功能**"——概念功能、人际功能、语篇功能,而且**三个功能同等重要**。她强调多功能的语言观有利于深入了解人类意识是怎样在社会语境中发展的。她释解了人类的语言能够将三种功能放在同一个句子中的原因——是语言的功能决定了词汇语法结构。这是功能语言学语法观的基础。她从功能语言学的角度阐述了教授语言的过程,还分析、解释了话语过程的功能意义,以及小句的具体功能。她探讨了三个语境变量对语义选择的功能控制,以及文体学的两个研究目的:(1)分析文学作品语言的内在功能结构;(2)揭示语言功能怎样表达作品的主题思想,即语言的运用与主题如何契合。

韩茹凯教授坚持认为,SFL是关于"语篇的理论"。她特别重视分析对话语篇,尤其是日常会话,因为这是了解言语与语境密切关系的重要途径。阅读她的文章的一个突出印象就是:她对分析母亲和幼童之间的对话情有独钟,或许与她是一位女性,特别是一位母亲的身份不无关系。她不仅分析对话的语境、词汇和语法的功能特点,还特别强调对语篇组织(texture)和结构特点的分析,因为它们是将词汇、语法单位衔接、连贯在一起的、关于语篇研究的两个基本要素。她从大量的实际话语中发现了新现象,甚至总结、提炼出语言学的规律。她也重视对句子的研究,但是这些句子一定是出现在语篇中的句子。她应用功能语言学的分析方法,剖析了叶芝的诗《临水自照的老人们》的韵律及其所表达的深刻含义,为文体分析提供了范例。

重视语篇分析是韩茹凯教授重视语言的社会功能和应用价值的体现。她认为"语言使用是语言系统在社会历史语境下的实例化"。她强调,语言"只有在应用中才能得到发展,获得进化"。语言学理论也只有在"应用中"才能被证实、才能得到发展。在论述语言教育的论文中她同样强调了这一点。她从心理人类学、社会人类学、教育社会学的角度,讨论、分析了写读教育和第二语言教学的定义、所涉及的因素,还展示了她的"第二语言教学综合模式"教学大纲,讨论了这个大纲的特点和这个看似符合逻辑的封闭模式的问题以及教师必须具备什么样的社会学观和语言学观。笔者相信,这是在通往"适用语言学"的道路上迈出的坚实的一步。

选集的第一个特点是既对SFL做了比较全面、精辟的论述,又从不同的角度、不同的学科观察、考证语言的方方面面,因为她相信,"一个无法在某个学科解决的问题,很可能借助另一个学科的洞察力找到解释或解决的方案"。韩茹凯教授堪称跨学科甚至超学科研究的典范。

纵观她的著作,可以看到马克思主义的世界观、阶级观和马克思主义辩证唯物主义思想和伯恩斯坦的社会学理论,对她的语言观和她的社会语言学认识观的深刻影响,这是选集的第二个特点。她指出,人们的日常会话被深深地打上了资本主义制度的经济基础和权力分配、权力控制的阶级烙印。这个论点也体现在讨论伯恩斯坦的社会结构成分预测语码分类、现实社会中工人阶级孩子语言教育和发展中国家第二语言教学的论述中。辩证唯物主义观深刻影响了她对社会化与语言的紧密关系的认识,也贯穿于诠释生理和社会相互生成的动态逻辑、社会中介与智力发展、语言系统与语言系统实例化、语境与语篇、语言理论与实践相互推动、相互依赖等等关系的论述中。

选集的第三个特点是韩茹凯教授对各个时代与语言研究有关的许多学者的思想做了反思性的或者批判性的评述。韩茹凯教授鼓励教师培养学生的批判性反思能力,而她自己就是在学术上极具批判性反思能力的一位学者。且略举数例。在评论维果茨基和巴赫金关于"语言"(langue)和"言语"(parole)的看法时,她指出他们都只关注"言语",而不重视"语言",与索绪尔只重视"语言"而不重视"言语"完全相反,都有偏颇。在论述维果茨基对"符号中介"在人的心智发展中做出的贡献时,她批评维果茨基理论只重视语言符号对高级智力发展的中介作用,忽视了日常会话在其中的协调作用,忽视了"平凡的日常知识内化"的价值,有站在"精英主义"立场的嫌疑;而且他只重视词汇,无视语篇意义和社会语境的影响。韩茹凯教授建议,维果茨基和巴赫金应当用韩礼德语言观和伯恩斯坦的社会学理论,来修正、补充、完善他们关于符号中介和话语语类(speech genre)的论述。在肯定了拉波夫对社会语言学的发展做出了杰出贡献的同时,韩茹凯教授批评他不应把语言变异现象排斥在社会语言学之外。她肯定了语料库语言学的革命性的贡献,但也指出了它的局限性——同维果茨基和拉波夫一样,都缺乏合适的语言学模型作为分析基础。她批评了很多专家不重视研究日常会话中表现出来的意识形态、权力问题,不重视研究语义变异现象,"更不用说从词汇-语法角度做实实在在的分析"工作了。她尖锐地批驳了乔姆斯基的"语言天生"和"语言自治"的形式主义语言学理论,更是用犀利的言辞揭露西方国家将"民主"再语义化,用来掩盖他们欺压贫穷国家的实质。她还分析了自由市场经济给教育管理带来的多种负面影响,她相信批判式"反思"教育可能有效改变这个制度带来的种种弊病。她强调"我们"生活在一个受"压迫"的社会中,所以作为语言学家,我们理应去"了解、揭发这样的压迫是如何维持的、处于特殊位置的人们在其中起了什么作用”，这样可能会“促进人类的进步”。

选集的另一个特点是它体现了一位严谨的语言学家在实证研究中观察入微、分析细致的特质。其首要特点是对语境的精密分析。她认为虽然 SFL 对语境和语篇的描述在当代“最为全面”，但仍然“没有一个完整的描述框架”。她身体力行，做出了含有七个层次的语场系统表，用精密度的概念讨论系统各个层次的语义特点。她不但解剖了语境配置特点，还讨论了由语篇组织（texture）结合形成的“语境集合体”、由语篇结构形成的“语境常规体”以及多个不同语篇的结构图，深入解析了系统与实例的关系。韩茹凯教授是语类结构潜势（GSP）的倡导者，选集中的有关论述分析了多个语类结构潜势，特别解释了“推理”过程中的词汇-语法和各个成分的特点，为语境研究做了开创性的探索。其次，她对小句的功能进行了详尽分析。她用大篇幅解构了“The teacher taught the student English”的句子意义，并用这个例子一步一步详细解释了韩礼德教授的及物系统的功能语义基础和可能产生的不同的意识形态，提供了剖析教学过程和教学实质的范例。第三，她对衔接、衔接和谐、连贯的描述和分析环环入扣。她的“衔接范畴”写于 70 年代初期，详尽地讨论了各种衔接纽带和与衔接有关的各种概念，充分展示了她对英语衔接理论的独特贡献。第四，她对系统网络做出了初步的实验性构建。韩茹凯教授非常清楚，SFL 要真正将语言描写成“意义潜势”，就必须构建语言系统网络。这是一项艰巨的任务，但是必须脚踏实地地一步一步去完成。她本人做出了示范性的努力：提出了八个假设，陈述了六个协调网络和体现语义的路径；还建构了九个词汇系统，并用精密度的概念详细描述了怎样从词汇系统选择相应的语义特征。她将她所做的这一切看作是“在把英语建构为语义潜势的道路上迈出的微小的一步”。

韩茹凯教授不仅从纷繁的语言学知识海洋中创造性地诠释、解读、梳理出 SFL 的精华，她还是一位永远行进在不断进取、不断发现问题、解决问题道路上的具有前瞻性思维的学者。虽然她认为“SFL 提供了最成熟的理论”框架，但是她清醒地认识到“语言结构极其复杂”，SFL 还远远“没有完成对整个语言的描述”，需要一代一代学者凝神聚力、克难攻艰。但是她坚信，SFL“已经开启了与语言相关的所有现象的研究大门”，总有一天能“实现韩礼德将整个语言形式都变成语法系统进行描述的梦想”。笔者相信，如果每个 SFL 研究者都能像韩茹凯教授那样目光如炬、勤奋敬业，SFL 终将能如她所愿**构建成融合符号学、社会学、社会心理学交叉的语言学理论**。

阅读原著，让我对韩茹凯教授的渊博知识、深邃的洞见、严谨的科研作风敬佩不已；参阅中译本，让我对彭宣维教授和李雪娇博士修改译文、甚至大量篇幅的重新翻译、艰辛统稿（如参考文献）所倾注的巨大精力充满敬意。谨以此序文向“热衷于社会研究的语言学家”韩茹凯教授和她的《韩茹凯论语言》致敬！向彭教授和所有参与翻译工作的同仁一并致谢！

方　琰

2015 年 3 月 11 日

于清华园

第三部分

语类分析及教学实践

Part Three

Genre Analysis and Teaching Practice

18

韩茹凯的语体结构潜势理论及其对语篇分析的贡献*

18.1 引　言

20 世纪 60 年代以后，许多语言学家逐渐认识到，仅对句子层次的分析研究，远远不能揭示语言及语言交际的本质，因为语言交际并不是由"无限的合乎语法的句子"（Chomsky 1957）构成的。人们开始对语篇的研究发生了浓厚的兴趣，对语篇的定义、结构展开了热烈的讨论。"语篇分析"激发了包括社会学家、人类学家、民族学家、心理学家、人工智能学家在内的许多人的兴趣。他们从不同的角度、以不同的方式对各类语篇进行了分析研究，获得了不少可喜的成果。

70 年代布拉格学派达内什在马泰修斯的"功能句法观"（即每个句子由主位"Theme"和述位"Rheme"两个功能成分组成）（Danes 1974）和菲尔巴斯的"交际动力"（Communicative Dynamism）（Firbas 1987）理论基础上，提出了主位"进程"（thematic progression）的理论，为已知信息即主位和新信息即述位，在语篇中的相互衔接的顺序，提出了五个具体的模

* 原登载于《外语学刊》，1995（1），本文做了一些修改。

式,对语篇的小结构顺序理论作出了贡献(刘鸿坤 1987)。韩礼德区分了主位-述位与已知-新信息的定义和它们之间的相互关系(1985)。虽然他的模式比较复杂,但对新信息的分布和标志主位的概念有其独到的见解。荷兰语言学家范戴克提出的篇章结构概念和树形图,发展了语篇大顺序的理论,"可以被看作篇章产生和解说的模式",虽然在理论上还有许多含糊不清之处(Halliday 1985),比如他注意到了不同的语体含有不同结构,然而他没有从总体的概念上讨论语篇结构的理论框架。

80 年代中,澳大利亚学者马丁和韩茹凯分别从语域和语体①(genre)两个角度讨论了语篇的结构,对话语分析和语篇学说两方面做出了各自的贡献。

马丁将韩礼德的主位-述位理论扩大到语篇的整体结构,发展了宏观主位(macro-Theme 即语篇主位)和超句主位(hyper-Theme 即段落主位)两个新概念(Halliday 1992),探讨了语篇主位怎样在段落和句子两个层次上得到发展和体现。他推进了韩礼德有关语域和主位-述位结构的理论。他的理论将另文介绍。

韩茹凯在与韩礼德合著的 *Language, Context and Text: Aspects of language in a social-semiotic perspective* (1985)一书中,集中讨论了语篇的语体及其结构成分的问题。她提出的 Generic Structure Potential(语体结构潜势),简称 GSP 理论,不仅发展了范戴克的语篇大顺序理论,而且还在语体理论和语篇整体结构理论框架两个方面,推动了语篇学说的研究。

本章将主要介绍韩茹凯的 GSP 理论,并简述它对语篇学说理论和应用两个方面的贡献。

18.2 语篇的定义和特点

韩茹凯同意韩礼德将语篇定义为"语义的单位",即"在某种情景中作

① 20 世纪 90 年代,普遍把这个词译为"语体",现在看来可能会与"语言的文体"相混淆。后来我根据 genre 被定义为"语篇的类型"(Hasan 1977),将该词译为"语类"(方琰 2001)。

某件事”的语言（胡壮麟 1988）。也就是说语篇和语境密切相关，它不能脱离语境独立存在。这与美国结构主义学派的“超句”的概念截然不同（H &H 1985）。

语篇有许多特点，最突出的是“结构的统一性”（unity of structure）和组织的统一性（unity of texture），虽然组织与结构相互之间有着密切的关系。GSP 主要探讨的是语篇信息形式的整体结构（the global structure of the message），也就是语篇结构的统一性。

18.3 语篇的结构

18.3.1 研究的对象

韩茹凯指出，无论哪种语体的整体结构都包含着不同的成分。韩茹凯将日常会话这种语体当作自己的研究对象，这是因为：（1）日常会话的结构鲜为人知；（2）对日常会话结构的研究，可以使人们更清楚地看到语言与现实生活之间密切的关系；（3）“日常会话的内容最广泛，结构最为复杂”（H &H 1985）。具体地说，GSP 以“市场会话”（service encounter），即顾客与卖主之间的对话为素材，探讨语篇的整体结构。

18.3.2 语篇和语境

韩茹凯强调语篇和语境两个概念是不可分的。语篇是语言在某个语境中的具体运用；而语境则是语篇得以产生的环境条件，因而可用来对一个社会中产生的许许多多的语篇加以解释。缺少其中一个概念，另一个概念也将会变得含混不清。它们之间相互作用，相互预测。语篇的语义可以揭示产生它的语境；而语境的某些特点，如语场（field）、语旨（tenor）、语式（mode），可以用来预测语篇的结构成分，也就是说，语境可以影响语篇的语体及其结构。

18.3.3 语境格式(Contextual Configuration，简称 CC)

韩茹凯将语境格式定义为“实现语场、语旨、语式的一组具体的值。”比如父母口头表扬孩子,或雇主口头责备雇员,均有一定的语境格式。前者的语场：表扬某人;语旨：父母与孩子的关系;语式：口语。后者的语场：责备某人;语旨：雇主与雇员的关系;语式：口语。两种语境格式中,实现语式的值相同,但实现语旨和语场的值均不相同。

18.3.4 语境格式与语篇结构

语境格式 CC 的主要作用就是使语篇结构保持统一。CC 能说明语言交往这一社会活动的主要特点,可以回答语篇结构中五个方面的问题：

(1) 哪些成分必须出现;
(2) 哪些成分可能出现;
(3) 这些成分必须在什么地方出现;
(4) 这些成分可能在什么地方出现;
(5) 这些成分出现的次数。

也就是说,CC 可以预测语境的必要成分、非必要成分、它们出现的顺序、相互之间的关系以及相互之间可能产生的影响。韩茹凯举了几个例子,分析了构成各个语篇 CC 的变量——语场、语旨和语式,然后讨论了它们的语篇结构。这里仅介绍其中两个例子,即语篇 1 和语篇 2 的语境格式(CC_1及 CC_2)以及它们的语篇结构(TS_1,及 TS_2)。

18.3.4.1 语篇的语境(CC_1)

构成 **CC_1**的变量具体的值如下：

语场：经济交易：购买零售商品：易坏水果……;

语旨：交易者：买者为主，卖者为辅；两者之间的社会距离：接近于最大。韩茹凯认为语旨总是包含一对参与者，它们或者属于不同的阶层如卖主与顾客，此时顾客享有更大的控制权；或者属于同一个层次，比如朋友之间。另外，两者之间的社会距离，即彼此熟悉的程度，将影响交际过程中使用的语言风格。

语式：语言作用：辅助性；渠道：语音；传播方式：伴有视觉接触的口语。韩茹凯指出，交易中的语言只用来伴随物与钱的交易活动；她将渠道（channel）与传播方式（medium）区分开来，原因是这两者虽然在通常情况下概念相一致，然而有时却并不一致。例如给朋友写信，用的是口语的方式，书面的渠道。

18.3.4.2 语篇$_1$的结构（TS_1）

C: Can I have ten oranges and a kilo of bananas please?	] SR
V: Yes, anything else? C: No, thanks.	] SC
V: That'll be a dollar forty.	] S
C: Two dollars.	] p
V: Sixty, eighty, two dollars. Thank you.	] PC

（V=Vendor（卖主，小贩）；C=Customer（顾客））

符号说明：

SR =Sale request（购物请求，出自买主之口）

SC = Sale compliance（应允或不应允）

S = Sale（销售）

P = Purchase（购买）

PC =Purchase closure（购买结束）

TS_1成分和顺序为 SR ^ SC ^ S ^ P ^ PC。（^表示“后接”，即 SC 位于 SR 之后，S 则在 SC 之后；以此类推。）

18.3.4.3 语篇$_2$的语境格式（CC_2）

完全与 CC_1 相同。

18.3.4.4 语篇$_2$的结构式(TS_2)

V：Who's next?（1）

C：I think I am.（2）[（1）（2）= **SI**] I'll have ten oranges and a kilo of bananas, please. [（3）= **SR₁**]

V：Yes, anything else?（4）

C：Yes.（5）[（4）（5）= **SC₁**] I wanted some strawberries but these don't look very ripe.（6）

V：O they're ripe all right.（7）They're just that colour kind a'greeny pink.（8）

C：Mm I see.（9）[（6）（7）（8）（9）= **SE₁**] Will they be OK for this evening?（10）

V：O yeah, they'll be fine;（11）I had some yesterday（12）and they're good very sweet and fresh.（13）[（10）（11）（12）（13）= **SE₂**]

C：O all right then, I'll take two. [（14）= **SR₂**]

V：You'll like them（15）cos they're good.（16）Will that be all?（17）

C：Yeah, thank you.（18）[（15）（16）（17）（18）= **SC₂**]

V：That'll be two dollars sixty-nine please. [（19）= **S**]

C：I can give you nine cents.（20 = **P**）

V：Yeah OK thanks（21）eighty, three dollars（22）and two is five.（23）Thank you.（24）[（21）（22）（22）（23）（24）= **PC**]
Have a nice day.（25）

C：See ya'.（26）[（25）（26）= **F**]

符号说明：

SI = Sale Initiation　　（销售起始，往往来自买方）
SE = Sale Enquiry　　（问询，出自买方）
F = Finis　　（结束语）

TS_2的成分和顺序为 $SI \wedge SR_1 \wedge SC_1 \wedge SE_1 \wedge SE_2 \wedge SR_2 \wedge SC_2 \wedge S \wedge P \wedge PC \wedge F$。显然 TS_2 比 TS_1 复杂。它不仅比 TS_1 多了 SI、SE 和 F 三个成分，还含有 SR、SE、SC 的重复成分。

18.3.4.5 必要成分和非必要成分

从上面 TS_1 和 TS_2 可以看出，它们有着相同的成分和一些不同的成分。Hasan 认为这些相同的成分是语篇中必须出现的成分，不同的成分则是不一定在语篇中出现的成分。

必须出现的成分被定义为必要成分，它们是构成语体（genre）的决定因素。比如 TS_1 和 TS_2 的语境格式 CC 相同（即 $CC_1 = CC_2$），都包含 SR（请求）、SC（应允）、S（销售）、P（购买）以及 PC（购买结束）这五个成分，而且它们的结构成分都是按照 SR ^ SC ^ S ^ P ^ PC 的顺序出现的。这些必要成分的存在和出现的顺序决定了 TS_1 和 TS_2 同属一个语体，即"市场会话"语体。

非必要成分的定义是"可以出现但并不是必须出现的成分"。例如 TS_2 中的 SI、SE 和 F 以及 SR、SC、SE 的重复成分都属非必要成分。非必要成分决定某个 CC 的变体。例如 CC_2 就是 CC_1 的变体，虽然它们同属一个 CC。这就是说，在同一个 CC 当中，可以存在某些结构上和风格上的差异。

18.4 语篇与语体、语体结构潜势（GSP）

在这个基础上，韩茹凯提出了一个适于 CC_1 的所有语篇的结构模式，它既包含必要成分又包括非必要成分。她称这个模式为 CC_1 的 GSP：

[（G）·（SI）^][（SE·）{**SR** ^ **SC** ^} ^ **S** ^] **P** ^ **PC**（^ **F**）

圆括号表示所包含的非必要成分为 G（= greeting，比如 Good morning, Mrs. X），SI、SE、F。这些成分可以单独或同时出现，但并不一定要出现在 CC_1 所包含的语篇中。两个成分之间的圆点"·"表明一个序列中出现的顺序不止一个。但顺序的排列并不完全自由。它们的顺序要求用方括号表示。因此第一个方括号包含下面几个意思：

（1）G 与 SI 可以/不一定单独或同时出现；

（2）如果两者均出现，G 可在 SI 之前或之后；

(3) G 和 SI 均不能出现在跟随 SI 的其他成分之后;

圆形箭头表示重复。因此(SE)表示:

(1) SE 为非必要成分;

(2) SE 只要不出现在 G 或 SI 之前或 P、PC、F 之后,则可出现在任何地方;

(3) SE 可重复。

即 SE 可出现于其他三个在方括号之内的成分 SR、SC 和 S 之前、之后或之间。

带有圆形箭头的大括号{}表示在括号内的成分的重复率是一致的。如果 SR 出现两次,那么 SC 也必须出现两次。

从 CC_1 的 GSP 的结构可以看出,GSP 是一个强大的机制,是一个可以用来实现许多不同变体的结构。TS_1 和 TS_2 已经证明了这一点。下面再举一例 TS_3:

V: Good morning, Miss Reid.

C: Good morning, Bob. (V 和 C 均为 G)

Can I have a couple of apples? (SR)

V: Is that all today?

C: Yes thank you. (V 和 C 均为 SC)

V: Sixty cents. (S)

C: Here y'are. (P)

V: Thank you. (PC)

Goo' day.

C: Bye. (Goo' day 和 Bye 均为 F)

TS_3 中的必要成分与 TS_1 和 TS_2 完全相同,但是由于它包括了 G 和 F 两个非必要成分,因此可以认为 T_3 是与 T_1,和 T_2 同属一个 GSP 的变体。

韩茹凯还举了另外一些 CC_1 的变体,说明它们虽然都有各自的实际结构,但却同属一个 GSP 框架。

当然,市场会话的结构是非常复杂的,有时有可能出现一些与市场这个语场无关的另外一些非必要成分。韩茹凯探讨了将这些非必要成分引入必要成分的各种策略。这里不详细叙述。

18.5 GSP 理论对语篇分析的贡献

18.5.1 对语体分类研究有着十分重要的意义

韩茹凯不是把语篇作为孤立的例子对语篇结构进行研究的。她是从存在于一定语境中的某种语体出发,来讨论语篇结构的。她的研究表明:"同属一个语体的语篇都是某个已知的 GSP 的可能实现",即如果语篇的 GSP 的框架相同,则这些语篇就同属一个语体。具体地说,如果同属一个 GSP 的语篇结构中的 CC 的必要成分及其分布相同,那么这些语篇的语体就相同。换句话说,必要成分及其分布是确认某个 CC 的决定因素,也是实现该 CC 的 GSP 的决定因素。这两个因素发生变化,语体也会发生根本变化。它们之间的关系可表示为(→表示"决定"):

CC 的必要成分及其分布→**GSP**→语体

在一定的文化语境中,GSP 为语体的划分奠定了理论基础。

18.5.2 可用来解释语体的变异现象

韩茹凯将同属一个 GSP 框架的 CC 中的必要成分与非必要成分区分开来,不仅为语体的辨认确定了标准,同时也为语体的变异现象提供了理论上的依据。非必要成分的改变是引起某个语体发生千变万化的根源,它们是丰富的文化和社会现象的反映。朱永生曾运用 GSP 理论对苏州地区市场会话结构进行过调查(1992)。他分析了三个国营商店及三个个体摊位上买主与卖主之间的对话。他得出的结论是:"国营商店内的会话结构比较短,非必要成分比较少;而个体摊头的会话结构则偏长,非必要成分(尤其是 SC 即应允)大量出现,这是两类结构之间的一个重大差异。"市场会话结构中,由于语场("国营商店"相对"个体摊位")发生变化,CC 的非必要成分也随之变化,就产生了市场会话变体。

18.5.3 对语篇教学具有重要意义

GSP 理论从社会符号学的角度探讨了语体结构与语境的关系，为语篇结构的分析和语体定性提出了一个明确的框架，对语篇教学产生了深刻的影响。韩茹凯本人就指出，"对语体结构的理解是教学取得成功的积极因素。"

GSP 理论对语篇阅读理解有一定的帮助。阅读是一个极为复杂的心理过程。近年来国内外一些阅读理论专家指出，最理想的阅读模式可能是将"自下而上"(Bottom-up)与"自上而下"(Top-down)两种模式相结合的"相互关联"(Interactive)模式。"自下而上"模式是读者从词汇的语义解码开始，逐渐达到对语篇的理解。"自上而下"模式的阅读过程与"自下而上"相反，是从语篇开始，逐渐深入到对语法、词汇的理解。同时强调读者运用自己头脑中已经具有的背景知识，不断对阅读的内容进行预测，达到理解语篇以及获取所需信息的目的(Devine 1986)。"相互关联"模式需要两方面的知识：非语言知识即背景知识和语言知识。背景知识包括社会知识和文化知识。语言知识包含三个层次方面的知识：(1) 语篇的语义与结构，比如 GSP 理论、主位进程信息分布(Danes 1974)等方面的知识；(2) 语法知识，比如句子的三种语义的纯理功能结构(Halliday 1985)或其他学派有关语法的见解；(3) 关于词汇的结构与语义方面的知识。

GSP 理论有助于读者对不同语体的不同结构的掌握，可以帮助读者对语篇具体结构特点的分析、理解以及对层次发展规律做出预测。阅读课教师应当尽力让学生接触各种不同语体的语篇，分析它们的结构特点，了解语篇发展的不同模式。这样不仅有利于对内容的记忆，也可促进学生阅读速度和理解能力的提高。GSP 理论对教授口语课或写作课也具有重要的指导作用。教师可以要求学生将在阅读课内学会的语体分析方法运用到口语/写作课，让学生按照不同语体的结构，就某个题目用口头或笔头进行表述。这样组织起来的语篇，结构清晰，易于被听者或读者接受。其次，学生不仅应掌握在学校中需要经常使用的语体，譬如概要、报告、议论文等等，还应当学会社会经济文化生活中其他经常使用的语体，譬如广告、新闻、合同等等，以便将来更好地为社会服务。

像其他有关语篇的理论一样，GSP 自问世以来，就受到许多语言学家和英语教师的重视，对指导一些国家的英语教师选编教材，进行课堂教学起了很好的作用（Matthiessen 1995）。它对我国外语语篇教学的实用性，有待通过具体的语篇分析研究工作和课堂教学得到验证。

19

浅谈语类*

19.1 引言：语境、语域、语类

语类与语境和语域两个概念密不可分(Halliday & Hasan,下称 H & H 1985),因而在分析语类之前有必要简单讨论语境和语域概念。

19.1.1 情景语境与文化语境

马林洛夫斯基在 20 世纪 30 年代,提出了情景语境和文化语境的概念。他在南太平洋 Trobrand 群岛做人类学研究时发现,如果要理解当地居民的话语,就必须了解当地的社会特点和话语的“情景语境”,以及蕴含该“情景语境”的“文化语境”(Malinowski 1935)。他还指出,要研究任何一种语言,必须同时研究说这种语言的人的文化和他们的生活环境。然而,马林洛夫斯基本人的主要兴趣,是研究不同人种和他们的文化,语言学不是他的主要课题,因而他没有对这两个概念与语言的关系做系统详

* 本章原刊载于《外国语》1998 年第 1 期。列为本章时做了修改和补充。

尽的研究。他对语言学的贡献仅仅在于“零星的评论”，而这些评论也是夹杂在对民族文化的分析当中（Firth 1957c）。

马林洛夫斯基的语境观点对他的学术好友弗斯产生了一定的影响。弗斯将语境概念发展成了“语义存在于语境”的理论（Eggins 1994）。他对语境学说的主要贡献有两个方面。第一，他指出，语言的使用与语境特别是情景语境有密切的关系，学习使用语言的过程就是“学习去说在一定的情景下另一个人期待我们说的话”。“一旦有人与你交谈，你就置身于一定的语境中，就没有自由去选择你愿意说的话了”（同上）。有些语言学家将这种看法称为语言的预期性（Linguistic Predictability）（同上）。第二，情景语境中有很多因素，但并非所有的因素都与说的话有关。弗斯提出了会影响语用的几个因素（详见 1957）。关于语境的特点，其他一些社会语言学家、言语行为学者和系统功能语言学家如海姆斯（Hymes 1962/1974）、甘柏兹（Gumperz 1968）、格雷戈里（Gregory 1967）、尤尔和埃利斯（Ure & Ellis 1977）、韩礼德（H & H 1985）等也进行过研究。其中格雷戈里、尤尔和埃利斯对语域理论作了较详细的论述（Eggins 1994）。而韩礼德则发展了弗斯的情景因素理论，对语言的组织及其特定的情景特征之间的相关性做出了有独到见解的研究。

韩礼德（H & H 1985）认为，在任何一个情景中，都会有三个变量影响语言的使用。这三个变量是“语场”（field）、语旨（tenor）及语式（mode）。如果将韩礼德与弗斯的情景语境因素相比较，韩礼德的模式有以下几个特点：（1）强调情景语境与语言之间的关系。凡是与语言无关的语言活动及情境的其他特点均不包括在内；（2）韩礼德部分继承了弗斯的模式。语场涵盖了语言活动，而语旨则与情景参与者相似，只是韩礼德在说明中强调了参与者之间的关系；（3）与所有话语分析者相同，韩礼德注重研究语境对语言的组织和表达方式的影响，这就是语式的功能。这几个变量不仅是情景语境的主要变量，它们的相互配置，也是决定语域及实现与文化语境密切相关的语类的主要因素（Hasan，in H & H 1985；Martin 1992）。

韩茹凯采纳了韩礼德的观点，提出了与情境配置同义的语境配置概念，即 Contextual Configuration，简称 CC。她认为每个 CC 都是“一组实现语场、语旨、语式的值”（H & H 1985：55－56）。她将这三个变量的定义具体化。语场不仅包括“发生的行为”，还涉及“它们的目的”；语旨不仅指“参与者的角色”，还包括“它们之间的社会距离”，语式不仅既指“语言的作用"(主导还是辅助),还具体涉及"渠道"(文字或语音)和"媒介"(笔头或口头)(同上,56-58),比如由语场 Praising、语旨 Parent 与 Child、语式 Speech 构成的 CC 的值,为 Parent Praising Child in Speech。

19.1.2 语域与情景语境

韩礼德从里德(Reid 1956)那里借用了语域这个术语,最早使用在 *Linguistic Science and Language Teaching* (Halliday et al. 1964: 89)一书中。语域指在某个情景中说话者对语言的使用。20 世纪 70 年代,他进一步明确了语域与语境的关系(1978): 语域是情景语境的具体表现。20 世纪 80 年代他将语域理解为"与某一情景配置语场、语旨、语式有关的语义配置"(H & H 1985: 35)。这就意味着: (1) 情景语境包含三个变量; (2) 语域是这三个变量的配置产生的语义集合。

马丁(Martin 1992: 502)则认为,语域是指"由语境变量语场、语旨、语式构成的符号系统"。他与韩礼德的共同点是: 语域与语境三个变量存在着密切的关系。不同点是: 马丁认为: (1) 语域就是由这三个变量构成的;(2) 语域处于比较抽象的系统潜势层面上,通过语言得到实现;韩礼德则认为,语境(即他的情景语境)本身就是一个符号系统,他的实现取决于语域。我们认为,讨论与语类的关系时,这两种看法并没有实质性的区别,因而我们似乎可以说,马丁的语域配置和韩礼德的情景配置及韩茹凯的语境配置 CC 大同小异,这也许就是一些系统功能语言学家(如 Eggins 1994) 将这几个术语混用的原因。

19.2 语 类

下面将阐述系统功能语言学家韩礼德、韩茹凯、马丁及埃金斯对语类的看法,及笔者对这个概念的粗浅认识。

19.2.1 语类的定义

语类的概念来自 genre 这个词。几本英语词典(如 Collins、Collins COBUILD、Webster's Ninth New Collegiate、Longman 等)对该词的定义大同小异,都包含了下面两个内容:(1)它通常是指具有相同风格、形式或内容的艺术、文学、音乐、绘画类型。(2)有时它的定义范围比较宽,如泛指类、型或种类。

在语言学中,对这个词的含义,不同的语言学家有不同的理解。

即使同一个语言学家,如韩礼德,在不同的时期对该词的理解也并不完全相同。1989 年他在给语式下定义时说,语式是“象征性的组织”,即“语言所担负的角色,包括渠道和修辞方式,是不同范畴的语篇如劝告、议论、教诲等所表述的方式。”由于劝告、议论、教诲均属不同的语类,因而似乎可以说韩礼德这里所指的语式中的修辞方式涵盖了 genre 的内容,与海姆斯的“渠道、风格、语类”(Hymes 1972)大致相同。可是在其他一些场合,韩礼德强调了 genre 的“修辞目的”,与语场、语旨、语式密切相关(Martin 1992: 501)。他同意格雷戈里和卡罗尔(Gregory & Carroll 1978: 44 - 45)“用语言的种类来描述 genre”的提法。

韩茹凯(Hasan 1977: 229)在描述 GSP(语类结构潜势)概念时指出,genre 是语篇的类型(type of discourse)。在讨论语篇结构成分时(H & H 1985: 62),她提出了“语类是由结构的必要成分来定义”的论断。由于必要成分主要与语境配置 CC 当中的语场有关,因而似乎语类的确定主要取决于语场(见 2.2.3)。

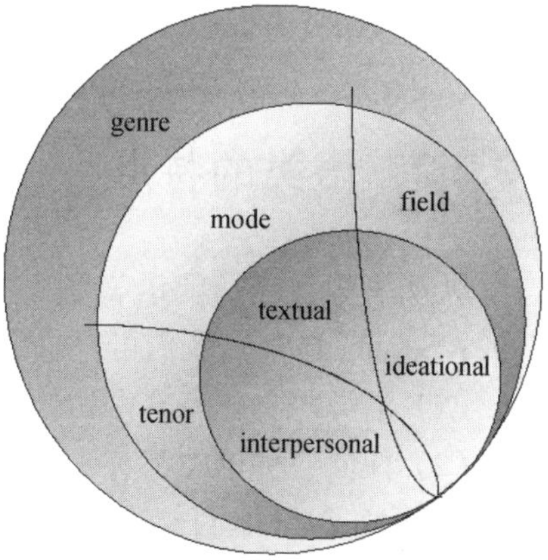

图 19 - 1 语类与语域(Martin & White 2005)

马丁对 genre 的定义和看法与韩茹凯有些不同。他似乎同意韩茹凯关于 genre 与语场、语旨、语式均有关系的看法(见图 19 - 1)。但他认为 genre 与这三个变量配置所产生的总体目标密切相关。他说:“语类是一种作为我们文化成员的说话者的有步骤的、有一定既定目标的、有目的的行为”(Martin 1985: 25)。1992 年他又进一步指出,genre 是“一个通过语域来实现的有步骤的、有一定目标的社会过程”(Martin 1992: 505)。

埃金斯(Eggins 1994: 27)关于 genre 的定义与马丁大致相同,它是“使用语言达到的有步骤的、有目的的活动类型”。她认为用这样的方法给 genre 下定义,会使我们发现,“在我们的文化中有多少种已被承认的社会行为,就会有多少种类型的 genre”。

由于这个词有不同的含义,曾有过不同的译法。在文学和写作课中,它被称为“体裁”。有些学者(胡 1994;方 1995)也曾译为“语体”。但“体裁”的含义较窄,而语体又容易与语式中的口笔语体或文体相混。以上四位语言学家除了马丁,都将 genre 与类型相联系,因而笔者认为在语言学中可将其译为“语类”,即语篇类型。妥否,请同行指正。例如,在英美文化中,存在着文学语类、流行的书写语类、教育语类等几个大语类(Eggins 1994)。而每个大语类又包含了子语类与子子语类。如文学语类可再分为小说、戏剧、诗歌等子语类,而小说又可分为侦探小说、浪漫小说、科幻小说等子子语类。教育语类又可分为讲座、报告、论文写作、考试、主持课堂讨论、教科书写作等子语类。

此外,还有一长串在日常生活中大量使用的语类:买卖东西、寻求和提供信息、讲故事、定约会、交流意见、面试、与朋友交谈……应当指出的是,日常生活语类在社会生活中广泛使用,但过去没有受到足够的重视,今后语言学家应当在这方面进行更深入的系统研究。

19.2.2 语类的特点

纵观一些系统功能语言学家关于语类的看法(H & H 1985; Martin 1992; Eggins 1994),我们可以总结出它的三个特点:

(1) 语类与文化有着密切的关系;

(2) 任何一种语类都有一个总体目标;

(3) 这个总体目标的实现与语境配置(Contextual Configuration,见 H & H 1985)或语域配置(register configuration,见 Martin 1992)有关。

下面将分别阐述这三个特点。

19.2.2.1 语类与文化语境

语言学家一致认为，语类与文化密不可分，语类具有很强的文化属性，它是某种文化特有的产物。例如：Sewamono（世話物，“世态剧”）以及它的子语类 Enkirimono（縁切物，“断缘剧”）只有在日本文化中才能找到（H & H 1985：53），而相声就是中国文化特有的语类，它包括说、学、逗、唱几种不同的形式，在翻译时，常被译作“Cross talk”。其实两者有很大差别，相声只反映中国文化，“Cross talk”反映的是英、美文化，而且形式也有所不同：后者一般不会有唱的形式，否则就不称其为“talk”。再如，如果说五言七律只存在于中国文化，那么十四行诗则是西方文化产生的特有的语类。类似的例子举不胜举。

正是由于语类的文化属性，导致埃金斯得出了下面的结论：“大部分的文化冲击，事实上就是语类冲击”，这是因为不仅两种文化的语类潜势（genre potential）不同，而且实现语类的方式也不同（Eggins 1994：35）。笔者认为这种说法似乎有些绝对化，因为理论上讲，文化冲击所包含的内容远远超过语类所包含的内容，比如意识形态的作用，可能不能小觑。当然，埃金斯强调语类冲击会带来文化冲击，也是有一定道理的。在一个陌生的环境，遇到许多异于自己文化中存在的语类，会使人感到很难融入那种文化。可能也正是由于语类的文化属性，埃金斯将语类与文化语境相提并论（Eggins 1994：34）。埃金斯用下图来说明语类、语境和语言的关系。这个图告诉我们：(1) 语言总是置于一定的情景语境当中，情景语境与语域同义，都是由语场、语旨、语式三个变量构成的；(2) 情景语境又置于一定的文化语境中，文化语境与语类处于同一层面，因而是同一个意思。

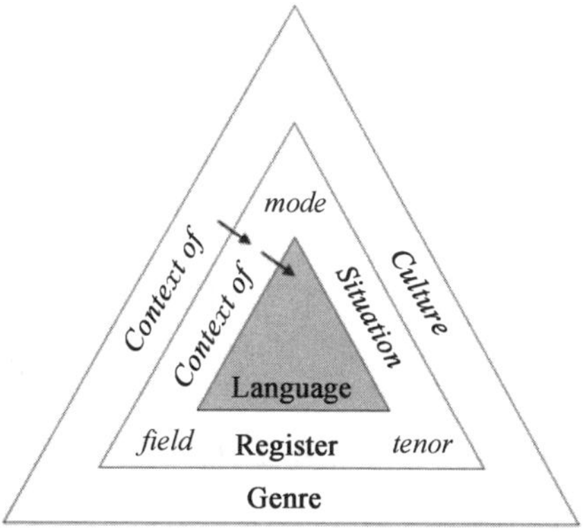

图 19-2 语类、语境、语言

马丁于 1992 年提出了与埃金斯不大相同的看法。他的文化语境包含了两个层次：意识形态和语类（Martin 1992：496）。意识形态指“编码方向系统，使人们能够根据他们的阶级、性别、民族和生活年代选择所要表达的语义”(Martin 1992: 581)。意识形态对语类的选择具有制约作用。或许这就是为什么韩礼德将语篇的文化语境定义为是:“一定的社会历史和意识形态产生一定的语篇,而该语篇又产生一定的社会历史和意识形态环境”(the socio-historical and ideological environment engendering, and engendered by the text)(Halliday 1978)。这里,他强调了语篇与社会-历史和意识形态环境因素之间的辩证关系。笔者在分析中国长卷画的文化语境时就使用了这个定义(Fang 2012, in Bowcher)。参考这个定义,她列出了几个问题将定义的内容具体化,不仅讨论了长卷画的历史、意识环境因素,也讨论了它对以后的绘画和社会生活产生的一些影响。不知妥否,请同行指正。这里再举一例说明意识形态对语类产生的影响。中华人民共和国成立后出现了一种特殊的语类——大字报,“文化大革命”中发展到顶峰。这种语类事实上就是当时的“阶级斗争为纲”的意识形态对语类选择的结果。如果将马丁和埃金斯的模式相比较,似乎在1992年马丁的模式中,文化语境包含的内容更丰富,层次更加分明。但是,在他后来发表的著作中,他的看法趋于与埃金斯一致,原因是意识形态很难定义(Martin & Rose 2008)。他将文化定义为“语类系统”(... Culture is a system of genres.)。这种将文化语境与语类等同起来的做法是否恰当值得商榷。因为文化语境是语言的文化符号系统,“而探索文化资源符号是一个永无止境的事业”(Martin 1992: 508)。文化语境专指语类,还是也包括其他层次,比如意识形态,需要我们进一步探索。

语类不仅取决于某个文化中存在的社会行为的种类,而且还会随着文化内容的变迁,在内容和形式上发生变化。随着西方文化的引入,一些1949年后在中国已不存在的语类,比如各种各样的广告也随之铺天盖地出现了。正如巴赫金(Bakhtin 1986: 60)所说的,“因为人类的活动是无限的”,因而“语类会随着它的活动范围的发展和复杂化而发生变化”。

19.2.2.2 语类的总体目标

马丁(Martin 1992)和埃金斯(Eggins 1994)都一再强调,任何一种语类都传达着一个总体目标或目的。总体目标不仅是语类定义的内容,也是区别语类的依据。虽然马丁一再声称韩茹凯对语类定义的依据与他的不同,他本人强调语境三个变量的配置与总体目标的关系,而韩茹凯则强调语场的作用。但我们看来,他们在语类的总体目标的认识上并无实质性的区别，因为韩茹凯的语场定义中不仅包含“发生的行为”，还包含“发生行为的目的”（H & H 1985：62），而马丁对语场的定义与韩礼德（H & H 1985）类同，范围较窄，仅指“发生的行为”。难怪他要补充提出语类所要达到的总体目标了。韩茹凯和马丁都认识到，只有当文化语境产生的语言具有一定的目的时，语言才有意义。

请看下面一段对话：

A：I forgot to tell you what Liu told me today.

B：What was it?

A：Dick and Jane are divorced.

不难看出，该对话的总体目的就是“论人是非”，因而属于 gossiping 语类。又如：

> “本报自扩为 4 开 16 版后，深受读者欢迎。第 209 期一上市便脱销。现应读者要求，予以加印，并交由北京天桥报刊门市部及北新桥、三里河、光明楼、海淀路、团结路等邮局零售，特此公告。”（《作家文摘》第 221 期）

显然，这个语篇的总体目的是“告诉读者该报将加印第 209 期”，因而属于“加印启事”语类。

19.2.2.3 语类的实现

以韩茹凯（H & H 1985）和马丁（Martin 1992）为代表，提出了两个相似又不完全相同的语类实现模式。

19.2.2.3.1 语类结构潜势理论（Generic Structure Potential）

韩茹凯认为语境配置 CC 的作用在于：它可以预测语篇的结构成分（必要成分或非必要成分）、成分出现的顺序与次数，即 CC 的三个变量在很大程度上，决定了“语类结构”（generic structure）成分。如在“加印启事”一例中，“加印决定”由语场“加印第 209 期”决定；语旨“出版者与读者”的关系决定了语篇可包含“读者反映”“加印原因”“销售单位及地点”三个成分；而语式“书面体”则决定了“结束语”——“特此公告”这样一个成分。

韩茹凯还认为，“语类是由语篇的必要成分来定义的”（H & H 1985：62）。由于“必要成分可从语场获得”（Martin 1992：504），因而在三个变量中,语场在确定语类时起了关键的作用。例如“加印启事”语类的确定,主要取决于语场“加印第209期”。其他两个变量将影响非必要成分的出现,非必要成分的异同导致属于同一语类的语篇的多样化。包含了某一语类所有的必要成分和非必要成分的结构表达式,可称为该语类的“结构潜势”。例如,商业交易语类结构潜势可表达为(Eggins 1994: 40):

(Sales Initiation)^{Sales Request ^ Sales Compliance ^ Purchase ^ (Price)} ^ Payment ^(Thanks)^(Change)^ Purchase Closure

这个表达式说明:(1) 属于这个语类的所有语篇都必须包含Sales Request、Sales Compliance、Purchase、Payment、Purchase Closure这几个必要成分;(2) ( )内的成分为非必要成分,它们是语篇多样化的依据;(3) 在{ }内的所有成分均可重复;(4) 所有的成分都是按一定的先后顺序排列的,位置不能相互颠倒。

笔者试用图19-3总结出CC与语类结构潜势GSP的关系以及GSP与它的语篇之间的关系:

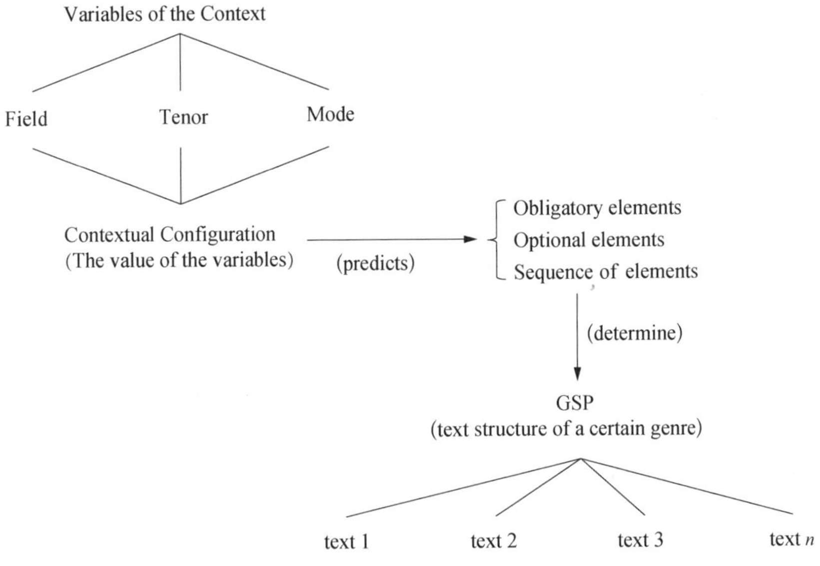

图19-3 语类结构潜势GSP与语篇之间的关系

这个图说明:情景语境的三个变量语场、语旨、语式构成了语境配置结构CC;而CC的值可用来预测语篇的必要成分、非必要成分和这些成分出现的顺序;从而决定了该语篇的结构潜势 GSP;因而所有具备这个结构潜势的语篇均属于这个语类。

理论上,所有的语类都应当有一个结构潜势。然而,由于不同语类的语篇在结构上的复杂程度不同,有可能涉及其他因素,这方面的研究还有待进一步深入。

文托拉(Ventola 1987: 75 - 76)在韩茹凯的“语类结构潜势”基础上,提出了一个商业交易系统图。马丁认为这是系统功能语法框架内对语类结构最为详细的描述(1992: 553)。由于本文篇幅有限,不在此详述。

19.2.2.3.2 纲要式结构理论(Schematic Structure)

有好几位语言学家都曾从不同的角度提出过纲要式结构理论(胡 1994)。本文主要讨论马丁的理论观点。

在马丁的理论中,“语域配置”代替了“语境配置”,“纲要式结构”代替了“语类结构”。

首先,语类与语域的关系被描述为语类/语域配置,即“语域是语类的表现形式”(1992: 495),语类通过语域配置得到实现。与韩茹凯不同的一点是:他强调语场、语旨、语式三个变量在确定语类时都起了作用。“语类是作为有着相互关联的社会过程的语场、语旨、语式产生的语义的集合”,而不是“只取决于语场”(Martin 1992)。比如,“现场直播足球评论”与“报刊足球评论”,两者的语场是相同的,都是足球评论。马丁认为由于语式不同(口语体相对于书写体),前者将球赛的“开始作为起点”,后者则将“比赛的结果”作为评论的起点,因而导致它们“属于不同的语类”(同上)。

笔者认为语场、语旨、语式在实现语类的过程中都起了作用,但它们的作用并不完全相同。似乎可以说语场可用于确定大的语类如“足球评论”,而语式或语旨可用于对该语类系统的子语类的划分,即:

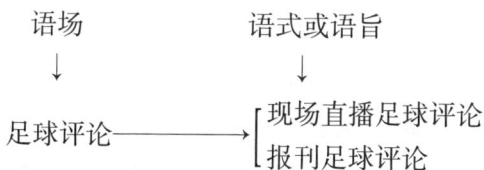

语场　　　　　　语式或语旨
↓　　　　　　　　↓
足球评论——→[现场直播足球评论
　　　　　　　　报刊足球评论

马丁指出,语类通过语域实现的模式具体表现在语篇的纲要式结构上。纲要式结构是语类的分阶段的、有步骤的组织结构(Eggins 1994)。用马丁的话来说,“它是从 A 到 B 的一种方法,按照这个方法,一个已知的文化就可完成某种语类在这个文化中要做的任何事情”;“语类的每一个步骤,对表达该语类想要表达的整体意义,都做出部分贡献”(Martin 1985: 251)。说本族语的人,只要听到某一个步骤,往往就能识别与之有关的语类。比如,当我们听到“昨天在回家的路上,我碰到了一件事”,马上就会猜到这是叙述个人经历的语类。

描述纲要式结构有两种方法:形式的和功能的(Eggins 1994)。前者指组成语篇的不同层次的语言单位(如章、段、句、词),但它不能揭示出该语类每个步骤对实现总体目标有什么贡献。正是由于这个原因,功能语言学家均采取后一种方法,将语篇划分为几个不同的功能部分。例如,上面的“论人是非”的纲要式结构可表达为“Preannouncement ^ enquiry ^ gossiping”;而“加印启事”的纲要式结构为“读者反映^加印原因^加印决定^销售单位及地址^结束语”。

不仅如此,语域还将决定属于某个语类的纲要式结构的每个步骤,及对语言的词汇-语法层(即词与语法结构)的选择。例如,“加印原因”与“加印决定”这两个步骤所使用的词汇、语法结构就不会完全相同。总之,语类、语域和语言的词汇-语法层之间存在着抽象意义上的实现关系,即语类↙语域↙词汇语法(↙意为“被实现”)。

当然,由于所有的语类及其步骤,都是用同一种语言具体表现出来的,它们对词汇和语法结构选择并不会全然不同。确切地说,它们之间的差异是通过不同的词汇和语法结构的不同组合表达出来的。如果将马丁的纲要式实现语类的模式与韩茹凯的 GSP 模式相比较,我们就会发现:(1) 两个模式均强调语类与语场、语旨、语式的关系,及成分或步骤的顺序;(2) 马丁的模式强调三个变量同时决定总体目标、决定语类,而韩茹凯的模式则强调语场是判断语类的决定因素;(3) 韩茹凯的模式将必要成分与非必要成分区分开来,并指出属于同一 GSP 语篇文体上的差异来源于非必要成分,而马丁的模式没有做过类似的区分;(4) 在马丁的模式中,语类是通过语域变量配置所决定的步骤在词汇-语法层上得到实现的,而在韩茹凯的模式中,语类是通过语境配置 CC 体现出来的。

19.3 结　语

以系统功能语言学创始人韩礼德为代表的一批学者，将语言看作具有代表某种文化意义潜势的符号系统。以这个认识为基础，他们在探索文化语境/情景语境的层次、变量方面做出了不懈的努力，对语类的研究只反映了这种努力的一个侧面。目前，这个领域的研究工作还在继续深入。这些学者在语境的内容、层次、语类实现模式方面存在一定的分歧，但在下面几个方面有着共识：(1) 语类是文化的反映，具有很强的社会属性；(2) 任何一种语类都有一个总体目标；(3) 语类是通过语境变量/语域变量配置所决定的成分或步骤，在词汇-语法层上得到实现或体现出来的。

理论应当而且必须与实践相结合，才会具有实际价值，理论也才能得到发展。马丁和韩茹凯的理论模式也不例外。这两个模式，尤其是马丁的理论自问世以来已经比较广泛地被澳大利亚学者和教师，应用于指导计算机语言学和语言教学研究，尤其是中小学的语言教学和其他与语言有关的课程教学，出版了不少教科书并建立了一个"读为学"的网站 www.readingtolearn.com.au，在国际上产生了较大的影响。笔者以及其所指导的研究生自 1994 年以来在该理论的指导下，在清华大学英语专业和大学英语写作课教学中先后做过三次实验。我们曾分别在第 22 次国际系统功能语言学会议和北京大学 1997 年大学英语国际会议上做过有关的实验报告，引起了与会者的兴趣。因本文主要讨论理论问题，教学实验将另文阐述。我们相信，对于这个领域的研究，不仅有助于进一步揭示语言与文化的关系，而且语类意识的建立，对语篇的文体分析、阅读课、写作课的教学均有着重要的实际指导意义。

20

语篇语类[①]研究[*]

20.1 引 言

对语篇的语类研究源远流长，可追溯到亚里士多德时期。他在《诗歌》一文中将其定义为文学类别，后来又在《论修辞》一书中将其定义为雄辩术类别（Devitt 2000）。18 世纪末以前，这个领域的研究一直在西方文学中占有重要的地位。但在以后的两个世纪中，由于人们的注意力转向了对文学作品和作者的研究，语类在文学中没有受到足够的重视。这种情况一直延续到 20 世纪 80 年代。近 20 年来，许多学者又重新开始对这个领域发生兴趣，研究者主要来自功能语言学界和应用语言学界。20 世纪 90 年代末期，非文学界在这个领域里的研究成果引起了文学界的关

---

* 原刊载于《清华大学学报（哲学社会科学版）》2002 年第 1 期（总第 17 卷）。列入本章时做了少许修改。

① 受亚里士多德的影响，西方文学界传统上都把 genre 看作是语篇类型形式上的分类，以前一直将其译为"体裁"。1977 年韩茹凯在语篇分析研究中提出了 genre 可定义为"types of discourse"的观点，并主要关注语篇的功能结构。笔者于 1998 年将其译为"语类"即语篇类型。这个词在不同的情境中有不同含义，可以有不止一种译法。我们认为"语类"更能体现当代语言学对语篇功能结构的研究成果，因而本章决定采用这个术语。

注，在文学界又一次掀起了研究高潮（Bawarshi 2000）。现在语类已成为多个学科研究的热门话题。本文除了简要介绍这个术语的来源之外，还将概述语类在语言学和应用语言学界的研究情况、西方文学界提出的挑战以及这个领域的研究走向。

20.2 语言学和应用语言学对语类的研究

20 世纪七八十年代，语言学的研究从句子扩展到了语篇层次，研究者开始关注语篇的结构和它的语义功能。这个时期，韩礼德的系统功能语言学理论也逐步成为西方功能语言学的代表，他的理论被视为当代最有影响的两大语言学学派之一。他对语言的功能观成为语类研究的重要理论支柱。后来，语类的研究又受到巴赫金的对话学理论（Bakhtin 1986）的影响，近年来还接受了吉登斯（Anthony Giddens）的结构理论以及俄国活动系统理论研究成果的影响，人们对语类有了新的认识。通过不同方法对不同语篇的研究，学者们已形成了既高深又复杂的看法（见 Devitt 2000）。

语言学和应用语言学对语类的研究经历了三个时期：（1）关注语类的社会/交际目的；（2）观察和分析语篇的语类结构；（3）探讨语类的多样性和复杂性。

20 世纪 80 年代初期，米勒提出将语类视为“典型的社会行为”（Miller 1984），即人们使用语类来做事，这些行为通过在重复的环境中一再出现而典型化。她还认为确定语类最重要的因素是社会目的。比伯（Douglas Biber）也认为外部的、非语言标准的交际目的是语类的主要界定方法（Biber 1988）。这被一些学者视为当前普遍被接受的看法。有的学者则进一步认为交际目的决定了语篇在社会中具有的功能或使用价值（Bawarshi 2000；Beebee 1994）。

受韩礼德（Halliday 1978）的直接影响，系统功能语言学家韩茹凯（H & H 1985）于 1985 年提出了一个分析原始/典型语篇语类的理论框架

GSP,即"Generic Structure Potential"(语类结构潜势)理论。由于这个理论具有较大的影响,这里简介它的框架和主要内容:(1)语类服务于社会的某个特别的目的;(2)语境配制 CC(Contextual Configuration),即"实现语场、语旨、语式的值",可以预测语篇的结构成分、成分出现的次数与顺序;(3)每个语类都有语类结构潜势,包含语篇的必要成分(obligatory elements)和非必要成分(optional elements),其结构遵循一定的次序——这就意味着 CC 的三个变量在很大程度上可以预测语类结构潜势;(4)"语类是由语篇的必要成分来定义的",具有相同必要成分的语篇属于同一个语类。非必要成分决定属于同一个语类的语篇变异现象。笔者将韩茹凯的语类结构潜势 GSP 与语篇之间的关系,总结出了一个模式表示出来(见"浅谈语类"图 19-3,方琰 1998)。

与韩茹凯的语类结构潜势相类似的框架,有马丁(Martin 1992)和埃金斯(Eggins 1994),他们都将语类定义为"使用语言达到的有步骤的、有目的的活动类型"。他们的框架被称为"纲要式结构",其中的"步骤"与韩茹凯的"结构成分"同义。这三位系统功能语言学家,都重视研究语篇语类结构的实现问题,都认为语域三个要素(语场、语旨、语式)的配置,是实现语类结构潜势/纲要式结构的关键。持相似看法的学者还有斯韦尔斯(John Swales)和巴蒂亚(Vijay Kumar Bhatia)(Devitt 2000)。

然而近年来,一些语言学家在研究中发现,将语类看作"语篇可以通过一系列步骤展开的一个框架"的认识(Leitch & Roper 1998),可能有些偏颇。费尔克拉夫(Fairclough 1995)觉得语类实际上比理想的模式更加"灵活"、更加"不可预测",更像一个"大杂烩"。他的研究认为可将语类看成具有"多面"(multi-faceted)的特性。

另有一部分研究者认为,无论是交际目的(communicative purpose),还是形式结构(formal structure),还是其他因素,语类用单一的条件是难以确定的。亨利和罗斯伯里(Henry & Roseberry 1997)指出,尽管"交际目的"在语类定义中具有主导地位,其他因素,如惯用结构,语言上的限制,甚至语言活动的参与者等,都对界定起着一定的作用。费尔克拉夫认为口气(voice)、文体(style)、语式(mode)、活动类型(activity type)以及它源于的语篇(the "discourses" which are drawn upon)都对语类的界定起一定的作用(Fairclough 1995)。斯科隆(Scollon 2000)在对比、分析《人民日报》三种不同的版本时,考虑了八个语类特征因素,包括标题、位置、结构框架、口吻、视角、引用、是否使用程式性的语言表达方式、词汇特点。但是,他没有明确划分语类的理论标准,导致他忽略了学者们较一致同意的最重要的因素——社会交际目的。借鉴系统功能语言学家和上述斯科隆的看法,笔者在探讨"文化大革命"当中《人民日报》的语类特征因素时,也考虑了多种因素,包含交际目的、结构潜势、标题、位置、口吻、字体、句法、词汇特点等等,发现其中**交际目的**和**结构潜势**最为重要(方琰 2003)。

帕尔特里奇(Brian Paltridge)于 1997 年(见 Hyon 2000)区分了原始类型(prototypes)与不那么典型的语类的例子(less clear-cut examples)。他指出,对"某个语类的表征越接近该语类的原始类型的形象,它的例子就会越清晰地表明它是这个语类的一个范例。"他还用韩茹凯的语类结构潜势的理论,分析了论文介绍部分的组成成分,发现只有两个成分为必要成分,而且成分的次序也相当灵活。因而他认为用这样的框架来定义原始类型的语类也有不足之处。他试着使用将韩礼德的系统功能语言学框架(Halliday 1985)与菲尔默的语义框架(semantic frame)(Fillmore 1968)理论相结合的方法划分语类。总之,他也认为对语类的划分,要建立在考虑多个或形形色色("myriad")因素的基础上。但是他的理论框架及实验结果,也提供了对韩茹凯(H & H, 1985)创导的用典型或原始类型划分语类方法的强有力的支持。

语类侵殖(genre colonization)的理论更清楚地说明了语类具有多元特性。1998 年利奇和罗珀(Leitch & Roper 1998) 在对比电视上的广告谈论(ad talk) 节目和电台谈话(talkback)节目之后,认为前者吸取了各种电台谈话的语篇组成形式,但是它却属于广告语类,因为它的交际目的是推销商品,即语篇的形式结构为 A,但其交际目的和功能结构潜势却为 B,因而其语类被确定为 B。在现代生活中语类侵殖现象颇为常见。毕比(Thomas O. Beebee)也认为,每个语篇都会涉及一个以上的语类,即使是隐性的(Devitt 2000)。斯科隆(Scollon 2000) 在分析报刊语篇时也发现有框架结构混杂在一起的现象。这类语类侵殖现象也可以叫作体裁互文性现象(辛斌 2000)。这种现象最典型的表现在文学语类中(Devitt 2000)。

20.3 文学语类理论

20 世纪 90 年代,从事文学研究方向的许多学者,受到语言学界和应用语言学界在语类方面的研究启示和冲击,又开始对这个领域产生兴趣,通过讨论和深入的观察,对语类的性质有了新的认识。文学研究者从比较文学、文化研究、历史研究以及其他文学流派的研究中对语类进行了重新审视,重新认识了它在文学研究中的地位。比如,德维特(Devitt 2000)指出,罗斯玛林(Adena Rosmarin)在 *Power of Genre*(1985)一书中认为语类可以重新被看作是“文学批评的工具”。珀洛夫(Marjorie Perloff)为当代研究语类主要的西方学者,在编辑后现代语类时,用后现代认知方法提供了一个审视所有语篇类型的论坛,讨论既包括文学语类也包括非文学语类的语篇,既包括语篇也包括非语篇。1993 年菲什洛夫(David Fishelov)出版了他的专著 *Metaphors of Genre: The Role of Analogies in Genre Theory*,回顾了语类研究的过去和最新发展状况,以便重新发现对理解语类有用的东西(Devitt 2000)。而毕比在他的 *The Ideology of Genre: A Comparative Study of Generic Instability*(1994)一书中,明确了语类的意识形态概念在文学研究中至关重要的地位。显然,语类又一次成为文学研究中的重要概念,文学理论家正在重新认识语类以便更好研究文学作品。这些新的看法在某些方面与语言学和应用语言学的语类观点有类似之处。两个研究方向都认为:(1) 应当从语类的语用功能来分析语篇的语类;(2) 都注重对标准性或一致性和多样性现象的研究(Devitt 2000)。

目前已有不少文学研究方向的语类学者,反驳了那种认为最好的文学作品是不属于任何语类的浪漫说法。比如,德里达就认为“不存在没有语类的语篇”(Devitt 2000),而菲什洛夫更明确指出,“即使在现代文学那些似乎语类规则不存在的领域内,语类规则仍然是文学交流情景至关重要的一部分”;“作者不会在真空里进行创作,一个不听话的孩子仍然是家里的一分子”(Devitt 2000)。

当然,由于研究的目的不同,语言学和应用语言学与文学在语类领域的研究存在着很大的区别:语言学和应用语言学理论研究者,主要寻找具有典型语类的语篇，审视作者如何遵循某个语类的规则，以及读者在预测语类中所扮演的角色；而文学语类研究者为了扩展文学领域，则更注重寻找打破语类常规的语篇，评价作者如何违反语类的规则，以及读者在对非常规语类特点的理解中所起的作用。此外，文学语类研究者对文学语篇语类的多样性给予极高的评价，认为最好的文学作品就是那些具有“原创性”或“创新”意义的作品(Devitt 2000)。如果说前者更注重一致性，那么后者则更注重用多元的观点来研究文学作品的特点。

但是，应当看到，两个研究方向在很多方面如语类的层次、语类与社会的关系、语类与意识形态的关系的看法越来越接近(Devitt 2000)。

20.4 语类的系统和层次

毕比(Beebee 1994)将“genre”和“text type”区分开来，区分的标准不仅考虑语篇的总体目的，还要考虑其具体目的、语篇是否具有相似的语言特点。这就使得属于不同 genre 的语篇可以规划为同一种 text type (Leitch & Roper 1998)，即如果各种 genre 的具体交际目的和语言特点相似，它们就可归类为同一种 text type。另一种看法是应用韩礼德的系统功能语言学理论来观察语类，认为属于某种文化的语类是一个系统，从大到小分为不同的层次，每个大语类都包含了子语类与子子语类(Eggins 1994；方琰 1998)。德维特也说过，“语类并不是独立存在的，它们被置于语类的层次和系统中，每一种语类的定义都会牵扯到整个系统及该系统的其他成员”(Devitt 2000)，它是与语类系统中其他语类相比较而存在的。比珀(Biber 1988)和埃金斯(Eggins 1994)具体指出，一个大的类别包含了多个语类，语篇的目的与分类层次相关。比如，文学语类又可进一步分为短篇小说、诗歌、杂文等等子语类。语域三个要素的配置在划分不同层次中的语类起了一定的作用。例如，电视新闻、广播新闻、报刊新闻总的交际目的都是传播新闻(语场相同)，也就是说它们都属于新闻语类，但由于三者的语旨(即传播的对象)、语式(传播的方式)不同，在第二个层次上的分类就不同了：电视新闻通过声音/画面或两种方式将新闻传播给观众，广播新闻只通过声音将新闻传播给听众，而报刊新闻则只通过文字将新闻传播给读者。可用下图表示：

语场　　语式或语旨
↓　　　↓
新闻　{电视新闻
　　　 广播新闻
　　　 报刊新闻

20.5 语类的变迁与社会的变迁

两个方向的研究人员，尤其是文学语类研究者都认识到，无论在文学作品或在非文学语篇中，语类或语篇意义都不是"客观的、一成不变的"，而是"动态的和不断变化的"（Cohen 1986，见 Devitt 2000）、都是通过一定的文化语境中的作者、读者、语篇、语境四种因素的相互交往而产生出来的。我们对语类的认识应当注重这些关系如何在某个文化中相互交往。这就是说，文化是语类产生和存在的前提。早在 1986 年巴赫金就说过，文化与语类有着密切的关系，语类会随着文化的变迁而变迁。而科恩（Ralph Cohen）（见 Devitt 2000）也明确指出"语类概念在理论和实践上会由于历史的原因而兴起、变化、衰落。"语类的丰富性、语类系统和它的层次及其语类的划分都会由于时代的变迁、情景的变化、不同社会的交际目的而发生变化。毕比（Beebee 1994）则说过，"语类变化源于社会和政治的变化，即社会的变迁是语类变迁的根源"。语类变化源于社会和政治的变化的例子很多，仅举中国政治批判中的大字报语类为例。它是在"以阶级斗争为纲"的意识形态中产生的，在"文化大革命"中发展到了顶点，后来随着改革开放的到来而逐渐衰落。语类还会随着文化内容的变迁、会随着它的活动范围的发展和复杂化，而在内容和形式上发生变化（Bakhtin 1986）。例如，随着西方文化的引入，一些 1949 年后在中国几乎不存在的语类，如各种各样的广告也随之铺天盖地地出现了，内容和形式也变得越来越复杂。

社会的变迁可以从各个方面反映出来：可以从经济的增长、生活方式的变化、政治改革、大众媒体的变化反映出来，也可以从文化艺术领域里文学、绘画、音乐、舞蹈，以及人们生活中的各种活动类型的变化反映出来。要认识了解某个社会、某种文化，只要看看这个社会、这种文化中有什么样的语类以及这些语类的特征就一目了然了。难怪埃金斯（Eggins 1994）认为"大部分的文化冲击事实上就是语类冲击"。

20.6 语类与意识形态

由于语类与文化、社会和政治休戚相关，就决定了语类与意识形态的密切关系。正如毕比（Beebee 1994）所说的"既然使用价值必然有其社会性，那么语类也就必然具有意识形态的特征"。巴瓦什（Bawarshi 2000）也指出，语类的"使用价值是由其社会属性来决定的，这样就使得语类部分成为文化的载体和再生产者——总之，是意识形态的再生产者"。有的学者甚至认为语类本身就是一种形式的意识形态（"Genre is a form of ideology."见 Pappas et al. 1998）。

笔者对"文化大革命"时期及其后一年《人民日报》（1966—1977）语类特点的分析，也发现这两者有着密切的关系（方琰 2003）。这个时期大多数的语篇含有强烈反映"文化大革命"时代特点的政治倾向和意识形态。从口号、专栏标题、毛泽东语录，到大批判专栏、时事报道、学习毛主席著作心得体会、政论文这些语类，到对被打倒对象的批判以及对被捍卫对象个人形象的神化、对毛泽东思想的颂扬、对"美帝""苏修"的批判和憎恨，这些语类所占的比例为绝对多数，完全可以说明这个时期的主导意识形态。这个时期毛主席语录几乎天天刊登，口号、专栏标题上报的频率也相当高。在所有的十几个语类中，大批判专栏、时事报道、学习毛主席著作心得体会、政论文这四个语类的比例就高达近 63%。虽然我们没有统计其他语类如人物典型介绍、介绍性文章、调查分析、会见等等,但只要翻开这个时期的《人民日报》就不难发现,这个时期绝大多数语类都与上述内容有关。在时事报道中,349 篇中有关“抓生产、促生产”的只有 27 篇,仅占 7.7%。

虽然这篇文章没有与现在的《人民日报》的语类做比较,但是只要稍稍注意一下,就可以发现“文化大革命”时期,它的语类要少得多。比如,跨越 12 年的 12 份报纸中没有任何文学副刊,也就是说,没有一篇属于文学语类的语篇,版面固化、内容单一,根本谈不上“百花齐放”,见不到多元、开放、包容的气息。

另外,这个时期的两个语类:天气预报和广告也很有意思。预报天气,只出现在 1966 年 5 月“文革”前的报上,列在第一版左面最上方,包含的内容也较丰富,其语类结构潜势为“日期^星期^农历日期^当天天气状况”。但“文化大革命”开始以后被取消,代之以毛主席语录。直到 1975 年开始恢复,但放在不引人瞩目的报纸下边框上。天气预报的目的是报告当天天气状况,为人们外出工作、旅游提供方便。“文化大革命”时期近 10 年中,这个语类的消失,说明媒体对人民生活的关心已经放到了很次要的地位上,也隐性地反映了阶级斗争是当时占有主导地位的意识形态。再如,这个时期的广告与现在广告的目的大不相同。那个时期是以宣传毛泽东思想为主,这可以从它的标题看出来,都是通告文艺演出或美术展览,文艺演出是清一色的样板戏,美术展览则是歌颂毛泽东思想或工农兵;而现在广告的主要目的是推销商品,是以营利为目的。当然,两个时期的广告还有其他一些不同的地方。譬如,售票处和票价在“文化大革命”时期不出现在广告内,而是出现在其他不明显处——这恐怕也与当时的意识形态有关,钱是人们在公开场合回避的话题。另外,演出常常是政治任务,不以营利为目的,因而以赠票居多。

20.7 研究的意义与目前关注的课题

如上所述,过去的二三十年,对语类的研究又重新受到学者们的关注，目前语类在文学批评、语篇分析、批评语言学、外语教学中占有很重要的地位（Devitt 2000；Hyon 1996），人们已越来越认识到它在这些学科的发展中的重要意义。比如，巴赫金甚至把语类当成“社会符号”来看待，认为语篇语类的结构形式，可以塑造和实现“言语计划或言语意愿”（Bakhtin 1986）。人们已经认识到语类知识是写作、理解语篇的先决条件。语类知识可以帮助人们建立起语类意识，可以培养人们对语篇语类的敏感性。语类知识已成为语篇研究人员、读者、作者、批评家分析语篇、解释语篇、评述和审视语篇的重要依据和工具（Bawarshi 2000）。在一部分地区，外语/二语教学中，以语类为基础的教学已经具有相当大的规模。比如在韩礼德的影响非常大的澳大利亚，由于语类专家处于教育领导岗位、由于研究者与广大教师有着密切的关系、由于系统功能语言学派内部的团结，以语类为基础的教学在中小学的语言教学中已占了主导地位（Hyon 1996）。

语篇分析，不论文学作品还是非文学作品，都可以把原始语类框架作为分析基础，虽然这个框架会不断变化。当然，在语篇分析中既要重视原始语类框架又要重视语类的侵殖性或互文性，根据语篇的实际情况分析语篇语类的特点。同时，注意语类的侵殖性或互文性及其与意识形态的密切关系，也可使作为读者的文学批评家对文学作品做出更准确的评价。

语类知识对读者至关重要。读者应当意识到，在试图理解文学作品或是日常生活语篇的过程中，都会受到语类的制约。原始语类框架知识和语类侵殖性知识，可帮助读者预测该语篇的语类框架及其特点，对语篇做出深入的分析和理解，使读者更好地欣赏文学作品。

语类概念对写作者也非常重要。它不仅能为学习写作的人提供原始语类的语义框架，为学习写作打下良好的基础。它还为他们提供了写作不同语类的语篇语义框架，为他们以后进行创造性的写作打下很好的基础。认识语类的多样性、复杂性、灵活性，可鼓励他们打破原始语类框架的束缚，拓展思维，开辟新的视角，写出具有原创性的作品。

语类概念对读者、写作者和评论家的重要性是与语类具有很强的生成作用分不开的。巴瓦什指出语类“在构建语篇（文学研究、文化研究、创造性写作、修辞研究、作文、应用语言学）的过程中起一定的作用”，因为“语类载有社会规定了的一系列适合一定场合的、可辨认行为的社会动机”，很像是语篇和作者之间建立起来的社会行为语码，可视为一种“语类合同”(Bawarshi 2000)。毕比则断言,“语篇、作者、语境以及作为读者的批评家”都离不开“语类对他们的塑造”,“这一点就更加充分地体现了语类所具有的力量”(Beebee 1994)。

到目前为止,语类理论的研究经历了三个阶段:(1) 从亚里士多德时期到18世纪末,比较注重研究语篇语类形式上的结构。从那以后对语类的探究进入低潮。(2) 20世纪80年代以来,系统功能语言学及应用语言学,开始重视探讨语篇语类的社会目的和功能结构,对语类的研究已从单一的描述阶段过渡到解释行为的阶段,从分类阶段过渡到审视语类的潜势阶段,从单一学科过渡到跨学科的研究阶段。人们还认识到语类不仅具有“限制功能”,它还对语篇的生成具有“构建功能”。这方面的研究成果对文学理论研究产生重大影响,成为这个研究方向的理论基础(Bawarshi 2000)。(3) 从90年代开始,语言学界、应用语言学界、文学语类理论对这个课题开展了热烈的讨论,甚至是激烈的争论。文学语类理论,在慎重地接受语言学和应用语言学有关语类研究的很多观点的同时,对后者提出了新的问题和新的挑战。文学语类理论研究者指出,虽然前者也讨论语类的多样性和复杂性,但它主要关注的是语类的一致性,往往对其多样性和复杂性的程度认识不足。一个比较完善的语类理论,不仅应当充分认识语类的一致性,还应当认识其多样性和复杂性,而且还应当充分估计它的变异性、不稳定性和灵活性。这种看法对语言学语类研究已经并将产生重大影响。

现在,对语篇语类的研究随着21世纪的到来,已进入了一个新的时期。不同方向的许多研究者都逐渐认识到,对语类的研究必须采用多元的观点,必须在语言学、应用语言学(主要是外语/二语教学)、批判语言学、文学评论、认知心理学、社会学等领域进行跨学科的研究,才能做到更客观、更深入,才能在研究的工作中取得更多更新的成果。人们还认识到,语类的研究不仅要关注其一致性,还要充分认识到它的多样性、复杂性、不稳定性和灵活性(见 Devitt 2000; Bawarshi 2000)。

当然对语类的性质、特点等方面问题还存在很多分歧,或者需要进一步深入讨论。比如,有一部分文学评论家就认为文学作品根本不属于任何语类,不受任何语类框架的约束,对非文学语类研究理论甚至采取“敌视”的态度(Bawarshi 2000),认为语类概念是对“文学作品和作家的威胁”,是对“语篇独立性”的“威胁”。目前有关语类概念、功能的研究和争论仍在继续。就是在系统功能学派内部也存在很大分歧。比如在应用以语类为基础的外语/二语教学中，对学生的读和写的教学效果、对是否要培养学生的批判能力的认识上就存在不同的看法(Hyon 1996)。语类与意识形态的关系已成为文学、批评语言学和语篇分析的关注对象，但是，对它们之间的关系如何影响语篇分析看法也不一致。人们正在理论和语篇分析的实践中继续更加深入地探讨。语类如何对语篇、作者、语境以及作为读者的批评家的塑造也有待于进一步揭示。另外，我们也看到，人们已经开始研究语类和语境之间的关系了。比如巴瓦什就说，我们不仅应当对语境在构建语篇的过程所起的作用有足够的认识，而且还应当充分认识语类在"构建语境"中所起的作用；用他的话来说，语类"提供了使得语篇行为成为可能，使得语篇成为有意义行为的条件"(Bawarshi 2000)。这就意味着，语类不仅受制于一定的文化语境，它还反过来为阅读、评论和写作构建某个相关的语境。这方面的研究还刚刚开始，有待于进一步深入。

20.8 结　语

本章概述了语类发展的脉络，也涉及目前争论的一些热门话题。由于篇幅有限，也由于这个领域内容丰富，涵盖面很宽，文章只讨论了其中部分笔者感兴趣的问题。我们期望在新世纪，对语类的研究方法、语类的社会和语篇功能、语类与文学作品的分析和评论、语类与意识形态的关系、语类与语境的关系等等方面会有更深入、更全面的探讨和研究。

21

报刊语类的界定与分析*

21.1 语类的概念

英语中"genre"是一个高度模糊的概念。在文学,修辞学,语言学等研究中,它有着不同的定义和内涵;即使单纯在西方语言学中,它的含义也存在很多分歧。有学者认为它往往与话语事件(speech events)偶合,但又需要独立分析(Hymes 1974)。另有学者则用它来指交际事件的类型,如笑话、故事、讲座、打招呼、交谈等(Saville-Troike 1989)。20 世纪七八十年代系统功能语言学理论也开始探讨这一概念(Halliday 1978)。韩茹凯早在 1977 年(229),就将语类定义为"语篇的类型"(type of discourse)。马丁的 genre 指的是:各种通过语言实现的行为类型,这些类型是各种文化语境的重要组成部分(Martin 1985:150)。库蒂尔(Barbara Couture)认为 genre 是语篇结构的层次,它指确定了语篇的开头、发展和结尾的条件(Couture 1986:82)。

由于这个词的多义性,在汉语中有不同的译法。传统的译法为"体裁",以文学作品和作文的形式结构来划分类别。但根据有些语言学家

---

* 本章原为方琰、高云莉合作的论文,刊登在《语言教学与研究》2001 年第 6 期。

将其定义为“types of discourse”（Hasan 1977）并主要关注语篇的功能结构，一些学者（方琰 1998；黄国文 1998）将其译为“语类”（即语篇类型）。我们认为，这个词在不同的情境中有不同含义，可以有不止一种译法。

自20世纪80年代后期，语类的概念逐渐明朗，尽管仍存在分歧。马丁和埃金斯都将语类定义为“使用语言达到的有步骤的、有目的的活动类型”（Martin 1992; Eggins 1994）。他们均强调语篇的目的，以及语篇一般具有纲要式结构或语类结构（schematic structure 或 generic structure），都提出语类结构通过语域的三个要素（语场、语旨、语式）的配置来实现的观点。韩茹凯于1985年提出语类结构潜势理论（H & H 1985）。亨利和罗斯伯里将韩茹凯对语类的论述总结为：（1）语类服务于社会的某个特别的目的（... serves a particular purpose in a society）；（2）语类由一些成分或步骤组成；（3）其中某些是必要成分（obligatory elements），而“语类是由语篇的必要成分来定义的”，这些成分决定了某个语类的语类结构潜势（generic structure potential）（H & H 1985）；其他成分为非必要成分，决定属于同一个语类的语篇变异现象（Henry & Roseberry 1998）。

对语类结构，近年来西方语言学界中的分析较多，如斯韦尔斯（Swales 1981）对学术论文引言部分的分析；汤普森（Thompson 1994）对讲座开场白的分析。此外，巴蒂亚（Bhatia 1993）做过促销信、申请书和法律文件的分析；亨利和罗斯伯里则分析过旅行介绍（Henry & Roseberry 1997）。埃金斯（Eggins 1994）对某些语类结构潜势也做过比较详细的分析。例如，她分析了英文食谱的结构，包括标题、诱导、成分、方法和供应人数。

21.2 语类的界定

然而，目前语类的界定仍然是最关键、也是最困难的问题；仍然是仁者见仁，智者见智，众说纷纭。黄国文（1998）在讨论语篇的分类时曾指出"要确定某一语言有多少个语篇类型是很难的。关于语篇类型的确定，……在实际操作上，问题并不那么简单。"确实如此。对于确定某一种语言有多少个语类在理论上似乎是可能的，但实际上是很难做到的。这是由于语类与文化具有密切的关系，在当今变幻莫测的世界，每一种文化都在发生迅猛变化的情况下，语类系统必定会像语言系统一样，也是动态的，需要不断地调整、补充和扩展。即使找到确定语类的标准，也很难勾画出某个文化语境中的语类系统。正如巴赫金（Bakhtin 1986：60）说的："因为人类活动是无限的"，因而"语类会随着它的活动范围的发展和复杂化而发生变化"。然而，语言学家并不因为确定语言系统有困难，就不去做这项工作，语类研究人员也没有因为确定语类的任务艰巨，而停止对这个领域的探索。相反，也许正因为对它的研究具有挑战性，很多学者才对这个课题产生了浓厚的兴趣，近年来发表了大量的论文。我们认为他们的研究对揭示语类的本质、对语类的界定有着重要意义。下面我们将粗略总结不同的学者对语类的界定的几种不同的看法。

21.2.1 对语类界定的不同看法

（1）用交际目的界定语类

米勒（Miller 1984）认为确定语类最重要的因素是社会目的，即在某个社会语境下的交际目的；比珀（Biber 1998）也认为外部的、非语言标准的交际目的是语类的主要界定方法。这被一些学者视为当前普遍被接受的看法（Forman & Jone 1999）。

（2）用交际目的和语篇的结构潜势界定语类

强调语类结构通过语域的三个要素（语场、语旨、语式）的配置来实现（H & H 1985；Martin 1992；Eggins 1994）。

（3）关于语类界定的多元观点

近年来，一些语言学家（如利奇和罗珀）在研究中发现，将语类看作"语篇可以通过一系列步骤展开的一个框架"的认识（Leitch & Roper 1998，下称 L & R），可能有些偏颇。费尔克拉夫（Fairclough 1995）觉得语类实际上比理想的模式更加"灵活"、更加"不可预测"，更像一个"大杂烩”。他的研究认为可将语类看成具有“多面”(multi-faceted)的特性。另有一部分研究者认为,无论是交际目的(communicative purpose),还是形式结构(formal structure),还是其他因素,语类用单一的条件是难以确定的。亨利和罗斯伯里指出,尽管“交际目的”在语类定义中具有主导地位,其他因素,如惯用结构,语言上的限制,甚至语言活动的参与者等,都对界定起着一定的作用(Henry & Roseberry 1997: 480)。帕尔特里奇于1997年(见Hyon 2000: 190)区分了原始类型(prototypes)与不那么典型的语类的例子(less clear-cut examples)。他指出,对“某个语类的表征越接近该语类的原始类型的形象,它的例子就会越清晰地表明它是这个语类的一个范例。”他还用韩茹凯的语类结构潜势的理论,分析了论文介绍部分的组成成分,发现只有两个成分为必要成分,而且成分的次序也相当灵活。因而他认为,用这样的框架来定义原始类型的语类也有不足之处。他试着使用将系统功能语言学框架(H & H 1985)与费尔默的语义框架(semantic frame)理论(Fillmore 1968)相结合的方法划分语类。总之,他也认为对语类的划分要建立在考虑多个或形形色色(“myriad”)的因素的基础上。但是他的理论框架及实验结果,也提供了对韩茹凯创导的用典型,或原始类型划分语类方法的强有力的支持。关于语类侵殖(genre colonization)的理论,更清楚地说明了语类具有多元特性。1998年利奇和罗珀在对比电视上的广告谈论(ad talk)节目和电台谈话(talkback)节目之后,认为前者吸取了各种电台谈话的语篇组成形式,但是它却属于广告语类,因为它的交际目的是推销商品,即语篇的形式结构为A,但其交际目的和功能结构潜势却为B,因而其语类被确定为电视广告。在现代生活中语类侵殖现象颇为常见。毕比也说,每个语篇都会涉及一个以上的语类,即使是隐性的(Beebee 1994)。斯科隆在分析报刊语篇时也发现有框架结构混杂在一起的现象(Scollon 2000)。这类语类侵殖现象也可以叫作体裁互文性现象(辛斌 2000)。这种现象最典型的表现在文学语类中(Devitt 2000)。

上面有关语类的界定的论述可分为三派:(1)认为语类的确定只需观察语类的交际目的;(2)认为某个语篇语类必须含有两个要素,即有一定的交际目的和一定的功能结构形式或结构潜势;(3)语类具有多元性、复杂性和灵活性,往往呈现侵殖或互文性现象。

21.2.2 用功能的观点来划分语类

(1) 交际目的对语类的划分最为重要,对具有侵殖或互文性现象的语篇尤其如此。如下面引自一本杂志的语篇:

> "4 月 25 日晴
>
> 今天心情特别好,因为听说今年的可伶可俐最佳拍档大招募就要开始了。正要去告诉小敏,她倒先对我说……"

接下去是以日记人的口吻,对活动时间、参加办法、奖品及吸引力的详细解释。在体裁上,它是一则日记,而语类上它是商业广告——以推销商品、诱导参加商业活动为目的的语篇。又如通俗读物《苏菲的故事》,尽管它以情节小说的体裁出现,实际却是以解释基本哲学概念为目的的阐释性语篇。

再如,一些学者对信件、日记的语类的划分,均取决于语篇的常规交际目的或仅参考其通常的体裁。如信件通常以告知对方、交流信息为目的,日记以记录个人见闻感受为目的。但在实际应用中,信件可以分为报刊发表的公开信、日后出版的半公开信、书信体散文、小说等等。日记也可以有私人日记、交换日记、供发表出版的日记(如作家日记)、日记体文学,甚至日记体广告等。它们的具体交际目的以及结构潜势都是有所不同的。因此我们认为,如果局限于上面提到的体裁或常规目的,也可以划分出书信语类、日记语类;但是一旦其交际目的落入了其他语类的范畴,就应该划归为其他语类,如上面所举的日记形式的广告语篇就属于这种情况。

(2) 交际目的与分类的层次密切相关。

有些语言学家(Biber 1998; Eggins 1994)指出,一个大的类别(superordinate category)包含了多种语类,因为一个语篇的目的与分类层次是相关的。比如,比珀在实际分类中,就把布道、大学讲座、法庭宣读和政治讲演等都归类为"有准备的讲话",然后再依据具体的交际目的和其他因素(如功能结构)细分出上面几个语类。同样,文学语类又可进一步分为短篇小说、诗歌、杂文等等。

(3) 语域三个要素的配置在划分不同层次中的语类起了一定的作用。

电视新闻、广播新闻、报刊新闻总的交际目的都是传播新闻(语场相同),但由于三者的语旨(即传播的对象)、语式(传播的方式)不同,在第两个层次上的分类就不同：

语场　　语式或语旨
↓　　　　↓
新闻　{电视新闻
　　　{广播新闻
　　　{报刊新闻

第一个层次的语域三个要素的配置为：语场：新闻；语旨：传播者与接受者；语式：大众媒介。第二个层次的语域三个要素的配置为：语场：传播新闻；语旨：作者/报告者与读者/观众或听众；语式：写的方式/说的方式。比如，《人民日报》在第一个层次上属于新闻语类，在第二个层次上就属于报刊语类。但它又可根据具体语篇的语场、语旨、语式的配置划分出它的子语类。

（4）功能结构潜势在界定语类时有重要作用。

具体语篇的语场、语旨、语式的配置结果，体现在语篇的结构上，因而语篇表层的功能结构，就成为判定语篇的语类的重要参数。从上面所举的日记形式的广告语篇和《苏菲的故事》这两个例子中我们不难发现，交际目的在语类的确定中至关重要，而且它们的"结构潜势"也是语类确定的重要因素。"结构潜势"往往并非指语篇体裁上的结构，尽管在大多数语篇中，二者往往密切相关，有所重合。例如在上面的日记形式的广告语篇例子中，决定语类的不是"日期＾天气＾正文"这种形式上的体裁结构，而是以说服参加、推销商品为交际目的的功能结构。这种目的具体体现在广告语篇的"说明＾诱导＾提供详细信息"这样的功能结构潜势中。

21.3　报刊语类的界定

21.3.1　报刊语类界定的最重要因素

斯科隆（Scollon 2000）曾对《人民日报》的国内版、海外版和英文版的某些语类特征因素进行过分析。他的语类特征因素包括语篇的标题、位置、口气、语篇框架(与结构潜势相似)、视角(三份不同的报纸,视角不同。)、语言特点等。他的文章对进一步深入探讨报刊语类特点有一定的启示。但文章存在一个比较大的问题:没有明确界定语类的参数,理论根据不清楚。比如他的语类特征因素,没有提到**交际目的**这个普遍被认为是界定语类的重要因素。

上面我们已经论证了四个可用来界定语类的因素。这四个因素是否也可以用来确定报刊比如《人民日报》的语类呢?上面我们已经确定了它在第一个层次上为新闻语类,在第二个层次上属于报刊语类。此时,它的层次已经确定,也就是说在这个层次上它的总体语场(新闻)、语旨(即传播的对象)、语式(传播的方式)已经明确,即它们的配置为**通过书面的形式向读者传播新闻**。因而在确定《人民日报》的各种语篇的语类时,就不必考虑上述第二、第三个因素了。但是在这个层次上,具体语篇的语场、语旨、语式的配置所体现出的结构仍是个未知数。因此我们认为从理论上看,界定这份报纸各种语篇的语类的最重要的参数有两个:(1)报刊语篇的具体的**交际目的**;(2)通过语域三要素配置所实现的**结构潜势**,它可作为语类界定的最重要的辅助因素,因为它既然是语篇的**功能性结构**,因而就与交际目的密切相关,有时甚至不可分割。标题、位置、口气、语言特点对文章的风格和特点的形成都有一定的贡献,我们另文讨论(方琰 2003)。由于篇幅所限,本章对它们不作分析。以下,我们将通过具体的语篇分析论证我们的看法。

21.3.2 语料和方法

我们采取的是以语料为基础的分析方法。选择了不同年代(自 20 世纪 60 年代中期至 1995 年)的《人民日报》,每年取样一份,逐篇分析文章的交际目的和它的结构潜势,尝试划分出它们的语篇类型,并列表说明。之所以选择《人民日报》作为分析的对象,是因为它一向被认为是中国官方最有权威也是最严肃的、最有代表性的报纸。

在分析当中我们发现,“文革”期间的报纸有一些非常特殊的语类,如口号、语录、批判等,是特殊年代的历史现象,需要另外详细分析(方琰 2003)。因而实际上本文以 1979、1980、1985、1990 和 1995 年报纸各一份为例,分析了全部242篇文章的交际目的和结构潜势。由于报纸上的广告和副刊的文学类文章较为复杂,可能体现语类侵殖/互文性现象,可自成体系,暂且不作重点讨论。

21.3.3 分析结果

分析结果初步证明依据语篇的**交际目的**和它的**结构潜势**,可以划分出《人民日报》不同的语类,具体地说,分出了九个类型的语篇。列表如下(^表示先后次序,( )内为非必要成分,* 表示自成体系,暂不详细分析):

表21-1 《人民日报》语类语篇的交际目的和结构潜势

语类	时事	议论	引用文	典型人物	会议报道	介绍性文章	调查分析	*文学副刊	*广告
交际目的	以告知时事为目的	以论证,指导为目的	以引用发言,使读者了解某人的某种观点为目的	以介绍人物,树立典型为目的	以告知会议情况和会议精神为目的	以传达知识、通报情况为目的	以说明、分析情况为目的	以娱乐为目的	以推销商品为目的
结构潜势	时间^地点^(人物)^事件经过	论点^论证^结论	引入^多段间接引语	人物介绍^人物事迹	时间^地点^会议名称^发言情况	引入^介绍	引入^调查情况^分析		
举例	青海粮食产量增长(80年11月17日)	发展集市贸易(85年4月15日)	强烈抗议美国(90年2月25日)	革新迷韩连喜(80年11月17日)	北京军区表彰大会(90年2月25日)	人造轻骨料(80年11月17日)	民间信用社(85年4月15日)		

21.3.4 说明与讨论

当然,上述分类只是多种分类层次中的一个层次,也只是根据语篇整体的主要交际目的和结构潜势来划分的,可能有不全面,不合理的地方。但是,通过考察语篇的语类,我们透过表层现象,观察了它们的目的,及其功能结构这些本质现象,能够揭示出一些内在的涵义。这里要特别说明一下“引用”这个语类。就所引用的内容来说,可能是说明(一个文件),或是议论(发表看法),但在报刊上以连续两次,或两次以上的平行结构,进行间接引用时(“某某说”“某某指出”等),它就有了一种传声、转达的目的,这与直接撰文说明或议论,在目的上是不同的,尽管内容相关甚至相近。首先,它表达的是第三方的解释或看法,表明这是第三方的意见;其次,它在一定程度上也反映了报纸的观点,但比较含蓄、隐蔽,因而也比较安全,含有一种间接表达的目的。斯科隆(Scollon 2000)也特别提到了引用的使用(use of quoted material),指出它对于文章作者和被引用人的区分作用,以及所取得的中立效果。亨利和罗斯伯里(Henry & Roseberry 1997: 489)在分析英文作文时,也提到“引用”(reported speech)的疏远效果。另外它有与其他语类不同的独特结构:引入^多段间接引语。我们认为,它有着可辨识的、与众不同的交际目的和语类结构,因而可以划分为一个单独的语类。

又如会议报道,虽然含有时事成分,但一般都有对会议主旨和会议精神的介绍,在一定程度上也带有传达某种观点的目的,但更为客观一些,而且也有自己的结构特点:时间^地点^会议名称^发言情况。又如人物典型,是以树立典型人物、提供范例、提倡向模范人物学习为目的的,如《革新迷韩连喜》,其典型结构或结构潜势为:人物介绍^人物事迹。如果单纯介绍人物生平或轶事,如《比利时首相马尔滕斯》,则属于介绍性文章类型。判断的标准,仍然是语篇的目的及其结构潜势。

21.4 报刊语类与社会变迁

由于语类以语篇的功能目的为内涵,它不可避免地反映了报刊的目的取向,从而在一个侧面可反映社会和意识形态的变迁。必须指出,许多语言学家都对语类和意识形态的密切关系作过论述(Devitt 2000)。有的认为语类(及语类理论)“必然具有意识形态的特性”(Beebee 1994);有的甚至认为实际上语类就是一种形式的意识形态(“Genre is a form of ideology.”)(Faircloth 1989; Lemke 1995;均见 Pappas & Pettegrew 1998)。从对《人民日报》各种语篇的分析,我们不仅可以看出语类和意识形态的密切关系,而且语类的变化往往成为反映社会和意识形态变迁的表征。下面将简单剖析20世纪70、80、90年代各个时期《人民日报》语篇语类,如何反映当时的时代特点及意识形态的变化的。

20世纪70年代的《人民日报》,人物典型占据了很大的比重。例如,在1979年3月10日的报道中,描写典型人物的文章约占30%。其中包括越南反击战英雄、柬埔寨反越英雄和罗马尼亚劳动模范,也包括几篇歌颂周总理的文章。这反映了六七十年代以来占主导地位的“榜样的力量是无穷的”传统的意识形态。

80年代初期,时事、介绍、议论比例都有所增加,调查分析所占比例也相对加大。例如,1980年11月17日的报道,讨论了农村修理电器难、小厂影响纺织工业发展、应当如何发挥优势等等问题。这反映了国家在动乱之后百废待兴,需要对各方面做出调查分析,并探讨解决问题的办法,也反映了实事求是的新态度。

到了80年代中期,会议报道明显增多。例如,1985年4月15日的新闻,报道了经委生产办公室会议、全国燃料管理工作会议、农垦系统宣传座谈会等,反映了这一时期对上情下达的需要。

进入90年代初期,会议报道和引用文所占的分量非常突出。例如,1990年2月25日的新闻中,出现多次引用文。《审计工作要制度化法制化规范化》,连续六段以“说”“指出”“强调”等引用了李鹏的讲话;《强烈抗议美政府侵犯中国主权》,以“发言人称”分三段引用抗议者的讲话;《北大学生寒假归来谈感受》,引用三位同学和“大家”的感想,谈对民主、自由、多党制的新认识;《香港工会联合会谈基本法》,用“提到”“表示”等引用工会的观点。如前所述,这种语类带有说明某人持某种观点,并含蓄表达报纸观点的目的,一定程度上反映了1989年政治风波后,报纸的认真、谨慎态度。

这个时期《人民日报》的另一个突出的特点是介绍性文章的增多。例如,在1995年12月3日的报道中,介绍了乌克兰总统库奇马、俄中友协会长阿尔希波夫、无线电百年、秘鲁的马丘比丘公园、国内艺术品拍卖、二胡演奏家周维等方面的知识，目的是拓宽读者的视野、扩展知识面。此外，议论语类相对减少。也就是说，报纸更多地以扩大读者对客观世界的认识和了解为目的，减少了直接的主观说教，反映了开放时代的走向和宏观趋势。

综观不同年代《人民日报》的语类，语篇类型的变化清楚地反映了社会和意识形态的变迁。这是传统的、以形式划分的体裁所不具备的特性，是语篇分析一个新的侧面，值得我们进一步研究。

21.5　结束语

本文讨论了目前中西方不同学者对语类概念和语类界定的不同看法，提出了用交际目的和结构潜势来界定报刊语类的假设。通过分析 20 世纪 70 年代到 90 年代不同年代的《人民日报》的二百多篇文章，证实了这两个因素可以作为报刊语类的界定方法。最后还讨论了语类的变化与社会和意识形态变迁的正向关系。

但由于我们的分析仅限于《人民日报》有限数量的语类，这样的界定报刊语类的方法是否具有普遍意义，尚需进一步论证。我们认为找到界定语类的方法，虽然较难却是非常重要的：不仅可以为划分语类提供参考的依据，还可以促进研究语类与文化的关系，如探讨“报刊语篇类型的变化与中国社会变化的关系”等课题。这也是深入研究语类与文化语境的其他层面，如意识形态以及它和语域的关系的基础。

22

Generic Changes and Social Changes

— A Survey of an Official Chinese Newspaper of 50 Years *

22.1 Introduction

22.1.1 Aim, Scope, and Significance

This chapter makes a diachronic study of the generic features of *The People's Daily* published in China since the 1950s. The purpose is to find out whether generic changes in one newspaper can reveal or construe the drastic social and cultural changes in China or to disclose the relations of the generic features and the social and the ideological features of the past five decades.

---

* The Chinese version of this chapter was published in *The Journal of Research in Foreign Language and Literature*, 2004(1).

We believe that it is significant to conduct this research project, not only because it may further testify the positive correlation between generic changes and social and cultural changes (Bakhtin 1986) but also because such a study has been rare. There have been only two authors so far who have conducted research as such①.

22.1.2 Research Method

As mentioned above, we adopt the method of a diachronic corpus-based study because we believe such a method may disclose gradual generic changes year by year. We have chosen ***The People's Daily*** as the data for our research as it is the most important official Chinese newspaper representing the voice of the government and regarded as the most serious authoritative newspaper in this country. We hypothesize that if we could observe drastic generic changes in this newspaper, then one would find many more such changes in the less serious newspapers as usually these newspapers would have more varieties of articles in terms of genre; and that if the generic changes in this newspaper could construe the changes in the society and culture, we would be able to observe a strong correlation between generic changes and social/cultural changes. Concretely speaking, we have randomly selected one copy published every year starting from 1950, the year right after the founding of the People's Republic of China, to the

① Scollon (2000) perhaps is among the few scholars to have studied the generic variations of ***The People's Daily***. He compares five days' publications of three versions of this newspaper (the English version for international readers, and the other two versions both in Chinese, one for domestic readers and the other for overseas Chinese readers). Having modified his defining features of genre, Fang Yan presented a paper entitled "**A Critical Study of the Generic Features of *The People's Daily* Published During the 'Cultural Revolution' in China**" at the 27th SFC in Ottawa in July, 2001. The Chinese version of this paper is collected in the book *Linguistics: China Keeping in Pace with the World*, edited by Qian Jun and published by Foreign Language Teaching and Research Press in 2003 (钱军,《语言学：中国与世界同步》，外语教学与研究出版社,2003).

year of 2001, thus resulting in collecting a corpus of 52 copies spanning five decades.

Following the arguments made by Halliday (1994), Crystal (1985 in Hu 1994) and Hu (1994) on the concept of discourse, we have found that there are two types of discourses in this newspaper: those with a generic or schematic structure (Hasan in H & H 1985; Martin 1992), which have beginnings, developments and endings, and those without, such as slogans, subtitles and short sayings by famous people. Our concern in this chapter is with the former. We shall make a brief discussion on different approaches in defining a genre, and propose some variables to define newspaper genres, the variables of which are looked at from the functional point of view. Then we shall make a detailed analysis of the changes of genres in this newspaper, in aspects of 1) changes in linguistics features; 2) changes in layout and placement; 3) changes of communicative purposes; 4) changes of generic structures, and 5) changes of the variety of genres in the past five decades. In our discussion, the focus will be on how the generic changes construe the social/cultural changes, esp. the correlation between generic changes and ideological changes.

22.2 Variables in defining the genres of a newspaper

22.2.1 Definition of "genre"

There are various viewpoints on the concept and the nature of genre. One school holds that genre, being a "typified social action", can be defined in terms of its communicative or social purpose (Miller 1984). Another school maintains that in defining genre, we have to examine the generic or schematic structure of the text under study apart from taking its communicative purpose into consideration (Hasan in H & H 1985; Swales 1990; Martin 1992; Eggins 1994). Some others think that genre is a complex concept, which may be defined by more variables than those just mentioned (Fairclough 1995; Henry & Roseberry 1997). Still others argue that genre is not a static concept (Cohen 1986; Hyon 2000), and we have to be aware of the existence of the phenomenon of genre colonization (Leitch & Roper 1998) or generic mixing (Scollon 2000).

22.2.2 Variables in Defining Newspaper Genres

Scollon (*ibid.*) finds eight features to be "significant features in a newspaper" which are used to signal generic identification. They are "placement, headline, textual frame, point of view, tone, quotation, formulas, vocabulary". We find, however, there are two weaknesses in his classification: 1) he hasn't presented a clear theoretical criterion in the classification of genres; 2) he has neglected one most important generic feature — the communicative purpose. Following Miller (1984) and Hasan (1985 in H & H) and taking into consideration the above Scollon's generic features, in one of my papers (Fang in Qian Jun 2003), I listed seven features as the most important to define a genre of a newspaper, including 1) **Communicative purpose (some discourses may have more than one purposes)**; 2) **Generic structure** (the obligatory and optional elements and their sequence, with **focus** on **the obligatory elements** — see Hasan in H & H 1985); 3) **Placement** (the most important articles usually appear **on the front page**); 4) **Typeface (bold or otherwise; often important articles printed in bold type)**; 5) **Tone (the neutral, authoritative, condemning tones, direct or indirect tone, etc.)**; 6) **Language (syntactic/grammatical or lexical features)**; and 7) **Headlines** (often reflecting **the focus** of the content). In the present chapter, we still apply these seven features in our discussion though we replace "language" with **linguistic**

features to refer to **the way of presentation** and **the type of characters.** There are three features shared by our classification and Scollon's: both include headlines, placement and tone. Yet there are obvious differences. We use the term generic structure to replace his frame structure though the two terms bear a similar meaning. We do not have the feature "point of view" or perspective as we are analyzing only one newspaper, which often has one perspective while he does three versions. We include the communicative purpose of an article, which Scollon does not. We do not consider "quotation" as a variable in defining genre as it itself can be a separate genre since it renders a different tone from the indirect speech. As the **layout** of the newspaper has to do with the **placement** of the articles of different genres, we discuss these two features together. Theoretically, we define the variables of a newspaper mainly from the functional perspective: the communicative purpose, placement and headlines construing the ideational function of the newspaper; the typeface and the tone the interpersonal, and the generic structure and linguistic features the textual. We do not deal with the phenomenon of genre colonization due to space limitation although we have noticed its existence in some genres (for instance, literary genres).

Applying these variables to analyzing the discourses, we have arrived at more than 30 genres in this newspaper. The most frequently appearing genre is "news report", followed by news commentary, editorial, report on meetings and receptions (including banqueting, arrival and farewell), speech, letter to the editor, statement, communique, regulation and rule, telegraph, advertisement, report of a person or a place, introductory information of a country or a person, revision, weather forecast, photo, cartoon, and literary genres such as poetry, prose, story, short drama, literary commentary, etc. Although some of the genres mentioned above can be further categorized into subtypes, we do not do so bearing in mind that our attention should be mainly given to addressing the correlation between the generic changes and social changes having taken place in the past decades.

22.3 Generic changes in the past decades

22.3.1 Changes in linguistic features

22.3.1.1 Changes in the way of presentation

The first conspicuous feature that catches the eyes of the reader of *The People's Daily* is its way to present the news: whether in the manner of top-down or from the left to the right.

From 1950 to 1955 in the Chinese mainland, the words in the news articles went from the top to the bottom in the form of columns, as is still the practice of many newspapers published in Hong Kong SAR, China and in Taiwan, China, which may be the influence coming from the writing path of Chinese since the ancient times.

Yet from 1956 to the present, the words of the news mainly go from the left to the right, with the most important reports appearing on the left or on the top of the right. But there are still articles written in the top-down fashion, either for novelty or for the change of style.

22.3.1.2 Changes in the type of characters

Before 1954, the newspaper used the complicated type of characters; after that year, the simplified characters① (The changes underwent three stages in accordance with the publications of the three groups of simplified characters. We do not include them here due to space limitation).

We have summarized changes in linguistic features in Table 22 – 1.

---

① The gradual adoption of the simplified characters was originally considered to be the first stage for the Romanization of the Chinese writing system but the attempt was unsuccessful. (See Fang 2011)

Table 22 – 1 Changes of Linguistic Features

Way of presentation	Top-down to left-right
Type of Character	Complex to simplified

The change of presenting words from *top-down* to *left-right* since the 1950s is an influence from the Western writing system. When New China was founded, there were two realities: on the one hand, the broad masses needed to be educated; on the other hand, the Chinese way of presentation of words in written works, and the use of complicated characters were big obstacles for them to learn how to read and write. These two changes are an indication of New China's intention to practice what was good and convenient for the broad masses. It also reflects the fact that China is open in learning what is good from other cultures and languages.

22.3.1.3 Changes in the layout and placement

The changes in layout and placement are most obvious on the **top** of the **first** page. In the following discussion, we shall look closely at the first page, with the focus on the top.

1) From 1950 to 1956

On the left was a photo reflecting the advancements of the new country, often with the title "Our Great Motherland", the purpose of which is clear: to inform the readers of the progress that China was making with each passing day.

The newspaper's title 人民日报 (*The People's Daily*) appeared in the middle of the top. These four characters, which remain up to now, were the handwriting of Mao Zedong, who has been known as one of the best contemporary calligraphers. With Mao's handwriting to be the title, the ideological implication is clear: the newspaper is an authoritative official newspaper representing the viewpoints of the Party and the government, and Mao Zedong Thought should be applied to guiding the orientation of this newspaper. Under these four characters was the information of this newspaper: the issue number, price, number of pages, address of the press, telephone numbers of three most important branches, locations for subscription.

On the right were the main contents of the pages, usually four.

2) From 1957 to 1966

On the left was the title of the newspaper and from 1958 on, its Roman alphabet representations or *pinyin* added below the title, under which were the issue number and the address of the newspaper.

In the middle were the main contents of the current issue. The newspaper usually covered eight pages, a special issue twelve; for instance, during the convention of the People's Congress, *The People's Daily* would have 12 pages as it would need more space for publicizing speeches made by the representatives.

On the right was weather forecast.

3) From 1967 to 1977

On the left and in the middle was the same information — the title of the newspaper and the main contents but on the right appeared a quotation from revolutionary leaders, most frequently from Mao Zedong. Weather forecast stopped appearing until 1975 when there was only a brief report at the bottom rim on Page 4.

4) From 1978 to early 1990s

The format is similar to the period of 1957 – 1966.

5) From the mid 1990s to the present:

On the left was still the title of the newspaper though in smaller characters.In the middle was weather forecast, in the same fashion as before 1966. On the right was the most important news, often news about the activities of top state leaders, e.g. those of the Chairman or the Premier of the State Council. The contents of the daily issue were arranged specially in a block on the second half of the first page.

We have summarized the changes in layout and placement in Table 22 – 2.

Table 22 - 2 **Changes in Layout and Placement**

Year/feature	left	middle	right
1950 - 1956	Photo (great motherland)	title (characters only)	contents
1957 - 1966	title with pinyin	contents	*weather forecast*
1967 - 1977	title with pinyin	contents	**quotes from Mao**
1978 - early 1990s	title with pinyin	contents	*weather forecast*
mid 1990s - now	title with pinyin	*weather forecast*	key news report

The disappearance of weather forecast from 1967 to 1975 mirrors covertly the dominance of the ideology of class struggle in the political life during the "Cultural Revolution", and also indicates that there was little concern for the livelihood of the people. For the purpose of this genre is to make life easier for people to go to work or to travel. But with the changes of the society, this genre has been restored and given a more prominent placement, not only appearing on Page 1 but also given a larger space on another page. This reflects the ideological change of the attitude of the newspaper to the everyday life of the readers: keen attention should be given to people's life. There are other features concerning the layout and placement of the newspaper:

1) It has been expanding from 4 and to 6 or 8 and now to 12 pages; some local editions 16 pages. Now important international and domestic news reports occupy 4 - 5 pages. This reflects the reality of the active involvement of China in international affairs as well as its development in various fields.

2) Since the middle of the 1990s, each page is devoted to a special field with indications on the top rim of every page. Take the issue of Dec. 21, 2001. There were 12 pages. Page 1 covered the most important domestic and international news, Page 2 important news, and Page 3 international news. Page 4 was devoted to important domestic news. What is interesting is that it had a special block reporting the weather, which included three elements: analysis of the tendency of weather, weather forecast of main cities at home

and abroad and weather forecast of tourist spots. Page 5 was focused on domestic economy, Page 6 on education, science and culture, Page 7 on less international news, Page 8 on physical culture, and Page 9 on theory (mainly Marxist theory). Page 10 was dedicated to letters to the editor, Page 11 to CPC Party life and the last page to creative writings of literary genres. Therefore, we can find issues concerning economy, education, science and culture, and sports, each of which had a special page exclusively about it. This may have the following implications: *a*) the chief mission for the whole country was turned to develop its economy and to further promote the country's economic boom; *b*) education and science and technology had become the basis for China's long term development; therefore, raising the level of people's awareness of the importance of science and technology had become an urgent mission of the country; *c*) to achieve the goal of building China into a strong country, it was of vital importance to raise the national physical build-up; *d*) the appearing of a variety of literary genres was an indication of a more colorful life that people were enjoying, and *e*) a page especially arranged for CPC Party life obviously had the aim to educate its members, whose number was as large as 60 million by then, in adopting a correct world outlook when they were challenged with great ideological changes brought about by the economic reform.

22.3.2 Changes of the communicative purposes of some genres

Due to space limitation, we shall only look at the communicative purposes of two genres: news reports and advertisements.

The genre of news reports takes up the largest proportion of all genres. But we find that in different periods, their communicative purposes vary. For instance, when the republic was newly founded, the purpose of many news reports was to mobilize the people to plunge into the reconstruction of the country and the struggle against the U.S. in the Korean War. Most news reports at present circle around the economic development or center on creating a peaceful environment for economic construction. At the same time, each news report may have its particular purpose. These changes are illustrated in Table 22 - 3.

Table 22 - 3 Changes of Communicative Purpose of News Report

1950s	To mobilize masses to plunge into reconstruction and the struggle against U.S. in Korean War
Now	To promote the economic development; to create a peaceful environment for the economic boom

Though the communicative purposes of news reports vary in different periods, yet they seem to be concurrent with the dominant ideology or the political situation of each period.

To illustrate further the correlation between the changes in communication purpose of a certain genre and social changes, we shall look at a special genre — ads — in three different periods.

The purpose of ads before and after the "Cultural Revolution" was for promoting services or the selling of goods no matter whether they were ads of products or of performances and movies. There was **a scarcity of variety** of ads, Table 22 - 4 is an illustration of changes of communicative purposes of advertisements.

Table 22 - 4 Changes of Communicative Purpose of Ads

Before and after "CR"	To promote services or the selling of goods.
During "CR"	Either to eulogize thoughts of the political leader or to sing the praise of workers, peasants and soldiers.

22.3.3 Changes of the generic structure of some genres

We shall discuss the changes of generic structure of only two genres: weather report and ads for short of space.

Before 1966, **the generic structure of weather report** included: date ^ day ^ date (according to the Lunar Calendar) ^ weather of that day (daytime ^ night ^ temperature). However, we find drastic changes when this genre reappeared on May 25, 1975. Instead of appearing at a prominent place on the front page, it was placed at the bottom rim of Page 4. There were other distinctive generic changes. For example, the Lunar Calendar date was missing. At the beginning of the 1980s, this genre was restored in its original place with its original structure. In the issue of September 13, 2000, we not only see a brief weather report on the top of the first page but also a more detailed weather forecast on Page 4, which included three elements: analysis of the tendency of weather, weather forecast of main cities at home and that in tourist places. Here we shall only look at the generic structure of the weather tendency, which consisted of title ^ duration ^ tendency analysis [information source ^ weather forecast ^ (whether suitable for sightseeing)]. We summarize the generic structure of the different periods of reporting the tendency of weather in Table 22 - 5.

Table 22 - 5 Generic Structure of Weather Report

Before 1966	date ^ day ^ date (Lunar Calendar) ^ weather of day [daytime ^ night ^ temperature]
Late 1966 - 1974	no such genre
1975 - late 1970s	without date according to Lunar Calendar
1980s - mid 1990s	the same as before 1966
Mid 1990s - 2001	the same as before 1966 + weather forecast of main cities at home and that in tourist places + analysis of weather tendency on another page, consisting of title ^ duration ^ tendency analysis [information source ^ weather forecast ^ whether suitable for sightseeing]

We have commented above that this newspaper had no weather report during the "Cultural Revolution". When it reappeared in 1975, it was given an unimportant placement without the element of Lunar Calendar date. This change was a piece of strong evidence of the negligence of agricultural production in the rural area. For Chinese farmers usually arrange their farming schedule according to the seasons made by the Lunar Calendar. Apparently, as far as the editors were concerned, people did not have to worry about their basic necessities at that time — to feed themselves. But the restoration of weather report and a special space devoted to a detailed forecast since the mid 1990s show that concern for the livelihood of the people has again become an important business for the newspaper considered to represent the government.

Finally, we shall look at the generic structure of another genre: that of ads: ads of journals and of performances.

We find that ads of journals in the 1950s (1954 - 02 - 20) had such a generic structure: name ^ issue number ^ contents ^ names of authors ^ price ^ publisher ^ issuing office ^ introduction to the journal. This genre disappeared in the late 1960s and 1970s. Ads of journals reappeared after the 1980s and with richer generic features. For example, we find three very interesting ads of a journal in the 1999 issue in the format of satire and humor. To begin with, the ads took a fairly large space. On the left was the ad proper, presented by the generic structure comprising general introduction ^ brief description ^ title ^ nature ^ history ^ year for the first issue ^ issuing office ^ price ^ effect ^ publication dates ^ number of issuing office ^ retail price, as shown in Table 22 - 6. On the right was additional information about the ad: 1) the main contents of the issues published in the past, and 2) the information for subscription in the past. For short of space, we shall omit a detailed description of its generic structure and contents.

Table 22 - 6 Generic Structure of Ads of Journals

1950s	title ^ issue number ^ contents ^ names of authors ^ price ^ publisher ^ issuing office ^ introduction to the journal
CR	no such genre
1999 (in the format of satire and humor)	The ad proper: general introduction ^ brief description ^ title ^ nature ^ history ^ year of first issue ^ issuing office ^ price ^ effect ^ publication dates ^ number of issuing office ^ retail price + additional information (contents of past issues and subscription)

As mentioned above, this genre was no longer existent in the late 1960s and 1970s. Also there was a very tight control on the publications of journals. At present, there have not only appeared many more kinds of journals and magazines but the generic structure of its ads is much more complex than that in the 1950s. This may be an indication of China being more open and more democratic in letting its people speak their minds. This is also an immediate reflection of the influence of the market economy, which follows the rule of competition among goods and services. In order for a journal to survive and to have a wider circulation, the modelling of the ads to be more informative is of vital importance.

Let's compare the generic structure of ads of performances in different periods. In the 1950s, its generic structure included unit ^ items ^ **actors** ^ time ^ place ^ (**booking office and time and place for booking**). During the "Cultural Revolution", however, we can only find two kinds, either ads of art exhibitions or of performances by art troupes, their generic structures simply including unit ^ items ^ time ^ place. The names of the performers and booking office did not, however, appear in the ads. In recent years, readers can also find the information of ads in its internet version, the generic structure of which is about the same as that in the 1950s. Table 22 – 7 is a summary of the changes of the generic structure of ads of performances.

Table 22 – 7 Generic Structure of Ads of Performances

1950s	unit ^ items ^ actors ^ time ^ place ^ (booking office and time and place for booking)
CR	unit ^ items ^ time ^ place
Now	unit ^ items ^ actors ^ time ^ place ^ (booking office and time and place for booking), also information of ads in the internet version

What is the reason for the names of actors included in the structure in the 1950s and now but for the disappearance of this element during the "Cultural Revolution"? The underlying ideology was that one should not pursue personal fame and therefore the names of actors should be neglected in an ad. What is more, the information in this period about booking office was put at the bottom of the frame on the same page and in smaller characters. We have also noticed that the element "price" never appeared in the generic structure in all the stages in the five decades, even now. The underlying ideology may be that money is not as important as other elements, so talking about money should be avoided in public life. It would be interesting to wait and see what will happen in the future①.

22.3.4 Changes of the variety of genres

One of the most conspicuous features of this newspaper is the change of the variety of genres. Let's first look at Table 22 - 8, which is a summary of the changes of the dominant genres, and then we shall discuss in detail the possible relations between the genres of a particular time and the prevailing ideology or social features of that period so that we can see how genres construe the social reality.

Table 22 - 8 Changes of the Variety of Genres

Year	Most representative genres
1950 - 1957	Government statements, decisions, telegraphs, instructions, announcements, letters to the editor
1958 - 1965	Averagely, 15 - 17 genres, e.g. 38 ads and literary genres such as poetry, literary commentary, poem + drawing, feature story (1958 issue)
1970s	Reporting on representative personalities
Early 1980s	Introductory genre, comments, investigations
Mid 1980s	Meetings and conferences

(Continued on the next page)

① Now when I am editing this chapter, I have noticed that "price" has become an obligatory element of this genre. For instance, there are two prices for seeing a Finish music performance at the National Theatre on May 24th, 2016: one for VIP (1280 yuan) and the other for ordinary viewer (1080 yuan) and with its discount information.

Year	Most representative genres
Early 1990s	Many quotes
Mid 1990s	Introductory genres
Mid 1990s – now	Meeting between leaders, visits, regulations on law, short satirical articles, letters to the editor, responses from the readers, literary genres such as reflections, fairy stories, traveling notes, personal notes, appreciation of food and dishes (Dec. 20th, 2001)

From 1950 to 1957, we see a great proportion of government statements, decisions, declarations, telegraphs, instructions and announcements. The appearance of these genres in a big amount explains the necessity of setting up new orders for the newly founded republic. From the 1950 and 1951 issues, we also find quite a lot of letters to the editor, which were suggestions such as how to promote production in different fields, the necessity of creating a new social environment in the new society, etc. The headlines of the news reports of the 1950 – 1954 issues covered news on economic construction, on the raising of the people's livelihood and especially on the 1950 – 1953 Korean War, particularly on the victories of the Chinese People's Volunteer Army and the defeats of American forces. It reflects the fact that despite the unfavorable international environment, the Chinese people had a high morale and were optimistic in making a great effort in building New China.

We have noticed two conspicuous features in the 1958 – 1965 issues: one is that the number of genres increased from an average of 8 – 9 to of 15 – 17. Take the April 12, 1958 issue. It has 25 genres with various literary genres such as literary commentary, poetry, poem + drawing, prose, feature story in addition to 38 ads on industrial products, journals, theatrical activities, films, etc. This directly reflected the social reality after 1958, in which the whole country was carrying out Mao's thought of "letting one hundred flowers blossom and one hundred schools contend". This resulted in more daring in thinking and in creating more works of literary genres.

There were fewer genres of this newspaper during the "Cultural

Revolution". For example, there was not a single article of any literary genre during the 12 years; the layout and format looked very boring, which was a true reflection of the monocultural social reality of that "revolutionary" period. There were almost no ads except those of art exhibition and performances by art troupes but their generic structure would be quite different from that before or after the "CR" (see 22.3.3). Articles of four genres were predominant, taking up about 63% of the total. The headlines tell us that they were all associated with the "propaganda" of the ideology of that period, that is, waging a class struggle against domestic and international revisionism and imperialism. In addition, it would not be hard to discover that most news reports were related to the prevailing ideology of the time if one just scanned the six pages of the newspaper. This is evidence of the view on the close relationship between genre and ideology (Devitt 2000; Beebee 1994; Fang in Qian 2003). In news reports, there were 27 articles out of 349 published in this period on "promoting revolution and production", taking up about only 7.7% of the total. Evidently, raising the livelihood of the people was not the main concern of the government during this period (Fang in Qian 2003).

In the 1970s, the genre of reporting representative personalities took a large proportion. For instance, in the issue of March 10th, 1979, articles of this genre took about 30%, including Vietnamese heroes in the Vietnam War Against American Aggression, Kampuchea heroes in the War Against Vietnamese Aggression, model workers in Romania, as well as articles singing the praise of the late Chinese Premier Zhou Enlai. This phenomenon reflected the dominant ideology in the 1970s that "heroes and model workers can exercise enormous influence on people".

At the beginning of the 1980s, there was an increase of news reports, introductory articles, comments and investigation. For instance, the issue of Nov. 17th, 1980 discussed and investigated on the difficulties in repairing electric gadgets in the rural areas, the phenomenon of how small plants had prevented the development of textile industry, the way how to develop the potential of an enterprise. This may well mirror the necessity of making investigations and analysis, and of exploring ways to solve the existing problems in China's economic development after the "CR". This also reflected the adoption of a new "down to earth" working attitude.

The issues published in the middle 1980s were marked with many meetings and conferences. For example, the issue of April 15th of 1985 reported meetings held respectively by the Production Office of National Economic Commission and by the National Fuel Management Conference, and a seminar held by the Ministry of Agriculture, etc. This was a reflection of the need for a direct interaction between the top leaders and those at the grass roots level so that the country's economy could be developed faster.

At the beginning of the 1990s, the proportion of quotations in the news reports was an outstanding feature. For instance, in the issue of Feb. 25th, 1990, there were quite a few quotes. In one article, there were six paragraphs quoting a leader's speech. In a protest statement against the U.S. invasion of China, the speaker was quoted three times. In a report of Beijing students returning from their hometowns in winter holidays, there were three direct quotations on their opinions on democracy, freedom and multiparty political system. We all know that quotations usually have the function of stating the speaker's own viewpoint and at the same time implying the attitude of the newspaper.

Yet in the mid 1990s, we see an increase of the introductory genre. On December 3rd, 1995, for instance, there were articles introducing the president of Ukraine, the chairman of Russian-China Friendship Association, the centenary of the invention of the wireless, a park in Peru, an auction of paintings in China, a Chinese *Erhu* (a string musical instrument) player, etc. The purpose of these articles could be to expand the vision and enrich the knowledge of the readers.

Since the 1980s, there has been a steady increase of the number and variety of genres. For example, the Dec. 20th, 2001 issue had 28 genres, including meetings between leaders, visits, regulations on law, short satirical articles, letters to the editor, responses from the readers, literary genres such as reflections, fairy stories, traveling notes, personal notes, appreciation of food and dishes, etc. These mirror the social fact that with the further opening of China's door to the outside world, there are more exchanges between China and other countries, and that China has made a great effort in building itself into a country governed by law. The variety of literary genres construes the reality that the society is more open, the life of the Chinese people is more colorful and they are freer in expressing themselves. If we look at the headlines and placements of the news reports, it is not difficult to notice that their contents have extended to cover many more areas.

22.4 Conclusion

From the above discussions on generic changes in many aspects of *The People's Daily* we can perhaps come to the following conclusions:

(1) There have been drastic generic changes in the past five decades in all aspects in *The People's Daily*: linguistic features, layout of pages and placement of articles of different genres, communicative purposes, generic structures as well as varieties of genres.

(2) The generic changes present a reverse shape of a saddle. The newspaper in the 1950s had quite a variety of genres and witnessed big changes in the layout and linguistic features as compared with those after this period. The generic structures then were richer and more complex than those in the years following this decade. During the "Cultural Revolution", there was a sharp decrease in the variety of genres, and news articles were written with simpler generic structures. However, when China decided to open its door to the outside world, there was a drastic change in all aspects of the genres. Now, there are many more types of genres in this newspaper, which is designed with a much richer format, a more lively layout and more complex generic structures so that it is able to better cater to the needs of the

readers.

(3) This study shows that generic changes in a society reflect the changes of the prevailing ideology in different periods and that these changes are closely bound with the changes of a society and a culture. Concretely, the generic changes of *The People's Daily* in the past five decades mirror the changes of China from fighting for her survival to adopting an extreme leftist ideology of class struggle and then to taking the development of economy as the center of the country's mission. The generic changes also show that the government has shifted from neglecting people's livelihood to focusing on the enhancement of people's educational level, the building up of their awareness of science and technology and the improvement of their livelihood. These changes indicate clearly the tendency or orientation of China's social development: changing from a mono-cultural society to a multi-cultural society.

(4) The findings in this corpus-based diachronic study may support the arguments that there is a close relationship between society and genre (Bakhtin 1986; Eggins 1994) and that "generic change" originates "in social and political change" (Beebee 1994).

Finally, we should point out that in this chapter we have only discussed the impact of social or cultural changes on generic changes but we have not touched upon the impact of generic changes on the society or culture, which needs to be dealt with in the future.

23

探索以语类为基础的英语写作教学模式*

23.1 引 言

语言的学习和研究离不开文化语境和情景语境。文化语境有一个重要的概念称为“语篇类型”(type of discourse)(Halliday & Hasan 1985),简称“语类”(genre,相当于文学中的“体裁”,但它也包含非文学体裁,特别是日常生活语篇的各种类型,比如书信、日记、日常会话等等)。20 世纪 90 年代初,笔者开始接触语类理论,系统阅读了韩茹凯和马丁(H & H 1985; Martin 1992)有关的书籍和学术论文,受到很大启发。当时笔者正给清华大学英语专业四年级学生上英语写作课,发现虽然学生已经学习了十几年的英语,但在半数以上学生的作文中,不仅还有相当多的基本语言错误,对一些实用性语类的写作也不知如何起笔。于是,笔者应用韩茹凯的语类结构潜势理论做了初步的实验和探讨,取

* 本章汇集了笔者过去十几年来撰写的有关语类教学路子的理论和教学实践的论文精要(见参考文献部分)。蔡慧萍对教学实验部分作了一些补充。

得了一定的效果;后来,指导了一名硕士研究生在非英语专业的学生中继续试验,也取得了较好的结果(方琰、兰青 1997)。2002 年笔者又与另一位研究生写了一篇论文(方琰、方艳华,2002),探讨应用文写作的教学路子。2003 年至 2007 年,笔者接受浙江海洋学院(现已改名为浙江海洋大学)的聘请,担任了该校外国语学院的名誉院长。调研教学问题时,碰到的第一个问题就是写作课教学存在比较大的问题。于是建议外国语学院的负责人蔡慧萍老师,对国内出版的十几本写作教科书和三个院校的五百多名大学生做了相关调研(蔡慧萍 2005;蔡慧萍、方琰 2006)。根据调研结果,决定应用"语类"理论在英语专业二年级学生中做教学实验。一年结束前,我们在实验班的同学们中又做了调研,反应相当好,而且学生在全国英语专业四、八级测试中,写作的成绩高于全国高校平均水平,对于一个当时在浙江省教学业绩考核排名在中下的省属高等教育普通本科二级院校而言,这是一个很好的成果(蔡慧萍、方琰 2007)。有了第一年的基础,我们第二年、第三年、第四年又扩大了实验范围,修改教案,改进教学方法,继续实验。后来形成了有八位老师组成的教学团队。经过五年在二年级全体同学中采取同样的教学方法授课,取得了非常好的教学成果,不仅写作水平有了很大的提高,更重要的是学生们对英语写作产生了兴趣,愿意表达,也初步学会了如何表达。笔者和蔡慧萍老师多次在国内外学术会议上与同行交流。2012 年 4 月,由笔者和一位外籍教师担任审校和顾问,由蔡慧萍等主编出版了一本写作教科书,题为《语类-过程英语写作教程》(以下称"教材")。从 2014 年开始,这个教学团队将实验扩大到阅读、听、说、视听课堂上,也取得了初步的成果。

有鉴于此,本章将进一步分析和探讨英语写作的教学路子,特别是应用文的写作模式。

首先我们将简略回顾写作教学的路子,然后讨论语类教学模式涉及的相关理论,并分析教学中必然接触到的两大语类:语篇语类(text genre)和课程语类(curriculum genre)(Rose 2006)。在对比这两种与课程有关的语类的基础上,文章将重点汇报当时在浙江海洋学院所做的教学实验以及实验引起的思考。

23.2 写作教学路子

过去几十年中,英语写作的一个突出的特点是从注重成品(product)转变为注重过程(process)(Yang 1995)。在中国,现在以语类为基础的路子也逐渐受到越来越多英语教师的关注(方琰、方艳华 2002;张德禄 2002;罗兴霞 2004)。

23.2.1 注重成品的教学路子

写作者将注意力放到对语言知识的运用方面,比如注重对词汇、句法、衔接手段的恰当应用。极端的看法是只要英语基础好,英语写作就没有问题。这种教学路子极不重视对学生写作整体规划能力的培养,也不重视对写作技巧,诸如起草、编辑的训练(Badge & White 2000)。

23.2.2 注重过程的教学路子

过程写作教学中,语言知识的运用是次要的,写作的整体规划是关注的焦点。虽然对写作过程的阶段有不同的看法,但一般都认为应包含预写、起草、修改、编辑四个步骤。不足之处是,似乎所有类型的写作过程都是一样的,不重视对不同类型语篇的写作训练(Badge & White 2000)。

23.2.3 以语类为基础的综合教学路子

自 20 世纪 80 年代以来,很多英语教师开始认识到前两个路子都有不全面的地方。随着语言学家对语类研究的深入,他们转向以语类为基础的教学路子,认为语类是教授英语写作的有重要影响的因素。悉尼的功能语言学家应用这个概念,指导、制定了当地中小学的母语和土著人第二语言教学的阅读与写作大纲,指导中小学各门课程老师应用语类教学路子,培养学生阅读和写作所学课程的能力,取得了非常好的效果(Christie 1999; Christie & Martin 1997; Rothery 1994; Rose 2004/2006)。此后,各国的语言学家纷纷借鉴他们的经验,开始研究将这个理论用于帮助人们学习外语。1996 年"新伦敦集团"强调,语言教学需要一个新的教学路子,指出,"学生需要有机会读、写他们日常学校生活碰到的各种语类"(Sengupta et al. 1999)。这个路子的目的是:(1) 帮助学习者提高语类意识;(2) "提高学习者对语类相关的修辞结构和语言特征的认识"(Henry & Roseberry 1998)。因而,与注重产出的路子相同,这个路子注重对语言的应用能力的培训;与之不同的是,它认为"写作随着产生它的社会语境的不同而有所变化"(Badge & White 2000),应尽可能多地让学生接触英语社会里不同的语类(Hasan in H & H 1985)。这个教学路子注重写作目的,有意识地提高学生对不同语类语义框架的认识,提高他们的整体写作能力,以便学会写作不同的语类语篇。同时,这个教学路子在教学过程中也重视写作过程中几个步骤的规划。也就是说这个路子能比较好地处理写作任务必须解决的三个问题:(1) 确定某个语类限定的内容(即语义框架);(2) 注重语篇的整体结构;(3) 选择适合这个语类的修辞手段和语言表达的方式;(4) 注重整个写作过程各种能力(预写、起草、修改、编辑等步骤)的培训。显然,这个教学路子结合了注重成品和注重过程两种教学路子的优点,是一个综合性的教学路子。我们所做的教学实验就是这样一个综合性的教学路子,它以韩茹凯和马丁的语类理论为基础的,也参考了与此相关的学者的研究成果。

23.3 语类理论

有许多语言学家研究语类理论,系统功能语言学家做出的贡献尤为突出(方琰 1998/2002)。韩茹凯(H & H 1985)和马丁(Martin 1985;1992)可能是系统功能语言学家中较早研究语类的学者。20 世纪 90 年代之后,埃金斯(Eggins 1994)、罗斯(Martin & Rose 2007;Rose 2006)等许多学者进一步发展或应用了这个理论。这里我们集中回顾韩茹凯和马丁两位语言学家的相关理论,也会讨论其他学者对这个教学路子做出的独特贡献。

23.3.1 韩茹凯的语类结构潜势理论(Generic Structure Potential)

系统功能语言学的核心思想是:语言是一种意义的源泉,是用来表达意义潜势的(meaning potential)。1985 年韩茹凯提出了语类结构潜势(Generic Structure Potential,后称 GSP)理论。GSP 是某个语类中所有语篇产生的源泉,包括语篇的必要成分、可选成分和重复成分。这个理论有三点值得注意:(1) 语境配置 CC(Contextual Configuration)的值,即"实现语场、语旨、语式的值",可以预测语篇的结构成分、成分出现的次数与顺序。她还将这三个变量的定义具体化,语场不仅包括"发生的行为",还涉及"它们的目的";语旨不仅指"参与者的角色",还包括"它们之间的社会距离";语式不仅既指"语言的作用"(主导还是辅助),还具体涉及"渠道"(文字或语音)和"媒介"(笔头或口头)(Hasan in H & H 1985)。(2) 每个语类的 GSP 都包含语篇的必要成分(obligatory elements)和非必要成分(optional elements),其结构遵照一定的次序进行排列。这就意味着 CC 的三个变量在很大程度上可以预测所涉及语类的 GSP。比如,要写一个人的简历,则要求其语场——简单介绍本人的概况、学习和工作经历,目的是求职或求学;语旨——作者与读者,互不认识,因而要求语言正式;语式——书写体。这三个成分就决定了简历的语境配置为"用正式的书写体和简洁的语言描述个人的经历"。(3) 语类是由"语篇结构的必要成分来定义的"(同上),也就是说具有相同必要成分的语篇属于同一个语类。非必要成分决定属于同一个语类的语篇变异现象。根据以上的叙述,笔者归纳出了语类结构潜势(GSP)与语篇之间的关系图,见图 19-3。

又如,已知语篇的语场为:Applying to Study in a University in a

Foreign Country, 这也是写作的目的; 它的语旨: writer and unknown foreign reader; 语式: written to be read; 其语境配置为"writing an application letter to an unknown person for studying in a foreign country",就决定了它的语类为"Writing an Application Letter,"要求的语篇结构成分包括: heading ^ inside address ^ date of writing ^ salutation ^ objective ^ education background ^ (other qualifications) ^ expectations and thanks ^ complimentary close ^ signature [( )内的成分为非必要成分,其他均为必要成分。]

23.3.2 马丁的纲要式结构理论(Schematic Structure Theory)

马丁同意韩茹凯(H & H 1985)关于语类与语域三个变量语场、语旨、语式均有关系的看法,都认为语言与产生它的文化语境和情景语境密切相关。但与韩茹凯也有些不同之处,他明确指出语类是由语域三个变量来实现的,而且与这三个变量配置所产生的总体目标密切相关。1985 年他提出了语类的纲要式结构理论(Schematic Structure Theory, 后称 SST)。他将语类定义为"一种我们作为某个文化成员的说话者的有步骤的、有一定既定目标的、有目的的行为"(1985: 25)。他认为任何一个语篇都是为了实现某一交际目的而产生的,不同的交际目的决定了不同的语类,会出现不同的语义成分和语言特征。也就是说,在不同的语类中,语言的三个纯理功能(metafunctions),即概念功能、人际功能和语篇功能(Halliday 1994; Thompson 1996)的配置也会随之不同(Martin 1992; Martin & Rose 2003)。1992 年他将语类进一步定义为:"一个通过语域来实现的有步骤的、有一定目标的社会过程"。"有步骤的"是因为每个语类语篇由不止一个步骤展开;"有目标的"是因为每个语篇都应有一个清晰的交际目的;"是一个社会过程"强调语类展开的过程就是社会交往的过程。语类、语域、语旨三大功能的关系可用图 19 - 1 表示。

不难看出,韩茹凯的语类只涉及由语言构成的语篇,对口语和书面语言构成的语篇的分析有独到之处。因此,她在分析中使用"elements"。然而,马丁的语类的概念不仅包含语言构成的语类,还包含所有的社会行为和社会活动。在他看来,任何社会行为或活动都有既定的目的,都有一定的步骤,即有一定的"stages",都是一个社会过程,因而都属于一定的语类。埃金斯(Eggins 1994)同意马丁的观点,她甚至认为"在我们的文化中有多少种已被承认的社会行为,就会有多少种类型的语类。"这个观点也可以用来说明,在不同的文化语境中,同属一个语类的过程的目的、步骤会有一些差异。比如,同为学术会议的开幕式,西方一般不包含照相(合影)这个步骤;但是在中国,这似乎是一个不可或缺的步骤。

马丁的这个定义,也为他的学生罗瑟里(J. Rothery)和罗斯(David Rose),对课堂教学语类过程的研究提供了理论基础。罗瑟里讨论了课堂学习,认为应当包括三个步骤:解构语篇、共同构建语篇、独立构建语篇(Rothery 1994)。这三个步骤在课堂学习中循环进行,即,"共同构建语篇"或"独立建构语篇"过程中,如果遇到问题,还可对所学语篇作第二次的"解构"。罗瑟里在实践中得到的经验是:这三个步骤都必须在一定的情景中进行,因而在教学过程中,必须要确立它的场景(setting context);而三个步骤的共同目的都是为了构建所学语类的语场(building field);而每个步骤又有各自的目的:"解构"和"独立构建"这两个步骤都是为了掌握所学的语类语篇,而"共同建构"不仅促进学生相互的交流,还鼓励他们学会用批评性的眼光审视所学语类的语篇。她的这三个循环步骤和它们各自的目的可用图 23-1 表示:

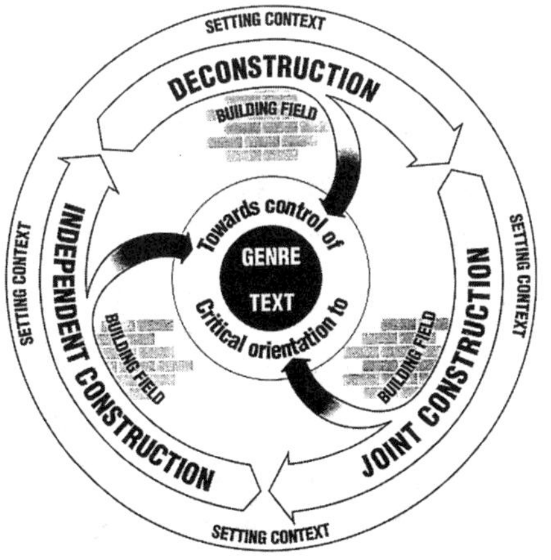

图 23-1　课堂学习的循环步骤(Rothery 1994)

罗斯于21世纪初,开始投身于“Reading to Learn”科研项目,而且还建立了网站www.readingtolearn.com.au,身体力行地将马丁的语类理论和罗瑟里的课堂循环模式,应用于中小学的读写教学当中,取得了可喜的成果(2004, 2006),而且在实践中进一步发展了这个理论。比如,他和马丁一起总结出了澳大利亚中学生学习的英语课程语类(curriculum genre)(Martin & Rose 2007)。英语课程学习的语类主要包括: recount, narrative, exemplum, anecdote, personal response, review, interpretation, critical response, exposition, discussion;而社会科学和自然科学学习的写作语类包括: autobiographical recount, biological recount, historical account, sequential explanation, factual explanation, consequential explanation, descriptive report, classifying report, compositional report, procedure, procedural recount等,两者加起来共有二十几个语类,他们还列出了各种语类的目的和步骤。根据语篇分析的需要,罗斯又提出了“语篇的语义层次”概念,认为有必要将语篇从功能的角度划分为genre(语类)、stage(步骤)、phase(阶段)、message(信息)四个层次(Rose 2006)。每个层次之间的关系是实现关系,即语类由它的步骤实现;步骤由构成它的阶段实现;最后,阶段由语言的信息单位实现。他以一个传统的印度口语故事为例,分析出这个语类包含的四个步骤:(1) Orientation;(2) Complication;(3) Evaluation;(4) Resolution。每个步骤由又不同的阶段构成。比如Orientation包含了setting、reaction、problem、solution四个阶段。Complication包含problem、reaction、problem三个阶段。Evaluation只包含reaction一个阶段。Resolution包含了setting、problem、solution三个阶段。他还讨论了这些阶段的逻辑-语义关系:应首先确定它们是“扩展”还是“投射”关系,然后进一步讨论如何“扩展”:是“增强”还是“阐述”;最后又讨论了“增强”的方式:是按照时间顺序“增强”,还是按照结果的重要性“增强”,等等。他以故事为例将这些关系的逻辑-语义关系做了总结,列表如下(见下页)。

这样,故事语类的语言阶段setting、description、events、effects、reaction、problem、solution、comments、reflection就会通过上述的逻辑-语义关系一步一步得到展开。相信这个模式对于教授故事语类写作的教师会有一定的启发。

表 23-1 **Common Options in Story Phases**

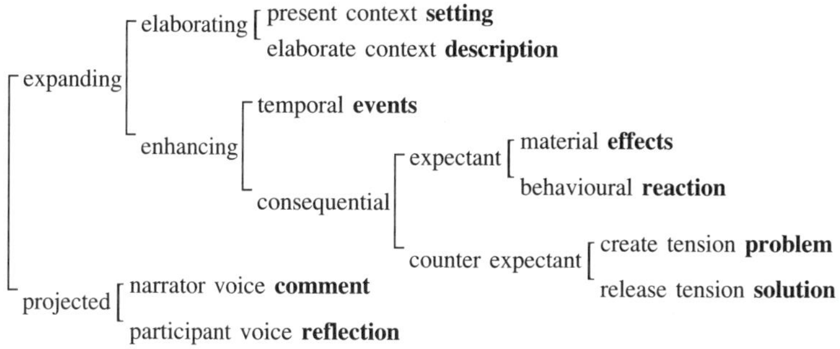

罗斯还较详细地探讨了课堂语类(curriculum genre),提供了设计这个语类的框架,包括分析学习活动的顺序(sequence of learning activities),和教学过程中的活动及教学双方的关系,如师生关系或母/父子关系(2006)。

23.3.3 关于语类划分的多元观点

近些年来,一些语言学家在研究中发现,将语类看作一定语义结构的认识可能有些偏颇。他们更倾向于将语类看成一个"大杂烩",具有"多面"(multi-faceted)的特性,认为对语类的划分应建立在多个因素的基础上(Fairclough 1995)。一个语篇可能形式上类似某个语类,但是内容却属于另一个语类。比如以日记的形式做的却是广告,这就是典型的跨语类现象,或语类侵殖现象,或互文性现象。在语类划分的问题上,很多学者都持多元观点(方琰 1998; 2002)。

23.4 以语类为基础的英语写作教学模式

23.4.1 模式

参考斯卡达马利亚(Marlene Scardamalia)和贝瑞特(Carl Bereiter)的

知识-转换模式(Scardamalia & Bereiter 1987),根据上面有关的语类理论框架,笔者和方艳华(2002)提出一个以语类为基础的英语写作教学模式:

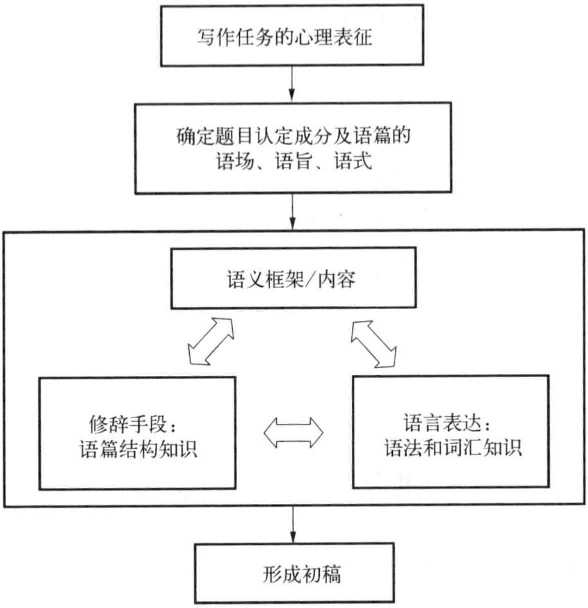

图 23-2 语类为基础的英语写作教学模式(方琰、方艳华 2002)

23.4.2 模式剖析

在此模式中,写作者应首先建立一个写作任务的心理表征,由此引向确定题目认定成分并分析语场、语旨、语式,从而确定写作任务和语类及其结构。若写作任务是"resume",题目认定成分很可能有"the name of the writer","the place where the writer has studied and worked, etc."。这些题目认定成分将激活记忆,搜索与该题目有关的活动和事实。与此同时,写作任务也应引向已选题目的语场、语旨、语式的确定。上面一节讨论的语类语境配置理论,为预测语类及其结构潜势和写作的语义/内容打下了基础,也为修辞手段和语言的运用定下了基调。又如:从写作任务"state your opinion on fast food",可以产生出对"state one's opinion"语类的选择,其必要成分包括 the statement of an opinion ^ giving evidence ^

inference。而修辞手段方面的要求是“清晰、衔接、有说服力”。修辞手段很可能包括对 thematic structure 和 cohesive devices 的灵活运用。总之,内容、修辞手段和语言运用这三个成分互相交互,促使写作者选择所需要的表达方式来完成写作任务。在这里,语言的表达方式取决于要说的内容,即内容→语言的运用;另一方面,语言的使用可能成功地完成内容确定的目的,但也可能不能完成。这往往是由于写作者的英语水平有限引起的。由于语言上的困难,写作者不得不选择不合适的表达方式(Ammon 1985),也就是说语言上和修辞上的问题会影响内容的表达。

在开始写作前,有一个内容、修辞、语言三个成分自上而下的交互过程,写作者应把内容列成一个大纲,注明修辞上的要求;在起草阶段也要注意它们之间的相互交往,直到做出选择,落在笔头上。修改草稿、编辑的过程中,这三方面的交互仍在继续,直到最后完成写作。而语类知识在整个过程中,一直起着纲领性的作用。还应当指出,它们之间的相互交往通常会受到文化背景和写作者心理状态的制约。比如,汉语的语篇逻辑与英语的语篇逻辑会有很大的不同(苏宁 1999)。又如,如果一个作者对某个题目很有兴趣,那么他的写作动机就会比较高,而且上面的三个因素的互交也会更加积极(Ammon 1985)。

此模式是以语类为基础的,它既重视过程也注重产出,所以比其他路子有一定的优越性。

模式首先要求写作者在正确地表征写作任务之后,必须选择所需的语类。这就要求写作者在开始写作时,脑子里储存足够的有关这个语类的知识。因此教师有必要让学生熟悉各种不同语类以及它们的结构。特别要引导学生学会对语类三要素的分析。

在交互过程中,三种知识都必须调动起来。为此,教师可能需要在教学工作中,注重写作课的筹划,以便帮助学生激活思维、产生语篇结构、选择所需的语言表达方式,以便使写作更容易驾驭(Silva 1993)。一般说来,语言在内容和修辞手段的实现方面,是一个瓶颈。显然,语言表达方式会随着不同的写作任务而不同,但是用来表达修辞要求的语言手段一般来说是有限的,也是比较稳定的,特别对于开始学习或处于中等阶段的学习者来说更是如此。教师有必要花一定的时间,向学生介绍实现某些语类可能使用的修辞手段,必要时可以配以各种练习。

当然,不可能对内容、修辞、语言这三个方面给予同样的注意,可以有步骤地引导学生起草各种写作任务。比如,一篇作文的重点是列出内容的框架，下一篇可以是训练对语言的运用（Silva 1993）。在开始阶段，可以在课堂上进行讨论，分析语境三要素，确定语境配置和语类，分析该语类的必要成分和其他成分，接着让学生勾勒出它的语类结构及写作大纲（在教学中，应尽量避免使用语言学术语），然后逐渐让学生讨论针对该语类可能使用的修辞手段和语言表达方式。从中级阶段开始，除了继续做上面的练习之外，还应当完成全篇文章。在这个阶段，特别是高级阶段，应当注意跨语类问题（方琰、方艳华 2002）。

以上所有这些从实践中发展出来的理论和教学模式，都对我们的英语写作教学研究和实验有着很大的启示。

23.5 以语类为基础的英语写作教学实践

23.5.1 调查研究

从 2005 年 9 月至今，我们以语类为理论基础的英语写作教学实践已经走过了十几个年头。我们在这里简单地向同仁们汇报整个实验的过程，希望得到批评和指正，也希望与其他院校的同仁们分享我们的收获。

首先汇报我们做的三个调查：写作教材、受试学生和写作课任课教师。

23.5.1.1 教材调查

我们在 2005 年，针对 1994 年 1 月至 2004 年 12 月间由国内外语教学与研究出版社、上海外语教育出版社、高等教育出版社、大连理工大学出版社、西安交通大学出版社和清华大学出版社 6 家重要出版社，出版发行的适合我国高校学生使用的 21 套英语写作教材，在编写原则、教学内容、教学重点三个方面进行了分析（蔡慧萍 2005），发现：(1) 当时已经出版的英语写作教材大都比较重视写作知识的教授，往往忽视了培养学生分析语篇的能力，编写原则仍然带有指令性和控制性，而且教学内容经常出现重复现象;(2)教材中所体现出来的语类意识淡薄,教材所涉及的语类不够广泛,绝大多数教材只把记叙文、描写文、说明文和议论文的写作作为教材的主要内容。对所涉及的语类写作指导也很少将该语篇的交际目的联系起来,“忽视了文章总是为一定的交际目的而写的,总在一定的语境中显示出自己的交际功能”(高芳 2002)这一事实。总之,绝大多数英语写作教材过于注重英语写作知识与技巧的教授,教学内容的重点以词、句子居多,写作教材的语类覆盖面不广,教材中不重视对语类意识的培养。

23.5.1.2 学生调查

我们采用问卷的调查方式。调查问卷、调查对象、详细的数据和素材分析方法、调查结果的详情不再重复,请参阅蔡慧萍、方琰 2006 年的论文《英语写作教学现状调查与思考》。这里只做简单的回顾。

调查问卷由笔者设计,于 2004 年 12 月在浙江海洋学院(2016 年更名“大学”)英语专业的 30 名大三学生中进行了一次预测。之后,笔者对预测的问卷结果进行了翔实的统计和分析,并对问卷调查的内容进行了调整,于 2005 年 6 月又分别在国内三所高校,发放 600 份问卷进行更大范围的调查。调查对象以英语专业本科生为主(335 人,占 62%),同时也调查了部分非英语专业本科生(98 人,18%)、硕士研究生以及博士生(分别为 56 人,10%;48 人,10%),参与者均为国内高校学完英语写作课程的大二以上的在校学生。重点是了解师生是否建立了语类意识、学生们的写作情况以及他们对写作课的看法。

我们运用 SPSS 10.1 对收回的 537 份有效问卷中的 22 个单项选择题,进行了描述性和统计学处理,然后分别对 4 个多项选择题运用相同的工具和方法进行单独处理,开放性问题则运用“主题一致”分析法进行了归纳,做出了提及次数(人数)。

通过问卷调查,我们发现喜欢英语写作课的学生数只占受试者的三分之一左右。同时我们还发现,当时学生在英语写作方面感到有困难的比例仍然很高,约有近一半同学表示英语写作有困难。主要集中在以下四个方面:英语词汇量少;不知道不同类型的文章对英语有不同的要求;不知如何下笔或不知写些什么;经常用汉语翻译;还有 7%的同学在语法上有很大问题。

为了了解学生在大学期间学习过的语类是否广泛，我们也设计了一个多项选择题。结果是：学生在大学期间，系统性地学过写说明文，议论文的学生最多，分别占受试学生的 55.3%和 52.7%。其次为个人简历、读书报告、课程论文、通知、叙事。学生普遍没有系统地学习过其他语类，尤其是应用文语类。

本次调查的结果，与蔡慧萍对写作教材调查中发现的结果基本一致：我国高校英语写作教材中，应用文体的涉及面不广，高校学生在大学期间学过的语类也很有限。

23.5.1.3 教师的写作教学状况

有关教师的写作教学方式，我们一共设计了 17 个问题，在清华大学任课教师中进行调研。这 17 个问题均采用单项选择题形式，了解教师在写作教学中是否能体现出较强的语类意识，比如教师是否经常同学生一起讨论不同语类的写作目的、不同语类的文章应包含哪些必要信息，以及可能会出现的语言现象等。调查中我们发现绝大多数教师在上写作课时，经常让学生分析范文的写作优点，也经常让学生分析有缺陷的作文中的问题，上课时也经常按写作的步骤进行教学。调研中还发现，目前写作教学的互动性明显增强，写作教学不再以教师讲解词汇、分析语法为主，而是师生互动式地进行探索性学习，这显然是写作教学中的一大进步。然而调研也发现，目前教师的英语的语类意识还不是很强，还未能运用相关理论来分析各种语类的语篇。比如不经常讨论文章的写作目的，不经常让学生列写作提纲，不经常讨论与作文命题相关的内容和信息，不经常讨论作文结构布局、组织方法，以及可能出现的语言现象等（详情见蔡慧萍、方琰 2006）。

23.5.1.4 调查结果与发现

通过调查与分析，我们发现以下四点：

（1）学生对英语写作教学的满意度低，兴趣不浓，缺少高水平的英语写作教师，外籍教师的写作教学水平也不高。

（2）学生在大学期间接受系统学习的语类不够丰富，教学内容的应用性不够突出，未能体现学以致用的原则。

（3）学生在英语写作中仍然存在着许多困难，英语词汇量少；不知道不同语类的文章在结构、内容以及语言表达上有什么要求，因此不知道该如何下笔；不能用英语思维，更多的是借助于汉语进行翻译写作。

（4）目前高校教师语类分析意识还不是很强，对范文语篇的分析及讨论缺乏理论指导，未能运用有关理论进行语篇分析或习作讲评（蔡慧萍、方琰 2006）。

23.5.2 确定在中国语境下英语专业大学生所需要学习的语类

要确定中国英语专业大学生需要学习的语类，不仅要充分考虑中国的语言环境和学生们的需求，还要领会高等学校外语专业教学指导委员会英语组，2000 年编写出版的《高等学校英语专业英语教学大纲》（以下简称《大纲》）的精神。根据《大纲》要求，学生应"能写各类体裁①的文章，做到内容充实，语言通顺，用词恰当，表达得体"（2000：10）。《大纲》对英语写作课的要求是："英语写作课的目的在于培养学生初步的英语写作能力，包括提纲、文章摘要、短文以及简单的应用文。……如有条件，还应进一步训练学生掌握各种文体及其篇章结构，如描写文，记叙文，说明文和议论文等"（2000：24）。考虑到《大纲》的要求和学生学习常用应用文体的强烈愿望，我们依照从易到难、学以致用的原则，筛选了 18 种常用应用语类，依次为：卡片写作、通知、便条（10 种不同情景下的便条）、求职信、个人简历、求助信、信件（私人信件和公函）、提要写作、书评或读书报告、事件陈述、人物描写、地点描写、议论文、五种运用不同写作方法的说明文，如例证说明文、过程分析说明文、因果分析说明文、比较对比说明文、分类说明文等。对比罗斯和马丁列出的二十几种澳大利亚中学生所学习的语类（Rose & Martin 2006），可以看出，这两组语类有相同的地方，也有相当大的区别。相同之处是，学生们都必须学会英语写作所需要的语类，虽然语类的名称稍有不同。不同的是，为了培养学生的审评和批评能力，

① "体裁"和"语类"都是从"genre"翻译过来的，但两个词汇的意思有些不同。"体裁"着重文学语篇的分类，"语类"比较注重一般日常语篇和社会活动类型的分类。教育部使用的是传统的分类方法，我们认为在语言教学实验中，学生应从应用文开始，再扩展到学习其他"体裁"，因而使用"语类"比较准确。

澳大利亚的学生还要求学写 interpretation 和 critical response。这不仅跟西方文化注重发展个人的独立思考能力有关,也与学生的英语水平有关。他们毕竟是生活在英语的环境当中,虽然是中学生,但他们平均的英语水平比中国大学生要高。另外一点不同的是:他们学习的语类可分为两组,一组是为英语学习拟定的,另一组是为学习其他学科拟定的。我们在其他课程当中没有安排英语写作的内容,虽然看起来这些语类对我们的学生将来的学习和工作也会有很大的作用。目前我们的语类教学还没有深入到这些科目。

23.5.3 教学实验

23.5.3.1 目的、受试、预测、理论

第一年的实验始于 2005 年 9 月,2006 年 7 月结束;第二年的实验于 2007 年夏季学期末完成。第一次实验是探索性的,目的是验证两个假设:(1) 建立语类意识有助于英语写作能力的提高;(2) 该理论同样适用于中国语境中的大学英语写作教学。第二次的实验扩大到了 6 个班,目的在于进一步验证上述两个假设,同时改进教学环节的各个部分,找出实验中的不足之处。现在语类教学法的实践更加成熟,实验已经进行了十一个年头,覆盖了整个二年级 200 多名学生,教学人员已增加到八位,实验的课程从写作课扩展到英语阅读、大学英语、英语视听、英语论文写作课与研究生英语等课程。下面具体汇报我们的教学实践,特别是第一年教学实验的情况。

教学实验的受试者为蔡慧萍所任教的浙江海洋学院英语专业大二学生,共 34 人,实验课程为"英语写作"。为了解受试学生对英语写作的认识以及他们真实的写作水平,我们在教学实验实施前,向他们发放了一个由 15 个调查项目组成的问卷和几个开放性的问题。调查结果显示,学生的建议和要求与我们在《英语写作现状调查与思考》(蔡慧萍,方琰 2006)一文中的调查结果相当一致,主要集中在以下两点:(1) 要求突出教学内容的应用性,教学内容的选取既要考虑到大纲的要求,也要考虑到学生的实际需求。(2) 要求教师多向学生提供各种语类的优秀范文,并要

求教师引导学生从内容、结构以及语言特征等方面学会分析所学的语篇,让学生明白该语篇为什么要这样组织,然后进行大量的课内外的写作练习。

为了更充分了解受试学生在教学实验之前的英语写作水平和存在的主要问题,我们要求受试的 34 位同学在第一节写作课内,写一篇 200 字左右的命题作文。结果发现了以下几个问题:(1) 内容不够切题、不够完整。(2) 结构不严谨、条理不清楚。应用语类理论分析,文章的起始段落应包括目的和背景,而受试者的习作中有 5 篇作文是无头无尾的一段式文章,另有 5 篇为只有开头和主体而无结尾的两段式文章。其余 24 篇作文,从形式上看似乎有开头、主体和结语三大部分,但每一部分的内容都与写作目的不完全吻合。(3) 语法错误多,语言表达不通顺,主要集中在时态、句法、连词、标点符号的误用或不当使用。

总体上看,受试学生在实验开始前审题能力差,语类意识淡薄,写作目的不明确,把握语篇必要语义成分的能力不强,语言表达能力弱,存在着想到什么就写什么,或能写什么就写什么的现象。

我们将 18 种语类(见 4.2)安排在两个学期进行,共计 32 个教学周,每周 2 学时,共 64 学时。第一学期以常用应用文语类写作为主,第二学期主要教学四大主要语类(描写文、叙述文、说明文、议论文)的写作。《大纲》中提到的论文写作,安排在四年级的后续课程"高级英语写作"中进行重点训练。

我们应用系统功能语言学为基础的语类教学路子作为教学实验的指导理念,包括"高级英语写作":其各个结构部分的教学也同样以语类结构潜势理论为指导理论。具体地说,我们的教学实验注重语篇语类的分析和课堂教学步骤的设计。课堂教学步骤的设计,我们参考了罗瑟里的"课堂学习的循环步骤"(Rothery 1994)以及笔者和方艳华的写作教学模式(方琰、方艳华 2002);语篇语类的分析,我们主要采用韩茹凯的"GSP"(H & H 1985)理论,也借鉴马丁的"SST"(1985)所描述的步骤和阶段的划分方法。

23.5.3.2 课程学习的步骤

我们重新设计了英语写作课的课堂教学步骤。考虑了中国学生的学习语境,我们采用的语类教学法,共由七个教学步骤组成:学前写作(prewriting）→ 课堂讨论（classroom discussion）→ 范文评析（sample commentary）→自我修正（self-revision）→小组交流（group interaction）→课外练习与自我评析（after class practice and self-evaluation）→教师评阅（teacher's evaluation，包括当面评改）。每一个教学步骤都有明确的目的。学前写作是学生建立“写作任务心理表征”（方琰、方艳华 2002）的过程，让学生思考这个语类有关的各种问题，特别是有关内容的选择和结构方面的问题；通过课堂讨论，使学生明了写作目的、语篇在社会交际中的作用、交际双方的关系、语篇的必要成分、内容的展开形式以及语言使用上的特征，以便建立起语类意识，逐步培养学生的语篇分析能力；通过范文评析，学生可以对比自己的写作初稿，发现存在的问题，可以更加深刻地认识语类结构的重要性，也可以实际了解什么是内容充实、结构合理、语言通顺、表达得体的好作文；自我修改初稿，学生可以找出自己写作中的问题，并针对性地加以改进；小组交流可以让学生们取长补短，逐渐学会帮助别人修改作文，同时也提高自己的写作和评判能力；课后练习与学生自我评析可进一步培养学生对语篇的分析能力；通过教师的评阅，特别是当面评改，学生可以全面了解自己取得的进步以及存在的问题。每一个语类的教学步骤在编写的教材《语类-过程英语写作》（2012）中都有详细描述，如想了解详情，敬请参阅。

与罗瑟里的“课堂学习的循环步骤”相同，这七个步骤的共同目的都是为了构建所学语类的语场（building field）、建立语类意识（building up genre awareness）。而且每个步骤又有各自的目的：“课堂讨论”、“范文评析”（相当于罗瑟里的“解构”）、“自我修正”、“课外练习与自我评析”（相当于罗瑟里的“独立构建”）这四个步骤都是为了掌握所学的语类语篇，而“课堂讨论”和“小组交流”（相当于罗瑟里的“共同建构”）是学会用批评性的眼光审视所学的语类语篇的问题。在整个写作过程中要求学生思考以下几个问题：（1）写作目的是什么？（2）交际双方是什么关系？（3）该语篇是属于什么语式？是为口头阅读还是书面阅读而写？（4）哪些应该是必要成分？哪些是可选成分？（5）语篇中的各种成分是如何组织及表达的？内容按照什么顺序展开的？“课堂讨论”和“小组讨论”步骤还可思考：（6）你觉得这篇习作有哪些主要问题？这几个问题都是按照 GSP 理论设计出来的。

23.5.3.3 语类的分析

每种语类的教学,我们都应用韩茹凯的 GSP 理论进行语篇分析。这里仅选取十个语类的语义成分的组合和排列顺序作为例子,以说明我们的分析方法(其余的语类的分析和例子,请参阅“教材”)。

(1) Cardwriting: Date ^ salutation ^ short message ^ complimentary close ^ signature;

(2) Notice writing: heading ^ body [purpose ^ detailed information] ^ organizer or signature ^ date;

(3) Business letter: heading ^ inside address ^ salutation ^ body [purpose and expectation] ^ complimentary close ^ signature;

(4) Resume writing: personal information ^ objective ^ education background ^ work or professional experiences ^ (awards/honors/interests) ^ references;

(5) News report writing: head ^ lead ^ body [elaboration and background] ^ conclusion (secondary material);

(6) Abstract writing (arranged in one of the following sequences):

a) (background) ^ purpose ^ scope/main content ^ (method) ^ results ^ (conclusion) ^ (recommendations or implication);

b) (background) ^ scope/main content ^ purpose ^ (method) ^ results ^ (conclusion) ^ (recommendations or implication);

c) purpose ^ (background) ^ (method) ^ scope/main content ^ results ^ (conclusion) ^ (recommendations or implication);

(7) Narration of an event: orientation ^ record of the event [who, what, when, where, how, why] ^ coda;

(8) Description of a place: (orientation) ^ detailed features [location ^ area ^ population ^ landscape ^ local customs ^ local specialties ^ history] (which to be chosen depends on the writing purpose) ^ coda;

(9) Cause-effect essay: introduction (the thesis statement, getting your reader to ask why or so what) ^ causes and/or effects of a certain event (depending on the writing purpose) ^ coda (making a conclusion or a summary);

（10）Argumentation essay：introduction [clarifying the controversy and stating your viewpoint] ^ body [sufficient evidence to support your point of view or refute the opposing views by using examples, facts, statistic findings, or personal experiences and observations] ^ conclusion/coda (restatement of your thesis)。

（注：有必要说明这些语义成分的排列符号：① 我们使用了韩茹凯的“成分”(element)来分析语篇的语义成分；② 在[ ]之内的成分(比如，在“body”内的成分)相当于罗斯的“Phase”或“阶段”，也可称为“子成分”；③ 在( )之内的成分属于可选成分。）

通过几个教学步骤反复分析和对比、分析学生自己所写的几稿的语篇和范文的语篇语义结构，学生逐步掌握了语篇语类分析方法。

在我们的教学七个教学环节或步骤中有一个特别的环节：教师评阅。这个步骤有两种形式：书面批改和当面批改。我们在下一节将比较详细地介绍这个环节。

23.5.3.4 教师评阅

无论哪种形式，我们都会依照在整个写作过程中要求学生思考的五六个问题（见 23.5.3.2）进行评阅，不仅要评阅学生习作的语法和词汇的用法，更要评阅习作的内容，即语义结构（语义成分、成分的顺序和排列等）中出现的问题。仅举一例（“教材”中，每一课都对一篇习作有详细的评阅。）。

这是一篇学生写的“抱怨”公函，因篇幅所限，习作略。这里只提及教师的评论。这位教师提出了四点评议：第一点关于写作目的：“This letter looks like a complaint letter and the writer's writing purpose is relatively clear. The writer complained ... However, the writer failed to obey (follow) the Westerners' thinking pattern and did not put the necessary semantic elements of the writing purpose at the very beginning. Instead he expressed it at the end of the letter, which is most likely influenced by his Chinese thinking mode.” 第二点和第三点分别讨论作者与阅读者的社会关系和公函的书写方式和格式，指出这封公函在这两方面的不足和问题。第四点回顾了公函的语义结构，详细列出了它应有的语义成分及它们的排列顺序，同时指出这篇习作在这方面的问题。（评阅原文，请参阅“教材”

第 69 页。)

当面批阅是我们教学环节中重要的一环。教师每周利用一个下午的时间,对三分之一的学生进行面对面的交流,以了解他们在学习中的困难,当面反馈习作中的问题,并鼓励学生看到自己的进步。学生对这种评阅方式非常赞赏。

语篇的写作当然必须重视语言的训练。考虑到我们的学生已经在中学几乎系统学习过所有的语法现象,因此我们根据所学习的语类,加强与这个语类有密切关系的语法内容的练习,更重视没有学习过的语法项目和修辞手段的训练。

23.5.3.5 语言训练

根据所学的语类,我们安排了语言训练项目(请参阅“教材”每一课的“Language Tips and Practice”)。这里仅举几例:

(1)“Card writing”这个语类,我们注重训练学生“祈使句”中“may”“wish”“hope”“with”的语法概念和使用方法;

(2)“Business letter”语类,要求学生的习作遵循七个“C”开头的词汇:completeness、concreteness、clarity、conciseness、courtesy、correctness和consideration(详情,请参阅“教材”)。我们不仅厘清各个词的概念,举例做具体说明,还安排了相关练习。

(3)“News report writing”语类,要求学生:*a*)学会根据不同的场合选择恰当的词汇组篇;*b*)能区别和逐渐学会运用正式语言和非正式语言;*c*)区别词汇的本意(denotation)和引申意义(connotation)。

(4)对“Narration of an event”语类,我们着重讲解和练习:*a*)各种过去时态的用法;*b*)表示时间顺序的词汇;*c*)描述事件和动作的动词。

(5)对“Description of a place”语类,要求学生学会:*a*)各种现在时态的用法;*b*)具体的描写感官的词汇以及比喻手段,以使描写更加生动;*c*)描述地方的具体词汇和用语。

(6)对“Division and classification essay”,我们安排了“衔接”(Cohesion)语法手段概念的讲解及练习,包括弄清它的语法概念,让学生学会使用各种连接词、过渡词、代词衔接、重复衔接等衔接手段;

(7)对“Process analysis”语类,我们列出了常用的表示时间顺序的词汇和表示重要性顺序的词汇,并附大量练习。

(8) 在"Cause and effect"的教学中,除了练习表示原因和效果的词汇外,还引进了"名词化"(nominalization)的语法概念和修辞手段的用法。这是一个新的语法项目,对它的掌握是写作成熟化的标志(Halliday 1985),为课程论文和毕业论文写作打下基础。

(9) 对"Argumentation essay",主要讨论、练习"主题句"(topic sentence)的概念及其作用。

(10) 对"Book report",通过"主位-述位"衔接模式和主位类型的讨论,进一步提高学生对衔接理念的理解和衔接手段的运用能力。

23.5.3.6 实验结果与分析

经过一学年的教学实践,我们发现实验班的学生发生了以下几个变化:

(1) 对写作课的兴趣变浓了。实验班中除 2 个同学表示不太喜欢英语写作课外,其余 32 个同学(94.1%)都明确表示喜欢或非常喜欢这种理念下的英语写作课程。写作不再是一个痛苦的过程,而是一种快乐的体验。

(2) 写作速度变快了。课程结束前,学生参加期终考试。绝大多数同学在开考一小时后就答完了卷并自信地纷纷交卷。显然,实验班的学生不再有不知如何入手的苦恼,从侧面反映了他们的写作能力提高了。

(3) 学生所学到的语类更加丰富了。学生不仅仅系统地学习了四大常用语类(描写文、记叙文、说明文和议论文)的写作,而且还学习了十几种常用应用语类的写作,充分体现了学以致用的原则。

(4) 学生的审题能力和对语篇的分析评价能力、自主写作意识明显提高。大多数的学生能够对英语作文从内容、结构、组织方式以及语言表达四个方面进行评价。厚厚的写作专用本上,可以看见学生对自己习作的批注以及修改稿。因课程涉及了近二十种语类写作,每个学生平均写了 50 篇左右的不同语类的语篇,包括初稿、修改稿和定稿。

一年结束前,我们在实验班的同学们中做了调研,反映相当好;而且在全国英语专业四、八级测试中写作的成绩高于全国高校平均水平,对于一个二级院校这是一个很好的成果(蔡慧萍、方琰 2007)。

然而,我们也发现了以下两个问题。

(1) 纸质教材或讲义只能提供极有限的范文,使学生过于依赖教师提供的范文。

(2) 教师对学生众多习作的批阅工作应接不暇。由于学生写作任务多,写作热情高涨,绝大多数学生都希望自己的作文能得到老师的认真批改。

有鉴于此,我们对第二轮教学实验在技术层面上进行了革新。我们借鉴了清华大学杨永林教授基于数字化教学理念的写作训练系统(杨永林等 2004),建立了我们自己的计算机写作语料库,还建立了我们的写作网站 http://61.153.216.116/ec3.0/C115/Course/Index.htm,为学生提供了更多的范文,以提高他们自主学习的能力。

这些年来我们不断修正和调整原来的教案和教学环节,教学队伍也不断扩大,教学质量得到进一步提高。2014 年 9 月,我们的写作教学系列成果荣获了浙江省政府颁发的省教学成果二等奖。

23.6 结论和启示

我们的实验验证了实验前做的两个假设:(1) 建立语类意识有助于英语写作能力的提高;(2) 该理论同样适用于中国语境中的大学英语写作教学,虽然教学需要根据中国的语境和各个院校的具体情况,在教学环节和方法上做适当调整。实验证明,语类教学路子在浙江海洋学院(已更名为浙江海洋大学)的写作课教学中取得了成功,不仅提高了这门课的教学质量,也提高了任课教师的理论水平和教学水平。我们认为,教学实验的成功有几个必需的条件:(1) 明确了以语类理论作为教学实验的指导理念;(2) 必须得到相关单位领导的大力支持。我们实验的过程中,学院的领导蔡慧萍老师亲自参与指导和实际的教学。她带头做了第一年的教学实验。她很用功,天天凌晨就起来备课、阅读相关的理论书刊、撰写教案。那一年,笔者和蔡老师几乎每天电子邮件来往,由笔者写出示范教案,并帮助她修改其教案,有时一课要修改多次;(3) 有一支团结、勤奋、不懈进取的教学队伍。

现在教学实践仍在进行,还需要全体参与教学的老师不断总结、积累经验,不断改进教学理念和教学方法,发现和解决新出现的问题,不断继续巩固写作课的教学成果,期待在听、说、读和视听教学中也取得好的成绩。

虽然我们将语类理论应用于写作教学已有十几个年头,但是由于各种原因,笔者原本的一些想法并未完全得到实现。本来笔者希望学生在二年级基本掌握语类写作路子之后,进一步加强对各种说明文和议论文的写作能力,并在三年级学习写作更多的语类,特别要学会写作各门课程的课程论文,甚至学写文学作品,目的是培养学生的跨语类分析能力和写作能力。然后在四年级上学期继续用语类理论,专门培训学生的毕业论文写作能力。这样,学生在三年半的学习期间,写作不断线,而且都以语类为基础理论学习写作,为毕业论文的写作和以后的就业和进一步的学习打下坚实的基础。但愿这个愿望能早日实现。

参考文献

Ammon, P. 1985. Helping children learn to write in English as a second language: some observation and hypothesis. In Freedman S. W. (ed.), *The Acquisition of Written Language: Response and Review.* Norwood, NJ: Ablex Publishing Corporation.

Badge, R. & G. White. 2000. A process genre approach in teaching writing, *ELT Journal*, (2).

Bakhtin, M. M. 1981. *The Dialogic Imagination* (translated by C. Emerson & M. Holquist). Austin: University of Texas Press.

Bakhtin, M. M. 1986. The problem of speech genres. In M. M. Bakhtin (ed.), *Speech Genres and Other Late Essays* (translated by V. McGee). Austin: University of Texas Press.

Bai, S. 2002. *An Outline of History of China*, Revised Edition. Beijing: Foreign Language Teaching and Research Press.

Bartlett, T. & G. O'Grady. 2017. *The Routledge Handbook of Systemic Functional Linguistics.* London: Routledge.

Bateman, J. A. 2008a. *Multimodality and Genre: A Foundation for the Systematic Analysis of Multi-modal Documents.* London: Palgrave Macmillan.

Bateman, J. A. 2008b. Systemic functional linguistics and the notion of linguistics structure: Unanswered questions, new possibilities. In J. J. Webster (ed.), 2008,

Meaning in Context: Strategies for Implementing Intelligent Applications of Language Studies. London: Continuum. 24 – 58.

Bateman, J. A. 2014. *Text and Image: A Critical Introduction to the Visual/Verbal Divide.* London: Routledge.

Bawarshi, A. 2000. The genre function. *College English* 62(3): 327 – 352.

Bednarek, M. 2006. *Evaluation in Media Discourse: Analysis of a Newspaper Corpus.* London/New York: Continuum.

Bednarek, M. 2007. Polyphony in appraisal: Typological and topological perspectives. *Linguistics and the Human Sciences* 3(2): 107 – 136.

Bednarek, M. 2008. *Emotion Talk Across Corpora.* London/New York: Palgrave Macmillan.

Bednarek, M. & J. R. Martin (eds.). 2010. *New Discourse on Language: Functional Perspectives on Multimodality, Identity and Affiliation.* London: Continuum.

Beebee, T. O. 1994. *The Ideology of Genre: A Comparative Study of Generic Instability.* University Park, PA: Pennsylvania State University Press.

Biber, D. 1998. *Variation Across Speech Writing.* Cambridge: Cambridge University Press.

Berry, M. 1977. *Introduction to Systemic Linguistics.* London: Batsford.

Bhatia, V. K. 1993. *Analyzing Genre: Language in Professional Settings.* London: Longman.

Bowcher, W. 2012. *Multimodal Texts from Around the World: Cultural and Linguistic Insights.* London: Palgrave.

Bowcher, W. L. & B. A. Smith (eds.). 2014. *Systemic Phonology: Recent Studies in English.* London: Equinox.

Brochure copy of *Qingming Shanghe Tu* (Kaifeng: Garden of *Qingming Shanghe Tu*), Printer and publisher unknown.

Brooks, E. & A. Brooks 1998. *The Original Analects.* New York: Columbia University Press.

Bureau of Language Application and Management of Ministry of Education (BLAMME), People's Republic of China, 2004.

Chafe, W. 1976. Givenness, contrasiveness, definiteness, subject, topics and point of view. In C.N. Li (ed.), *Subject and Topic.* New York: Academic Press.

Caffarel, A., J. R. Martin & C. M. I. M. Matthiessen (eds.). 2004. *Language Typology: A Functional Perspective.* Amsterdam: John Benjamins.

Chao, Yuenren. 1968. *A Grammar of Spoken Chinese.* Berkeley & Los Angeles: University of California Press.

Carter, R. & B. Deidre (eds.). 1982. *Literary Criticism.* London: Edward Arnold.

Chinaonline http://www.chinaonlinemusium.com/painting-along-theriver. php (accessed April 10, 2011).

Chomsky, N. 1957. *Syntactic Structures.* The Hague: Mouton.

Chomsky, N. 1965. *Aspects of the Theory of Syntax.* Cambridge, MA: The MIT Press.

Christie, F. (ed.). 1999. *Pedagogy and Linguistic and Social Process.* London: Cassell.

Christie, F. & J.R. Martin. 1997. *Genres and Institutions: Social Practices in the Workplace and School.* London: Cassell.

Chu, C. C. 1997. Aboutness and clause-linking: Two separate functions of topic in Mandarin. *Tsinghua Journal of Chinese Studies*, New Series XXVII., 1: 37 – 50.

Cohen, R. 1988. Do postmodern genres exist? In M. Perloff (ed.), *Postmodern Genres.* Norman: University of Oklahoma Press.

Confucius. *Lunyu* (*The Analects*). Reprinted in about 1978. Qufu: The Cultural Relics Committee of Qufu City.

Coutune, B. 1986. Effective ideation in written text: a functional approach to clarify and exigence. In B. Coutune (ed.), *Functional Approaches to Writing: Research Perspective.* Norwood, NJ: Ablex.

Creel, H. G. 1949. *Confucius: The Man and the Myth.* New York: The John Day Company.

Crystal, D. A. 1991. *Dictionary of Linguistics and Phonetics.* New York: Basil Blackwell.

Crystal, D. 2003. *English as a Global Language.* Cambridge, UK/New York: Cambridge University Press. See also culture.china.com.cn 2010 – 3 – 2 & 2010 – 3 – 24.

Daneš, F. 1964. A three-level approach to syntax. *Travaux Linguistiques de Prague* 1. 225 – 240.

Daneš, F. 1970. On instance of Prague school methodology: functional analysis of utterances and text. In L. G. Paul, (ed.), *Method and Theory in Linguistics.* The Hague: Moutou.

Daneš, F. 1974. Functional sentence perspective and organization of the text. In F.

Daneš (ed.), *Papers on Functional Sentence Perspective.* Prague: Academia.

Daneš, F. (ed.). 1974. *Papers on Functional Sentence Perspective.* Prague: Academia.

Devine, Thomas G. 1986. *Teaching Reading Comprehension: From Theory to Practice.* University of Lowell, U.S.A: Allyn Bacon Company.

Devitt, A. J. 2000. Integrating rhetorical and literary theories of genre. *College English*, *62/6:* 696-718.

Eggins, S. 1994. *An Introduction to Systemic Functional Linguistics.* London: Pinter.

Ellis, J. & J. Ure. 1969. Language varieties: Register. In A. R. Meetham (ed.), *Encyclopedia of Linguistics: Information and Control.* Oxford: Pergamon. 251-259.

Fang, Y. 1989. A tentative study of theme and rheme in Chinese. *Journal of Tsinghua University*, No. 2. 66-72.

Fang, Y. 1990. On subject in Chinese — "subject", "actor' and "theme". In Hu Zhuanglin (ed.), *Language*, *System and Function.* Beijing: Peking University Press. 53-62.

Fang, Y. 1993. A contrastive study of Theme and Rheme structures in English and Chinese. In Keqi Hao, Hermann Bluhme & Renzhi Li (eds.), *Proceedings of the International Conference on Texts and Language Research*, Xi'an: Xi'an Jiaotong University Press.

Fang, Y. 1998. A tentative study of genre. *Foreign languages*, No.1.

Fang, Y. 2003. A critical study of the generic features of *The People's Daily* published during the cultural revolution in China. In Qian J. (ed.), *Linguistics: China Keeping in Pace with the World.* Beijing: Foreign Language Teaching and Research Press. See also culture.china.com.cn 2010-3-2 & 2010-3-24.

Fang, Y. 2006. Constructing a harmonious world — linguistic studies on the Analects of Confucius. *The Journal of English Studies* (4).

Fang, Y. 2007. A study of topical theme in Chinese. In Jonathan J. Webster (ed.), *Meaning in Context — Strategies in Implementing Intelligent Applications of Language Studies.* London and New York: Continuum.

Fang, Y. 2011. A systemic functional perspective on the growth of Chinese. In Huang Guowen et al. (eds.), *Studies in Functional Linguistics and Discourse Analysis* (III). Beijing: Higher Education Press.

Fang, Y. 2012. A multisemiotic analysis of a Chinese long scroll painting. In Wendy

Bowcher (ed.), *Multimodal Texts from Around The World: Cultural and Linguistic Insight. Basingstoke, England: Palgrave Macmillan.*

Fang, Y. & Ai X. 1995. Analysis of thematic progression in Chinese discourse, *Journal of Foreign Language Research*, 2. 20 – 24.

Fang, Y et al. 2001. *Evaluations of Episodes in English Classic Films.* Beijing: Tsinghua University Press.

Fang, Y., E. McDonald, Cheng M. 1995. On theme in Chinese from clause to discourse. In Hasan and Fries (eds.), *On Subject and Theme.* Amsterdam: John Benjamins.

Fang, Y. & Shen M. 1997. A functional trend in the study of Chinese. In Hu Z. & Fang Y. (eds.), *Advances in Functional Linguistics in China.* Beijing: Tsinghua University Press.

Fang, Y. & J. Webster. 2014. *Developing Systemic Functional Linguistics: Theory and Application.* London: Equinox.

Fairclough, N. 1989. *Language and Power.* London: Longman.

Fairclough, N. 1995. *Critical Discourse Analysis.* London and NY: Longman.

Fawcett, R. 1980. *Cognitive Linguistics and Social Interaction: Towards an Integrated Model of a Systemic Functional Grammar and the Other Components of an Interacting Mind.* Heidelberg: Julius Gross.

Fillmore, C. J. 1968. The case for case. In E. Bach and R. T. Harms (eds.), *Universals in Language.* New York: Holt, Rinehart & Winston. 1 – 88.

Firbas, J. 1964. On defining the theme in functional sentence perspective, *Travaux Linguistiques de Prague* 1. 267 – 280.

Firbas, J. 1987. On two starting points of communication. In R. Steel and J. Threadgold (eds.), *Language Topics: Essays in honor of Michael Halliday*, Vol. I.

Fingarette, H. 1972. *Confucius: The Secular as Sacred.* New York: Harper & Row.

Firth, J. R. 1957a. A synopsis of linguistic theory, 1930 – 1955. In *Studies in Linguistic Analysis* (Special Volume of the Philological Society). London: Blackwell. 1 – 31. [Reprinted in F. R. Palmer, 1968. Selected papers of J. R. Firth 1952 –1959. 168 – 205, London: Longman.]

Firth, J. R. 1957b. *Papers in Linguistics, 1934 – 1951.* London: Oxford University Press.

Firth, J. R. 1957c. Ethnographic analysis and language with reference to Malinowski's views. In R. W. Firth (ed.), *Man and culture: An Evaluation of the Work of Bronislaw Malinowski.* London: Routledge and Kegan Paul. 93 – 118. [Reprinted in F. R. Palmer, 1968. *Selected Papers of J. R. Firth 1952 – 1959.* London: Longman. 137 – 167.]

Forman, J. & R. Jone. 1999. The genre of the Harvard Case method, *Journal of Business and Technical Communication* 13/4: 373 – 400.

Fowler, R. 1991. *Language in the News: Discourse and Ideology in the Press.* London & New York: Routledge.

Fries, P. H. 1981. On the status of Theme in English: Arguments from discourse. *Forum Linguisticum*, 6.1, 1 – 38.

Fries, P. H. 1992. The structuring of information in written English text. *Language Sciences* 14.4, 4614 – 4688.

Fries, P. H. 1992. Themes, methods of development and texts. A paper presented at the 19th International Systemic-Functional Congress (ISFG), held in July 1992 at Macquarie University, Sydney, Australia.

Gao, H. 1984. Focus in the information structure of English and Chinese, *Foreign Language Teaching and Research* 1. 7 – 13.

Garcia, A., W. J. Sullivan, & S. Tsiang. 2017. *An Introduction to Relational Network Theory.* London: Equinox.

Gleason, H. A. Jr. 1965. *Linguistics and English grammar.* New York: Holt, Rinehart & Winston.

Gleason, H. A. Jr. 1968. *Contrastive Analysis in Discourse Structure*, *Monograph Series on Languages and Linguistics*, 21 (Georgetown University Institute of Languages and Linguistics). [Reprinted in Makkai & Lockwood 1973: 258 – 276].

Gong, Q. 1987. *History of Chinese Grammar.* Beijing: Language and Culture Press.// 龚千炎. 1987. 中国语法学史稿. 北京: 语文出版社.

Gregory, M. 1967. Aspects of varieties differentiation. *Journal of Linguistics* 3. 177 – 198.

Gregory, M., & S. Carroll. 1978. *Language and Situation: Language Varieties and Their Social Contexts.* London: Routledge & Kegan Paul.

Gumperz, J. 1968. The speech community. In *International Encyclopedia of the Social Sciences.* New York: Macmillan.

Guo, X. 1999. *Sociolinguistics in China.* Nanjing: Nanjing University Press.

Guo, X. 2006. On the research of 'Huayu'. *Applied Linguistics*, 2. 22 – 28.

Halliday, M. A. K. 1961. Categories of the theory of grammar, *WORD* 17.3. 241 - 292. [Reprinted in J. J. Webster (ed.), *On grammar*. (Vol. 1 in *The Collected Works of M. A. K. Halliday*). London: Continuum. 37 - 94.]

Halliday, M. A. K. et al. 1964. *Linguistics Sciences and Language Teaching*. London: Longman.

Halliday, M. A. K. 1964 Syntax and the consumer. In *Georgetown Monograph Series in Languages and Linguistics*, 17. Georgetown, D. C.: Georgetown University Press. [Reprinted in Halliday & Martin, (eds.). 1981. *Readings in Systemic Linguistics*. London: Batsford. 21 - 28; and in J. J. Webster (ed.), 2003. *On language and linguistics*. (Vol. 3 in *The Collected Works of M. A. K. Halliday*). London: Continuum. 36 - 49.]

Halliday, M. A. K. 1966. Lexis as a linguistic level. In C. E. Bazell, J. C. Catford & M. A. K. Halliday (eds.), *In memory of J. R. Firth*. London: Longman. 148 - 162. [Reprinted in J. J. Webster (ed.), 2002. *On grammar*. 158 - 172 (Vol. 1 in *The Collected Works of M. A. K. Halliday*). London: Continuum.]

Halliday, M. A. K. 1967a. Notes on transitivity and theme in English: Part 1, *Journal of Linguistics*, 3.1. 37 - 81. [Reprinted in J. J. Webster (ed.), 2005. *Studies in English language*. (Vol. 7 in *The Collected Works of M. A. K. Halliday*). London: Continuum. 5 - 54.]

Halliday, M. A. K. 1967b. Notes on transitivity and theme in English: Part 2, *Journal of Linguistics*, 3.2. 199 - 244. [Reprinted in J. J. Webster (ed.), 2005. *Studies in English language*. (Vol. 6 in *The Collected Works of M. A. K. Halliday*). London: Continuum. 55 - 109.]

Halliday, M. A. K. 1967c. *Intonation and Grammar in British English*. The Hague: Mouton.

Halliday, M. A. K. 1968. Notes on transitivity and theme in English: Part 3, *Journal of Linguistics* 4.2, 179 - 215. [Reprinted in J. J. Webster (ed.), 2005. *Studies in English Language*. (Vol. 6 in *The Collected Works of M. A. K. Halliday*). London: Continuum. 110 - 153.]

Halliday, M. A. K. 1969. Options and functions in the English clause. *Brno Studies in English* 8. 81 - 88. [Reprinted in Halliday & Martin (ed.), 1981. *Readings in Systemic Linguistics*. London: Batsford. 138 - 145.]

Halliday, M. A. K. 1970a. Functional diversity in language, as seen from a consideration of modality and mood in English, *Foundations of Language*, 6(3):

322 – 361. [Reprinted in part as "Modality and modulation in English". In G. Kress (ed.), 1976. *Halliday: System and function in language*. Oxford: OUP 189 – 213; and in J. J. Webster (ed.), 2005. *Studies in English language*. (Vol. 6 in *The Collected Works of M. A. K. Halliday*). London: Continuum. 164 – 204.]

Halliday, M. A. K. 1970b. *A Course in Spoken English: Intonation.* London: Oxford University Press.

Halliday, M. A. K. 1970c. Language structure and language function, In J. Lyons (ed.), *New Horizons in Linguistics.* Harmondsworth: Penguin. 140 – 165. [Reprinted in J. J. Webster (ed.), 2002. *On grammar*. (Vol. 1 in *The Collected Works of M. A. K. Halliday*). London: Continuum. 173 – 195.]

Halliday, M. A. K. 1973. *Exploration in the Functions of Language.* London: Arnold.

Halliday, M. A. K. 1975. Language as social semiotic. In A. Makkai & V. B. Makkai (eds.), *The First LACUS Forum.* Columbia, S.C.: Hornbeam Press. 241 – 292. [Reprinted in J. J. Webster (ed.), 2007. *Language and society*. (Vol. 10 in *The Collected Works of M. A. K. Halliday*). London: Continuum. 169 – 201.]

Halliday, M. A. K. 1977. Text as semantic choice in social contexts. In T. van Dijk & J. Petofi (eds.), *Grammars and Descriptions*. Berlin: Walter de Gruyter.

Halliday, M. A. K. 1978. *Language as Social Semiotic: The Social Interpretation of Language and Meaning*. London: Edward Arnold.

Halliday, M. A. K. 2002. Modes of meaning and modes of expression: Types of grammatical structure, and their determination by different semantic functions. In D. J. Allerton, E. Carney & D. Holcroft (eds.), *Function and Context in Linguistics Analysis: Essays Offers to William Haas.* Cambridge: Cambridge University Press. 57 – 79. [Reprinted in J. J. Webster (ed.), *On grammar*. (Vol. 1 of *The Collected Works of M. A. K. Halliday*) London: Continuum. 196 – 218.]

Halliday, M. A. K. 1983. 在北京外国语学院学员报告录音.

Halliday, M. A. K. 1985. *An Introduction to Functional Grammar.* London: Edward Arnold. [Revised 2nd edition 1994; revised 3rd edition, with C. M. I. M. Matthiessen 2004; revised 4th edition, by C. M. I. M. Matthiessen 2014].

Halliday, M. A. K. 1985/1994. *A Short Introduction to Functional Grammar.* London: Edward Arnold.

Halliday, M. A. K. 1992. A systemic interpretation of Peking syllable finals. In Tench 1992: 98 – 121. [Reprinted in J. J. Webster (ed.), 2005. *Studies in Chinese Language*. (Vol. 8 in *The Collected Works of M. A. K. Halliday*). London:

Continuum. 294 – 320.]

Halliday, M. A. K. 1994. An *Introduction to Functional Grammar* (2nd edition). London: Edward Arnold.

Halliday, M. A. K. 1998. Things and relations: regrammaticizing experience as technical knowledge. In J. R. Martin and R. Veel (eds.), *Reading Science: Critical and functional perspective on discourse of science.* London & New York: Routledge.

Halliday, M. A. K. 2002. Computing meaning: Some reflections on past experience and present prospects. In G. W. Huang & Z. Y. Wang (eds.), *Discourse and Language Functions.* Beijing: Foreign Language Teaching and Research Press. 3 – 25. [Reprinted in J. J. Webster (ed.) 2005. *Computational and quantitative studies.* (Vol. 6 in *The Collected Works of M. A. K. Halliday*). London: Continuum. 239 – 267.]

Halliday, M. A. K. 2002. Linguistic studies of text and discourse. In *The Collected Works of M. A. K. Halliday.* London & New York: Continuum.

Halliday, M. A. K. 2003a. *On Language and Linguistics.* London & New York: Continuum.

Halliday, M. A. K. 2003b. Written language, standard language, global language. *World Englishes*, Vol. 22: 405 – 418.

Halliday, M. A. K. 2003c. Language as code and language as behaviour: A systemic-functional interpretation of the nature and ontogenesis of dialogue. Originally in R. Fawcett, M. A. K. Halliday, S. M. Lamb & A. Makkai (eds.), *The Semiotics of Language and Culture*, Vol. 1: Language as social semiotic. London: Pinter, 1984. 3 – 35. [Reprinted in J. J. Webster (ed.), *The language of early childhood.* (Vol. 4 in *The Collected Works of M. A. K. Halliday*). London: Continuum. 227 – 250.]

Halliday, M. A. K. 2004. *The Language of Science* (Vol. 5 in *The Collected Works of M. A. K. Halliday*). London: Continuum.

Halliday, M. A. K. & C. M. I. M. Matthiessen. 2004. An *Introduction to Functional Grammar*, 3rd revised edition. London: Edward Arnold.

Halliday, M. A. K. 2005. *Studies in Chinese Language.* London & New York: Continuum.

Halliday, M. A. K. 2008a. Working with meaning: Towards an appliable linguistics. In J. J. Webster (ed.), *Meaning in Context: Strategies for Implementing Intelligent Applications of Language Studies.* London: Continuum. 7 – 23.

Halliday, M. A. K. 2008b. *Complementarities in Language.* Beijing: The Commercial

Press.

Halliday, M. A. K. 2008c. Working with meaning: Towards an appliable linguistics. In J. J. Webster, (ed.) *Meaning in Context.* London & New York: Continuum.

Halliday, M. A. K. 2014. Some systemic functional reflexions on the history of meaning. In Fang Yan & J. J. Webster (eds.), *Developing Systemic Functional Linguistics.* London: Equinox.

Halliday, M. A. K. & W. S. Greaves. 2008. *Intonation in the Grammar of English.* London: Equinox.

Halliday, M. A. K. & R. Hasan. 1976. *Cohesion in English.* London: Longman.

Halliday, M. A. K. & R. Hasan. 1980. Text and context: Aspects of language in a social-semiotic perspective. *Sophia Linguistica* VI. Tokyo: The Graduate School of Languages and Linguistics & the Linguistic Institute for International Communication, Sophia University, 1980. [New edition published as M. A. K. Halliday & R. Hasan. 1985. *Language, Context, and Text: Aspects of language in a social-semiotic perspective.* Geelong, Victoria: Deakin University Press] [Republished in 1989 by Oxford University Press].

Halliday, M. A. K., & R. Hasan. 1985. *Language, Context and Text: Aspects of Language in a Social-Semiotic Perspective.* Victoria: Deaken University Press.

Halliday, M. A. K. & J. R. Martin. 1993. *Writing Science: Literacy & Discursive Power.* London: Falmer; and Pittsburgh: University of Pittsburgh Press.

Halliday, M. A. K. & C. M. I. M. Matthiessen. 1999. *Constructing Experience through Meaning: A Language-based Approach to Cognition.* London and New York: Cassell.

Halliday, M. A. K., A. McIntosh & P. Strevens. 1964. *The Linguistic Sciences and Language Teaching.* London: Longman (Longman's Linguistics Library).

Halliday, M. A. K. & J. J. Webster (eds.). 2009. *Continuum Companion to Systemic Functional Linguistics.* London: Continuum.

Hasan, R. 1977. Text in the systemic-functional model. In W. Dressler (ed.). *Current Trends in Text Linguistics.* 228 – 246. Berlin: Walter de Gruyter.

Hasan, R. 1987. The grammarian's dream: Lexis as most delicate grammar. In M. A. K. Halliday & R. P. Fawcett (eds.), *New Developments in Systemic Linguistics*, Vol. 1: *Theory and Description.* London: Pinter, 1987. 184 – 211. [Reprinted in R. Hasan, *Ways of Saying: Ways of Meaning*, 1966. (*Selected Papers of Ruqaiya Hasan* edited by C. Cloran, D. Butt & G. Williams). London: Cassell. 73 – 103].

Hasan, R. 2009. *Semantic Variation: Meaning in Society and Sociolinguistics.* London: Equinox, (Vol. 2 in the *Collected Works of Ruqaiya Hasan*, edited by J. J. Webster).

Hasan, R. & P. Fries. 1995. *On the Subject and Theme: A Discourse Functional Perspective.* Amsterdam & Philadelphia: John Benjamins Publishing Company.

Hasan, R., C. M. I. M. Matthiessen & J. J. Webster (eds.). 2005. *Continuing Discourse on Language: A Functional Perspective*, Vol. 1. London: Equinox.

Hasan, R., C. M. I. M. Matthiessen & J. J. Webster (eds.). 2007. *Continuing Discourse on Language: A Functional Perspective.* Vol. 2. London: Equinox.

Hasan, R. & P. Fries. 1995. *On Subject and Theme.* Amsterdam: John Benjamins.

Henry, A. & R. L. Roseberry. 1997. An investigation of the functions, strategies and linguistic features of the introductions and conclusions of essays, *System* 25/4: 479 - 495.

Henry & Roseberry, 1998. An evaluation of a genre-based approach to the teaching of EAP/ESP writing, *TESOL Quarterly* 32/1: 147 - 156.

Hjelmslev, L. 1947. Structural analysis of language, *Studia Linguistica* 1. 69 - 78.

Hjelmslev, L. 1961. *Prolegomena to a Theory of Language.* Madison, WI: University of Wisconsin Press.

Hockett, C. F. 1958. *A Course in Linguistics.* New York: MacMillan.

Hood, S. 2004. *Appraising Research: Taking a Stance in Academic Writing.* University of Technology Sydney PhD. Thesis.

Hooker, R., 2005. http://www.friesian.com/confuci.htm.

Hu, Y. 1987. *Modern Chinese.* Shanghai: Shanghai Education Press.

Hu, Z. L. 1994. *Cohesion and Coherence of Discourse*, Shanghai: Shanghai Education Press.

Hu, Z. L. & Jiang, W. 2006. *Linguistics: A Course Book.* Beijing: Peking University Press.

Huang, Y. 1986. Lexical reiteration in modern standard Chinese, *JCLTA*, No. 3.

Huang G. 2001. *Theory and Practice of Discourse Analysis: A Study in Advertising Discourse*, Shanghai: Shanghai Foreign Language Education Press.

Hymes, D. (ed.), 1972. *Directions in Sociolinguistics: The Ethnography of Communication.* New York: Holt, Rinehart & Winston.

Hymes, D. 1974. *Foundations in Sociolinguistics: An Ethnographic Approach.* Philadelphia, PA: University of Pennsylvania Press.

Hymes, D. 1962/1974. The ethnography of speaking. In B. G. Blount (ed.) *Language, Culture and Society*. Cambridge, MA: Winthrop.

Hyon, S. 1996. Genre in three traditions: implications for ESL. *TESOL Quarterly*, 30. 4.

Hyon, S. 2000. Book review on *Genre, Frames and Writing in Research Settings*. *English for Specific Purposes*, 19: 189 – 192.

Interview — M. A. K. Halliday May 1986 by Gunther Kress, Ruqaiya Hasan and J.R. Martin. In *Social Semiotics*, Vol. 2, 1992.

Interviewing Professor M. A. K. Halliday by Hu Zhuanglin and Zhu Yongsheng, 2010(6).

Jovanovich, Makkai A., & D. Lockwood. 1973. *Readings in Stratificational Linguistics*. University Park, AL: Alabama University Press.

Kachru, B. B. 1989. Teaching World Englishes. *Indian Journal of Applied Linguistics*, 15: 1.

Kress G. & T. Leeuwen 1996/2006. *Reading Images: The Grammar of Visual Design*. London: Routledge.

Lamb, M. & A. Makkai (eds.) 1984. *The Semiotics of Language and Culture: Vol. 1: Language as Social Semiotic*, 3 – 35. London: Pinter. [Reprinted in J. J. Webster (ed.) 2003. *The language of early childhood*. (Vol. 4 in *The Collected Works of M. A. K. Halliday*). London: Continuum. 227 – 250.]

Lamb, S. 1966. Epilegomena to a theory of language. *Romance Philology*, 19: 531 – 573.

Language Application Institute of China National Language Committee (LAICNLC), 2006.

Lei J. P. 1982. 孔雀开屏 (*Kongque Kai Ping*, the peacock opens its 'screen').

Lei, S. 2008. *Commentary on 'Along the River During the Qingming Festival'*. Jinan: Shandong Pictorial Press.

Leitch, S. & J. Roper. 1998. Genre colonization as a strategy: a framework for research and practice. *Public Relations Review*, 24(2).

Lemke, J. L. 1985. Ideology, intertextuality and the notion of register. In J. D. Benson & W. S. Greaves (eds.), *Systemic Perspectives on Discourse, Vol. 1: Selected theoretical papers from the 9th International Systemic Workshop*. Norwood, NJ: Ablex. 275 – 294.

Lemke, J. L. 1995. *Textual Politics: Discourse and Social Dynamics*. London:

Taylor & Francis.
Lemke, J. L. 1998. Multiplying meaning: visual and verbal semiotics in scientific text. In J.R. Martin & R. Veel (eds.), *Reading Science*. London: Routledge. 87 - 113.
Leys, S. 1998. *The Analects of Confucius.* Emeryville, CA: Alibris.
Li, C. N. & S. A. Thompson. 1978. Grammatical relations in languages without grammatical signals. *Proceedings of the Twelfth International Congress of Linguists*, edited by Wolfgang U. Dressler and Wolfgang Meid. Innsbruck. 687 - 691.
Li, C. N. & S. A Thompson. 1981. *Mandarin Chinese: A Functional Reference Grammar.* Berkeley: University of California Press.
Li, Eden. 2007. *Systemic Functional Grammar of Chinese.* London: Equinox.
Li, J. 2005. A study of the translation of synonyms in Chinese borrowed from other languages. *Applied Linguistics*, Nov. 4: 32 - 36.
Li, Y. C. 1971. *An Investigation of Case in Chinese Grammar.* South Orange, NJ: Seton Hall University Press.
Li, Y. 2002. The applications of "Theme" in translation studies. *Foreign Languages and Their Teaching*, 7: 19 - 22.
Lockwood, D. G. 1972. *Introduction to Stratificational Linguistics.* New York: Harcourt, Brace.
Long, R. 1981. *Transitivity in Chinese.* M. A. Dissertation. Sydney: University of Sydney.
Lu, J. 2006. A tentative commentary on the purpose of language studies. *Applied Linguistics*, 2: 7 - 12.
Lü S. 1984. Issues on Grammatical analysis in Chinese. In *Proceedings of Chinese Grammar.* Beijing: The Commercial Press.
Lü S. 1990. *Selected Works of Lü Shuxiang.* Beijing: The Commercial Press.
Lyons, J. 1981. *Language and Linguistics.* New York: Cambridge University Press.
Ma, J. 1983. *Ma's Grammar.* Beijing: The Commercial Press.
Malinowski, B. 1923. The problem of meaning in primitive languages, Supplement I to C. K. Ogden & I. A. Richards, *The Meaning of Meaning.* New York: Harcourt Brace & World. 296 - 336.
Malinowski, B. 1935. *Coral Gardens and Their Magic.* London: Allen & Unwin.
McDonald, E. 1992. Outline of a functional grammar of Chinese for teaching purposes. *Language Sciences* 14.4, 435 - 458.
Mei, R. & Wang L. 1995. *Advanced English* (Students' Book 1). Beijing: Foreign

Language Teaching and Research Press.

Martin, J. R., Language, register and genre. 2001. In F. Christie (ed.), 1984. *Children Writing: Reader*. 21 – 30. Geelong: Deakin University Press. (ECT language studies: Children writing) [Revised for A. Burns & C. Coffin (eds.), *Analyzing English in a Global Context: A Reader*. Clevedon: Routledge. 149 – 166. (Teaching English Language Worldwide)] [Japanese translation by Hiro Tsukada published in *Shidonii Gakuha no SFL: Haridei Gengo Riron no Tenkai*. Tokyo: Liber Press. 2005.] [Further revised for C. Coffin, T. Lillis & K. O'Halloran (eds.), 2010. *Applied Linguistics Methods: A Reader*. London: Routledge. 12 – 32.] [Reprinted in J. R. Martin, 2012. *Genre studies*. 47 – 68. (Volume 3 in *The Collected Works of J. R. Martin*, edited by Wang Zhenhua). Shanghai: Shanghai Jiao Tong University Press.]

Martin, J. R. 1985. Process and text: two aspects of semiotics. In J. Benson and W. Greaves, *Systemic Perspectives on Discourse*, Vol. I. 248 – 274.

Martin, J. R. 1992. *English Text: System and Structure*. Philadelphia/Amsterdam: John Benjamins Publishing Company.

Martin, J. R. 1996. Types of structure: Deconstructing notions of constituency in clause and text. In E. H. Hovy & D. R. Scott (ed.), *Computational and Conversational Discourse: Burning Issues — An Interdisciplinary Account*. 39 – 66. Heidelberg: Springer. (NATO Advanced Science Institute Series F — Computer and Systems Sciences, Vol. 151) [Reprinted in J. R. Martin, 2010. *SFL Theory*. 343 – 385. (Vol. 1 in *The Collected Works of J. R. Martin*, edited by Wang Zhenhua). Shanghai: Shanghai Jiaotong University Press.]

Martin, J. R. 1999. Modelling context: The crooked path of progress in contextual linguistics (Sydney SFL). In M. Ghadessy (ed.), *Text and Context in Functional Linguistics*. 25 – 61. Amsterdam: Benjamins. (CILT Series IV) [Reprinted in J. R. Martin, 2012. *Genre studies*. 222 – 247. (Vol. 3 in *The Collected Works of J. R. Martin*, edited by Wang Zhenhua). Shanghai: Shanghai Jiaotong University Press.]

Martin, J. R. 2001. A context for genre: Modelling social processes in functional linguistics. In J. Devilliers & R. Stainton (eds.), *Communication in Linguistics: Papers in Honour of Michael Gregory*. 287 – 328. Toronto: GREF. (Theoria Series 10). [Reprinted in Martin, 2012. *Genre studies*. 248 – 277.] (Volume 3 in *The Collected Works of J. R. Martin*, edited by Wang Zhenhua). Shanghai: Shanghai Jiao Tong University Press.

Martin, J. R. 2001. Cohesion and texture. In D. Schiffrin, D. Tannen & H. Hamilton (eds.), *Handbook of Discourse Analysis.* Oxford: Blackwell. 35 – 53.

Martin, J. R. 2010. Discourse semantics. In Wang Zhenhua (ed.), *The Collected Works of J. R. Martin*, Vol. 2. Shanghai: Shanghai Jiao Tong University Press.

Martin, J. R. 2011. Multimodal semiotics: Theoretical challenges. In S. Dreyfus, S. Hood & M. Stenglin (eds.), *Semiotic Margins: Reclaiming Meaning.* London: Continuum. 243 – 270. [Reprinted in J. R. Martin & Y. J. Doran, 2015c: 352 – 78]

Martin, J. R. 2012. *Language in Education* (Vol. 7 in *The Collected Works of J. R. Martin*, edited by Wang Zhenhua). Shanghai: Shanghai Jiao Tong University Press.

Martin, J. R., (ed.). 2013a. *Interviews with Michael Halliday: Language Turned back on Himself.* London: Bloomsbury.

Martin, J. R. 2013b. Modelling context: Matter as meaning. In C. Gouveia & M. Alexandre (eds.), *Languages, Metalanguages, Modalities, Cultures: Functional and Socio-discursive Perspectives.* Lisbon: BonD & ILTEC. 10 – 64.

Martin, J. R. 2014. Evolving systemic functional linguistics: Beyond the clause. *Functional Linguistics* 1.3. http://functionallinguistics.springeropen.com/

Martin, J. R. 2017. Meaning beyond the clause: Co-textual relations. In X. T. Cheng, X. W. Peng & J. J. Webster (eds.), *The Making of Meaning: Grammar, Society and Consciousness.* London: Bloomsbury.

Martin, J. R. In Press. One of three traditions: Genre, functional linguistics and the 'Sydney School'. In N. Artemeva & A. Freedman (eds.), *Trends and Traditions in Genre Studies.* Edmonton, AB: Inkshed Publications.

Martin, J. R. & Y. J. Doran (eds.). 2015a. *Grammatics.* London: Routledge. (Critical concepts in linguistics: Systemic functional linguistics, Vol. 1).

Martin, J. R. & Y. J. Doran (eds.). 2015b. *Grammatical Descriptions.* London: Routledge. (Critical concepts in linguistics: Systemic functional linguistics, Vol. 2).

Martin, J. R. & Y. J. Doran (eds.). 2015c. *Around Grammar: Phonology, Discourse Semantics and Multimodality.* London: Routledge. (Critical concepts in linguistics: Systemic functional linguistics, Vol. 3).

Martin, J. R. & Y. J. Doran (eds.). 2015d. *Context: Register and Genre.* London: Routledge. (Critical concepts in linguistics: Systemic functional linguistics, Vol. 4).

Martin, J. R. & Y. J. Doran (eds.). 2015e. *Language in Education.* London: Routledge. (Critical concepts in linguistics: Systemic functional linguistics,

Vol. 5).

Martin, J. R. & K. Maton. 2013. Cumulative knowledge-building in secondary schooling, *Special Issue of Linguistics and Education*, 24.1.

Martin, J. R. &C. M. I. M. Matthiessen, Systemic typology and topology. 1990. In F. Christie (ed.), *Literacy in Social Processes: Papers from the Inaugural Australian Systemic Linguistics Conference*, held at Deakin University, 345 – 383. Darwin: Centre for Studies in Language in Education, Northern Territory University. 1991. [Reprinted in Martin, 2010. *SFL Theory*. 343 – 385. (Vol. 1 in *The Collected Works of J. R. Martin*, edited by Wang Zhenhua). Shanghai: Shanghai Jiaotong University Press. 167 – 215].

Martin, J. R., C. M. I. M Matthiessen, &C. Painter. 1997. *Working with Functional Grammar*. Santa Cruz, CA: Arnold.

Martin, J. R. & D. Rose. 2003/2007. *Working with Discourse: Meaning Beyond the Clause* (2nd revised edition). London: Continuum.

Martin, J. R. &D. Rose. 2008. *Genre Relations: Mapping Culture*. London: Equinox.

Martin, J. R. & P. White. 2005. *The Language of Evaluation: Appraisal in English*. London: Palgrave Macmillan.

Martin, J. R., Y. S. Zhu & P. Wang. 2013. *Systemic Functional Grammar: A Next Step into the Theory — Axial Relations*. Beijing: Higher Education Press.

Martinec, R. 2005. Topics in multimodality, in R. Hasan, J. Webster and C. Matthiessen (eds.), *Continuing Discourse on Language*, Vol. 1. London: Equinox.

Mathesius, V. 1929. Zur saptzperspektive im modernen English. In *Archiv für das Studium der Neueren Sprachen und Literature*.

Matthiessen, C. 1992. Interpreting the textual metafunction. In M. Davies &L. Ravelli (eds.). *Advances in Systemic Linguistics*. London: Pinter.

Matthiessen, C. 1993. Instantial system and logogenesis, a paper presented at SF Symposium, Hangzhou (June 17 – 20).

Matthiessen, C. 1995. THEME as a resource in ideational 'knowledge' construction. In M. Ghadessy (ed.), *Thematic Developments in English Texts*. London: Pinter.

Matthiessen, C. M. I. M. 1995. *Lexicogrammatical Cartography: English Systems*. Tokyo: International Language Sciences.

Matthiessen, C. M. I. M. 2007a. The 'architecture' of language according to systemic functional theory: Developments since the 1970s. In R. Hasan et al. (eds.), *Continuing Discourse on Language: A Functional Perspective*, Vol. 2. London:

Equinox. 505 – 562.

Matthiessen, C. M. I. M. 2007b. Lexicogrammar in systemic functional linguistics: Descriptive and theoretical developments in the "IFG" tradition since the 1970s. In R. Hasan et al. (eds.). London: Equinox. 765 – 858.

Matthiessen, C. M. I. M. 2009. Ideas and new directions. In M. A. K. Halliday & J. J. Webster (eds.), *Continuum Companion to Systemic Functional Linguistics*, 12 – 58. London: Continuum.

Matthiessen, C. M. I. M. 2010. Systemic functional linguistics developing. *Annual Review of Functional Linguistics*, 2. 64 – 93. Beijing: Higher Education Press.

Matthiessen, C. M. I. M. 2014. Extending the description of process type within the system of transitivity in delicacy based on Levinian verb classes. *Functions of Language*, (21): 2.

Matthiessen, M.I.M. 2014. Appliable Discourse Analysis. In Fang Y. & J. Webster (eds.), *Developing Systemic Functional Linguistics: Theory and Application.* London: Equinox, 138 – 208.

Matthiessen, C. M. I. M. 2015. Halliday on language, In J. J. Webster (ed.), *The Bloomsbury Companion to M. A. K. Halliday.* London: Bloomsbury. 137 – 202.

Matthiessen, C. M. I. M & J. Bateman. 1991. *Text Generation and Systemic-Functional Linguistics.* London: Pinter.

Matthiessen, C. M. I. M. & M. A. K. Halliday. 2009. *Systemic Functional Grammar: A First Step into the Theory.* Beijing: Higher Education Press.

Matthiessen, C. M. I. M., K. Teruya & M. Lam. 2010. *Key Terms in Systemic Functional Linguistics.* London: Continuum.

Matthiessen, C. M. I. M., K. Teruya & C. Wu. 2008. Multilingual studies as a multi-dimensional space of interconnected language studies, In J. J. Webster (ed.), *Meaning in Context: Strategies for Implementing Intelligent Applications of Language Studies.* London: Continuum. 146 – 220.

Meng, Z. & Wei, J. 2008. *The Chinese Seal.* Beijing: Contemporary China Publishing House.

Miller, C. 1984. Genre as social action, *Quarterly Journal of Speech*, 70. 2.

O'Halloran, K. L. 2004. *Multimodal Discourse Analysis: Systemic Functional Perspectives.* London and New York: Continuum.

O'Halloran, K. L., S. Tan & K. L. E. Marissa. 2015. Multimodal semiosis and semiotics. In J. J. Webster (ed.), *The Bloomsbury Companion to M. A. K.*

Halliday. London: Bloomsbury. 386 – 411.

O'Toole, M. 1994. *The Language of Displayed Art*. London: Leicester University Press. [2nd revised edition, Routledge, 2011].

Ouyang, J. 2010. 名闻遐迩的稀世珍宝——《清明上河图》传世之谜 (*Mingwenxia'er de xishizhenbao — Qingming shanghe tu chuanshi zhimi*), *Archives World* 5: 28 – 31.

Ouyang, X. 1986. *Clause Complex in Chinese*. M. A. Dissertation. Sydney: Linguistics, University of Sydney.

Painter, C. & J. R. Martin. 2011. Intermodal complementarity: modelling affordances across image and verbiage in children's picture books. In Huang Guowen, et. al. (eds.), *Studies in Functional Linguistics and Discourse Analysis III*. Beijing: Higher Education Press.

Painter, C., J. R. Martin & L. Unsworth. 2013. *Reading Visual Narratives: Image Analysis in Children's Picture Books*. London: Equinox.

Palmer, F. R. (ed.). 1970. *Prosodic Analysis*. London: Oxford University Press.

Pappas, C. C. & B. S. Pettegrew. 1998. The role of genre in the psycholinguistic guessing game of reading. *Language Arts*, 75. 1.

Qian, J. 2003. *Linguistics: China in Pace of the World*. Beijing: Foreign Language Teaching and Research Press.

Qu, C. 1999. The Y-movements and its inverted order in English from the perspective of focus and topic in Chinese. *Journal of Learning*, No.4: 1 – 13.

Reid, T. B. W. 1956. Linguistics, structuralism, philology. In *Archivum Linguisticum*, 8.

Richards, J., et al. (eds.). 1985. *Longman Dictionary of Applied Linguistics*. N P: Longman Group Limited.

Rong Bao Zhai Press. 1999. *The Scroll of 'Along the River During the Qingming Festival'*.

Rose, D. 2004. Sequencing and pacing of hidden curriculum: How indigenous children are left out of the chain. In J. Muller, B. Davies & A. Morais (eds.), *Reading Bernstein, Researching Bernstein*. London: Routledge Falmer.

Rose, D. 2006. Reading Genre: a new wave of analysis. *Linguistics and the Human Sciences*, 2: 1.

Rose, D. & J. R. Martin. 2012. *Learning to Write, Reading to Learn: Genre, Knowledge and Pedagogy in the Sydney School*. London: Equinox.

Rothery, J. 1994. *Exploring Literacy in School English (Write it right Resources for Literacy and Learning)*. Sydney: Metropolitan East Disadvantaged Schools Program.

Sampson, G. 1980. *Schools of Linguistics: Competition and Evolution.* London: Hutchinson.

Saville-Troike, M. 1989. *The Ethnography of Communication.* Oxford: Blackwell.

Saussure, F. 1916/1966. *Course in General Linguistics.* New York: McGraw-Hill.

Scheffcyzyk, A. 1986. Function. In T. A. Sebeok (ed.), *Encyclopedia Dictionary of Semiotics.* Berlin/New York: Mouton de Gruyter.

Scollon, R. 2000. Generic variation in news stories in Chinese and English: acontrastive study of five days' newspaper. *Journal of Pragmatics*, 32.

Sengupta, S. et al. 1999. Supporting effective English communication within the context of teaching and research in a tertiary institute: developing a genre model for conscientious raising. *English for Specific Purposes*, (18).

Silva, T. 1993. Toward an understanding of a distinct nature of L2 writing: the EST research and its implications. *TESOL Quarterly*, (4).

Simon-Vandenbergen, A-M., M. Taverniers & L. J. Ravelli (eds.). 2003. *Grammatical Metaphor: Systemic and Functional Perspectives.* Amsterdam: John Benjamins.

Sinclair, J. McH. 1966. Beginning the study of lexis. In C. E. Bazell, J. C. Catford & M. A. K. Halliday (eds.), *In Memory of J. R. Firth.* London: Longman. 410-430.

Sinclair, J. McH. 1991. *Corpus, Concordance, Collocation.* Oxford: Oxford University Press, 1991.

Souza, L. M. de. F. 2010. Interlingual Re-instantiation: A Model for a New and More Comprehensive Systemic Functional Perspective on Translation. PhD thesis. Santa Catarina: Universidade Federal de Santa Catarina.

Shen, J. 1999. *On Irregularity and Markedness.* Nanchang: Jiangxi Education Press.

Shi, Y. 2001. Subject and topic in Chinese, *Journal of Language Research*, No. 2. 82-91.

Spencer, J. & M. J. Gregory. 1964. An approach to the study of style. In N. E. Enkvist, J. Spencer & M. J. Gregory (eds.), *Linguistics and Style.* London: Oxford University Press. 57-105.

Steiner, E. & C. Yallop (eds.). 2001. *Exploring Translation and Multilingual Text Production: Beyond Content.* Berlin/New York: Mouton de Gruyter.

Swales, J. 1981. Aspects of article introductions, *Aston ESP Research Report No. 1.* Birmingham: Language Studies Unit, University of Aston in Birmingham.

Swales, J. 1990. *Genre Analysis: English in Academic and Research Settings.* Cambridge: Cambridge University Press.

Tam, M. A. 1979. Grammatical Description of Transitivity in Mandarin Chinese with Special Reference to the Correspondences with English Based on a Study of Texts in Translation, Ph.D. Dissertation. London: University of London.

Tang, T. Charles. 1972. *A Case Grammar of Spoken Chinese.* Taipei: Hai-Guo Book Company.

Tench, P. (ed.). 1992. *Studies in Systemic Phonology.* London: Pinter Publishers.

Teng, S. 1975. *A Semantic Study of Transitivity Relations in Chinese.* Berkeley: University of California Press. Reprinted 1982 in Taipei: Student Book Co.

Teruya, K. & C. M. I. M. Matthiessen. 2015. Halliday in relation to language comparison and typology, In J. J. Webster (ed.), *The Bloomsbury Companion to M. A. K. Halliday.* London: Bloomsbury. 427 – 452.

Thompson, G. 1996/2004. *Introducing Functional Grammar.* London: Arnold.

Thompson, S. A. 1992. *Functional Grammar, International Encyclopedia of Linguistics II*, Ed. by W. Bright. Oxford: Oxford University Press.

Thompson, S. 1994. Frameworks and context: a genre-based approach to analyzing lecture introductions. *English for Specific Purposes*, 13: 171 – 186.

Thompson, G. (ed.). 2013. *Text & Talk* 33. 4 – 5. (Special Issue in Honour of Michael Halliday).

Thompson, T., W. Boucher, L. Fontaine & D. Schönthal (eds.). 2019. *The Cambridge Handbook of Systemic Functional Linguistics.* Cambridge: Cambridge University Press.

Tucker, G. 2007. Between lexis and grammar: Towards a systemic functional approach to phraseology. In R. Hasan et al. (eds.), *Continuing Discourse on Language: A Functional Perspective.* London: Equinox. 953 – 978.

Trask, R. L. 1993. *A Dictionary of Grammatical Terms in Linguisitcs.* New York: Routledge.

Tsao, F. 1980. *A Functional Study of Topic in Chinese: The First Step Towards Discourse Analysis.* Taipei: Student Book Co. (Reprinted 1988).

Turner, G. J. 1973. Social class and children's language of control. In B. Bernstein (ed.), *Class, Codes and Control 2: Applied Studies Towards a Sociology of*

Language. London: Routledge & Kegan Paul. 135 – 201. (Primary socialisation, language and education).

Ure, J & Ellis, J. 1977. Register in descriptive linguistics and linguistic sociology. In O. Uribe-Villas (ed.), *Issues in Sociolinguistics*. The Hague: Mouton.

Vachek, J. (ed.). 1964. *A Prague School Reader in Linguistics*. Bloomington: Indiana University Press.

Vachek, J. 1966. *The Linguistic School of Prague: An Introduction to Its Theory and Practice*. Bloomington: Indiana University Press.

Ventola, E. 1987. *The Structure of Social Interaction: A Systemic Approach to Semiotics of Service Encounter*. London: Pinter.

Wang, B. 2009. *History of Chinese Painting*. Beijing: Culture and Art Publishing House.

Wang, Li. 1985. *Modern Chinese Grammar*. Beijing: The Commercial Press.

Wang, L. 2006. The internalization of Chinese and its dissemination and maintenance. *Applied Linguistics*, No. 3: 41.

Wang, N. 2004. Comparative literature and globalism: A Chinese cultural and literary strategy, *Comparative Literature Studies*, Vol. 41, No. 4.

Wang, Jiali et al. 1997. *Modern Chinese* (*Xiandai Hanyu*). Beijing: The Commercial Press.

Wang, S. 1998. *A General Introduction to China*. Beijing: Peking University Press.

Webster, J. J. (ed.). 2015. *The Bloomsbury Companion to M. A. K. Halliday*. London: Bloomsbury.

Wen, J. 2005. *Government Work Report at the National People's Congress*. Beijing, China.

Whorf, B. L. 1942/1956. *Language, Thought and Reality: Selected Writings*. Cambridge, MA: The MIT Press.

Wilhelm, R. (tr.). 1931. *Confucius and Confucianism*. London: Harcourt Brace Jovanovich, Inc. Reprinted in 1972 by Routledge & Kegan Paul Ltd.

Wu, Y. 2003. The rise of Huayu as a global language and challenges. *Chinese Language Review*, No. 73.

Wu, Z. 2001. A tentative study on theme-rheme structure in Chinese clause. *Journal of Language Teaching and Research*, No. 3: 11 – 17.

Xiang, Xi. 1993. *A Concise History of Chinese*. Beijing: Higher Education Press.

Xinjingbao (New Capital Newspaper), June 17, 2005.

Xinjingbao, August 17, 2007.

Xu, T. 1990. *On Language.* Changchun: Northeast Normal University Press.

Xu, Z. 2000. *Interpretation of the Analects.* Beijing: The People's Literature Publishing House.

Xu, Z. 2000. *Translation of the Analects* (from the classical Chinese to the modern Chinese). Beijing: The People's Literature Publishing House.

Yang, R. L. 1995. Trends in the teaching of writing. *Language Learning Journal*, (12).

Yang, Y. 2007. *Grammatical Metaphor in Chinese* (PhD thesis). National University of Singapore, unpublished.

Yu, J. 2005. A study of the issues related to new word clusters in the real estate and their entries to dictionaries, *Applied Linguistics*, No. 4, 66-72.

Yu, J. 2006. On Chinese standardization and standardized Chinese, *Applied Linguistics*, No. 3: 26-33.

Zhang, A. 1962. *On 'Along the River During the Qingming Festival'*. Beijing: Zhaohua Art Press.

Zhou, B. 1997. *Along the River During the Qingming Festival and Studies Related to It.* Kaifeng: Henan University Press.

Zhang, B. & Fang M. 1994. On thematic structure in oral Chinese. *Journal of Peking University*, No. 2, 66-71.

Zhang, D. 1992. Text coherence and information structure: On the conditions of text coherence. *Foreign Languages Research*, No. 3.

Zhang, Xi & Liu, R. 2006. On the study of foreign policy on language dissemination to encourage the spread of Chinese. *Applied Linguistics*, No. 1: 39-47.

Zhao, J. 2005. Let our mother tongue go on to the world stage. *Applied Linguistics*, No.3: 28-30.

Zhejiang Daily, July 22nd, 2005.

Zhou, Q. 2005. On the harmony of language. *Applied Linguistics*, No. 3: 24-26.

Zhu, D. 1981. *A Grammar Course.* Beijing: The Commercial Press.

蔡慧萍. 2005. 我国高教英语写作教材的现状调查与思考. 外语与外语教学(6).

蔡慧萍，方琰. 2006. 英语写作教学现状调查与分析. 外语教学(9).

蔡慧萍，方琰. 2007. 语类结构潜势理论与英语写作教学模式实践研究. 外语与外语教学(4).

蔡慧萍等. 2012. 语类-过程英语写作教程. 浙江:浙江大学出版社.

陈脑冲. 1988. 英语主语及其功能探索(A Study of Subject in English and Its Functions). 北京大学英语系硕士学位论文.
陈望道. 1978. 文法简论. 上海:上海教育出版社.
陈望道. 1980. 陈望道语文论集. 复旦大学语言研究室编. 上海:上海教育出版社.
陈望道. 1982. 修辞学发凡. 上海:上海教育出版社.
方琰. 1986. 主位述位初探. 大学英语教学研究(2).
方琰. 1989a. 试论汉语的主位、述位结构. 清华大学学报 4(2).
方琰. 1989b. 试论汉语的主位述位结构——兼与英语的主位述位结构相比较. 大学英语教学与研究(2).
方琰. 1990. 浅谈汉语的主语——主语、施事、主位. 语言系统与功能. 胡壮麟主编. 北京:北京大学出版社.
方琰. 1995. Hasan 的语体结构潜势理论及它对语篇分析的贡献. 外语学刊(1).
方琰. 1998. 浅谈语类. 外国语(1).
方琰. 2002. 语篇语类研究. 清华大学学报(哲学社会学版)17(SL).
方琰. 2003. "文化大革命"中《人民日报》语类的语类特点. 语言学:中国与世界同步. 钱军主编. 北京:外语教学与研究出版社.
方琰. 2005. 系统功能语法与语篇分析. 外语教学(6).
方琰. 2010. 第三十六届国际系统功能语言学大会对中国学者的启示. 中国外语(6).
方琰. 2011. 迈进系统功能语言学的门槛. 系统功能语言学研究群言集. 黄国文等主编. 北京:高等教育出版社.
方琰,曹莉,孙郁根. 2001. 经典影片精彩片段语言评析(*Evaluations of Episodes in English Classic Films*). 北京:清华大学出版社.
方琰, 方艳华. 2002. 以语类为基础的应用文英语写作教学模式. 外语与外语教学(1).
方琰, 高云莉. 2001. 浅谈报刊语类的界定. 语言教学与研究(6).
方琰, 兰青. 1997. Hasan 的语类结构潜势理论在英语应用文写作教学中的应用. 功能语言学在中国的进展. 胡壮麟、方琰主编. 北京:清华大学出版社.
高晨阳. 1994. 中国传统思维方式研究. 济南:山东大学出版社.
高等学校外语专业教学指导委员会英语组. 2000. 高等学校英语专业英语教学大纲. 北京:高等教育出版社.
韩茹凯. 2011. 韩茹凯应用语言学自选集. 北京:外语教学与研究出版社. 2011.
韩茹凯. 2015. 韩茹凯论语言. 北京:北京大学出版社.
胡裕树. 1987. 现代汉语. 上海:上海教育出版社.

胡裕树，范晓. 1985. 试论语法的三个平面. 新疆师范大学学报.
胡壮麟. 1989. 从语义功能角度谈汉语语序. 西安国际应用语言学会议论文.
胡壮麟. 1990. 语言系统与功能. 北京:北京大学出版社.
胡壮麟. 1991. 王力与韩礼德. 北京大学学报(1).
胡壮麟. 1994. 语篇衔接与连贯. 上海:上海外语教育出版社.
胡壮麟等. 1988. 语言学教程. 北京:北京大学出版社.
胡壮麟，朱永生，张德禄. 1989. 系统功能语法概论. 长沙:湖南教育出版社.
胡壮麟，方琰. 1997. 功能语言学在中国的进展. 北京:清华大学出版社.
黄国文. 1998. 语篇分析中的语篇类型研究. 外语研究(2).
黄国文. 2004. 功能语言学与语篇分析. 外国艺术教育研究(功能语言学与语篇分析专号)导读.
黄国文. 2010. 对“胡-朱与 Halliday 访谈”的解读. 中国外语(6).
黄国文,常晨光,廖海青. 2011. 系统功能语言学研究群言集. 北京：高等教育出版社.
黄衍. 1985. 试论英语主位和述位. 外国语(5).
蒋锦彪. 2012. 可游可居——赏析黄公望的《富春山居图》. 群文天地(7).
蒋勋. 2012. 富春山居图. 北京:新星出版社.
黎锦熙. 1954. 新著国语文法. 上海:商务印书馆.
李传全. 1991. High Context：Chinese Language and Culture. 清华大学外语系硕士学位论文.
李临定. 1983. 宾语使用情况考察. 语文研究(2).
李临定. 1984. 施事、受事和句法分析. 语文研究(4).
李临定. 1985. 工具格和目的格. 语法研究和探索(三). 中国语文杂志社编. 北京：北京大学出版社.
李临定. 1994. 主语的语法地位. 李临定自选集. 郑州:河南教育出版社.
李淑静，胡壮麟. 1990. 语气与汉语的疑问语气系统. 语言系统与功能. 胡壮麟主编. 北京:北京大学出版社.
刘鸿绅. 1987. 篇章语言学的发展史及其研究领域. 国外语言学(3—4).
刘宽平. 2003. 提高中国学生英语写作能力的有效途径. 外语教学(6).
罗兴霞. 2004. 哈桑的 GSP 理论与英语写作教学. 政法学刊(6).
鲁川，林杏光. 1989. 现代汉语语法的格关系. 汉语学习(5).
吕叔湘. 1979. 汉语语法分析问题. 北京:商务印书馆.
吕叔湘. 1984. 汉语语法论文集(*Selective Papers of Chinese Grammar*). 北京:商务印书馆.

吕叔湘. 1985. 中国文法要略. 北京:商务印书馆.
吕叔湘. 1990a. 吕叔湘文集第一卷:中国文法要略. 北京:商务印书馆.
吕叔湘. 1990b. 吕叔湘文集第二卷:中国文法要略. 北京:商务印书馆.
吕叔湘. 1992. 歧义举例. 语境研究论文集. 西槙光正编. 北京:北京语言学院出版社.
吕叔湘、朱德熙. 1951. 语法修辞讲话. 北京:中国青年出版社.
马建忠. 1898/1998. 马氏文通. 北京:商务印书馆.
马建忠著, 章锡琛校注. 1988. 马氏文通校注. 北京:中华书局.
孟琮, 郑怀德等. 1987. 动词用法词典. 上海:上海辞书出版社.
庞玉厚, 方琰, 刘世生. 2010. 系统功能语言学的发展和面临的挑战. 外语与外语教学研究(2).
钱军. 2003. 语言学:中国与世界同步. 北京: 外语教学与研究出版社.
钱乃荣. 1990. 现代汉语. 北京:高等教育出版社.
秦秀白. 2000. 体裁教学法评述. 外语教学与研究(1).
申小龙. 1988. 中国句法文化. 长春:东北师范大学出版社.
申小龙. 1991. 中国句型文化. 长春:东北师范大学出版社.
申小龙. 1993. 汉语与中国文化的结构通约. 光明日报 1993 年 12 月 13 日.
石云孙. 1992. 论语境. 语境研究论文集. 西槙光正编,北京:北京语言学院出版社.
王福祥. 1984. 俄语实际切分句法. 北京:外语教学与研究出版社.
王还. 1986. 有关汉外语法对比的三个问题 (Three Issues Concerning the Comparison of the Grammars of Chinese and Foreign Language). 语言教学与研究(1).
王力. 1982. 王力文选(第一卷). 南宁:广西人民出版社.
王力. 1984. 王力文集(第一卷):中国语法理论. 济南:山东教育出版社.
王力. 1985. 中国现代语法. 北京:商务印书馆.
王耀庭. 2014.12.02. www.news.cn.
文炼(张斌), 胡附. 1984. 汉语语序研究中的几个问题. 中国语文(3).
辛斌. 2000. 语篇互文性的批评性分析. 苏州:苏州大学出版社.
徐杰. 1986. 工具范畴和容纳工具范畴的句法结构. 华中师范大学学报(5).
许慎. 1989. 说文解字. 北京:中国书店.
徐盛桓. 1982. 主位和述位. 外语教学与研究(1).
徐盛桓. 1985. 再论主位和述位. 外语教学与研究(4).
杨永林, 罗立胜, 张文霞. 2004. 一种基于数字化教学理念的写作训练系统. 外语电化教学(8).

张传真,张德禄. 1992. 情景—语篇—情景——高年级英语阅读课教改探微. 外语界 46(2):7－10+14.

张德禄. 2002. 论实用文体语类结构潜势. 山东外语教学(1).

张志公. 1982. 现代汉语. 北京:人民教育出版社.

赵秋菊. 2010. 曹春雷. 魅力中国 8(2).

周晓康. 1986. 汉语动词的及物性系统初探,浙江省语言学会 1986 年年会论文.

周晓康. 1990. 从及物性系统看汉语动词的语法—语义结构. 语言系统与功能. 胡壮麟主编. 北京:北京大学出版社.

朱德熙. 1984. 语法讲义. 北京:商务印书馆.

朱德熙. 1985. 语法答问. 北京:商务印书馆.

朱永生. 1992. 汉语市场会话结构研究(Structure of Chinese Service Encounter). 第二届全国话语分析研讨会论文.

朱永生. 1993. 语言・语篇・语境. 北京:清华大学出版社.

作家文摘(第 211 期).

附 录

各章中英文摘要

0

意义至关重要

——系统功能语言学简史

摘　要：本章呈现系统功能语言学(Systemic Functional Linguistics，缩称SFL)简史，以韩礼德1961年刊登于《词》(*Word*)上的论文“语法理论范畴”为出发点，勾勒出SFL发展的关键思想要点。论述聚焦于：(1) SFL被称为“系统”、“功能”以及“系统功能”语言学的原因；(2) SFL如何沿着这个方向，在音系学、词汇-语法学、语篇语义学逐步发展；(3) SFL如何将其视角扩展到语境模式(语域和语类)以及多模态领域(将语言之外的交流模式考虑在内)。文末简述了该理论的最新进展，并对自身定位为“适用语言学”的SFL有关理论和实践的辩证关系，做出自己的评论。

关键词：系统功能语言学；层次；纯理功能；纵轴；语境

Meaning Matters

— A Short History of Systemic Functional Linguistics

Abstract: This chapter presents a brief history of systemic functional linguistics (hereafter SFL), taking Halliday's 1961 *WORD* paper, 'Categories of the theory of grammar', as point of departure. It outlines the key strands of thought which have informed the development of SFL, focusing on (i) why it is referred to as systemic, as functional and as systemic functional, (ii) how it developed this orientation with reference to phonology, lexicogrammar and discourse semantics, and (iii) how it has extended this perspective to models of context (*register* and *genre*) and multimodality (taking into consideration modalities of communication beyond language). The chapter ends with a brief note on recent developments and a comment on the dialectic of theory and practice through which SFL positions itself as an appliable linguistics.

Key words: Systemic Functional Linguistics; stratification; metafunction; axis; context

1

主位和述位初探

摘　要：本章从韩礼德创立的功能语言学的角度出发，讨论主位和述位诸多方面的问题。首先提出了主位和述位的划分、主位的定义、主位的位置等问题；继而回顾了主位-述位理论的创立过程，概述了韩礼德对该理论的发展所做的贡献、主位-述位结构与新信息结构的关系、主位与主语在各种语气小句中的关系以及单项主位、复项主位、句项主位；随后分析了科技英语中主位-述位结构的特点，探讨了科技英语语篇中主位-述位进程模式；最后阐述对英语教学中应用主位-述位结构的一些认识。

关键词：功能语言学；主位；述位；新信息；主语；科技英语

A Study on Theme and Rheme

Abstract: This chapter discusses various issues concerning *Theme* and *Rheme* from the perspective of Functional Linguistics. It begins with the division of

Theme and Rheme, and the definition and the position of Theme, followed by an elaboration on the contributions made by Halliday on the theory of Theme, the relation of the Theme-Rheme structure and the Given-New structure, the relation of Theme and Subject in various mood clauses, and on Simple Theme, Multiple Theme and Clause Theme. After that, it makes an analysis of some distinctive features of the Theme-Rheme structure in scientific English texts, and presents six models of Thematic Progression in texts of this register. Finally, some views on the application of this theory in English teaching are elaborated.
Key words: Functional Linguistics; Theme; Rheme; new information; subject; scientific English

2

浅谈汉语的"主语"

——"主语""施事""主位"

摘　要：本章从韩礼德的功能语言学理论的角度，将汉语与英语做了比较，讨论了汉语的"主语"概念。文中认为，目前汉语语法对主语的定义缺乏科学性，主语担负了太多的语法功能。建议用"主语"表示被（谓语）陈述的对象，用"施事"表示动作者，用"主位"表示信息的出发点，即用三个表示不同功能的术语来代替传统语法中的"主语"。
关键词：功能语言学；主语；施事；主位

A Tentative Study on "Subject" in Chinese

— "Subject", "Actor" and "Theme"

Abstract: This chapter discusses the concept of "Subject" based on the traditional Chinese linguistics from the perspective of Halliday's Functional Linguistics. Comparing Chinese with English, the author argues that the definition of "Subject" derived from the traditional Chinese linguistics lacks scientific basis and that this term takes too many grammatical functions. It

suggests that we could apply three terms — *Subject*, *Doer* and *Theme* to replace the three functions performed by the traditional term "Subject".
Key words: traditional Chinese Linguistics; Functional Linguistics; subject; doer; theme

3

英汉主位-述位结构对比研究△

摘　要：本章从韩礼德对主位和述位的定义出发，首先确定汉语的语法分析有必要引进"主位"概念，继而对汉语和英语的陈述句、疑问句、复合句中的主位成分做了比较分析。
关键词：主位；述位；语法分析；比较研究

A Contrastive Study of Theme and Rheme Structure in English and Chinese

Abstract: The chapter begins with the definition of "Theme" and "Rheme" in English made by Halliday. Then it argues that there is a necessity of introducing the concept of "Theme" to the grammatical analysis of the Chinese language, which is followed by making a comparative study of the thematic elements in declarative, interrogative and complex sentences in the Chinese and English languages.
Key words: theme; rheme; grammatical analysis; comparative study

4

汉语主位进程结构分析

摘　要：本章应用韩礼德关于主位的定义、达内什的主位进程模式理论、钱乃荣关于句群的概念以及方琰等提出的主位-述位链的分析方法，并将马丁的语篇主位和段落主位与达内什关于主位的论述结合起来，选择了

10 篇不同语类的汉语语篇,对其主位进程结构进行了分析。分析结果论证了主位进程结构对形成语篇有着重要贡献。这样的语法分析有助于理解语篇内容和语篇表达内容的手段,也有助于初步领略语篇创作成功的原因。
关键词: 主位;主位进程模式;句群;主位-述位链;语篇主位;段落主位

An Analysis of Thematic Progression in Chinese

Abstract: This chapter has chosen 10 Chinese texts of different genres and analyzed their patterns of thematic progression by following Halliday's definition on theme, Daneš's theory of Thematic Progression, Qian Nairong's concept of sentence cluster and of the Theme-Rheme chain proposed by Fang Yan et. al., and the combination of Martin's concept of text theme and paragraph theme with Danes' theory on theme. It proves that the theory of Thematic Progression makes a significant contribution to the construction of a text. This method of analysis can be helpful in understanding the content of a text, the devices to construct a text as well as the reasons of the success of a text.
Key words: theme; thematic progression; sentence cluster; theme-rheme chain; text theme; paragraph theme

5

汉语主位系统初探[△]

摘　要: 本章分析了 10 篇不同语类的语篇,初步总结出汉语小句和小句复合句的主位网络系统。用于语篇分析的理论主要是韩礼德和他的同事们所代表的功能语言学。文中认为,对汉语主位系统的描述研究有着重要意义:(1) 汉语聚合关系的研究很大程度上受到忽视;(2) 主位系统的产生有助于部分提供汉语分析的语法框架。
关键词: 语篇分析;主位网络系统;功能语言学;汉语小句及小句复合句

A Tentative Thematic Network in Chinese

Abstract: This chapter has generalized the tentative thematic networks of clause and clause complex in Chinese, which is based on the analysis of 10 written texts in various genres. The theory informing the text analysis is that of functional linguistics of various branches but the main theory comes from the one represented by Halliday and his colleagues. The author argues that it is significant to do research in the description of the **Theme** system in Chinese: 1) Paradigmatic study in Chinese has very much been ignored; 2) Working out the **Theme** system will help to provide part of a grammatical framework for Chinese text analysis.
Key words: text analysis; thematic network; functional linguistics; clause and clause complex in Chinese

6

汉语的主位

——从小句到语篇[△]

摘　要：汉语小句结构理论和布拉格功能主义有关小句结构的理论，对汉语小句的分析均做出了很有启发性的贡献，但也都有一定的局限性。本章试图说明应用系统功能语言学理论框架，也许可以更全面解释汉语小句结构。文章探索了突出及物性结构在小句中位置的各种可能性，还应用该理论的多功能观点、主位进程及逻辑-语义关系，解释汉语复合句的主位结构。
关键词：汉语小句及小句复合句结构；系统功能语言学；主位结构；信息结构；及物性系统；主位进程；逻辑-语义关系

On Theme in Chinese

— From Clause to Discourse

Abstract: In this chapter, it is attempted to show that the insights about clause structure embodied in Chinese linguistics and Prague School

Linguistics can be more comprehensively developed within the framework of Systemic-Functional theory. Applying the multifunctional framework of this school in explaining the clause and clause complex structures in Chinese, the author has explored the possibilities of making the transitivity functions prominent in a clause, and also discussed thematic progression and the logic-semantic relations in a clause and clause complex.
Key words: clause and clause complex structure in Chinese; Systemic-Functional Linguistics; thematic structure; information structure; transitivity structure; thematic progression; logic-semantic relation

7

从系统功能语言学的视角 对汉语主题主位的研究△

摘　要：本章首先说明采用功能语言学研究汉语以及选择这个论题的原因，接着讨论了几个与论题相关的问题，包括：（1）阐述传统汉语语言学和功能语言学对汉语小句结构的研究视角；（2）主位的概念；（3）主题主位。主题主位的定义、主题主位的种类、主题主位的功能、主题主位的实现以及主位与语境的关系得到了深入探讨。
关键词：主题；主题主位；传统汉语语言学；功能语言学；小句结构；语境

A Study of Topical Theme in Chinese
— An SFL Perspective

Abstract: In the chapter, the reasons are first stated for taking the functional approach to studying Chinese and for choosing this topic. Then several issues relevant to the study of Topical Theme are addressed: 1) clause structure from both the traditional Chinese linguistics perspective and the functional perspective; 2) the concept of theme; and 3) Topical theme. The definition, types, and functions of Topical Theme, along with the realization of Topical Theme, and the relation between theme and context, are carefully discussed and analyzed.

Key words: topic; topical theme; traditional Chinese linguistics; functional approach; clause structure; context

8

汉语研究的功能倾向△

摘 要:本章旨在论证对汉语研究的一个假设——汉语研究可能一直存在着功能主义倾向。开篇首先厘清了用于论证的功能主义概念,接着勾勒出在汉语语言学研究的四个阶段中功能主义倾向的发展情况,最后对功能主义理论应用于汉语研究的现状做了评论性的总结。

关键词:假设;功能主义倾向;汉语语言学传统;系统功能语法

A Functional Trend in the Study of Chinese

Abstract: The chapter addresses itself to the verification of the hypothesis that a functional trend may exist in the study of Chinese. It begins with the clarification of the concept of functionalism applied in the elaboration, which is followed by the sketching of the development of the functional trend in four periods in the tradition of Chinese linguistic study: the embryonic period, the imitation period, the reform period and the flourishing period. Finally, the chapter makes a summary with a comment on the study of Chinese applying functional theories at present.

Key words: hypothesis; functional trend; tradition of Chinese linguistics; systemic-functional grammar

9

从系统功能语言学的视角观察汉语的演变△

摘 要:本章从系统功能语言学视角,研究汉语发展或进化带来的语言方面的诸多变化。全文首先讨论了语言的性质及韩礼德提出的引起语言变化的因素，其中重点讨论了这些因素产生的汉语系统意义潜势的扩展状况；接着阐述了汉语进化与社会变迁的辩证关系；最后在调查部分清华大学留学生的基础上，预测了汉语未来的发展。研究结论是：汉语已是世界性语言，但是否会成为全球性的语言，取决于中国全面发展的情况。

关键词：系统功能语言学视角；汉语的发展；促使语言扩展的因素；意义潜势；系统的扩展；调查

A Systemic-Functional Perspective on the Growth of Chinese

Abstract: This chapter takes the systemic-functional perspective to study some aspects of the changes brought about by the growth or evolution of Chinese. It first clarifies the nature of language, and then elaborates on factors contributing to the changes or the growth of a language proposed by Halliday in 2003. The focus is put at discussing the expansion of meaning potential along the paradigmatic axis in Chinese resulted from these factors, which is followed by a discussion of the dialectical relation between the evolution of Chinese and social-cultural changes. The chapter finally deals with the prospect on the future development of Chinese based on a survey made among international students of Tsinghua University, which concludes that whether Chinese, being a world language, will become a global language depends on China's development in all aspects.

Key words: systemic functional perspective; growth of Chinese; factors contributing to the expansion of a language; meaning potential; systemic expansion; survey

10

系统功能语法与语篇分析

摘　要：本章首先讨论了系统功能语法的框架，包括语言的层次及其实现关系、纯理功能系统和有关的子系统和功能、语篇分析的两个层面;然后使用“语境-语篇-评论”的分析方法,分析了三个语篇,用来说明系统功能语法对语篇分析的应用价值;最后提出了语篇分析的入项条件选择问题。
关键词: 系统功能语法;语言层次;语篇分析;分析方法;入项条件

Systemic Functional Linguistics and Discourse Analysis

Abstract: The chapter first discusses the framework of Systemic-Functional Grammar, including the levels of language, the relationship of realization between these levels, the system of meta-functions and their sub-systems and functions, and also the two levels for discourse analysis (Halliday; 1985). Then applying the method of “context — discourse — commentary”, the author analyzes three discourses in order to illustrate the applicability of this grammatical framework. Finally it raises the issue of selecting entry conditions for discourse analysis.
Key words: Systemic-Functional Grammar; levels of language; discourse analysis; method of analysis; entry condition

11

系统功能语言学与电影语篇分析[△]

摘　要: 本章试图应用韩礼德的功能语言学,分析和阐释一些经典英语电影语篇。分析涉及两个层次:“理解语篇”和“评价语篇”(韩礼德 1985)。讨论的重点是揭示这些语篇里纯理功能特征的含义。我们发现分析这些纯理功能,有助于理解电影语篇的深刻含义,也有助于理解语篇的语义和文体特征。这是阐释和欣赏电影语篇的重要环节。
关键词: 经典英语电影;功能语言学;语篇分析;纯理功能;阐释;语义和文体特征

Systemic-Functional Linguistics and Film Discourse Analysis

Abstract: This chapter presents an attempt of applying Halliday's Functional Linguistics to the interpretation of some classical English film discourses. The interpretation involves two levels: "the understanding of the text" and "the evaluation of the text" (Halliday 1985). The focus of the discussion is on the revelation of implications of features of meta-functions in these discourses. We have discovered that analysis of the meta-functions may help in disclosing the profound meanings of a film discourse and in understanding the semantic and stylistic features of that discourse, which is essential for the interpretation and appreciation of a film discourse.

Key words: classical English films; Functional Linguistics; discourse analysis; metafunctions; interpretation; semantic and stylistic features

12

经典英语电影精彩对话分析

摘　要：本章延续第 11 章的研究方法，应用系统功能语言学理论，选择、分析了四部美国经典影片(《卡萨布兰卡》《罗马假日》《克莱默夫妇》《金色池塘》)中一些对话的语言特点及其含义，进一步论证了该理论适用于揭示影片的内涵和分析人物的性格。

关键词：美国经典影片；系统功能语言学；对话含义；语言特点

Analysis of Impressive Dialogues in Classical English Films

Abstract: Continuing with the analytical method used in Chapter 11, the author applies the theory of Systemic Functional Linguistics to analyzing some representative dialogues in four classical American films (*Casablanca*, *Roman Holiday*, *Kramer versus Kramer*, and *On Golden Pond*). The

analysis has disclosed some distinctive linguistic features and their implications. It has verified again the applicability of this theory in revealing the profound implied meanings of these dialogues and the vivid description of the characters in the films.
Key words: classical American films; Systemic-Functional Linguistics; implied meanings in a dialogue; linguistic features

13

构建一个和谐的世界

——《论语》的语言学研究[△]

摘　要：本章运用系统功能语言学框架分析了《论语》，论证了这个框架也适用于揭示这部作品一些重要的语义内涵和语言特点，并展现其中有关的基本伦理。在简要介绍了产生这部作品的社会文化背景和情景语境之后，文章将重点放在分析作品的一些词汇和语法特征上，如语言范式和关键词汇的重复、动词过程、投射、情态的特点等。研究认为，这些手段的应用，成功地揭示了作品的要点和性质。文章最后讨论了书中孔子的价值观和伦理观对现实的中国和世界的意义。
关键词：《论语》；系统功能语言学框架；词汇-语法特点；孔子的价值观和伦理观

Constructing a Harmonious World

— Linguistic Studies on *The Analects of Confucius*

Abstract: An illustration is made in this chapter that the systemic-functional linguistic framework can also be applied to the revelation of some important semantic and linguistic features and of some basic ethics of *The Analects*. After giving a brief introduction to the social-cultural environment and situational context "engendering" the book, the author focuses on the linguistic analysis of some of its lexico-grammatical features, such as repetition of linguistic patterns and key words, features of process, projection and modality. The application of these lexico-grammatical means successfully disclose the main gist and characteristics of the book. Finally the chapter discusses the significance of Confucius' values and ethics contained in the book for the present China and world.

Key words: *The Analects*; systemic-functional linguistic framework; lexico-grammatical features; Confucius' values and ethics

14

孔子传记短评的"态度"分析△

摘　要：本章主要对一篇由一位西方学者撰写的有关孔子的短评进行分析，包含若干步骤。全文采取自上而下的分析方法，首先根据韩礼德 1960 年提出的关于文化语境的定义，分析了语篇的文化语境，继而分析了该语篇的情景语境的三个变量；然后，应用评价理论详细分析了该语篇的人际态度特点，具体从判定、欣赏、分级几个方面，分析和评述每个步骤对孔子的态度。研究发现，在此类语篇中没有"感情波动"特点的例子，作者往往从正面或积极的方面，对孔子和他的生平做出"判断"和"欣赏"。这说明语篇作者对孔子的人品及其贡献持有很高的评价；为强化其正面评价，作者采用加强力度和多声道的策略，旨在使读者对孔子持有与作者相同的评价态度。本章最后对这些特点的语义内涵作了综合性的评述。

关键词：孔子；积极语篇分析；评价理论；文化语境；情景语境；态度特征

An Analysis of the "Attitudes" in a Discourse on Confucius

Abstract: Adopting the "top-down" model, the chapter analyzes a discourse on Confucius written by a Western scholar. The genre of the discourse is defined as a biological commentary which divides into several stages. It first discusses the features of its context of culture by referring to Halliday's definition offered in the early 1960's, which is followed by an analysis of the three variables of the context of situation of this discourse. After that, the author elaborates on attitudinal features of the discourse in terms of the theory of appraisal. Concretely, the analysis is made stage by stage from the perspective of judgment, appreciation and graduation. It is found that there is no example of "affect" in this type of discourse, and the judgment and appreciation are mainly made from the positive perspective, which is a demonstration of the high evaluation of the author on both the personality of and contribution by Confucius. In order to strengthen his positive evaluation, the author employs both the strategies of amplification of force and engagement of multiple voices with the aim to align the reader attitudinally into sharing his evaluation of Confucius. Finally, based on these features, the author gives a rather detailed evaluation on the semantic implication of the discourse.

Key words: Confucius; positive discourse analysis; appraisal theory; context of culture; context of situation; attitudinal feature

15

一幅中国长卷画的多符号分析△

摘　要：本章尝试分析800多年前北宋时期张择端创作的中国长卷画《清明上河图》。文章首先说明选用这幅画作为分析素材的原因,并简单阐述用作分析绘画的系统功能语言学理论框架,然后讨论了分析这个多符号意义语篇的目的。分析确认了这个作品的视觉和语言上的语义特点,揭示出不同的符号意义如何共同创造语篇意义,探索了产生这个多符号意义语篇的文化语境,并证实了马丁内克的论点:赋予作品的视觉和语言信息在"很大程度上是社会构建的,又依赖于文化"。

关键词:中国长卷画;清明节;北宋;系统功能语言学;多符号意义分析

A Multisemiotic Analysis of a Chinese Long Scroll Painting

Abstract: This chapter is an attempt to analyze a classical Chinese long

scroll painting ***Along the River During the Qingming Festival*** (《清明上河图》,*qingming shang he tu*), produced by Zhang Zeduan about 800 years ago in the Northern Song Dynasty. It begins with stating reasons to choose this painting as the analytical datum. Then it elaborates on the theory informing the analysis: that of Systemic-Functional Linguistics (SFL). What follows are the discussion of the purposes of analyzing this multisemiotic discourse, and the analysis of this great work of art, which has identified semantic features of visual and verbal modes of this artefact, revealed how the semiotic resources work together to create meanings and explored the cultural context or the "cultural environment" for "engendering" this multisemiosis. Our analysis has verified that meanings "ascribed" to visual and verbal information "are to a large extent socially constructed and culturally dependent".
Key words: Chinese long scroll painting; the Qingming Festival; the Northern Song Dynasty; Systemic-Functional Linguistics; multisemiotic analysis

16

中国长卷画的多符号分析框架与参数

摘　要:本章使用两幅多符号意义长卷画——《富春江居图》为主,《清明上河图》为辅,作为分析的素材,比较详细讨论了基于系统功能语言学的理论框架和框架中的各个参数,并应用这些参数分析了绘画本身表达的概念功能意义、人际功能意义和语篇功能意义。文章继而分析了《富春江居图》的题词、跋和印章的功能和含义,其中对黄公望的题跋的画外人际关系和语类结构做了比较详细的讨论;对比分析了两幅长卷画的文化语境——通过对绘画多符号、多模态分析,再一次论证了系统功能语言学的"适用性"。这一理论框架,不仅可以有效地分析文字语篇,也同样可以有效地分析其他符号、其他模态的语篇。
关键词:《富春江居图》;系统功能语言学;参数;多符号、多模态分析;文化语境

A Study of the Analytical Framework and Parameters of Chinese Long Scrolls

Abstract: Using two multisemiotic long-scroll paintings— mainly ***Dwelling in the Fuchun Mountains*** (《富春江居图》), and ***Along the River During the Qingming Festival*** (《清明上河图》) as the analytical data, the chapter discusses in rather detail the Systemic-Functional theoretical framework and the concrete parameters based on it. It then applies the parameters to analyzing the ideational, the interpersonal and the textual meanings contained in the first painting, followed by an elaboration on the functions and meanings of its title, the postscript and the seals. An analysis is made on the external interpersonal relation and the generic structure of the postscript. Afterwards, a comparison is made between the two long scroll paintings in their contexts of culture. The analysis of the multisemiotic and multimodal discourses has again testified the appliability of Systemic Functional Linguistics, which is effective in decoding written texts as well as other semiotic discourses.

Key words: ***Dwelling in the Fuchun Mountains***; Systemic Functional Linguistics; parameter; multisemiotic and multimodal analysis; context of culture

17

为韩茹凯撰写的序言

摘　要:本章辑录先后为韩茹凯(Ruqaiya Hasan)的两本论著所做的中文序言。一本是《韩茹凯应用语言学自选集》,为韩茹凯的英语原著,2011 年由外语教学与研究出版社出版;一本是《韩茹凯论语言》,由北京师范大学彭宣维教授领衔、组织一批高校从事 SFL 研究的女性学者译成中文,2015 年由北京大学出版社出版。两个序言均介绍了韩茹凯对系统功能语言学和应用语言学的重要贡献、两本论著主要章节的内容、论著的特点、韩茹凯与中国功能语言学界深厚的渊源。在第二篇序言中笔者还对韩茹凯的为人和对她的学术贡献做了简要的评论，对韩茹凯深邃的洞见、严谨的科研作风和译者所倾注的巨大精力表达了深深的敬意。
关键词：韩茹凯；系统功能语言学；应用语言学；内容；特点；贡献

Prefaces Written for Ruqaiya Hasan

Abstract: This chapter covers two prefaces dedicated to two books written by Ruqaiya Hasan. One is entitled ***Selected Works of Ruqaiya Hasan on Applied Linguistics***, and the other ***Ruqaiya Hasan on Language***, the former published by Foreign Language Teaching and Research Press and the latter by Peking University Press. The second book is translated by a group of women researchers on SFL organized by Professor Peng Xuanwei of Beijing Normal University. The prefaces introduce unique contributions made by Ruqaiya Hasan to SFL and applied linguistics, the contents and characteristics of the books, the profound friendship between this scholar and systemic-functional linguists in China. In the second preface, the author makes a brief commentary on her academic contributions, and expresses her great admiration on the outstanding scholarship of Ruqaiya Hasan and the enormous efforts exerted by the translators.
Key words: Ruqaiya Hasan; systemic-functional linguistics; applied linguistics; content; characteristic; contribution

18

韩茹凯的语体结构潜势理论及其对语篇分析的贡献

摘　要：本章在简要概述了诸多语言学家对语篇理论的贡献后，重点介绍了韩茹凯的语体结构潜势（GSP）理论。文章简述了该学者对语篇学说理论和应用两个方面的贡献，介绍了韩茹凯以“市场会话”为素材，分析了语境格式（CC）概念，探讨了语篇与语境、语境格式的关系以及语篇结构、语篇、语类与语体结构潜势的关系。结尾是对语体结构潜势在语篇分析和语言教学方面所做贡献的几点评论。
关键词: 语篇理论;语体;语体结构潜势;语境格式;语篇分析;语言教学

Hasan's GSP Theory and Its Contribution to Discourse Analysis

Abstract: After introducing the contributions made by several linguists to discourse theory, the chapter focuses on the discussion of Hasan's theory of Generic Structural Potential (GSP). It makes an elaboration on her discourse theory and its application. Taking "Service Encounter" as her analytical datum, Hasan discusses the concept of "Contextual Configuration (CC)" and analyzes the relations between discourse and context, between CC and discourse structure, and between discourse structure, discourse and generic structural potential. In the last part, the author makes short comments on the contributions of GSP to discourse analysis and language teaching.
Key words: discourse theory; genre; generic structure potential; contextual configuration; discourse analysis; language teaching

19

浅谈语类

提　要: 本章认为语类概念存在两种观点:将语类定义为"语篇类型",或"通过语域实现的有步骤的、有一定目标的社会过程"。文中总结了"语类"的三个特点:(1)与文化紧密相关,可能是文化语境的一个层面:(2)任何语类都有一个总体目标:(3)语类的实现与其语境配置或语域配置有关,而语境配置可用来预期该语类的结构潜势。文中还探讨了语类结构潜势理论,用所列出的一个图表来说明语境配置与语类结构潜势的关系,以及语类结构潜势与可能产生的语篇之间的关系。最后是对理论与实践的关系的讨论。

关键词： 语类；文化语境；语境配置；语类结构潜势

A Tentative Study on Genre

Abstract: The chapter argues that there exist two points of view on the concept of genre, one of which defines genre as a "type of discourse", and the other as "a staged, goal-oriented social process realized through register". The author has summarized three features of genre: 1) genre is closely associated with culture, possibly as a plane at the stratum of the context of culture; 2) a genre would have an ultimate purpose or goal; and 3) the realization of a certain genre may be related to its contextual configuration (CC) or its register configuration, which can predict the GSP (Generic Structure Potential) of that genre. Based on this, the chapter elaborates on the GSP theory and works out a diagram illustrating the relation between CC and GSP, and that between GSP and its possible texts. Finally, the author discusses the relation between theory and practice.
Key words: genre; context of culture; contextual configuration; generic structure potential

20

语篇语类研究

摘　要： 本章简要介绍了"语类"这个术语的来源，概述语类在语言学和应用语言学界以及西方文学界的研究情况，讨论了语类的层次、语类与文化的关系、语类与意识形态的关系，最后涉及语类的研究意义以及语类领域目前关注的课题。
关键词： 语类；原始语类；交际目的；语类结构；意识形态；语类侵殖

A Study of Genre in Discourse

Abstract: This chapter first introduces the origin of the term of ***genre***

and the study of genre in linguistics, applied linguistics and Western literary circle. It then discusses the levels of genre, the relation between genre and culture and that between genre and ideology. It finally touches upon the significance of research on genre and the areas being focused on.

Key words: genre; proto-type; purpose of communication; generic structure; ideology; genre colonization

21

报刊语类的界定与分析

摘　要:本章总结了语言学界对语类的概念和各种界定方式的讨论。文章借助功能语言学的观点,试探性分析了《人民日报》200 多个语篇,论证了报刊语类的界定主要依据语篇的交际目的以及语类结构潜势。文章还初步讨论了语类变化与社会文化变迁的关系。
关键词:语类;语类界定;交际目的;语类结构潜势;社会文化变迁

Defining and Analyzing Newspaper Genres

— A Functional Perspective

Abstract: The chapter first summarizes the much-debated issue among linguists and discourse analysts concerning the concept of genre and the approaches to defining genre. Based on the analyses of over 200 articles of the *People's Daily*, this chapter proposes a functional perspective to define the various genres of newspaper discourses, taking the communicative purpose and the generic structure as the norm. It also finds that there is a close relationship between social changes and the diachronic variations of genres.
Key Words: genre; the defining of genre; communicative purpose; generic structure potential; social and cultural changes

22

语类变化与社会变迁

——对中国《人民日报》50 年语类变化的调查△

摘　要：本章对《人民日报》52 年中的语类特点做了一个历时的语料研究，目的是找出报纸的语类变化与中国巨大的社会和文化变化之间的关系。具体地说，论文从 1950 年到 2001 年的《人民日报》中每年选择一份，根据七个特点将所有的文章划分为不同的语类。我们发现在中国从单一文化向多元文化变化的同时，这份报纸的语篇类型有大幅度的增加，我们还发现某个时期某些语类的出现或存在可以从这个时期的主导意识形态中找到解释。这些发现进一步证实了以下论点的正确性，即社会与语类有着密切的关系，“语类变化”源于“社会和政治变化”。

关键词：语料；语类；语类变化；《人民日报》；社会或文化变化；意识形态

Generic Changes and Social Changes

— A Survey of an Official Chinese Newspaper of 50 Years

Abstract: We have made a corpus-based diachronic study of the generic features of the *People's Daily* published in the past 52 years. The purpose is to find out how generic changes in one newspaper reveal the drastic social and cultural changes in China. Concretely speaking, we have selected one copy every year spanning from 1950 to 2002 and then classified all the genres according to seven generic features. We have discovered that with China changing from the mono-cultural society to the multi-cultural society, there is a dramatic increase of genres in this newspaper, and that the existence of some genres in certain periods can find explanations in the then prevailing ideologies. These discoveries well support the arguments concerning the relation between genre and society/culture, and that between generic changes and social and political changes.

Key words: corpus; genre; generic feature; *People's Daily*; social/cultural change; ideology

23

探索以语类为基础的英语写作教学模式

摘　要：本章分析、探索了中国语境下，英语写作教学的模式和教学路子。文章首先讨论了不同的英语写作教学路子，特别是语类理论和基于语类理论的教学路子；重点报告了一所中国大学英语写作的教学实验，实验始于2005年，一直延续至今。实验报告比较详细地叙述了实验的背景、用于实验的理论——韩茹凯的语类潜势理论和马丁的纲要式结构理论；汇报了实验的设计、执行实验的情况、取得的成果以及现阶段扩展实验的领域。实验论证了语类理论在中国大学英语写作教学的适用性。文章最后表达了对继续进行和改进这个实验的期望。

关键词：英语写作；中国大学；语类结构潜势理论；纲要式结构理论；实验

Explorations in the Models and Approaches to Teaching English Writing in the Chinese Context

Abstract: This chapter analyzes and explores the models of and approaches to teaching English writing in the Chinese context. It begins with the discussion on the different approaches to the teaching of English writing, and then elaborates on related theories, particularly the genre theories and genre-based teaching approaches. The focus, however, is put on the presentation of a report of a teaching experiment of English writing at the tertiary level at a Chinese college, which has been implemented since 2005. The report first discusses the background of the experiment, followed by the mentioning of the theoretical basis of the experiment — the GSP theory and the Schematic Structure Theory proposed by Hasan and Martin respectively, and then by elaborations on the designing of the project, the details concerning the implementation of the experiment, the results gathered from it and the expanded research areas. Our experiment has testified the feasibility of the genre theory for teaching English writing in the context of Chinese colleges. Finally, the chapter expresses an expectation for continuing and further improving the implementation of this teaching model.

Key words: English writing; Chinese college; GSP theory; Schematic Structure Theory; experiment